MICROECONOMICS

CANADA IN THE GLOBAL ENVIRONMENT

EIGHTH EDITION

The moment you know

It's that inspired moment when something makes perfect sense.
MyEconLab for Parkin and Bade, *Economics: Canada in the Global Environment,* **Eighth Edition**

MyEconLab is a dynamic online tool that helps you reach that moment, time and again.

- Chapter tests generate your personal study plan and an assignment tool lets your instructor guide your learning toward those moments of true understanding.

- Practise problems directly from the textbook's Review Quiz and end-of-chapter Problems and Applications in your personal Study Plan with links to online learning resources.

- "Help-Me-Solve-This" breaks down a problem and guides you through the steps to solve it.

- Links to the eText guide you to revisit a concept or explanation when needed.

- Animated graphs with audio explanations reinforce your reading.

- The graphing tool enables you to build and manipulate graphs to understand how concepts, numbers, and graphs connect.

- Unlimited Practice: Hundreds of practice questions ensure that you get as much practice as you need, and as you work on each exercise, instant feedback helps you understand and apply the concepts.

Study on the Go
Scan the QR code at the end of each chapter to link to resources you can use on your smart-phone. Study on the Go provides a convenient and unprecedented integration between text and online content:

- Glossary flashcards
- Audio summaries
- Quizzes to make the most of your time when you're on the move

MICHAEL PARKIN   ROBIN BADE

MICROECONOMICS

CANADA IN THE GLOBAL ENVIRONMENT

EIGHTH EDITION

PEARSON

Toronto

Vice-President, Editorial Director: Gary Bennett
Editor-in-Chief: Nicole Lukach
Acquisitions Editor: Claudine O'Donnell
Senior Marketing Manager: Leigh-Anne Graham
Developmental Editor: Karen Townsend
Lead Project Manager: Söğüt Y. Güleç
Manufacturing Manager: Susan Johnson
Production Editor: Leanne Rancourt
Copy Editor: Trish O'Reilly

Proofreader: Sally Glover
Compositor: Nelson Gonzalez
Technical Illustrator: Richard Parkin
Permissions Researcher: Rema Celio
Photo Researchers: Rema Celio and Dominic Farrell
Art Director: Julia Hall
Cover and Interior Designer: Anthony Leung
Cover Image: Getty Images

10 9 8 7 6 5 4 3 2 1 [CKV]

Library and Archives Canada Cataloguing in Publication

Parkin, Michael, 1939–
    Microeconomics : Canada in the global environment / Michael Parkin, Robin Bade. — 8th ed.

Includes index.
ISBN 978-0-321-77808-6

    1. Microeconomics—Textbooks. 2. Canada—Economic Conditions—1991– —Textbooks. I. Bade, Robin II. Title.

HB172.P37 2013   338.5   C2011-906095-7

ISBN 978-0-321-77808-6

TO

OUR STUDENTS

Michael Parkin

Michael Parkin received his training as an economist at the Universities of Leicester and Essex in England. He is Professor Emeritus in the Department of Economics at the University of Western Ontario, Canada. Professor Parkin has held faculty appointments at Brown University, the University of Manchester, the University of Essex, and Bond University. He is a past president of the Canadian Economics Association and has served on the editorial boards of the *American Economic Review* and the *Journal of Monetary Economics* and as managing editor of the *Canadian Journal of Economics*. Professor Parkin's research on macroeconomics, monetary economics, and international economics has resulted in over 160 publications in journals and edited volumes, including the *American Economic Review,* the *Journal of Political Economy,* the *Review of Economic Studies,* the *Journal of Monetary Economics,* and the *Journal of Money, Credit and Banking.* He became most visible to the public with his work on inflation that discredited the use of wage and price controls. Michael Parkin also spearheaded the movement towards European monetary union.

Robin Bade

Robin Bade earned degrees in mathematics and economics at the University of Queensland and her Ph.D. at the Australian National University. She has held faculty appointments at the University of Edinburgh in Scotland, at Bond University in Australia, and at the Universities of Manitoba, Toronto, and Western Ontario in Canada. Her research on international capital flows appears in the *International Economic Review* and the *Economic Record.*

Professor Parkin and Dr. Bade are the joint authors of *Foundations of Economics* (Addison Wesley), *Modern Macroeconomics* (Pearson Education Canada), an intermediate text, and have collabrated on many research and textbook writing projects. They are both experienced and dedicated teachers of introductory economics.

BRIEF CONTENTS

The future is always uncertain. But at some times, and now is one such time, the range of possible futures is enormous. The major sources of this great uncertainty are economic policy and global macroeconomic forces. There is uncertainty about the way in which international trade policy will evolve as protectionism and trade agreements clash for centre stage. There is uncertainty about exchange rate policy as competitive devaluation rears its head. There is extraordinary uncertainty about monetary policy with the Bank of Canada holding interest rates at historical lows in an attempt to stimulate a flagging economy. And there is uncertainty about fiscal policy as federal and provincial budget deficits seem ever harder to control. In the global economy, the European debt crisis is the dominant source of uncertainty. But whether or when economic growth in China and India will slow and dampen the growth of the rest of the world is a big unknown.

Since the global financial crisis of August 2007 moved economics from the business report to the front page, justified fear has gripped producers, consumers, financial institutions, and governments.

Even the *idea* that the market is an efficient mechanism for allocating scarce resources came into question as some political leaders trumpeted the end of capitalism and the dawn of a new economic order in which tighter regulation reigned in unfettered greed.

Rarely do teachers of economics have such a rich feast on which to draw. And rarely are the principles of economics more surely needed to provide the solid foundation on which to think about economic events and navigate the turbulence of economic life.

Although thinking like an economist can bring a clearer perspective to and deeper understanding of today's events, students don't find the economic way of thinking easy or natural. *Microeconomics* seeks to put clarity and understanding in the grasp of the student through its careful and vivid exploration of the tension between self-interest and the social interest, the role and power of incentives—of opportunity cost and marginal benefit—and demonstrating the possibility that markets supplemented by other mechanisms might allocate resources efficiently.

Parkin and Bade students begin to think about issues the way real economists do and learn how to explore difficult policy problems and make more-informed decisions in their own economic lives.

◆ The Eighth Edition Revision

Simpler where possible, stripped of some technical detail, more copiously illustrated with well-chosen photographs, reinforced with improved chapter summaries and problem sets, and even more tightly integrated with MyEconLab: These are the hallmarks of this eighth edition of *Microeconomics: Canada in the Global Environment*.

This comprehensive revision also incorporates and responds to the detailed suggestions for improvements made by reviewers and users, both in the broad architecture of the text and in each chapter.

The revision builds on the improvements achieved in previous editions and retains its thorough and detailed presentation of the principles of economics, its emphasis on real-world examples and applications, its development of critical thinking skills, its diagrams renowned for pedagogy and precision, and its path-breaking technology.

Most chapters have been fine-tuned to achieve even greater clarity and to present the material in a more straightforward, visual, and intuitive way. Some chapters have been thoroughly reworked to cover new issues, particularly those that involve current policy problems. These changes are aimed at better enabling students to learn how to use the economic toolkit to analyze their own decisions and understand the events and issues they are confronted with in the media and at the ballot box.

Current issues organize each chapter. News stories about today's major economic events tie each chapter together, from new briefer chapter-opening questions to end-of-chapter problems and online practice. Each chapter includes a discussion of a critical issue of our time to demonstrate how economic theory can be applied to explore a particular debate or question. Among the many issues covered are

- The gains from trade, globalization, and protectionism in Chapters 2 and 7
- How ethanol competes with food and drives its price up in Chapter 2

- The fluctuating price of coffee in Chapter 3
- The efficiency of the global market for roses in Chapter 5
- Why movie-going and DVD rentals and downloads have all increased in Chapter 9
- How smart meters even out the use and cost of electricity in Chapter 11
- Climate change and a carbon tax in Chapter 16
- Today's tragedy of the commons—overfishing—in Chapter 17
- Increasing inequality in Canada and decreasing inequality across the nations in Chapter 19

Real-world examples and applications appear in the body of each chapter and in the end-of-chapter problems and applications, which are available in MyEconLab for assignment as homework, quizzes, or tests.

A selection of questions that appear daily in MyEconLab in *Economics in the News* are also available for assignment as homework, quizzes, or tests.

Highpoints of the Revision

In addition to being thoroughly updated and revised to include the topics and features just described, the chapters feature the following five notable changes:

1. **What Is Economics?** (Chapter 1): We have reworked the explanation of the economic way of thinking around six key ideas, all illustrated with student-relevant choices. The graphing appendix to this chapter has an increased focus on scatter diagrams and their interpretation and on understanding shifts of curves.

2. **Utility and Demand** (Chapter 8): This chapter has a revised explanation of the marginal utility model of consumer choice that now begins with the budget line and consumption possibilities. It then returns to the budget line to explain and illustrate the utility-maximizing rule—equalize the marginal utility per dollar for all goods. The dramatic changes in the market for recorded music illustrate the theory in action.

3. **Possibilities, Preferences, and Choices** (Chapter 9): Students find the analysis of the income effect and the substitution effect difficult and we have reworked this material to make the explanation clearer. We have omitted the work–leisure choice coverage of earlier editions and given the chapter a student-friendly application on choices about movies and DVDs.

4. **Oligopoly** (Chapter 15): We have omitted the kinked demand curve and dominant firm coverage of earlier editions and given the chapter a stronger game theory focus. A Gillette–Schick battle for the razor market illustrates game theory in action.

5. **Economic Inequality** (Chapter 19): This chapter now includes a section on inequality in the world economy and compares Canadian inequality with that in nations at the two extremes of equality and inequality. This new section also looks at the trend in global inequality and the contrast between increasing inequality within countries and decreasing inequality across countries. The section on the sources of inequality now includes an explanation of the superstar contest idea. This idea is used to explain the remarkable increase in inequality *among* members of the highest quintile and the rising share of the richest few.

◆ Features to Enhance Teaching and Learning

Reading Between the Lines

This Parkin and Bade hallmark helps students think like economists by connecting chapter tools and concepts to the world around them. In *Reading Between the Lines*, which appears at the end of each chapter, students apply the tools they have just learned by analyzing an article from a newspaper or news Web site. Each article sheds additional light on the questions first raised in the Chapter Opener. Questions about the article also appear with the end-of-chapter problems and applications.

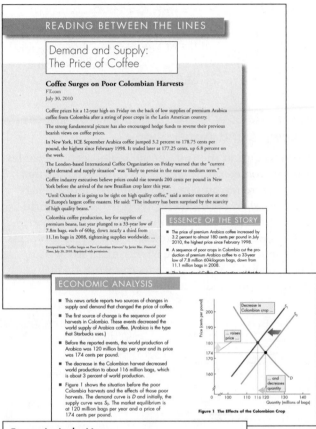

Economics in the News

32. After you have studied *Reading Between the Lines* on pp. 74–75, answer the following questions.

a. What happened to the price of coffee in 2010?

b. What substitutions do you expect might have been made to decrease the quantity of coffee demanded?

c. What influenced the demand for coffee in 2010 and what influenced the quantity of coffee demanded?

Diagrams That Show the Action

Through the past seven editions, this book has set new standards of clarity in its diagrams; the eighth edition continues to uphold this tradition. Our goal has always been to show "where the economic action is." The diagrams in this book continue to generate an enormously positive response, which confirms our view that graphical analysis is the most powerful tool available for teaching and learning economics.

Because many students find graphs hard to work with, we have developed the entire art program with the study and review needs of the student in mind.

The diagrams feature

- Original curves consistently shown in blue
- Shifted curves, equilibrium points, and other important features highlighted in red
- Colour-blended arrows to suggest movement
- Graphs paired with data tables
- Diagrams labelled with boxed notes
- Extended captions that make each diagram and its caption a self-contained object for study and review

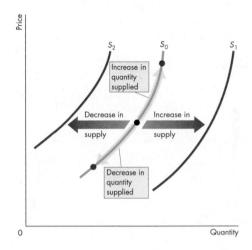

Chapter Objectives

Each chapter begins with a list of learning objectives, which enables students to see exactly where the chapter is going and to set their goals before they embark on their detailed study.

Chapter Openers

Each chapter opens with a carefully chosen photograph, question, and student-friendly vignette designed to give the student a quick sense of what the chapter is about and how it connects with their own economic world and experience. The chapter-opening story is woven into the body of the chapter and explored further in the *Reading Between the Lines* feature that ends the chapter.

Economics in Action Boxes

This new feature uses boxes within the chapter to address current events and economic occurrences that highlight and amplify the topics covered in the chapter. Instead of simply reporting the current events, the material in the boxes applies the event to an economics lesson, enabling students to see how economics plays a part in the world around them as they read through the chapter.

Some of the many issues covered in these boxes include the global market for crude oil, the best affordable choice of movies and DVDs, the cost of selling a pair of shoes, how Apple doesn't make the iPhone, the trends and cycles in real GDP and the price level, and the size of the fiscal stimulus multiplier. A complete list can be found on the inside back cover.

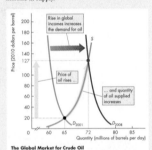

Economics in Action
The Global Market for Crude Oil
The demand and supply model provides insights into all competitive markets. Here, we'll apply what you've learned about the effects of an increase in demand to the global market for crude oil.

Crude oil is like the life-blood of the global economy. It is used to fuel our cars, airplanes, trains, and buses, to generate electricity, and to produce a wide range of plastics. When the price of crude oil rises, the costs of transportation, power, and materials all increase.

In 2001, the price of a barrel of oil was $20 (using the value of money in 2010). In 2008, before the global financial crisis ended a long period of economic expansion, the price peaked at $127 a barrel.

While the price of oil was rising, the quantity of oil produced and consumed also increased. In 2001, the world produced 65 million barrels of oil a day. By 2008, that quantity was 72 million barrels.

Who or what has been raising the price of oil? Is it the action of greedy oil producers? Oil producers might be greedy, and some of them might be big enough to withhold supply and raise the price, but it wouldn't be in their self-interest to do so. The higher price would bring forth a greater quantity supplied from other producers and the profit of the producer limiting supply would fall.

Oil producers could try to cooperate and jointly withhold supply. The Organization of Petroleum Exporting Countries, OPEC, is such a group of producers. But OPEC doesn't control the *world* supply and its members' self-interest is to produce the quantities that give them the maximum attainable profit.

So even though the global oil market has some big players, they don't fix the price. Instead, the actions of thousands of buyers and sellers and the forces of demand and supply determine the price of oil.

So how have demand and supply changed?

Because both the price and the quantity have increased, the demand for oil must have increased. Supply might have changed, too, but here we'll suppose that supply has remained the same.

The global demand for oil has increased for one major reason: World income has increased. The increase has been particularly large in the emerging economies of Brazil, China, and India. Increased world income has increased the demand for oil-using goods such as electricity, gasoline, and plastics, which in turn has increased the demand for oil.

The figure illustrates the effects of the increase in demand on the global oil market. The supply of oil remained constant along supply curve *S*. The demand for oil in 2001 was D_{2001}, so in 2001 the price was $20 a barrel and the quantity was 65 million barrels per day. The demand for oil increased and by 2008 it had reached D_{2008}. The price of oil increased to $127 a barrel and the quantity increased to 72 million barrels a day. The increase in the quantity is an *increase in the quantity supplied*, not an increase in supply.

The Global Market for Crude Oil

Key Terms
Highlighted terms simplify the student's task of learning the vocabulary of economics. Each highlighted term appears in an end-of-chapter list with its page number, in an end-of-book glossary with its page number, boldfaced in the index, and in MyEconLab in the interactive glossary and flashcards.

End-of-Chapter Summary
Each chapter closes with a concise summary organized by major topics and list of key terms with page references. These learning tools provide students with a summary for review and exam preparation.

In-Text Review Quizzes and End-of-Chapter Problems and Applications
A review quiz at the end of each major section enables students to determine whether a topic needs further study before moving on, and problems and applications at the end of each chapter provide an opportunity to practice and apply the topics of the chapter.

All the review quizzes and end-of-chapter problems and applications are in the MyEconLab study plan (shown below), where students can work them and receive instant feedback and explanations.

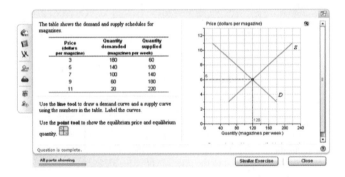

Interviews with Economists
Each major part of the text closes with a summary feature that includes an interview with a leading economist whose research and expertise correlates to what the student has just learned. These interviews explore the background, education, and research that these prominent economists have conducted, as well as advice for those who want to continue the study of economics.

For the Instructor

This book enables you to focus on the economic way of thinking and choose your own course structure in your principles course.

Focus on the Economic Way of Thinking

As an instructor, you know how hard it is to encourage a student to think like an economist. But that is your goal. Consistent with this goal, the text focuses on and repeatedly uses the central ideas of choice; tradeoff; opportunity cost; the margin; incentives; the gains from voluntary exchange; the forces of demand, supply, and equilibrium; the pursuit of economic rent; the tension between self-interest and the social interest; and the scope and limitations of government actions.

Flexible Structure

You have preferences for how you want to teach your course. We have organized this book to enable you to do so. The flexibility chart on p. xxiii illustrate the book's flexibility. By following the arrows through the charts you can select the path that best fits your preference for course structure. Whether you want to teach a traditional course that blends theory and policy, or one that takes a fast-track through either theory or policy issues, *Microeconomics: Canada in the Global Environment* gives you the choice.

Supplemental Resources

Instructor's Manual We have streamlined and reorganized the Instructor's Manual to reflect the focus and intuition of the eighth edition. The Instructor's Manual integrates the teaching and learning package and serves as a guide to all the supplements.

Each chapter contains

- A chapter overview
- A list of what's new in the eighth edition
- Ready-to-use lecture notes

A new user can walk into a classroom armed to deliver a polished lecture. The lecture notes provide an outline of the chapter; concise statements of key material; alternative tables and figures; key terms and definitions; boxes that highlight key concepts, provide an interesting anecdote, or suggest how to handle a difficult idea; and additional discussion questions. The PowerPoint® lecture notes incorporate the chapter outlines and teaching suggestions.

Solutions Manual For ease of use and instructor reference, a comprehensive Solutions Manual provides instructors with detailed solutions to the Review Quizzes and the end-of-chapter Study Plan Problems and Applications as well as Additional Problems and Applications. The Solutions Manual is available electronically on the Instructor's Resource Centre DVD (IRDVD), in the Instructor's Resources section of MyEconLab, and on the Instructor's Resource Centre.

Test Bank The eighth edition test bank (Test Item File), with more than 3,000 multiple-choice questions, has been prepared by Jeannie Gillmore of the University of Western Ontario. Jeannie has reviewed and edited all existing questions to ensure their clarity and consistency with the eighth edition and incorporated new questions. The new questions follow the style and format of the end-of-chapter text problems and provide the instructor with a whole new set of testing opportunities and/or homework assignments. Test Item File questions are available in MyEconLab for instructors to use in a test, quiz, or as homework.

TestGen Pearson TestGen enables instructors to view and edit test bank questions, generate tests, and print them in a variety of formats. Powerful search and sort functions make it easy to locate questions and arrange them in any order desired. TestGen also enables instructors to administer tests on a local area network, have tests graded electronically, and have the results prepared in electronic or printed reports. Pearson TestGen is compatible with Windows® or Macintosh® systems. This test bank is also available as a Test Item File in Microsoft Word® and Adobe Acrobat® formats.

PowerPoint® Resources Robin Bade has developed the full-colour Microsoft PowerPoint Lecture Presentation for each chapter, which includes the figures and tables from the text, animated graphs, and speaking notes. The lecture notes in the Instructor's Manual and the slide outlines are correlated, and the speaking notes are based on the Instructor's Manual teaching suggestions.

A separate set of PowerPoint files containing large-scale versions of all the text's figures (most of them animated) and tables are also available. The presentations can be used electronically in the classroom or printed to create hard-copy transparency masters. This item is available for Macintosh and Windows.

Clicker-Ready PowerPoint Resources (PRS Questions) Each chapter of the text includes 10 multiple-choice questions that test important concepts. Instructors can use these questions as in-class assignments or review quizzes.

Instructor's Resource Centre DVD (IRDVD) Fully compatible with Windows and Macintosh, this IRDVD contains files of every instructor supplement. Files included are Adobe PDF files of the Instructor's Manual, Test Item File, and Solutions Manual; PowerPoint resources; clicker-ready resources; and the TestGen. Add this useful resource to your exam copy bookbag or locate your local Pearson Canada sales representative at http://catalogue.pearsoned.ca/educator to request a copy of the IRDVD.

Instructors can download supplements from a secure, instructor-only source via the Pearson Canada Higher Education Instructor Resource Centre Web page (www.pearsonhighered.com/irc).

Economics Videos and Assignable Questions Featuring NEWS Economics videos featuring ABC News enliven your course with short news clips featuring real-world issues. These videos, available in MyEconLab, feature news footage and commentary by economists. Questions for each video clip are available for assignment in MyEconLab.

CourseSmart CourseSmart goes beyond traditional expectations—providing instant, online access to the textbooks and course materials you need at a lower cost for students. And even as students save money, you can save time and hassle with a digital eTextbook that allows you to search for the most relevant content at the very moment you need it. Whether it's evaluating textbooks or creating lecture notes to help students with difficult concepts, CourseSmart can make life a little easier. See how when you visit www.coursesmart.com/instructors.

Technology Specialists Pearson's Technology Specialists work with faculty and campus course designers to ensure that Pearson technology products, assessment tools, and online course materials are tailored to meet your specific needs. This highly qualified team is dedicated to helping schools take full advantage of a wide range of educational resources by assisting in the integration of a variety of instructional materials and media formats. Your local Pearson Canada sales representative can provide you with more details on this service program.

◆ For the Student

Study Guide

The eighth edition Study Guide by Avi Cohen of York University and Harvey King of the University of Regina is carefully coordinated with the text, MyEconLab, and the Test Item File. Each chapter of the Study Guide contains key concepts, helpful hints, true/false/uncertain questions, multiple-choice questions, and short-answer questions. Each Part Wrapup contains questions that go across chapters, which gives students an opportunity to test their cumulative understanding and to work a sample midterm test.

Study on the Go

Pearson's Study on the Go is an unprecedented mobile integration between text and online content. Students link to Study on the Go content directly from their smartphones, allowing them to study whenever and wherever they wish! Go to one of the sites below to see how you can download an app to your smartphone for free. Once the app is installed, scan the QR code on the summary page of each chapter to link to Study on the Go content, which includes the popular study tools: glossary, flashcards, audio summaries, and multiple-choice quizzes.

ScanLife: http://getscanlife.com
NeoReader: http://get.neoreader.com
QuickMark: www.quickmark.com.tw

PowerPoint Lecture Notes

Robin Bade has developed the full-colour Microsoft PowerPoint Lecture Notes for each chapter, which include animated versions of the textbook figures. Take these notes to class and edit them to create your own personal summary for review.

CourseSmart

CourseSmart goes beyond traditional expectations—providing instant, online access to the textbooks and course materials you need at an average saving of 60 percent. With instant access from any computer and the ability to search your text, you'll find the content you need quickly, no matter where you are. And with online tools such as highlighting and note-taking, you can save time and study efficiently. See all the benefits at www.coursesmart.com/students.

MyEconLab

MyEconLab's powerful assessment and tutorial system works hand-in-hand with *Microconomics: Canada in the Global Enviroment*. With comprehensive homework, quiz, test, and tutorial options, instructors can manage all assessment needs in one program.

- All of the Review Quiz questions and end-of-chapter Problems and Applications are assignable and automatically graded.
- Students can work the Review Quiz questions and end-of-chapter Study Plan Problems and Applications as part of the MyEconLab Study Plan.
- Instructors can assign the end-of-chapter Additional Problems and Applications as auto-graded assignments. These Problems and Applications are not available to students in MyEconLab unless assigned by the instructor.
- Many of the problems and applications are algorithmic, draw-graph, and numerical exercises.
- Test Item File questions are available for assignment as homework.
- The Custom Exercise Builder gives instructors the flexibility of creating their own problems for assignment.
- The powerful Gradebook records each student's performance and time spent on Tests, the Study Plan, and Homework and generates reports by student or by chapter.
- *Economics in the News* is a turn-key solution to bringing daily news into the classroom. Updated weekly during the academic year, we upload two relevant articles (one micro, one macro) and provide links for further information and questions that may be assigned for homework or for classroom discussion.

Experiments in MyEconLab

Experiments are a fun and engaging way to promote active learning and mastery of important economic concepts. Pearson's Experiments program is flexible and easy for instructors and students to use.

- Single-player experiments allow your students to play against virtual players from anywhere at any time with an Internet connection.
- Multiplayer experiments allow you to assign and manage a real-time experiment with your class.
- Pre- and post-questions for each experiment are available for assignment in MyEconLab.

MyEconLab Also Includes

- Enhanced Pearson eText, available within the online course materials and offline via an iPad app, allows instructors and students to highlight, bookmark, and take notes.
- Advanced Communication Tools enable students and instructors communication through email, discussion board, chat, and ClassLive.
- Customization options provide new and enhanced ways to share documents, add content, and rename menu items.
- Prebuilt courses offer a turn-key way for instructors to create a course that includes pre-built assignments distributed by chapter.
- Temporary Access for students who are awaiting financial aid provides a 17-day grace period of temporary access.
- A comprehensive suite of ABC News videos, which address current topics such as education, energy, U.S. Federal Reserve policy, and business cycles, is available for classroom use. Video-specific exercises are available for instructor assignment.

Robin and Michael, assisted by Jeannie Gillmore and Laurel Davies, author and oversee all of the MyEconLab content for *Economics*. Our peerless MyEconLab team has worked hard to ensure that it is tightly integrated with the book's content and vision. A more detailed walk-through of the student benefits and features of MyEconLab can be found on the inside front cover. Visit www.myeconlab.com for more information and an online demonstration of instructor and student features.

Acknowledgments

We thank our current and former colleagues and friends at the University of Western Ontario who have taught us so much. They are Jim Davies, Jeremy Greenwood, Ig Horstmann, Peter Howitt, Greg Huffman, David Laidler, Phil Reny, Chris Robinson, John Whalley, and Ron Wonnacott. We also thank Doug McTaggart and Christopher Findlay, co-authors of the Australian edition, and Melanie Powell and Kent Matthews, co-authors of the European edition. Suggestions arising from their adaptations of earlier editions have been helpful to us in preparing this edition.

We thank the several thousand students whom we have been privileged to teach. The instant response that comes from the look of puzzlement or enlightenment has taught us how to teach economics.

It is a special joy to thank the many outstanding editors, media specialists, and others at Pearson Canada who contributed to the concerted publishing effort that brought this edition to completion. Allan Reynolds, President and CEO; Steve O'Hearn, President Higher Education; Gary Bennett, Vice-President and Editorial Director for Higher Education; and Nicole Lukach, Editor-in-Chief Business and Economics have provided outstanding corporate direction. They have built a culture that brings out the best in its editors and authors.

Claudine O'Donnell, Acquisitions Editor for Economics and our sponsoring editor, played a major role in shaping this revision and the many outstanding supplements that accompany it. Claudine brings intelligence and insight to her work and is Canada's pre-eminent economics editor. Karen Townsend, Developmental Editor, managed the supplements' authors and reviewers. Victoria Naik, Media Content Developer, ensured that all our media assets were correctly assembled. Leigh-Anne Graham provided inspired marketing strategy and direction.

Our Production Editor, Leanne Rancourt, under the direction of Sögüt Güleç, Lead Project Manager, again kept her eye to the production process and its contributors. Trish O'Reilly, Sally Glover, and Kit Pasula provided a careful, consistent copy edit, proofread, and accuracy check. Anthony Leung designed the cover and package and yet again surpassed the challenge of ensuring that we meet the highest design standards.

We thank our talented eighth edition supplements authors and contributors—Avi Cohen, Laurel Davies, Jeannie Gillmore, and Harvey King.

We thank the many exceptional reviewers who have shared their insights through the various editions of this book. Their contribution has been invaluable.

We thank the people who work directly with us. Jeannie Gillmore provided outstanding research assistance on many topics, including the *Reading Between the Lines* news articles. Richard Parkin created the electronic art files and offered many ideas that improved the figures in this book. And Laurel Davies managed an ever-growing and ever more complex MyEconLab database.

Classroom experience will test the value of this book. We would appreciate hearing from instructors and students about how we can continue to improve it in future editions.

Michael Parkin
Robin Bade
London, Ontario, Canada
michael.parkin@uwo.ca
robin@econ100.com

 Reviewers

Syed Ahmed, Red Deer Community College
Ather H. Akbari, Saint Mary's University
Doug Allen, Simon Fraser University
Benjamin Amoah, University of Guelph
Torben Andersen, Red Deer College
Terri Anderson, Fanshawe College
Syed Ashan, Concordia University
Fred Aswani, McMaster University
Iris Au, University of Toronto, Scarborough
Keith Baxter, Bishop's University
Andy Baziliauskas, University of Winnipeg
Dick Beason, University of Alberta
Karl Bennett, University of Waterloo
Ronald Bodkin, University of Ottawa
Caroline Boivin, Concordia University
Paul Booth, University of Alberta
John Boyd, University of British Columbia
John Brander, University of New Brunswick
Larry Brown, Selkirk College
Sam Bucovetsky, York University
Bogdan Buduru, Concordia University
Lutz-Alexander Busch, University of Waterloo
Beverly J. Cameron, University of Manitoba
Norman Cameron, University of Manitoba
Emanuel Carvalho, University of Waterloo
Francois Casas, University of Toronto
Alan Tak Yan Chan, Atlantic Baptist University
Robert Cherneff, University of Victoria
Jason Childs, University of New Brunswick, Saint John
Saud Choudhry, Trent University
Louis Christofides, University of Guelph
Kam Hon Chu, Memorial University of Newfoundland
George Churchman, University of Manitoba
Avi J. Cohen, York University
Constantin Colonescu, Grant MacEwan University
Ryan A. Compton, University of Manitoba
Marilyn Cottrell, Brock University
Rosilyn Coulson, Douglas College
Brian Coulter, University College of the Fraser Valley
Stanya Cunningham, Concordia University College of Alberta
Douglas Curtis, Trent University
Garth Davies, Olds College
Ajit Dayanandan, University of Northern British Columbia
Carol Derksen, Red River College
David Desjardins, John Abbott College
Vaughan Dickson, University of New Brunswick (Fredericton)
Livio Di Matteo, Lakehead University
Mohammed Dore, Brock University
Torben Drewes, Trent University

Byron Eastman, Laurentian University
Fahira Eston, Humber College
Sigrid Ewender, Kwantlen Polytechnic University
Brian Ferguson, University of Guelph
Len Fitzpatrick, Carleton University
Peter Fortura, Algonquin College
Oliver Franke, Athabasca University
Bruno Fullone, George Brown College
Donald Garrie, Georgian College
Philippe Ghayad, Dawson College and Concordia University
David Gray, University of Ottawa
Sandra Hadersbeck, Okanagan College
Rod Hill, University of New Brunswick
Eric Kam, Ryerson University
Susan Kamp, University of Alberta
Cevat Burc Kayahan, University of Guelph
Peter Kennedy, Simon Fraser University
Harvey King, University of Regina
Patricia Koss, Concordia University
Robert Kunimoto, Mt. Royal University
David Johnson, Wilfrid Laurier University
Cliff Jutlah, York University, Glendon Campus
Michael G. Lanyi, University of Lethbridge
Eva Lau, University of Waterloo
Gordon Lee, University of Alberta
Byron Lew, Trent University
Anastasia M. Lintner, University of Guelph
Scott Lynch, Memorial University
Dan MacKay, SIAST
Leigh MacDonald, University of Western Ontario
Keith MacKinnon, York University
Mohammad Mahbobi, Thompson Rivers University
S. Manchouri, University of Alberta
Christian Marfels, Dalhousie University
Raimo Martalla, Malaspina University College
Perry Martens, University of Regina
Roberto Martínez-Espíneira, St. Francis Xavier University
Dennis McGuire, Okanagan University College
Rob Moir, University of New Brunswick, Saint John
Saeed Moshiri, University of Manitoba
Joseph Muldoon, Trent University
David Murrell, University of New Brunswick, Fredericton
Robin Neill, Carleton University
A. Gyasi Nimarko, Vanier College

Sonia Novkovic, Saint Mary's University
John O'Brien, Concordia University
Arne Paus-Jenssen, University of Saskatchewan
Andrea Podhorsky, York University
Derek Pyne, Memorial University of Newfoundland
Stephen Rakoczy, Humber College
Don Reddick, Kwantlen University College
June Riley, John Abbott College
E. Riser, Memorial University
Roberta Robb, Brock University
Nick Rowe, Carleton University
Michael Rushton, University of Regina
Balbir Sahni, Concordia University
Brian Scarfe, University of Regina
Marlyce Searcy, SIAST Palliser
Jim Sentance, University of Prince Edward Island
Lance Shandler, Kwantlen University College
Stan Shedd, University of Calgary
Chandan Shirvaikar, Red Deer College
Peter Sinclair, Wilfrid Laurier University
Ian Skaith, Fanshawe College
Scott Skjei, Acadia University
Judith Skuce, Georgian College
George Slasor, University of Toronto
Norman Smith, Georgian College
Bert Somers, John Abbott College
Lewis Soroka, Brock University
Glen Stirling, University of Western Ontario
Brennan Thompson, Ryerson University
Irene Trela, University of Western Ontario
Russell Uhler, University of British Columbia
Brian VanBlarcom, Acadia University
Marianne Vigneault, Bishop's University
Jane Waples, Memorial University of Newfoundland
Tony Ward, Brock University
Bruce Wilkinson, University of Alberta
Christopher Willmore, University of Victoria
Andrew Wong, Grant MacEwan University
Peter Wylie, University of British Columbia, Okanagan
Arthur Younger, Humber College Institute of Technology and Advanced Learning
Ayoub Yousefi, University of Western Ontario
Weiqiu Yu, University of New Brunswick, Fredericton

Micro Flexibility

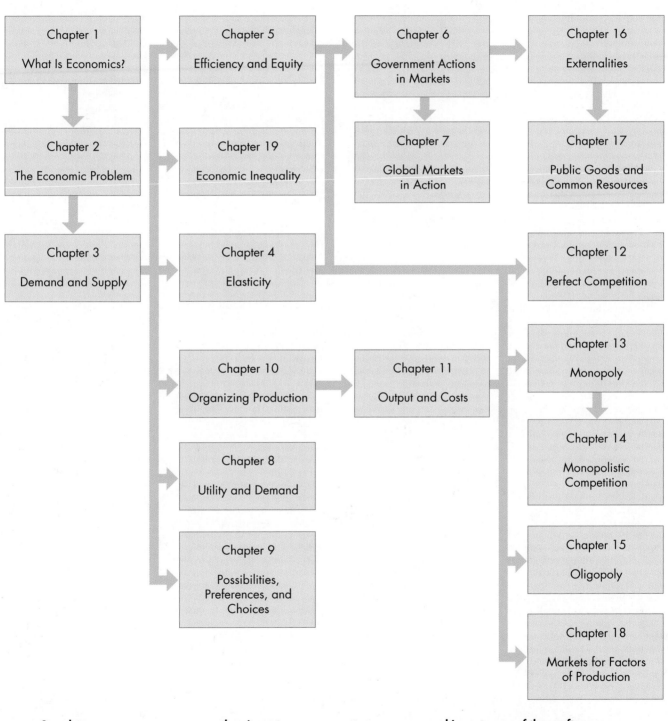

Chapter 1 What Is Economics?	**Chapter 5** Efficiency and Equity	**Chapter 6** Government Actions in Markets	**Chapter 16** Externalities
Chapter 2 The Economic Problem	**Chapter 19** Economic Inequality	**Chapter 7** Global Markets in Action	**Chapter 17** Public Goods and Common Resources
Chapter 3 Demand and Supply	**Chapter 4** Elasticity		**Chapter 12** Perfect Competition
	Chapter 10 Organizing Production	**Chapter 11** Output and Costs	**Chapter 13** Monopoly
	Chapter 8 Utility and Demand		**Chapter 14** Monopolistic Competition
	Chapter 9 Possibilities, Preferences, and Choices		**Chapter 15** Oligopoly
			Chapter 18 Markets for Factors of Production

Start here ...   **... then jump to any of these ...**   **... and jump to any of these after doing the prerequisites indicated**

TABLE OF CONTENTS

PART 4
FIRMS AND MARKETS 227

**PART 6
FACTOR MARKETS AND
INEQUALITY** 415

MICROECONOMICS

CANADA IN THE GLOBAL ENVIRONMENT

EIGHTH EDITION

CHAPTER

1

What Is Economics?

After studying this chapter, you will be able to

◆ Define economics and distinguish between microeconomics and macroeconomics

◆ Explain the two big questions of economics

◆ Explain the key ideas that define the economic way of thinking

◆ Explain how economists go about their work as social scientists and policy advisers

You are studying economics at a time of enormous challenge and change. Every day, new businesses are born and old ones die; new jobs are created and old ones disappear. Nations, businesses, and individuals must find ways of coping with economic change.

Your life will be shaped by the challenges that *you* face and the opportunities that *you* create. But to face those challenges and seize the opportunities they present, you must understand the powerful forces at play. The economics that you're about to learn will become your most reliable guide. This chapter gets you started. It describes the questions that economists try to answer and the ways in which they think as they search for the answers.

◆ Definition of Economics

A fundamental fact dominates our lives: We want more than we can get. Our inability to get everything we want is called **scarcity**. Scarcity is universal. It confronts all living things. Even parrots face scarcity!

Not only do I want a cracker—we all want a cracker!

© Frank Modell/The New Yorker Collection/www.cartoonbank.com

Think about the things that *you* want and the scarcity that *you* face. You want to live a long and healthy life. You want to go to a good school, college, or university. You want to live in a well-equipped, spacious, and comfortable home. You want the latest smart phone and a faster Internet connection for your laptop or iPad. You want some sports and recreational gear—perhaps some new skates or skis, or a new bike. And you want more time, much more than is available, to go to class, do your homework, play sports and games, read novels, go to the movies, listen to music, travel, and hang out with your friends.

What you can afford to buy is limited by your income and by the prices you must pay. And your time is limited by the fact that your day has 24 hours.

You want some other things that only governments provide. You want to live in a peaceful and secure world and safe neighbourhood and enjoy the benefits of clean air, lakes, and rivers.

What governments can afford is limited by the taxes they collect. Taxes lower people's incomes and compete with the other things they want to buy.

What everyone can get—what *society* can get—is limited by the productive resources available. These resources are the gifts of nature, human labour and ingenuity, and all the previously produced tools and equipment.

Because we can't get everything we want, we must make *choices*. You can't afford *both* a laptop *and* an iPhone, so you must *choose* which one to buy. You can't spend tonight *both* studying for your next test *and* going to the movies, so again, you must *choose* which one to do. Governments can't spend a tax dollar on *both* national defence *and* environmental protection, so they must *choose* how to spend that dollar.

Your choices must somehow be made consistent with the choices of others. If you choose to buy a laptop, someone else must choose to sell it. Incentives reconcile choices. An **incentive** is a reward that encourages an action or a penalty that discourages one. Prices act as incentives. If the price of a laptop is too high, more will be offered for sale than people want to buy. And if the price is too low, fewer will be offered for sale than people want to buy. But there is a price at which choices to buy and sell are consistent.

> **Economics** is the social science that studies the *choices* that individuals, businesses, governments, and entire societies make as they cope with *scarcity* and the *incentives* that influence and reconcile those choices.

The subject has two parts:

- Microeconomics
- Macroeconomics

Microeconomics is the study of the choices that individuals and businesses make, the way these choices interact in markets, and the influence of governments. Some examples of microeconomic questions are: Why are people downloading more movies? How would a tax on e-commerce affect eBay?

Macroeconomics is the study of the performance of the national economy and the global economy. Some examples of macroeconomic questions are: Why is the Canadian unemployment rate so high? Can the Bank of Canada make our economy expand by cutting interest rates?

◼ REVIEW QUIZ

1 List some examples of the scarcity that you face.
2 Find examples of scarcity in today's headlines.
3 Find an illustration of the distinction between microeconomics and macroeconomics in today's headlines.

You can work these questions in Study Plan 1.1 and get instant feedback.

 MyEconLab ◆

Two Big Economic Questions

Two big questions summarize the scope of economics:

■ How do choices end up determining *what, how,* and *for whom* goods and services are produced?

■ Can the choices that people make in the pursuit of their own *self-interest* also promote the broader *social interest*?

What, How, and For Whom?

Goods and services are the objects that people value and produce to satisfy human wants. *Goods* are physical objects such as cell phones and automobiles. *Services* are tasks performed for people such as cellphone service and auto-repair service.

What? What we produce varies across countries and changes over time. In Canada today, agriculture accounts for 2 percent of total production, manufactured goods for 20 percent, and services (retail and wholesale trade, health care, and education are the biggest ones) for 78 percent. In contrast, in China today, agriculture accounts for 10 percent of total production, manufactured goods for 46 percent, and services for 44 percent. Figure 1.1 shows these numbers and also the percentages for Brazil, which fall between those for Canada and China.

What determines these patterns of production? How do choices end up determining the quantities of cell phones, automobiles, cellphone service, auto-repair service, and the millions of other items that are produced in Canada and around the world?

How? Goods and services are produced by using productive resources that economists call **factors of production**. Factors of production are grouped into four categories:

■ Land
■ Labour
■ Capital
■ Entrepreneurship

Land The "gifts of nature" that we use to produce goods and services are called **land**. In economics, land is what in everyday language we call *natural resources*. It includes land in the everyday sense together with minerals, oil, gas, coal, water, air, forests, and fish.

FIGURE 1.1 What Three Countries Produce

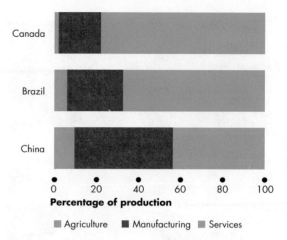

Percentage of production

■ Agriculture   ■ Manufacturing   ■ Services

Agriculture and manufacturing are small percentages of production in rich countries such as Canada and large percentages of production in poorer countries such as China. Most of what is produced in Canada is services. The percentages for Brazil lie between those for Canada and China.

Source of data: Central Intelligence Agency, CIA Factbook 2011.

———————————————— MyEconLab   animation ◆

Our land surface and water resources are renewable and some of our mineral resources can be recycled. But the resources that we use to create energy are nonrenewable—they can be used only once.

Labour The work time and work effort that people devote to producing goods and services is called **labour**. Labour includes the physical and mental efforts of all the people who work on farms and construction sites and in factories, shops, and offices.

The *quality* of labour depends on **human capital**, which is the knowledge and skill that people obtain from education, on-the-job training, and work experience. You are building your own human capital right now as you work on your economics course, and your human capital will continue to grow as you gain work experience.

Human capital expands over time. Today, 93 percent of the adult population of Canada have completed high school and 23 percent have a university degree and a further 40 percent have some post-secondary education. Figure 1.2 shows these measures of human capital in Canada since 1975.

FIGURE 1.2 A Measure of Human Capital

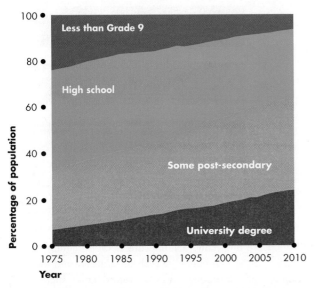

In 2009 (the most recent data), 23 percent of the adult population had a university degree. A further 40 percent had some post-secondary education, and 93 percent had completed high school.

Source of data: Statistics Canada.

MyEconLab   animation ◆

Capital   The tools, instruments, machines, buildings, and other constructions that businesses use to produce goods and services are called **capital**.

In everyday language, we talk about money, stocks, and bonds as being "capital." These items are *financial* capital. Financial capital plays an important role in enabling businesses to borrow the funds that they use to buy physical capital. But because financial capital is not used to produce goods and services, it is not a productive resource.

Entrepreneurship   The human resource that organizes labour, land, and capital is called **entrepreneurship**. Entrepreneurs come up with new ideas about what and how to produce, make business decisions, and bear the risks that arise from these decisions.

What determines the quantities of factors of production that are used to produce goods and services?

For Whom?   Who consumes the goods and services that are produced depends on the incomes that people earn. People with large incomes can buy a wide range of goods and services. People with small incomes have fewer options and can afford a smaller range of goods and services.

People earn their incomes by selling the services of the factors of production they own:

- Land earns **rent**.
- Labour earns **wages**.
- Capital earns **interest**.
- Entrepreneurship earns **profit**.

Which factor of production earns the most income? The answer is labour. Wages and fringe benefits are around 70 percent of total income. Land, capital, and entrepreneurship share the rest. These percentages have been remarkably constant over time.

Knowing how income is shared among the factors of production doesn't tell us how it is shared among individuals. And the distribution of income among individuals is extremely unequal. You know of some people who earn very large incomes: Mike Lazaridis of RIM, the maker of the BlackBerry, earned $4.6 million in 2010 and he was only 437th on *Forbes* World's Richest People list.

You know of even more people who earn very small incomes. Servers at Tim Horton's earn about $9 an hour; checkout clerks, cleaners, and textile and leather workers all earn less than $10 an hour.

You probably know about other persistent differences in incomes. Men, on average, earn more than women; whites earn more than minorities; college graduates earn more than high-school graduates.

We can get a good sense of who consumes the goods and services produced by looking at the percentages of total income earned by different groups of people. The 20 percent of people with the lowest incomes earn about 5 percent of total income, while the richest 20 percent earn close to 50 percent of total income. So on average, people in the richest 20 percent earn more than 10 times the incomes of those in the poorest 20 percent.

Why is the distribution of income so unequal? Why do women and minorities earn less than white males?

Economics provides some answers to all these questions about what, how, and for whom goods and services are produced and much of the rest of this book will help you to understand those answers.

We're now going to look at the second big question of economics: Can the pursuit of self-interest promote the social interest? This question is a difficult one both to appreciate and to answer.

Can the Pursuit of Self-Interest Promote the Social Interest?

Every day, you and 33 million other Canadians, along with 7 billion people in the rest of the world, make economic choices that result in *what, how*, and *for whom* goods and services are produced.

Self-Interest A choice is in your **self-interest** if you think that choice is the best one available for you. You make most of your choices in your self-interest. You use your time and other resources in the ways that make the most sense to you, and you don't think too much about how your choices affect other people. You order a home delivery pizza because you're hungry and want to eat. You don't order it thinking that the delivery person needs an income. And when the pizza delivery person shows up at your door, he's not doing you a favour. He's pursuing his self-interest and hoping for a good tip.

Social Interest A choice is in the **social interest** if it leads to an outcome that is the best for society as a whole. The social interest has two dimensions: efficiency and equity (or fairness). What is best for society is an efficient and fair use of resources.

Economists say that **efficiency** is achieved when the available resources are used to produce goods and services at the lowest possible cost and in the quantities that give the greatest possible value or benefit. We will make the concept of efficiency precise and clear in Chapter 2. For now, just think of efficiency as a situation in which resources are put to their best possible use.

Equity or fairness doesn't have a crisp definition. Reasonable people, both economists and others, have a variety of views about what is fair. There is always room for disagreement and a need to be careful and clear about the notion of fairness being used.

The Big Question Can we organize our economic lives so that when each one of us makes choices that are in our self-interest, we promote the social interest? Can trading in free markets achieve the social interest? Do we need government action to achieve the social interest? Do we need international cooperation and treaties to achieve the global social interest?

Questions about the social interest are hard ones to answer and they generate discussion, debate, and disagreement. Let's put a bit of flesh on these questions with four examples.

The examples are

- Globalization
- The information-age economy
- Climate change
- Economic instability

Globalization The term *globalization* means the expansion of international trade, borrowing and lending, and investment.

Globalization is in the self-interest of those consumers who buy low-cost goods and services produced in other countries; and it is in the self-interest of the multinational firms that produce in low-cost regions and sell in high-price regions. But is globalization in the self-interest of the low-wage worker in Malaysia who sews your new running shoes and the displaced shoemaker in Toronto? Is it in the social interest?

Economics in Action
Life in a Small and Ever-Shrinking World

When Nike produces sports shoes, people in Malaysia get work; and when China buys new regional jets, Canadians who work at Bombardier in Toronto build them. While globalization brings expanded production and job opportunities for some workers, it destroys many Canadian jobs. Workers in manufacturing industries must learn new skills, take service jobs—which are often lower paid—or retire earlier than previously planned.

The Information-Age Economy The technological change of the past 40 years has been called the *Information Revolution.*

The information revolution has clearly served your self-interest: It has provided your cell phone, laptop, loads of handy applications, and the Internet. It has also served the self-interest of Bill Gates of Microsoft and Gordon Moore of Intel, both of whom have seen their wealth soar.

But did the information revolution best serve the social interest? Did Microsoft produce the best possible Windows operating system and sell it at a price that was in the social interest? Did Intel make the right quality of chips and sell them in the right quantities for the right prices? Or was the quality too low and the price too high? Would the social interest have been better served if Microsoft and Intel had faced competition from other firms?

Climate Change Climate change is a huge political issue today. Every serious political leader is acutely aware of the problem and of the popularity of having proposals that might lower carbon emissions.

Every day, when you make self-interested choices to use electricity and gasoline, you contribute to carbon emissions; you leave your carbon footprint. You can lessen your carbon footprint by walking, riding a bike, taking a cold shower, or planting a tree.

But can each one of us be relied upon to make decisions that affect the Earth's carbon-dioxide concentration in the social interest? Must governments change the incentives we face so that our self-interested choices are also in the social interest? How can governments change incentives? How can we encourage the use of wind and solar power to replace the burning of fossil fuels that brings climate change?

Economics in Action
Chips and Windows

Gordon Moore, who founded the chip-maker Intel, and Bill Gates, a co-founder of Microsoft, held privileged positions in the *Information Revolution.*

For many years, Intel chips were the only available chips and Windows was the only available operating system for the original IBM PC and its clones. The PC and Apple's Mac competed, but the PC had a huge market share.

An absence of competition gave Intel and Microsoft the power and ability to sell their products at prices far above the cost of production. If the prices of chips and Windows had been lower, many more people would have been able to afford a computer and would have chosen to buy one.

Economics in Action
Greenhouse Gas Emissions

Burning fossil fuels to generate electricity and to power airplanes, automobiles, and trucks pours a staggering 28 billions tonnes (4 tonnes per person) of carbon dioxide into the atmosphere each year.

Two-thirds of the world's carbon emissions comes from the United States, China, the European Union, Russia, and India. The fastest growing emissions are coming from India and China.

The amount of global warming caused by economic activity and its effects are uncertain, but the emissions continue to grow and pose huge risks.

Economic Instability The years between 1993 and 2007 were a period of remarkable economic stability, so much so that they've been called the *Great Moderation*. During those years, the Canadian and global economies were on a roll. Incomes in Canada increased by 30 percent and incomes in China tripled.

Economics in Action
A Credit Crunch

Flush with funds and offering record low interest rates, U.S. banks went on a lending spree to home buyers. Rapidly rising home prices made home owners feel well off and they were happy to borrow and spend. Home loans were bundled into securities that were sold and resold to banks around the world.

In 2006, as interest rates began to rise and the rate of rise in home prices slowed, borrowers defaulted on their loans. What started as a trickle became a flood. As more people defaulted, banks took losses that totalled billions of dollars by mid-2007.

Global credit markets stopped working, and people began to fear a prolonged slowdown in economic activity. Some even feared the return of the economic trauma of the *Great Depression* of the 1930s. The U.S. Federal Reserve and the Bank of Canada, determined to avoid a catastrophe, started lending on a very large scale to troubled banks.

The Bank of Canada avoided a catastrophe, but many people did lose their jobs and some were forced to sell their homes.

There was a short-lived financial crisis in some Asian economies in 1997 but nothing serious enough to upset sustained global income growth.

But in August 2007, a period of financial stress began. A bank in France was the first to feel the pain that soon would grip the entire global financial system.

Banks take in people's deposits and get more funds by borrowing from each other and from other firms. Banks use these funds to make loans. All the banks' choices to borrow and lend and the choices of people and businesses to lend to and borrow from banks are made in self-interest. But does this lending and borrowing serve the social interest? Is there too much borrowing and lending that needs to be reined in, or is there too little and a need to stimulate more?

When the banks got into trouble in 2008, they received bailout loans from governments and central banks such as the U.S. Federal Reserve and the Bank of Canada. Did the bailout of troubled banks in the global financial crisis serve the social interest?

Banks weren't the only recipients of public funds. General Motors was saved by U.S. and Canadian government bailouts. GM makes its decisions in its self-interest. Did the bailouts of GM serve the social interest?

REVIEW QUIZ

1 Describe the broad facts about *what*, *how*, and *for whom* goods and services are produced.
2 Use headlines from the recent news to illustrate the potential for conflict between self-interest and the social interest.

You can work these questions in Study Plan 1.2 and get instant feedback.
——————— MyEconLab ◆

We've looked at four topics and asked many questions that illustrate the big question: Can choices made in the pursuit of self-interest also promote the social interest? We've asked questions but not answered them because we've not yet explained the economic principles needed to do so.

By working through this book, you will discover the economic principles that help economists figure out when the social interest is being served, when it is not, and what might be done when it is not being served. We will return to each of the unanswered questions in future chapters.

◆ The Economic Way of Thinking

The questions that economics tries to answer tell us about the *scope of economics,* but they don't tell us how economists *think* and go about seeking answers to these questions. You're now going to see how economists go about their work.

We're going to look at six key ideas that define the *economic way of thinking.* These ideas are

- A choice is a *tradeoff.*
- People make *rational choices* by comparing *benefits* and *costs.*
- *Benefit* is what you gain from something.
- *Cost* is what you *must give up* to get something.
- Most choices are "*how-much*" choices made at the *margin.*
- Choices respond to *incentives.*

A Choice Is a Tradeoff

Because we face scarcity, we must make choices. And when we make a choice, we select from the available alternatives. For example, you can spend Saturday night studying for your next economics test or having fun with your friends, but you can't do both of these activities at the same time. You must choose how much time to devote to each. Whatever choice you make, you could have chosen something else.

You can think about your choices as tradeoffs. A **tradeoff** is an exchange—giving up one thing to get something else. When you choose how to spend your Saturday night, you face a tradeoff between studying and hanging out with your friends.

Making a Rational Choice

Economists view the choices that people make as rational. A **rational choice** is one that compares costs and benefits and achieves the greatest benefit over cost for the person making the choice.

Only the wants of the person making a choice are relevant to determine its rationality. For example, you might like your coffee black and strong but your friend prefers his milky and sweet. So it is rational for you to choose espresso and for your friend to choose cappuccino.

The idea of rational choice provides an answer to the first question: *What* goods and services will be

produced and in what quantities? The answer is those that people rationally choose to buy!

But how do people choose rationally? Why do more people choose a BlackBerry rather than an iPhone? Why don't CNR and CPR build high-speed tracks so that VIA Rail can run Bombardier's super-fast trains like those used in Europe? The answers turn on comparing benefits and costs.

Benefit: What You Gain

The **benefit** of something is the gain or pleasure that it brings and is determined by **preferences**—by what a person likes and dislikes and the intensity of those feelings. If you get a huge kick out of "Guitar Hero," that video game brings you a large benefit. And if you have little interest in listening to Yo Yo Ma playing a Vivaldi cello concerto, that activity brings you a small benefit.

Some benefits are large and easy to identify, such as the benefit that you get from being in school: A big piece of that benefit is the goods and services that you will be able to enjoy with the boost to your earning power when you graduate. Some benefits are small, such as the benefit you get from a slice of pizza.

Economists measure benefit as the most that a person is *willing to give up* to get something. You are willing to give up a lot to be in school. But you would give up only an iTunes download for a slice of pizza.

Cost: What You *Must* Give Up

The **opportunity cost** of something is the highest-valued alternative that must be given up to get it.

To make the idea of opportunity cost concrete, think about *your* opportunity cost of being in school. It has two components: the things you can't afford to buy and the things you can't do with your time.

Start with the things you can't afford to buy. You've spent all your income on tuition, residence fees, books, and a laptop. If you weren't in school, you would have spent this money on tickets to ball games and movies and all the other things that you enjoy. But that's only the start of your opportunity cost. You've also given up the opportunity to get a job. Suppose that the best job you could get if you weren't in school is working at the Royal Bank of Canada as a teller and earning $25,000 a year. Another part of your opportunity cost of being in school is all the things that you could buy with the extra $25,000 you would have had.

As you well know, being a student eats up many hours in class time, doing homework assignments, preparing for tests, and so on. To do all these school activities, you must give up many hours of what would otherwise be leisure time spent with your friends.

So the opportunity cost of being in school is all the good things that you can't afford and don't have the spare time to enjoy. You might want to put a dollar value on that cost or you might just list all the items that make up the opportunity cost.

The examples of opportunity cost that we've just considered are all-or-nothing costs—you're either in school or not in school. Most situations are not like this one. They involve choosing *how much* of an activity to do.

How Much? Choosing at the Margin

You can allocate the next hour between studying and instant messaging your friends, but the choice is not all or nothing. You must decide how many minutes to allocate to each activity. To make this decision, you compare the benefit of a little bit more study time with its cost—you make your choice at the **margin**.

The benefit that arises from an increase in an activity is called **marginal benefit**. For example, your marginal benefit from one more night of study before a test is the boost it gives to your grade. Your marginal benefit doesn't include the grade you're already achieving without that extra night of work.

The *opportunity cost* of an *increase* in an activity is called **marginal cost**. For you, the marginal cost of studying one more night is the cost of not spending that night on your favourite leisure activity.

To make your decisions, you compare marginal benefit and marginal cost. If the marginal benefit from an extra night of study exceeds its marginal cost, you study the extra night. If the marginal cost exceeds the marginal benefit, you don't study the extra night.

Choices Respond to Incentives

Economists take human nature as given and view people as acting in their self-interest. All people—you, other consumers, producers, politicians, and public servants—pursue their self-interest.

Self-interested actions are not necessarily *selfish* actions. You might decide to use your resources in ways that bring pleasure to others as well as to yourself. But a self-interested act gets the most benefit for *you* based on *your* view about benefit.

The central idea of economics is that we can predict the self-interested choices that people make by looking at the *incentives* they face. People undertake those activities for which marginal benefit exceeds marginal cost; and they reject options for which marginal cost exceeds marginal benefit.

For example, your economics instructor gives you a problem set and tells you these problems will be on the next test. Your marginal benefit from working these problems is large, so you diligently work them. In contrast, your math instructor gives you a problem set on a topic that she says will never be on a test. You get little marginal benefit from working these problems, so you decide to skip most of them.

Economists see incentives as the key to reconciling self-interest and social interest. When our choices are *not* in the social interest, it is because of the incentives we face. One of the challenges for economists is to figure out the incentives that result in self-interested choices being in the social interest.

Economists emphasize the crucial role that institutions play in influencing the incentives that people face as they pursue their self-interest. Laws that protect private property and markets that enable voluntary exchange are the fundamental institutions. You will learn as you progress with your study of economics that where these institutions exist, self-interest can indeed promote the social interest.

REVIEW QUIZ

1 Explain the idea of a tradeoff and think of three tradeoffs that you have made today.

2 Explain what economists mean by rational choice and think of three choices that you've made today that are rational.

3 Explain why opportunity cost is the best forgone alternative and provide examples of some opportunity costs that you have faced today.

4 Explain what it means to choose at the margin and illustrate with three choices at the margin that you have made today.

5 Explain why choices respond to incentives and think of three incentives to which you have responded today.

You can work these questions in Study Plan 1.3 and get instant feedback.

MyEconLab ◆

Economics as Social Science and Policy Tool

Economics is both a social science and a toolkit for advising on policy decisions.

Economist as Social Scientist

As social scientists, economists seek to discover how the economic world works. In pursuit of this goal, like all scientists, economists distinguish between positive and normative statements.

Positive Statements A *positive* statement is about what *is*. It says what is currently believed about the way the world operates. A positive statement might be right or wrong, but we can test it by checking it against the facts. "Our planet is warming because of the amount of coal that we're burning" is a positive statement. We can test whether it is right or wrong.

A central task of economists is to test positive statements about how the economic world works and to weed out those that are wrong. Economics first got off the ground in the late 1700s, so it is a young science compared with, for example, physics, and much remains to be discovered.

Normative Statements A *normative* statement is about what *ought to be*. It depends on values and cannot be tested. Policy goals are normative statements. For example, "We ought to cut our use of coal by 50 percent" is a normative policy statement. You may agree or disagree with it, but you can't test it. It doesn't assert a fact that can be checked.

Unscrambling Cause and Effect Economists are particularly interested in positive statements about cause and effect. Are computers getting cheaper because people are buying them in greater quantities? Or are people buying computers in greater quantities because they are getting cheaper? Or is some third factor causing both the price of a computer to fall and the quantity of computers bought to increase?

To answer such questions, economists create and test economic models. An **economic model** is a description of some aspect of the economic world that includes only those features that are needed for the purpose at hand. For example, an economic model of a cellphone network might include features such as the prices of calls, the number of cellphone users, and the volume of calls. But the model would ignore cellphone colours and ringtones.

A model is tested by comparing its predictions with the facts. But testing an economic model is difficult because we observe the outcomes of the simultaneous change of many factors. To cope with this problem, economists look for natural experiments (situations in the ordinary course of economic life in which the one factor of interest is different and other things are equal or similar); conduct statistical investigations to find correlations; and perform economic experiments by putting people in decision-making situations and varying the influence of one factor at a time to discover how they respond.

Economist as Policy Adviser

Economics is useful. It is a toolkit for advising governments and businesses and for making personal decisions. Some of the most famous economists work partly as policy advisers.

For example, Jagdish Bhagwati of Columbia University, whom you will meet on pp. 52–54, has advised governments and international organizations on trade and economic development issues. And leading Canadian economists David Laidler of the University of Western Ontario and Christopher Ragan of McGill University have spent time advising the Bank of Canada and the Department of Finance.

All the policy questions on which economists provide advice involve a blend of the positive and the normative. Economics can't help with the normative part—the policy goal. But for a given goal, economics provides a method of evaluating alternative solutions—comparing marginal benefits and marginal costs and finding the solution that makes the best use of the available resources.

REVIEW QUIZ

1 Distinguish between a positive statement and a normative statement and provide examples.
2 What is a model? Can you think of a model that you might use in your everyday life?
3 How do economists try to disentangle cause and effect?
4 How is economics used as a policy tool?

You can work these questions in Study Plan 1.4 and get instant feedback.

—— MyEconLab ◆

SUMMARY

Key Points

Definition of Economics (p. 2)

- All economic questions arise from scarcity—from the fact that wants exceed the resources available to satisfy them.
- Economics is the social science that studies the choices that people make as they cope with scarcity.
- The subject divides into microeconomics and macroeconomics.

Working Problem 1 will give you a better understanding of the definition of economics.

Two Big Economic Questions (pp. 3–7)

- Two big questions summarize the scope of economics:
    1. How do choices end up determining *what*, *how*, and *for whom* goods and services are produced?
    2. When do choices made in the pursuit of *self-interest* also promote the *social interest*?

Working Problems 2 and 3 will give you a better understanding of the two big questions of economics.

The Economic Way of Thinking (pp. 8–9)

- Every choice is a tradeoff—exchanging more of something for less of something else.
- People make rational choices by comparing benefit and cost.
- Benefit is the gain you get from something.
- Cost—*opportunity cost*—is what you must give up to get something.
- Most choices are made at the *margin* by comparing marginal benefit and marginal cost.
- Choices respond to incentives.

Working Problems 4 and 5 will give you a better understanding of the economic way of thinking.

Economics as Social Science and Policy Tool (p. 10)

- Economists distinguish between positive statements—what is—and normative statements—what ought to be.
- To explain the economic world, economists create and test economic models.
- Economics is a toolkit used to provide advice on government, business, and personal economic decisions.

Working Problem 6 will give you a better understanding of economics as social science and policy tool.

Key Terms

Benefit, 8	Margin, 9	SCAN THIS
Capital, 4	Marginal benefit, 9	
Economic model, 10	Marginal cost, 9	
Economics, 2	Microeconomics, 2	
Efficiency, 5	Opportunity cost, 8	
Entrepreneurship, 4	Preferences, 8	
Factors of production, 3	Profit, 4	
Goods and services, 3	Rational choice, 8	
Human capital, 3	Rent, 4	
Incentive, 2	Scarcity, 2	
Interest, 4	Self-interest, 5	
Labour, 3	Social interest, 5	
Land, 3	Tradeoff, 8	
Macroeconomics, 2	Wages, 4	

STUDY PLAN PROBLEMS AND APPLICATIONS

MyEconLab ◆ You can work Problems 1 to 6 in Chapter 1 Study Plan and get instant feedback.

Definition of Economics (Study Plan 1.1)

1. Apple Inc. decides to make iTunes freely available in unlimited quantities.
   a. Does Apple's decision change the incentives that people face?
   b. Is Apple's decision an example of a microeconomic or a macroeconomic issue?

Two Big Economic Questions (Study Plan 1.2)

2. Which of the following pairs does not match?
   a. Labour and wages
   b. Land and rent
   c. Entrepreneurship and profit
   d. Capital and profit

3. Explain how the following news headlines concern self-interest and the social interest.
   a. Starbucks Expands in China
   b. McDonald's Moves into Salads
   c. Food Must Be Labelled with Nutrition Data

The Economic Way of Thinking (Study Plan 1.3)

4. The night before an economics test, you decide to go to the movies instead of staying home and working your MyEconLab Study Plan. You get 50 percent on your test compared with the 70 percent that you normally score.
   a. Did you face a tradeoff?
   b. What was the opportunity cost of your evening at the movies?

5. **Costs Soar for London Olympics**
   The regeneration of East London, the site of the 2012 Olympic Games, is set to add extra £1.5 billion to taxpayers' bill.
   Source: *The Times*, London, July 6, 2006
   Is the cost of regenerating East London an opportunity cost of hosting the 2012 Olympic Games? Explain why or why not.

Economics as Social Science and Policy Tool (Study Plan 1.4)

6. Which of the following statements is positive, which is normative, and which can be tested?
   a. Russia to lift grain export ban.
   b. China is the largest trading partner of Canada.
   c. The federal government should increase the production of biofuels.

ADDITIONAL PROBLEMS AND APPLICATIONS

MyEconLab ◆ You can work these problems in MyEconLab if assigned by your instructor.

Definition of Economics

7. **Hundreds Line up for 5 p.m. Ticket Giveaway**
   By noon, hundreds of Eminem fans had lined up for a chance to score free tickets to the concert.
   Source: *Detroit Free Press*, May 18, 2009
   When Eminem gave away tickets, what was free and what was scarce? Explain your answer.

Two Big Economic Questions

8. How does the creation of a successful movie influence *what*, *how*, and *for whom* goods and services are produced?

9. How does a successful movie illustrate self-interested choices that are also in the social interest?

The Economic Way of Thinking

10. Last fall, Costco opened its gas bar at a busy intersection just off Highway 401 in Toronto. Since then the neighbourhood has been swamped with cars, as drivers come from far and away for discounts of 10 cents a litre.
    a. What is the opportunity cost of a litre of gas? Explain.
    b. To control the crowd, Costco hires traffic police. What is the tradeoff that Costco faces?

11. What might be an incentive for you to take a class in summer school? List some of the benefits and costs involved in your decision. Would your choice be rational?

Economics as Social Science and Policy Tool

12. Look at today's *Financial Post*. What is the leading economic news story? With which of the big economic questions does it deal and what tradeoffs does it discuss or imply?

13. Provide two microeconomic statements and two macroeconomic statements. Classify your statements as positive or normative. Explain why.

APPENDIX

Graphs in Economics

After studying this appendix, you will be able to

◆ Make and interpret a scatter diagram

◆ Identify linear and nonlinear relationships and relationships that have a maximum and a minimum

◆ Define and calculate the slope of a line

◆ Graph relationships among more than two variables

◆ Graphing Data

A graph represents a quantity as a distance on a line. In Fig. A1.1, a distance on the horizontal line represents temperature, measured in degrees Celsius. A movement from left to right shows an increase in temperature. The point 0 represents zero degrees Celsius. To the right of 0, the temperature is positive. To the left of 0, the temperature is negative (as indicated by the minus sign). A distance on the vertical line represents height, measured in thousands of metres. The point 0 represents sea level. Points above 0 represent metres above sea level. Points below 0 represent metres below sea level (indicated by a minus sign).

In Fig. A1.1, the two scale lines are perpendicular to each other and are called *axes*. The vertical line is the *y*-axis, and the horizontal line is the *x*-axis. Each axis has a zero point, which is shared by the two axes and called the *origin*.

To make a two-variable graph, we need two pieces of information: the value of the variable *x* and the value of the variable *y*. For example, off the coast of British Columbia, the temperature is 10 degrees—the value of *x*. A fishing boat is located at 0 metres above sea level—the value of *y*. These two bits of information appear as point *A* in Fig. A1.1. A climber at the top of Mount McKinley on a cold day is 6,194 metres above sea level in a zero-degree gale. These two pieces of information appear as point *B*. On a warmer day, a climber might be at the peak of Mt. McKinley when the temperature is 10 degrees, at point *C*.

We can draw two lines, called *coordinates*, from point *C*. One, called the *x*-coordinate, runs from

---

FIGURE A1.1   Making a Graph

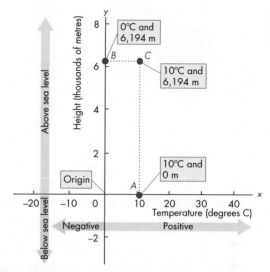

Graphs have axes that measure quantities as distances. Here, the horizontal axis (*x*-axis) measures temperature, and the vertical axis (*y*-axis) measures height. Point *A* represents a fishing boat at sea level (0 on the *y*-axis) on a day when the temperature is 10°C. Point *B* represents a climber at the top of Mt. McKinley, 6,194 metres above sea level in a zero-degree gale. Point *C* represents a climber at the top of Mt. McKinley, 6,194 metres above sea level, at a temperature of 10°C.

———————————— MyEconLab   animation ◆

C to the vertical axis. This line is called "the *x*-coordinate" because its length is the same as the value marked off on the *x*-axis. The other, called the *y*-coordinate, runs from *C* to the horizontal axis. This line is called "the *y*-coordinate" because its length is the same as the value marked off on the *y*-axis.

We describe a point on a graph by the values of its *x*-coordinate and its *y*-coordinate. For example, at point *C*, *x* is 10 degrees and *y* is 6,194 metres.

A graph like that in Fig. A1.1 can be made using any quantitative data on two variables. The graph can show just a few points, like Fig. A1.1, or many points. Before we look at graphs with many points, let's reinforce what you've just learned by looking at two graphs made with economic data.

Economists measure variables that describe *what, how,* and *for whom* goods and services are produced. These variables are quantities produced and prices. Figure A1.2 shows two examples of economic graphs.

FIGURE A1.2   Two Graphs of Economic Data

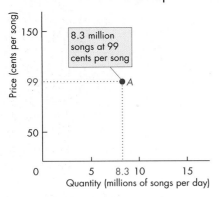

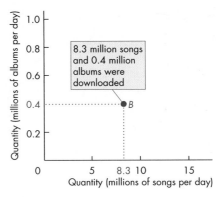

The graph in part (a) tells us that in January 2010, 8.3 million songs per day were downloaded from the iTunes store at a price of 99 cents a song.

The graph in part (b) tells us that in January 2010, 8.3 million songs per day and 0.4 million albums per day were downloaded from the iTunes store.

(a) iTunes downloads: quantity and price

(b) iTunes downloads: songs and albums

MyEconLab   animation

Figure A1.2(a) is a graph about iTunes song downloads in January 2010. The *x*-axis measures the quantity of songs downloaded per day and the *y*-axis measures the price of a song. Point *A* tells us what the quantity and price were. You can "read" this graph as telling you that in January 2010, 8.3 million songs a day were downloaded at a price of 99¢ per song.

Figure A1.2(b) is a graph about iTunes song and album downloads in January 2010. The *x*-axis measures the quantity of songs downloaded per day and the *y*-axis measures the quantity of albums downloaded per day. Point *B* tells us what these quantities were. You can "read" this graph as telling you that in January 2010, 8.3 million songs and 0.4 million albums a day were downloaded.

The three graphs that you've just seen tell you how to make a graph and how to read a data point on a graph, but they don't improve on the raw data. Graphs become interesting and revealing when they contain a number of data points because then you can visualize the data.

Economists create graphs based on the principles in Figs. A1.1 and A1.2 to reveal, describe, and visualize the relationships among variables. We're now going to look at some examples. These graphs are called scatter diagrams.

Scatter Diagrams

A **scatter diagram** is a graph that plots the value of one variable against the value of another variable for a number of different values of each variable. Such a graph reveals whether a relationship exists between two variables and describes their relationship.

Movies and DVDs The table in Fig. A1.3 shows some data on two variables: the number of tickets sold at the box office and the number of DVDs sold for eight of the most popular movies in 2009.

What is the relationship between these two variables? Does a big box office success generate a large volume of DVD sales? Or does a box office success mean that fewer DVDs are sold?

We can answer these questions by making a scatter diagram. We do so by graphing the data in the table. In the graph in Fig. A1.3, each point shows the number of box office tickets sold (the *x* variable) and the number of DVDs sold (the *y* variable) of one of the movies. There are eight movies, so there are eight points "scattered" within the graph.

The point labelled *A* tells us that *Star Trek* sold 34 million tickets at the box office and 6 million DVDs. The points in the graph form a pattern, which reveals that larger box office sales are associated with larger DVD sales. But the points also tell us that this association is weak. You can't predict DVD sales with any confidence by knowing only the number of tickets sold at the box office.

Two Economic Examples Figure A1.4 shows two scatter diagrams of economic variables. Part (a) shows the relationship between income and expenditure in Canada from 2001 to 2010. Each point represents income and expenditure in a given year. For example, point *A* shows that in 2006, income was $26,000 and expenditure was $24,000. This graph shows that as income increases, so does expenditure, and the relationship is a close one.

FIGURE A1.3   Scatter Diagram

Movie	Tickets	DVDs
	(millions)	
Twilight	38	10
Transformers: Revenge of the Fallen	54	9
Up	39	8
Harry Potter and the Half-Blood Prince	40	7
Star Trek	34	6
The Hangover	37	6
Ice Age: Dawn of the Dinosaurs	26	5
The Proposal	22	5

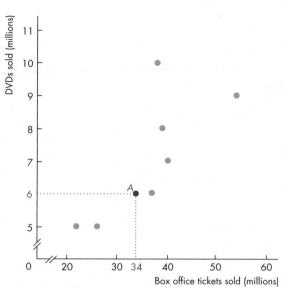

The table lists the number of tickets sold at the box office and the number of DVDs sold for eight popular movies. The scatter diagram reveals the relationship between these two variables. Each point shows the values of the two variables for a specific movie. For example, point A shows the point for *Star Trek*, which sold 34 million tickets at the box office and 6 million DVDs. The pattern formed by the points shows that there is a tendency for large box office sales to bring greater DVD sales. But you couldn't predict how many DVDs a movie would sell just by knowing its box office sales.

MyEconLab   animation

Figure A1.4(b) shows a scatter diagram of Canadian unemployment and inflation from 2000 to 2010. In 2005, the unemployment rate was 7 percent and the inflation rate was 1.6 percent at point *B*. The data here show a loose negative relationship between the two variables. Higher unemployment is loosely associated with lower inflation.

You can see that a scatter diagram conveys a wealth of information, and it does so in much less space than we have used to describe only some of its features. But you do have to "read" the graph to obtain all this information.

FIGURE A1.4   Two Economic Scatter Diagrams

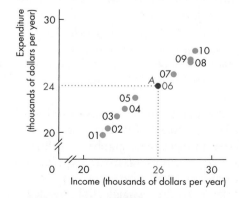

(a) Income and expenditure

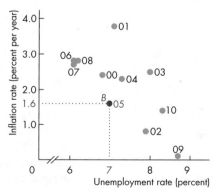

(b) Unemployment and inflation

The scatter diagram in part (a) shows the relationship between income and expenditure from 2001 to 2010. Point A shows that in 2006, income was $26,000 on the x-axis and expenditure was $24,000 on the y-axis. This graph shows that as income increases, so does expenditure, and the relationship is a close one.

The scatter diagram in part (b) shows a loose negative relationship between unemployment and inflation in Canada during the 2000s.

MyEconLab   animation

Breaks in the Axes The graph in Fig. A1.4(a) has breaks in its axes, as shown by the small gaps. The breaks indicate that there are jumps from the origin, 0, to the first values recorded.

The breaks are used because the lowest values of income and expenditure exceed $18,000. If we made this graph with no breaks in its axes, there would be a lot of empty space, all the points would be crowded into the top right corner, and it would be difficult to see whether a relationship exists between these two variables. By breaking the axes, we are able to bring the relationship into view.

Putting a break in one or both axes is like using a zoom lens to bring the relationship into the centre of the graph and magnify it so that the relationship fills the graph.

Misleading Graphs Breaks can be used to highlight a relationship, but they can also be used to mislead—to make a graph that lies. The most common way of making a graph lie is to put a break in the axis and either to stretch or compress the scale. For example, suppose that in Fig. A1.4(a), the *y*-axis that measures expenditure ran from zero to $30,000 while the *x*-axis was the same as the one shown. The graph would now create the impression that despite a huge increase in income, expenditure had barely changed.

To avoid being misled, it is a good idea to get into the habit of always looking closely at the values and the labels on the axes of a graph before you start to interpret it.

Correlation and Causation A scatter diagram that shows a clear relationship between two variables, such as the one in Fig. A1.4(a), tells us that the two variables have a high correlation. When a high correlation is present, we can predict the value of one variable from the value of the other variable. But correlation does not imply causation.

Sometimes a high correlation is a coincidence, but sometimes it does arise from a causal relationship. It is likely, for example, that rising income causes rising expenditure (Fig. A1.4a) and that a high unemployment rate makes for a slack economy in which prices don't rise quickly, so the inflation rate is low (Fig. A1.4b).

You've now seen how we can use graphs in economics to show economic data and to reveal relationships. Next, we'll learn how economists use graphs to construct and display economic models.

◆ Graphs Used in Economic Models

The graphs used in economics are not always designed to show real-world data. Often they are used to show general relationships among the variables in an economic model.

An *economic model* is a stripped-down, simplified description of an economy or of a component of an economy such as a business or a household. It consists of statements about economic behaviour that can be expressed as equations or as curves in a graph. Economists use models to explore the effects of different policies or other influences on the economy in ways that are similar to the use of model airplanes in wind tunnels and models of the climate.

You will encounter many different kinds of graphs in economic models, but there are some repeating patterns. Once you've learned to recognize these patterns, you will instantly understand the meaning of a graph. Here, we'll look at the different types of curves that are used in economic models, and we'll see some everyday examples of each type of curve. The patterns to look for in graphs are the following four cases:

- Variables that move in the same direction
- Variables that move in opposite directions
- Variables that have a maximum or a minimum
- Variables that are unrelated

Let's look at these four cases.

Variables That Move in the Same Direction

Figure A1.5 shows graphs of the relationships between two variables that move up and down together. A relationship between two variables that move in the same direction is called a **positive relationship** or a **direct relationship**. A line that slopes upward shows such a relationship.

Figure A1.5 shows three types of relationships: one that has a straight line and two that have curved lines. All the lines in these three graphs are called curves. Any line on a graph—no matter whether it is straight or curved—is called a *curve*.

A relationship shown by a straight line is called a **linear relationship**. Figure A1.5(a) shows a linear relationship between the number of kilometres travelled in 5 hours and speed. For example, point *A* shows that we will travel 200 kilometres in 5 hours if our speed is 40 kilometres an hour. If we double our speed to 80 kilometres an hour, we will travel 400 kilometres in 5 hours.

Figure A1.5(b) shows the relationship between distance sprinted and recovery time (the time it takes the heart rate to return to its normal resting rate). This relationship is an upward-sloping one that starts out quite flat but then becomes steeper as we move along the curve away from the origin. The reason this curve becomes steeper is that the additional recovery time needed from sprinting an additional 100 metres increases. It takes less than 5 minutes to recover from sprinting 100 metres but more than 10 minutes to recover from 200 metres.

Figure A1.5(c) shows the relationship between the number of problems worked by a student and the amount of study time. This relationship is an upward-sloping one that starts out quite steep and becomes flatter as we move along the curve away from the origin. Study time becomes less productive as the student spends more hours studying and becomes more tired.

Variables That Move in Opposite Directions

Some variables move in opposite directions. Figure A1.6 shows relationships between such variables. When variables move in opposite directions there is a **negative relationship** or an **inverse relationship**.

Figure A1.6(a) shows the relationship between the hours spent playing squash and the hours spent playing tennis when the total time available is 5 hours. One extra hour spent playing tennis means one hour less spent playing squash and vice versa. This relationship is negative and linear.

Figure A1.6(b) shows the relationship between the cost per kilometre travelled and the length of a journey. The longer the journey, the lower is the cost per kilometre. But as the journey length increases, even though the cost per kilometre decreases, the fall in the cost is smaller the longer the journey. This feature of the relationship is shown by the fact that the curve slopes downward, starting out steep at a short journey length and then becoming flatter as the journey length increases. This relationship arises because some of the costs are fixed, such as auto insurance, and the fixed costs are spread over a longer journey.

FIGURE A1.5   Positive (Direct) Relationships

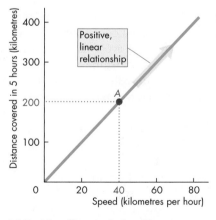

(a) Positive, linear relationship

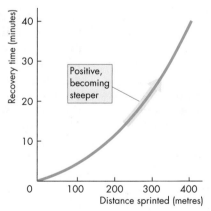

(b) Positive, becoming steeper

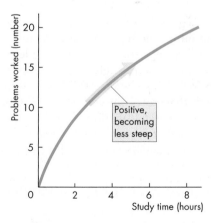

(c) Positive, becoming less steep

Each part shows a positive (direct) relationship between two variables. That is, as the value of the variable measured on the x-axis increases, so does the value of the variable measured on the y-axis. Part (a) shows a linear positive relationship—as the two variables increase together, we move along a straight line.

Part (b) shows a positive relationship such that as the two variables increase together, we move along a curve that becomes steeper.

Part (c) shows a positive relationship such that as the two variables increase together, we move along a curve that becomes flatter.

FIGURE A1.6   Negative (Inverse) Relationships

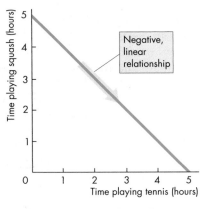

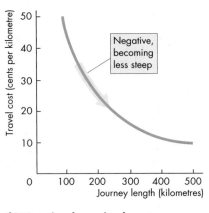

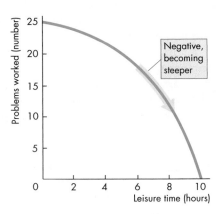

(a) Negative, linear relationship   **(b) Negative, becoming less steep**   **(c) Negative, becoming steeper**

Each part shows a negative (inverse) relationship between two variables. Part (a) shows a linear negative relationship. The total time spent playing tennis and squash is 5 hours. As the time spent playing tennis increases, the time spent playing squash decreases, and we move along a straight line.

Part (b) shows a negative relationship such that as the journey length increases, the travel cost decreases as we move along a curve that becomes less steep.

Part (c) shows a negative relationship such that as leisure time increases, the number of problems worked decreases as we move along a curve that becomes steeper.

MyEconLab   animation ◆

Figure A1.6(c) shows the relationship between the amount of leisure time and the number of problems worked by a student. Increasing leisure time produces an increasingly large reduction in the number of problems worked. This relationship is a negative one that starts out with a gentle slope at a small number of leisure hours and becomes steeper as the number of leisure hours increases. This relationship is a different view of the idea shown in Fig. A1.5(c).

Variables That Have a Maximum or a Minimum

Many relationships in economic models have a maximum or a minimum. For example, firms try to make the maximum possible profit and to produce at the lowest possible cost. Figure A1.7 shows relationships that have a maximum or a minimum.

Figure A1.7(a) shows the relationship between rainfall and wheat yield. When there is no rainfall, wheat will not grow, so the yield is zero. As the rainfall increases up to 10 days a month, the wheat yield increases. With 10 rainy days a month, the wheat

yield reaches its maximum at 2 tonnes per hectare (point *A*). Rain in excess of 10 days a month starts to lower the yield of wheat. If every day is rainy, the wheat suffers from a lack of sunshine and the yield decreases to zero. This relationship is one that starts out sloping upward, reaches a maximum, and then slopes downward.

Figure A1.7(b) shows the reverse case—a relationship that begins sloping downward, falls to a minimum, and then slopes upward. Most economic costs are like this relationship. An example is the relationship between the gasoline cost per kilometre and speed for a car trip. At low speeds, the car is creeping in a traffic snarl-up. The number of kilometres per litre is low, so the gasoline cost per kilometre is high. At high speeds, the car is travelling faster than its efficient speed, using a large quantity of gasoline, and again the number of kilometres per litre is low and the gasoline cost per kilometre is high. At a speed of 100 kilometres an hour, the gasoline cost per kilometre is at its minimum (point *B*). This relationship is one that starts out sloping downward, reaches a minimum, and then slopes upward.

FIGURE A1.7   Maximum and Minimum Points

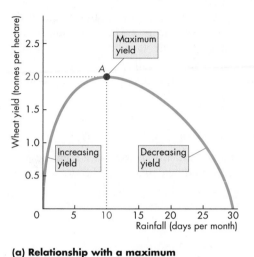

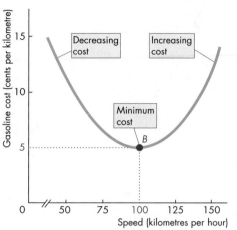

(a) Relationship with a maximum

(b) Relationship with a minimum

Part (a) shows a relationship that has a maximum point, *A*. The curve slopes upward as it rises to its maximum point, is flat at its maximum, and then slopes downward.

Part (b) shows a relationship with a minimum point, *B*. The curve slopes downward as it falls to its minimum, is flat at its minimum, and then slopes upward.

MyEconLab animation ◆

Variables That Are Unrelated

There are many situations in which no matter what happens to the value of one variable, the other variable remains constant. Sometimes we want to show the independence between two variables in a graph. Figure A1.8 shows two ways of achieving this.

In describing the graphs in Fig. A1.5 through Fig. A1.7, we have talked about curves that slope upward or downward, and curves that become less steep or steeper. Let's spend a little time discussing exactly what we mean by *slope* and how we measure the slope of a curve.

FIGURE A1.8   Variables That Are Unrelated

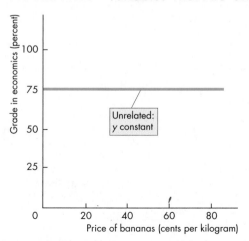

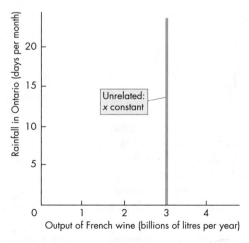

(a) Unrelated: *y* constant

(b) Unrelated: *x* constant

This figure shows how we can graph two variables that are unrelated. In part (a), a student's grade in economics is plotted at 75 percent on the *y*-axis regardless of the price of bananas on the *x*-axis. The curve is horizontal.

In part (b), the output of the vineyards of France on the *x*-axis does not vary with the rainfall in Ontario on the *y*-axis. The curve is vertical.

MyEconLab animation ◆

◆ The Slope of a Relationship

We can measure the influence of one variable on another by the slope of the relationship. The **slope** of a relationship is the change in the value of the variable measured on the *y*-axis divided by the change in the value of the variable measured on the *x*-axis. We use the Greek letter Δ (*delta*) to represent "change in." Thus Δ*y* means the change in the value of the variable measured on the *y*-axis, and Δ*x* means the change in the value of the variable measured on the *x*-axis. Therefore the slope of the relationship is

$$\text{Slope} = \frac{\Delta y}{\Delta x}.$$

If a large change in the variable measured on the *y*-axis (Δ*y*) is associated with a small change in the variable measured on the *x*-axis (Δ*x*), the slope is large and the curve is steep. If a small change in the variable measured on the *y*-axis (Δ*y*) is associated with a large change in the variable measured on the *x*-axis (Δ*x*), the slope is small and the curve is flat.

We can make the idea of slope clearer by doing some calculations.

The Slope of a Straight Line

The slope of a straight line is the same regardless of where on the line you calculate it. The slope of a straight line is constant. Let's calculate the slope of the positive relationship in Fig. A1.9. In part (a),

FIGURE A1.9   The Slope of a Straight Line

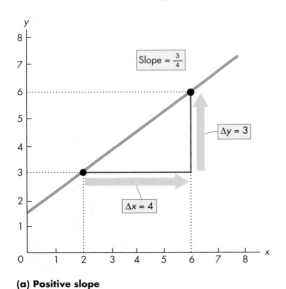

(a) Positive slope

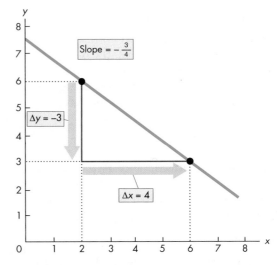

(b) Negative slope

To calculate the slope of a straight line, we divide the change in the value of the variable measured on the *y*-axis (Δ*y*) by the change in the value of the variable measured on the *x*-axis (Δ*x*) as we move along the line.

　　Part (a) shows the calculation of a positive slope. When *x* increases from 2 to 6, Δ*x* equals 4. That change

in *x* brings about an increase in *y* from 3 to 6, so Δ*y* equals 3. The slope (Δ*y*/Δ*x*) equals 3/4.

　　Part (b) shows the calculation of a negative slope. When *x* increases from 2 to 6, Δ*x* equals 4. That increase in *x* brings about a decrease in *y* from 6 to 3, so Δ*y* equals –3. The slope (Δ*y*/Δ*x*) equals –3/4.

MyEconLab animation ◆

when x increases from 2 to 6, y increases from 3 to 6. The change in x is +4—that is, Δx is 4. The change in y is +3—that is, Δy is 3. The slope of that line is

$$\frac{\Delta y}{\Delta x} = \frac{3}{4}.$$

In part (b), when x increases from 2 to 6, y decreases from 6 to 3. The change in y is *minus* 3—that is, y is −3. The change in x is *plus* 4—that is, Δx is 4. The slope of the curve is

$$\frac{\Delta y}{\Delta x} = \frac{-3}{4}.$$

Notice that the two slopes have the same magnitude (3/4), but the slope of the line in part (a) is positive (+3/+4 = 3/4) while that in part (b) is negative (−3/+4 = −3/4). The slope of a positive relationship is positive; the slope of a negative relationship is negative.

The Slope of a Curved Line

The slope of a curved line is trickier. The slope of a curved line is not constant, so the slope depends on where on the curved line we calculate it. There are two ways to calculate the slope of a curved line: You can calculate the slope at a point, or you can calculate the slope across an arc of the curve. Let's look at the two alternatives.

Slope at a Point To calculate the slope at a point on a curve, you need to construct a straight line that has the same slope as the curve at the point in question. Figure A1.10 shows how this is done. Suppose you want to calculate the slope of the curve at point A. Place a ruler on the graph so that the ruler touches point A and no other point on the curve, then draw a straight line along the edge of the ruler. The straight red line is this line, and it is the tangent to the curve at point A. If the ruler touches the curve only at point A, then the slope of the curve at point A must be the same as the slope of the edge of the ruler. If the curve and the ruler do not have the same slope, the line along the edge of the ruler will cut the curve instead of just touching it.

Now that you have found a straight line with the same slope as the curve at point A, you can calculate the slope of the curve at point A by calculating the slope of the straight line. Along the straight line, as x

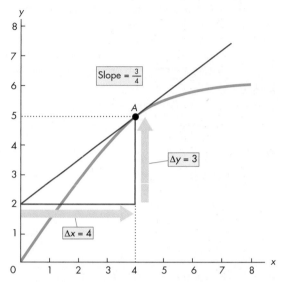

FIGURE A1.10   Slope at a Point

Slope = $\frac{3}{4}$

$\Delta y = 3$

$\Delta x = 4$

To calculate the slope of the curve at point A, draw the red line that just touches the curve at A—the tangent. The slope of this straight line is calculated by dividing the change in y by the change in x along the red line. When x increases from 0 to 4, Δx equals 4. That change in x is associated with an increase in y from 2 to 5, so Δy equals 3. The slope of the red line is 3/4, so the slope of the curve at point A is 3/4.

——————— MyEconLab   animation ◆

increases from 0 to 4 (Δx is 4) y increases from 2 to 5 (Δy is 3). Therefore the slope of the straight line is

$$\frac{\Delta y}{\Delta x} = \frac{3}{4}.$$

So the slope of the curve at point A is 3/4.

Slope Across an Arc An arc of a curve is a piece of a curve. Figure A1.11 shows the same curve as in Fig. A1.10, but instead of calculating the slope at point A, we are now going to calculate the slope across the arc from point B to point C. You can see that the slope of the curve at point B is greater than at point C. When we calculate the slope across an arc, we are calculating the average slope between two points. As we move along the arc from B to C, x increases from 3 to 5 and y increases from 4.0 to 5.5. The change in x is 2 (Δx is 2), and the change in y is 1.5 (Δy is 1.5).

FIGURE A1.11   Slope Across an Arc

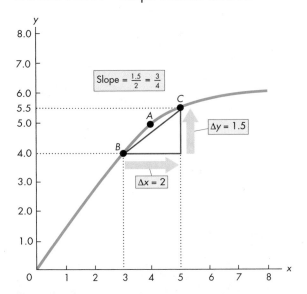

To calculate the average slope of the curve along the arc *BC*, draw a straight line from point *B* to point *C*. The slope of the line *BC* is calculated by dividing the change in *y* by the change in *x*. In moving from *B* to *C*, the increase in *x* is 2 (Δ*x* equals 2) and the change in *y* is 1.5 (Δ*y* equals 1.5). The slope of the line *BC* is 1.5 divided by 2, or 3/4. So the slope of the curve across the arc *BC* is 3/4.

─────── MyEconLab animation ◆

Therefore the slope is

$$\frac{\Delta y}{\Delta x} = \frac{1.5}{2} = \frac{3}{4}.$$

So the slope of the curve across the arc *BC* is 3/4.

This calculation gives us the slope of the curve between points *B* and *C*. The actual slope calculated is the slope of the straight red line from *B* to *C*. This slope approximates the average slope of the curve along the arc *BC*. In this particular example, the slope across the arc *BC* is identical to the slope of the curve at point *A*, but the calculation of the slope of a curve does not always work out so neatly. You might have fun constructing some more examples and a few counter examples.

You now know how to make and interpret a graph. So far, we've limited our attention to graphs of two variables. We're now going to learn how to graph more than two variables.

Graphing Relationships Among More Than Two Variables

We have seen that we can graph the relationship between two variables as a point formed by the *x*- and *y*-coordinates in a two-dimensional graph. You might be thinking that although a two-dimensional graph is informative, most of the things in which you are likely to be interested involve relationships among many variables, not just two. For example, the amount of ice cream consumed depends on the price of ice cream and the temperature. If ice cream is expensive and the temperature is low, people eat much less ice cream than when ice cream is inexpensive and the temperature is high. For any given price of ice cream, the quantity consumed varies with the temperature; and for any given temperature, the quantity of ice cream consumed varies with its price.

Figure A1.12 shows a relationship among three variables. The table shows the number of litres of ice cream consumed each day at two different temperatures and at a number of different prices of ice cream. How can we graph these numbers?

To graph a relationship that involves more than two variables, we use the *ceteris paribus* assumption.

Ceteris Paribus

Ceteris paribus (often shortened to *cet par*) means "if all other relevant things remain the same." To isolate the relationship of interest in a laboratory experiment, a scientist holds everything constant except for the variable whose effect is being studied. Economists use the same method to graph a relationship that has more than two variables.

Figure A1.12 shows an example. There, you can see what happens to the quantity of ice cream consumed when the price of ice cream varies but the temperature is held constant.

The curve labelled 21°C shows the relationship between ice cream consumption and the price of ice cream if the temperature remains at 21°C. The numbers used to plot that curve are those in the first two columns of the table. For example, if the temperature is 21°C, 10 litres of ice cream are consumed when the price is $2.75 a scoop and 18 litres are consumed when the price is $2.25 a scoop.

The curve labelled 32°C shows the relationship between ice cream consumption and the price of ice cream if the temperature remains at 32°C. The

FIGURE A1.12   Graphing a Relationship Among Three Variables

Price (dollars per scoop)	Ice cream consumption (litres per day)	
	21°C	**32°C**
2.00	25	50
2.25	18	36
2.50	13	26
2.75	**10**	**20**
3.00	7	14
3.25	5	10
3.50	3	6

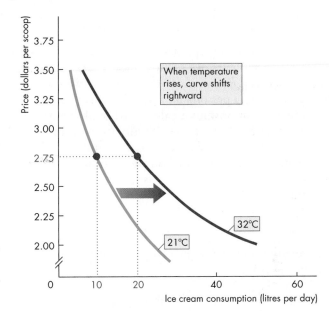

Ice cream consumption depends on its price and the temperature. The table tells us how many litres of ice cream are consumed each day at different prices and two different temperatures. For example, if the price is $2.75 a scoop and the temperature is 21°C, 10 litres of ice cream are consumed.

To graph a relationship among three variables, the value of one variable is held constant. The graph shows the relationship between price and consumption when temperature is held constant. One curve holds temperature at 21°C and the other holds it at 32°C.

A change in the price of ice cream brings a movement along one of the curves—along the blue curve at 21°C and along the red curve at 32°C.

When the temperature *rises* from 21°C to 32°C, the curve that shows the relationship between consumption and price *shifts* rightward from the blue curve to the red curve.

MyEconLab   animation ◆

numbers used to plot that curve are those in the first and third columns of the table. For example, if the temperature is 32°C, 20 litres are consumed when the price is $2.75 a scoop and 36 litres are consumed when the price is $2.25 a scoop.

When the price of ice cream changes but the temperature is constant, you can think of what happens in the graph as a movement along one of the curves. At 21°C there is a movement along the blue curve; at 32°C there is a movement along the red curve.

When Other Things Change

The temperature is held constant along each of the curves in Fig. A1.12, but in reality the temperature changes. When that event occurs, you can think of

what happens in the graph as a shift of the curve. When the temperature rises from 21°C to 32°C, the curve that shows the relationship between ice cream consumption and the price of ice cream shifts rightward from the blue curve to the red curve.

You will encounter these ideas of movements along and shifts of curves at many points in your study of economics. Think carefully about what you've just learned and make up some examples (with assumed numbers) about other relationships.

With what you have learned about graphs, you can move forward with your study of economics. There are no graphs in this book that are more complicated than those that have been explained in this appendix.

MATHEMATICAL NOTE

Equations of Straight Lines

If a straight line in a graph describes the relationship between two variables, we call it a linear relationship. Figure 1 shows a *linear relationship* between two economic variables: a person's income and expenditure.

All linear relationships are described by the same general equation. We call the quantity that is measured on the horizontal axis (or *x*-axis) *x*, and we call the quantity that is measured on the vertical axis (or *y*-axis) *y*. In the case of Fig. 1, *x* is income and *y* is expenditure.

A Linear Equation

The equation that describes a straight-line relationship between *x* and *y* is

$$y = a + bx.$$

In this equation, *a* and *b* are fixed numbers and they are called *constants*. The values of *x* and *y* vary, so these numbers are called *variables*. Because the equation describes a straight line, the equation is called a linear equation.

The equation tells us that when the value of *x* is zero, the value of *y* is *a*. We call the constant *a* the *y*-axis intercept. The reason is that on the graph the straight line hits the *y*-axis at a value equal to *a*. Figure 1 illustrates the *y*-axis intercept.

For positive values of *x*, the value of *y* exceeds *a*. The constant *b* tells us by how much *y* increases above *a* as *x* increases. The constant *b* is the slope of the line.

Slope of Line

As we explain in the chapter, the slope of a relationship is the change in the value of *y* divided by the change in the value of *x*. We use the Greek letter Δ (delta) to represent "change in." So Δy means the change in the value of the variable measured on the *y*-axis, and Δx means the change in the value of the variable measured on the *x*-axis. Therefore the slope of the relationship is

$$\text{Slope} = \frac{\Delta y}{\Delta x}.$$

To see why the slope is *b*, suppose that initially the value of *x* is x_1, or $200 in Fig. 2. The corresponding value of *y* is y_1, also $200 in Fig. 2. The equation of the line tells us that

$$y_1 = a + bx_1. \tag{1}$$

Now the value of Δx increases by *x* to $x_1 + \Delta x$ (or $400 in Fig. 2). And the value of *y* increases by Δy to $y_1 + \Delta y$ (or $300 in Fig. 2).

The equation of the line now tells us that

$$y_1 + \Delta y = a + b(x_1 + \Delta x). \tag{2}$$

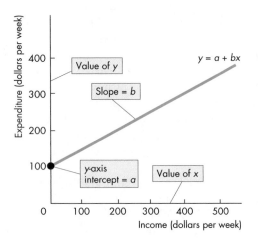

Figure 1 Linear relationship

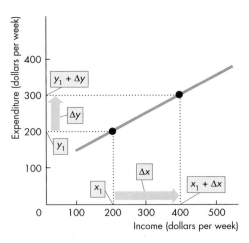

Figure 2 Calculating slope

To calculate the slope of the line, subtract equation (1) from equation (2) to obtain

$$\Delta y = b\Delta x \qquad (3)$$

and now divide equation (3) by x to obtain

$$\Delta y/\Delta x = b.$$

So the slope of the line is b.

Position of Line

The y-axis intercept determines the position of the line on the graph. Figure 3 illustrates the relationship between the y-axis intercept and the position of the line. In this graph, the y-axis measures saving and the x-axis measures income.

When the y-axis intercept, a, is positive, the line hits the y-axis at a positive value of y—as the blue line does. Its y-axis intercept is 100. When the y-axis intercept, a, is zero, the line hits the y-axis at the origin—as the purple line does. Its y-axis intercept is 0. When the y-axis intercept, a, is negative, the line hits the y-axis at a negative value of y—as the red line does. Its y-axis intercept is –100.

As the equations of the three lines show, the value of the y-axis intercept does not influence the slope of the line. All three lines have a slope equal to 0.5.

Positive Relationships

Figure 1 shows a positive relationship—the two variables x and y move in the same direction. All positive relationships have a slope that is positive. In the equation of the line, the constant b is positive. In this example, the y-axis intercept, a, is 100. The slope b equals $\Delta y/\Delta x$, which in Fig. 2 is 100/200 or 0.5. The equation of the line is

$$y = 100 + 0.5x.$$

Negative Relationships

Figure 4 shows a negative relationship—the two variables x and y move in opposite directions. All negative relationships have a slope that is negative. In the equation of the line, the constant b is negative. In the example in Fig. 4, the y-axis intercept, a, is 30. The slope, b, equals $\Delta y/\Delta x$, which is –20/2 or –10. The equation of the line is

$$y = 30 + (-10)x$$

or

$$y = 30 - 10x.$$

Example

A straight line has a y-axis intercept of 50 and a slope of 2. What is the equation of this line?

The equation of a straight line is

$$y = a + bx$$

where a is the y-axis intercept and b is the slope. So the equation is

$$y = 50 + 2x.$$

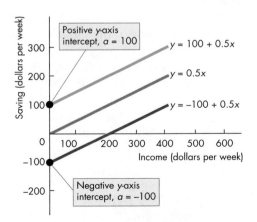

Figure 3 The y-axis intercept

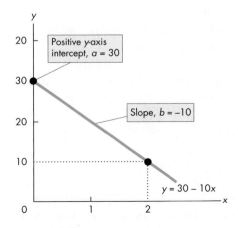

Figure 4 Negative relationship

REVIEW QUIZ

1 Explain how we "read" the three graphs in Figs. A1.1 and A1.2.
2 Explain what scatter diagrams show and why we use them.
3 Explain how we "read" the three scatter diagrams in Figs. A1.3 and A1.4.
4 Draw a graph to show the relationship between two variables that move in the same direction.
5 Draw a graph to show the relationship between two variables that move in opposite directions.
6 Draw a graph to show the relationship between two variables that have a maximum and a minimum.

7 Which of the relationships in Questions 4 and 5 is a positive relationship and which is a negative relationship?
8 What are the two ways of calculating the slope of a curved line?
9 How do we graph a relationship among more than two variables?
10 Explain what change will bring a *movement along* a curve.
11 Explain what change will bring a *shift* of a curve.

You can work these questions in Study Plan 1.A and get instant feedback.

——————————————————— MyEconLab ◆

SUMMARY

Key Points

Graphing Data (pp. 13–16)

■ A graph is made by plotting the values of two variables x and y at a point that corresponds to their values measured along the x-axis and the y-axis.

■ A scatter diagram is a graph that plots the values of two variables for a number of different values of each.

■ A scatter diagram shows the relationship between the two variables. It shows whether they are positively related, negatively related, or unrelated.

Graphs Used in Economic Models (pp. 16–19)

■ Graphs are used to show relationships among variables in economic models.

■ Relationships can be positive (an upward-sloping curve), negative (a downward-sloping curve), positive and then negative (have a maximum point), negative and then positive (have a minimum point), or unrelated (a horizontal or vertical curve).

The Slope of a Relationship (pp. 20–22)

■ The slope of a relationship is calculated as the change in the value of the variable measured on the y-axis divided by the change in the value of the variable measured on the x-axis—that is, $\Delta y/\Delta x$.

■ A straight line has a constant slope.

■ A curved line has a varying slope. To calculate the slope of a curved line, we calculate the slope at a point or across an arc.

Graphing Relationships Among More Than Two Variables (pp. 22–23)

■ To graph a relationship among more than two variables, we hold constant the values of all the variables except two.

■ We then plot the value of one of the variables against the value of another.

■ A *cet par* change in the value of a variable on an axis of a graph brings a movement along the curve.

■ A change in the value of a variable held constant along the curve brings a shift of the curve.

Key Terms

Ceteris paribus, 22
Direct relationship, 16
Inverse relationship, 17
Linear relationship, 16

Negative relationship, 17
Positive relationship, 16
Scatter diagram, 14
Slope, 20

SCAN THIS

STUDY PLAN PROBLEMS AND APPLICATIONS

MyEconLab ◆ You can work Problems 1 to 11 in Chapter 1A Study Plan and get instant feedback.

Use the following spreadsheet to work Problems 1 to 3. The spreadsheet provides the economic data: Column A is the year, column B is the inflation rate, column C is the interest rate, column D is the growth rate, and column E is the unemployment rate.

	A	B	C	D	E
1	2000	2.4	4.3	5.7	6.8
2	2001	3.8	3.5	3.1	7.1
3	2002	0.8	2.4	2.1	7.9
4	2003	2.5	2.5	2.7	8.0
5	2004	2.3	1.8	1.8	7.3
6	2005	1.6	2.1	3.3	7.0
7	2006	2.8	2.8	3.9	6.1
8	2007	2.7	2.9	1.5	6.1
9	2008	2.8	2.1	1.7	6.2
10	2009	0.1	0.8	–2.5	8.7
11	2010	1.4	1.0	2.2	8.3

1. Draw a scatter diagram of the inflation rate and the interest rate. Describe the relationship.

2. Draw a scatter diagram of the growth rate and the unemployment rate. Describe the relationship.

3. Draw a scatter diagram of the interest rate and the unemployment rate. Describe the relationship.

Use the following news clip to work Problems 4 to 6.

Clash of the Titans Tops Box Office With Sales of $61.2 Million:

Movie	Theatres (number)	Revenue (dollars per theatre)
Clash of the Titans	3,777	16,213
Tyler Perry's Why Did I Get Married	2,155	13,591
How To Train Your Dragon	4,060	7,145
The Last Song	2,673	5,989

Source: Bloomberg.com, April 5, 2010

4. Draw a graph of the relationship between the revenue per theatre on the *y*-axis and the number of theatres on the *x*-axis. Describe the relationship.

5. Calculate the slope of the relationship between 4,060 and 2,673 theatres.

6. Calculate the slope of the relationship between 2,155 and 4,060 theatres.

7. Calculate the slope of the following relationship.

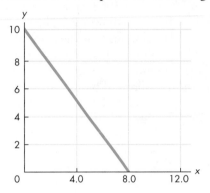

Use the following relationship to work Problems 8 and 9.

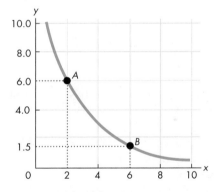

8. Calculate the slope of the relationship at point *A* and at point *B*.

9. Calculate the slope across the arc *AB*.

Use the following table to work Problems 10 and 11. The table gives the price of a balloon ride, the temperature, and the number of rides a day.

Price (dollars per ride)	Balloon rides (number per day)		
	10°C	20°C	30°C
5	32	40	50
10	27	32	40
15	18	27	32

10. Draw a graph to show the relationship between the price and the number of rides, when the temperature is 20°C. Describe this relationship.

11. What happens in the graph in Problem 10 if the temperature rises to 30°C?

ADDITIONAL ASSIGNABLE PROBLEMS AND APPLICATIONS

MyEconLab ◆ You can work these problems in MyEconLab if assigned by your instructor.

Use the following spreadsheet to work Problems 12 to 14. The spreadsheet provides data on oil and gasoline: Column A is the year, column B is the price of oil (dollars per barrel), column C is the price of gasoline (cents per litre), column D is quantity of crude oil produced, and column E is the quantity of gasoline refined (both in millions of barrels per day).

	A	B	C	D	E
1	1999	24	29	5.9	8.1
2	2000	30	38	5.8	8.2
3	2001	17	37	5.8	8.3
4	2002	24	35	5.7	8.4
5	2003	27	40	5.7	8.5
6	2004	37	47	5.4	8.7
7	2005	49	58	5.2	8.7
8	2006	56	65	5.1	8.9
9	2007	86	71	5.1	9.0
10	2008	43	82	5.0	8.9
11	2009	76	60	4.9	8.9

12. Draw a scatter diagram of the price of oil and the quantity of crude oil produced. Describe the relationship.

13. Draw a scatter diagram of the price of gasoline and the quantity of gasoline refined. Describe the relationship.

14. Draw a scatter diagram of the quantity of crude oil produced and the quantity of gasoline refined. Describe the relationship.

Use the following data to work Problems 15 to 17. Draw a graph that shows the relationship between the two variables x and y:

x	0	1	2	3	4	5
y	25	24	22	18	12	0

15. a. Is the relationship between the two variables positive or negative?
    b. Does the slope of the relationship become steeper or flatter as the value of x increases?
    c. Think of some economic relationships that might be similar to this one.

16. Calculate the slope of the relationship between the two variables when x equals 3.

17. Calculate the slope of the relationship across the arc as x increases from 4 to 5.

18. Calculate the slope of the curve at point A.

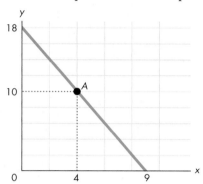

Use the following curve to work Problems 19 and 20.

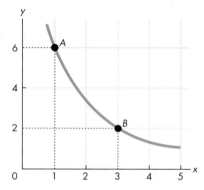

19. Calculate the slope at point A and at point B.

20. Calculate the slope across the arc AB.

Use the following table to work Problems 21 to 23. The table gives the price of an umbrella, the number purchased, and rainfall in millimetres (mm).

Price	Umbrellas purchased (number per day)		
(dollars per umbrella)	0 mm	200 mm	400 mm
20	4	7	8
30	2	4	7
40	1	2	4

21. Draw a graph to show the relationship between the price and the number of umbrellas purchased, holding the amount of rainfall constant at 200 mm. Describe this relationship.

22. What happens in the graph in Problem 21 if the price rises and rainfall is constant?

23. What happens in the graph in Problem 21 if the rainfall increases from 200 mm to 400 mm?

Grown for Biofuel

The Economic Problem

After studying this chapter,
you will be able to

◆ Define the production possibilities
frontier and use it to calculate opportunity
cost

◆ Distinguish between production possibilities and preferences and define efficiency

◆ Explain how current production choices
expand future production possibilities

◆ Explain how specialization and trade
expand production possibilities

◆ Describe the economic institutions that
coordinate decisions

Why does food cost much more today than it did a few years ago? One
reason is that we're using corn to produce biofuel—ethanol. Another is that
droughts have cut global grain production.

In this chapter, you will study an *economic model*—the production
possibilities frontier—that explains how ethanol and drought raise the
cost of producing food; that makes clear what it means to say that production is efficient or inefficient; that shows how we expand our production
possibilities and how we gain by trading with others.

At the end of the chapter, in *Reading Between the Lines*, we return to
explaining how producing ethanol has raised the cost of food.

◆ Production Possibilities and Opportunity Cost

Every working day, in mines, factories, shops, and offices and on farms and construction sites across Canada, 17 million people produce a vast variety of goods and services valued at $5 billion. But the quantities of goods and services that we can produce are limited both by our available resources and by technology. And if we want to increase our production of one good, we must decrease our production of something else—we face a tradeoff. You are going to learn about the production possibilities frontier, which describes the limit to what we can produce and provides a neat way of thinking about and illustrating the idea of a tradeoff.

The **production possibilities frontier** (*PPF*) is the boundary between those combinations of goods and services that can be produced and those that cannot. To illustrate the *PPF*, we focus on two goods at a time and hold the quantities produced of all the other goods and services constant. That is, we look at a *model* economy in which everything remains the same except for the production of the two goods we are considering.

Let's look at the production possibilities frontier for cola and pizza, which represent *any* pair of goods or services.

Production Possibilities Frontier

The *production possibilities frontier* for cola and pizza shows the limits to the production of these two goods, given the total resources and technology available to produce them. Figure 2.1 shows this production possibilities frontier. The table lists some combinations of the quantities of pizza and cola that can be produced in a month given the resources available. The figure graphs these combinations. The *x*-axis shows the quantity of pizzas produced, and the *y*-axis shows the quantity of cola produced.

The *PPF* illustrates *scarcity* because we cannot attain the points outside the frontier. These points describe wants that can't be satisfied. We can produce at any point *inside* the *PPF* or *on* the *PPF*. These points are attainable. Suppose that in a typical month, we produce 4 million pizzas and 5 million cans of cola. Figure 2.1 shows this combination as point *E* and as possibility *E* in the table. The figure

FIGURE 2.1   Production Possibilities Frontier

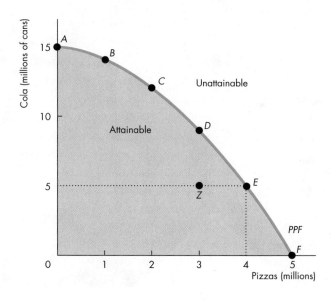

Possibility	Pizzas (millions)		Cola (millions of cans)
A	0	and	15
B	1	and	14
C	2	and	12
D	3	and	9
E	4	and	5
F	5	and	0

The table lists six production possibilities for cola and pizzas. Row *A* tells us that if we produce no pizzas, the maximum quantity of cola we can produce is 15 million cans. Points *A, B, C, D, E,* and *F* in the figure represent the rows of the table. The curve passing through these points is the production possibilities frontier (*PPF*).

The *PPF* separates the attainable from the unattainable. Production is possible at any point *inside* the orange area or *on* the frontier. Points outside the frontier are unattainable. Points inside the frontier, such as point *Z,* are inefficient because resources are wasted or misallocated. At such points, it is possible to use the available resources to produce more of either or both goods.

also shows other production possibilities. For example, we might stop producing pizza and move all the people who produce it into producing cola. Point *A* in the figure and possibility *A* in the production table show this case. The quantity of cola produced increases to 15 million cans, and pizza dries up. Alternatively, we might close the cola factories and switch all the resources into producing pizza. In this situation, we produce 5 million pizzas. Point *F* in the figure and possibility *F* in the table show this case.

Production Efficiency

We achieve **production efficiency** if we produce goods and services at the lowest possible cost. This outcome occurs at all the points *on* the *PPF*. At points *inside* the *PPF*, production is inefficient because we are giving up more than necessary of one good to produce a given quantity of the other good.

For example, at point *Z* in Fig. 2.1, we produce 3 million pizzas and 5 million cans of cola. But we have enough resources to produce 3 million pizzas and 9 million cans of cola. Our pizzas cost more cola than necessary. We can get them for a lower cost. Only when we produce *on* the *PPF* do we incur the lowest possible cost of production.

Production is *inefficient* inside the *PPF* because resources are either *unused* or *misallocated* or both.

Resources are *unused* when they are idle but could be working. For example, we might leave some of the factories idle or some workers unemployed.

Resources are *misallocated* when they are assigned to tasks for which they are not the best match. For example, we might assign skilled pizza chefs to work in a cola factory and skilled cola producers to work in a pizza shop. We could get more pizzas *and* more cola from these same workers if we reassigned them to the tasks that more closely match their skills.

Tradeoff Along the *PPF*

Every choice *along* the *PPF* involves a *tradeoff*. On the *PPF* in Fig. 2.1, we trade off cola for pizzas.

Tradeoffs arise in every imaginable real-world situation in which a choice must be made. At any given point in time, we have a fixed amount of labour, land, capital, and entrepreneurship. By using our available technologies, we can employ these resources to produce goods and services, but we are limited in what we can produce. This limit defines a boundary between what we can attain and what we cannot attain. This boundary is the real-world's production possibilities frontier, and it defines the tradeoffs that we must make. On our real-world *PPF*, we can produce more of any one good or service only if we produce less of some other goods or services.

When doctors want to spend more on AIDS and cancer research, they face a tradeoff: more medical research for less of some other things. When Parliament wants to spend more on education and health care, it faces a tradeoff: more education and health care for less national defence or for higher taxes and less personal spending. When an environmental group argues for less logging, it is suggesting a tradeoff: greater conservation of endangered wildlife for less paper. When you want to study more, you face a tradeoff: more study time for less leisure or sleep.

All tradeoffs involve a cost—an opportunity cost.

Opportunity Cost

The **opportunity cost** of an action is the highest-valued alternative forgone. The *PPF* makes this idea precise and enables us to calculate opportunity cost. Along the *PPF*, there are only two goods, so there is only one alternative forgone: some quantity of the other good. Given our current resources and technology, we can produce more pizzas only if we produce less cola. The opportunity cost of producing an additional pizza is the cola we *must* forgo. Similarly, the opportunity cost of producing an additional can of cola is the quantity of pizzas we must forgo.

In Fig. 2.1, if we move from point *C* to point *D*, we get 1 million more pizzas but 3 million fewer cans of cola. The additional 1 million pizzas *cost* 3 million cans of cola, so one pizza costs 3 cans of cola.

If we move in the opposite direction from point *D* to point *C*, the quantity of cola produced increases by 3 million cans and the quantity of pizzas produced decreases by 1 million. The additional 3 million cans of cola *cost* 1 million pizzas, so one can of cola costs 1/3 of a pizza. The opportunity cost of producing an additional can of cola is equal to the *inverse* of the opportunity cost of producing an additional pizza.

Opportunity Cost Is a Ratio   Opportunity cost is a ratio. It is the decrease in the quantity produced of one good divided by the increase in the quantity produced of another good as we move along the production possibilities frontier.

Increasing Opportunity Cost The opportunity cost of a pizza increases as the quantity of pizzas produced increases. The outward-bowed shape of the *PPF* reflects increasing opportunity cost. When we produce a large quantity of cola and a small quantity of pizza—between points *A* and *B* in Fig. 2.1—the frontier has a gentle slope. An increase in the quantity of pizzas costs a small decrease in the quantity of cola—the opportunity cost of a pizza is a small quantity of cola.

When we produce a large quantity of pizzas and a small quantity of cola—between points *E* and *F* in Fig. 2.1—the frontier is steep. A given increase in the quantity of pizzas *costs* a large decrease in the quantity of cola, so the opportunity cost of a pizza is a large quantity of cola.

Economics in Action
Increasing Opportunity Cost at Hydro One

Hydro One, Ontario's electric power producer, faces increasing opportunity cost. At low output rates, it costs 2.3 cents per kilowatt hour (kWh) to produce electricity using hydro-powered generators and 3.2 cents per kWh using nuclear generators. As Hydro One increases its output rate, the opportunity cost increases to 4.1 cents per kWh using coal and 6.6 cents per kWh using gas and oil turbines. The figure shows Hydro One's increasing opportunity cost. (Because nuclear plants can't be turned on and off, they produce some electricity alongside hydro all the time.)

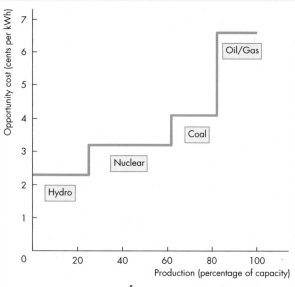

The Increasing Opportunity Cost of Producing Electricity

The *PPF* is bowed outward because resources are not all equally productive in all activities. People with many years of experience working for PepsiCo are good at producing cola but not very good at making pizzas. So if we move some of these people from PepsiCo to Domino's, we get a small increase in the quantity of pizzas but a large decrease in the quantity of cola.

Similarly, people who have spent years working at Domino's are good at producing pizzas, but they have no idea how to produce cola. So if we move some of these people from Domino's to PepsiCo, we get a small increase in the quantity of cola but a large decrease in the quantity of pizzas. As we produce more of one good, we must use resources that are less suited to that activity and more suited to producing the other good, so we face increasing opportunity cost.

Increasing opportunity cost is a universal phenomenon. When the rate of production increases, so does the opportunity cost of production. *Economics in Action* shows the increasing opportunity cost of producing electricity as Ontario's Hydro One power producer steps up its output rate to meet peak demand.

REVIEW QUIZ

1 How does the production possibilities frontier illustrate scarcity?
2 How does the production possibilities frontier illustrate production efficiency?
3 How does the production possibilities frontier show that every choice involves a tradeoff?
4 How does the production possibilities frontier illustrate opportunity cost?
5 Why is opportunity cost a ratio?
6 Why does the *PPF* bow outward and what does that imply about the relationship between opportunity cost and the quantity produced?

You can work these questions in Study Plan 2.1 and get instant feedback.

———————————— MyEconLab ◆

We've seen that what we can produce is limited by the production possibilities frontier. We've also seen that production on the *PPF* is efficient. But we can produce many different quantities on the *PPF*. How do we choose among them? How do we know which point on the *PPF* is the best one?

Using Resources Efficiently

We achieve *production efficiency* at every point on the *PPF*, but which point is best? The answer is the point on the *PPF* at which goods and services are produced in the quantities that provide the greatest possible benefit. When goods and services are produced at the lowest possible cost and in the quantities that provide the greatest possible benefit, we have achieved **allocative efficiency**.

The questions that we raised when we reviewed the four big issues in Chapter 1 are questions about allocative efficiency. To answer such questions, we must measure and compare costs and benefits.

The *PPF* and Marginal Cost

The **marginal cost** of a good is the opportunity cost of producing one more unit of it. We calculate marginal cost from the slope of the *PPF*. As the quantity of pizzas produced increases, the *PPF* gets steeper and the marginal cost of a pizza increases. Figure 2.2 illustrates the calculation of the marginal cost of a pizza.

Begin by finding the opportunity cost of producing pizzas in blocks of 1 million pizzas. The cost of the first million pizzas is 1 million cans of cola; the cost of the second million pizzas is 2 million cans of cola; the cost of the third million pizzas is 3 million cans of cola, and so on. The bars in part (a) illustrate these calculations.

The bars in part (b) show the cost of an average pizza in each of the 1 million pizza blocks. Focus on the third million pizzas—the move from *C* to *D* in part (a). Because this block of 1 million pizzas cost 3 million cans of cola, one of these pizzas, on average, costs 3 cans of cola—the height of the bar in part (b).

Next, find the opportunity cost of each additional pizza—the marginal cost of producing a pizza. The marginal cost of producing a pizza increases as the quantity of pizzas produced increases. The marginal cost at point *C* is less than it is at point *D*. On average over the range from *C* to *D*, the marginal cost of a pizza is 3 cans of cola. But it exactly equals 3 cans of cola only in the middle of the range between *C* and *D*.

The red dot in part (b) indicates that the marginal cost of producing a pizza is 3 cans of cola when 2.5 million pizzas are produced. Each black dot in part (b) is interpreted in the same way. The red curve that passes through these dots, labelled *MC*, is the marginal cost curve. It shows the marginal cost of producing a pizza at each quantity of pizzas as we move along the *PPF*.

FIGURE 2.2   The *PPF* and Marginal Cost

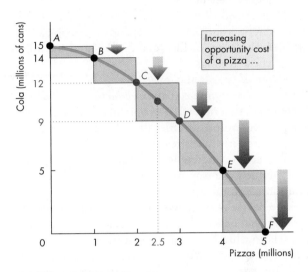

(a) *PPF* and opportunity cost

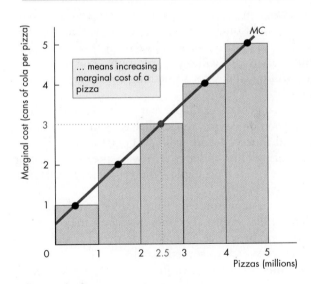

(b) Marginal cost

Marginal cost is calculated from the slope of the *PPF*. As the quantity of pizzas produced increases, the *PPF* gets steeper and the marginal cost of producing a pizza increases. The bars in part (a) show the opportunity cost of pizza in blocks of 1 million pizzas. The bars in part (b) show the cost of an average pizza in each of these 1 million blocks. The red curve, *MC*, shows the marginal cost of producing a pizza at each point along the *PPF*. This curve passes through the centre of each of the bars in part (b).

Preferences and Marginal Benefit

The **marginal benefit** from a good or service is the benefit received from consuming one more unit of it. This benefit is subjective. It depends on people's **preferences**—people's likes and dislikes and the intensity of those feelings.

Marginal benefit and *preferences* stand in sharp contrast to *marginal cost* and *production possibilities.* Preferences describe what people like and want and the production possibilities describe the limits or constraints on what is feasible.

We need a concrete way of illustrating preferences that parallels the way we illustrate the limits to production using the *PPF.*

The device that we use to illustrate preferences is the **marginal benefit curve**, which is a curve that shows the relationship between the marginal benefit from a good and the quantity consumed of that good. Note that the *marginal benefit curve* is *unrelated* to the *PPF* and cannot be derived from it.

We measure the marginal benefit from a good or service by the most that people are *willing to pay* for an additional unit of it. The idea is that you are willing to pay less for a good than it is worth to you but you are not willing to pay more: The most you are willing to pay for something is its marginal benefit.

It is a general principle that the more we have of any good or service, the smaller is its marginal benefit and the less we are willing to pay for an additional unit of it. This tendency is so widespread and strong that we call it a principle—the *principle of decreasing marginal benefit.*

The basic reason why marginal benefit decreases is that we like variety. The more we consume of any one good or service, the more we tire of it and would prefer to switch to something else.

Think about your willingness to pay for a pizza. If pizza is hard to come by and you can buy only a few slices a year, you might be willing to pay a high price to get an additional slice. But if pizza is all you've eaten for the past few days, you are willing to pay almost nothing for another slice.

You've learned to think about cost as opportunity cost, not as a dollar cost. You can think about marginal benefit and willingness to pay in the same way. The marginal benefit, measured by what you are willing to pay for something, is the quantity of other goods and services that you are willing to forgo. Let's continue with the example of cola and pizza and illustrate preferences this way.

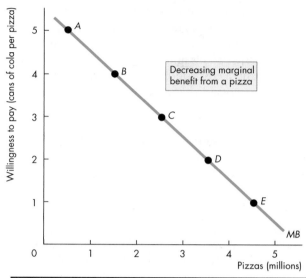

FIGURE 2.3   Preferences and the Marginal Benefit Curve

Decreasing marginal benefit from a pizza

Possibility	Pizzas (millions)	Willingness to pay (cans of cola per pizza)
A	0.5	5
B	1.5	4
C	2.5	3
D	3.5	2
E	4.5	1

The larger the quantity of pizzas available, the less cola people are willing to give up for an additional pizza. With 0.5 million pizzas available, people are willing to pay 5 cans of cola per pizza, but with 4.5 million pizzas, people are willing to pay only 1 can of cola per pizza. Willingness to pay measures marginal benefit. A universal feature of people's preferences is that as the quantity consumed increases, marginal benefit decreases.

——— MyEconLab   animation ◆

Figure 2.3 illustrates preferences as the willingness to pay for pizza in terms of cola. In row *A,* with 0.5 million pizzas available, people are willing to pay 5 cans of cola per pizza. As the quantity of pizzas increases, the amount that people are willing to pay for a pizza falls. With 4.5 million pizzas available, people are willing to pay only 1 can of cola per pizza.

Let's now use the concepts of marginal cost and marginal benefit to describe allocative efficiency.

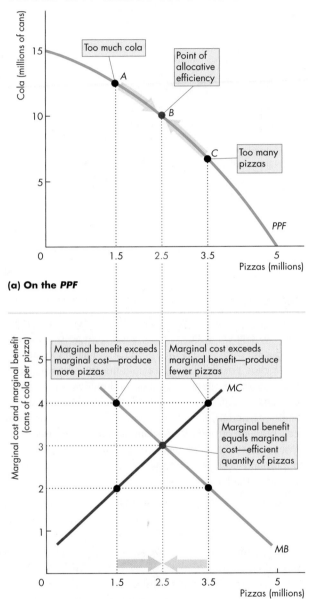

FIGURE 2.4   Efficient Use of Resources

(a) On the PPF

(b) Marginal benefit equals marginal cost

The greater the quantity of pizzas produced, the smaller is the marginal benefit (MB) from a pizza—the less cola people are willing to give up to get an additional pizza. But the greater the quantity of pizzas produced, the greater is the marginal cost (MC) of a pizza—the more cola people must give up to get an additional pizza. When marginal benefit equals marginal cost, resources are being used efficiently.

———— MyEconLab   animation   ◆

Allocative Efficiency

At *any* point on the *PPF*, we cannot produce more of one good without giving up some other good. At the *best* point on the *PPF*, we cannot produce more of one good without giving up some other good that provides greater benefit. We are producing at the point of allocative efficiency—the point on the *PPF* that we prefer above all other points.

Suppose in Fig. 2.4, we produce 1.5 million pizzas. The marginal cost of producing a pizza is 2 cans of cola, and the marginal benefit from a pizza is 4 cans of cola. Because someone values an additional pizza more highly than it costs to produce, we can get more value from our resources by moving some of them out of producing cola and into producing pizza.

Now suppose we produce 3.5 million pizzas. The marginal cost of a pizza is now 4 cans of cola, but the marginal benefit from a pizza is only 2 cans of cola. Because the additional pizza costs more to produce than anyone thinks it is worth, we can get more value from our resources by moving some of them away from producing pizza and into producing cola.

Suppose we produce 2.5 million pizzas. Marginal cost and marginal benefit are now equal at 3 cans of cola. This allocation of resources between pizzas and cola is efficient. If more pizzas are produced, the forgone cola is worth more than the additional pizzas. If fewer pizzas are produced, the forgone pizzas are worth more than the additional cola.

REVIEW QUIZ

1 What is marginal cost? How is it measured?
2 What is marginal benefit? How is it measured?
3 How does the marginal benefit from a good change as the quantity produced of that good increases?
4 What is allocative efficiency and how does it relate to the production possibilities frontier?
5 What conditions must be satisfied if resources are used efficiently?

You can work these questions in Study Plan 2.2 and get instant feedback.
———————————————— MyEconLab   ◆

You now understand the limits to production and the conditions under which resources are used efficiently. Your next task is to study the expansion of production possibilities.

Economic Growth

During the past 30 years, production per person in Canada has doubled. The expansion of production possibilities is called **economic growth**. Economic growth increases our *standard of living*, but it doesn't overcome scarcity and avoid opportunity cost. To make our economy grow, we face a tradeoff—the faster we make production grow, the greater is the opportunity cost of economic growth.

The Cost of Economic Growth

Economic growth comes from technological change and capital accumulation. **Technological change** is the development of new goods and of better ways of producing goods and services. **Capital accumulation** is the growth of capital resources, including *human capital*.

Technological change and capital accumulation have vastly expanded our production possibilities. We can produce automobiles that provide us with more transportation than was available when we had only horses and carriages. We can produce satellites that provide global communications on a much larger scale than that available with the earlier cable technology. But if we use our resources to develop new technologies and produce capital, we must decrease our production of consumption goods and services. New technologies and new capital have an opportunity cost. Let's look at this opportunity cost.

Instead of studying the *PPF* of pizzas and cola, we'll hold the quantity of cola produced constant and examine the *PPF* for pizzas and pizza ovens. Figure 2.5 shows this *PPF* as the blue curve PPF_0. If we devote no resources to producing pizza ovens, we produce at point *A*. If we produce 3 million pizzas, we can produce 6 pizza ovens at point *B*. If we produce no pizza, we can produce 10 ovens at point *C*.

The amount by which our production possibilities expand depends on the resources we devote to technological change and capital accumulation. If we devote no resources to this activity (point *A*), our *PPF* remains the blue curve PPF_0 in Fig. 2.5. If we cut the current pizza production and produce 6 ovens (point *B*), then in the future, we'll have more capital and our *PPF* will rotate outward to the position shown by the red curve PPF_1. The fewer resources we use for producing pizza and the more resources we use for producing ovens, the greater is the expansion of our future production possibilities.

FIGURE 2.5   Economic Growth

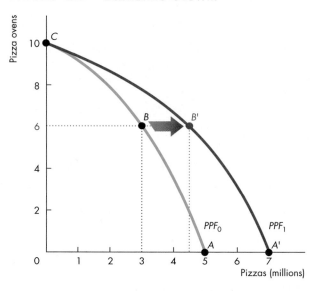

PPF_0 shows the limits to the production of pizzas and pizza ovens, with the production of all other goods and services remaining the same. If we devote no resources to producing pizza ovens and produce 5 million pizzas, our production possibilities will remain the same at PPF_0. But if we decrease pizza production to 3 million and produce 6 ovens, at point *B*, our production possibilities expand. After one period, the *PPF* rotates outward to PPF_1 and we can produce at point *B'*, a point outside the original PPF_0. We can rotate the *PPF* outward, but we cannot avoid opportunity cost. The opportunity cost of producing more pizzas in the future is fewer pizzas today.

—————————— MyEconLab   animation   ◆

Economic growth brings enormous benefits in the form of increased consumption in the future, but it is not free and it doesn't abolish scarcity.

In Fig. 2.5, to make economic growth happen we must use some resources to produce new ovens, which leaves fewer resources to produce pizzas. To move to *B'* in the future, we must move from *A* to *B* today. The opportunity cost of more pizzas in the future is fewer pizzas today. Also, on the new *PPF*, we still face a tradeoff and opportunity cost.

The ideas about economic growth that we have explored in the setting of the pizza industry also apply to nations. Hong Kong and Canada provide a striking case study.

Economics in Action
Hong Kong Overtakes Canada

In 1960, the production possibilities per person in Canada were more than three times those in Hong Kong (see the figure). Canada devotes one-fifth of its resources to accumulating capital and in 1960, Canada was at point *A* on its *PPF*. Hong Kong devotes one-third of its resources to accumulating capital and in 1960, Hong Kong was at point *A* on its *PPF*.

Since 1960, both economies have experienced economic growth, but because Hong Kong devotes a bigger fraction of its resources to accumulating capital, its production possibilities have expanded more quickly.

By 2010, production possibilities per person in Hong Kong were *greater* than those in Canada. Hong Kong has overtaken Canada.

If Hong Kong continues to devote more resources to accumulating capital than Canada does (at point *B* on its 2010 *PPF*), Hong Kong will continue to grow more rapidly. But if it devotes fewer resources to capital accumulation (moving to point *D* on its 2010 *PPF*), then Hong Kong's economic growth rate will slow.

Hong Kong is typical of the fast-growing Asian economies. In China, India, Taiwan, Thailand, and South Korea, production possibilities are expanding at rates of between 5 percent and 10 percent a year.

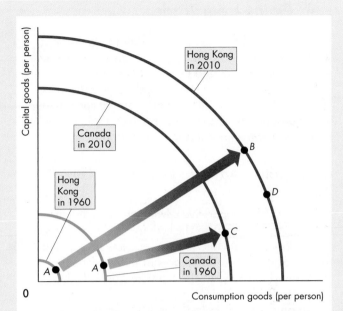

Economic Growth in Canada and Hong Kong

If such high economic growth rates are maintained, these other Asian countries will continue to close the gap between themselves and Canada, and, as Hong Kong has done, eventually overtake Canada. To catch up with Hong Kong, Canada would need to devote a larger part of production to accumulating physical and human capital.

A Nation's Economic Growth

The experiences of Canada and Hong Kong make a striking example of the effects of our choices about consumption and capital goods on the rate of economic growth.

If a nation devotes all its factors of production to producing consumption goods and services and none to advancing technology and accumulating capital, its production possibilities in the future will be the same as they are today.

To expand production possibilities in the future, a nation must devote fewer resources to producing current consumption goods and services and some resources to accumulating capital and developing new technologies. As production possibilities expand, consumption in the future can increase. The decrease in today's consumption is the opportunity cost of tomorrow's increase in consumption.

 REVIEW QUIZ

1 What generates economic growth?
2 How does economic growth influence the production possibilities frontier?
3 What is the opportunity cost of economic growth?
4 Why has Hong Kong experienced faster economic growth than Canada?
5 Does economic growth overcome scarcity?

You can work these questions in Study Plan 2.3 and get instant feedback.

————————————————— MyEconLab ◆

Next, we're going to study another way in which we expand our production possibilities—the amazing fact that *both* buyers and sellers gain from specialization and trade.

◆ Gains from Trade

People can produce for themselves all the goods and services that they consume, or they can produce one good or a few goods and trade with others. Producing only one good or a few goods is called *specialization*. We are going to learn how people gain by specializing in the production of the good in which they have a *comparative advantage* and trading with others.

Comparative Advantage and Absolute Advantage

A person has a **comparative advantage** in an activity if that person can perform the activity at a lower opportunity cost than anyone else. Differences in opportunity costs arise from differences in individual abilities and from differences in the characteristics of other resources.

No one excels at everything. One person is an outstanding pitcher but a poor catcher; another person is a brilliant lawyer but a poor teacher. In almost all human endeavours, what one person does easily, someone else finds difficult. The same applies to land and capital. One plot of land is fertile but has no mineral deposits; another plot of land has outstanding views but is infertile. One machine has great precision but is difficult to operate; another is fast but often breaks down.

Although no one excels at everything, some people excel and can outperform others in a large number of activities—perhaps even in all activities. A person who is more productive than others has an **absolute advantage**.

Absolute advantage involves comparing productivities—production per hour—whereas comparative advantage involves comparing opportunity costs.

A person who has an absolute advantage does not have a *comparative* advantage in every activity. John Grisham is a better lawyer and a better author of fast-paced thrillers than most people. He has an absolute advantage in these two activities. But compared to others, he is a better writer than lawyer, so his *comparative* advantage is in writing.

Because ability and resources vary from one person to another, people have different opportunity costs of producing various goods. These differences in opportunity cost are the source of comparative advantage.

Let's explore the idea of comparative advantage by looking at two smoothie bars: one operated by Liz and the other operated by Joe.

Liz's Smoothie Bar Liz produces smoothies and salads. In Liz's high-tech bar, she can turn out either a smoothie or a salad every 2 minutes—see Table 2.1. If Liz spends all her time making smoothies, she can produce 30 an hour. And if she spends all her time making salads, she can also produce 30 an hour. If she splits her time equally between the two, she can produce 15 smoothies and 15 salads an hour. For each additional smoothie Liz produces, she must decrease her production of salads by one, and for each additional salad she produces, she must decrease her production of smoothies by one. So

> Liz's opportunity cost of producing 1 smoothie is 1 salad,

and

> Liz's opportunity cost of producing 1 salad is 1 smoothie.

Liz's customers buy smoothies and salads in equal quantities, so she splits her time equally between the two items and produces 15 smoothies and 15 salads an hour.

Joe's Smoothie Bar Joe also produces smoothies and salads, but his bar is smaller than Liz's. Also, Joe has only one blender, and it's a slow, old machine. Even if Joe uses all his resources to produce smoothies, he can produce only 6 an hour—see Table 2.2. But Joe is good at making salads. If he uses all his resources to make salads, he can produce 30 an hour.

Joe's ability to make smoothies and salads is the same regardless of how he splits an hour between the two tasks. He can make a salad in 2 minutes or a smoothie in 10 minutes. For each additional smoothie

---

TABLE 2.1   Liz's Production Possibilities

Item	Minutes to produce 1	Quantity per hour
Smoothies	2	30
Salads	2	30

TABLE 2.2   Joe's Production Possibilities

Item	Minutes to produce 1	Quantity per hour
Smoothies	10	6
Salads	2	30

Joe produces, he must decrease his production of salads by 5. And for each additional salad he produces, he must decrease his production of smoothies by 1/5 of a smoothie. So

> Joe's opportunity cost of producing 1 smoothie is 5 salads,

and

> Joe's opportunity cost of producing 1 salad is 1/5 of a smoothie.

Joe's customers, like Liz's, buy smoothies and salads in equal quantities. So Joe spends 50 minutes of each hour making smoothies and 10 minutes of each hour making salads. With this division of his time, Joe produces 5 smoothies and 5 salads an hour.

Liz's Comparative Advantage   In which of the two activities does Liz have a comparative advantage? Recall that comparative advantage is a situation in which one person's opportunity cost of producing a good is lower than another person's opportunity cost of producing that same good. Liz has a comparative advantage in producing smoothies. Her opportunity cost of a smoothie is 1 salad, whereas Joe's opportunity cost of a smoothie is 5 salads.

Joe's Comparative Advantage   If Liz has a comparative advantage in producing smoothies, Joe must have a comparative advantage in producing salads. Joe's opportunity cost of a salad is 1/5 of a smoothie, whereas Liz's opportunity cost of a salad is 1 smoothie.

Achieving the Gains from Trade

Liz and Joe run into each other one evening in a singles bar. After a few minutes of getting acquainted, Liz tells Joe about her amazing smoothie business. Her only problem, she tells Joe, is that she would like to produce more because potential customers leave when her lines get too long.

Joe is hesitant to risk spoiling his chances by telling Liz about his own struggling business, but he takes the risk. Joe explains to Liz that he spends 50 minutes of every hour making 5 smoothies and 10 minutes making 5 salads. Liz's eyes pop. "Have I got a deal for you!" she exclaims.

Here's the deal that Liz sketches on a paper napkin. Joe stops making smoothies and allocates all his time to producing salads; Liz stops making salads and allocates all her time to producing smoothies. That is, they both specialize in producing the good in which they have a comparative advantage. Together they produce 30 smoothies and 30 salads in an hour—see Table 2.3(b).

They then trade. Liz sells Joe 10 smoothies and Joe sells Liz 20 salads—the price of a smoothie is 2 salads—see Table 2.3(c).

After the trade, Joe has 10 salads—the 30 he produces minus the 20 he sells to Liz. He also has the 10 smoothies that he buys from Liz. So Joe now has increased the quantities of smoothies and salads that he can sell to his customers—see Table 2.3(d).

TABLE 2.3   Liz and Joe Gain from Trade

(a) Before trade	Liz	Joe
Smoothies	15	5
Salads	15	5

(b) Specialization	Liz	Joe
Smoothies	30	0
Salads	0	30

(c) Trade	Liz	Joe
Smoothies	sell 10	buy 10
Salads	buy 20	sell 20

(d) After trade	Liz	Joe
Smoothies	20	10
Salads	20	10

(e) Gains from trade	Liz	Joe
Smoothies	+5	+5
Salads	+5	+5

Liz has 20 smoothies—the 30 she produces minus the 10 she sells to Joe. She also has the 20 salads that she buys from Joe. Liz has increased the quantities of smoothies and salads that she can sell to her customers—see Table 2.3(d). Liz and Joe both gain 5 smoothies and 5 salads an hour—see Table 2.3(e).

To illustrate her idea, Liz grabs a fresh napkin and draws the graphs in Fig. 2.6. The blue *PPF* in part (a) shows Joe's production possibilities. Before trade, he is producing 5 smoothies and 5 salads an hour at point *A*. The blue *PPF* in part (b) shows Liz's production possibilities. Before trade, she is producing 15 smoothies and 15 salads an hour at point *A*.

Liz's proposal is that they each specialize in producing the good in which they have a comparative advantage. Joe produces 30 salads and no smoothies at point *B* on his *PPF*. Liz produces 30 smoothies and no salads at point *B* on her *PPF*.

Liz and Joe then trade smoothies and salads at a price of 2 salads per smoothie or 1/2 a smoothie per salad. Joe gets smoothies for 2 salads each, which is less than the 5 salads it costs him to produce a smoothie. Liz gets salads for 1/2 a smoothie each, which is less than the 1 smoothie that it costs her to produce a salad.

With trade, Joe has 10 smoothies and 10 salads at point *C*—a gain of 5 smoothies and 5 salads. Joe moves to a point *outside* his *PPF*.

With trade, Liz has 20 smoothies and 20 salads at point *C*—a gain of 5 smoothies and 5 salads. Liz moves to a point *outside* her *PPF*.

Despite Liz being more productive than Joe, both of them gain from specializing—producing the good in which they have a comparative advantage—and trading.

FIGURE 2.6   The Gains from Trade

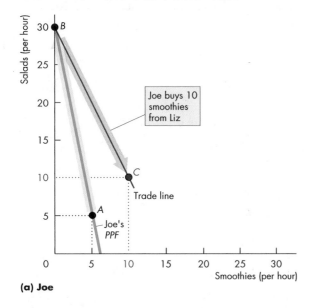

(a) Joe

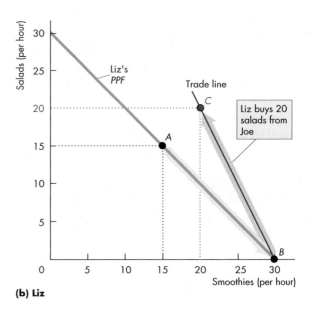

(b) Liz

Initially, Joe produces at point *A* on his *PPF* in part (a), and Liz produces at point *A* on her *PPF* in part (b). Joe's opportunity cost of producing a salad is less than Liz's, so Joe has a comparative advantage in producing salads. Liz's opportunity cost of producing a smoothie is less than Joe's, so Liz has a comparative advantage in producing smoothies.

If Joe specializes in making salads, he produces 30 salads and no smoothies at point *B* on his *PPF*. If Liz specializes

in making smoothies, she produces 30 smoothies and no salads at point *B* on her *PPF*. They exchange salads for smoothies along the red "Trade line." Liz buys salads from Joe for less than her opportunity cost of producing them. Joe buys smoothies from Liz for less than his opportunity cost of producing them. Each goes to point *C*—a point outside his or her *PPF*. With specialization and trade, Joe and Liz gain 5 smoothies and 5 salads each with no extra resources.

MyEconLab   animation   ◆

Economics in Action
Canada and China Gain from Trade

In Chapter 1 (see p. 5), we asked whether globalization is in the social interest. What you have just learned about the gains from trade provides a big part of the answer. We gain from specialization and trade.

The gains that we achieve from *international* trade are similar to those achieved by Joe and Liz. When Canadians buy clothes that are manufactured in China and when China buys Bombardier regional jets manufactured in Canada, the people of both countries gain.

We could slide along our *PPF* producing fewer regional jets and more jackets. Similarly, China could slide along its *PPF* producing more regional jets and fewer jackets. But everyone would lose. The opportunity cost of our jackets and China's opportunity cost of regional jets would rise.

By specializing in regional jets and trading with China, Canadians get their jackets at a lower cost than that at which Canada can produce them, and China gets its aircraft at a lower cost than that at which it can produce them.

 REVIEW QUIZ

1   What gives a person a comparative advantage?
2   Distinguish between comparative advantage and absolute advantage.
3   Why do people specialize and trade?
4   What are the gains from specialization and trade?
5   What is the source of the gains from trade?

You can work these questions in Study Plan 2.4 and get instant feedback.

————————————————— MyEconLab ◆

◆ Economic Coordination

People gain by specializing in the production of those goods and services in which they have a comparative advantage and then trading with each other. Liz and Joe, whose production of salads and smoothies we studied earlier in this chapter, can get together and make a deal that enables them to enjoy the gains from specialization and trade. But for billions of individuals to specialize and produce millions of different goods and services, their choices must somehow be coordinated.

Two competing economic coordination systems have been used: central economic planning and decentralized markets.

Central economic planning was tried in Russia and China and is still used in Cuba and North Korea. This system works badly because government economic planners don't know people's production possibilities and preferences. Resources get wasted, production ends up *inside* the *PPF*, and the wrong things get produced.

Decentralized coordination works best but to do so it needs four complementary social institutions. They are

- Firms
- Markets
- Property rights
- Money

Firms

A **firm** is an economic unit that hires factors of production and organizes those factors to produce and sell goods and services. Examples of firms are Canadian Tire, Tim Hortons, and General Motors.

Firms coordinate a huge amount of economic activity. For example, Canadian Tire buys or rents buildings, equips them with storage shelves and checkout lanes, hires labour, and decides what goods to buy and sell.

Canadian Tire doesn't produce the goods that it sells. It could do so. It could own and coordinate production of all the goods it sells. But John W. and Alfred J. Billes succeeded by specializing in providing good service and retailing supplies from other firms that specialize (just as Liz and Joe did). This trade between firms takes place in markets.

Markets

In ordinary speech, the word *market* means a place where people buy and sell goods such as fish, meat, fruits, and vegetables. In economics, a *market* has a more general meaning. A **market** is any arrangement that enables buyers and sellers to get information and to do business with each other. An example is the market in which oil is bought and sold—the world oil market. The world oil market is not a place. It is the network of oil producers, oil users, wholesalers, and brokers who buy and sell oil. In the world oil market, decision makers do not meet physically. They make deals by telephone, fax, and direct computer link.

Markets have evolved because they facilitate trade. Without organized markets, we would miss out on a substantial part of the potential gains from trade. Enterprising individuals and firms, each pursuing their own self-interest, have profited from making markets—standing ready to buy or sell the items in which they specialize. But markets can work only when property rights exist.

Property Rights

The social arrangements that govern the ownership, use, and disposal of anything that people value are called **property rights**. *Real property* includes land and buildings—the things we call property in ordinary speech—and durable goods such as plant and equipment. *Financial property* includes stocks and bonds and money in the bank. *Intellectual property* is the intangible product of creative effort. This type of property includes books, music, computer programs, and inventions of all kinds and is protected by copyrights and patents.

Where property rights are enforced, people have the incentive to specialize and produce the goods in which they have a comparative advantage. Where people can steal the production of others, resources are devoted not to production but to protecting possessions. Without property rights, we would still be hunting and gathering like our Stone Age ancestors.

Money

Money is any commodity or token that is generally acceptable as a means of payment. Liz and Joe didn't use money in the example above. They exchanged salads and smoothies. In principle, trade in markets can exchange any item for any other item. But you can perhaps imagine how complicated life would be if we exchanged goods for other goods. The "invention" of money makes trading in markets much more efficient.

Circular Flows Through Markets

Figure 2.7 shows the flows that result from the choices that households and firms make. Households specialize and choose the quantities of labour, land, capital, and entrepreneurial services to sell or rent to firms. Firms choose the quantities of factors of production to hire. These (red) flows go through the *factor markets*. Households choose the quantities of goods and services to buy, and firms choose the quantities to produce. These (red) flows go through the *goods markets*. Households receive incomes and make expenditures on goods and services (the green flows).

How do markets coordinate all these decisions?

Coordinating Decisions

Markets coordinate decisions through price adjustments. To see how, think about your local market for hamburgers. Suppose that too few hamburgers are available and some people who want to buy hamburgers are not able to do so. To make buying and selling plans the same, either more hamburgers must be offered for sale or buyers must scale down their appetites (or both). A rise in the price of a hamburger produces this outcome. A higher price encourages producers to offer more hamburgers for sale. It also encourages some people to change their lunch plans. Fewer people buy hamburgers, and more buy hot dogs. More hamburgers (and more hot dogs) are offered for sale.

Alternatively, suppose that more hamburgers are available than people want to buy. In this case, to make the choices of buyers and sellers compatible, more hamburgers must be bought or fewer hamburgers must be offered for sale (or both). A fall in the price of a hamburger achieves this outcome. A lower price encourages people to buy more hamburgers. It also encourages firms to produce a smaller quantity of hamburgers.

FIGURE 2.7   Circular Flows in the Market Economy

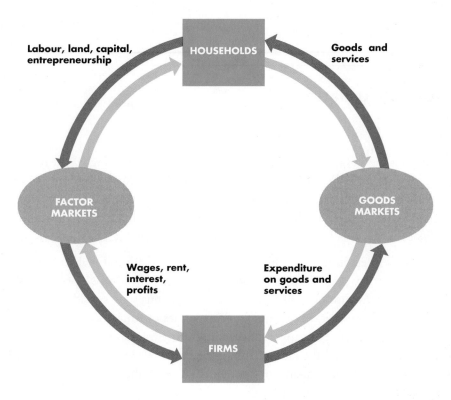

Households and firms make economic choices and markets coordinate these choices.

Households choose the quantities of labour, land, capital, and entrepreneurial services to sell or rent to firms in exchange for wages, rent, interest, and profits. Households also choose how to spend their incomes on the various types of goods and services available.

Firms choose the quantities of factors of production to hire and the quantities of goods and services to produce.

Goods markets and factor markets coordinate these choices of households and firms.

The counterclockwise red flows are real flows—the flow of factors of production from households to firms and the flow of goods and services from firms to households.

The clockwise green flows are the payments for the red flows. They are the flow of income from firms to households and the flow of expenditure on goods and services from households to firms.

MyEconLab   animation ◆

REVIEW QUIZ

1   Why are social institutions such as firms, markets, property rights, and money necessary?
2   What are the main functions of markets?
3   What are the flows in the market economy that go from firms to households and the flows from households to firms?

You can work these questions in Study Plan 2.5 and get instant feedback.

MyEconLab ◆

◆ You have now begun to see how economists approach economic questions. Scarcity, choice, and divergent opportunity costs explain why we specialize and trade and why firms, markets, property rights, and money have developed. You can see all around you the lessons you've learned in this chapter. *Reading Between the Lines* on pp. 44–45 provides an opportunity to apply the *PPF* model to deepen your understanding of the reasons for the increase in the cost of food associated with the increase in corn production.

The Rising Opportunity Cost of Food

The Meaning of Agflation

Investors Chronicle
August 11, 2010

The response of the Russian government to a lousy 2010 harvest and soaring wheat prices was as predictable as it was bone-headed. Predictable, because the Russian government has form—by imposing a ban on wheat exports, it was repeating what it did in 2007–08 after a poor harvest. Bone-headed, because in the long run Russia's action will distort markets to the detriment of its consumers—effectively an export ban tells farmers to grow less wheat.

Still, it's not as if Russia's rulers have a monopoly on distorting agricultural markets. In the Land of the Free, they're pretty good at it, too. Take the egregious effect of US politicians' love affair with ethanol production from maize. Thanks to generous state subsidies, this inefficient way of making ethanol now accounts for 85m tonnes of America's annual maize production. While production of maize approaches 300m tonnes most years, that might not matter too much. Except that to fill the tank of a gas-guzzling SUV just once takes as much grain as will feed a person for a year. Small wonder that the U.S. is already giving over more maize to ethanol production than to export. ...

It takes a lot of grain to produce meat. So it is cheaper to eat the stuff as, say, bread, though perhaps it's more appetising to eat it as pork or beef. The trouble is, 3 lbs of grain are needed to raise 1 lb of pork and for beef the ratio is more like eight to one. Yet, thanks to China's economic transformation, the average Chinese is now eating well over 100 lbs of meat a year; maybe three times more than he did 30 years ago. Meat consumption rising at that sort of rate will always mean higher input costs and higher inflation. ...

ESSENCE OF THE STORY

- Grain production is not keeping up with the amount people want to use as food and fuel.

- Rising global incomes lead to more meat consumption, which increases the amount of grain used to feed animals.

- Ethanol mills use close to one-third of U.S. grain production.

- A drought in Russia in 2010 decreased production.

- All grain prices are likely to keep rising in a process the news article calls "Agflation."

ECONOMIC ANALYSIS

- The United States produces 53 percent of the world's ethanol and Brazil produces 33 percent. Canada produces a bit more than 1 percent (see Fig. 1).

- In Brazil, ethanol is made from sugar but in the United States it is made from corn, so ethanol and food compete to use the same resources.

- To produce more ethanol, U.S. farmers have increased the number of hectares devoted to corn production.

- The amount of land devoted to corn production has also increased in other regions of the world.

- Figure 2 shows the U.S. production possibilities frontier, PPF, for corn and other goods and services.

- The increase in the production of corn is illustrated by a movement along the PPF in Fig. 1 from point A in 2009 to point B in 2010.

- In moving from point A to point B, the United States incurs a higher opportunity cost of producing corn, as the greater slope of the PPF at point B indicates.

- In other regions of the world, despite the fact that more land was devoted to corn production, the amount of corn produced fell slightly.

- The reason is that droughts in South America and Eastern Europe lowered the crop yield per hectare in those regions.

- Figure 3 shows the rest of the world's PPF for corn and other goods and services in 2009 and 2010.

- The increase in the amount of land devoted to producing corn is illustrated by a movement along PPF_{09}.

- With a decrease in the crop yield, production possibilities decrease and the PPF rotates inward.

- The rotation from PPF_{09} to PPF_{10} illustrates this decrease in production possibilities.

- The opportunity cost of producing corn in the rest of the world increased for two reasons: the movement along its PPF and the inward rotation of the PPF.

- With a higher opportunity cost of producing corn, the cost of both ethanol and food increases.

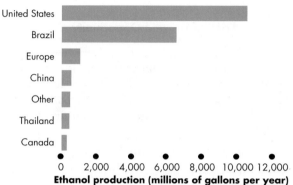

Figure 1 Ethanol Production in 2009

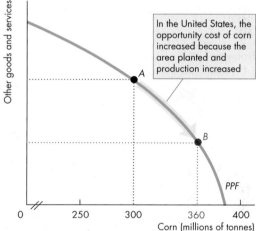

In the United States, the opportunity cost of corn increased because the area planted and production increased

Figure 2 U.S. PPF

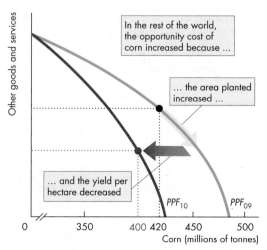

In the rest of the world, the opportunity cost of corn increased because …

… the area planted increased …

… and the yield per hectare decreased

Figure 3 Rest of the World PPF

45

SUMMARY

Key Points

Production Possibilities and Opportunity Cost

(pp. 30–32)

- The production possibilities frontier is the boundary between production levels that are attainable and those that are not attainable when all the available resources are used to their limit.
- Production efficiency occurs at points on the production possibilities frontier.
- Along the production possibilities frontier, the opportunity cost of producing more of one good is the amount of the other good that must be given up.
- The opportunity cost of all goods increases as the production of the good increases.

Working Problems 1 to 3 will give you a better understanding of production possibilities and opportunity cost.

Using Resources Efficiently (pp. 33–35)

- Allocative efficiency occurs when goods and services are produced at the least possible cost and in the quantities that bring the greatest possible benefit.
- The marginal cost of a good is the opportunity cost of producing one more unit of it.
- The marginal benefit from a good is the benefit received from consuming one more unit of it and is measured by the willingness to pay for it.
- The marginal benefit from a good decreases as the amount of the good available increases.
- Resources are used efficiently when the marginal cost of each good is equal to its marginal benefit.

Working Problems 4 to 10 will give you a better understanding of the efficient use of resources.

Economic Growth (pp. 36–37)

- Economic growth, which is the expansion of production possibilities, results from capital accumulation and technological change.
- The opportunity cost of economic growth is forgone current consumption.
- The benefit of economic growth is increased future consumption.

Working Problem 11 will give you a better understanding of economic growth.

Gains from Trade (pp. 38–41)

- A person has a comparative advantage in producing a good if that person can produce the good at a lower opportunity cost than everyone else.
- People gain by specializing in the activity in which they have a comparative advantage and trading with others.

Working Problems 12 to 17 will give you a better understanding of the gains from trade.

Economic Coordination (pp. 41–43)

- Firms coordinate a large amount of economic activity, but there is a limit to the efficient size of a firm.
- Markets coordinate the economic choices of people and firms.
- Markets can work efficiently only when property rights exist.
- Money makes trading in markets more efficient.

Working Problem 18 will give you a better understanding of economic coordination.

Key Terms

Absolute advantage, 38
Allocative efficiency, 33
Capital accumulation, 36
Comparative advantage, 38
Economic growth, 36
Firm, 41
Marginal benefit, 34
Marginal benefit curve, 34
Marginal cost, 33

Market, 42
Money, 42
Opportunity cost, 31
Preferences, 34
Production efficiency, 31
Production possibilities frontier, 30
Property rights, 42
Technological change, 36

SCAN THIS

STUDY PLAN PROBLEMS AND APPLICATIONS

MyEconLab ◆ You can work Problems 1 to 21 in Chapter 2 Study Plan and get instant feedback.

Production Possibilities and Opportunity Cost

(Study Plan 2.1)

Use the following data to work Problems 1 to 3.

Brazil produces ethanol from sugar, and the land used to grow sugar can be used to grow food crops. Suppose that Brazil's production possibilities for ethanol and food crops are as follows:

Ethanol (barrels per day)		Food crops (tonnes per day)
70	and	0
64	and	1
54	and	2
40	and	3
22	and	4
0	and	5

1. a. Draw a graph of Brazil's *PPF* and explain how your graph illustrates scarcity.
   b. If Brazil produces 40 barrels of ethanol a day, how much food must it produce to achieve production efficiency?
   c. Why does Brazil face a tradeoff on its *PPF*?

2. a. If Brazil increases its production of ethanol from 40 barrels per day to 54 barrels per day, what is the opportunity cost of the additional ethanol?
   b. If Brazil increases its production of food crops from 2 tonnes to 3 tonnes per day, what is the opportunity cost of the additional food?
   c. What is the relationship between your answers to parts (a) and (b)?

3. Does Brazil face an increasing opportunity cost of ethanol? What feature of Brazil's *PPF* illustrates increasing opportunity cost?

Using Resources Efficiently (Study Plan 2.2)

Use the above table to work Problems 4 and 5.

4. Define marginal cost and calculate Brazil's marginal cost of producing a tonne of food when the quantity produced is 2.5 tonnes per day,

5. Define marginal benefit, explain how it is measured, and explain why the data in the table does not enable you to calculate Brazil's marginal benefit from food.

6. Distinguish between *production efficiency* and *allocative efficiency*. Explain why many production possibilities achieve production efficiency but only one achieves allocative efficiency.

Use the following graphs to work Problems 7 to 10. Harry enjoys tennis but wants a high grade in his economics course. The graphs show his *PPF* for these two "goods" and his *MB* curve from tennis.

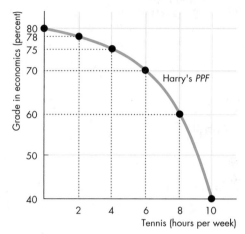

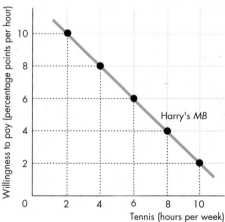

7. What is Harry's marginal cost of tennis if he plays for (i) 3 hours a week; (ii) 5 hours a week; and (iii) 7 hours a week?

8. a. If Harry uses his time to achieve allocative efficiency, what is his economics grade and how many hours of tennis does he play?
   b. Explain why Harry would be worse off getting a grade higher than your answer to part (a).

9. If Harry becomes a tennis superstar with big earnings from tennis, what happens to his *PPF*, his *MB* curve, and his efficient time allocation?

10. If Harry suddenly finds high grades in economics easier to attain, what happens to his *PPF*, his *MB* curve, and his efficient time allocation?

Economic Growth (Study Plan 2.3)

11. A farm grows wheat and produces pork. The marginal cost of producing each of these products increases as more of it is produced.

    a. Make a graph that illustrates the farm's *PPF*.

    b. The farm adopts a new technology that allows it to use fewer resources to fatten pigs. Use your graph to illustrate the impact of the new technology on the farm's *PPF*.

    c. With the farm using the new technology described in part (b), has the opportunity cost of producing a tonne of wheat increased, decreased, or remained the same? Explain and illustrate your answer.

    d. Is the farm more efficient with the new technology than it was with the old one? Why?

Gains from Trade (Study Plan 2.4)

Use the following data to work Problems 12 and 13.

12. In an hour, Sue can produce 40 caps or 4 jackets and Tessa can produce 80 caps or 4 jackets.

    a. Calculate Sue's opportunity cost of producing a cap.

    b. Calculate Tessa's opportunity cost of producing a cap.

    c. Who has a comparative advantage in producing caps?

    d. If Sue and Tessa specialize in producing the good in which each has a comparative advantage, and then trade jackets and caps, who gains from the specialization and trade?

13. Suppose that Tessa buys a new machine for making jackets that enables her to make 20 jackets an hour. (She can still make only 80 caps per hour.)

    a. Who now has a comparative advantage in producing jackets?

    b. Can Sue and Tessa still gain from trade?

Use the following data to work Problems 14 to 17.

Imports accounted for about 70 percent of sales of pork meat in Australia. Pork imports from Denmark, Canada, and the United States rose 48 percent in the past year. Australian producers receive about $2.30 per kilogram, which costs $3 to produce.

14. What does this data suggest about Australia's comparative advantage in pork meat production?

15. Pork imports had grown rapidly in the previous four years. What does this suggest about the change in Australia's comparative advantage in this product and why might that change have occurred?

16. Canada is an important supplier of pork meat to Australia, while Australia exports wine to Canada. Construct both an Australian and a Canadian *PPF* for wine and pork that are consistent with this pattern of trade.

17. The pork industry had sought restrictions on imports but the government decided that there was no case for restricting imports. What would have been the effect of restrictions on imports on production efficiency in Australia?

Economic Coordination (Study Plan 2.5)

18. For 50 years, Cuba has had a centrally planned economy in which the government made the decisions on how resources were allocated.

    a. Why would you expect Cuba's production possibilities (per person) to be smaller than those of Canada?

    b. What are the social institutions that Cuba might lack that help Canada to achieve allocative efficiency?

Economics in the News (Study Plan 2.EN)

Use the following data to work Problems 19 to 21.

Brazil produces ethanol from sugar at a cost of 83 cents per gallon. The United States produces ethanol from corn at a cost of $1.14 per gallon. Sugar grown on one acre of land produces twice the quantity of ethanol as the corn grown on an acre. The United States imports 5 percent of the ethanol it uses and produces the rest itself. Since 2003, U.S. ethanol production has more than doubled and U.S. corn production has increased by 45 percent.

19. a. Does Brazil or the United States have a comparative advantage in producing ethanol?

    b. Sketch the *PPF* for ethanol and other goods and services for the United States.

    c. Sketch the *PPF* for ethanol and other goods and services for Brazil.

20. a. Do you expect the opportunity cost of producing ethanol in the United States to have increased since 2003? Explain why.

    b. Do you think the United States has achieved production efficiency in its manufacture of ethanol? Explain why or why not.

    c. Do you think the United States has achieved allocative efficiency in its manufacture of ethanol? Explain why or why not.

21. Sketch a figure similar to Fig. 2.6 on p. 40 to show how both the United States and Brazil can gain from specialization and trade.

ADDITIONAL PROBLEMS AND APPLICATIONS

MyEconLab ◆ You can work these problems in MyEconLab if assigned by your instructor.

Production Possibilities and Opportunity Cost

Use the following table to work Problems 22 to 23.

The people of Leisure Island have 50 hours of labour a day that can be used to produce entertainment and good food. The table shows the maximum quantity of either entertainment or good food that Leisure Island can produce with different quantities of labour.

Labour (hours)	Entertainment (units per month)		Good food (units per month)
0	0	or	0
10	20	or	30
20	40	or	50
30	60	or	60
40	80	or	65
50	100	or	67

22. Is an output of 50 units of entertainment and 50 units of good food attainable and efficient? With a production of 50 units of entertainment and 50 units of good food, do the people of Leisure Island face a tradeoff?

23. What is the opportunity cost of producing an additional unit of entertainment? Explain how the opportunity cost of a unit of entertainment changes as more entertainment is produced.

Use the following table to work Problems 24 and 25.

Suppose that Sunland's production possibilities are

Food (kilograms per month)		Sunscreen (litres per month)
300	and	0
200	and	50
100	and	100
0	and	150

24. a. Draw a graph of Sunland's *PPF* and explain how your graph illustrates a tradeoff.
  b. If Sunland produces 150 kilograms of food per month, how much sunscreen must it produce if it achieves production efficiency?
  c. What is Sunland's opportunity cost of producing 1 kilogram of food?
  d. What is Sunland's opportunity cost of producing 1 litre of sunscreen?
  e. Explain the relationship between your answers to parts (c) and (d).

25. What feature of a *PPF* illustrates increasing opportunity cost? Explain why the country's opportunity cost does or does not increase.

Using Resources Efficiently

26. In Problem 24, what is the marginal cost of a kilogram of food in Sunland when the quantity produced is 150 kilograms per day? What is special about Sunland's marginal cost of food?

27. The table describes the preferences in Sunland.

Sunscreen (litres per month)	Willingness to pay (kilograms of food per litre)
25	3
75	2
125	1

  a. What is the marginal benefit from sunscreen and how is it measured?
  b. Draw a graph of Sunland's marginal benefit from sunscreen.

Economic Growth

28. Capital accumulation and technological change bring economic growth, which means that the *PPF* keeps shifting outward: Production that was unattainable yesterday becomes attainable today; production that is unattainable today will become attainable tomorrow. Why doesn't this process of economic growth mean that scarcity is being defeated and will one day be gone?

Gains from Trade

Use the following data to work Problems 29 and 30.

Kim can produce 40 pies or 400 cakes an hour. Liam can produce 100 pies or 200 cakes an hour.

29. a. Calculate Kim's opportunity cost of a pie and Liam's opportunity cost of a pie.
  b. If each spends 30 minutes of each hour producing pies and 30 minutes producing cakes, how many pies and cakes does each produce?
  c. Who has a comparative advantage in producing pies? Who has a comparative advantage in producing cakes?

30. a. Draw a graph of Kim's *PPF* and Liam's *PPF.*
  b. On your graph, show the point at which each produces when they spend 30 minutes of each hour producing pies and 30 minutes producing cakes.
  c. On your graph, show what Kim produces and what Liam produces when they specialize.
  d. When they specialize and trade, what are the total gains from trade?

e. If Kim and Liam share the total gains equally, what trade takes place between them?

31. Tony and Patty produce skis and snowboards. The tables show their production possibilities. Tony produces 5 snowboards and 40 skis a week; Patty produces 10 snowboards and 5 skis a week.

Tony's Production Possibilities

Snowboards (per week)		Skis (per week)
25	and	0
20	and	10
15	and	20
10	and	30
5	and	40
0	and	50

Patty's Production Possibilities

Snowboards (per week)		Skis (per week)
20	and	0
10	and	5
0	and	10

a. Who has a comparative advantage in producing snowboards? And who has a comparative advantage in producing skis?

b. If Tony and Patty specialize and trade 1 snowboard for 1 ski, what are the gains from trade?

Economic Coordination

32. Indicate on a graph of the circular flows in the market economy, the real and money flows in which the following items belong:

a. You buy an iPad from the Apple Store.

b. Apple Inc. pays the designers of the iPad.

c. Apple Inc. decides to expand and rents an adjacent building.

d. You buy a new e-book from Amazon.

e. Apple Inc. hires a student as an intern during the summer.

Economics in the News

33. After you have studied *Reading Between the Lines* on pp. 44–45, answer the following questions.

a. How does an increase in the use of corn to produce ethanol affect the opportunity cost of corn?

b. How would you expect an increase in the quantity of corn produced to influence the opportunity cost of producing corn?

c. Why did the cost of producing corn increase in the rest of the world?

d. Is it possible that the increased quantity of corn produced, despite the higher cost of production, represents a move towards allocative efficiency?

34. **Malaria Eradication Back on the Table**

In response to the Gates Malaria Forum in October 2007, countries are debating the pros and cons of eradication. Dr. Arata Kochi of the World Health Organization believes that with enough money malaria cases could be cut by 90 percent, but he believes that it would be very expensive to eliminate the remaining 10 percent of cases. He concluded that countries should not strive to eradicate malaria.

Source: *The New York Times*, March 4, 2008

a. Is Dr. Kochi talking about *production efficiency* or *allocative efficiency* or both?

b. Make a graph with the percentage of malaria cases eliminated on the *x*-axis and the marginal cost and marginal benefit from driving down malaria cases on the *y*-axis. On your graph:

(i) Draw a marginal cost curve that is consistent with Dr. Kochi's opinion.

(ii) Draw a marginal benefit curve that is consistent with Dr. Kochi's opinion.

(iii) Identify the quantity of malaria eradicated that achieves allocative efficiency.

35. **Lots of Little Screens**

Inexpensive broadband access has created a generation of television producers for whom the Internet is their native medium. As they redirect the focus from TV to computers, cell phones, and iPods, the video market is developing into an open digital network.

Source: *The New York Times*, December 2, 2007

a. How has inexpensive broadband changed the production possibilities of video entertainment and other goods and services?

b. Sketch a *PPF* for video entertainment and other goods and services before broadband.

c. Show how the arrival of inexpensive broadband has changed the *PPF*.

d. Sketch a marginal benefit curve for video entertainment.

e. Show how the new generation of TV producers for whom the Internet is their native medium might have changed the marginal benefit from video entertainment.

f. Explain how the efficient quantity of video entertainment has changed.

Your Economic Revolution

Three periods in human history stand out as ones of economic revolution. The first, the *Agricultural Revolution*, occurred 10,000 years ago. In what is today Iraq, people learned to domesticate animals and plant crops. People stopped roaming in search of food and settled in villages, towns, and cities where they specialized in the activities in which they had a comparative advantage and developed markets in which to exchange their products. Wealth increased enormously.

You are studying economics at a time that future historians will call the *Information Revolution*. Over the entire world, people are embracing new information technologies and prospering on an unprecedented scale.

Economics was born during the *Industrial Revolution*, which began in England during the 1760s. For the first time, people began to apply science and create new technologies for the manufacture of textiles and iron, to create steam engines, and to boost the output of farms.

During all three economic revolutions, many have prospered but many have been left behind. It is the range of human progress that poses the greatest question for economics and the one that Adam Smith addressed in the first work of economic science: What causes the differences in wealth among nations?

Many people had written about economics before **Adam Smith**, *but he made economics a science. Born in 1723 in Kirkcaldy, a small fishing town near Edinburgh, Scotland, Smith was the only child of the town's customs officer. Lured from his professorship (he was a full professor at 28) by a wealthy Scottish duke who gave him a pension of £300 a year—10 times the average income at that time—Smith devoted 10 years to writing his masterpiece:* An Inquiry into the Nature and Causes of the **Wealth of Nations**, *published in 1776.*

Why, Adam Smith asked, are some nations wealthy while others are poor? He was pondering these questions at the height of the Industrial Revolution, and he answered by emphasizing the role of the division of labour and free markets.

To illustrate his argument, Adam Smith described two pin factories. In the first, one person, using the hand tools available in the 1770s, could make 20 pins a day. In the other, by using those same hand tools but breaking the process into a number of individually small operations in which people specialize—by the division of labour—10 people could make a staggering 48,000 pins a day.

> It is not from the benevolence of the butcher, the brewer, or the baker that we expect our dinner, but from their regard to their own interest.
>
> **ADAM SMITH**
> *The Wealth of Nations*

One draws out the wire, another straightens it, a third cuts it, a fourth points it, a fifth grinds it. Three specialists make the head, and a fourth attaches it. Finally, the pin is polished and packaged.

But a large market is needed to support the division of labour: One factory employing 10 workers would need to sell more than 15 million pins a year to stay in business!

Professor Bhagwati, what attracted you to economics?
When you come from India, where poverty hits the eye, it is easy to be attracted to economics, which can be used to bring prosperity and create jobs to pull up the poor into gainful employment.

I learned later that there are two broad types of economist: those who treat the subject as an arid mathematical toy and those who see it as a serious social science.

If Cambridge, where I went as an undergraduate, had been interested in esoteric mathematical economics, I would have opted for something else. But the Cambridge economists from whom I learned—many among the greatest figures in the discipline—saw economics as a social science. I therefore saw the power of economics as a tool to address India's poverty and was immediately hooked.

Who had the greatest impact on you at Cambridge?
Most of all, it was Harry Johnson, a young Canadian of immense energy and profound analytical gifts. Quite unlike the shy and reserved British dons, Johnson was friendly, effusive, and supportive of students who flocked around him. He would later move to Chicago, where he became one of the most influential members of the market-oriented Chicago school. Another was Joan Robinson, arguably the world's most impressive female economist.

When I left Cambridge for MIT, going from one Cambridge to the other, I was lucky to transition from one phenomenal set of economists to another. At MIT, I learned much from future Nobel laureates Paul Samuelson and Robert Solow. Both would later become great friends and colleagues when I joined the MIT faculty in 1968.

After Cambridge and MIT, you went to Oxford and then back to India. What did you do in India?
I joined the Planning Commission in New Delhi, where my first big job was to find ways of raising the bottom 30 percent of India's population out of poverty to a "minimum income" level.

And what did you prescribe?
My main prescription was to "grow the pie." My research suggested that the share of the bottom 30 percent of the pie did not seem to vary dramatically with differences in economic and political systems. So growth in the pie seemed to be the principal

(but not the only) component of an antipoverty strategy. To supplement growth's good effects on the poor, the Indian planners were also dedicated to education, health, social reforms, and land reforms. Also, the access of the lowest-income and socially disadvantaged groups to the growth process and its benefits was to be improved in many ways, such as extension of credit without collateral.

> My main prescription was to "grow the pie" … Much empirical work shows that where growth has occurred, poverty has lessened.

Today, this strategy has no rivals. Much empirical work shows that where growth has occurred, poverty has lessened. It is nice to know that one's basic take on an issue of such central importance to humanity's well-being has been borne out by experience!

You left India in 1968 to come to the United States and an academic job at MIT. Why?
While the decision to emigrate often reflects personal factors—and they were present in my case—the offer of a professorship from MIT certainly helped me

JAGDISH BHAGWATI is University Professor at Columbia University. Born in India in 1934, he studied at Cambridge University in England, MIT, and Oxford University before returning to India. He returned to teach at MIT in 1968 and moved to Columbia in 1980. A prolific scholar, Professor Bhagwati also writes in leading newspapers and magazines throughout the world. He has been much honoured for both his scientific work and his impact on public policy. His greatest contributions are in international trade but extend also to developmental problems and the study of political economy.

Michael Parkin talked with Jagdish Bhagwati about his work and the progress that economists have made in understanding the benefits of economic growth and international trade since the pioneering work of Adam Smith.

make up my mind. At the time, it was easily the world's most celebrated department. Serendipitously, the highest-ranked departments at MIT were not in engineering and the sciences but in linguistics (which had Noam Chomsky) and economics (which had Paul Samuelson). Joining the MIT faculty was a dramatic breakthrough: I felt stimulated each year by several fantastic students and by several of the world's most creative economists.

We hear a lot in the popular press about fair trade and level playing fields. What's the distinction between free trade and fair trade? How can the playing field be unlevel?

Free trade simply means allowing no trade barriers such as tariffs, subsidies, and quotas. Trade barriers make domestic prices different from world prices for traded goods. When this happens, resources are not being used efficiently. Basic economics from the time of Adam Smith tells us why free trade is good for us and why barriers to trade harm us, though our understanding of this doctrine today is far more nuanced and profound than it was at its creation.

Fair trade, on the other hand, is almost always a sneaky way of objecting to free trade. If your rivals are hard to compete with, you are not likely to get protection simply by saying that you cannot hack it. But if you say that your rival is an "unfair" trader, that is an easier sell! As international competition has grown fiercer, cries of "unfair trade" have therefore multiplied. The lesser rogues among the protectionists ask for "free and fair trade," whereas the worst ones ask for "fair, not free, trade."

> Fair trade ... is almost always a sneaky way of objecting to free trade.

At the end of World War II, the General Agreement on Tariffs and Trade (GATT) was established and there followed several rounds of multilateral trade negotiations and reductions in barriers to trade. How do you assess the contribution of GATT and its successor, the World Trade Organization (WTO)?

The GATT has made a huge contribution by overseeing massive trade liberalization in industrial goods among the developed countries. GATT rules, which "bind" tariffs to negotiated ceilings, prevent the raising of tariffs and have prevented tariff wars like those of the 1930s in which mutual and retaliatory tariff barriers were raised, to the detriment of everyone.

The GATT was folded into the WTO at the end of the Uruguay Round of trade negotiations, and the WTO is institutionally stronger. For instance, it has a binding dispute settlement mechanism, whereas the GATT had no such teeth. It is also more ambitious in its scope, extending to new areas such as the environment, intellectual property protection, and investment rules.

Running alongside the pursuit of multilateral free trade has been the emergence of bilateral trade agreements such as NAFTA and the European Union (EU). How do you view the bilateral free trade areas in today's world?

Unfortunately, there has been an explosion of bilateral free trade areas today. By some estimates, the ones in place and others being plotted approach 400! Each bilateral agreement gives preferential treatment to its trading partner over others. Because there are now so many bilateral agreements, such as those between the United States and Israel and between the United States and Jordan, the result is a chaotic pattern of different tariffs depending on where a product comes from. Also, "rules of origin" must be agreed upon to determine whether a product is, say, Jordanian or Taiwanese if Jordan qualifies for a preferential tariff but Taiwan does not and Taiwanese inputs enter the Jordanian manufacture of the product.

I have called the resulting crisscrossing of preferences and rules of origin the "spaghetti bowl" problem. The world trading system is choking under these proliferating bilateral deals. Contrast this complexity with the simplicity of a multilateral system with common tariffs for all WTO members.

We now have a world of uncoordinated and inefficient trade policies. The EU makes bilateral free trade agreements with different non-EU countries, so the United States follows with its own bilateral agreements; and with Europe and the United States doing it, the Asian countries, long wedded to multilateralism, have now succumbed to the mania.

> **We now have a world of uncoordinated and inefficient trade policies.**

Instead, if the United States had provided leadership by rewriting rules to make the signing of such bilateral agreements extremely difficult, this plague on the trading system today might well have been averted.

Is the "spaghetti bowl" problem getting better or worse?
Unquestionably it is getting worse. Multilateralism is retreating and bilateralism is advancing. The 2010 G-20 meeting in Canada was a disappointment. At the insistence of the United States, a definite date for completing the Doha Round was dropped and instead, unwittingly rubbing salt into the wound, President Barack Obama announced his administration's willingness to see the U.S.–South Korea free trade agreement through.

There are distressing recent reports that the U.S. Commerce Department is exploring ways to strengthen the bite of anti-dumping actions, which are now generally agreed to be a form of discriminatory protectionism aimed selectively at successful exporting nations and firms.

Equally distressing is Obama's decision to sign a bill that raises fees on some temporary work visas in order to pay for higher border-enforcement expenditures. Further, it was asserted that a tax on foreign workers would reduce the numbers coming in and "taking jobs away" from U.S. citizens. Many supporters of the proposal claimed, incoherently, that it would simultaneously discourage foreign workers from entering the United States and increase revenues.

Obama's surrender exemplified the doctrine that one retreat often leads to another, with new lobbyists following in others' footsteps. Perhaps the chief mistake, as with recent "Buy American" provisions in U.S. legislation, was to allow the Employ American Workers Act (EAWA) to be folded into the stimulus bill. This act makes it harder for companies to get governmental support to hire skilled immigrants with H1(b) visas: They must first show that they have not laid off or do not plan to lay off U.S. workers in similar occupations. Whatever the shortcomings of such measures in economic-policy terms, the visa-fee-enhancement provision is de facto discriminatory, and thus violates WTO rules against discrimination between domestic and foreign firms, or between foreign firms from different WTO countries.

While the visa-fee legislation is what lawyers call "facially" non-discriminatory, its design confers an advantage on U.S. firms vis-à-vis foreign firms. Such acts of discrimination in trade policies find succor in the media and in some of America's prominent think tanks. For example, in the wake of the vast misery brought by flooding to the people of Pakistan, the U.S. and other governments have risen to the occasion with emergency aid. But there have also been proposals to grant duty-free access to Pakistan's exports. But this would be discriminatory towards developing countries that do not have duty-free access, helping Pakistan at their expense.

What advice do you have for a student who is just starting to study economics? Is economics a good subject in which to major?
I would say enormously so. In particular, we economists bring three unique insights to good policymaking.

First, economists look for second- and subsequent-round effects of actions.

Second, we correctly emphasize that a policy cannot be judged without using a counterfactual. It is a witticism that an economist, when asked how her husband was, said, "Compared to what?"

Third, we uniquely and systematically bring the principle of social cost and social benefit to our policy analysis.

CHAPTER

3

Demand and Supply

After studying this chapter, you will be able to

◆ Describe a competitive market and think about a price as an opportunity cost

◆ Explain the influences on demand

◆ Explain the influences on supply

◆ Explain how demand and supply determine prices and quantities bought and sold

◆ Use the demand and supply model to make predictions about changes in prices and quantities

What makes the price of coffee double in just two years and then fall by 50 percent? This chapter enables you to answer this and similar questions.

You know that economics is about the choices people make to cope with scarcity and how those choices respond to incentives. Prices act as incentives. You're going to see how people respond to prices and how prices get determined by demand and supply.

The demand and supply model that you study in this chapter is the main tool of economics.

At the end of the chapter, in *Reading Between the Lines*, we'll apply the model to the market for coffee and explain why its price fluctuates so much.

◆ Markets and Prices

When you need a new pair of running shoes, want a bagel and a latte, plan to upgrade your cell phone, or look for a winter break in the sun, you must find a place where people sell those items or offer those services. The place in which you find them is a *market.* You learned in Chapter 2 (p. 42) that a market is any arrangement that enables buyers and sellers to get information and to do business with each other.

A market has two sides: buyers and sellers. There are markets for *goods* such as apples and hiking boots, for *services* such as haircuts and tennis lessons, for *factors of production* such as computer programmers and earthmovers, and for other manufactured *inputs* such as memory chips and auto parts. There are also markets for money such as Japanese yen and for financial securities such as Yahoo! stock. Only our imagination limits what can be traded in markets.

Some markets are physical places where buyers and sellers meet and where an auctioneer or a broker helps to determine the prices. Examples of this type of market are live car auctions and the wholesale fish, meat, and produce markets.

Some markets are groups of people spread around the world who never meet and know little about each other but are connected through the Internet or by telephone and fax. Examples are the e-commerce markets and the currency markets.

But most markets are unorganized collections of buyers and sellers. You do most of your trading in this type of market. An example is the market for basketball shoes. The buyers in this $3-billion-a-year market are the 45 million Canadians and Americans who play basketball (or who want to make a fashion statement). The sellers are the tens of thousands of retail sports equipment and footwear stores. Each buyer can visit several different stores, and each seller knows that the buyer has a choice of stores.

Markets vary in the intensity of competition that buyers and sellers face. In this chapter, we're going to study a **competitive market**—a market that has many buyers and many sellers, so no single buyer or seller can influence the price.

Producers offer items for sale only if the price is high enough to cover their opportunity cost. And consumers respond to changing opportunity cost by seeking cheaper alternatives to expensive items.

We are going to study how people respond to *prices* and the forces that determine prices. But to pursue these tasks, we need to understand the relationship between a price and an opportunity cost.

In everyday life, the *price* of an object is the number of dollars that must be given up in exchange for it. Economists refer to this price as the **money price**.

The *opportunity cost* of an action is the highest-valued alternative forgone. If, when you buy a cup of coffee, the highest-valued thing you forgo is some gum, then the opportunity cost of the coffee is the *quantity* of gum forgone. We can calculate the quantity of gum forgone from the money prices of the coffee and the gum.

If the money price of coffee is $1 a cup and the money price of gum is 50¢ a pack, then the opportunity cost of one cup of coffee is two packs of gum. To calculate this opportunity cost, we divide the price of a cup of coffee by the price of a pack of gum and find the *ratio* of one price to the other. The ratio of one price to another is called a **relative price**, and a *relative price is an opportunity cost.*

We can express the relative price of coffee in terms of gum or any other good. The normal way of expressing a relative price is in terms of a "basket" of all goods and services. To calculate this relative price, we divide the money price of a good by the money price of a "basket" of all goods (called a *price index*). The resulting relative price tells us the opportunity cost of the good in terms of how much of the "basket" we must give up to buy it.

The demand and supply model that we are about to study determines *relative prices,* and the word "price" means *relative* price. When we predict that a price will fall, we do not mean that its *money* price will fall—although it might. We mean that its *relative* price will fall. That is, its price will fall *relative* to the average price of other goods and services.

REVIEW QUIZ

1 What is the distinction between a money price and a relative price?
2 Explain why a relative price is an opportunity cost.
3 Think of examples of goods whose relative price has risen or fallen by a large amount.

You can work these questions in Study Plan 3.1 and get instant feedback.

━━━━━━━━━━━━━━ MyEconLab ◆

Let's begin our study of demand and supply, starting with demand.

Demand

If you demand something, then you

1. Want it,
2. Can afford it, and
3. Plan to buy it.

Wants are the unlimited desires or wishes that people have for goods and services. How many times have you thought that you would like something "if only you could afford it" or "if it weren't so expensive"? Scarcity guarantees that many—perhaps most—of our wants will never be satisfied. Demand reflects a decision about which wants to satisfy.

The **quantity demanded** of a good or service is the amount that consumers plan to buy during a given time period at a particular price. The quantity demanded is not necessarily the same as the quantity actually bought. Sometimes the quantity demanded exceeds the amount of goods available, so the quantity bought is less than the quantity demanded.

The quantity demanded is measured as an amount per unit of time. For example, suppose that you buy one cup of coffee a day. The quantity of coffee that you demand can be expressed as 1 cup per day, 7 cups per week, or 365 cups per year.

Many factors influence buying plans, and one of them is the price. We look first at the relationship between the quantity demanded of a good and its price. To study this relationship, we keep all other influences on buying plans the same and we ask: How, other things remaining the same, does the quantity demanded of a good change as its price changes?

The law of demand provides the answer.

The Law of Demand

The **law of demand** states

> Other things remaining the same, the higher the price of a good, the smaller is the quantity demanded; and the lower the price of a good, the greater is the quantity demanded.

Why does a higher price reduce the quantity demanded? For two reasons:

- Substitution effect
- Income effect

Substitution Effect When the price of a good rises, other things remaining the same, its *relative* price—its opportunity cost—rises. Although each good is unique, it has *substitutes*—other goods that can be used in its place. As the opportunity cost of a good rises, the incentive to economize on its use and switch to a substitute becomes stronger.

Income Effect When a price rises, other things remaining the same, the price rises *relative* to income. Faced with a higher price and an unchanged income, people cannot afford to buy all the things they previously bought. They must decrease the quantities demanded of at least some goods and services. Normally, the good whose price has increased will be one of the goods that people buy less of.

To see the substitution effect and the income effect at work, think about the effects of a change in the price of an energy bar. Several different goods are substitutes for an energy bar. For example, an energy drink could be consumed instead of an energy bar.

Suppose that an energy bar initially sells for $3.00 and then its price falls to $1.50. People now substitute energy bars for energy drinks—the substitution effect. And with a budget that now has some slack from the lower price of an energy bar, people buy even more energy bars—the income effect. The quantity of energy bars demanded increases for these two reasons.

Now suppose that an energy bar initially sells for $3 and then the price doubles to $6. People now buy fewer energy bars and more energy drinks—the substitution effect. And faced with a tighter budget, people buy even fewer energy bars—the income effect. The quantity of energy bars demanded decreases for these two reasons.

Demand Curve and Demand Schedule

You are now about to study one of the two most used curves in economics: the demand curve. You are also going to encounter one of the most critical distinctions: the distinction between *demand* and *quantity demanded*.

The term **demand** refers to the entire relationship between the price of a good and the quantity demanded of that good. Demand is illustrated by the demand curve and the demand schedule. The term *quantity demanded* refers to a point on a demand curve—the quantity demanded at a particular price.

Figure 3.1 shows the demand curve for energy bars. A **demand curve** shows the relationship between the quantity demanded of a good and its price when all other influences on consumers' planned purchases remain the same.

The table in Fig. 3.1 is the demand schedule for energy bars. A *demand schedule* lists the quantities demanded at each price when all the other influences on consumers' planned purchases remain the same. For example, if the price of a bar is 50¢, the quantity demanded is 22 million a week. If the price is $2.50, the quantity demanded is 5 million a week. The other rows of the table show the quantities demanded at prices of $1.00, $1.50, and $2.00.

We graph the demand schedule as a demand curve with the quantity demanded on the *x*-axis and the price on the *y*-axis. The points on the demand curve labelled *A* through *E* correspond to the rows of the demand schedule. For example, point *A* on the graph shows a quantity demanded of 22 million energy bars a week at a price of 50¢ a bar.

Willingness and Ability to Pay Another way of looking at the demand curve is as a willingness-and-ability-to-pay curve. The willingness and ability to pay is a measure of *marginal benefit.*

If a small quantity is available, the highest price that someone is willing and able to pay for one more unit is high. But as the quantity available increases, the marginal benefit of each additional unit falls and the highest price that someone is willing and able to pay also falls along the demand curve.

In Fig. 3.1, if only 5 million energy bars are available each week, the highest price that someone is willing to pay for the 5 millionth bar is $2.50. But if 22 million energy bars are available each week, someone is willing to pay 50¢ for the last bar bought.

A Change in Demand

When any factor that influences buying plans changes, other than the price of the good, there is a **change in demand**. Figure 3.2 illustrates an increase in demand. When demand increases, the demand curve shifts rightward and the quantity demanded at each price is greater. For example, at $2.50 a bar, the quantity demanded on the original (blue) demand curve is 5 million energy bars a week. On the new (red) demand curve, at $2.50 a bar, the quantity demanded is 15 million bars a week. Look closely at the numbers in the table and check that the quantity demanded at each price is greater.

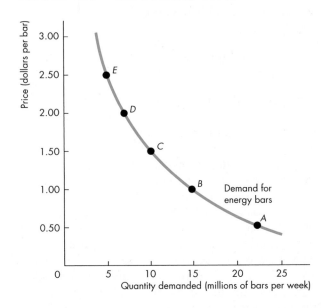

FIGURE 3.1   The Demand Curve

	Price (dollars per bar)	Quantity demanded (millions of bars per week)
A	0.50	22
B	1.00	15
C	1.50	10
D	2.00	7
E	2.50	5

The table shows a demand schedule for energy bars. At a price of 50¢ a bar, 22 million bars a week are demanded; at a price of $1.50 a bar, 10 million bars a week are demanded. The demand curve shows the relationship between quantity demanded and price, other things remaining the same. The demand curve slopes downward: As the price falls, the quantity demanded increases.

The demand curve can be read in two ways. For a given price, the demand curve tells us the quantity that people plan to buy. For example, at a price of $1.50 a bar, people plan to buy 10 million bars a week. For a given quantity, the demand curve tells us the maximum price that consumers are willing and able to pay for the last bar available. For example, the maximum price that consumers will pay for the 15 millionth bar is $1.00.

MyEconLab   animation

FIGURE 3.2   An Increase in Demand

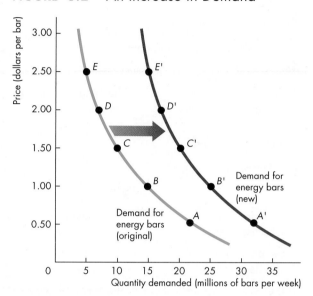

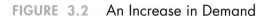

Original demand schedule Original income		New demand schedule New higher income		
	Price (dollars per bar)	Quantity demanded (millions of bars per week)	Price (dollars per bar)	Quantity demanded (millions of bars per week)
A	0.50	22	A' 0.50	32
B	1.00	15	B' 1.00	25
C	1.50	10	C' 1.50	20
D	2.00	7	D' 2.00	17
E	2.50	5	E' 2.50	15

A change in any influence on buying plans other than the price of the good itself results in a new demand schedule and a shift of the demand curve. A change in income changes the demand for energy bars. At a price of $1.50 a bar, 10 million bars a week are demanded at the original income (row C of the table) and 20 million bars a week are demanded at the new higher income (row C'). A rise in income increases the demand for energy bars. The demand curve shifts *rightward*, as shown by the shift arrow and the resulting red curve.

————— MyEconLab animation ◆

Six main factors bring changes in demand. They are changes in

- The prices of related goods
- Expected future prices
- Income
- Expected future income and credit
- Population
- Preferences

Prices of Related Goods The quantity of energy bars that consumers plan to buy depends in part on the prices of substitutes for energy bars. A **substitute** is a good that can be used in place of another good. For example, a bus ride is a substitute for a train ride; a hamburger is a substitute for a hot dog; and an energy drink is a substitute for an energy bar. If the price of a substitute for an energy bar rises, people buy less of the substitute and more energy bars. For example, if the price of an energy drink rises, people buy fewer energy drinks and more energy bars. The demand for energy bars increases.

The quantity of energy bars that people plan to buy also depends on the prices of complements with energy bars. A **complement** is a good that is used in conjunction with another good. Hamburgers and fries are complements, and so are energy bars and exercise. If the price of an hour at the gym falls, people buy more gym time *and more* energy bars.

Expected Future Prices If the expected future price of a good rises and if the good can be stored, the opportunity cost of obtaining the good for future use is lower today than it will be in the future when people expect the price to be higher. So people retime their purchases—they substitute over time. They buy more of the good now before its price is expected to rise (and less afterward), so the demand for the good today increases.

For example, suppose that a Florida frost damages the season's orange crop. You expect the price of orange juice to rise, so you fill your freezer with enough frozen juice to get you through the next six months. Your current demand for frozen orange juice has increased, and your future demand has decreased.

Similarly, if the expected future price of a good falls, the opportunity cost of buying the good today is high relative to what it is expected to be in the future. So again, people retime their purchases. They buy less of the good now before its price is expected to fall, so the demand for the good decreases today and increases in the future.

Computer prices are constantly falling, and this fact poses a dilemma. Will you buy a new computer now, in time for the start of the school year, or will you wait until the price has fallen some more? Because people expect computer prices to keep falling, the current demand for computers is less (and the future demand is greater) than it otherwise would be.

Income   Consumers' income influences demand. When income increases, consumers buy more of most goods; and when income decreases, consumers buy less of most goods. Although an increase in income leads to an increase in the demand for *most* goods, it does not lead to an increase in the demand for *all* goods. A **normal good** is one for which demand increases as income increases. An **inferior good** is one for which demand decreases as income increases. As incomes increase, the demand for air travel (a normal good) increases and the demand for long-distance bus trips (an inferior good) decreases.

Expected Future Income and Credit   When expected future income increases or credit becomes easier to get, demand for the good might increase now. For example, a salesperson gets the news that she will receive a big bonus at the end of the year, so she goes into debt and buys a new car now, rather than wait until she receives the bonus.

Population   Demand also depends on the size and the age structure of the population. The larger the population, the greater is the demand for all goods and services; the smaller the population, the smaller is the demand for all goods and services. For example, the demand for parking spaces or movies or just about anything that you can imagine is much greater in the Greater Toronto Area (population 5.6 million) than it is in Thunder Bay (population 124,000).

Also, the larger the proportion of the population in a given age group, the greater is the demand for the goods and services used by that age group. For example, in 2010, there were 2.3 million 20- to 24-year-olds in Canada compared with 2.1 million in 2000. As a result, the demand for university places in 2010 was greater than in 2000. Over this same period, the number of Canadians aged 90 years more than doubled to exceed 200,000. As a result, the demand for nursing home services increased.

TABLE 3.1   The Demand for Energy Bars

The Law of Demand

The quantity of energy bars demanded

Decreases if:	Increases if:
■ The price of an energy bar rises	■ The price of an energy bar falls

Changes in Demand

The demand for energy bars

Decreases if:	Increases if:
■ The price of a substitute falls	■ The price of a substitute rises
■ The price of a complement rises	■ The price of a complement falls
■ The expected future price of an energy bar falls	■ The expected future price of an energy bar rises
■ Income falls*	■ Income rises*
■ Expected future income falls or credit becomes harder to get*	■ Expected future income rises or credit becomes easier to get*
■ The population decreases	■ The population increases

*An energy bar is a normal good.

Preferences   Demand depends on preferences. *Preferences* determine the value that people place on each good and service. Preferences depend on such things as the weather, information, and fashion. For example, greater health and fitness awareness has shifted preferences in favour of energy bars, so the demand for energy bars has increased.

Table 3.1 summarizes the influences on demand and the direction of those influences.

A Change in the Quantity Demanded Versus a Change in Demand

Changes in the influences on buying plans bring either a change in the quantity demanded or a change in demand. Equivalently, they bring either a movement along the demand curve or a shift of the demand curve. The distinction between a change in the quantity demanded and a change in demand is the same as that between a movement along the demand curve and a shift of the demand curve.

A point on the demand curve shows the quantity demanded at a given price, so a movement along the demand curve shows a **change in the quantity demanded**. The entire demand curve shows demand, so a shift of the demand curve shows a *change in demand*. Figure 3.3 illustrates these distinctions.

Movement Along the Demand Curve If the price of the good changes but no other influence on buying plans changes, we illustrate the effect of the price change as a movement along the demand curve.

A fall in the price of a good increases the quantity demanded of it. In Fig. 3.3, we illustrate the effect of a fall in price as a movement down along the demand curve D_0.

A rise in the price of a good decreases the quantity demanded of it. In Fig. 3.3, we illustrate the effect of a rise in price as a movement up along the demand curve D_0.

A Shift of the Demand Curve If the price of a good remains constant but some other influence on buying plans changes, there is a change in demand for that good. We illustrate a change in demand as a shift of the demand curve. For example, if more people work out at the gym, consumers buy more energy bars regardless of the price of a bar. That is what a rightward shift of the demand curve shows— more energy bars are demanded at each price.

In Fig. 3.3, there is a *change in demand* and the demand curve shifts when any influence on buying plans changes, other than the price of the good. Demand *increases* and the demand curve *shifts right-ward* (to the red demand curve D_1) if the price of a substitute rises, the price of a complement falls, the expected future price of the good rises, income increases (for a normal good), expected future income or credit increases, or the population increases. Demand *decreases* and the demand curve *shifts leftward* (to the red demand curve D_2) if the price of a substitute falls, the price of a complement rises, the expected future price of the good falls, income decreases (for a normal good), expected future income or credit decreases, or the population decreases. (For an inferior good, the effects of changes in income are in the opposite direction to those described above.)

FIGURE 3.3   A Change in the Quantity Demanded Versus a Change in Demand

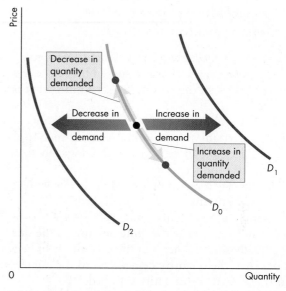

When the price of the good changes, there is a movement along the demand curve and *a change in the quantity demanded*, shown by the blue arrows on demand curve D_0. When any other influence on buying plans changes, there is a shift of the demand curve and a *change in demand*. An increase in demand shifts the demand curve rightward (from D_0 to D_1). A decrease in demand shifts the demand curve leftward (from D_0 to D_2).

MyEconLab   animation ◆

REVIEW QUIZ

1 Define the quantity demanded of a good or service.
2 What is the law of demand and how do we illustrate it?
3 What does the demand curve tell us about the price that consumers are willing to pay?
4 List all the influences on buying plans that change demand, and for each influence, say whether it increases or decreases demand.
5 Why does demand not change when the price of a good changes with no change in the other influences on buying plans?

You can work these questions in Study Plan 3.2 and get instant feedback.

MyEconLab ◆

Supply

If a firm supplies a good or service, the firm

1. Has the resources and technology to produce it,
2. Can profit from producing it, and
3. Plans to produce it and sell it.

A supply is more than just having the *resources* and the *technology* to produce something. *Resources and technology* are the constraints that limit what is possible.

Many useful things can be produced, but they are not produced unless it is profitable to do so. Supply reflects a decision about which technologically feasible items to produce.

The **quantity supplied** of a good or service is the amount that producers plan to sell during a given time period at a particular price. The quantity supplied is not necessarily the same amount as the quantity actually sold. Sometimes the quantity supplied is greater than the quantity demanded, so the quantity sold is less than the quantity supplied.

Like the quantity demanded, the quantity supplied is measured as an amount per unit of time. For example, suppose that GM produces 1,000 cars a day. The quantity of cars supplied by GM can be expressed as 1,000 a day, 7,000 a week, or 365,000 a year. Without the time dimension, we cannot tell whether a particular quantity is large or small.

Many factors influence selling plans, and again one of them is the price of the good. We look first at the relationship between the quantity supplied of a good and its price. Just as we did when we studied demand, to isolate the relationship between the quantity supplied of a good and its price, we keep all other influences on selling plans the same and ask: How does the quantity supplied of a good change as its price changes when other things remain the same?

The law of supply provides the answer.

The Law of Supply

The **law of supply** states:

> Other things remaining the same, the higher the price of a good, the greater is the quantity supplied; and the lower the price of a good, the smaller is the quantity supplied.

Why does a higher price increase the quantity supplied? It is because *marginal cost increases.* As the quantity produced of any good increases, the marginal cost of producing the good increases. (See Chapter 2, p. 33 to review marginal cost.)

It is never worth producing a good if the price received for the good does not at least cover the marginal cost of producing it. When the price of a good rises, other things remaining the same, producers are willing to incur a higher marginal cost, so they increase production. The higher price brings forth an increase in the quantity supplied.

Let's now illustrate the law of supply with a supply curve and a supply schedule.

Supply Curve and Supply Schedule

You are now going to study the second of the two most used curves in economics: the supply curve. You're also going to learn about the critical distinction between *supply* and *quantity supplied.*

The term **supply** refers to the entire relationship between the price of a good and the quantity supplied of it. Supply is illustrated by the supply curve and the supply schedule. The term *quantity supplied* refers to a point on a supply curve—the quantity supplied at a particular price.

Figure 3.4 shows the supply curve of energy bars. A **supply curve** shows the relationship between the quantity supplied of a good and its price when all other influences on producers' planned sales remain the same. The supply curve is a graph of a supply schedule.

The table in Fig. 3.4 sets out the supply schedule for energy bars. A *supply schedule* lists the quantities supplied at each price when all the other influences on producers' planned sales remain the same. For example, if the price of an energy bar is 50¢, the quantity supplied is zero—in row *A* of the table. If the price of an energy bar is $1.00, the quantity supplied is 6 million energy bars a week—in row *B*. The other rows of the table show the quantities supplied at prices of $1.50, $2.00, and $2.50.

To make a supply curve, we graph the quantity supplied on the *x*-axis and the price on the *y*-axis. The points on the supply curve labelled *A* through *E* correspond to the rows of the supply schedule. For example, point *A* on the graph shows a quantity supplied of zero at a price of 50¢ an energy bar. Point *E* shows a quantity supplied of 15 million bars at $2.50 an energy bar.

FIGURE 3.4   The Supply Curve

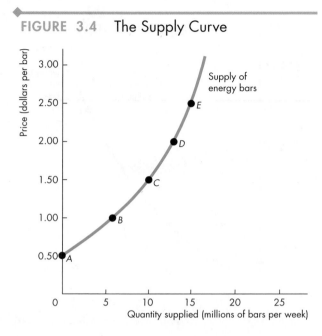

	Price (dollars per bar)	Quantity supplied (millions of bars per week)
A	0.50	0
B	1.00	6
C	1.50	10
D	2.00	13
E	2.50	15

The table shows the supply schedule of energy bars. For example, at a price of $1.00, 6 million bars a week are supplied; at a price of $2.50, 15 million bars a week are supplied. The supply curve shows the relationship between the quantity supplied and the price, other things remaining the same. The supply curve slopes upward: As the price of a good increases, the quantity supplied increases.

A supply curve can be read in two ways. For a given price, the supply curve tells us the quantity that producers plan to sell at that price. For example, at a price of $1.50 a bar, producers are planning to sell 10 million bars a week. For a given quantity, the supply curve tells us the minimum price at which producers are willing to sell one more bar. For example, if 15 million bars are produced each week, the lowest price at which a producer is willing to sell the 15 millionth bar is $2.50.

—————— MyEconLab   animation   ◆

Minimum Supply Price   The supply curve can be interpreted as a minimum-supply-price curve—a curve that shows the lowest price at which someone is willing to sell. This lowest price is the *marginal cost.*

If a small quantity is produced, the lowest price at which someone is willing to sell one more unit is low. But as the quantity produced increases, the marginal cost of each additional unit rises, so the lowest price at which someone is willing to sell an additional unit rises along the supply curve.

In Fig. 3.4, if 15 million bars are produced each week, the lowest price at which someone is willing to sell the 15 millionth bar is $2.50. But if 10 million bars are produced each week, someone is willing to accept $1.50 for the last bar produced.

A Change in Supply

When any factor that influences selling plans other than the price of the good changes, there is a **change in supply**. Six main factors bring changes in supply. They are changes in

- The prices of factors of production
- The prices of related goods produced
- Expected future prices
- The number of suppliers
- Technology
- The state of nature

Prices of Factors of Production   The prices of the factors of production used to produce a good influence its supply. To see this influence, think about the supply curve as a minimum-supply-price curve. If the price of a factor of production rises, the lowest price that a producer is willing to accept for that good rises, so supply decreases. For example, during 2008, as the price of jet fuel increased, the supply of air travel decreased. Similarly, a rise in the minimum wage decreases the supply of hamburgers.

Prices of Related Goods Produced   The prices of related goods that firms produce influence supply. For example, if the price of energy gel rises, firms switch production from bars to gel. The supply of energy bars decreases. Energy bars and energy gel are *substitutes in production*—goods that can be produced by using the same resources. If the price of beef rises, the supply of cowhide increases. Beef and cowhide are *complements in production*—goods that must be produced together.

Expected Future Prices If the expected future price of a good rises, the return from selling the good in the future increases and is higher than it is today. So supply decreases today and increases in the future.

The Number of Suppliers The larger the number of firms that produce a good, the greater is the supply of the good. As new firms enter an industry, the supply in that industry increases. As firms leave an industry, the supply in that industry decreases.

Technology The term "technology" is used broadly to mean the way that factors of production are used to produce a good. A technology change occurs when a new method is discovered that lowers the cost of producing a good. For example, new methods used in the factories that produce computer chips have lowered the cost and increased the supply of chips.

The State of Nature The state of nature includes all the natural forces that influence production. It includes the state of the weather and, more broadly, the natural environment. Good weather can increase the supply of many agricultural products and bad weather can decrease their supply. Extreme natural events such as earthquakes, tornadoes, and hurricanes can also influence supply.

Figure 3.5 illustrates an increase in supply. When supply increases, the supply curve shifts rightward and the quantity supplied at each price is larger. For example, at $1.00 per bar, on the original (blue) supply curve, the quantity supplied is 6 million bars a week. On the new (red) supply curve, the quantity supplied is 15 million bars a week. Look closely at the numbers in the table in Fig. 3.5 and check that the quantity supplied is larger at each price.

Table 3.2 summarizes the influences on supply and the directions of those influences.

A Change in the Quantity Supplied Versus a Change in Supply

Changes in the influences on selling plans bring either a change in the quantity supplied or a change in supply. Equivalently, they bring either a movement along the supply curve or a shift of the supply curve.

A point on the supply curve shows the quantity supplied at a given price. A movement along the supply curve shows a **change in the quantity supplied**. The entire supply curve shows supply. A shift of the supply curve shows a *change in supply*.

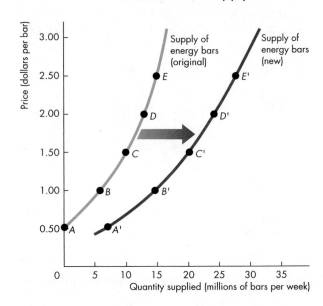

FIGURE 3.5   An Increase in Supply

| Original supply schedule | | | New supply schedule | | |
Old technology			New technology		
	Price (dollars per bar)	Quantity supplied (millions of bars per week)		Price (dollars per bar)	Quantity supplied (millions of bars per week)
A	0.50	0	A'	0.50	7
B	1.00	6	B'	1.00	15
C	1.50	10	C'	1.50	20
D	2.00	13	D'	2.00	25
E	2.50	15	E'	2.50	27

A change in any influence on selling plans other than the price of the good itself results in a new supply schedule and a shift of the supply curve. For example, a new, cost-saving technology for producing energy bars changes the supply of energy bars. At a price of $1.50 a bar, 10 million bars a week are supplied when producers use the old technology (row C of the table) and 20 million energy bars a week are supplied when producers use the new technology (row C'). An advance in technology *increases* the supply of energy bars. The supply curve shifts *rightward*, as shown by the shift arrow and the resulting red curve.

MyEconLab   animation

Figure 3.6 illustrates and summarizes these distinctions. If the price of the good changes and other things remain the same, there is a *change in the quantity supplied* of that good. If the price of the good falls, the quantity supplied decreases and there is a movement down along the supply curve S_0. If the price of the good rises, the quantity supplied increases and there is a movement up along the supply curve S_0. When any other influence on selling plans changes, the supply curve shifts and there is a *change in supply*. If supply increases, the supply curve shifts rightward to S_1. If supply decreases, the supply curve shifts leftward to S_2.

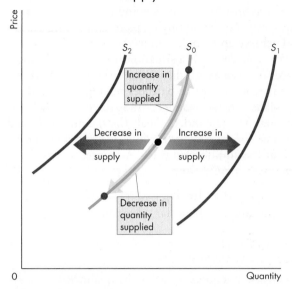

FIGURE 3.6   A Change in the Quantity Supplied Versus a Change in Supply

When the price of the good changes, there is a movement along the supply curve and *a change in the quantity supplied*, shown by the blue arrows on supply curve S_0. When any other influence on selling plans changes, there is a shift of the supply curve and a *change in supply*. An increase in supply shifts the supply curve rightward (from S_0 to S_1), and a decrease in supply shifts the supply curve leftward (from S_0 to S_2).

MyEconLab   animation

TABLE 3.2   The Supply of Energy Bars

The Law of Supply

The quantity of energy bars supplied

Decreases if:	Increases if:
■ The price of an energy bar falls	■ The price of an energy bar rises

Changes in Supply

The supply of energy bars

Decreases if:	Increases if:
■ The price of a factor of production used to produce energy bars rises	■ The price of a factor of production used to produce energy bars falls
■ The price of a substitute in production rises	■ The price of a substitute in production falls
■ The price of a complement in production falls	■ The price of a complement in production rises
■ The expected future price of an energy bar rises	■ The expected future price of an energy bar falls
■ The number of suppliers of bars decreases	■ The number of suppliers of bars increases
■ A technology change decreases energy bar production	■ A technology change increases energy bar production
■ A natural event decreases energy bar production	■ A natural event increases energy bar production

---

REVIEW QUIZ

1 Define the quantity supplied of a good or service.
2 What is the law of supply and how do we illustrate it?
3 What does the supply curve tell us about the producer's minimum supply price?
4 List all the influences on selling plans, and for each influence, say whether it changes supply.
5 What happens to the quantity of cell phones supplied and the supply of cell phones if the price of a cell phone falls?

You can work these questions in Study Plan 3.3 and get instant feedback.

MyEconLab ◆

Now we're going to combine demand and supply and see how prices and quantities are determined.

◆ Market Equilibrium

We have seen that when the price of a good rises, the quantity demanded *decreases* and the quantity supplied *increases*. We are now going to see how the price adjusts to coordinate buying plans and selling plans and achieve an equilibrium in the market.

An *equilibrium* is a situation in which opposing forces balance each other. Equilibrium in a market occurs when the price balances buying plans and selling plans. The **equilibrium price** is the price at which the quantity demanded equals the quantity supplied. The **equilibrium quantity** is the quantity bought and sold at the equilibrium price. A market moves towards its equilibrium because

- Price regulates buying and selling plans.
- Price adjusts when plans don't match.

Price as a Regulator

The price of a good regulates the quantities demanded and supplied. If the price is too high, the quantity supplied exceeds the quantity demanded. If the price is too low, the quantity demanded exceeds the quantity supplied. There is one price at which the quantity demanded equals the quantity supplied. Let's work out what that price is.

Figure 3.7 shows the market for energy bars. The table shows the demand schedule (from Fig. 3.1) and the supply schedule (from Fig. 3.4). If the price is 50¢ a bar, the quantity demanded is 22 million bars a week but no bars are supplied. There is a shortage of 22 million bars a week. The final column of the table shows this shortage. At a price of $1.00 a bar, there is still a shortage but only of 9 million bars a week.

If the price is $2.50 a bar, the quantity supplied is 15 million bars a week but the quantity demanded is only 5 million. There is a surplus of 10 million bars a week.

The one price at which there is neither a shortage nor a surplus is $1.50 a bar. At that price, the quantity demanded equals the quantity supplied: 10 million bars a week. The equilibrium price is $1.50 a bar, and the equilibrium quantity is 10 million bars a week.

Figure 3.7 shows that the demand curve and the supply curve intersect at the equilibrium price of $1.50 a bar. At each price *above* $1.50 a bar, there is a surplus of bars. For example, at $2.00 a bar, the surplus is 6 million bars a week, as shown by the

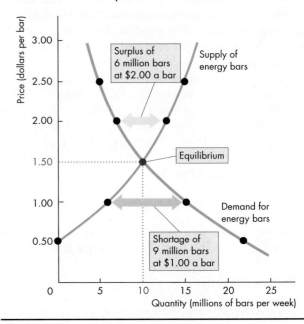

FIGURE 3.7   Equilibrium

Price (dollars per bar)	Quantity demanded	Quantity supplied	Shortage (−) or surplus (+)
	(millions of bars per week)		
0.50	22	0	−22
1.00	15	6	−9
1.50	**10**	**10**	**0**
2.00	7	13	+6
2.50	5	15	+10

The table lists the quantity demanded and the quantity supplied as well as the shortage or surplus of bars at each price. If the price is $1.00 a bar, 15 million bars a week are demanded and 6 million bars are supplied. There is a shortage of 9 million bars a week, and the price rises.

If the price is $2.00 a bar, 7 million bars a week are demanded and 13 million bars are supplied. There is a surplus of 6 million bars a week, and the price falls.

If the price is $1.50 a bar, 10 million bars a week are demanded and 10 million bars are supplied. There is neither a shortage nor a surplus, and the price does not change. The price at which the quantity demanded equals the quantity supplied is the equilibrium price, and 10 million bars a week is the equilibrium quantity.

MyEconLab   animation ◆

blue arrow. At each price *below* $1.50 a bar, there is a shortage of bars. For example, at $1.00 a bar, the shortage is 9 million bars a week, as shown by the red arrow.

Price Adjustments

You've seen that if the price is below equilibrium, there is a shortage and that if the price is above equilibrium, there is a surplus. But can we count on the price to change and eliminate a shortage or a surplus? We can, because such price changes are beneficial to both buyers and sellers. Let's see why the price changes when there is a shortage or a surplus.

A Shortage Forces the Price Up Suppose the price of an energy bar is $1. Consumers plan to buy 15 million bars a week, and producers plan to sell 6 million bars a week. Consumers can't force producers to sell more than they plan, so the quantity that is actually offered for sale is 6 million bars a week. In this situation, powerful forces operate to increase the price and move it towards the equilibrium price. Some producers, noticing lines of unsatisfied consumers, raise the price. Some producers increase their output. As producers push the price up, the price rises towards its equilibrium. The rising price reduces the shortage because it decreases the quantity demanded and increases the quantity supplied. When the price has increased to the point at which there is no longer a shortage, the forces moving the price stop operating. The price comes to rest at its equilibrium.

A Surplus Forces the Price Down Suppose the price of a bar is $2. Producers plan to sell 13 million bars a week, and consumers plan to buy 7 million bars a week. Producers cannot force consumers to buy more than they plan, so the quantity that is actually bought is 7 million bars a week. In this situation, powerful forces operate to lower the price and move it towards the equilibrium price. Some producers, unable to sell the quantities of energy bars they planned to sell, cut their prices. In addition, some producers scale back production. As producers cut the price, the price falls towards its equilibrium. The falling price decreases the surplus because it increases the quantity demanded and decreases the quantity supplied. When the price has fallen to the point at which there is no longer a surplus, the forces moving the price stop operating. The price comes to rest at its equilibrium.

The Best Deal Available for Buyers and Sellers

When the price is below equilibrium, it is forced upward. Why don't buyers resist the increase and refuse to buy at the higher price? The answer is because they value the good more highly than its current price and they can't satisfy their demand at the current price. In some markets—for example, the markets that operate on eBay—the buyers might even be the ones who force the price up by offering to pay a higher price.

When the price is above equilibrium, it is bid downward. Why don't sellers resist this decrease and refuse to sell at the lower price? The answer is because their minimum supply price is below the current price and they cannot sell all they would like to at the current price. Sellers willingly lower the price to gain market share.

At the price at which the quantity demanded and the quantity supplied are equal, neither buyers nor sellers can do business at a better price. Buyers pay the highest price they are willing to pay for the last unit bought, and sellers receive the lowest price at which they are willing to supply the last unit sold.

When people freely make offers to buy and sell and when demanders try to buy at the lowest possible price and suppliers try to sell at the highest possible price, the price at which trade takes place is the equilibrium price—the price at which the quantity demanded equals the quantity supplied. The price coordinates the plans of buyers and sellers, and no one has an incentive to change it.

◗ REVIEW QUIZ

1 What is the equilibrium price of a good or service?

2 Over what range of prices does a shortage arise? What happens to the price when there is a shortage?

3 Over what range of prices does a surplus arise? What happens to the price when there is a surplus?

4 Why is the price at which the quantity demanded equals the quantity supplied the equilibrium price?

5 Why is the equilibrium price the best deal available for both buyers and sellers?

You can work these questions in Study Plan 3.4 and get instant feedback.

─────────────── MyEconLab ◆

Predicting Changes in Price and Quantity

The demand and supply model that we have just studied provides us with a powerful way of analyzing influences on prices and the quantities bought and sold. According to the model, a change in price stems from a change in demand, a change in supply, or a change in both demand and supply. Let's look first at the effects of a change in demand.

An Increase in Demand

If more people join health clubs, the demand for energy bars increases. The table in Fig. 3.8 shows the original and new demand schedules for energy bars as well as the supply schedule of energy bars.

The increase in demand creates a shortage at the original price and to eliminate the shortage, the price must rise.

Figure 3.8 shows what happens. The figure shows the original demand for and supply of energy bars. The original equilibrium price is $1.50 an energy bar, and the equilibrium quantity is 10 million energy bars a week. When demand increases, the demand curve shifts rightward. The equilibrium price rises to $2.50 an energy bar, and the quantity supplied increases to 15 million energy bars a week, as highlighted in the figure. There is an *increase in the quantity supplied* but *no change in supply*—a movement along, but no shift of, the supply curve.

A Decrease in Demand

We can reverse this change in demand. Start at a price of $2.50 a bar with 15 million energy bars a week being bought and sold, and then work out what happens if demand decreases to its original level. Such a decrease in demand might arise if people switch to energy gel (a substitute for energy bars). The decrease in demand shifts the demand curve leftward. The equilibrium price falls to $1.50 a bar, the quantity supplied decreases, and the equilibrium quantity decreases to 10 million bars a week.

We can now make our first two predictions:

1. When demand increases, the price rises and the quantity increases.
2. When demand decreases, the price falls and the quantity decreases.

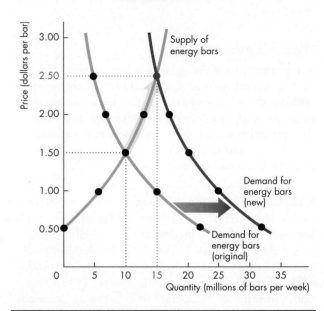

FIGURE 3.8   The Effects of a Change in Demand

Price (dollars per bar)	Quantity demanded (millions of bars per week)		Quantity supplied (millions of bars per week)
	Original	New	
0.50	22	32	0
1.00	15	25	6
1.50	**10**	20	**10**
2.00	7	17	13
2.50	**5**	**15**	**15**

Initially, the demand for energy bars is the blue demand curve. The equilibrium price is $1.50 a bar, and the equilibrium quantity is 10 million bars a week. When more health-conscious people do more exercise, the demand for energy bars increases and the demand curve shifts rightward to become the red curve.

At $1.50 a bar, there is now a shortage of 10 million bars a week. The price of a bar rises to a new equilibrium of $2.50. As the price rises to $2.50, the quantity supplied increases—shown by the blue arrow on the supply curve—to the new equilibrium quantity of 15 million bars a week. Following an increase in demand, the quantity supplied increases but supply does not change—the supply curve does not shift.

MyEconLab   animation

Economics in Action
The Global Market for Crude Oil

The demand and supply model provides insights into all competitive markets. Here, we'll apply what you've learned about the effects of an increase in demand to the global market for crude oil.

Crude oil is like the life-blood of the global economy. It is used to fuel our cars, airplanes, trains, and buses, to generate electricity, and to produce a wide range of plastics. When the price of crude oil rises, the costs of transportation, power, and materials all increase.

In 2001, the price of a barrel of oil was $20 (using the value of money in 2010). In 2008, before the global financial crisis ended a long period of economic expansion, the price peaked at $127 a barrel.

While the price of oil was rising, the quantity of oil produced and consumed also increased. In 2001, the world produced 65 million barrels of oil a day. By 2008, that quantity was 72 million barrels.

Who or what has been raising the price of oil? Is it the action of greedy oil producers? Oil producers might be greedy, and some of them might be big enough to withhold supply and raise the price, but it wouldn't be in their self-interest to do so. The higher price would bring forth a greater quantity supplied from other producers and the profit of the producer limiting supply would fall.

Oil producers could try to cooperate and jointly withhold supply. The Organization of Petroleum Exporting Countries, OPEC, is such a group of producers. But OPEC doesn't control the *world* supply and its members' self-interest is to produce the quantities that give them the maximum attainable profit.

So even though the global oil market has some big players, they don't fix the price. Instead, the actions of thousands of buyers and sellers and the forces of demand and supply determine the price of oil.

So how have demand and supply changed?

Because both the price and the quantity have increased, the demand for oil must have increased. Supply might have changed, too, but here we'll suppose that supply has remained the same.

The global demand for oil has increased for one major reason: World income has increased. The increase has been particularly large in the emerging economies of Brazil, China, and India. Increased world income has increased the demand for oil-using goods such as electricity, gasoline, and plastics, which in turn has increased the demand for oil.

The figure illustrates the effects of the increase in demand on the global oil market. The supply of oil remained constant along supply curve S. The demand for oil in 2001 was D_{2001}, so in 2001 the price was $20 a barrel and the quantity was 65 million barrels per day. The demand for oil increased and by 2008 it had reached D_{2008}. The price of oil increased to $127 a barrel and the quantity increased to 72 million barrels a day. The increase in the quantity is an *increase in the quantity supplied*, not an increase in supply.

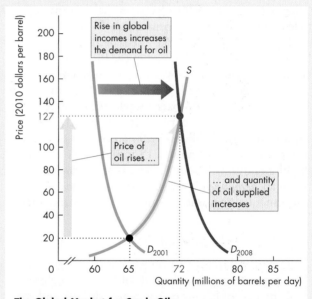

The Global Market for Crude Oil

An Increase in Supply

When Nestlé (the producer of PowerBar) and other energy bar producers switch to a new cost-saving technology, the supply of energy bars increases. Figure 3.9 shows the new supply schedule (the same one that was shown in Fig. 3.5). What are the new equilibrium price and quantity? The price falls to $1.00 a bar, and the quantity increases to 15 million bars a week. You can see why by looking at the quantities demanded and supplied at the old price of $1.50 a bar. The new quantity supplied at that price is 20 million bars a week, and there is a surplus. The price falls. Only when the price is $1.00 a bar does the quantity supplied equal the quantity demanded.

Figure 3.9 illustrates the effect of an increase in supply. It shows the demand curve for energy bars and the original and new supply curves. The initial equilibrium price is $1.50 a bar, and the equilibrium quantity is 10 million bars a week. When supply increases, the supply curve shifts rightward. The equilibrium price falls to $1.00 a bar, and the quantity demanded increases to 15 million bars a week, highlighted in the figure. There is an *increase in the quantity demanded* but *no change in demand*—a movement along, but no shift of, the demand curve.

A Decrease in Supply

Start out at a price of $1.00 a bar with 15 million bars a week being bought and sold. Then suppose that the cost of labour or raw materials rises and the supply of energy bars decreases. The decrease in supply shifts the supply curve leftward. The equilibrium price rises to $1.50 a bar, the quantity demanded decreases, and the equilibrium quantity decreases to 10 million bars a week.

We can now make two more predictions:

1. When supply increases, the price falls and the quantity increases.
2. When supply decreases, the price rises and the quantity decreases.

You've now seen what happens to the price and the quantity when either demand or supply changes while the other one remains unchanged. In real markets, both demand and supply can change together. When this happens, to predict the changes in price and quantity, we must combine the effects that you've just seen. That is your final task in this chapter.

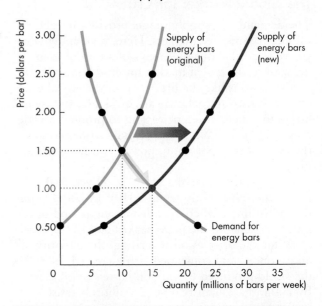

FIGURE 3.9   The Effects of a Change in Supply

Price (dollars per bar)	Quantity demanded (millions of bars per week)	Quantity supplied (millions of bars per week)	
		Original	New
0.50	22	0	7
1.00	15	6	15
1.50	10	10	20
2.00	7	13	25
2.50	5	15	27

Initially, the supply of energy bars is shown by the blue supply curve. The equilibrium price is $1.50 a bar, and the equilibrium quantity is 10 million bars a week. When the new cost-saving technology is adopted, the supply of energy bars increases and the supply curve shifts rightward to become the red curve.

At $1.50 a bar, there is now a surplus of 10 million bars a week. The price of an energy bar falls to a new equilibrium of $1.00 a bar. As the price falls to $1.00, the quantity demanded increases—shown by the blue arrow on the demand curve—to the new equilibrium quantity of 15 million bars a week. Following an increase in supply, the quantity demanded increases but demand does not change—the demand curve does not shift.

MyEconLab   animation ◆

Economics in Action
The Market for Strawberries

California produces 85 percent of North America's strawberries and its crop, which starts to increase in March, is in top flight by April. During the winter months of January and February, Florida is the main strawberry producer.

In a normal year, the supplies from these two regions don't overlap much. As California's production steps up in March and April, Florida's production falls off. The result is a steady supply of strawberries and not much seasonal fluctuation in the price of strawberries.

But 2010 wasn't a normal year. Florida had exceptionally cold weather, which damaged the strawberry fields, lowered crop yields, and delayed the harvests. The result was unusually high strawberry prices.

With higher-than-normal prices, Florida farmers planted strawberry varieties that mature later than their normal crop and planned to harvest this fruit during the spring. Their plan worked perfectly and good growing conditions delivered a bumper crop by late March.

On the other side of the nation, while Florida was freezing, Southern California was drowning under unusually heavy rains. This wet weather put the strawberries to sleep and delayed their growth. But when the rains stopped and the temperature began to rise, California joined Florida with a super abundance of fruit.

With an abundance of strawberries, the price tumbled. Strawberry farmers in both regions couldn't hire enough labour to pick the super-sized crop, so some fruit was left in the fields to rot.

The figure explains what was happening in the market for strawberries.

Demand, shown by the demand curve, D, didn't change. In January, the failed Florida crop kept supply low and the supply curve was $S_{January}$. The price was high at $7.60 per kilogram and production was 2.50 million kilograms per day.

In April, the bumper crops in both regions increased supply to S_{April}. This increase in supply lowered the price to $2.40 per kilogram and increased the quantity demanded—a movement along the demand curve—to 2.75 million kilograms per day.

You can also see in the figure why farmers left fruit in the field to rot. At the January price of $7.60 a kilogram, farmers would have been paying top wages to hire the workers needed to pick fruit at the rate of 3 million kilograms per day. This is the quantity on supply curve S_{April} at $7.60 a pound.

But with the fall in price to $2.40 a kilogram, growers were not able to make a profit by picking more than 2.75 million kilograms.

For some growers the price wasn't high enough to cover the cost of hiring labour, so they opened their fields to anyone who wanted to pick their own strawberries for free.

The events we've described here in the market for strawberries illustrate the effects of a change in supply with no change in demand.

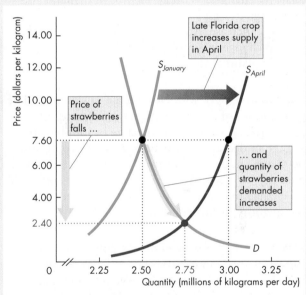

The Market for Strawberries

All the Possible Changes in Demand and Supply

Figure 3.10 brings together and summarizes the effects of all the possible changes in demand and supply. With what you've learned about the effects of a change in *either* demand or supply, you can predict what happens if *both* demand and supply change together. Let's begin by reviewing what you already know.

Change in Demand with No Change in Supply The first row of Fig. 3.10, parts (a), (b), and (c), summarizes the effects of a change in demand with no change in supply. In part (a), with no change in either demand or supply, neither the price nor the quantity changes. With an *increase* in demand and no change in supply in part (b), both the price and quantity increase. And with a *decrease* in demand and no change in supply in part (c), both the price and the quantity decrease.

Change in Supply with No Change in Demand The first column of Fig. 3.10, parts (a), (d), and (g), summarizes the effects of a change in supply with no change in demand. With an *increase* in supply and no change in demand in part (d), the price falls and quantity increases. And with a *decrease* in supply and no change in demand in part (g), the price rises and the quantity decreases.

Increase in Both Demand and Supply You've seen that an increase in demand raises the price and increases the quantity. And you've seen that an increase in supply lowers the price and increases the quantity. Fig. 3.10(e) combines these two changes. Because either an increase in demand or an increase in supply increases the quantity, the quantity also increases when both demand and supply increase. But the effect on the price is uncertain. An increase in demand raises the price and an increase in supply lowers the price, so we can't say whether the price will rise or fall when both demand and supply increase. We need to know the magnitudes of the changes in demand and supply to predict the effects on price. In the example in Fig. 3.10(e), the price does not change. But notice that if demand increases by slightly more than the amount shown in the figure, the price will rise. And if supply increases by slightly more than the amount shown in the figure, the price will fall.

Decrease in Both Demand and Supply Figure 3.10(i) shows the case in which demand and supply *both decrease*. For the same reasons as those we've just reviewed, when both demand and supply decrease, the quantity decreases, and again the direction of the price change is uncertain.

Decrease in Demand and Increase in Supply You've seen that a decrease in demand lowers the price and decreases the quantity. And you've seen that an increase in supply lowers the price and increases the quantity. Fig. 3.10(f) combines these two changes. Both the decrease in demand and the increase in supply lower the price, so the price falls. But a decrease in demand decreases the quantity and an increase in supply increases the quantity, so we can't predict the direction in which the quantity will change unless we know the magnitudes of the changes in demand and supply. In the example in Fig. 3.10(f), the quantity does not change. But notice that if demand decreases by slightly more than the amount shown in the figure, the quantity will decrease; if supply increases by slightly more than the amount shown in the figure, the quantity will increase.

Increase in Demand and Decrease in Supply Figure 3.10(h) shows the case in which demand increases and supply decreases. Now, the price rises, and again the direction of the quantity change is uncertain.

REVIEW QUIZ

What is the effect on the price and quantity of MP3 players (such as the iPod) if

1 The price of a PC falls or the price of an MP3 download rises? (Draw the diagrams!)
2 More firms produce MP3 players or electronics workers' wages rise? (Draw the diagrams!)
3 Any two of the events in questions 1 and 2 occur together? (Draw the diagrams!)

You can work these questions in Study Plan 3.5 and get instant feedback.

———————————————— MyEconLab ◆

To complete your study of demand and supply, take a look at *Reading Between the Lines* on pp. 74–75, which explains why the price of coffee increased in 2010. Try to get into the habit of using the demand and supply model to understand the movements in prices in your everyday life.

FIGURE 3.10   The Effects of All the Possible Changes in Demand and Supply

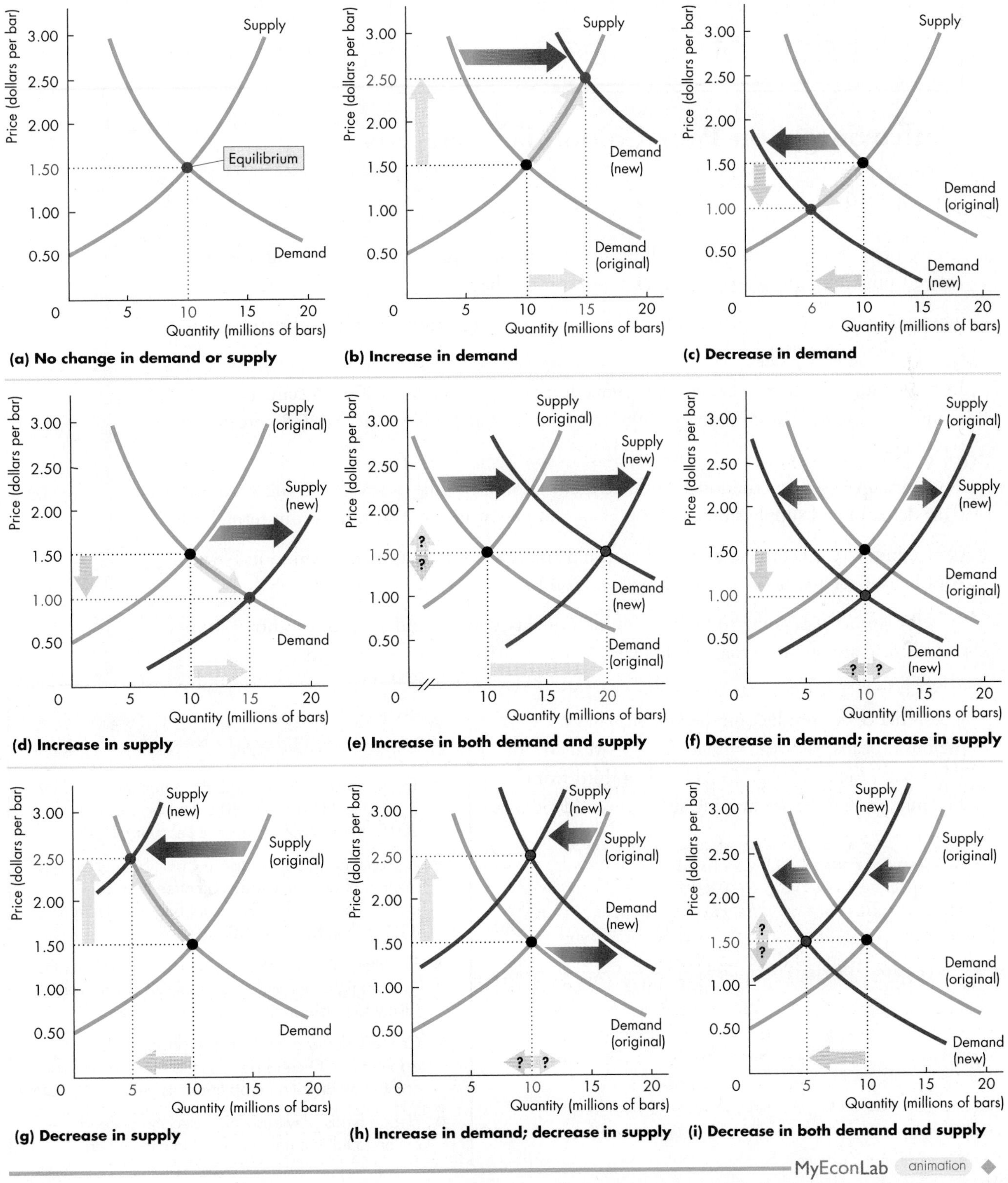

(a) No change in demand or supply

(b) Increase in demand

(c) Decrease in demand

(d) Increase in supply

(e) Increase in both demand and supply

(f) Decrease in demand; increase in supply

(g) Decrease in supply

(h) Increase in demand; decrease in supply

(i) Decrease in both demand and supply

MyEconLab   animation

Demand and Supply: The Price of Coffee

Coffee Surges on Poor Colombian Harvests

FT.com

July 30, 2010

Coffee prices hit a 12-year high on Friday on the back of low supplies of premium Arabica coffee from Colombia after a string of poor crops in the Latin American country.

The strong fundamental picture has also encouraged hedge funds to reverse their previous bearish views on coffee prices.

In New York, ICE September Arabica coffee jumped 3.2 percent to 178.75 cents per pound, the highest since February 1998. It traded later at 177.25 cents, up 6.8 percent on the week.

The London-based International Coffee Organization on Friday warned that the "current tight demand and supply situation" was "likely to persist in the near to medium term."

Coffee industry executives believe prices could rise towards 200 cents per pound in New York before the arrival of the new Brazilian crop later this year.

"Until October it is going to be tight on high quality coffee," said a senior executive at one of Europe's largest coffee roasters. He said: "The industry has been surprised by the scarcity of high quality beans."

Colombia coffee production, key for supplies of premium beans, last year plunged to a 33-year low of 7.8m bags, each of 60kg, down nearly a third from 11.1m bags in 2008, tightening supplies worldwide. ...

Excerpted from "Coffee Surges on Poor Colombian Harvests" by Javier Blas. *Financial Times*, July 30, 2010. Reprinted with permission.

ESSENCE OF THE STORY

- The price of premium Arabica coffee increased by 3.2 percent to almost 180 cents per pound in July 2010, the highest price since February 1998.

- A sequence of poor crops in Colombia cut the production of premium Arabica coffee to a 33-year low of 7.8 million 60-kilogram bags, down from 11.1 million bags in 2008.

- The International Coffee Organization said that the "current tight demand and supply situation" was "likely to persist in the near to medium term."

- Coffee industry executives say prices might approach 200 cents per pound before the arrival of the new Brazilian crop later this year.

- Hedge funds previously expected the price of coffee to fall but now expect it to rise further.

ECONOMIC ANALYSIS

- This news article reports two sources of changes in supply and demand that changed the price of coffee.

- The first source of change is the sequence of poor harvests in Colombia. These events decreased the world supply of Arabica coffee. (Arabica is the type that Starbucks uses.)

- Before the reported events, the world production of Arabica was 120 million bags per year and its price was 174 cents per pound.

- The decrease in the Colombian harvest decreased world production to about 116 million bags, which is about 3 percent of world production.

- Figure 1 shows the situation before the poor Colombia harvests and the effects of those poor harvests. The demand curve is D and initially, the supply curve was S_0. The market equilibrium is at 120 million bags per year and a price of 174 cents per pound.

- The poor Colombian harvests decreased supply and the supply curve shifted leftward to S_1. The price increased to 180 cents per pound and the quantity decreased to 116 million bags.

- The second source of change influenced both supply and demand. It is a change in the expected future price of coffee.

- The hedge funds referred to in the news article are speculators that try to profit from buying at a low price and selling at a high price.

- With the supply of coffee expected to remain low, the price was expected to rise further—a rise in the expected future price of coffee.

- When the expected future price of coffee rises, some people want to buy more coffee (so they can sell it later)—an increase in the demand today. And some people offer less coffee for sale (so they can sell it later for a higher price)—a decrease in the supply today.

- Figure 2 shows the effects of these changes in the demand and supply today.

- Demand increases and the demand curve shifts from D_0 to D_1. Supply decreases and the supply curve shifts from S_1 to S_2.

- Because demand increases and supply decreases, the price rises. In this example, it rises to 200 cents per pound.

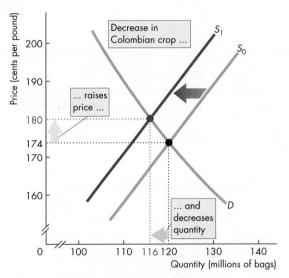

Figure 1 The Effects of the Colombian Crop

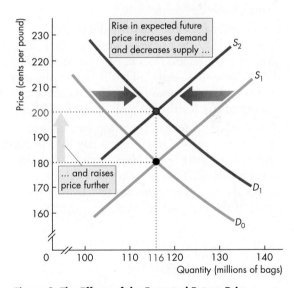

Figure 2 The Effects of the Expected Future Price

- Also, because demand increases and supply decreases, the change in the equilibrium quantity can go in either direction.

- In this example, the increase in demand equals the decrease in supply, so the equilibrium quantity remains constant at 116 million bags per year.

◆ MATHEMATICAL NOTE

Demand, Supply, and Equilibrium

Demand Curve

The law of demand says that as the price of a good or service falls, the quantity demanded of that good or service increases. We can illustrate the law of demand by drawing a graph of the demand curve or writing down an equation. When the demand curve is a straight line, the following equation describes it:

$$P = a - bQ_D,$$

where P is the price and Q_D is the quantity demanded. The a and b are positive constants.

The demand equation tells us three things:

1. The price at which no one is willing to buy the good (Q_D is zero). That is, if the price is a, then the quantity demanded is zero. You can see the price a in Fig. 1. It is the price at which the demand curve hits the y-axis—what we call the demand curve's "y-intercept."

2. As the price falls, the quantity demanded increases. If Q_D is a positive number, then the price P must be less than a. As Q_D gets larger, the price P becomes smaller. That is, as the quantity increases, the maximum price that buyers are willing to pay for the last unit of the good falls.

3. The constant b tells us how fast the maximum price that someone is willing to pay for the good falls as the quantity increases. That is, the constant b tells us about the steepness of the demand curve. The equation tells us that the slope of the demand curve is $-b$.

Supply Curve

The law of supply says that as the price of a good or service rises, the quantity supplied of that good or service increases. We can illustrate the law of supply by drawing a graph of the supply curve or writing down an equation. When the supply curve is a straight line, the following equation describes it:

$$P = c + dQ_S,$$

where P is the price and Q_S is the quantity supplied. The c and d are positive constants.

The supply equation tells us three things:

1. The price at which sellers are not willing to supply the good (Q_S is zero). That is, if the price is c, then no one is willing to sell the good. You can see the price c in Fig. 2. It is the price at which the supply curve hits the y-axis—what we call the supply curve's "y-intercept."

2. As the price rises, the quantity supplied increases. If Q_S is a positive number, then the price P must be greater than c. As Q_S increases, the price P becomes larger. That is, as the quantity increases, the minimum price that sellers are willing to accept for the last unit rises.

3. The constant d tells us how fast the minimum price at which someone is willing to sell the good rises as the quantity increases. That is, the constant d tells us about the steepness of the supply curve. The equation tells us that the slope of the supply curve is d.

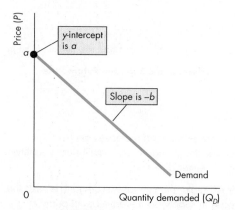

Figure 1 Demand curve

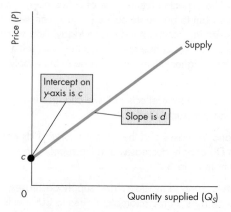

Figure 2 Supply curve

Market Equilibrium

Demand and supply determine market equilibrium. Figure 3 shows the equilibrium price (P^*) and equilibrium quantity (Q^*) at the intersection of the demand curve and the supply curve.

We can use the equations to find the equilibrium price and equilibrium quantity. The price of a good adjusts until the quantity demanded Q_D equals the quantity supplied Q_S. So at the equilibrium price (P^*) and equilibrium quantity (Q^*),

$$Q_D = Q_S = Q^*.$$

To find the equilibrium price and equilibrium quantity, substitute Q^* for Q_D in the demand equation and Q^* for Q_S in the supply equation. Then the price is the equilibrium price (P^*), which gives

$$P^* = a - bQ^*$$
$$P^* = c + dQ^*.$$

Notice that

$$a - bQ^* = c + dQ^*.$$

Now solve for Q^*:

$$a - c = bQ^* + dQ^*$$
$$a - c = (b + d)Q^*$$
$$Q^* = \frac{a - c}{b + d}.$$

To find the equilibrium price, (P^*), substitute for Q^* in either the demand equation or the supply equation.

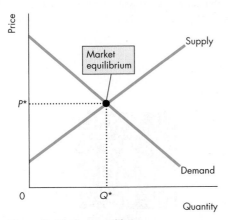

Price

Market equilibrium

Supply

P^*

Demand

0   Q^*

Quantity

Figure 3 Market equilibrium

Using the demand equation, we have

$$P^* = a - b\left(\frac{a - c}{b + d}\right)$$
$$P^* = \frac{a(b + d) - b(a - c)}{b + d}$$
$$P^* = \frac{ad + bc}{b + d}.$$

Alternatively, using the supply equation, we have

$$P^* = c + d\left(\frac{a - c}{b + d}\right)$$
$$P^* = \frac{c(b + d) + d(a - c)}{b + d}$$
$$P^* = \frac{ad + bc}{b + d}.$$

An Example

The demand for ice cream cones is

$$P = 800 - 2Q_D.$$

The supply of ice cream cones is

$$P = 200 + 1Q_S.$$

The price of a cone is expressed in cents, and the quantities are expressed in cones per day.

To find the equilibrium price (P^*) and equilibrium quantity (Q^*), substitute Q^* for Q_D and Q_S and P^* for P. That is,

$$P^* = 800 - 2Q^*$$
$$P^* = 200 + 1Q^*.$$

Now solve for Q^*:

$$800 - 2Q^* = 200 + 1Q^*$$
$$600 = 3Q^*$$
$$Q^* = 200.$$

And

$$P^* = 800 - 2(200)$$
$$= 400.$$

The equilibrium price is $4 a cone, and the equilibrium quantity is 200 cones per day.

SUMMARY

Key Points

Markets and Prices (p. 56)

- A competitive market is one that has so many buyers and sellers that no single buyer or seller can influence the price.
- Opportunity cost is a relative price.
- Demand and supply determine relative prices.

Working Problem 1 will give you a better understanding of markets and prices.

Demand (pp. 57–61)

- Demand is the relationship between the quantity demanded of a good and its price when all other influences on buying plans remain the same.
- The higher the price of a good, other things remaining the same, the smaller is the quantity demanded—the law of demand.
- Demand depends on the prices of related goods (substitutes and complements), expected future prices, income, expected future income and credit, the population, and preferences.

Working Problems 2 to 5 will give you a better understanding of demand.

Supply (pp. 62–65)

- Supply is the relationship between the quantity supplied of a good and its price when all other influences on selling plans remain the same.
- The higher the price of a good, other things remaining the same, the greater is the quantity supplied—the law of supply.

- Supply depends on the prices of factors of production used to produce a good, the prices of related goods produced, expected future prices, the number of suppliers, technology, and the state of nature.

Working Problems 6 to 9 will give you a better understanding of supply.

Market Equilibrium (pp. 66–67)

- At the equilibrium price, the quantity demanded equals the quantity supplied.
- At any price above the equilibrium price, there is a surplus and the price falls.
- At any price below the equilibrium price, there is a shortage and the price rises.

Working Problems 10 and 11 will give you a better understanding of market equilibrium.

Predicting Changes in Price and Quantity (pp. 68–73)

- An increase in demand brings a rise in the price and an increase in the quantity supplied. A decrease in demand brings a fall in the price and a decrease in the quantity supplied.
- An increase in supply brings a fall in the price and an increase in the quantity demanded. A decrease in supply brings a rise in the price and a decrease in the quantity demanded.
- An increase in demand and an increase in supply bring an increased quantity but an uncertain price change. An increase in demand and a decrease in supply bring a higher price but an uncertain change in quantity.

Working Problems 12 to 14 will give you a better understanding of predicting changes in price and quantity.

Key Terms

Change in demand, 58
Change in supply, 63
Change in the quantity demanded, 61
Change in the quantity supplied, 64
Competitive market, 56
Complement, 59
Demand, 57
Demand curve, 58
Equilibrium price, 66
Equilibrium quantity, 66

Inferior good, 60
Law of demand, 57
Law of supply, 62
Money price, 56
Normal good, 60
Quantity demanded, 57
Quantity supplied, 62
Relative price, 56
Substitute, 59
Supply, 62
Supply curve, 62

SCAN THIS

STUDY PLAN PROBLEMS AND APPLICATIONS

MyEconLab ◆ You can work Problems 1 to 17 in Chapter 3 Study Plan and get instant feedback.

Markets and Prices (Study Plan 3.1)

1. William Gregg owned a mill in South Carolina. In December 1862, he placed a notice in the *Edgehill Advertiser* announcing his willingness to exchange cloth for food and other items. Here is an extract:

   1 yard of cloth for 1 pound of bacon

   2 yards of cloth for 1 pound of butter

   4 yards of cloth for 1 pound of wool

   8 yards of cloth for 1 bushel of salt

   a. What is the relative price of butter in terms of wool?

   b. If the money price of bacon was 20¢ a pound, what do you predict was the money price of butter?

   c. If the money price of bacon was 20¢ a pound and the money price of salt was $2.00 a bushel, do you think anyone would accept Mr. Gregg's offer of cloth for salt?

Demand (Study Plan 3.2)

2. The price of food increased during the past year.

   a. Explain why the law of demand applies to food just as it does to all other goods and services.

   b. Explain how the substitution effect influences food purchases and provide some examples of substitutions that people might make when the price of food rises and other things remain the same.

   c. Explain how the income effect influences food purchases and provide some examples of the income effect that might occur when the price of food rises and other things remain the same.

3. Place the following goods and services into pairs of likely substitutes and pairs of likely complements. (You may use an item in more than one pair.) The goods and services are coal, oil, natural gas, wheat, corn, rye, pasta, pizza, sausage, skateboard, roller blades, video game, laptop, iPod, cell phone, text message, e-mail, phone call, voice mail.

4. During 2010, the average income in China increased by 10 percent. Compared to 2009, how do you expect the following would change:

   a. The demand for beef. Explain your answer.

   b. The demand for rice. Explain your answer.

5. In May 2010, the price of gasoline was 99.6 cents per litre. By May 2011, the price had increased to 132 cents per litre. Assume that there were no changes in average income, population, or any other influence on buying plans. Explain how the rise in the price of gasoline would affect

   a. The demand for gasoline.

   b. The quantity of gasoline demanded.

Supply (Study Plan 3.3)

6. From May 2010 to February 2011, the price of corn increased by 100 percent and some barley growers on the Prairies stopped planting barley and started to grow corn.

   a. Does this fact illustrate the law of demand or the law of supply? Explain your answer.

   b. Why would a barley farmer grow corn?

Use the following information to work Problems 7 to 9.

Dairies make low-fat milk from full-cream milk. In making low-fat milk, the dairies produce cream, which is made into ice cream. In the market for low-fat milk, the following events occur one at a time:

   (i)   The wage rate of dairy workers rises.

   (ii) The price of cream rises.

   (iii) The price of low-fat milk rises.

   (iv) With the period of low rainfall extending, dairies raise their expected price of low-fat milk next year.

   (v)   With advice from health-care experts, dairy farmers decide to switch from producing full-cream milk to growing vegetables.

   (vi) A new technology lowers the cost of producing ice cream.

7. Explain the effect of each event on the supply of low-fat milk.

8. Use a graph to illustrate the effect of each event.

9. Does any event (or events) illustrate the law of supply?

Market Equilibrium (Study Plan 3.4)

10. "As more people buy computers, the demand for Internet service increases and the price of Internet service decreases. The fall in the price of Internet service decreases the supply of Internet service." Explain what is wrong with this statement.

11. The demand and supply schedules for gum are

Price (cents per pack)	Quantity demanded	Quantity supplied
	(millions of packs a week)	
20	180	60
40	140	100
60	100	140
80	60	180
100	20	220

   a. Draw a graph of the market for gum and mark in the equilibrium price and quantity.

   b. Suppose that the price of gum is 70¢ a pack. Describe the situation in the gum market and explain how the price adjusts.

   c. Suppose that the price of gum is 30¢ a pack. Describe the situation in the gum market and explain how the price adjusts.

Predicting Changes in Price and Quantity
(Study Plan 3.5)

12. The following events occur one at a time:
   (i)   The price of crude oil rises.
   (ii) The price of a car rises.
   (iii) All speed limits on highways are abolished.
   (iv) Robots cut car production costs.

   Which of these events will increase or decrease (state which occurs)
   a. The demand for gasoline?
   b. The supply of gasoline?
   c. The quantity of gasoline demanded?
   d. The quantity of gasoline supplied?

13. In Problem 11, a fire destroys some factories that produce gum and the quantity of gum supplied decreases by 40 million packs a week at each price.

   a. Explain what happens in the market for gum and draw a graph to illustrate the changes.

   b. If at the time the fire occurs there is an increase in the teenage population, which increases the quantity of gum demanded by 40 million packs a week at each price, what are the new equilibrium price and quantity of gum? Illustrate these changes on your graph.

14. **Tim Hortons' Risk**
   Tim Hortons has exploded to become a dominant player among quick-serve restaurants. In 2001, it took the risk by switching to centralized production of baked goods, which lowered its labour costs and increased its sales volume.
   Source: *Financial Post*, August 12, 2010
   Draw a graph to show the effect of lower labour costs on the price of Tims' baked goods and the quantity sold.

Economics in the News (Study Plan 3.EN)

15. **Don't Look for Cheap Food Anytime Soon**
   Global food prices probably will rise in the first half of this century because of an expanding population and higher incomes and slower crop-yield growth.
   Source: *National Post*, March 9, 2011
   Explain the effect on food prices of
   a. Expanding population and rising incomes.
   b. Slower crop-yield growth.

16. **Frigid Florida Winter Is Bad News for Tomato Lovers**
   An unusually cold January in Florida destroyed entire fields of tomatoes and forced many farmers to delay their harvest. Florida's growers are shipping only a quarter of their usual 2.5 million kilograms a week. The price has risen from $13.00 for a 12.5-kilogram box a year ago to $60 now.
   Source: *USA Today*, March 3, 2010
   a. Make a graph to illustrate the market for tomatoes in January 2009 and January 2010.
   b. On the graph, show how the events in the news clip influence the market for tomatoes.
   c. Why is the news "bad for tomato lovers"?

17. **Gas Prices Jump Across Canada amid Libya Unrest** Oil prices shot up to US$103 a barrel as traders were forced to question how bad the Libyan situation would get and whether the instability could spread to other oil-rich nations. In Toronto, the gas price jumped 3.7 percent to 121.4 cents per litre and after it rose 2 cents a litre earlier in the week.
   Source: CTV News, June 6, 2011
   a. Does demand for or the supply of gasoline or both change when the price of oil soars?
   b. Use a graph to illustrate what happens to the equilibrium price of gasoline and the equilibrium quantity of gasoline bought when the price of oil soars.

ADDITIONAL PROBLEMS AND APPLICATIONS

MyEconLab ◆ You can work these problems in MyEconLab if assigned by your instructor.

Markets and Prices

18. What features of the world market for crude oil make it a competitive market?

19. The money price of a textbook is $90 and the money price of the Wii game *Super Mario Galaxy* is $45.

    a. What is the opportunity cost of a textbook in terms of the Wii game?

    b. What is the relative price of the Wii game in terms of textbooks?

Demand

20. The price of gasoline has increased during the past year.

    a. Explain why the law of demand applies to gasoline just as it does to all other goods and services.

    b. Explain how the substitution effect influences gasoline purchases and provide some examples of substitutions that people might make when the price of gasoline rises and other things remain the same.

    c. Explain how the income effect influences gasoline purchases and provide some examples of the income effects that might occur when the price of gasoline rises and other things remain the same.

21. Think about the demand for the three game consoles: Xbox, PS3, and Wii. Explain the effect of the following events on the demand for Xbox games and the quantity of Xbox games demanded, other things remaining the same.

    a. The price of an Xbox falls.

    b. The prices of a PS3 and a Wii fall.

    c. The number of people writing and producing Xbox games increases.

    d. Consumers' incomes increase.

    e. Programmers who write code for Xbox games become more costly to hire.

    f. The expected future price of an Xbox game falls.

    g. A new game console that is a close substitute for Xbox comes onto the market.

Supply

22. Classify the following pairs of goods and services as substitutes in production, complements in production, or neither.

    a. Bottled water and health club memberships

    b. French fries and baked potatoes

    c. Leather purses and leather shoes

    d. Hybrids and SUVs

    e. Diet coke and regular coke

23. As the global financial crisis hit, the prices of homes fell across the United States and the number of homes offered for sale decreased.

    a. Does this fact illustrate the law of demand or the law of supply? Explain your answer.

    b. Why would home owners decide not to sell?

24. **G.M. Cuts Production for Quarter**
    General Motors cut its fourth-quarter production schedule by 10 percent because Ford Motor, Chrysler, and Toyota sales declined in August.

    Source: *The New York Times*, September 5, 2007

    Explain whether this news clip illustrates a change in the supply of cars or a change in the quantity supplied of cars.

Market Equilibrium

Use the following figure to work Problems 25 and 26.

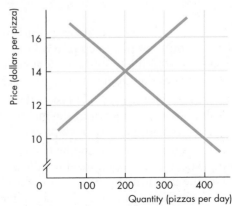

25. a. Label the curves. Which curve shows the willingness to pay for a pizza?

    b. If the price of a pizza is $16, is there a shortage or a surplus and does the price rise or fall?

c. Sellers want to receive the highest possible price, so why would they be willing to accept less than $16 a pizza?

26. a. If the price of a pizza is $12, is there a shortage or a surplus and does the price rise or fall?

b. Buyers want to pay the lowest possible price, so why would they be willing to pay more than $12 for a pizza?

27. The demand and supply schedules for potato chips are

Price (cents per bag)	Quantity demanded	Quantity supplied
	(millions of bags per week)	
50	160	130
60	150	140
70	140	150
80	130	160
90	120	170
100	110	180

a. Draw a graph of the potato chip market and mark in the equilibrium price and quantity.

b. If the price is 60¢ a bag, is there a shortage or a surplus, and how does the price adjust?

Predicting Changes in Price and Quantity

28. In Problem 27, a new dip increases the quantity of potato chips that people want to buy by 30 million bags per week at each price.

a. How does the demand and/or supply of chips change?

b. How does the price and quantity of chips change?

29. In Problem 27, if a virus destroys potato crops and the quantity of potato chips produced decreases by 40 million bags a week at each price, how does the supply of chips change?

30. If the virus in Problem 29 hits just as the new dip in Problem 28 comes onto the market, how does the price and quantity of chips change?

31. The world's largest instant-noodle maker said soaring wheat prices have forced noodle prices up. Despite the rising price, Asia's middle class, with their increasing incomes, are eating more wheat products as they try to diversify their diets from rice and save time with processed foods.

a. Explain the effect of soaring wheat prices on the market for noodles, other things remaining the same.

b. Explain the effect of the middle class switching its diet from rice to noodles on the market for noodles, other things remaining the same.

c. Explain the combined effect of soaring wheat prices and rising incomes on the equilibrium price and quantity of noodles.

d. As the middle class in Asia continues to grow, how might the price of rice change?

Economics in the News

32. After you have studied *Reading Between the Lines* on pp. 74–75, answer the following questions.

a. What happened to the price of coffee in 2010?

b. What substitutions do you expect might have been made to decrease the quantity of coffee demanded?

c. What influenced the demand for coffee in 2010 and what influenced the quantity of coffee demanded?

d. What influenced the supply of coffee during 2010 and how did the supply of coffee change?

e. How did the combination of the factors you have noted in parts (c) and (d) influence the price and quantity of coffee?

f. Was the change in the quantity of coffee a change in the quantity demanded or a change in the quantity supplied?

33. **Strawberry Prices Drop as Late Harvest Hits Market**
Shoppers bought strawberries in March for $1.25 a pound rather than the $3.49 a pound they paid last year. With the price so low, some growers plowed over their strawberry plants to make way for spring melons; others froze their harvests and sold them to juice and jam makers.
Source: *USA Today*, April 5, 2010

a. Explain how the market for strawberries would have changed if growers had not plowed in their plants but offered locals "you pick for free."

b. Describe the changes in demand and supply in the market for strawberry jam.

34. **"Popcorn Movie" Experience Gets Pricier**
Cinemas are raising the price of popcorn. Demand for field corn, which is used for animal feed, corn syrup, and ethanol, has increased and its price has exploded. That's caused some farmers to shift from growing popcorn to easier-to-grow field corn.
Source: *USA Today*, May 24, 2008

Explain and illustrate graphically the events described in the news clip in the market for

a. Popcorn

b. Movie tickets

CHAPTER

4

Elasticity

After studying this chapter, you will be able to

◆ Define, calculate, and explain the factors that influence the price elasticity of demand

◆ Define, calculate, and explain the factors that influence the cross elasticity of demand and the income elasticity of demand

◆ Define, calculate, and explain the factors that influence the elasticity of supply

When the price of gasoline soars, you complain a lot but keep on filling your tank and spending more on gas. Would you react the same way if a Florida frost wiped out a tomato crop, driving the price of tomatoes to five times its normal level?

How can we compare the effects of price changes on buying plans for different goods such as gasoline and tomatoes?

This chapter introduces you to elasticity: a tool that addresses these quantitative questions.

At the end of the chapter, in *Reading Between the Lines*, we'll use elasticity to explain what was happening in the market for fresh winter tomatoes from Florida during the severe winter of 2010. But we'll begin by explaining elasticity in another familiar setting: the market for pizza.

Price Elasticity of Demand

You know that when supply increases, the equilibrium price falls and the equilibrium quantity increases. But does the price fall by a large amount and the quantity increase by a little? Or does the price barely fall and the quantity increase by a large amount?

The answer depends on the responsiveness of the quantity demanded to a change in price. You can see why by studying Fig. 4.1, which shows two possible scenarios in a local pizza market. Figure 4.1(a) shows one scenario, and Fig. 4.1(b) shows the other.

In both cases, supply is initially S_0. In part (a), the demand for pizza is shown by the demand curve D_A. In part (b), the demand for pizza is shown by the demand curve D_B. Initially, in both cases, the price is $20 a pizza and the equilibrium quantity is 10 pizzas an hour.

Now a large pizza franchise opens up, and the supply of pizza increases. The supply curve shifts rightward to S_1. In case (a), the price falls by an enormous $15 to $5 a pizza, and the quantity increases by only 3 to 13 pizzas an hour. In contrast, in case (b), the price falls by only $5 to $15 a pizza, and the quantity increases by 7 to 17 pizzas an hour.

The different outcomes arise from differing degrees of responsiveness of the quantity demanded to a change in price. But what do we mean by responsiveness? One possible answer is slope. The slope of demand curve D_A is steeper than the slope of demand curve D_B.

In this example, we can compare the slopes of the two demand curves, but we can't always make such a comparison. The reason is that the slope of a demand curve depends on the units in which we measure the price and quantity. And we often must compare the demand for different goods and services that are measured in unrelated units. For example, a pizza producer might want to compare the demand for pizza with the demand for soft drinks. Which quantity demanded is more responsive to a price change? This question can't be answered by comparing the slopes of two demand curves. The units of measurement of pizza and soft drinks are unrelated. The question can be answered with a measure of responsiveness that is independent of units of measurement. Elasticity is such a measure.

The **price elasticity of demand** is a units-free measure of the responsiveness of the quantity demanded of a good to a change in its price when all other influences on buying plans remain the same.

FIGURE 4.1   How a Change in Supply
Changes Price and Quantity

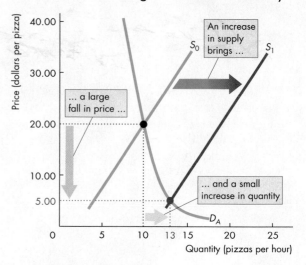

(a) Large price change and small quantity change

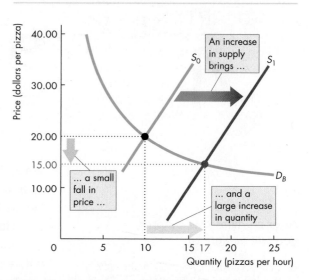

(b) Small price change and large quantity change

Initially, the price is $20 a pizza and the quantity sold is 10 pizzas an hour. Then supply increases from S_0 to S_1. In part (a), the price falls by $15 to $5 a pizza, and the quantity increases by 3 to 13 pizzas an hour. In part (b), the price falls by only $5 to $15 a pizza, and the quantity increases by 7 to 17 pizzas an hour. The price change is smaller and the quantity change is larger in case (b) than in case (a). The quantity demanded is more responsive to the change in the price in case (b) than in case (a).

MyEconLab   animation ◆

Calculating Price Elasticity of Demand

We calculate the *price elasticity of demand* by using the formula:

$$\text{Price elasticity of demand} = \frac{\text{Percentage change in quantity demanded}}{\text{Percentage change in price}}.$$

To calculate the price elasticity of demand for pizza, we need to know the quantity demanded of pizza at two different prices, when all other influences on buying plans remain the same.

Figure 4.2 zooms in on the demand curve for pizza and shows how the quantity demanded responds to a small change in price. Initially, the price is $20.50 a pizza and 9 pizzas an hour are demanded—the original point. The price then falls to $19.50 a pizza, and the quantity demanded increases to 11 pizzas an hour—the new point. When the price falls by $1 a pizza, the quantity demanded increases by 2 pizzas an hour.

To calculate the price elasticity of demand, we express the change in price as a percentage of the *average price* and the change in the quantity demanded as a percentage of the *average quantity*. By using the average price and average quantity, we calculate the elasticity at a point on the demand curve midway between the original point and the new point.

The original price is $20.50 and the new price is $19.50, so the price change is $1 and the average price is $20 a pizza. Call the percentage change in the price $\%\Delta P$, then

$$\%\Delta P = (\Delta P/P_{ave}) \times 100 = (\$1/\$20) \times 100 = 5\%.$$

The original quantity demanded is 9 pizzas and the new quantity demanded is 11 pizzas, so the quantity change is 2 pizzas and the average quantity demanded is 10 pizzas. Call the percentage change in the quantity demanded $\%\Delta Q$, then

$$\%\Delta Q = (\Delta Q/Q_{ave}) \times 100 = (2/10) \times 100 = 20\%.$$

The price elasticity of demand equals the percentage change in the quantity demanded (20 percent) divided by the percentage change in price (5 percent) and is 4. That is,

$$\text{Price elasticity of demand} = \frac{\%\Delta Q}{\%\Delta P}$$
$$= \frac{20\%}{5\%} = 4.$$

FIGURE 4.2   Calculating the Elasticity of Demand

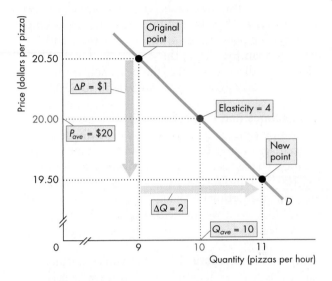

The elasticity of demand is calculated by using the formula:*

$$\text{Price elasticity of demand} = \frac{\text{Percentage change in quantity demanded}}{\text{Percentage change in price}}$$
$$= \frac{\%\Delta Q}{\%\Delta P}$$
$$= \frac{\Delta Q/Q_{ave}}{\Delta P/P_{ave}}$$
$$= \frac{2/10}{1/20} = 4.$$

This calculation measures the elasticity at an average price of $20 a pizza and an average quantity of 10 pizzas an hour.

* In the formula, the Greek letter delta (Δ) stands for "change in" and %Δ stands for "percentage change in."

MyEconLab   animation

Average Price and Quantity Notice that we use the *average* price and *average* quantity. We do this because it gives the most precise measurement of elasticity—at the midpoint between the original price and the new price. If the price falls from $20.50 to $19.50, the $1 price change is 4.9 percent of $20.50. The 2 pizza change in quantity is 22.2 percent of 9 pizzas, the original quantity. So if we use these numbers, the price elasticity of demand is 22.2 divided by 4.9, which equals 4.5. If the price rises from $19.50 to $20.50, the $1 price change is 5.1 percent of $19.50. The 2 pizza change in quantity is 18.2 percent of 11 pizzas, the original quantity. So if we use these numbers, the price elasticity of demand is 18.2 divided by 5.1, which equals 3.6.

By using percentages of the *average* price and *average* quantity, we get the same value for the elasticity regardless of whether the price falls from $20.50 to $19.50 or rises from $19.50 to $20.50.

Percentages and Proportions   Elasticity is the ratio of two percentage changes, so when we divide one percentage change by another, the 100s cancel. A percentage change is a *proportionate* change multiplied by 100. The proportionate change in price is $\Delta P/P_{ave}$, and the proportionate change in quantity demanded is $\Delta Q/Q_{ave}$. So if we divide $\Delta Q/Q_{ave}$ by $\Delta P/P_{ave}$ we get the same answer as we get by using percentage changes.

A Units-Free Measure   Now that you've calculated a price elasticity of demand, you can see why it is a *units-free measure*. Elasticity is a units-free measure because the percentage change in each variable is independent of the units in which the variable is measured. The ratio of the two percentages is a number without units.

Minus Sign and Elasticity   When the price of a good *rises*, the quantity demanded *decreases*. Because a *positive* change in price brings a *negative* change in the quantity demanded, the price elasticity of demand is a negative number. But it is the magnitude, or *absolute value*, of the price elasticity of demand that tells us how responsive the quantity demanded is. So to compare price elasticities of demand, we use the *magnitude* of the elasticity and ignore the minus sign.

Inelastic and Elastic Demand

Figure 4.3 shows three demand curves that cover the entire range of possible elasticities of demand. In Fig. 4.3(a), the quantity demanded is constant regardless of the price. If the quantity demanded remains constant when the price changes, then the price elasticity of demand is zero and the good is said to have a **perfectly inelastic demand**. One good that has a very low price elasticity of demand (perhaps zero over some price range) is insulin. Insulin is of such importance to some diabetics that if the price rises or falls, they do not change the quantity they buy.

If the percentage change in the quantity demanded equals the percentage change in the price, then the price elasticity equals 1 and the good is said to have a **unit elastic demand**. The demand in Fig. 4.3(b) is an example of a unit elastic demand.

Between the cases shown in Fig. 4.3(a) and Fig. 4.3(b) is the general case in which the percentage change in the quantity demanded is less than the percentage change in the price. In this case, the price elasticity of demand is between zero and 1 and the good is said to have an **inelastic demand**. Food and shelter are examples of goods with inelastic demand.

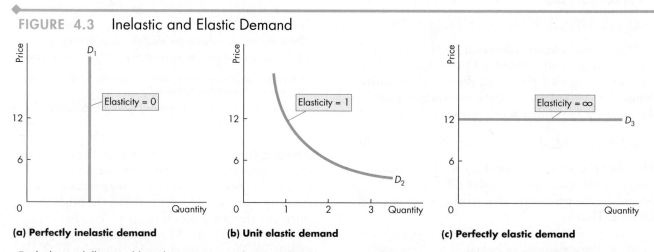

FIGURE 4.3   Inelastic and Elastic Demand

(a) Perfectly inelastic demand   **(b) Unit elastic demand**   **(c) Perfectly elastic demand**

Each demand illustrated here has a constant elasticity. The demand curve in part (a) illustrates the demand for a good that has a zero elasticity of demand. The demand curve in part (b) illustrates the demand for a good with a unit elasticity of demand. And the demand curve in part (c) illustrates the demand for a good with an infinite elasticity of demand.

MyEconLab   animation

If the quantity demanded changes by an infinitely large percentage in response to a tiny price change, then the price elasticity of demand is infinity and the good is said to have a **perfectly elastic demand**. Figure 4.3(c) shows a perfectly elastic demand. An example of a good that has a very high elasticity of demand (almost infinite) is a soft drink from two campus machines located side by side. If the two machines offer the same soft drinks for the same price, some people buy from one machine and some from the other. But if one machine's price is higher than the other's, by even a small amount, no one buys from the machine with the higher price. Drinks from the two machines are perfect substitutes. The demand for a good that has a perfect substitute is perfectly elastic.

Between the cases in Fig. 4.3(b) and Fig. 4.3(c) is the general case in which the percentage change in the quantity demanded exceeds the percentage change in price. In this case, the price elasticity of demand is greater than 1 and the good is said to have an **elastic demand**. Automobiles and furniture are examples of goods that have elastic demand.

Elasticity Along a Linear Demand Curve

Elasticity and slope are not the same. A linear demand curve has a constant slope but a varying elasticity. Let's see why.

The demand curve in Fig. 4.4 is linear. A $5 fall in the price brings an increase of 10 pizzas an hour no matter what the initial price and quantity.

Let's now calculate some elasticities along this demand curve.

At the midpoint of the demand curve, the price is $12.50 and the quantity is 25 pizzas per hour. When the price falls from $15 to $10 a pizza, the quantity demanded increases from 20 to 30 pizzas an hour and the average price and average quantity are at the midpoint of the demand curve. So

$$\text{Price elasticity of demand} = \frac{10/25}{5/12.25}$$

$$= 1.$$

That is, at the midpoint of a linear demand curve, the price elasticity of demand is 1.

At prices *above* the midpoint, demand is elastic. For example, when the price falls from $25 to $15 a pizza, the quantity demanded increases from zero to

20 pizzas an hour. The average price is $20 a pizza, and the average quantity is 10 pizzas. So

$$\text{Price elasticity of demand} = \frac{\Delta Q/Q_{ave}}{\Delta P/P_{ave}}$$

$$= \frac{20/10}{10/20}$$

$$= 4.$$

That is, the price elasticity of demand at an average price of $20 a pizza is 4.

At prices *below* the midpoint, demand is inelastic. For example, when the price falls from $10 a pizza to zero, the quantity demanded increases from 30 to 50 pizzas an hour. The average price is now $5 and the average quantity is 40 pizzas an hour. So

$$\text{Price elasticity of demand} = \frac{20/40}{10/5}$$

$$= 1/4.$$

That is, the price elasticity of demand at an average price of $5 a pizza is 1/4.

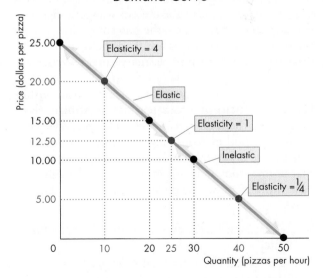

FIGURE 4.4   Elasticity Along a Linear Demand Curve

On a linear demand curve, demand is unit elastic at the midpoint (elasticity is 1), elastic above the midpoint, and inelastic below the midpoint.

MyEconLab   animation   ◆

Total Revenue and Elasticity

The **total revenue** from the sale of a good equals the price of the good multiplied by the quantity sold. When a price changes, total revenue also changes. But a cut in the price does not always decrease total revenue. The change in total revenue depends on the elasticity of demand in the following ways:

- If demand is elastic, a 1 percent price cut increases the quantity sold by more than 1 percent and total revenue increases.
- If demand is inelastic, a 1 percent price cut increases the quantity sold by less than 1 percent and total revenue decreases.
- If demand is unit elastic, a 1 percent price cut increases the quantity sold by 1 percent and total revenue does not change.

In Fig. 4.5(a), over the price range from $25 to $12.50, demand is elastic. Over the price range from $12.50 to zero, demand is inelastic. At a price of $12.50, demand is unit elastic.

Figure 4.5(b) shows total revenue. At a price of $25, the quantity sold is zero, so total revenue is zero. At a price of zero, the quantity demanded is 50 pizzas an hour and total revenue is again zero. A price cut in the elastic range brings an increase in total revenue—the percentage increase in the quantity demanded is greater than the percentage decrease in price. A price cut in the inelastic range brings a decrease in total revenue—the percentage increase in the quantity demanded is less than the percentage decrease in price. At unit elasticity, total revenue is at a maximum.

Figure 4.5 shows how we can use this relationship between elasticity and total revenue to estimate elasticity using the total revenue test. The **total revenue test** is a method of estimating the price elasticity of demand by observing the change in total revenue that results from a change in the price, when all other influences on the quantity sold remain the same.

- If a price cut increases total revenue, demand is elastic.
- If a price cut decreases total revenue, demand is inelastic.
- If a price cut leaves total revenue unchanged, demand is unit elastic.

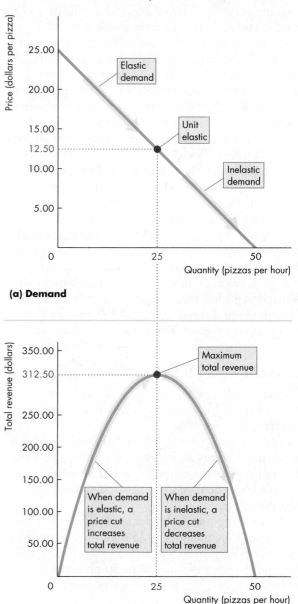

FIGURE 4.5   Elasticity and Total Revenue

(a) Demand

(b) Total revenue

When demand is elastic, in the price range from $25 to $12.50, a decrease in price (part a) brings an increase in total revenue (part b). When demand is inelastic, in the price range from $12.50 to zero, a decrease in price (part a) brings a decrease in total revenue (part b). When demand is unit elastic, at a price of $12.50 (part a), total revenue is at a maximum (part b).

MyEconLab   animation

Your Expenditure and Your Elasticity

When a price changes, the change in your expenditure on the good depends on *your* elasticity of demand.

- If your demand is elastic, a 1 percent price cut increases the quantity you buy by more than 1 percent and your expenditure on the item increases.
- If your demand is inelastic, a 1 percent price cut increases the quantity you buy by less than 1 percent and your expenditure on the item decreases.
- If your demand is unit elastic, a 1 percent price cut increases the quantity you buy by 1 percent and your expenditure on the item does not change.

So if you spend more on an item when its price falls, your demand for that item is elastic; if you spend the same amount, your demand is unit elastic; and if you spend less, your demand is inelastic.

The Factors That Influence the Elasticity of Demand

The elasticity of demand for a good depends on
- The closeness of substitutes
- The proportion of income spent on the good
- The time elapsed since the price change

Closeness of Substitutes The closer the substitutes for a good or service, the more elastic is the demand for it. Oil from which we make gasoline has no close substitutes (imagine a steam-driven, coal-fuelled car). So the demand for oil is inelastic. Plastics are close substitutes for metals, so the demand for metals is elastic.

The degree of substitutability depends on how narrowly (or broadly) we define a good. For example, a personal computer has no close substitutes, but a Dell PC is a close substitute for a Hewlett-Packard PC. So the elasticity of demand for personal computers is lower than the elasticity of demand for a Dell or a Hewlett-Packard.

In everyday language we call goods such as food and shelter *necessities* and goods such as exotic vacations *luxuries*. A necessity has poor substitutes and is crucial for our well-being. So a necessity generally has an inelastic demand. A luxury usually has many substitutes, one of which is not buying it. So a luxury generally has an elastic demand.

Proportion of Income Spent on the Good Other things remaining the same, the greater the proportion of income spent on a good, the more elastic (or less inelastic) is the demand for it.

Economics in Action
Elastic and Inelastic Demand

The real-world price elasticities of demand in the table range from 1.52 for metals, the item with the most elastic demand in the table, to 0.05 for oil, the item with the most inelastic demand in the table. The demand for food is also inelastic.

Oil and food, which have poor substitutes and inelastic demand, might be classified as necessities. Furniture and motor vehicles, which have good substitutes and elastic demand, might be classified as luxuries.

Price Elasticities of Demand

Good or Service	Elasticity
Elastic Demand	
Metals	1.52
Electrical engineering products	1.39
Mechanical engineering products	1.30
Furniture	1.26
Motor vehicles	1.14
Instrument engineering products	1.10
Professional services	1.09
Transportation services	1.03
Inelastic Demand	
Gas, electricity, and water	0.92
Chemicals	0.89
Drinks	0.78
Clothing	0.64
Tobacco	0.61
Banking and insurance services	0.56
Housing services	0.55
Agricultural and fish products	0.42
Books, magazines, and newspapers	0.34
Food	0.12
Oil	0.05

Sources of data: Ahsan Mansur and John Whalley, "Numerical Specification of Applied General Equilibrium Models: Estimation, Calibration, and Data," in *Applied General Equilibrium Analysis,* eds. Herbert E. Scarf and John B. Shoven (New York: Cambridge University Press, 1984), 109, and Henri Theil, Ching-Fan Chung, and James L. Seale, Jr., *Advances in Econometrics, Supplement I, 1989, International Evidence on Consumption Patterns* (Greenwich, Conn.: JAI Press Inc., 1989), and Geoffrey Heal, Columbia University, Web site.

Economics in Action
Price Elasticities of Demand for Food

The price elasticity of demand for food in the United States is estimated to be 0.12. This elasticity is an average over all types of food. The demand for most food items is inelastic, but there is a wide range of elasticities, as the figure below shows for a range of fruits, vegetables, and meats.

The demand for grapes and beef is elastic. The demand for oranges is unit elastic. These food items have many good substitutes. Florida winter tomatoes have closer substitutes than tomatoes in general, so the demand for the Florida winter variety is more elastic (less inelastic) than the demand for tomatoes.

Carrots and cabbage, on which we spend a very small proportion of income, have an almost zero price elasticity of demand.

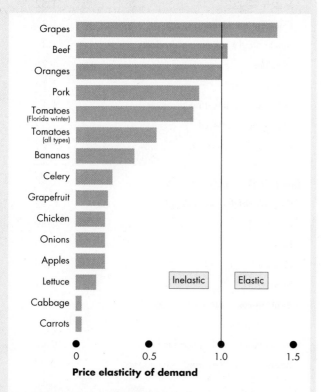

Price Elasticities of Demand for Food

Sources of data: Kuo S. Huang, *U.S. demand for food: A complete system of price and income effects* U.S. Dept. of Agriculture, Economic Research Service, Washington, DC, 1985 and J. Scott Shonkwiler and Robert D. Emerson, "Imports and the Supply of Winter Tomatoes: An Application of Rational Expectations", *American Journal of Agricultural Economics*, Vol. 64, No. 4 (Nov., 1982), pp. 634-641 and Kuo S. Huang, "A Further Look at Flexibilities and Elasticities", *American Journal of Agricultural Economics*, Vol. 76, No. 2 (May, 1994), pp. 313–317.

Think about your own elasticity of demand for chewing gum and housing. If the price of gum doubles, you consume almost as much as before. Your demand for gum is inelastic. If apartment rents double, you look for more students to share accommodation with you. Your demand for housing is not as inelastic as your demand for gum. Why the difference? Housing takes a large proportion of your budget, and gum takes only a tiny proportion. You don't like either price increase, but you hardly notice the higher price of gum, while the higher rent puts your budget under severe strain.

Time Elapsed Since Price Change The longer the time that has elapsed since a price change, the more elastic is demand. When the price of oil increased by 400 percent during the 1970s, people barely changed the quantity of oil and gasoline they bought. But gradually, as more efficient auto and airplane engines were developed, the quantity bought decreased. The demand for oil became more elastic as more time elapsed following the huge price hike.

REVIEW QUIZ

1 Why do we need a units-free measure of the responsiveness of the quantity demanded of a good or service to a change in its price?
2 Define the price elasticity of demand and show how it is calculated.
3 What is the total revenue test? Explain how it works.
4 What are the main influences on the elasticity of demand that make the demand for some goods elastic and the demand for other goods inelastic?
5 Why is the demand for a luxury generally more elastic (or less inelastic) than the demand for a necessity?

You can work these questions in Study Plan 4.1 and get instant feedback.

——————————————————— MyEconLab ◆

You've now completed your study of the *price* elasticity of demand. Two other elasticity concepts tell us about the effects of other influences on demand. Let's look at these other elasticities of demand.

More Elasticities of Demand

Back at the pizzeria, you are trying to work out how a price rise by the burger shop next door will affect the demand for your pizza. You know that pizzas and burgers are substitutes. You also know that when the price of a substitute for pizza rises, the demand for pizza increases. But by how much?

You also know that pizza and soft drinks are complements. And you know that if the price of a complement of pizza rises, the demand for pizza decreases. So you wonder, by how much will a rise in the price of a soft drink decrease the demand for your pizza?

To answer these questions, you need to calculate the cross elasticity of demand. Let's examine this elasticity measure.

Cross Elasticity of Demand

We measure the influence of a change in the price of a substitute or complement by using the concept of the cross elasticity of demand. The **cross elasticity of demand** is a measure of the responsiveness of the demand for a good to a change in the price of a substitute or complement, other things remaining the same. We calculate the *cross elasticity of demand* by using the formula:

$$\text{Cross elasticity of demand} = \frac{\text{Percentage change in quantity demanded}}{\text{Percentage change in price of a substitute or complement}}.$$

The cross elasticity of demand can be positive or negative. It is *positive* for a *substitute* and *negative* for a *complement.*

Substitutes Suppose that the price of pizza is constant and people buy 9 pizzas an hour. Then the price of a burger rises from $1.50 to $2.50. No other influence on buying plans changes and the quantity of pizzas bought increases to 11 an hour.

The change in the quantity demanded is +2 pizzas—the new quantity, 11 pizzas, minus the original quantity, 9 pizzas. The average quantity is 10 pizzas. So the quantity of pizzas demanded increases by 20 percent. That is,

$$(\Delta Q/Q_{ave}) \times 100 = (+2/10) \times 100 = +20\%.$$

The change in the price of a burger, a substitute for pizza, is +$1—the new price, $2.50, minus the original price, $1.50. The average price is $2 a burger. So the price of a burger rises by 50 percent. That is,

$$(\Delta P/P_{ave}) \times 100 = (+\$1/\$2) \times 100 = +50\%.$$

So the cross elasticity of demand for pizza with respect to the price of a burger is

$$\frac{+20\%}{+50\%} = 0.4.$$

Figure 4.6 illustrates the cross elasticity of demand. Pizza and burgers are substitutes. Because they are substitutes, when the price of a burger rises, the demand for pizza increases. The demand curve for pizza shifts rightward from D_0 to D_1. Because a *rise* in the price of a burger brings an *increase* in the demand for pizza, the cross elasticity of demand for pizza with respect to the price of a burger is *positive*. Both the price and the quantity change in the same direction.

FIGURE 4.6   Cross Elasticity of Demand

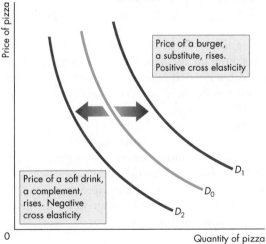

A burger is a *substitute* for pizza. When the price of a burger rises, the demand for pizza increases and the demand curve for pizza shifts rightward from D_0 to D_1. The cross elasticity of demand is *positive*.

A soft drink is a *complement* of pizza. When the price of a soft drink rises, the demand for pizza decreases and the demand curve for pizza shifts leftward from D_0 to D_2. The cross elasticity of demand is *negative*.

MyEconLab animation

Complements Now suppose that the price of pizza is constant and 11 pizzas an hour are bought. Then the price of a soft drink rises from $1.50 to $2.50. No other influence on buying plans changes and the quantity of pizzas bought decreases to 9 an hour.

The change in the quantity demanded is the opposite of what we've just calculated: The quantity of pizzas demanded decreases by 20 percent (–20%).

The change in the price of a soft drink, a complement of pizza, is the same as the percentage change in the price of a burger that we've just calculated. The price rises by 50 percent (+50%). So the cross elasticity of demand for pizza with respect to the price of a soft drink is

$$\frac{-20\%}{+50\%} = -0.4.$$

Because pizza and soft drinks are complements, when the price of a soft drink rises, the demand for pizza decreases. The demand curve for pizza shifts leftward from D_0 to D_2. Because a *rise* in the price of a soft drink brings a *decrease* in the demand for pizza, the cross elasticity of demand for pizza with respect to the price of a soft drink is *negative*. The price and quantity change in *opposite* directions.

The magnitude of the cross elasticity of demand determines how far the demand curve shifts. The larger the cross elasticity (absolute value), the greater is the change in demand and the larger is the shift in the demand curve.

If two items are close substitutes, such as two brands of spring water, the cross elasticity is large. If two items are close complements, such as movies and popcorn, the cross elasticity is large.

If two items are somewhat unrelated to each other, such as newspapers and orange juice, the cross elasticity is small—perhaps even zero.

Income Elasticity of Demand

Suppose the economy is expanding and people are enjoying rising incomes. This prosperity brings an increase in the demand for most types of goods and services. But by how much will the demand for pizza increase? The answer depends on the **income elasticity of demand**, which is a measure of the responsiveness of the demand for a good or service to a change in income, other things remaining the same.

The income elasticity of demand is calculated by using the formula:

$$\text{Income elasticity of demand} = \frac{\text{Percentage change in quantity demanded}}{\text{Percentage change in income}}.$$

Income elasticities of demand can be positive or negative and they fall into three interesting ranges:

- Greater than 1 (*normal* good, income elastic)
- Positive and less than 1 (*normal* good, income inelastic)
- Negative (*inferior* good)

Income Elastic Demand Suppose that the price of pizza is constant and 9 pizzas an hour are bought. Then incomes rise from $975 to $1,025 a week. No other influence on buying plans changes and the quantity of pizzas sold increases to 11 an hour.

The change in the quantity demanded is +2 pizzas. The average quantity is 10 pizzas, so the quantity demanded increases by 20 percent. The change in income is +$50 and the average income is $1,000, so incomes increase by 5 percent. The income elasticity of demand for pizza is

$$\frac{20\%}{5\%} = 4.$$

The demand for pizza is income elastic. The percentage increase in the quantity of pizza demanded exceeds the percentage increase in income. *When the demand for a good is income elastic, the percentage of income spent on that good increases as income increases.*

Income Inelastic Demand If the income elasticity of demand is positive but less than 1, demand is income inelastic. The percentage increase in the quantity demanded is positive but less than the percentage increase in income. *When the demand for a good is income inelastic, the percentage of income spent on that good decreases as income increases.*

Inferior Goods If the income elasticity of demand is negative, the good is an *inferior* good. The quantity demanded of an inferior good and the amount spent on it *decrease* when income increases. Goods in this category include small motorcycles, potatoes, and rice. Low-income consumers buy most of these goods.

Economics in Action
Necessities and Luxuries

The table shows estimates of some real-world income elasticities of demand. The demand for a necessity such as food or clothing is income inelastic, while the demand for a luxury such as transportation, which includes airline and foreign travel, is income elastic.

But what is a necessity and what is a luxury depends on the level of income. For people with a low income, food and clothing can be luxuries. So the level of income has a big effect on income elasticities of demand. The figure shows this effect on the income elasticity of demand for food in 10 countries. In countries with low incomes, such as Tanzania and India, the income elasticity of demand for food is high. In countries with high incomes, such as Canada, the income elasticity of demand for

food is low. That is, as income increases, the income elasticity of demand for food decreases. Low-income consumers spend a larger percentage of any increase in income on food than do high-income consumers.

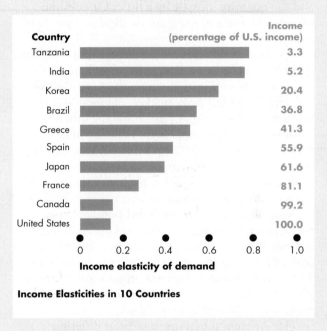

Income Elasticities in 10 Countries

Some Real-World Income Elasticities of Demand

Income Elastic Demand

Airline travel	5.82
Movies	3.41
Foreign travel	3.08
Electricity	1.94
Restaurant meals	1.61
Local buses and trains	1.38
Haircuts	1.36
Automobiles	1.07

Income Inelastic Demand

Tobacco	0.86
Alcoholic drinks	0.62
Furniture	0.53
Clothing	0.51
Newspapers and magazines	0.38
Telephone	0.32
Food	0.14

Sources of data: H.S. Houthakker and Lester D. Taylor, *Consumer Demand in the United States* (Cambridge, Mass.: Harvard University Press, 1970), and Henri Theil, Ching-Fan Chung, and James L. Seale, Jr., *Advances in Econometrics, Supplement 1, 1989, International Evidence on Consumption Patterns* (Greenwich, Conn.: JAI Press, Inc., 1989).

REVIEW QUIZ

1 What does the cross elasticity of demand measure?
2 What does the sign (positive versus negative) of the cross elasticity of demand tell us about the relationship between two goods?
3 What does the income elasticity of demand measure?
4 What does the sign (positive versus negative) of the income elasticity of demand tell us about a good?
5 Why does the level of income influence the magnitude of the income elasticity of demand?

You can work these questions in Study Plan 4.2 and get instant feedback.

━━━━━━━━━━━━━━━━━ MyEconLab ◆

You've now completed your study of the *cross elasticity* of demand and the *income elasticity* of demand. Let's look at the other side of the market and examine the elasticity of supply.

Elasticity of Supply

You know that when demand increases, the equilibrium price rises and the equilibrium quantity increases. But does the price rise by a large amount and the quantity increase by a little? Or does the price barely rise and the quantity increase by a large amount?

The answer depends on the responsiveness of the quantity supplied to a change in price. You can see why by studying Fig. 4.7, which shows two possible scenarios in a local pizza market. Figure 4.7(a) shows one scenario, and Fig. 4.7(b) shows the other.

In both cases, demand is initially D_0. In part (a), supply is shown by the supply curve S_A. In part (b), supply is shown by the supply curve S_B. Initially, in both cases, the price is $20 a pizza and the equilibrium quantity is 10 pizzas an hour.

Now increases in incomes and population increase the demand for pizza. The demand curve shifts rightward to D_1. In case (a), the price rises by $10 to $30 a pizza, and the quantity increases by only 3 to 13 pizzas an hour. In contrast, in case (b), the price rises by only $1 to $21 a pizza, and the quantity increases by 10 to 20 pizzas an hour.

The different outcomes arise from differing degrees of responsiveness of the quantity supplied to a change in price. We measure the degree of responsiveness by using the concept of the elasticity of supply.

Calculating the Elasticity of Supply

The **elasticity of supply** measures the responsiveness of the quantity supplied to a change in the price of a good when all other influences on selling plans remain the same. It is calculated by using the formula:

$$\text{Elasticity of supply} = \frac{\text{Percentage change in quantity supplied}}{\text{Percentage change in price}}.$$

We use the same method that you learned when you studied the elasticity of demand. (Refer back to p. 85 to check this method.) Let's calculate the elasticity of supply along the supply curves in Fig. 4.7.

In Fig. 4.7(a), when the price rises from $20 to $30, the price rise is $10 and the average price is $25, so the price rises by 40 percent of the average price. The quantity increases from 10 to 13 pizzas an

---

FIGURE 4.7   How a Change in Demand Changes Price and Quantity

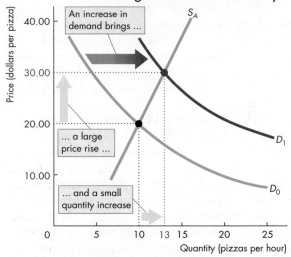

(a) Large price change and small quantity change

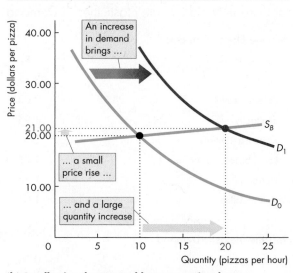

(b) Small price change and large quantity change

Initially, the price is $20 a pizza, and the quantity sold is 10 pizzas an hour. Then the demand for pizza increases. The demand curve shifts rightward to D_1. In part (a), the price rises by $10 to $30 a pizza, and the quantity increases by 3 to 13 pizzas an hour. In part (b), the price rises by only $1 to $21 a pizza, and the quantity increases by 10 to 20 pizzas an hour. The price change is smaller and the quantity change is larger in case (b) than in case (a). The quantity supplied is more responsive to a change in the price in case (b) than in case (a).

—————— MyEconLab animation ◆

hour, so the increase is 3 pizzas, the average quantity is 11.5 pizzas an hour, and the quantity increases by 26 percent. The elasticity of supply is equal to 26 percent divided by 40 percent, which equals 0.65.

In Fig. 4.7(b), when the price rises from $20 to $21, the price rise is $1 and the average price is $20.50, so the price rises by 4.9 percent of the average price. The quantity increases from 10 to 20 pizzas an hour, so the increase is 10 pizzas, the average quantity is 15 pizzas, and the quantity increases by 67 percent. The elasticity of supply is equal to 67 percent divided by 4.9 percent, which equals 13.67.

Figure 4.8 shows the range of elasticities of supply. If the quantity supplied is fixed regardless of the price, the supply curve is vertical and the elasticity of supply is zero. Supply is perfectly inelastic. This case is shown in Fig. 4.8(a). A special intermediate case occurs when the percentage change in price equals the percentage change in quantity. Supply is then unit elastic. This case is shown in Fig. 4.8(b). No matter how steep the supply curve is, if it is linear and passes through the origin, supply is unit elastic. If there is a price at which sellers are willing to offer any quantity for sale, the supply curve is horizontal and the elasticity of supply is infinite. Supply is perfectly elastic. This case is shown in Fig. 4.8(c).

The Factors That Influence the Elasticity of Supply

The elasticity of supply of a good depends on

- Resource substitution possibilities
- Time frame for the supply decision

Resource Substitution Possibilities Some goods and services can be produced only by using unique or rare productive resources. These items have a low, perhaps even a zero, elasticity of supply. Other goods and services can be produced by using commonly available resources that could be allocated to a wide variety of alternative tasks. Such items have a high elasticity of supply.

A Van Gogh painting is an example of a good with a vertical supply curve and a zero elasticity of supply. At the other extreme, wheat can be grown on land that is almost equally good for growing corn, so it is just as easy to grow wheat as corn. The opportunity cost of wheat in terms of forgone corn is almost constant. As a result, the supply curve of wheat is almost horizontal and its elasticity of supply is very large. Similarly, when a good is produced in many different countries (for example, sugar and beef), the supply of the good is highly elastic.

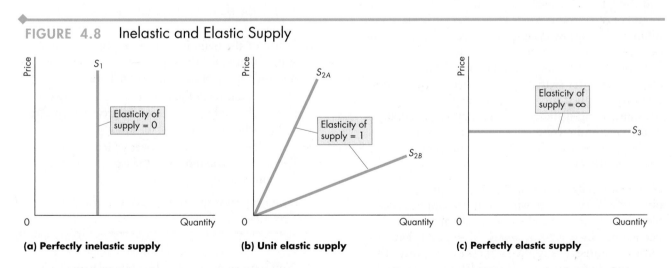

FIGURE 4.8   Inelastic and Elastic Supply

(a) Perfectly inelastic supply

(b) Unit elastic supply

(c) Perfectly elastic supply

Each supply illustrated here has a constant elasticity. The supply curve in part (a) illustrates the supply of a good that has a zero elasticity of supply. The supply curve in part (b) illustrates the supply of a good with a unit elasticity of supply. All linear supply curves that pass through the origin illustrate supplies that are unit elastic. The supply curve in part (c) illustrates the supply of a good with an infinite elasticity of supply.

The supply of most goods and services lies between these two extremes. The quantity produced can be increased but only by incurring a higher cost. If a higher price is offered, the quantity supplied increases. Such goods and services have an elasticity of supply between zero and infinity.

Time Frame for the Supply Decision   To study the influence of the amount of time elapsed since a price change, we distinguish three time frames of supply:

- Momentary supply
- Short-run supply
- Long-run supply

Momentary Supply   When the price of a good changes, the immediate response of the quantity supplied is determined by the *momentary supply* of that good.

Some goods, such as fruits and vegetables, have a perfectly inelastic momentary supply—a vertical supply curve. The quantities supplied depend on crop-planting decisions made earlier. In the case of oranges, for example, planting decisions have to be made many years in advance of the crop being available. Momentary supply is perfectly inelastic because, on a given day, no matter what the price of oranges, producers cannot change their output. They have picked, packed, and shipped their crop to market, and the quantity available for that day is fixed.

In contrast, some goods have a perfectly elastic momentary supply. Long-distance phone calls are an example. When many people simultaneously make a call, there is a big surge in the demand for telephone cables, computer switching, and satellite time. The quantity supplied increases, but the price remains constant. Long-distance carriers monitor fluctuations in demand and reroute calls to ensure that the quantity supplied equals the quantity demanded without changing the price.

Short-Run Supply   The response of the quantity supplied to a price change when only *some* of the possible adjustments to production can be made is determined by *short-run supply*. Most goods have an inelastic short-run supply. To increase output in the short run, firms must work their labour force overtime and perhaps hire additional workers. To decrease their output in the short run, firms either lay off workers or reduce their hours of work. With the passage of time, firms can make more adjustments, perhaps training additional workers or buying additional tools and other equipment.

For the orange grower, if the price of oranges falls, some pickers can be laid off and oranges left on the trees to rot. Or if the price of oranges rises, the grower can use more fertilizer and improved irrigation to increase the yields of their existing trees.

But an orange grower can't change the number of trees producing oranges in the short run.

Long-Run Supply   The response of the quantity supplied to a price change after *all* the technologically possible ways of adjusting supply have been exploited is determined by *long-run supply*. For most goods and services, long-run supply is elastic and perhaps perfectly elastic.

For the orange grower, the long run is the time it takes new tree plantings to grow to full maturity—about 15 years. In some cases, the long-run adjustment occurs only after a completely new production plant has been built and workers have been trained to operate it—typically a process that might take several years.

REVIEW QUIZ

1 Why do we need a units-free measure of the responsiveness of the quantity supplied of a good or service to a change in its price?
2 Define the elasticity of supply and show how it is calculated.
3 What are the main influences on the elasticity of supply that make the supply of some goods elastic and the supply of other goods inelastic?
4 Provide examples of goods or services whose elasticities of supply are (a) zero, (b) greater than zero but less than infinity, and (c) infinity.
5 How does the time frame over which a supply decision is made influence the elasticity of supply? Explain your answer.

You can work these questions in Study Plan 4.3 and get instant feedback.

─────────────────────── MyEconLab ◆

◆   You have now learned about the elasticities of demand and supply. Table 4.1 summarizes all the elasticities that you've met in this chapter. In the next chapter, we study the efficiency of competitive markets. But first study *Reading Between the Lines* on pp. 98–99, which puts the elasticity of demand to work and looks at the market for winter tomatoes.

TABLE 4.1   A Compact Glossary of Elasticities

Price Elasticities of Demand

A relationship is described as	When its magnitude is	Which means that
Perfectly elastic	Infinity	The smallest possible increase in price causes an infinitely large decrease in the quantity demanded*.
Elastic	Less than infinity	The percentage decrease in the quantity demanded exceeds the percentage increase in price.
Unit elastic	1	The percentage decrease in the quantity demanded equals the percentage increase in price.
Inelastic	Less than 1 but greater than zero	The percentage decrease in the quantity demanded is less than the percentage increase in price.
Perfectly inelastic	Zero	The quantity demanded is the same at all prices.

Cross Elasticities of Demand

A relationship is described as	When its value is	Which means that
Close substitutes	Large	The smallest possible increase in the price of one good causes an infinitely large increase in the quantity demanded of the other good.
Substitutes	Positive	If the price of one good increases, the quantity demanded of the other good also increases.
Unrelated goods	Zero	If the price of one good increases, the quantity demanded of the other good remains the same.
Complements	Negative	If the price of one good increases, the quantity demanded of the other good decreases.

Income Elasticities of Demand

A relationship is described as	When its value is	Which means that
Income elastic (normal good)	Greater than 1	The percentage increase in the quantity demanded is greater than the percentage increase in income.
Income inelastic (normal good)	Less than 1 but greater than zero	The percentage increase in the quantity demanded is greater than zero but less than the percentage increase in income.
Negative (inferior good)	Less than zero	When income increases, quantity demanded decreases.

Elasticities of Supply

A relationship is described as	When its magnitude is	Which means that
Perfectly elastic	Infinity	The smallest possible increase in price causes an infinitely large increase in the quantity supplied.
Elastic	Less than infinity but greater than 1	The percentage increase in the quantity supplied exceeds the percentage increase in the price.
Unit elastic	1	The percentage increase in the quantity supplied equals the percentage increase in the price.
Inelastic	Greater than zero but less than 1	The percentage increase in the quantity supplied is less than the percentage increase in the price.
Perfectly inelastic	Zero	The quantity supplied is the same at all prices.

*In each description, the directions of change may be reversed. For example, in this case, the smallest possible *decrease* in price causes an infinitely large *increase* in the quantity demanded.

The Elasticities of Demand and Supply for Tomatoes

Florida's Pain Is Now Ontario's Gain

The Toronto Star
March 20, 2010

Ontario consumers won't have to chop tomatoes from their burgers or BLTs, despite a big chill that destroyed most of Florida's winter crop.

Tomatoes grown in greenhouses across the province are in bountiful supply and available in produce aisles, according to the Ontario Greenhouse Vegetable Growers Association. ...

In 2009, association members produced 177 million kilograms of tomatoes. Seventy-five percent of the crop is exported to the U.S. with the rest consumed in Ontario.

Since the deep freeze in Florida, Gilvesy [general manager of the Ontario Greenhouse Vegetable Growers Association] said the association has had calls from concerned consumers and fast food outlets, which typically buy field products and are currently looking for new suppliers. He expects locally grown greenhouse tomatoes will help meet demand created in Florida after an 11-day freeze in January destroyed nearly 70 percent of the crop.

Plunging temperatures prevented farmers in the Sunshine State from replanting the winter crop. As a result, the average wholesale price of an 11-kilogram box of Florida tomatoes hit $30 from $6.50 last year. Florida produces about 75 percent of tomatoes in the United States.

The shortage south of the border will be a boost for local growers who will be able to meet increased demands. "We don't wish any producer ill, but this is the nature of agriculture," Gilvesy said.

ESSENCE OF THE STORY

- Florida produces 75 percent of tomatoes in the United States.

- Tomatoes are grown in greenhouses in Ontario and in 2009 production was 177 million kilograms, of which 75 percent was exported to the United States.

- In January 2010, an 11-day freeze wiped out 70 percent of the Florida crop.

- The average wholesale price of an 11-kilogram box of tomatoes rose from $6.50 in 2009 to $30.00 in 2010.

- Ontario growers were able to "meet increased demands."

ECONOMIC ANALYSIS

- According to J. Scott Shonkwiler and Robert D. Emerson, two agricultural economists at the University of Florida, the price elasticity of demand for tomatoes is 0.8.

- A 1 percent rise in the price of tomatoes brings a 0.8 percent decrease in the quantity demanded, other things remaining the same.

- According to the news article, in a normal period, the price of tomatoes was $6.50 a box (11 kilograms). From other sources, we know that tomato growers normally ship 1 million boxes a week.

- With the information just stated, we can determine the demand for tomatoes. It is the curve D in Figs. 1 and 2. This demand curve passes through the point that shows that 1 million boxes are demanded at a price of $6.50 a box and the elasticity of demand for tomatoes is 0.8.

- Figure 2 shows the calculation that confirms the price elasticity of demand is 0.8. When the price rises from $6.50 to $30.00 a box, as it did in 2010, the quantity demanded decreases from 1 million boxes to 320,000 (or 0.32 million) boxes. Use the numbers and the midpoint formula to confirm that the elasticity of demand is 0.8.

- Figures 1 and 3 show the supply of tomatoes. The news article says that Florida growers (the main U.S. producers of tomatoes in winter) lost 70 percent of their production. So assume that they shipped 300,000 boxes (0.3 million boxes) a week.

- Other growers (including those in Ontario using greenhouses) make up the difference between what the Florida growers supply and the quantity demanded.

- The supply curve in normal times, S_0, must pass through the equilibrium point at 1 million boxes and $6.50 a box.

- The supply curve in 2010, S_1, must pass through the equilibrium point at that time of 0.32 million boxes and $30 a box. It also passes through the point 0.3 million boxes and $6.50 a box because that is the quantity that Florida growers would ship even if the price remained at $6.50 a box.

- We can calculate the elasticity of supply by using the numbers in Fig. 3 and the midpoint formula. The elasticity of supply is 0.05, which means that supply is extremely inelastic.

- The very small elasticity of supply isn't surprising. It means that it is difficult to increase production quickly.

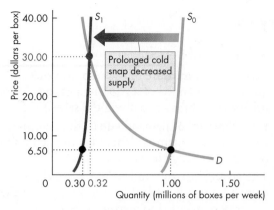

Figure 1 The Market for Tomatoes

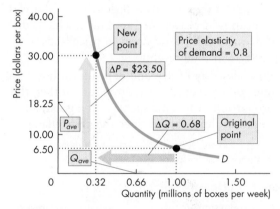

Figure 2 Price Elasticity of Demand for Tomatoes

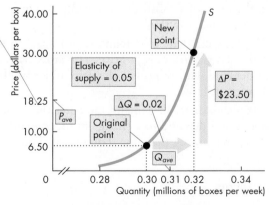

Figure 3 Price Elasticity of Supply of Tomatoes

- The Ontario growers are not so much able to "meet increased demands," as sell their crop for a much higher price.

SUMMARY

Key Points

Price Elasticity of Demand (pp. 84–90)

- Elasticity is a measure of the responsiveness of the quantity demanded of a good to a change in its price, other things remaining the same.
- Price elasticity of demand equals the percentage change in the quantity demanded divided by the percentage change in the price.
- The larger the magnitude of the price elasticity of demand, the greater is the responsiveness of the quantity demanded to a given price change.
- If demand is elastic, a cut in price leads to an increase in total revenue. If demand is unit elastic, a cut in price leaves total revenue unchanged. And if demand is inelastic, a cut in price leads to a decrease in total revenue.
- Price elasticity of demand depends on how easily one good serves as a substitute for another, the proportion of income spent on the good, and the length of time elapsed since the price change.

Working Problems 1 to 7 will give you a better understanding of the price elasticity of demand.

More Elasticities of Demand (pp. 91–93)

- Cross elasticity of demand measures the responsiveness of the demand for one good to a change in the price of a substitute or a complement, other things remaining the same.
- The cross elasticity of demand with respect to the price of a substitute is positive. The cross elasticity of demand with respect to the price of a complement is negative.
- Income elasticity of demand measures the responsiveness of demand to a change in income, other things remaining the same. For a normal good,

the income elasticity of demand is positive. For an inferior good, the income elasticity of demand is negative.

- When the income elasticity of demand is greater than 1 (income elastic demand), the percentage of income spent on the good increases as income increases.
- When the income elasticity of demand is less than 1 (income inelastic demand or the demand for an inferior good), the percentage of income spent on the good decreases as income increases.

Working Problems 8 to15 will give you a better understanding of cross and income elasticities of demand.

Elasticity of Supply (pp. 94–97)

- Elasticity of supply measures the responsiveness of the quantity supplied of a good to a change in its price, other things remaining the same.
- The elasticity of supply is positive and ranges between zero (vertical supply curve) and infinity (horizontal supply curve).
- Supply decisions have three time frames: momentary, short run, and long run.
- Momentary supply refers to the response of the quantity supplied to a price change at the instant that the price changes.
- Short-run supply refers to the response of the quantity supplied to a price change after some of the technologically feasible adjustments in production have been made.
- Long-run supply refers to the response of the quantity supplied to a price change when all the technologically feasible adjustments in production have been made.

Working Problems 16 and 17 will give you a better understanding of the elasticity of supply.

Key Terms

Cross elasticity of demand, 91
Elastic demand, 87
Elasticity of supply, 94
Income elasticity of demand, 92
Inelastic demand, 86
Perfectly elastic demand, 87

Perfectly inelastic demand, 86
Price elasticity of demand, 84
Total revenue, 88
Total revenue test, 88
Unit elastic demand, 86

SCAN THIS

MyEconLab ◆ You can work Problems 1 to 18 in Chapter 4 Study Plan and get instant feedback.

Price Elasticity of Demand (Study Plan 4.1)

1. Rain spoils the strawberry crop, the price rises from $4 to $6 a box, and the quantity demanded decreases from 1,000 to 600 boxes a week.
   a. Calculate the price elasticity of demand over this price range.
   b. Describe the demand for strawberries.

2. If the quantity of dental services demanded increases by 10 percent when the price of dental services falls by 10 percent, is the demand for dental services inelastic, elastic, or unit elastic?

3. The demand schedule for hotel rooms is

Price (dollars per night)	Quantity demanded (millions of rooms per night)
200	100
250	80
400	50
500	40
800	25

   a. What happens to total revenue when the price falls from $400 to $250 a night and from $250 to $200 a night?
   b. Is the demand for hotel rooms elastic, inelastic, or unit elastic?

4. The figure shows the demand for pens.

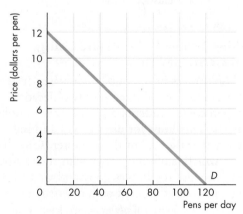

Calculate the elasticity of demand when the price rises from $4 to $6 a pen. Over what price range is the demand for pens elastic?

5. In 2003, when music downloading first took off, Universal Music slashed the average price of a CD from $21 to $15. The company expected the price cut to boost the quantity of CDs sold by 30 percent, other things remaining the same.

   a. What was Universal Music's estimate of the price elasticity of demand for CDs?
   b. If you were making the pricing decision at Universal Music, what would be your pricing decision? Explain your decision.

6. The demand for illegal drugs is inelastic. Much of the expenditure on illegal drugs comes from crime. Assuming these statements to be correct,
   a. How will a successful campaign that decreases the supply of drugs influence the price of illegal drugs and the amount spent on them?
   b. What will happen to the amount of crime?
   c. What is the most effective way of decreasing the quantity of illegal drugs bought and decreasing the amount of drug-related crime?

7. **The Grip of Gas**
   U.S. drivers are ranked as the least sensitive to changes in the price of gasoline. For example, if the price rose from $3 to $4 per gallon and stayed there for a year U.S. purchases of gasoline would fall only about 5 percent.
   Source: *Slate*, September 27, 2005
   a. Calculate the price elasticity of demand for gasoline. Is the demand for gasoline elastic, unit elastic, or inelastic?
   b. Explain how the price rise from $3 to $4 a gallon changes the total revenue from gasoline sales.

More Elasticities of Demand (Study Plan 4.2)

8. If a 12 percent rise in the price of orange juice decreases the quantity of orange juice demanded by 22 percent and increases the quantity of apple juice demanded by 14 percent, calculate the
   a. Price elasticity of demand for orange juice
   b. Cross elasticity of demand for apple juice with respect to the price of orange juice

9. When Judy's income increased from $130 to $170 a week, she increased her demand for concert tickets by 15 percent and decreased her demand for bus rides by 10 percent. Calculate Judy's income elasticity of demand for (a) concert tickets and (b) bus rides.

10. If a 5 percent rise in the price of sushi decreases the quantity of soy sauce demanded by 2 percent and decreases the quantity of sushi demanded by 1 percent, calculate the
    a. Price elasticity of demand for sushi

b. Cross elasticity of demand for soy sauce with respect to the price of sushi

11. **Spam Sales Rise as Food Costs Soar**

Sales of Spam are rising as consumers realize that Spam and other lower-cost foods can be substituted for costlier cuts of meat as a way of controlling their already stretched food budgets.

Source: *AOL Money & Finance*, May 28, 2008

a. Is Spam a normal good or an inferior good? Explain.

b. Would the income elasticity of demand for Spam be negative or positive? Explain.

Use the following information to work Problems 12 to 14.

As Gas Costs Soar, Buyers Flock to Small Cars

Faced with high gas prices, Americans are substituting smaller cars for SUVs. In April 2008, Toyota Yaris sales increased 46 percent and Ford Focus sales increased 32 percent from a year earlier. Sales of SUVs decreased by more than 25 percent in 2008 and Chevrolet Tahoe sales fell 35 percent. Full-size pickup sales decreased more than 15 percent in 2008 and Ford F-Series pickup sales decreased by 27 percent in April 2008. The effect of a downsized vehicle fleet on fuel consumption is unknown. In California, gasoline consumption decreased by 4 percent in January 2008 from a year earlier. The price of gasoline in January 2008 increased by about 30 percent from a year earlier.

Source: *The New York Times*, May 2, 2009

12. Calculate the price elasticity of demand for gasoline in California.

13. Calculate the cross elasticity of demand for
    a. Toyota Yaris with respect to the price of gasoline
    b. Ford Focus with respect to the price of gasoline

14. Calculate the cross elasticity of demand for
    a. Chevrolet Tahoe with respect to the price of gasoline
    b. A full-size pickup with respect to the price of gasoline

15. **Home Depot Earnings Hammered**

As gas and food prices increased and home prices slumped, people had less extra income to spend on home improvements. And the improvements that they made were on small inexpensive types of repairs and not major big-ticket items.

Source: CNN, May 20, 2008

a. What does this news clip imply about the income elasticity of demand for big-ticket home-improvement items?

b. Would the income elasticity of demand be greater or less than 1? Explain.

Elasticity of Supply (Study Plan 4.3)

16. The table sets out the supply schedule of jeans.

Price (dollars per pair)	Quantity supplied (millions of pairs per year)
120	24
125	28
130	32
135	36

Calculate the elasticity of supply when
a. The price rises from $125 to $135 a pair
b. The average price is $125 a pair

17. You are told that a 10 percent increase in the price of a good has led to a 1 percent increase in the quantity supplied of the good after one month and a 25 percent increase in the quantity supplied after 1 year.

a. Is the supply of this good elastic, unit elastic, or inelastic? Is this good likely to be produced using factors of production that are easily obtained? What is the elasticity of supply of this good?

b. What is the elasticity of supply after 1 year? Has the supply of this good become more elastic or less elastic? Why?

Economics in the News (Study Plan 4.EN)

18. **Swelling Textbook Costs Have College Students Saying "Pass"**

Textbook prices have doubled and risen faster than average prices for the past two decades. Sixty percent of students do not buy textbooks. Some students hunt for used copies and sell them back at the end of the semester; some buy online, which is often cheaper than the campus store; some use the library copy and wait till it's free; some share the book with a classmate.

Source: *Washington Post*, January 23, 2006

Explain what this news clip implies about

a. The price elasticity of demand for textbooks

b. The income elasticity of demand for college textbooks

c. The cross elasticity of demand for college textbooks from the campus bookstore with respect to the online price of a textbook

ADDITIONAL PROBLEMS AND APPLICATIONS

MyEconLab ◆ You can work these problems in MyEconLab if assigned by your instructor.

Price Elasticity of Demand

19. With higher fuel costs, airlines raised their average fare from 75¢ to $1.25 per passenger kilometre and the number of passenger kilometres decreased from 2.5 million a day to 1.5 million a day.
    a. What is the price elasticity of demand for air travel over this price range?
    b. Describe the demand for air travel.

20. The figure shows the demand for DVD rentals.

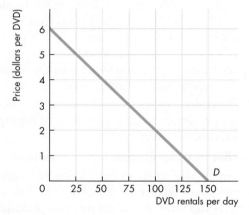

    a. Calculate the elasticity of demand when the price of a DVD rental rises from $3 to $5.
    b. At what price is the elasticity of demand for DVD rentals equal to 1?

Use the following table to work Problems 21 to 23. The demand schedule for computer chips is

Price (dollars per chip)	Quantity demanded (millions of chips per year)
200	50
250	45
300	40
350	35
400	30

21. a. What happens to total revenue if the price falls from $400 to $350 a chip and from $350 to $300 a chip?
    b. At what price is total revenue at a maximum?

22. At an average price of $350, is the demand for chips elastic, inelastic, or unit elastic? Use the total revenue test to answer this question.

23. At $250 a chip, is the demand for chips elastic or inelastic? Use the total revenue test to answer this question.

24. Your price elasticity of demand for bananas is 4. If the price of bananas rises by 5 percent, what is
    a. The percentage change in the quantity of bananas you buy?
    b. The change in your expenditure on bananas?

25. When heavy rain ruined the banana crop in Central America, the price of bananas rose from $1 a kilogram to $2 a kilogram. Banana growers sold fewer bananas, but their total revenue remained unchanged.
    a. By how much did the quantity of bananas demanded change?
    b. Is the demand for bananas from Central America elastic or inelastic?

26. In May 2009, iTunes raised the price of 33 songs from 99¢ per download to $1.29 per download. In the week following the price rise, the quantity of downloads of these 33 songs fell 35 percent.
    a. Calculate the price elasticity of demand for these 33 songs.
    b. How did iTunes' revenue from downloads of these 33 songs change?

More Elasticities of Demand

27. When Alex's income was $3,000, he bought 4 bagels and 12 doughnuts a month. Now his income is $5,000 and he buys 8 bagels and 6 doughnuts a month.
    a. Calculate Alex's income elasticity of demand for bagels.
    b. Calculate Alex's income elasticity of demand for doughnuts.

28. A 5 percent fall in the price of chocolate sauce increases the quantity of chocolate sauce demanded by 10 percent; and with no change in the price of ice cream, the quantity of ice cream demanded increases by 15 percent.
    a. Calculate the price elasticity of demand for chocolate sauce.
    b. Calculate the cross elasticity of demand for ice cream with respect to the price of chocolate sauce.
    c. Are ice cream and chocolate sauce substitutes or complements? Why?

29. A 10 percent rise in the price of peanut butter decreases the quantity of peanut butter

demanded by 5 percent; and with no change in the price of jam, the quantity of jam demanded decreases by 3 percent.

a. Calculate the price elasticity of demand for peanut butter.

b. Calculate the cross elasticity of demand for jam with respect to the price of peanut butter.

c. Are peanut butter and jam substitutes or complements? Why?

30. A drought cuts the quantity of wheat grown by 2 percent.

a. If the price elasticity of demand for wheat is 0.5, by how much will the price of wheat rise?

b. If pasta makers estimate that this change in the price of wheat will increase the price of pasta by 25 percent and decrease the quantity demanded of pasta by 8 percent, what is the pasta makers' estimate of the price elasticity of demand for pasta?

c. If pasta sauce makers estimate that, with the change in the price of pasta, the quantity of pasta sauce demanded will decrease by 5 percent, what is the pasta sauce makers' estimate of the cross elasticity of demand for pasta sauce with respect to the price of pasta?

Elasticity of Supply

31. The table sets out the supply schedule of long-distance phone calls.

Price (cents per minute)	Quantity supplied (millions of minutes per day)
10	200
20	400
30	600
40	800

Calculate the elasticity of supply when

a. The price falls from 40¢ to 30¢ a minute

b. The average price is 20¢ a minute

32. **Weak Coal Prices Hit China's Third-Largest Coal Miner**

The chairman of Yanzhou Coal Mining reported that the recession had decreased the demand for coal, with its sales falling by 11.9 percent to 7.92 million tons from 8.99 million tons a year earlier, despite a 10.6 percent cut in the price.

Source: Dow Jones, April 27, 2009

Calculate the elasticity of supply of coal. Is the supply of coal elastic or inelastic?

Economics in the News

33. After you have studied *Reading Between the Lines* on pp. 98–99, answer the following questions.

a. Which do you expect to be more price elastic and why: the demand for tomatoes in general or the demand for tomatoes grown in Ontario greenhouses?

b. When cold weather destroyed the Florida crop and more tomatoes came from Ontario greenhouses, what happened to the supply of tomatoes and the quantity of tomatoes supplied?

c. Mr. Gilvesy, general manager of the Ontario Greenhouse Vegetable Growers Association, says that "The shortage south of the border will be a boost for local growers who will be able to meet increased demands." What does this statement mean? Provide an alternative statement that is consistent with the facts and the supply and demand model.

d. What does the response of Ontario tomato growers imply about the elasticity of supply of Ontario tomatoes to Florida?

34. **Netflix to Offer Online Movie Viewing**

Online movie rental service Netflix has introduced a new feature to allow customers to watch movies and television series on their personal computers. Netflix competes with video rental retailer Blockbuster, which added an online rental service to the in-store rental service.

Source: CNN, January 16, 2007

a. How will online movie viewing influence the price elasticity of demand for in-store movie rentals?

b. Would the cross elasticity of demand for online movies and in-store movie rentals be negative or positive? Explain.

c. Would the cross elasticity of demand for online movies with respect to high-speed Internet service be negative or positive? Explain.

35. Statistics Canada reported the price elasticity of demand for the following travel classes:

Long-haul international business: 0.265

Long-haul international leisure: 1.04

Short-haul business: 0.7

Short-haul leisure: 1.5

CP24 reported that in the past year, Air Canada ticket prices jumped by 34 percent.

Calculate the percentage change in the number of passengers in each travel class.

Efficiency and Equity

After studying this chapter, you will be able to

◆ Describe the alternative methods of allocating scarce resources

◆ Explain the connection between demand and marginal benefit and define consumer surplus; and explain the connection between supply and marginal cost and define producer surplus

◆ Explain the conditions under which markets are efficient and inefficient

◆ Explain the main ideas about fairness and evaluate claims that markets result in unfair outcomes

Every time you decide to buy something, whether it's an everyday pizza or a Valentine's Day rose, you express your view about how scarce resources should be used and you make choices in your *self-interest*. A pizza cook one block away and a Colombian rose grower thousands of kilometres away make *their* self-interested choices about what to produce. Markets coordinate these self-interested choices, but do they allocate resources between pizza and roses, and everything else, efficiently and fairly in the *social interest*?

You will learn how economists approach and answer this question by studying a model market for pizza and then, at the end of the chapter, in *Reading Between the Lines*, by asking if the global market for roses is efficient.

◆ Resource Allocation Methods

The goal of this chapter is to evaluate the ability of markets to allocate resources efficiently and fairly. But to see whether the market does a good job, we must compare it with its alternatives. Resources are scarce, so they must be allocated somehow. Trading in markets is just one of several alternative methods.

Resources might be allocated by

- Market price
- Command
- Majority rule
- Contest
- First-come, first-served
- Lottery
- Personal characteristics
- Force

Let's briefly examine each method.

Market Price

When a market price allocates a scarce resource, the people who are willing and able to pay that price get the resource. Two kinds of people decide not to pay the market price: those who can afford to pay but choose not to buy and those who are too poor and simply can't afford to buy.

For many goods and services, distinguishing between those who choose not to buy and those who can't afford to buy doesn't matter. But for a few items, it does matter. For example, poor people can't afford to pay school fees and doctors' fees. Because poor people can't afford items that most people consider to be essential, these items are usually allocated by one of the other methods.

Command

A **command system** allocates resources by the order (command) of someone in authority. In the Canadian economy, the command system is used extensively inside firms and government departments. For example, if you have a job, most likely someone tells you what to do. Your labour is allocated to specific tasks by a command.

A command system works well in organizations in which the lines of authority and responsibility are clear and it is easy to monitor the activities being performed. But a command system works badly when the range of activities to be monitored is large and when it is easy for people to fool those in authority. North Korea uses a command system and it works so badly that it even fails to deliver an adequate supply of food.

Majority Rule

Majority rule allocates resources in the way that a majority of voters choose. Societies use majority rule to elect representative governments that make some of the biggest decisions. For example, majority rule decides the tax rates that end up allocating scarce resources between private use and public use. And majority rule decides how tax dollars are allocated among competing uses such as education and health care.

Majority rule works well when the decisions being made affect large numbers of people and self-interest must be suppressed to use resources most effectively.

Contest

A contest allocates resources to a winner (or a group of winners). Sporting events use this method. Andy Roddick competes with other tennis professionals, and the winner gets the biggest payoff. But contests are more general than those in a sports arena, though we don't normally call them contests. For example, Bill Gates won a contest to provide the world's personal computer operating system.

Contests do a good job when the efforts of the "players" are hard to monitor and reward directly. When a manager offers everyone in the company the opportunity to win a big prize, people are motivated to work hard and try to become the winner. Only a few people end up with a big prize, but many people work harder in the process of trying to win. The total output produced by the workers is much greater than it would be without the contest.

First-Come, First-Served

A first-come, first-served method allocates resources to those who are first in line. Many casual restaurants won't accept reservations. They use first-come, first-served to allocate their scarce tables. Highway space is allocated in this way too: The first to arrive at the on-ramp gets the road space. If too many vehicles enter the highway, the speed slows and people wait in line for some space to become available.

First-come, first-served works best when, as in the above examples, a scarce resource can serve just one user at a time in a sequence. By serving the user who arrives first, this method minimizes the time spent waiting for the resource to become free.

Lottery

Lotteries allocate resources to those who pick the winning number, draw the lucky cards, or come up lucky on some other gaming system. Provincial lotteries and casinos reallocate millions of dollars worth of goods and services every year.

But lotteries are more widespread than jackpots and roulette wheels in casinos. They are used to allocate landing slots to airlines at some airports, places in the New York and London marathons, and have been used to allocate fishing rights and the electromagnetic spectrum used by cell phones.

Lotteries work best when there is no effective way to distinguish among potential users of a scarce resource.

Personal Characteristics

When resources are allocated on the basis of personal characteristics, people with the "right" characteristics get the resources. Some of the resources that matter most to you are allocated in this way. For example, you will choose a marriage partner on the basis of personal characteristics. But this method can also be used in unacceptable ways. Allocating the best jobs to white, Anglo-Saxon males and discriminating against visible minorities and women is an example.

Force

Force plays a crucial role, for both good and ill, in allocating scarce resources. Let's start with the ill.

War, the use of military force by one nation against another, has played an enormous role historically in allocating resources. The economic supremacy of European settlers in the Americas and Australia owes much to the use of this method.

Theft, the taking of the property of others without their consent, also plays a large role. Both large-scale organized crime and small-scale petty crime collectively allocate billions of dollars worth of resources annually.

But force plays a crucial positive role in allocating resources. It provides the state with an effective method of transferring wealth from the rich to the poor, and it provides the legal framework in which voluntary exchange in markets takes place.

A legal system is the foundation on which our market economy functions. Without courts to enforce contracts, it would not be possible to do business. But the courts could not enforce contracts without the ability to apply force if necessary. The state provides the ultimate force that enables the courts to do their work.

More broadly, the force of the state is essential to uphold the principle of the rule of law. This principle is the bedrock of civilized economic (and social and political) life. With the rule of law upheld, people can go about their daily economic lives with the assurance that their property will be protected—that they can sue for violations against their property (and be sued if they violate the property of others).

Free from the burden of protecting their property and confident in the knowledge that those with whom they trade will honour their agreements, people can get on with focusing on the activity in which they have a comparative advantage and trading for mutual gain.

REVIEW QUIZ

1 Why do we need methods of allocating scarce resources?
2 Describe the alternative methods of allocating scarce resources.
3 Provide an example of each allocation method that illustrates when it works well.
4 Provide an example of each allocation method that illustrates when it works badly.

You can work these questions in Study Plan 5.1 and get instant feedback.

━━━━━━━━━━━━━━━━━━━━ MyEconLab ◆

In the next sections, we're going to see how a market can achieve an efficient use of resources, examine the obstacles to efficiency, and see how sometimes an alternative method might improve on the market. After looking at efficiency, we'll turn our attention to the more difficult issue of fairness.

◆ Benefit, Cost, and Surplus

Resources are allocated efficiently and in the *social interest* when they are used in the ways that people value most highly. You saw in Chapter 2 that this outcome occurs when the quantities produced are at the point on the *PPF* at which marginal benefit equals marginal cost (see pp. 33–35). We're now going to see whether competitive markets produce the efficient quantities.

We begin on the demand side of a market.

Demand, Willingness to Pay, and Value

In everyday life, we talk about "getting value for money." When we use this expression, we are distinguishing between *value* and *price*. Value is what we get, and price is what we pay.

The value of one more unit of a good or service is its marginal benefit. We measure marginal benefit by the maximum price that is willingly paid for another unit of the good or service. But willingness to pay determines demand. *A demand curve is a marginal benefit curve.*

In Fig. 5.1(a), Lisa is willing to pay $1 for the 30th slice of pizza and $1 is her marginal benefit from that slice. In Fig. 5.1(b), Nick is willing to pay $1 for the 10th slice of pizza and $1 is his marginal benefit from that slice. But at what quantity is the market willing to pay $1 for the marginal slice? The answer is provided by the *market demand curve*.

Individual Demand and Market Demand

The relationship between the price of a good and the quantity demanded by one person is called *individual demand*. And the relationship between the price of a good and the quantity demanded by all buyers is called *market demand*.

> The market demand curve is the horizontal sum of the individual demand curves and is formed by adding the quantities demanded by all the individuals at each price.

Figure 5.1(c) illustrates the market demand for pizza if Lisa and Nick are the only people in the market. Lisa's demand curve in part (a) and Nick's demand curve in part (b) sum horizontally to the market demand curve in part (c).

FIGURE 5.1   Individual Demand, Market Demand, and Marginal Social Benefit

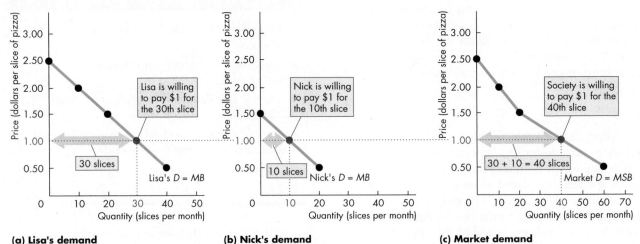

(a) Lisa's demand   **(b) Nick's demand**   **(c) Market demand**

At a price of $1 a slice, the quantity demanded by Lisa is 30 slices and the quantity demanded by Nick is 10 slices, so the quantity demanded by the market is 40 slices. Lisa's demand

curve in part (a) and Nick's demand curve in part (b) sum horizontally to the market demand curve in part (c). The market demand curve is the marginal social benefit curve, *MSB*.

At a price of $1 a slice, Lisa demands 30 slices and Nick demands 10 slices, so the market quantity demanded at $1 a slice is 40 slices.

For Lisa and Nick, their demand curves are their marginal benefit curves. For society, the market demand curve is the marginal benefit curve. We call the marginal benefit to the entire society *marginal social benefit*. So the market demand curve is also the *marginal social benefit curve, MSB*.

Consumer Surplus

We don't always have to pay as much as we are willing to pay. We get a bargain. When people buy something for less than it is worth to them, they receive a consumer surplus. **Consumer surplus** is the excess of the benefit received from a good over the amount paid for it. We can calculate consumer surplus as the marginal benefit (or value) of a good minus its price, summed over the quantity bought.

Figure 5.2(a) shows Lisa's consumer surplus from pizza when the price is $1 a slice. At this price, she buys 30 slices a month because the 30th slice is worth exactly $1 to her. But Lisa is willing to pay $2 for the 10th slice, so her marginal benefit from this

slice is $1 more than she pays for it—she receives a surplus of $1 on the 10th slice.

Lisa's consumer surplus is the sum of the surpluses on *all of the slices she buys*. This sum is the area of the green triangle—the area below the demand curve and above the market price line. The area of this triangle is equal to its base (30 slices) multiplied by its height ($1.50) divided by 2, which is $22.50. The area of the blue rectangle in Fig. 5.2(a) shows what Lisa pays for 30 slices of pizza.

Figure 5.2(b) shows Nick's consumer surplus, and part (c) shows the consumer surplus for the market. The consumer surplus for the market is the sum of the consumer surpluses of Lisa and Nick.

All goods and services have decreasing marginal benefit, so people receive more benefit from their consumption than the amount they pay.

Supply and Marginal Cost

Your next task is to see how market supply reflects marginal cost. The connection between supply and cost closely parallels the related ideas about demand and benefit that you've just studied. Firms are in business to make a profit. To do so, they must sell

---

FIGURE 5.2   Demand and Consumer Surplus

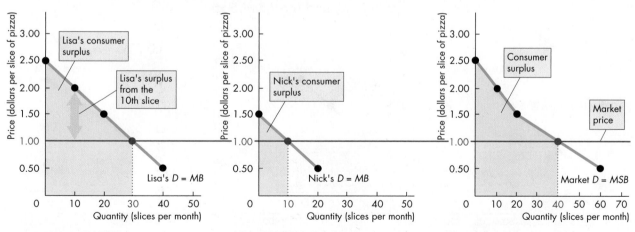

(a) Lisa's consumer surplus   **(b) Nick's consumer surplus**   **(c) Market consumer surplus**

Lisa is willing to pay $2 for her 10th slice of pizza in part (a). At a market price of $1 a slice, Lisa receives a surplus of $1 on the 10th slice. The green triangle shows her consumer surplus on the 30 slices she buys at $1 a slice. The

green triangle in part (b) shows Nick's consumer surplus on the 10 slices that he buys at $1 a slice. The green area in part (c) shows the consumer surplus for the market. The blue rectangles show the amounts spent on pizza.

MyEconLab animation

their output for a price that exceeds the cost of production. Let's investigate the relationship between cost and price.

Supply, Cost, and Minimum Supply-Price

Firms make a profit when they receive more from the sale of a good or service than the cost of producing it. Just as consumers distinguish between value and price, so producers distinguish between *cost* and *price*. Cost is what a firm gives up when it produces a good or service and price is what a firm receives when it sells the good or service.

The cost of producing one more unit of a good or service is its marginal cost. Marginal cost is the minimum price that producers must receive to induce them to offer one more unit of a good or service for sale. But the minimum supply-price determines supply. *A supply curve is a marginal cost curve.*

In Fig. 5.3(a), Maria is willing to produce the 100th pizza for $15, her marginal cost of that pizza. In Fig. 5.3(b), Mario is willing to produce the 50th pizza for $15, his marginal cost of that pizza.

What quantity is this market willing to produce for $15 a pizza? The answer is provided by the *market supply curve*.

Individual Supply and Market Supply

The relationship between the price of a good and the quantity supplied by one producer is called *individual supply*. And the relationship between the price of a good and the quantity supplied by all producers is called *market supply*.

> The market supply curve is the horizontal sum of the individual supply curves and is formed by adding the quantities supplied by all the producers at each price.

Figure 5.3(c) illustrates the market supply of pizzas if Maria and Mario are the only producers. Maria's supply curve in part (a) and Mario's supply curve in part (b) sum horizontally to the market supply curve in part (c).

At a price of $15 a pizza, Maria supplies 100 pizzas and Mario supplies 50 pizzas, so the quantity supplied by the market at $15 a pizza is 150 pizzas.

For Maria and Mario, their supply curves are their marginal cost curves. For society, the market supply curve is the marginal cost curve. We call society's marginal cost *marginal social cost*. So the market supply curve is also the *marginal social cost curve, MSC*.

FIGURE 5.3   Individual Supply, Market Supply, and Marginal Social Cost

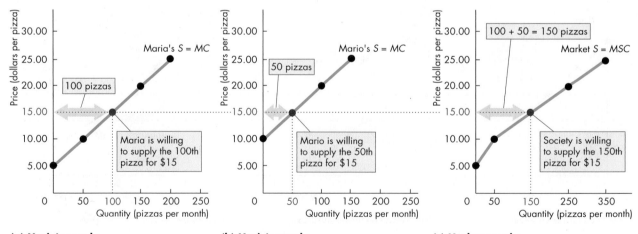

(a) Maria's supply

(b) Mario's supply

(c) Market supply

At a price of $15 a pizza, the quantity supplied by Maria is 100 pizzas and the quantity supplied by Mario is 50 pizzas, so the quantity supplied by the market is 150 pizzas. Maria's supply curve in part (a) and Mario's supply curve in part (b) sum horizontally to the market supply curve in part (c). The market supply curve is the marginal social cost curve, *MSC*.

MyEconLab   animation

Producer Surplus

When price exceeds marginal cost, the firm receives a producer surplus. **Producer surplus** is the excess of the amount received from the sale of a good or service over the cost of producing it. It is calculated as the price received minus the marginal cost (or minimum supply-price), summed over the quantity sold.

Figure 5.4(a) shows Maria's producer surplus from pizza when the price is $15 a pizza. At this price, she sells 100 pizzas a month because the 100th pizza costs her $15 to produce. But Maria is willing to produce the 50th pizza for her marginal cost, which is $10, so she receives a surplus of $5 on this pizza.

Maria's producer surplus is the sum of the surpluses on the pizzas she sells. This sum is the area of the blue triangle—the area below the market price and above the supply curve. The area of this triangle is equal to its base (100) multiplied by its height ($10) divided by 2, which is $500.

The red area below the supply curve in Fig. 5.4(a) shows what it costs Maria to produce 100 pizzas.

The area of the blue triangle in Fig. 5.4(b) shows Mario's producer surplus and the blue area in Fig. 5.4(c) shows the producer surplus for the market.

The producer surplus for the market is the sum of the producer surpluses of Maria and Mario.

Consumer surplus and producer surplus can be used to measure the efficiency of a market. Let's see how we can use these concepts to study the efficiency of a competitive market.

REVIEW QUIZ

1 What is the relationship between marginal benefit, value, and demand?
2 What is the relationship between individual demand and market demand?
3 What is consumer surplus? How is it measured?
4 What is the relationship between marginal cost, minimum supply-price, and supply?
5 What is the relationship between individual supply and market supply?
6 What is producer surplus? How is it measured?

You can work these questions in Study Plan 5.2 and get instant feedback.

———————————— MyEconLab ◆

FIGURE 5.4   Supply and Producer Surplus

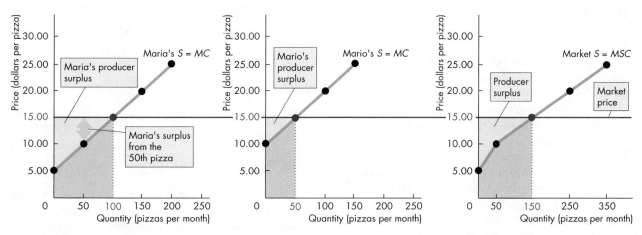

(a) Maria's producer surplus   **(b) Mario's producer surplus**   **(c) Market producer surplus**

Maria is willing to produce the 50th pizza for $10 in part (a). At a market price of $15 a pizza, Maria gets a surplus of $5 on the 50th pizza. The blue triangle shows her producer surplus on the 100 pizzas she sells at $15 each. The

blue triangle in part (b) shows Mario's producer surplus on the 50 pizzas he sells at $15 each. The blue area in part (c) shows the producer surplus for the market. The red areas show the cost of producing the pizzas sold.

———————————— MyEconLab   animation ◆

Is the Competitive Market Efficient?

Figure 5.5(a) shows the market for pizza. The market forces that you studied in Chapter 3 (pp. 66–67) pull the pizza market to its equilibrium price of $15 a pizza and equilibrium quantity of 10,000 pizzas a day. Buyers enjoy a consumer surplus (green area) and sellers enjoy a producer surplus (blue area), but is this competitive equilibrium efficient?

Efficiency of Competitive Equilibrium

You've seen that the market demand curve for a good or service tells us the marginal social benefit from it. You've also seen that the market supply curve of a good or service tells us the marginal social cost of producing it.

Equilibrium in a competitive market occurs when the quantity demanded equals the quantity supplied at the intersection of the demand curve and the supply curve. At this intersection point, marginal social benefit on the demand curve equals marginal social cost on the supply curve. This equality is the condition for allocative efficiency. So in equilibrium, a competitive market achieves allocative efficiency.

Figure 5.5 illustrates the efficiency of competitive equilibrium. The demand curve and the supply curve intersect in part (a) and marginal social benefit equals marginal social cost in part (b).

If production is less than 10,000 pizzas a day, the marginal pizza is valued more highly than it costs to produce. If production exceeds 10,000 pizzas a day, the marginal pizza costs more to produce than the value that consumers place on it. Only when 10,000 pizzas a day are produced is the marginal pizza worth exactly what it costs.

The competitive market pushes the quantity of pizzas produced to its efficient level of 10,000 a day. If production is less than 10,000 pizzas a day, a shortage raises the price, which increases production. If production exceeds 10,000 pizzas a day, a surplus of pizzas lowers the price, which decreases production. So a competitive pizza market is efficient.

Figure 5.5(a) also shows the consumer surplus and producer surplus. The sum of consumer surplus and producer surplus is called **total surplus**. When the efficient quantity is produced, total surplus is maximized. Buyers and sellers acting in their self-interest end up promoting the social interest.

FIGURE 5.5 An Efficient Market for Pizza

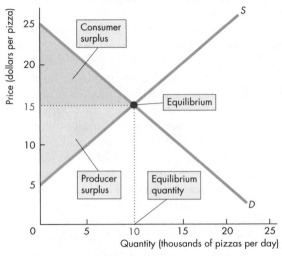

(a) Equilibrium and surpluses

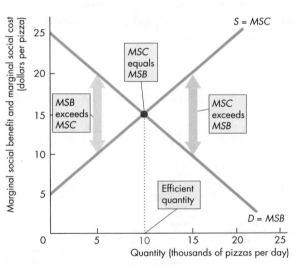

(b) Efficiency

Competitive equilibrium in part (a) occurs when the quantity demanded equals the quantity supplied. Resources are used efficiently in part (b) when marginal social benefit, *MSB*, equals marginal social cost, *MSC*. Total surplus, which is the sum of consumer surplus (the green triangle) and producer surplus (the blue triangle) is maximized.

The efficient quantity in part (b) is the same as the equilibrium quantity in part (a). The competitive pizza market produces the efficient quantity of pizzas.

MyEconLab animation

Economics in Action

The Invisible Hand

Writing in his *Wealth of Nations* in 1776, Adam Smith was the first to suggest that competitive markets send resources to the uses in which they have the highest value (see p. 51). Smith believed that each participant in a competitive market is "led by an invisible hand to promote an end [the efficient use of resources] which was no part of his intention."

You can see the invisible hand at work in the cartoon and in the world today.

Umbrella for Sale The cold drinks vendor has cold drinks and shade and he has a marginal cost and a minimum supply-price of each. The reader on the park bench has a marginal benefit from each and a willingness to pay for it. The reader's marginal benefit from shade exceeds the vendor's marginal cost; but the vendor's marginal cost of a cold drink exceeds the reader's marginal benefit. They trade the umbrella. The vendor gets a producer surplus from selling the shade for more than its marginal cost, and the reader gets a consumer surplus from buying the shade for less than its marginal benefit. Both the vendor and the reader are better off and the umbrella has moved to its highest-valued use.

The Invisible Hand at Work Today The market economy relentlessly performs the activity illustrated in the cartoon to achieve an efficient allocation of resources.

An Ontario frost cuts the supply of grapes. With fewer grapes available, the marginal social benefit increases. A shortage of grapes raises their price, so the market allocates the smaller quantity available to the people who value them most highly.

A new technology cuts the cost of producing a smart phone. With a lower production cost, the supply of smart phones increases and the price of a smart phone falls. The lower price encourages an increase in the quantity demanded of this now less-costly tool. The marginal social benefit from a smart phone is brought to equality with its marginal social cost.

Market Failure

Markets do not always achieve an efficient outcome. We call a situation in which a market delivers an inefficient outcome one of **market failure**. Market failure can occur because too little of an item is produced (underproduction) or too much is produced (overproduction). We'll describe these two market failure outcomes and then see why they arise.

Underproduction In Fig. 5.6(a), the quantity of pizzas produced is 5,000 a day. At this quantity, consumers are willing to pay $20 for a pizza that costs only $10 to produce. By producing only 5,000 pizzas a day, total surplus is smaller than its maximum possible level. The quantity produced is inefficient—there is underproduction.

We measure the scale of inefficiency by **deadweight loss**, which is the decrease in total surplus that results

FIGURE 5.6   Underproduction and Overproduction

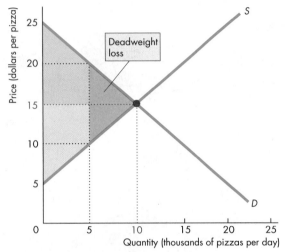

(a) Underproduction

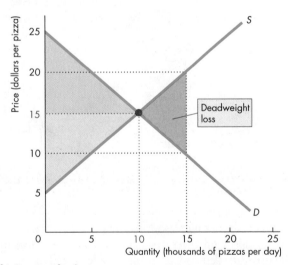

(b) Overproduction

If 5,000 pizzas a day are produced, in part (a), total surplus (the sum of the green and blue areas) is smaller than its maximum by the amount of the deadweight loss (the grey triangle). At all quantities below 10,000 pizzas a day, the benefit from one more pizza exceeds its cost.

If 15,000 pizzas a day are produced, in part (b), total surplus is also smaller than its maximum by the amount of the deadweight loss. At all quantities in excess of 10,000 pizzas a day, the cost of one more pizza exceeds its benefit.

MyEconLab   animation

from an inefficient level of production. The grey triangle in Fig. 5.6(a) shows the deadweight loss.

Overproduction   In Fig. 5.6(b), the quantity of pizzas produced is 15,000 a day. At this quantity, consumers are willing to pay only $10 for a pizza that costs $20 to produce. By producing the 15,000th pizza, $10 of resources are wasted. Again, the grey triangle shows the deadweight loss, which reduces the total surplus to less than its maximum.

Inefficient production creates a deadweight loss that is borne by the entire society: It is a social loss.

Sources of Market Failure

Obstacles to efficiency that bring market failure and create deadweight losses are

- Price and quantity regulations
- Taxes and subsidies
- Externalities
- Public goods and common resources
- Monopoly
- High transactions costs

Price and Quantity Regulations   *Price regulations* that put a cap on the rent a landlord is permitted to charge and laws that require employers to pay a minimum wage sometimes block the price adjustments that balance the quantity demanded and the quantity supplied and lead to underproduction. *Quantity regulations* that limit the amount that a farm is permitted to produce also lead to underproduction.

Taxes and Subsidies   *Taxes* increase the prices paid by buyers and lower the prices received by sellers. So taxes decrease the quantity produced and lead to underproduction. *Subsidies*, which are payments by the government to producers, decrease the prices paid by buyers and increase the prices received by sellers. So subsidies increase the quantity produced and lead to overproduction.

Externalities   An *externality* is a cost or a benefit that affects someone other than the seller or the buyer. An *external cost* arises when an electric utility burns coal and emits carbon dioxide. The utility doesn't consider the cost of climate change when it decides how much power to produce. The result is overproduction. An *external benefit* arises when a condomium owner installs a smoke detector and decreases her neighbour's fire risk. She doesn't consider the benefit to her neighbour when she decides how many detectors to install. The result is underproduction.

Public Goods and Common Resources A *public good* is a good or service that is consumed simultaneously by everyone even if they don't pay for it. National defence is an example. Competitive markets would underproduce national defence because it is in each person's interest to free ride on everyone else and avoid paying for her or his share of such a good.

A *common resource* is owned by no one but is available to be used by everyone. Atlantic salmon is an example. It is in everyone's self-interest to ignore the costs they impose on others when they decide how much of a common resource to use. The result is that the resource is overused.

Monopoly A *monopoly* is a firm that is the sole provider of a good or service. Local water supply and cable television are supplied by firms that are monopolies. The monopoly's self-interest is to maximize its profit. Because the monopoly has no competitors, it can set the price to achieve its self-interested goal. To achieve its goal, a monopoly produces too little and charges too high a price. It leads to underproduction.

High Transactions Costs When you go to Starbucks, you pay for more than the coffee. You pay your share of the cost of the barista's time, the espresso maker, and the decor. When you buy your first condominium, you will pay for more than the condominium. You will buy the services of a realtor and a lawyer. Economists call the costs of the services that enable a market to bring buyers and sellers together **transactions costs**.

It is costly to operate *any* market, so to use market price to allocate resources, it must be worth bearing the transactions costs. Some markets are too costly to operate. For example, it is too costly to operate a market in time slots on a local tennis court. Instead of a market, the court uses first-come, first-served: You hang around until the court becomes vacant and "pay" with your waiting time. When transactions costs are high, the market might underproduce.

You now know the conditions under which resource allocation is efficient. You've seen how a competitive market can be efficient, and you've seen some obstacles to efficiency. Can alternative allocation methods improve on the market?

Alternatives to the Market

When a market is inefficient, can one of the alternative nonmarket methods that we described at the beginning of this chapter do a better job? Sometimes it can.

Often, majority rule might be used in an attempt to improve the allocation of resources. But majority rule has its own shortcomings: A group that pursues the self-interest of its members can become the majority. For example, a price or quantity regulation that creates inefficiency is almost always the result of a self-interested group becoming the majority and imposing costs on the minority. Also, with majority rule, votes must be translated into actions by bureaucrats who have their own agendas based on their self-interest.

Managers in firms issue commands and avoid the transactions costs that they would incur if they went to a market every time they needed a job done.

First-come, first-served works best in some situations. Think about the scene at a busy ATM. Instead of waiting in line people might trade places at a "market" price. But someone would need to ensure that trades were honoured. At a busy ATM, first-come, first-served is the most efficient arrangement.

There is no one efficient mechanism that allocates all resources efficiently. But markets, when supplemented by other mechanisms such as majority rule, command systems, and first-come, first-served, do an amazingly good job.

REVIEW QUIZ

1 Do competitive markets use resources efficiently? Explain why or why not.
2 What is deadweight loss and under what conditions does it occur?
3 What are the obstacles to achieving an efficient allocation of resources in the market economy?

You can work these questions in Study Plan 5.3 and get instant feedback.

——————————— MyEconLab ◆

Is an efficient allocation of resources also a fair allocation? Does the competitive market provide people with fair incomes for their work? Do people always pay a fair price for the things they buy? Don't we need the government to step into some competitive markets to prevent the price from rising too high or falling too low? Let's now study these questions.

◆ Is the Competitive Market Fair?

When a natural disaster strikes, such as a severe winter storm or a flood, the prices of many essential items jump. The reason prices jump is that the demand and willingness to pay for these items has increased, but the supply has not changed. So the higher prices achieve an efficient allocation of scarce resources. News reports of these price hikes almost never talk about efficiency. Instead, they talk about equity or fairness. The claim that is often made is that it is unfair for profit-seeking dealers to cheat the victims of natural disaster.

Similarly, when low-skilled people work for a wage that is below what most would regard as a "living wage," the media and politicians talk of employers taking unfair advantage of their workers.

How do we decide whether something is fair or unfair? You know when you *think* something is unfair, but how do you *know?* What are the *principles* of fairness?

Philosophers have tried for centuries to answer this question. Economists have offered their answers too. But before we look at the proposed answers, you should know that there is no universally agreed upon answer.

Economists agree about efficiency. That is, they agree that it makes sense to make the economic pie as large as possible and to produce it at the lowest possible cost. But they do not agree about equity. That is, they do not agree about what are fair shares of the economic pie for all the people who make it. The reason is that ideas about fairness are not exclusively economic ideas. They touch on politics, ethics, and religion. Nevertheless, economists have thought about these issues and have a contribution to make. Let's examine the views of economists on this topic.

To think about fairness, think of economic life as a game—a serious game. All ideas about fairness can be divided into two broad groups. They are

- It's not fair if the *result* isn't fair.
- It's not fair if the *rules* aren't fair.

It's Not Fair If the *Result* Isn't Fair

The earliest efforts to establish a principle of fairness were based on the view that the result is what matters. The general idea was that it is unfair if people's incomes are too unequal. For example, it is unfair that a bank president earns millions of dollars a year

while a bank teller earns only thousands of dollars. It is unfair that a store owner makes a larger profit and her customers pay higher prices in the aftermath of a winter storm.

During the nineteenth century, economists thought they had made the incredible discovery: Efficiency requires equality of incomes. To make the economic pie as large as possible, it must be cut into equal pieces, one for each person. This idea turns out to be wrong. But there is a lesson in the reason that it is wrong, so this idea is worth a closer look.

Utilitarianism The nineteenth-century idea that only equality brings efficiency is called *utilitarianism*. **Utilitarianism** is a principle that states that we should strive to achieve "the greatest happiness for the greatest number." The people who developed this idea were known as utilitarians. They included the most eminent thinkers, such as Jeremy Bentham and John Stuart Mill.

Utilitarians argued that to achieve "the greatest happiness for the greatest number," income must be transferred from the rich to the poor up to the point of complete equality—to the point at which there are no rich and no poor.

They reasoned in the following way: First, everyone has the same basic wants and a similar capacity to enjoy life. Second, the greater a person's income, the smaller is the marginal benefit of a dollar. The millionth dollar spent by a rich person brings a smaller marginal benefit to that person than the marginal benefit that the thousandth dollar spent brings to a poorer person. So by transferring a dollar from the millionaire to the poorer person, more is gained than is lost. The two people added together are better off.

Figure 5.7 illustrates this utilitarian idea. Tom and Jerry have the same marginal benefit curve, *MB*. (Marginal benefit is measured on the same scale of 1 to 3 for both Tom and Jerry.) Tom is at point *A*. He earns $5,000 a year, and his marginal benefit from a dollar is 3 units. Jerry is at point *B*. He earns $45,000 a year, and his marginal benefit from a dollar is 1 unit. If a dollar is transferred from Jerry to Tom, Jerry loses 1 unit of marginal benefit and Tom gains 3 units. So together, Tom and Jerry are better off—they are sharing the economic pie more efficiently. If a second dollar is transferred, the same thing happens: Tom gains more than Jerry loses. And the same is true for every dollar transferred until they both reach point *C*. At point *C*, Tom and Jerry have $25,000

FIGURE 5.7 Utilitarian Fairness

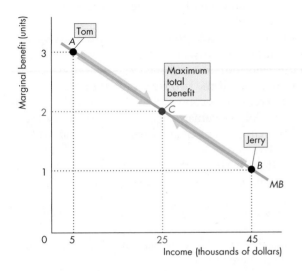

Tom earns $5,000 and has 3 units of marginal benefit at point A. Jerry earns $45,000 and has 1 unit of marginal benefit at point B. If income is transferred from Jerry to Tom, Jerry's loss is less than Tom's gain. Only when each of them has $25,000 and 2 units of marginal benefit (at point C) can the sum of their total benefit increase no further.

——————— MyEconLab animation ◆

each and a marginal benefit of 2 units. Now they are sharing the economic pie in the most efficient way. It brings the greatest happiness to Tom and Jerry.

The Big Tradeoff One big problem with the utilitarian ideal of complete equality is that it ignores the costs of making income transfers. Recognizing the costs of making income transfers leads to what is called the **big tradeoff**, which is a tradeoff between efficiency and fairness.

The big tradeoff is based on the following facts. Income can be transferred from people with high incomes to people with low incomes only by taxing the high incomes. Taxing people's income from employment makes them work less. It results in the quantity of labour being less than the efficient quantity. Taxing people's income from capital makes them save less. It results in the quantity of capital being less than the efficient quantity. With smaller quantities of both labour and capital, the quantity of goods and services produced is less than the efficient quantity. The economic pie shrinks.

The tradeoff is between the size of the economic pie and the degree of equality with which it is shared. The greater the amount of income redistribution through income taxes, the greater is the inefficiency—the smaller is the economic pie.

There is a second source of inefficiency. A dollar taken from a rich person does not end up as a dollar in the hands of a poorer person. Some of the dollar is spent on administration of the tax and transfer system. The cost of tax-collecting agencies, such as the Canada Revenue Agency (CRA), and welfare-administering agencies, such as Human Resources and Skills Development Canada, must be paid with some of the taxes collected. Also, taxpayers hire accountants, auditors, and lawyers to help them ensure that they pay the correct amount of taxes. These activities use skilled labour and capital resources that could otherwise be used to produce goods and services that people value.

When all these costs are taken into account, taking a dollar from a rich person does not give a dollar to a poor person. It is possible that with high taxes, people with low incomes might end up being worse off. Suppose, for example, that highly taxed entrepreneurs decide to work less hard and shut down some of their businesses. Low-income workers get fired and must seek other, perhaps even lower-paid, work.

Today, because of the big tradeoff, no one says that fairness requires equality of incomes.

Make the Poorest as Well Off as Possible A new solution to the big-tradeoff problem was proposed by philosopher John Rawls in a classic book entitled *A Theory of Justice*, published in 1971. Rawls says that, taking all the costs of income transfers into account, the fair distribution of the economic pie is the one that makes the poorest person as well off as possible. The incomes of rich people should be taxed, and after paying the costs of administering the tax and transfer system, what is left should be transferred to the poor. But the taxes must not be so high that they make the economic pie shrink to the point at which the poorest person ends up with a smaller piece. A bigger share of a smaller pie can be less than a smaller share of a bigger pie. The goal is to make the piece enjoyed by the poorest person as big as possible. Most likely, this piece will not be an equal share.

The "fair results" idea requires a change in the results after the game is over. Some economists say that these changes are themselves unfair and propose a different way of thinking about fairness.

It's Not Fair If the *Rules* Aren't Fair

The idea that it's not fair if the rules aren't fair is based on a fundamental principle that seems to be hardwired into the human brain: the symmetry principle. The **symmetry principle** is the requirement that people in similar situations be treated similarly. It is the moral principle that lies at the centre of all the big religions and that says, in some form or other, "Behave towards other people in the way you expect them to behave towards you."

In economic life, this principle translates into *equality of opportunity*. But equality of opportunity to do what? This question is answered by the philosopher Robert Nozick in a book entitled *Anarchy, State, and Utopia*, published in 1974.

Nozick argues that the idea of fairness as an outcome or result cannot work and that fairness must be based on the fairness of the rules. He suggests that fairness obeys two rules:

1. The state must enforce laws that establish and protect private property.
2. Private property may be transferred from one person to another only by voluntary exchange.

The first rule says that everything that is valuable must be owned by individuals and that the state must ensure that theft is prevented. The second rule says that the only legitimate way a person can acquire property is to buy it in exchange for something else that the person owns. If these rules, which are the only fair rules, are followed, then the result is fair. It doesn't matter how unequally the economic pie is shared, provided that the pie is made by people, each one of whom voluntarily provides services in exchange for the share of the pie offered in compensation.

These rules satisfy the symmetry principle. If these rules are not followed, the symmetry principle is broken. You can see these facts by imagining a world in which the laws are not followed.

First, suppose that some resources or goods are not owned. They are common property. Then everyone is free to participate in a grab to use them. The strongest will prevail. But when the strongest prevails, the strongest effectively *owns* the resources or goods in question and prevents others from enjoying them.

Second, suppose that we do not insist on voluntary exchange for transferring ownership of resources from one person to another. The alternative is *involuntary* transfer. In simple language, the alternative is theft.

Both of these situations violate the symmetry principle. Only the strong acquire what they want. The weak end up with only the resources and goods that the strong don't want.

In a majority-rule political system, the strong are those in the majority or those with enough resources to influence opinion and achieve a majority.

In contrast, if the two rules of fairness are followed, everyone, strong and weak, is treated in a similar way. All individuals are free to use their resources and human skills to create things that are valued by themselves and others and to exchange the fruits of their efforts with all others. This set of arrangements is the only one that obeys the symmetry principle.

Fairness and Efficiency If private property rights are enforced and if voluntary exchange takes place in a competitive market, resources will be allocated efficiently if there are no

1. Price and quantity regulations
2. Taxes and subsidies
3. Externalities
4. Public goods and common resources
5. Monopolies
6. High transactions costs

And according to the Nozick rules, the resulting distribution of income and wealth will be fair. Let's study an example to check the claim that if resources are allocated efficiently, they are also allocated fairly.

Case Study: A Water Shortage in a Natural Disaster

An earthquake has broken the pipes that deliver drinking water to a city. Bottled water is available, but there is no tap water. What is the fair way to allocate the bottled water?

Market Price Suppose that if the water is allocated by market price, the price jumps to $8 a bottle—five times its normal price. At this price, the people who own water can make a large profit by selling it. People who are willing and able to pay $8 a bottle get the water. And because most people can't afford the $8 price, they end up either without water or consuming just a few drops a day.

You can see that the water is being used efficiently. There is a fixed amount available, some people are willing to pay $8 to get a bottle, and the water goes to those people. The people who own and sell water receive a large producer surplus and total surplus is maximized.

In the rules view, the outcome is fair. No one is denied the water they are willing to pay for. In the results view, the outcome would most likely be regarded as unfair. The lucky owners of water make a killing, and the poorest end up the thirstiest.

Nonmarket Methods Suppose that by a majority vote, the citizens decide that the government will buy all the water, pay for it with a tax, and use one of the nonmarket methods to allocate the water to the citizens. The possibilities now are

Command Someone decides who is the most deserving and needy. Perhaps everyone is given an equal share. Or perhaps government officials and their families end up with most of the water.

Contest Bottles of water are prizes that go to those who are best at a particular contest.

First-come, first-served Water goes to the first off the mark or to those who place the lowest value on their time and can afford to wait in line.

Lottery Water goes to those in luck.

Personal characteristics Water goes to those with the "right" characteristics. Perhaps the old, the young, or pregnant women get the water.

Except by chance, none of these methods delivers an allocation of water that is either fair or efficient. It is unfair in the rules view because the distribution involves involuntary transfers of resources among citizens. It is unfair in the results view because the poorest don't end up being made as well off as possible.

The allocation is inefficient for two reasons. First, resources have been used to operate the allocation scheme. Second, some people are willing to pay for more water than the quantity they have been allocated and others have been allocated more water than they are willing to pay for.

The second source of inefficiency can be overcome if, after the nonmarket allocation, people are permitted to trade water at its market price. Those who value the water they have at less than the market price sell, and people who are willing to pay the market price to obtain more water buy. Those who value the water most highly are the ones who consume it.

Market Price with Taxes Another approach is to allocate the scarce water using the market price but then to alter the redistribution of buying power by taxing the sellers and providing benefits to the poor.

Suppose water owners are taxed on each bottle sold and the revenue from these taxes is given to the poorest people. People are then free, starting from this new distribution of buying power, to trade water at the market price.

Because the owners of water are taxed on what they sell, they have a weaker incentive to offer water for sale and the supply decreases. The equilibrium price rises to more than $8 a bottle. There is now a deadweight loss in the market for water—similar to the loss that arises from underproduction on pp. 113–114. (We study the effects of a tax and show its inefficiency in Chapter 6 on pp. 133–138.)

So the tax is inefficient. In the rules view, the tax is also unfair because it forces the owners of water to make a transfer to others. In the results view, the outcome might be regarded as being fair.

This brief case study illustrates the complexity of ideas about fairness. Economists have a clear criterion of efficiency but no comparably clear criterion of fairness. Most economists regard Nozick as being too extreme and want a fair tax system, but there is no consensus about what a fair tax system looks like.

REVIEW QUIZ

1 What are the two big approaches to thinking about fairness?
2 What is the utilitarian idea of fairness and what is wrong with it?
3 Explain the big tradeoff. What idea of fairness has been developed to deal with it?
4 What is the idea of fairness based on fair rules?

You can work these questions in Study Plan 5.4 and get instant feedback.
━━━━━━━━━━━━━━━━━━━━━━ MyEconLab ◆

◆ You've now studied efficiency and equity (fairness), the two biggest issues that run through the whole of economics. *Reading Between the Lines* on pp. 120–121 looks at an example of an efficient market in our economy today. At many points throughout this book—and in your life—you will return to and use the ideas you've learned in this chapter. We start in the next chapter where we study some sources of *in*efficiency and *un*fairness.

Is the Global Market for Roses Efficient?

More Ash Fallout: 10 Million Roses Ruined

www.cbsnews.com

April 19, 2010

NAIROBI, Kenya—Daniel Oyier has been eating only once a day since an ash-belching volcano more than 5,000 miles away caused him to be laid off from his $4-a-day job packing red roses and white lilies for export to Paris and Amsterdam.

Some 5,000 day labourers in Kenya have been without work since the ash cloud from Iceland shut down air traffic across Europe, showing how one event can have drastic consequences in distant lands in today's global economy. ...

Kenya has thrown away 10 million flowers—mostly roses—since the volcano eruption. ...

The world's biggest flower auction in the Dutch town of Aalsmeer saw a drop of 15 percent in flowers sold on Monday as a result of flight disruptions from the volcanic ash cloud. ...

Farmers have been forced to find alternative routes to get their products to market—even at a loss. They flew 1,000 tonnes of flowers to Spain on Monday, from where it would be transported by road to Paris and Amsterdam. ...

Other flower-growing regions have seen sales fall because of the eruption. ...

Willem Verhoogt [a South African exporter said his firm was] ... supposed to export 11,000 pounds of fresh cut flowers mainly to Europe, and to the United States via flights through Europe.

"All together, it could be between 10 to 15 tonnes that won't go in the end," he said. "We've advised farmers not to pick flowers anymore."

ESSENCE OF THE STORY

- In April 2010, the global fresh flower market was disrupted by the ash cloud from an erupting volcano in Iceland that shut down Europe's air traffic.

- Many of the world's flowers are traded at auction in the Dutch town of Aalsmeer, which saw a drop of 15 percent in the quantity of flowers sold.

- 5,000 workers in Kenya who pick and pack flowers were without work.

- Kenya's flower growers threw away 10 million flowers—mostly roses.

- South African flower growers were prevented from shipping as much as 15 tonnes of fresh cut flowers to Europe and the United States.

- Some farmers found alternative but more costly routes to get their flowers to market.

ECONOMIC ANALYSIS

- Roses are traded in a global market.

- Most of the roses sold in North America come from Colombia and Ecuador, but the world's largest cut flower market is in Aalsmeer, Holland, where 75 percent of the world's flowers are traded every day.

- On a normal day, flowers arrive by air from Africa, Central and South America, the Middle East, and Asia and are traded at auction, and then delivered by air to the United States, Canada, and other destinations.

- Figure 1 illustrates the market on a normal day. The demand and marginal benefit curve is $D_0 = MSB_0$; the supply and marginal cost curve is $S_0 = MSC_0$; and the auction finds the equilibrium and efficient outcome.

- April 19, 2010, was not a normal day. The eruption of a volcano in Iceland closed northern Europe's air transportation. Flowers could not be transported either in or out of Holland by air.

- Alternative but more costly arrangements were quickly made to fly flowers in and out of Athens (Greece) and Madrid (Spain) and transport them by truck from these cities to Aalsmeer.

- Figure 2 shows the situation on April 19. Supply decreased because the cost of inbound transportation increased. Demand decreased because the cost of outbound transportation increased.

- The demand and marginal benefit curve is $D_1 = MSB_1$; the supply and marginal cost curve is $S_1 = MSC_1$; and the auction finds the new equilibrium and efficient outcome.

- It turned out that the quantity decreased by 20 percent (from 20 million to 16 million), but the price was unchanged. Both demand and supply were influenced by the loss of air transportation and decreased by the same amount.

- Consumer surplus (the green triangle) and producer surplus (the blue triangle) shrank on April 19, but the total surplus was at its maximum given the circumstances.

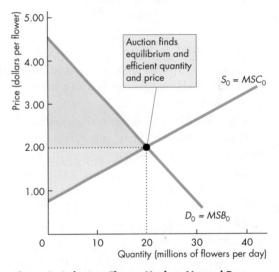

Figure 1 Aalsmeer Flower Market: Normal Day

Traders in the flower auction at Aalsmeer, Holland, find the equilibrium prices.

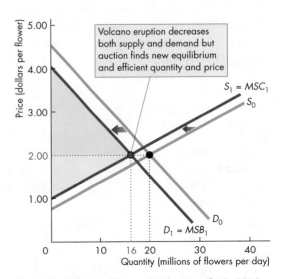

Figure 2 Aalsmeer Flower Market: April 19, 2010

121

SUMMARY

Key Points

Resource Allocation Methods (pp. 106–107)

- Because resources are scarce, some mechanism must allocate them.
- The alternative allocation methods are market price; command; majority rule; contest; first-come, first-served; lottery; personal characteristics; and force.

Working Study Plan Problems 1 and 2 will give you a better understanding of resource allocation methods.

Benefit, Cost, and Surplus (pp. 108–111)

- The maximum price willingly paid is marginal benefit, so a demand curve is also a marginal benefit curve.
- The market demand curve is the horizontal sum of the individual demand curves and is the marginal social benefit curve.
- Value is what people are *willing to* pay; price is what people *must* pay.
- Consumer surplus is the excess of the benefit received from a good or service over the amount paid for it.
- The minimum supply-price is marginal cost, so a supply curve is also a marginal cost curve.
- The market supply curve is the horizontal sum of the individual supply curves and is the marginal social cost curve.
- Cost is what producers pay; price is what producers receive.

- Producer surplus is the excess of the amount received from the sale of a good or service over the cost of producing it.

Working Study Plan Problems 3 to 10 will give you a better understanding of benefit, cost, and surplus.

Is the Competitive Market Efficient? (pp. 112–115)

- In a competitive equilibrium, marginal social benefit equals marginal social cost and resource allocation is efficient.
- Buyers and sellers acting in their self-interest end up promoting the social interest.
- Total surplus, consumer surplus plus producer surplus, is maximized.
- Producing less than or more than the efficient quantity creates deadweight loss.
- Price and quantity regulations; taxes and subsidies; externalities; public goods and common resources; monopoly; and high transactions costs can lead to market failure.

Working Study Plan Problems 11 to 13 will give you a better understanding of the efficiency of competitive markets.

Is the Competitive Market Fair? (pp. 116–119)

- Ideas about fairness can be divided into two groups: fair *results* and fair *rules*.
- Fair-results ideas require income transfers from the rich to the poor.
- Fair-rules ideas require property rights and voluntary exchange.

Working Study Plan Problems 14 and 15 will give you a better understanding of the fairness of competitive markets.

Key Terms

Big tradeoff, 117
Command system, 106
Consumer surplus, 109
Deadweight loss, 113
Market failure, 113

Producer surplus, 111
Symmetry principle, 118
Total surplus, 112
Transactions costs, 115
Utilitarianism, 116

SCAN THIS

STUDY PLAN PROBLEMS AND APPLICATIONS

MyEconLab ◆ You can work Problems 1 to 17 in Chapter 5 Study Plan and get instant feedback.

Resource Allocation Methods (Study Plan 5.1)

Use the following information to work Problems 1 and 2.

1. At West, recognized as the "jewel in Vancouver's culinary crown," reservations are essential. At Le Bistro Chez Michel, a restaurant in North Vancouver, reservations are recommended. At Vij's, a restaurant not too far from the University of British Columbia, reservations are not accepted.
   a. Describe the method of allocating scarce table resources at these three restaurants.
   b. Why do you think restaurants have different reservations policies?

2. Why do you think restaurants don't use the market price to allocate their tables?

Benefit, Cost, and Surplus (Study Plan 5.2)

Use the following table to work Problems 3 to 5. The table gives the demand schedules for train travel for the only buyers in the market, Ann, Beth, and Cy.

Price (dollars per kilometre)	Quantity demanded (kilometres)		
	Ann	Beth	Cy
3	30	25	20
4	25	20	15
5	20	15	10
6	15	10	5
7	10	5	0
8	5	0	0
9	0	0	0

3. a. Construct the market demand schedule.
   b. What are the maximum prices that Ann, Beth, and Cy are willing to pay to travel 20 kilometres? Why?

4. a. What is the marginal social benefit when the total distance travelled is 60 kilometres?
   b. What is the marginal private benefit for each person when they travel a total distance of 60 kilometres and how many kilometres does each of the people travel?

5. a. What is each traveller's consumer surplus when the price is $4 a kilometre?
   b. What is the market consumer surplus when the price is $4 a kilometre?

Use the following table to work Problems 6 to 8. The table gives the supply schedules of hot air balloon rides for the only sellers in the market, Xavier, Yasmin, and Zack.

Price (dollars per ride)	Quantity supplied (rides per week)		
	Xavier	Yasmin	Zack
100	30	25	20
90	25	20	15
80	20	15	10
70	15	.10	5
60	10	5	0
50	5	0	0
40	0	0	0

6. a. Construct the market supply schedule.
   b. What are the minimum prices that Xavier, Yasmin, and Zack are willing to accept to supply 20 rides? Why?

7. a. What is the marginal social cost when the total number of rides is 30?
   b. What is the marginal cost for each supplier when the total number of rides is 30 and how many rides does each of the sellers supply?

8. When the price is $70 a ride,
   a. What is each firm's producer surplus?
   b. What is the market producer surplus?

Use the following news clip to work Problems 9 and 10.

eBay Saves Billions for Bidders

If you think you would save money by bidding on eBay auctions, you would likely be right. Two University of Maryland researchers calculated the difference between the actual purchase price paid for auction items and the top price bidders stated they were willing to pay. They found that the difference averaged at least $4 per auction.

Source: *Information Week*, January 28, 2008

9. What method is used to allocate goods on eBay? How does the allocation method used by eBay auctions influence consumer surplus?

10. a. Can an eBay auction give the seller a surplus?
    b. On a graph, show the consumer surplus and producer surplus from an eBay auction.

Is the Competitive Market Efficient? (Study Plan 5.3)

11. The figure illustrates the competitive market for cell phones.

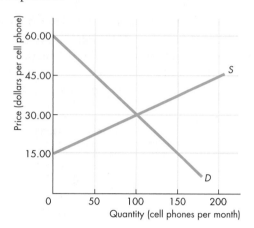

a. What are the equilibrium price and equilibrium quantity of cell phones?

b. Shade in and label the consumer surplus at the competitive equilibrium.

c. Shade in and label the producer surplus at the competitive equilibrium.

d. Calculate total surplus at the competitive equilibrium.

e. Is the competitive market for cell phones efficient?

12. The table gives the demand and supply schedules for sunscreen.

Price (dollars per bottle)	Quantity demanded	Quantity supplied
	(bottles per day)	
0	400	0
5	300	100
10	200	200
15	100	300
20	0	400

Sunscreen factories are required to limit production to 100 bottles a day.

a. What is the maximum price that consumers are willing to pay for the 100th bottle?

b. What is the minimum price that producers are willing to accept for the 100th bottle?

c. Describe the situation in this market.

13. Explain why each restaurant in Problem 1 might be using an efficient allocation method.

Is the Competitive Market Fair? (Study Plan 5.4)

14. Explain why the allocation method used by each restaurant in Problem 1 is fair or not fair.

15. In Problem 12, how can the 100 bottles available be allocated to beach-goers? Which possible methods would be fair and which would be unfair?

Economics in the News (Study Plan 5.EN)

16. **The World's Largest Tulip and Flower Market**

Every day 20 million tulips, roses, and other cut flowers are auctioned at the Dutch market called *The Bloemenveiling*. Each day 55,000 Dutch auctions take place, matching buyers and sellers.

Source: Tulip-Bulbs.com

A Dutch auction is one in which the auctioneer starts by announcing the highest price. If no one offers to buy the flowers, the auctioneer lowers the price until a buyer is found.

a. What method is used to allocate flowers at the Bloemenveiling?

b. How does a Dutch flower auction influence consumer surplus and producer surplus?

c. Are the flower auctions at the Bloemenveiling efficient?

17. **Wii Sells Out Across Japan**

After a two-month TV-ad blitz for Wii in Japan, demand was expected to be much higher than supply. Yodobashi Camera was selling Wii games on a first-come, first-served basis. Eager customers showed up early and those who tried to join the line after 6 or 7 a.m. were turned away—many rushed off to the smaller stores that were holding raffles to decide who got a Wii.

Source: *Gamespot News*, December 1, 2006

a. Why was the quantity demanded of Wii expected to exceed the quantity supplied?

b. Did Nintendo produce the efficient quantity of Wii? Explain.

c. Can you think of reasons why Nintendo might want to underproduce and leave the market with fewer Wii than people want to buy?

d. What are the two methods of resource allocation described in the news clip? Is either method of allocating Wii efficient?

e. What do you think some of the people who managed to buy a Wii did with it?

f. Explain which is the fairer method of allocating the Wii: the market price or the two methods described in the news clip.

ADDITIONAL PROBLEMS AND APPLICATIONS

MyEconLab ◆ You can work these problems in MyEconLab if assigned by your instructor.

Resource Allocation Methods

18. At the Stratford Festival Theatre no reservations are accepted on the day of the performance; at matinees, reservations are accepted; at opening night performances reservations are essential. Describe the method of allocating seats in these three performances. Why do you think the Startford Festival Theatre has different reservations policies?

Benefit, Cost, and Surplus

Use the following table to work Problems 19 to 22. The table gives the supply schedules for jet-ski rides by the only suppliers: Rick, Sam, and Tom.

Price	Quantity supplied (rides per day)		
(dollars per ride)	Rick	Sam	Tom
10.00	0	0	0
12.50	5	0	0
15.00	10	5	0
17.50	15	10	5
20.00	20	15	10

19. What is each owner's minimum supply-price of 10 rides a day?
20. Which owner has the largest producer surplus when the price of a ride is $17.50? Explain.
21. What is the marginal social cost of 45 rides a day?
22. Construct the market supply schedule of jet-ski rides.

Use the following table to work Problems 23 and 24. The table gives the demand and supply schedules for sandwiches.

Price	Quantity demanded	Quantity supplied
(dollars per sandwich)	(sandwiches per hour)	
0	300	0
1	250	50
2	200	100
3	150	150
4	100	200
5	50	250
6	0	300

23. a. What is the maximum price that consumers are willing to pay for the 200th sandwich?

b. What is the minimum price that producers are willing to accept for the 200th sandwich?

c. If 200 sandwiches a day are available, what is the total surplus?

Is the Competitive Market Efficient?

24. a. If the sandwich market is efficient, what is the consumer surplus, what is the producer surplus, and what is the total surplus?

b. If the demand for sandwiches increases and sandwich makers produce the efficient quantity, what happens to producer surplus and deadweight loss?

Use the following news clip to work Problems 25 to 27.

The Right Price for Digital Music

Apple's $1.29-for-the-latest-songs model isn't perfect and isn't it too much to pay for music that appeals to just a few people? What we need is a system that will be profitable but fair to music lovers. The solution: Price song downloads according to demand. The more people who download a particular song, the higher will be the price of that song; The fewer people who buy a particular song, the lower will be the price of that song. That is a free-market solution—the market would determine the price.

Source: *Slate*, December 5, 2005

Assume that the marginal social cost of downloading a song from the iTunes Store is zero. (This assumption means that the cost of operating the iTunes Store doesn't change if people download more songs.)

25. a. Draw a graph of the market for downloadable music with a price of $1.29 for all the latest songs. On your graph, show consumer surplus and producer surplus.

b. With a price of $1.29 for all the latest songs, is the market efficient or inefficient? If it is inefficient, show the deadweight loss on your graph.

26. If the pricing scheme described in the news clip were adopted, how would consumer surplus, producer surplus, and the deadweight loss change?

27. a. If the pricing scheme described in the news clip were adopted, would the market be efficient or inefficient? Explain.

b. Is the pricing scheme described in the news clip a "free-market solution"? Explain.

28. Only 1 percent of the world supply of water is fit for human consumption. Some places have more water than they can use; some could use much more than they have. The 1 percent available would be sufficient if only it were in the right place.
    a. What is the major problem in achieving an efficient use of the world's water?
    b. If there were a global market in water, like there is in oil, how do you think the market would be organized?
    c. Would a free world market in water achieve an efficient use of the world's water resources? Explain why or why not.

Is the Competitive Market Fair?

29. Use the information in Problem 28. Would a free world market in water achieve a fair use of the world's water resources? Explain why or why not and be clear about the concept of fairness that you are using.

30. The winners of the men's and women's tennis singles at the Canadian Open are paid twice as much as the runners-up, but it takes two players to have a singles final. Is the compensation arrangement fair?

Economics in the News

31. After you have studied *Reading Between the Lines* on pp. 120–121, answer the following questions.
    a. What is the method used to allocate the world's cut flowers?
    b. Who benefits from this method of resource allocation: buyers, sellers, or both? Explain your answer using the ideas of marginal social benefit, marginal social cost, consumer surplus, and producer surplus.
    c. On April 19, 2010, when the equilibrium quantity of cut flowers decreased by 20 percent, why was the outcome still efficient? Why was there not underproduction and a deadweight loss?
    d. If the government of Holland placed a limit of 15 million a day on the quantity of flowers traded at Aalsmeer, would there be underproduction and a deadweight loss created? Explain your answer.

32. **Fight over Water Rates; Escondido Farmers Say Increase Would Put Them out of Business**
    Agricultural users of water pay less than residential and business users. Since 1993, water rates have increased by more than 90 percent for residential customers and by only 50 percent for agricultural users.
    Source: *The San Diego Union-Tribune*, June 14, 2006
    a. Do you think that the allocation of water between agricultural and residential users is likely to be efficient? Explain your answer.
    b. If agricultural users paid a higher price, would the allocation of resources be more efficient?
    c. If agricultural users paid a higher price, what would happen to consumer surplus and producer surplus from water?
    d. Is this pricing policy fair?

33. **Ticketmaster Accused of "Price Gouging" in Canada**
    Ticketmaster has to deal with accusations of "price gouging" by angry Elton John fans in Saskatchewan. When tickets went on sale, fans discovered that Ticketmaster had already sold out of their allotment, and instead recommended fans try to buy tickets at Tickets Now, a secondary ticketing site owned by Ticketmaster. Not only did Tickets Now already have tickets for sale, but they were also demanding much higher prices than originally posted on Ticketmaster, leading fans to accuse the company of scalping. …
    Ticketmaster said they were not aware they were shuffling fans to Tickets Now and has since removed the link. Ticketmaster said that the inventory belongs to the promoter and artist, and the artist determines who has what privileges in advance of the public on sale or not, like fan clubs for instance.
    Source: *Rolling Stone*, July 14, 2008
    a. What is "price gouging"? Is price gouging in the social interest or self-interest?
    b. Explain the effect of the company's "scalping" on consumer surplus and producer surplus.
    c. Evaluate the "fairness" of Ticketmaster "shuffling fans to Tickets Now" when the concert tickets went on sale to the public.
    d. Describe the allocation method used when "the artist determines who has what privileges in advance of the public on sale or not, like fan clubs for instance."

Government Actions in Markets

After studying this chapter, you will be able to

◆ Explain how rent ceilings create housing shortages and inefficiency

◆ Explain how minimum wage laws create unemployment and inefficiency

◆ Explain the effects of a tax

◆ Explain the effects of production quotas and subsidies on production, costs, and prices

◆ Explain how markets for illegal goods work

In Vancouver, where beverage servers and grocery clerks earn $10 an hour, you'd be hard pressed to find a condominium for rent at less than $1,000 a month. Can governments help low-income Canadians by boosting pay and capping condominium rents? You're going to learn about the effects of these types of government actions. And in *Reading Between the Lines* at the end of the chapter, we apply what you've learned to the market for low-skilled labour in British Columbia. You'll also learn about the effects of taxes, production quotas and subsidies, and laws that make trading in some things illegal.

◆ A Housing Market with a Rent Ceiling

We spend more of our income on housing than on any other good or service, so it isn't surprising that rents can be a political issue. When rents are high, or when they jump by a large amount, renters might lobby the government for limits on rents.

A government regulation that makes it illegal to charge a price higher than a specified level is called a **price ceiling** or **price cap**.

The effects of a price ceiling on a market depend crucially on whether the ceiling is imposed at a level that is above or below the equilibrium price.

A price ceiling set *above the equilibrium price* has no effect. The reason is that the price ceiling does not constrain the market forces. The force of the law and the market forces are not in conflict. But a price ceiling *below the equilibrium price* has powerful effects on a market. The reason is that the price ceiling attempts to prevent the price from regulating the quantities demanded and supplied. The force of the law and the market forces are in conflict.

When a price ceiling is applied to a housing market, it is called a rent ceiling. A **rent ceiling** set below the equilibrium rent creates

- A housing shortage
- Increased search activity
- A black market

A Housing Shortage

At the equilibrium price, the quantity demanded equals the quantity supplied. In a housing market, when the rent is at the equilibrium level, the quantity of housing supplied equals the quantity of housing demanded and there is neither a shortage nor a surplus of housing.

But at a rent set below the equilibrium rent, the quantity of housing demanded exceeds the quantity of housing supplied—there is a shortage. So if a rent ceiling is set below the equilibrium rent, there will be a shortage of housing.

When there is a shortage, the quantity available is the quantity supplied and somehow, this quantity must be allocated among the frustrated demanders. One way in which this allocation occurs is through increased search activity.

Increased Search Activity

The time spent looking for someone with whom to do business is called search activity. We spend some time in **search activity** almost every time we make a purchase. When you're shopping for the latest hot new cell phone, and you know four stores that stock it, how do you find which store has the best deal? You spend a few minutes on the Internet, checking out the various prices. In some markets, such as the housing market, people spend a lot of time checking the alternatives available before making a choice.

When a price is regulated and there is a shortage, search activity increases. In the case of a rent-controlled housing market, frustrated would-be renters scan the newspapers, not only for housing ads but also for death notices! Any information about newly available housing is useful, and condominium seekers race to be first on the scene when news of a possible supplier breaks.

The *opportunity cost* of a good is equal not only to its price but also to the value of the search time spent finding the good. So the opportunity cost of housing is equal to the rent (a regulated price) plus the time and other resources spent searching for the restricted quantity available. Search activity is costly. It uses time and other resources, such as phone calls, automobiles, and gasoline, that could have been used in other productive ways.

A rent ceiling controls only the rent portion of the cost of housing. The cost of increased search activity might end up making the full cost of housing *higher* than it would be without a rent ceiling.

A Black Market

A rent ceiling also encourages illegal trading in a **black market**, an illegal market in which the equilibrium price exceeds the price ceiling. Black markets occur in rent-controlled housing and many other markets. For example, scalpers run black markets in tickets for big sporting events and rock concerts.

When a rent ceiling is in force, frustrated renters and landlords constantly seek ways of increasing rents. One common way is for a new tenant to pay a high price for worthless fittings, such as charging $2,000 for threadbare drapes. Another is for the tenant to pay an exorbitant price for new locks and keys—called "key money."

The level of a black market rent depends on how tightly the rent ceiling is enforced. With loose enforcement, the black market rent is close to the unregulated rent. But with strict enforcement, the black market rent is equal to the maximum price that a renter is willing to pay.

Figure 6.1 illustrates the effects of a rent ceiling. The demand curve for housing is *D* and the supply curve is *S*. A rent ceiling is imposed at $800 a month. Rents that exceed $800 a month are in the grey-shaded illegal region in the figure. You can see that the equilibrium rent, where the demand and supply curves intersect, is in the illegal region.

At a rent of $800 a month, the quantity of housing supplied is 60,000 units and the quantity demanded is 100,000 units. So with a rent of $800 a month, there is a shortage of 40,000 units of housing.

To rent the 60,000th unit, someone is willing to pay $1,200 a month. They might pay this amount by incurring search costs that bring the total cost of housing to $1,200 a month, or they might pay a black market price of $1,200 a month. Either way, they end up incurring a cost that exceeds what the equilibrium rent would be in an unregulated market.

Inefficiency of a Rent Ceiling

A rent ceiling set below the equilibrium rent results in an inefficient underproduction of housing services. The *marginal social benefit* of housing exceeds its *marginal social cost* and a deadweight loss shrinks the producer surplus and consumer surplus (Chapter 5, pp. 112–114).

Figure 6.2 shows this inefficiency. The rent ceiling ($800 per month) is below the equilibrium rent ($1,000 per month) and the quantity of housing supplied (60,000 units) is less than the efficient quantity (80,000 units).

Because the quantity of housing supplied (the quantity available) is less than the efficient quantity, there is a deadweight loss, shown by the grey triangle. Producer surplus shrinks to the blue triangle and consumer surplus shrinks to the green triangle. The red rectangle represents the potential loss from increased search activity. This loss is borne by consumers and the full loss from the rent ceiling is the sum of the deadweight loss and the increased cost of search.

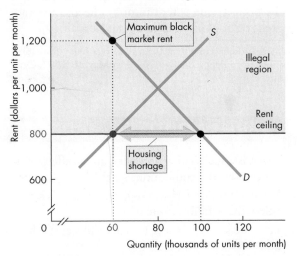

FIGURE 6.1   A Rent Ceiling

A rent above the rent ceiling of $800 a month is illegal (in the grey-shaded illegal region). At a rent of $800 a month, the quantity of housing supplied is 60,000 units. Frustrated renters spend time searching for housing and they make deals with landlords in a black market. Someone is willing to pay $1,200 a month for the 60,000th unit.

MyEconLab animation ◆

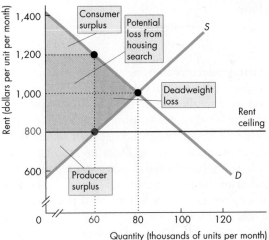

FIGURE 6.2   The Inefficiency of a Rent Ceiling

With no rent ceiling, the market produces an efficient 80,000 units of housing at a rent of $1,000 a month. A rent ceiling of $800 a month decreases the quantity of housing supplied to 60,000 units. Producer surplus and consumer surplus shrink and a deadweight loss arises. The area of the red rectangle represents the cost of resources used in increased search activity. The full loss from the rent ceiling equals the sum of the area of the red rectangle and the grey triangle.

MyEconLab animation ◆

Are Rent Ceilings Fair?

Rent ceilings might be inefficient, but don't they achieve a fairer allocation of scarce housing? Let's explore this question.

Chapter 5 (pp. 116–118) reviews two key ideas about fairness. According to the *fair rules* view, anything that blocks voluntary exchange is unfair, so rent ceilings are unfair. But according to the *fair result* view, a fair outcome is one that benefits the less well off. So according to this view, the fairest outcome is the one that allocates scarce housing to the poorest. To see whether rent ceilings help to achieve a fairer outcome in this sense, we need to consider how the market allocates scarce housing resources in the face of a rent ceiling.

Blocking rent adjustments doesn't eliminate scarcity. Rather, because it decreases the quantity of housing available, it creates an even bigger challenge for the housing market. Somehow, the market must ration a smaller quantity of housing and allocate that housing among the people who demand it.

When the rent is not permitted to allocate scarce housing, what other mechanisms are available, and are *they* fair? Some possible mechanisms are

- A lottery
- First-come, first-served
- Discrimination

A lottery allocates housing to those who are lucky, not to those who are poor. First-come, first-served (a method used to allocate housing in England after World War II) allocates housing to those who have the greatest foresight and who get their names on a list first, not to the poorest. Discrimination allocates scarce housing based on the views and self-interest of the owner of the housing. In the case of public housing, what counts is the self-interest of the bureaucracy that administers the allocation.

In principle, self-interested owners and bureaucrats could allocate housing to satisfy some criterion of fairness, but they are not likely to do so. Discrimination based on friendship, family ties, and criteria such as race, ethnicity, or sex is more likely to enter the equation. We might make such discrimination illegal, but we cannot prevent it from occurring.

It is hard, then, to make a case for rent ceilings on the basis of fairness. When rent adjustments are blocked, other methods of allocating scarce housing resources operate that do not produce a fair outcome.

Economics in Action

Rent Control Winners: The Rich and Famous

New York, San Francisco, London, and Paris, four of the world's great cities, have rent ceilings in some part of their housing markets. Winnipeg has rent ceilings and Toronto had them until the late 1990s. Other Canadian cities including Calgary, Edmonton, and Vancouver do not have rent ceilings.

To see the effects of rent ceilings in practice we can compare the housing markets in cities with ceilings with those without ceilings. We learn two main lessons from such a comparison.

First, rent ceilings definitely create a housing shortage. Second, they do lower the rents for some but raise them for others.

A survey[*] conducted in the United States in 1997 showed that the rents of housing units *actually available for rent* were 2.5 times the average of all rents in New York City, but equal to the average rent in Philadelphia, where there is no rent ceiling. The winners from rent ceilings in New York City are the families that have lived there for a long time, including some rich and famous ones. The voting power of the winners keeps the rent ceilings in place, while mobile newcomers are the losers in a city with rent ceilings.

The bottom line is that in principle and in practice, rent ceilings are inefficient and unfair.

[*] William Tucker, "How Rent Control Drives Out Affordable Housing," Cato Policy Analysis No. 274, May 21, 1997, Cato Institute.

REVIEW QUIZ

1 What is a rent ceiling and what are its effects if it is set above the equilibrium rent?
2 What are the effects of a rent ceiling that is set below the equilibrium rent?
3 How are scarce housing resources allocated when a rent ceiling is in place?
4 Why does a rent ceiling create an inefficient and unfair outcome in the housing market?

You can work these questions in Study Plan 6.1 and get instant feedback.

────────────────────────── MyEconLab ◆

You now know how a price ceiling (rent ceiling) works. Next, we'll learn about the effects of a price floor by studying a minimum wage in a labour market.

A Labour Market with a Minimum Wage

For each one of us, the labour market is the market that influences the jobs we get and the wages we earn. Firms decide how much labour to demand, and the lower the wage rate, the greater is the quantity of labour demanded. Households decide how much labour to supply, and the higher the wage rate, the greater is the quantity of labour supplied. The wage rate adjusts to make the quantity of labour demanded equal to the quantity supplied.

When wage rates are low, or when they fail to keep up with rising prices, labour unions might turn to governments and lobby for a higher wage rate.

A government regulation that makes it illegal to charge a price lower than a specified level is called a **price floor**.

The effects of a price floor on a market depend crucially on whether the floor is imposed at a level that is above or below the equilibrium price.

A price floor set *below the equilibrium price* has no effect. The reason is that the price floor does not constrain the market forces. The force of the law and the market forces are not in conflict. But a price floor *above the equilibrium price* has powerful effects on a market. The reason is that the price floor attempts to prevent the price from regulating the quantities demanded and supplied. The force of the law and the market forces are in conflict.

When a price floor is applied to a labour market, it is called a **minimum wage**. A minimum wage imposed at a level that is above the equilibrium wage creates unemployment. Let's look at the effects of a minimum wage.

Minimum Wage Brings Unemployment

At the equilibrium price, the quantity demanded equals the quantity supplied. In a labour market, when the wage rate is at the equilibrium level, the quantity of labour supplied equals the quantity of labour demanded: There is neither a shortage of labour nor a surplus of labour.

But at a wage rate above the equilibrium wage, the quantity of labour supplied exceeds the quantity of labour demanded—there is a surplus of labour. So when a minimum wage is set above the equilibrium wage, there is a surplus of labour. The demand for labour determines the level of employment, and the surplus of labour is unemployed.

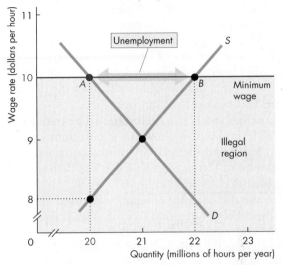

FIGURE 6.3 Minimum Wage and Unemployment

The minimum wage rate is set at $10 an hour. Any wage rate below $10 an hour is illegal (in the grey-shaded illegal region). At the minimum wage of $10 an hour, 20 million hours are hired but 22 million hours are available. Unemployment—*AB*—of 2 million hours a year is created. With only 20 million hours demanded, someone is willing to supply the 20 millionth hour for $8.

MyEconLab animation ◆

Figure 6.3 illustrates the effect of the minimum wage on unemployment. The demand for labour curve is *D* and the supply of labour curve is *S*. The horizontal red line shows the minimum wage set at $10 an hour. A wage rate below this level is illegal, in the grey-shaded illegal region of the figure. At the minimum wage rate, 20 million hours of labour are demanded (point *A*) and 22 million hours of labour are supplied (point *B*), so 2 million hours of available labour are unemployed.

With only 20 million hours demanded, someone is willing to supply that 20 millionth hour for $8. Frustrated unemployed workers spend time and other resources searching for hard-to-find jobs.

Inefficiency of a Minimum Wage

In the labour market, the supply curve measures the marginal social cost of labour to workers. This cost is leisure forgone. The demand curve measures the marginal social benefit from labour. This benefit is the value of the goods and services produced. An unregulated labour market allocates the economy's scarce labour resources to the jobs in which they are valued most highly. The market is efficient.

The minimum wage frustrates the market mechanism and results in unemployment and increased job search. At the quantity of labour employed, the marginal social benefit of labour exceeds its marginal social cost and a deadweight loss shrinks the firms' surplus and the workers' surplus.

Figure 6.4 shows this inefficiency. The minimum wage ($10 an hour) is above the equilibrium wage ($9 an hour) and the quantity of labour demanded and employed (20 million hours) is less than the efficient quantity (21 million hours).

Because the quantity of labour employed is less than the efficient quantity, there is a deadweight loss, shown by the grey triangle. The firms' surplus shrinks to the blue triangle and the workers' surplus shrinks to the green triangle. The red rectangle shows the potential loss from increased job search, which is borne by workers. The full loss from the minimum wage is the sum of the deadweight loss and the increased cost of job search.

FIGURE 6.4   The Inefficiency of a Minimum Wage

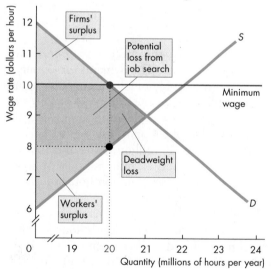

A minimum wage decreases employment. Firms' surplus (blue area) and workers' surplus (green area) shrink and a deadweight loss (grey area) arises. Job search increases and the red area shows the loss from this activity.

———————— MyEconLab animation ◆

Is the Minimum Wage Fair?

The minimum wage is unfair on both views of fairness: It delivers an unfair *result* and imposes an unfair *rule*.

The *result* is unfair because only those people who have jobs and keep them benefit from the minimum wage. The unemployed end up worse off than they would be with no minimum wage. Some of those who search for jobs and find them end up worse off because of the increased cost of job search they incur. Also those who find jobs aren't always the least well off. When the wage rate doesn't allocate labour, other mechanisms determine who finds a job. One such mechanism is discrimination, which is yet another source of unfairness.

The minimum wage imposes an unfair *rule* because it blocks voluntary exchange. Firms are willing to hire more labour and people are willing to work more, but they are not permitted by the minimum wage law to do so.

But two prominent economists have challenged this view. David Card of the University of California at Berkeley (see pp. 484–486) and Alan Krueger of Princeton University say that increases in the U.S. minimum wage have *increased* teenage employment and *decreased* unemployment.

They say that a higher wage *increases* employment by making workers more productive and less likely to quit, which lowers costly labour turnover.

According to Daniel Hamermesh of the University of Texas at Austin, Card and Krueger got the timing wrong. Hamermesh says that firms cut employment *before* the minimum wage is increased in anticipation of the increase, so looking for the effects of an increase *after* it has occurred misses its main effects.

Finis Welch of Texas A&M University and Kevin Murphy of the University of Chicago say the employment effects that Card and Krueger found are caused by regional differences in economic growth, not by changes in the minimum wage.

Card and Krueger have not broken the consensus that the minimum wage destroys jobs.

---

* Michele Campolieti, Tony Fang, and Morley Gunderson, "Minimum Wage Impacts on Youth Employment Transitions, 1993–1999," *Canadian Journal of Economics*, Vol. 38, No. 1, February 2005, pp. 81–104.

◆ REVIEW QUIZ

1 What is a minimum wage and what are its effects if it is set above the equilibrium wage?
2 What are the effects of a minimum wage set below the equilibrium wage?
3 Explain how scarce jobs are allocated when a minimum wage is in place.
4 Explain why a minimum wage creates an inefficient allocation of labour resources.
5 Explain why a minimum wage is unfair.

You can work these questions in Study Plan 6.2 and get instant feedback.

──────────────── MyEconLab ◆

Next we're going to study a more widespread government action in markets: taxes. We'll see how taxes change prices and quantities. You will discover the surprising fact that while the government can impose a tax, it can't decide who will pay it! You will also see that a tax creates a deadweight loss.

◆ Taxes

Everything you earn and almost everything you buy is taxed. Income taxes and social security taxes are deducted from your earnings and sales taxes (GST or HST) are added to the bill when you buy something. Employers also pay a social security tax for their workers, and producers of tobacco products, alcoholic drinks, and gasoline pay a tax every time they sell something.

Who *really* pays these taxes? Because the income tax and social security tax are deducted from your pay, and the sales tax is added to the prices that you pay, isn't it obvious that *you* pay these taxes? And isn't it equally obvious that your employer pays the employer's contribution to the social security tax and that tobacco producers pay the tax on cigarettes?

You're going to discover that it isn't obvious who *really* pays a tax and that lawmakers don't make that decision. We begin with a definition of tax incidence.

Tax Incidence

Tax incidence is the division of the burden of a tax between buyers and sellers. When the government imposes a tax on the sale of a good,* the price paid by buyers might rise by the full amount of the tax, by a lesser amount, or not at all. If the price paid by buyers rises by the full amount of the tax, then the burden of the tax falls entirely on buyers—the buyers pay the tax. If the price paid by buyers rises by a lesser amount than the tax, then the burden of the tax falls partly on buyers and partly on sellers. And if the price paid by buyers doesn't change at all, then the burden of the tax falls entirely on sellers.

Tax incidence does not depend on the tax law. The law might impose a tax on sellers or on buyers, but the outcome is the same in either case. To see why, let's look at the tax on cigarettes in Ontario.

A Tax on Sellers

On February 1, 2006, Ontario upped the tax on the sale of cigarettes to $3.09 for a pack of 25. To work out the effects of this tax (rounded to $3) on the sellers of cigarettes, we begin by examining the effects on demand and supply in the market for cigarettes.

---

* These propositions also apply to services and factors of production (land, labour, and capital).

In Fig. 6.5, the demand curve is *D*, and the supply curve is *S*. With no tax, the equilibrium price is $6 per pack and 350 million packs a year are bought and sold.

A tax on sellers is like an increase in cost, so it decreases supply. To determine the position of the new supply curve, we add the tax to the minimum price that sellers are willing to accept for each quantity sold. You can see that without the tax, sellers are willing to offer 350 million packs a year for $6 a pack. So with a $3 tax, they will offer 350 million packs a year only if the price is $9 a pack. The supply curve shifts to the red curve labelled *S + tax on sellers*.

Equilibrium occurs where the new supply curve intersects the demand curve at 325 million packs a year. The price paid by buyers rises by $2 to $8 a pack. And the price received by sellers falls by $1 to $5 a pack. So buyers pay $2 of the tax and sellers pay the other $1.

A Tax on Buyers

Suppose that instead of taxing sellers, Ontario taxes cigarette buyers $3 a pack.

A tax on buyers lowers the amount they are willing to pay sellers, so it decreases demand and shifts the demand curve leftward. To determine the position of this new demand curve, we subtract the tax from the maximum price that buyers are willing to pay for each quantity bought. You can see, in Fig. 6.6, that without the tax, buyers are willing to buy 350 million packs a year for $6 a pack. So with a $3 tax, they are willing to buy 350 million packs a year only if the price including the tax is $6 a pack, which means that they're willing to pay sellers only $3 a pack. The demand curve shifts to become the red curve labelled *D – tax on buyers*.

Equilibrium occurs where the new demand curve intersects the supply curve at a quantity of 325 million packs a year. The price received by sellers is $5 a pack, and the price paid by buyers is $8.

Equivalence of Tax on Buyers and Sellers

You can see that the tax on buyers in Fig. 6.6 has the same effects as the tax on sellers in Fig. 6.5. In both cases, the equilibrium quantity decreases to 325 million packs a year, the price paid by buyers rises to $8 a pack, and the price received by sellers falls to $5 a pack. Buyers pay $2 of the $3 tax, and sellers pay the other $1 of the tax.

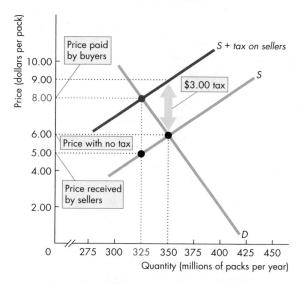

FIGURE 6.5   A Tax on Sellers

With no tax, 350 million packs a year are bought and sold at $6 a pack. A tax on sellers of $3 a pack shifts the supply curve from *S* to *S + tax on sellers*. The equilibrium quantity decreases to 325 million packs a year, the price paid by buyers rises to $8 a pack, and the price received by sellers falls to $5 a pack. The tax raises the price paid by buyers by less than the tax and lowers the price received by sellers, so buyers and sellers share the burden of the tax.

——— MyEconLab   animation ◆

Can We Share the Burden Equally?   Suppose that the Government of Ontario wants the burden of the cigarette tax to fall equally on buyers and sellers and declares that a $1.50 tax be imposed on each. Is the burden of the tax then shared equally?

You can see that it is not. The tax is still $3 a pack. You've seen that the tax has the same effect regardless of whether it is imposed on sellers or buyers. So imposing half the tax on sellers and half on buyers is like an average of the two cases you've just examined. (Draw the demand–supply graph and work out what happens in this case. The demand curve shifts downward by $1.50 and the supply curve shifts upward by $1.50. The new equilibrium quantity is still 325 million packs a year. Buyers pay $8 a pack, of which $1.50 is tax. Sellers receive $6.50 from buyers, but pay a $1.50 tax, so sellers net $5 a pack.)

When a transaction is taxed, there are two prices: the price paid by buyers, which includes the tax; and the price received by sellers, which excludes the tax.

FIGURE 6.6   A Tax on Buyers

With no tax, 350 million packs a year are bought and sold at $6 a pack. A tax on buyers of $3 a pack shifts the demand curve from D to D – tax on buyers. The equilibrium quantity decreases to 325 million packs a year, the price paid by buyers rises to $8 a pack, and the price received by sellers falls to $5 a pack. The tax raises the price paid by buyers by less than the tax and lowers the price received by sellers, so buyers and sellers share the burden of the tax.

——— MyEconLab   animation ◆

Buyers respond to the price that *includes* the tax and sellers respond to the price that *excludes* the tax.

A tax is like a wedge between the price buyers pay and the price sellers receive. The size of the wedge determines the effects of the tax, not the side of the market on which the government imposes the tax.

The Employment Insurance Tax The Employment Insurance tax is an example of a tax that the federal government imposes equally on *both* buyers (employers) and sellers (workers) of labour. But the principles you've just learned apply to this tax too. The market for labour, not the federal government, decides how the burden of the Employment Insurance tax is divided between firms and workers.

In the Ontario cigarette tax example, buyers bear twice the burden of the tax borne by sellers. In special cases, either buyers or sellers bear the entire burden. Let's see what determines this division of the burden of a tax between buyers and sellers.

Tax Incidence and Elasticity of Demand

The division of the tax between buyers and sellers depends in part on the elasticity of demand. There are two extreme cases:

- Perfectly inelastic demand—buyers pay.
- Perfectly elastic demand—sellers pay.

Perfectly Inelastic Demand Figure 6.7 shows the market for insulin, a vital daily medication for those with diabetes. Demand is perfectly inelastic at 100,000 doses a day, regardless of the price, as shown by the vertical demand curve D. That is, a diabetic would sacrifice all other goods and services rather than not consume the insulin dose that provides good health. The supply curve of insulin is S. With no tax, the price is $2 a dose and the quantity is 100,000 doses a day.

If insulin is taxed at 20¢ a dose, we must add the tax to the minimum price at which drug companies are willing to sell insulin. The result is the new supply curve S + *tax*. The price rises to $2.20 a dose, but the quantity does not change. Buyers pay the entire tax of 20¢ a dose.

FIGURE 6.7   Tax with Perfectly Inelastic Demand

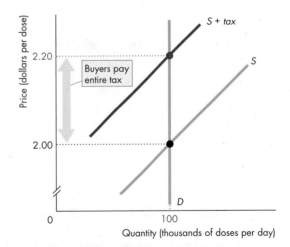

In this market for insulin, demand is perfectly inelastic. With no tax, the price is $2 a dose and the quantity is 100,000 doses a day. A tax of 20¢ a dose shifts the supply curve to S + *tax*. The price rises to $2.20 a dose, but the quantity bought does not change. Buyers pay the entire tax.

——— MyEconLab   animation ◆

Perfectly Elastic Demand   Figure 6.8 shows the market for pink marker pens. Demand is perfectly elastic at $1 a pen, as shown by the horizontal demand curve *D*. If pink pens are less expensive than the other colours, everyone uses pink. If pink pens are more expensive than other colours, no one uses pink. The supply curve is *S*. With no tax, the price of a pink pen is $1 and the quantity is 4,000 pens a week.

Suppose that the government imposes a tax of 10¢ a pen on pink marker pens but not on other colours. The new supply curve is *S + tax*. The price remains at $1 a pen, and the quantity decreases to 1,000 pink pens a week. The 10¢ tax leaves the price paid by buyers unchanged but lowers the amount received by sellers by the full amount of the tax. Sellers pay the entire tax of 10¢ a pink pen.

We've seen that when demand is perfectly inelastic, buyers pay the entire tax, and when demand is perfectly elastic, sellers pay the entire tax. In the usual case, demand is neither perfectly inelastic nor perfectly elastic and the tax is split between buyers and sellers. But the division depends on the elasticity of demand: The more inelastic the demand, the larger is the amount of the tax paid by buyers.

FIGURE 6.8   Tax with Perfectly Elastic Demand

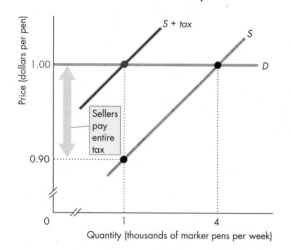

In this market for pink pens, demand is perfectly elastic. With no tax, the price of a pen is $1 and the quantity is 4,000 pens a week. A tax of 10¢ a pink pen shifts the supply curve to *S + tax*. The price remains at $1 a pen, and the quantity of pink pens sold decreases to 1,000 a week. Sellers pay the entire tax.

———— MyEconLab ⬤ animation ◆

Tax Incidence and Elasticity of Supply

The division of the tax between buyers and sellers also depends, in part, on the elasticity of supply. Again, there are two extreme cases:

■ Perfectly inelastic supply—sellers pay.
■ Perfectly elastic supply—buyers pay.

Perfectly Inelastic Supply   Figure 6.9(a) shows the market for water from a mineral spring that flows at a constant rate that can't be controlled. Supply is perfectly inelastic at 100,000 bottles a week, as shown by the supply curve *S*. The demand curve for the water from this spring is *D*. With no tax, the price is 50¢ a bottle and the quantity is 100,000 bottles.

Suppose this spring water is taxed at 5¢ a bottle. The supply curve does not change because the spring owners still produce 100,000 bottles a week, even though the price they receive falls. But buyers are willing to buy the 100,000 bottles only if the price is 50¢ a bottle, so the price remains at 50¢ a bottle. The tax reduces the price received by sellers to 45¢ a bottle, and sellers pay the entire tax.

Perfectly Elastic Supply   Figure 6.9(b) shows the market for sand from which computer-chip makers extract silicon. Supply of this sand is perfectly elastic at a price of 10¢ a kilogram, as shown by the supply curve *S*. The demand curve for sand is *D*. With no tax, the price is 10¢ a kilogram and 5,000 kilograms a week are bought.

If this sand is taxed at 1¢ a kilogram, we must add the tax to the minimum supply-price. Sellers are now willing to offer any quantity at 11¢ a kilogram along the curve *S + tax*. A new equilibrium is determined where the new supply curve intersects the demand curve: at a price of 11¢ a kilogram and a quantity of 3,000 kilograms a week. The tax has increased the price buyers pay by the full amount of the tax—1¢ a kilogram—and has decreased the quantity sold. Buyers pay the entire tax.

We've seen that when supply is perfectly inelastic, sellers pay the entire tax, and when supply is perfectly elastic, buyers pay the entire tax. In the usual case, supply is neither perfectly inelastic nor perfectly elastic and the tax is split between buyers and sellers. But how the tax is split depends on the elasticity of supply: The more elastic the supply, the larger is the amount of the tax paid by buyers.

FIGURE 6.9   Tax and the Elasticity of Supply

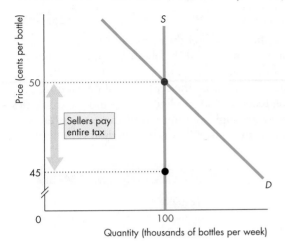

(a) Perfectly inelastic supply

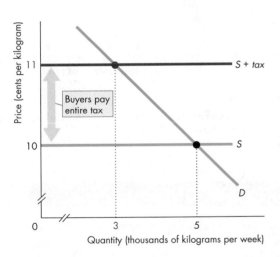

(b) Perfectly elastic supply

Part (a) shows the market for water from a mineral spring. Supply is perfectly inelastic. With no tax, the price is 50¢ a bottle. With a tax of 5¢ a bottle, the price remains at 50¢ a bottle. The number of bottles bought remains the same, but the price received by sellers decreases to 45¢ a bottle. Sellers pay the entire tax.

Part (b) shows the market for sand. Supply is perfectly elastic. With no tax, the price is 10¢ a kilogram. A tax of 1¢ a kilogram increases the minimum supply-price to 11¢ a kilogram. The supply curve shifts to S + tax. The price increases to 11¢ a kilogram. Buyers pay the entire tax.

MyEconLab   animation ◆

Taxes and Efficiency

A tax drives a wedge between the buying price and the selling price and results in inefficient underproduction. The price buyers pay is also the buyers' willingness to pay, which measures *marginal social benefit*. The price sellers receive is also the sellers' minimum supply-price, which equals *marginal social cost*.

A tax makes marginal social benefit exceed marginal social cost, shrinks the producer surplus and consumer surplus, and creates a deadweight loss.

Figure 6.10 shows the inefficiency of a tax on MP3 players. The demand curve, *D*, shows marginal social benefit, and the supply curve, *S*, shows marginal social cost. Without a tax, the market produces the efficient quantity (5,000 players a week).

With a tax, the sellers' minimum supply-price rises by the amount of the tax and the supply curve shifts to *S* + *tax*. This supply curve does *not* show marginal social cost. The tax component isn't a *social*

FIGURE 6.10   Taxes and Efficiency

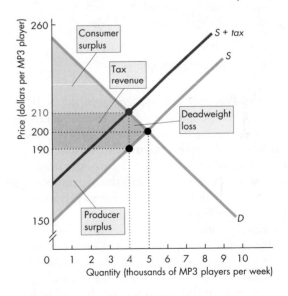

With no tax, 5,000 players a week are produced. With a $20 tax, the buyers' price rises to $210, the sellers' price falls to $190, and the quantity decreases to 4,000 players a week. Consumer surplus shrinks to the green area, and producer surplus shrinks to the blue area. Part of the loss of consumer surplus and producer surplus goes to the government as tax revenue (the purple area) and part becomes a deadweight loss (the grey area).

MyEconLab   animation ◆

cost of production. It is a transfer of resources to the government. At the new equilibrium quantity (4,000 players a week), both consumer surplus and producer surplus shrink. Part of each surplus goes to the government in tax revenue—the purple area; part becomes a deadweight loss—the grey area.

Only in the extreme cases of perfectly inelastic demand and perfectly inelastic supply does a tax not change the quantity bought and sold so that no deadweight loss arises.

Taxes and Fairness

We've examined the incidence and the efficiency of taxes. But when political leaders debate tax issues, it is fairness, not incidence and efficiency, that gets the most attention. The NDP complains that tax cuts are unfair because they give the benefits of lower taxes to the rich. Conservatives counter that it is fair that the rich get most of the tax cuts because they pay most of the taxes. No easy answers are available to the questions about the fairness of taxes.

Economists have proposed two conflicting principles of fairness to apply to a tax system:

- The benefits principle
- The ability-to-pay principle

The Benefits Principle   The *benefits principle* is the proposition that people should pay taxes equal to the benefits they receive from the services provided by government. This arrangement is fair because it means that those who benefit most pay the most taxes. It makes tax payments and the consumption of government-provided services similar to private consumption expenditures.

The benefits principle can justify high fuel taxes to pay for highways, high taxes on alcoholic beverages and tobacco products to pay for public healthcare services, and high rates of income tax on high incomes to pay for the benefits from law and order and from living in a secure environment, from which the rich might benefit more than the poor.

The Ability-to-Pay Principle   The *ability-to-pay principle* is the proposition that people should pay taxes according to how easily they can bear the burden of the tax. A rich person can more easily bear the burden than a poor person can, so the ability-to-pay principle can reinforce the benefits principle to justify high rates of income tax on high incomes.

Economics in Action
Workers and Consumers Pay the Most Tax

Because the elasticity of the supply of labour is low and the elasticity of demand for labour is high, workers pay most of the personal income taxes and most of the social security taxes. Because the elasticities of demand for alcohol, tobacco, and gasoline are low and the elasticities of supply are high, the burden of these taxes (excise taxes) falls more heavily on buyers than on sellers.

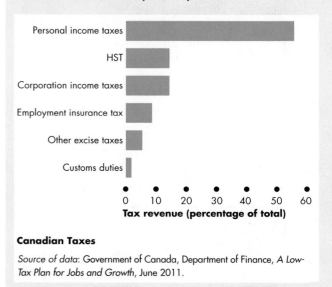

Canadian Taxes

Source of data: Government of Canada, Department of Finance, *A Low-Tax Plan for Jobs and Growth*, June 2011.

REVIEW QUIZ

1   How does the elasticity of demand influence the incidence of a tax, the tax revenue, and the deadweight loss?
2   How does the elasticity of supply influence the incidence of a tax, the quantity bought, the tax revenue, and the deadweight loss?
3   Why is a tax inefficient?
4   When would a tax be efficient?
5   What are the two principles of fairness that are applied to tax systems?

You can work these questions in Study Plan 6.3 and get instant feedback.

───────────────────────────── MyEconLab ◆

Your next task is to study the tools that governments use to influence the markets for farm products: production quotas and subsidies.

◆ Production Quotas and Subsidies

An early or late frost, a hot dry summer, and a wet spring present just a few of the challenges that fill the lives of farmers with uncertainty and sometimes with economic hardship. Fluctuations in the weather bring fluctuations in farm output and prices and sometimes leave farmers with low incomes. To help farmers avoid low prices and low incomes, governments intervene in the markets for farm products.

Price floors that work a bit like the minimum wage that you've already studied might be used. But as you've seen, this type of government action creates a surplus and is inefficient. These same conclusions apply to the effects of a price floor for farm products.

Governments often use two other methods of intervention in the markets for farm products:

- Production quotas
- Subsidies

Production Quotas

In the markets for milk, eggs, and poultry (among others), governments have, from time to time, imposed production quotas. A **production quota** is an upper limit to the quantity of a good that may be produced in a specified period. To discover the effects of a production quota, let's look at what a quota does to the market for milk.

Suppose that the milk farmers want to limit total production to get a higher price. They persuade the government to introduce a production quota on milk.

The effect of the production quota depends on whether it is set below or above the equilibrium quantity. If the government introduced a production quota above the equilibrium quantity, nothing would change because milk farmers would already be producing less than the quota. But a production quota set *below the equilibrium quantity* has big effects, which are

- A decrease in supply
- A rise in price
- A decrease in marginal cost
- Inefficient underproduction
- An incentive to cheat and overproduce

Figure 6.11 illustrates these effects.

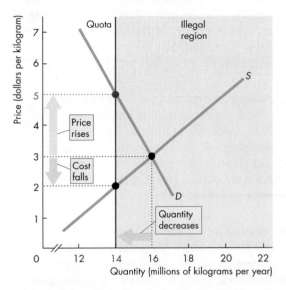

FIGURE 6.11   The Effects of a Production Quota

With no quota, farmers produce 16 million kilograms of milk (powder) a year and the price is $3 a kilogram. A production quota of 14 million kilograms a year restricts total production to that amount. The quantity produced decreases to 14 million kilograms a year, the price rises to $5 a kilogram. Because marginal social cost (on the supply curve) is less than marginal social benefit (on the demand curve), a deadweight loss arises from the underproduction.

═══════════════ MyEconLab   animation   ◆

A Decrease in Supply   A production quota on milk decreases the supply of milk. Each farmer is assigned a production limit that is less than the amount that would be produced—and supplied—without the quota. The total of the farmers' limits equals the quota, and any production in excess of the quota is illegal.

The quantity supplied becomes the amount permitted by the production quota, and this quantity is fixed. The supply of milk powder becomes perfectly inelastic at the quantity permitted under the quota.

In Fig. 6.11, with no quota, farmers would produce 16 million kilograms of milk (powder) a year—the market equilibrium quantity. With a production quota set at 14 million kilograms a year, the grey-shaded area shows the illegal region. As in the case of price ceilings and price floors, market forces and political forces are in conflict in this illegal region.

The vertical red line labelled "Quota" becomes the supply curve of milk at prices above $2 a kilogram.

A Rise in Price The production quota raises the price of milk. When the government sets a production quota, it leaves market forces free to determine the price. Because the quota decreases the supply of milk, it raises the price. In Fig. 6.11, with no quota, the price is $3 a kilogram. With a quota of 14 million kilograms, the price rises to $5 a kilogram.

A Decrease in Marginal Cost The production quota lowers the marginal cost of producing milk. Marginal cost decreases because farmers produce less and stop using the resources with the highest marginal cost. Milk farmers slide down their supply (and marginal cost) curves. In Fig. 6.11, marginal cost decreases to $2 a kilogram.

Inefficiency The production quota results in inefficient underproduction. Marginal social benefit at the quantity produced is equal to the market price, which has risen. Marginal social cost at the quantity produced has decreased and is less than the market price. So marginal social benefit exceeds marginal social cost and a deadweight loss arises.

An Incentive to Cheat and Overproduce The production quota creates an incentive for farmers to cheat and produce more than their individual production limit. With the quota, the price exceeds marginal cost, so the farmer can get a larger profit by producing one more unit. Of course, if all farmers produce more than their assigned limit, the production quota becomes ineffective, and the price falls to the equilibrium (no quota) price.

To make the production quota effective, farmers must set up a monitoring system to ensure that no one cheats and overproduces. But it is costly to set up and operate a monitoring system and it is difficult to detect and punish producers who violate their quotas.

Because of the difficulty of operating a quota, producers often lobby governments to establish a quota and provide the monitoring and punishment systems that make it work.

Subsidies

In Canada, the European Union, and the United States, the producers of many farm products, including grain, meat, milk, and eggs, receive subsidies. A **subsidy** is a payment made by the government to a producer.

The effects of a subsidy are similar to the effects of a tax, but they go in the opposite directions. These effects are

■ An increase in supply
■ A fall in price and increase in quantity produced
■ An increase in marginal cost
■ Payments by government to farmers
■ Inefficient overproduction

Figure 6.12 illustrates the effects of a subsidy to grain farmers.

An Increase in Supply In Fig. 6.12, with no subsidy, the demand curve D and the supply curve S determine the price of grain at $40 a tonne and the quantity of grain at 40 million tonnes a year.

Suppose that the government introduces a subsidy of $20 a tonne to grain farmers. A subsidy is like a negative tax. A tax is equivalent to an increase in cost, so a subsidy is equivalent to a decrease in cost. The subsidy brings an increase in supply.

To determine the position of the new supply curve, we subtract the subsidy from the farmers' minimum supply-price. In Fig. 6.12, with no subsidy, farmers are willing to offer 40 million tonnes a year at a price of $40 a tonne. With a subsidy of $20 a tonne, they will offer 40 million tonnes a year if the price is as low as $20 a tonne. The supply curve shifts to the red curve labelled $S - subsidy$.

A Fall in Price and Increase in Quantity Produced The subsidy lowers the price of grain and increases the quantity produced. In Fig. 6.12, equilibrium occurs where the new supply curve intersects the demand curve at a price of $30 a tonne and a quantity of 60 million tonnes a year.

An Increase in Marginal Cost The subsidy lowers the price paid by consumers but increases the marginal cost of producing grain. Marginal cost increases because farmers grow more grain, which means that they must begin to use some resources that are less ideal for growing grain. Farmers slide up their supply (and marginal cost) curves. In Fig. 6.12, marginal cost increases to $50 a tonne.

Payments by Government to Farmers The government pays a subsidy to farmers on each tonne of grain produced. In this example, farmers increase production to 60 million tonnes a year and receive a

FIGURE 6.12   The Effects of a Subsidy

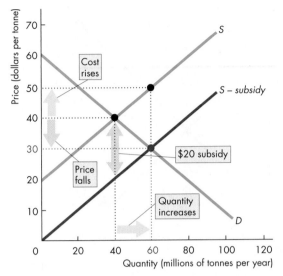

With no subsidy, farmers produce 40 million tonnes a year at $40 a tonne. A subsidy of $20 a tonne shifts the supply curve rightward to *S – subsidy*. The equilibrium quantity increases to 60 million tonnes a year, the price falls to $30 a tonne, and the price plus the subsidy received by farmers rises to $50 a tonne. In the new equilibrium, marginal social cost (on the supply curve) exceeds marginal social benefit (on the demand curve) and the subsidy results in inefficient overproduction.

 MyEconLab   animation ◆

subsidy of $20 a tonne. So grain farmers receive payments from the government that total $1,200 million a year.

Inefficient Overproduction The subsidy results in inefficient overproduction. At the quantity produced with the subsidy, marginal social benefit is equal to the market price, which has fallen. Marginal social cost has increased and it exceeds the market price. Because marginal social cost exceeds marginal social benefit, the increased production brings inefficiency.

Subsidies spill over to the rest of the world. Because a subsidy lowers the domestic market price, subsidized farmers will offer some of their output for sale on the world market. The increase in supply on the world market lowers the price in the rest of the world. Faced with lower prices, farmers in other countries decrease production and receive smaller revenues.

Economics in Action
Rich, High-Cost Farmers the Winners

Farm subsidies are a major obstacle to achieving an efficient use of resources in the global markets for farm products and are a source of tension between rich and developing nations.

Canada, the United States, and the European Union pay their farmers subsidies, which create inefficient overproduction of food in these rich economies.

One international study concluded that Canadians would be better off if they imported *all* their food rather than produce any themselves!

At the same time, U.S. and European subsidies make it more difficult for farmers in the developing nations of Africa, Asia, and Central and South America to compete in global food markets. Farmers in these countries can often produce at a lower opportunity cost than Canadian, U.S. and European farmers.

Two rich countries, Australia and New Zealand, have stopped subsidizing farmers. The result has been an improvement in the efficiency of farming in these countries. New Zealand is so efficient at producing lamb and dairy products that it has been called the Saudi Arabia of milk (an analogy to Saudi Arabia's huge oil reserve and production).

International opposition to farm subsidies is strong. Opposition to farm subsidies inside Canada, the European Union, and the United States is growing, but it isn't as strong as the pro-farm lobby, so don't expect an early end to these subsidies.

REVIEW QUIZ

1 Summarize the effects of a production quota on the market price and the quantity produced.
2 Explain why a production quota is inefficient.
3 Explain why a voluntary production quota is difficult to operate.
4 Summarize the effects of a subsidy on the market price and the quantity produced.
5 Explain why a subsidy is inefficient.

You can work these questions in Study Plan 6.4 and get instant feedback.

━━━━━━━━━━━━━━━━━ MyEconLab ◆

Governments intervene in some markets by making it illegal to trade in a good. Let's now see how these markets work.

◆ Markets for Illegal Goods

The markets for many goods and services are regulated, and buying and selling some goods is illegal. The best-known examples of such goods are drugs, such as marijuana, cocaine, ecstasy, and heroin.

Despite the fact that these drugs are illegal, trade in them is a multibillion-dollar business. This trade can be understood by using the same economic model and principles that explain trade in legal goods. To study the market for illegal goods, we're first going to examine the prices and quantities that would prevail if these goods were not illegal. Next, we'll see how prohibition works. Then we'll see how a tax might be used to limit the consumption of these goods.

A Free Market for a Drug

Figure 6.13 shows the market for a drug. The demand curve, D, shows that, other things remaining the same, the lower the price of the drug, the larger is the quantity of the drug demanded. The supply curve, S, shows that, other things remaining the same, the lower the price of the drug, the smaller is the quantity supplied. If the drug were not illegal, the quantity bought and sold would be Q_C and the price would be P_C.

A Market for an Illegal Drug

When a good is illegal, the cost of trading in the good increases. By how much the cost increases and who bears the cost depend on the penalties for violating the law and the degree to which the law is enforced. The larger the penalties and the better the policing, the higher are the costs. Penalties might be imposed on sellers, buyers, or both.

Penalties on Sellers   Drug dealers in Canada face large penalties if their activities are detected. For example, a marijuana dealer caught with less than 3 kilograms could serve a 5-year-less-a-day prison term. A heroin dealer or a marijuana dealer caught with more than 3 kilograms could be imprisoned for life. These penalties are part of the cost of supplying illegal drugs, and they bring a decrease in supply—a leftward shift in the supply curve. To determine the new supply curve, we add the cost of breaking the law to the minimum price that drug dealers are willing to accept. In Fig. 6.13, the cost of breaking the

FIGURE 6.13   A Market for an Illegal Good

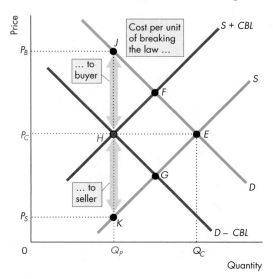

The demand curve for drugs is D, and the supply curve is S. If drugs are not illegal, the quantity bought and sold is Q_C at a price of P_C—point E. If selling drugs is illegal, the cost of breaking the law by selling drugs (CBL) is added to the minimum supply-price and supply decreases to S + CBL. The market moves to point F. If buying drugs is illegal, the cost of breaking the law is subtracted from the maximum price that buyers are willing to pay, and demand decreases to D – CBL. The market moves to point G. With both buying and selling illegal, the supply curve and the demand curve shift and the market moves to point H. The market price remains at P_C, but the market price plus the penalty for buying rises—point J—and the market price minus the penalty for selling falls—point K.

MyEconLab   animation ◆

law by selling drugs (*CBL*) is added to the minimum price that dealers will accept and the supply curve shifts leftward to S + *CBL*. If penalties were imposed only on sellers, the market equilibrium would move from point E to point F.

Penalties on Buyers   In Canada, it is illegal to *possess* drugs such as marijuana, cocaine, ecstasy, and heroin. Possession of marijuana can bring a prison term of 6 months and a fine of $1,000. Possession of heroin can bring a prison term of 7 years. Penalties fall on buyers, and the cost of breaking the law must be subtracted from the value of the good to determine the maximum price buyers are willing to pay for the drugs. Demand decreases, and the demand curve shifts leftward. In Fig. 6.13, the demand curve shifts to $D - CBL$. If penalties were imposed only on buyers, the market equilibrium would move from point E to point G.

Penalties on Both Sellers and Buyers If penalties are imposed on both sellers *and* buyers, both supply and demand decrease and both the supply curve and the demand curve shift. In Fig. 6.13, the costs of breaking the law are the same for both buyers and sellers, so both curves shift leftward by the same amount. The market equilibrium moves to point H. The market price remains at the competitive market price P_C, but the quantity bought decreases to Q_P. Buyers pay P_C plus the cost of breaking the law, which equals P_B. Sellers receive P_C minus the cost of breaking the law, which equals P_S.

The larger the penalties and the greater the degree of law enforcement, the larger is the decrease in demand and/or supply. If the penalties are heavier on sellers, the supply curve shifts farther than the demand curve and the market price rises above P_C. If the penalties are heavier on buyers, the demand curve shifts farther than the supply curve and the market price falls below P_C. In Canada, the penalties on sellers are larger than those on buyers, so the quantity of drugs traded decreases and the market price increases compared with a free market.

With high enough penalties and effective law enforcement, it is possible to decrease demand and/or supply to the point at which the quantity bought is zero. But in reality, such an outcome is unusual. It does not happen in Canada in the case of illegal drugs. The key reason is the high cost of law enforcement and insufficient resources for the police to achieve effective enforcement. Because of this situation, some people suggest that drugs (and other illegal goods) should be legalized and sold openly but also taxed at a high rate in the same way that legal drugs such as alcohol are taxed. How would such an arrangement work?

Legalizing and Taxing Drugs

From your study of the effects of taxes, it is easy to see that the quantity bought of a drug could be decreased if the drug was legalized and taxed. Imposing a sufficiently high tax could decrease the supply, raise the price, and achieve the same decrease in the quantity bought as does a prohibition on drugs. The government would collect a large tax revenue.

Illegal Trading to Evade the Tax It is likely that an extremely high tax rate would be needed to cut the quantity of drugs bought to the level prevailing with a prohibition. It is also likely that many drug dealers and consumers would try to cover up their activities to evade the tax. If they did act in this way, they would face the cost of breaking the law: the tax law. If the penalty for tax law violation is as severe and as effectively policed as drug-dealing laws, the analysis we've already conducted applies also to this case. The quantity of drugs bought would depend on the penalties for law breaking and on the way in which the penalties are assigned to buyers and sellers.

Taxes Versus Prohibition: Some Pros and Cons Which is more effective: prohibition or taxes? In favour of taxes and against prohibition is the fact that the tax revenue can be used to make law enforcement more effective. It can also be used to run a more effective education campaign against illegal drug use. In favour of prohibition and against taxes is the fact that prohibition sends a signal that might influence preferences, decreasing the demand for illegal drugs. Also, some people intensely dislike the idea of the government profiting from trade in harmful substances.

◢ REVIEW QUIZ

1 How does the imposition of a penalty for selling an illegal drug influence demand, supply, price, and the quantity of the drug consumed?

2 How does the imposition of a penalty for possessing an illegal drug influence demand, supply, price, and the quantity of the drug consumed?

3 How does the imposition of a penalty for selling *or* possessing an illegal drug influence demand, supply, price, and the quantity of the drug consumed?

4 Is there any case for legalizing drugs?

You can work these questions in Study Plan 6.5 and get instant feedback.

━━━━━━━━━━━━━━━━━━━━━━━━ MyEconLab ◆

◆ You now know how to use the demand and supply model to predict prices, to study government actions in markets, and to study the sources and costs of inefficiency. In *Reading Between the Lines* on pp. 144–145, you will see how to apply what you've learned to the youth labour market in British Columbia and see the effect on unemployment of raising the minimum wage.

Government Actions in Labour Markets

B.C.'s Minimum Wage Increased Sunday

Vancouver Sun
May 2, 2011

VANCOUVER—The minimum wage hike in B.C. went into effect Sunday, raising the amount by 75 cents to $8.75, but it will still be the lowest in the country. That is until it is raised again to $10.25 in May 2012.

Last month, Premier Christy Clark ended an almost decade-long freeze to B.C.'s minimum wage and put an end to the controversial training wage which paid new workers $6 per hour.

Although the government has eliminated the training wage, it has also set a lower increase for alcohol servers. Those workers will see an increase of only 50 cents an hour, with a cap of $9 an hour by next year.

Ian Tostenson, president and CEO of the B.C. Restaurant and Food Services Association, has said that the sharp increases have left many business owners concerned they will have to reduce staff.

Jim Sinclair, president of the B.C. Federation of Labour, has dismissed this argument. He argues that good wages help employers because people with money in their pockets spend it in small businesses.

The B.C. Federation of Labour has called on the government to index future minimum wage increases beyond May 2012 to the cost of living. On Nov. 1, it will rise again to $9.50 and then $10.25 next year.

ESSENCE OF THE STORY

- On May 2, 2011, the minimum wage in British Columbia increased by 75 cents to $8.75.

- The BC minimum wage is the lowest in the country. That is, until it is raised again to $10.25 in May 2012.

- It is almost 10 years since British Columbia changed its minimum wage.

- The B.C. Restaurant and Food Services Association says many businesses will reduce staff.

- The B.C. Federation of Labour wants further increases beyond 2012 and says good wages help employers because people spend the increase on things produced by small businesses.

ECONOMIC ANALYSIS

- In mid-2011, the minimum wage rates in Canada ranged from $8.75 an hour in British Columbia to $11.00 an hour in Nunavut. Figure 1 shows the data.

- The minimum wage affects younger low-skilled workers more than older and more skilled workers.

- The May 2011 rise in the minimum wage rate in British Columbia reported in the news article can be expected to decrease employment and increase unemployment among young workers in 2011.

- The planned 2012 rise in the minimum wage rate to $10.25 can be expected to decrease employment and increase unemployment among young workers even more during 2012.

- Figures 2 and 3 show the British Columbia labour market for young workers. The demand curve is *LD* and the supply curve is *LS*.

- The assumed elasticity of demand is 0.4, which is that estimated by Michele Campolieti, Morley Gunderson, and Tony Fang (see *Economics in Action* on pp. 132–133). The assumed elasticity of supply is 0.2.

- Figure 2 shows the market in 2011. At the start of the year, the minimum wage rate was $8.00 an hour: 322,000 young people were employed and 52,000 were unemployed.

- With the assumed elasticities of demand and supply, the rise in the minimum wage from $8.00 to $8.75 decreases the quantity of labour demanded, increases the quantity of labour supplied, and increases the unemployment of young workers to 70,000.

- If the elasticities are smaller than those assumed, unemployment will increase by a smaller amount.

- Figure 3 shows the market in 2012. At the start of the year, the minimum wage rate was $8.75 an hour. With our assumed elasticities of demand and supply, at that minimum wage rate, 311,000 young people are employed and 70,000 are unemployed.

- With the assumed elasticities of demand and supply, the 2012 rise in the minimum wage to $10.25 will decrease the quantity of labour demanded, increase the quantity of labour supplied, and increase the unemployment of young workers to 101,000.

- Based on the research that we describe on pp.132–133, it is very unlikely that the B.C. Federation of Labour is correct and that employment will not suffer.

- The idea that higher wages help small business by increasing the demand for their products is not correct. The higher cost of labour is certain to exceed any increase in revenue.

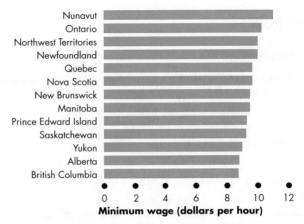

Figure 1 Minimum Wage Rates Across Canada

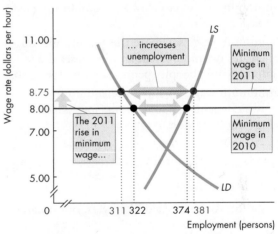

Figure 2 BC's Labour Market for Young Workers in 2011

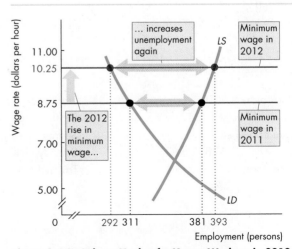

Figure 3 BC's Labour Market for Young Workers in 2012

145

SUMMARY

Key Points

A Housing Market with a Rent Ceiling (pp. 128–130)

- A rent ceiling that is set above the equilibrium rent has no effect.
- A rent ceiling that is set below the equilibrium rent creates a housing shortage, increased search activity, and a black market.
- A rent ceiling that is set below the equilibrium rent is inefficient and unfair.

Working Problems 1 to 6 will give you a better understanding of a housing market with a rent ceiling.

A Labour Market with a Minimum Wage (pp. 131–133)

- A minimum wage set below the equilibrium wage rate has no effect.
- A minimum wage set above the equilibrium wage rate creates unemployment and increases the amount of time people spend searching for a job.
- A minimum wage set above the equilibrium wage rate is inefficient, unfair, and hits low-skilled young people hardest.

Working Problems 7 to 12 will give you a better understanding of a labour market with a minimum wage.

Taxes (pp. 133–138)

- A tax raises the price paid by buyers, but usually by less than the tax.
- The elasticity of demand and the elasticity of supply determine the share of a tax paid by buyers and sellers.

- The less elastic the demand or the more elastic the supply, the larger is the share of the tax paid by buyers.
- If demand is perfectly elastic or supply is perfectly inelastic, sellers pay the entire tax. And if demand is perfectly inelastic or supply is perfectly elastic, buyers pay the entire tax.

Working Problems 13 to 15 will give you a better understanding of taxes.

Production Quotas and Subsidies (pp. 139–141)

- A production quota leads to inefficient underproduction, which raises the price.
- A subsidy is like a negative tax. It lowers the price, increases the cost of production, and leads to inefficient overproduction.

Working Problems 16 and 17 will give you a better understanding of production quotas and subsidies.

Markets for Illegal Goods (pp. 142–143)

- Penalties on sellers increase the cost of selling the good and decrease the supply of the good.
- Penalties on buyers decrease their willingness to pay and decrease the demand for the good.
- Penalties on buyers and sellers decrease the quantity of the good, raise the price buyers pay, and lower the price sellers receive.
- Legalizing and taxing can achieve the same outcome as penalties on buyers and sellers.

Working Problem 18 will give you a better understanding of markets for illegal goods.

Key Terms

Black market, 128
Minimum wage, 131
Price cap, 128
Price ceiling, 128
Price floor, 131

Production quota, 139
Rent ceiling, 128
Search activity, 128
Subsidy, 140
Tax incidence, 133

SCAN THIS

STUDY PLAN PROBLEMS AND APPLICATIONS

MyEconLab ◆ You can work Problems 1 to 18 in Chapter 6 Study Plan and get instant feedback.

A Housing Market with a Rent Ceiling (Study Plan 6.1)
Use the following graph of the market for rental housing in Townsville to work Problems 1 and 2.

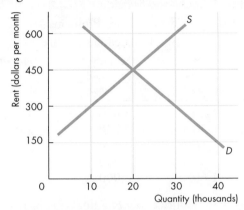

1. a. What are the equilibrium rent and equilibrium quantity of rental housing?
   b. If a rent ceiling is set at $600 a month, what is the quantity of housing rented and what is the shortage of housing?

2. If a rent ceiling is set at $300 a month, what is the quantity of housing rented, the shortage of housing, and the maximum price that someone is willing to pay for the last unit of housing available?

Use the following news clip to work Problems 3 to 6.

Rising Fertilizer Prices

Prospects for the fertilizer sector are exceptional this year. Grain prices have sky rocketed, stimulating greater plantings of grain and greater demand for fertilizer. The price of fertilizer has soared from US$350 to more than US$600 per tonne during the past year.
Source: *National Post*, June 21, 2011

Suppose that the government tries to halt the fertilizer price rise and sets a price ceiling below the equilibrium price.

3. How would the price ceiling influence the quantity of fertilizer supplied and the quantity demanded?

4. How would the price ceiling influence
   a. The quantity of fertilizer sold and the shortage or surplus of fertilizer?
   b. The maximum price that a farmer is willing to pay for the last tonne of fertilizer available on a black market?

5. Draw a graph to illustrate the effects of a price ceiling set below the equilibrium price in the market for fertilizer.

6. Explain the various ways in which a price ceiling on fertlizer that is set below the equilibrium price would make buyers and sellers of fertilizer better off or worse off. What would happen to total surplus and deadweight loss in this market?

A Labour Market with a Minimum Wage (Study Plan 6.2)
Use the following data to work Problems 7 to 9.
The table gives the demand and supply schedules of teenage labour.

Wage rate (dollars per hour)	Quantity demanded	Quantity supplied
	(hours per month)	
4	3,000	1,000
5	2,500	1,500
6	2,000	2,000
7	1,500	2,500
8	1,000	3,000

7. Calculate the equilibrium wage rate, the number of hours worked, and the quantity of unemployment.

8. If a minimum wage for teenagers is set at $5 an hour, how many hours do they work and how many hours of teenage labour are unemployed?

9. If a minimum wage for teenagers is set at $7 an hour,
   a. How many hours do teenagers work and how many hours are unemployed?
   b. Demand for teenage labour increases by 500 hours a month. What is the wage rate paid to teenagers and how many hours of teenage labour are unemployed?

Use the following news clip to work Problems 10 to 12.

India Steps Up Pressure for Minimum Wage for Its Workers in the Gulf

Oil-rich countries in the [Persian] Gulf, already confronted by strong labour protests, are facing renewed pressure from India to pay minimum wages for unskilled workers. With five million immigrant workers in the region, India is trying to win better conditions for their citizens.
Source: *International Herald Tribune*, March 27, 2008

Suppose that the Gulf countries paid a minimum wage above the equilibrium wage to Indian workers.

10. How would the market for labour be affected in the Gulf countries? Draw a supply and demand graph to illustrate your answer.

11. How would the market for labour be affected in India? Draw a supply and demand graph to illustrate your answer. [Be careful: The minimum wage is in the Gulf countries, not in India.]

12. Would migrant Indian workers be better off or worse off or unaffected by this minimum wage?

Taxes (Study Plan 6.3)

13. The table gives the demand and supply schedules for chocolate brownies.

Price (cents per brownie)	Quantity demanded	Quantity supplied
	(millions per day)	
50	5	3
60	4	4
70	3	5
80	2	6
90	1	7

a. If brownies are not taxed, what is the price of a brownie and how many are bought?

b. If sellers are taxed 20¢ a brownie, what is the price? How many are sold? Who pays the tax?

c. If buyers are taxed 20¢ a brownie, what is the price? How many are bought? Who pays the tax?

14. **Junk-Food Tax Needed to Fight Obesity**

A Canadian Health Measures Survey found more than 60% of adults were overweight or obese. A junk-food tax could help reduce the consumption of high-fat foods and drinks. Despite the prospect of a public outcry if a junk-food tax were implemented, people will eventually come to realize the tax is in their best interest.

Source: *Postmedia News*, April 27, 2011

a. Would buyers or sellers of "junk food" pay more of the junk-food tax?

b. Explain why a junk-food tax would generate a public outcry. What would determine how much tax revenue would be collected?

15. **Air Canada Adds Fuel Surcharge on U.S. Flights**

Air Canada announced on Friday that it's imposing fuel surcharges of $10 one-way for economy-class flights between Canada and the United States, and $15 one-way in the executive cabin.

Source: *Globe and Mail*, March 4, 2011

Would the total price of an economy ticket rise by $10? How would consumer surplus change? Explain your answers.

Production Quotas and Subsidies (Study Plan 6.4)

Use the following data to work Problems 16 and 17. The demand and supply schedules for rice are

Price (dollars per box)	Quantity demanded	Quantity supplied
	(boxes per week)	
1.20	3,000	1,500
1.30	2,750	2,000
1.40	2,500	2,500
1.50	2,250	3,000
1.60	2,000	3,500

16. Calculate the price, the marginal cost of rice, and the quantity produced if the government sets a production quota of 2,000 boxes a week.

17. Calculate the price, the marginal cost of rice, and the quantity produced if the government introduces a subsidy of $0.30 a box.

Markets for Illegal Goods (Study Plan 6.5)

18. The figure illustrates the market for a banned substance.

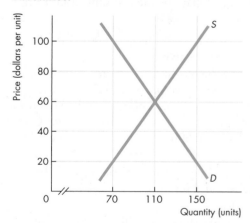

Calculate the market price and the quantity consumed if a penalty of $20 a unit is imposed on

a. Sellers only

b. Buyers only

c. Both sellers and buyers

ADDITIONAL PROBLEMS AND APPLICATIONS

MyEconLab ◆ You can work these problems in MyEconLab if assigned by your instructor.

A Housing Market with a Rent Ceiling

Use the following table to work Problems 19 to 21.
The table shows the demand and supply schedules
for on-campus housing.

Rent (dollars per room)	Quantity demanded	Quantity supplied
	(rooms per term)	
500	2,500	2,000
550	2,250	2,000
600	2,000	2,000
650	1,750	2,000
700	1,500	2,000

19. If the college puts a rent ceiling of $650 a month on rooms, what is the rent paid, how many rooms are rented, and is the on-campus housing market efficient?

20. If the college strictly enforced a rent ceiling of $550 a month, what is the rent paid, how many rooms are rented, and is the on-campus housing market efficient?

21. Suppose that with a strictly enforced rent ceiling of $550 a month, a black market develops. How high might the black market rent be? Would the on-campus housing market be fair? Explain your answer.

A Labour Market with a Minimum Wage

Use the following news clip to work Problems 22 and 23.

2011 Ontario Minimum Wage Rate Set—Highest Provincial Minimum Wage

After seven consecutive increases, the Ontario minimum wage rate will remain at $10.25 per hour in 2011, the highest provincial minimum wage in Canada. The Ontario minimum wage has increased by 50 percent over the last seven years. These increases in part make up for a nine year minimum wage freeze between 1995 and 2004.

Source: news.ontario.com, February 11, 2011

22. On a graph of the market for low-skilled labour, show the effect of the 50-percent increase in the minimum wage over the past seven years on the quantity of low-skilled labour employed.

23. Explain the effects of the 50-percent increase in the minimum wage over seven years on the workers' surplus and the firms' surplus. Has the

labour market become more efficient or less efficient? Explain.

Taxes

24. The demand and supply schedules for tulips are

Price (dollars per bunch)	Quantity demanded	Quantity supplied
	(bunches per week)	
10	100	40
12	90	60
14	80	80
16	70	100
18	60	120

a. If tulips are not taxed, what is the price and how many bunches are bought?

b. If tulips are taxed $6 a bunch, what are the price and quantity bought? Who pays the tax?

25. **Cigarette Taxes, Black Markets, and Crime: Lessons from New York's 50-Year Losing Battle**

New York City has the highest cigarette taxes in the United States. During the four months following the recent tax hike, sales of taxed cigarettes in the city fell by more than 50 percent as consumers turned to the city's bustling black market. The thriving illegal market for cigarettes has diverted billions of dollars from legitimate businesses and governments to criminals.

Source: Cato Institute, February 6, 2003

a. How has the market for cigarettes in New York City responded to the high cigarette taxes?

b. How does the emergence of a black market impact the elasticity of demand in a legal market?

c. Why might an increase in the tax rate actually cause a decrease in the tax revenue?

Production Quotas and Subsidies

26. **Battling Foreign Farm Subsidies**

On the farm subsidy front, farmers in Europe received subsidies of about $6 a bushel, U.S. farmers got $2.50 a bushel, Canadian farmers received subsidies of only 40 cents a bushel.

Source: CBC News, August 6, 2004

In which market do you think the surplus (as a percentage of equilibrium output) is largest and which market is the most inefficient?

Use the following figure, which shows the market for tomatoes, to work Problems 27 and 28.

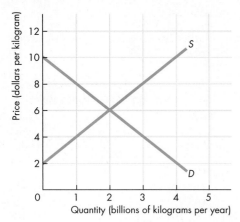

27. a. What are the equilibrium price and quantity of tomatoes? Is the market for tomatoes efficient?
   b. If the government subsidizes tomato growers at $4 per kilogram, what is the quantity of tomatoes produced, the quantity demanded, and the subsidy received by all growers?

28. If the government subsidizes tomato growers at $4 a kilogram, is the market for tomatoes efficient? Who gains and who loses from the subsidy and what is the deadweight loss? Could the subsidy be regarded as being fair?

Markets for Illegal Goods

29. The table gives the demand and supply schedules for an illegal drug.

Price (dollars per unit)	Quantity demanded	Quantity supplied
	(units per day)	
50	500	300
60	400	400
70	300	500
80	200	600
90	100	700

   a. If there are no penalties on buying or selling the drug, what is the price and how many units are consumed?
   b. If the penalty on sellers is $20 a unit, what are the price and quantity consumed?
   c. If the penalty on buyers is $20 a unit, what are the price and quantity consumed?

Economics in the News

30. After you have studied *Reading Between the Lines* on pp. 144–145, answer the following questions.
   a. What is the range of minimum wage rates across the provinces and what are the changes in the minimum wage in British Columbia?
   b. Does a minimum wage change the demand for labour, the supply of labour, or neither?
   c. How does the elasticity of demand for labour and the elasticity of supply of labour influence the magnitude of the effect of a rise in the minimum wage on unemployment?
   d. Explain what is wrong with the idea that higher wages help small business by increasing the demand for their products.
   e. Can you suggest an alternative policy to the minimum wage that might increase both the average wage rate and the employment of teenage workers?

Use the following news clip to work Problems 31 to 33.

Coal Shortage at China Plants

Chinese power plants have run short of coal, an unintended effect of government-mandated price controls designed to shield the public from rising global energy costs. Beijing has also frozen retail prices of gasoline and diesel. That helped farmers and the urban poor, but it has spurred sales of gas-guzzling luxury cars and propelled double-digit annual growth in fuel consumption. At the same time, oil refiners are suffering heavy losses and some have begun cutting production, causing fuel shortages.

Source: CNN, May 20, 2008

31. a. Are China's price controls described in the news clip price floors or price ceilings?
   b. Explain how China's price controls have created shortages or surpluses in the markets for coal, gasoline, and diesel.
   c. Illustrate your answer to part (b) graphically by using the supply and demand model.

32. Explain how China's price controls have changed consumer surplus, producer surplus, total surplus, and the deadweight loss in the markets for coal, gasoline, and diesel.

33. Show on a graph the change in consumer surplus, producer surplus, total surplus, and the deadweight loss in the markets for coal, gasoline, and diesel.

Global Markets in Action

After studying this chapter, you will be able to

◆ Explain how markets work with international trade

◆ Identify the gains from international trade and its winners and losers

◆ Explain the effects of international trade barriers

◆ Explain and evaluate arguments used to justify restricting international trade

iPods, Wii games, and Nike shoes are just three of the items you might buy that are not produced in Canada. In fact, most of the things that you buy are produced abroad, often in Asia, and transported here in container ships and FedEx cargo jets. International trade is part of the sometimes controversial globalization process that is having a profound effect on our lives.

Why do we go to such lengths to trade and communicate with others in faraway places? You will find some answers in this chapter. And in *Reading Between the Lines* at the end of the chapter, you can apply what you've learned and examine the effects of a Canadian tariff on ski jackets imported from China.

◆ How Global Markets Work

Because we trade with people in other countries, the goods and services that we can buy and consume are not limited by what we can produce. The goods and services that we buy from other countries are our **imports**; and the goods and services that we sell to people in other countries are our **exports**.

International Trade Today

Global trade today is enormous. In 2010, global exports and imports were $37 trillion, which is 58 percent of the value of global production. The United States is the world's largest international trader and accounts for 10 percent of world exports and 13 percent of world imports. Germany and China, which rank second and third behind the United States, lag by a large margin.

In 2010, total Canadian exports were $478 billion, which is about 30 percent of the value of Canadian production. Total Canadian imports were $509 billion, which is about 31 percent of total expenditure in Canada.

We trade both goods and services. In 2010, exports of services were about 17 percent of total exports and imports of services were about 21 percent of total imports.

What Drives International Trade?

Comparative advantage is the fundamental force that drives international trade. Comparative advantage (see Chapter 2, p. 38) is a situation in which a person can perform an activity or produce a good or service at a lower opportunity cost than anyone else. This same idea applies to nations. We can define *national comparative advantage* as a situation in which a nation can perform an activity or produce a good or service at a lower opportunity cost than any other nation.

The opportunity cost of producing a T-shirt is lower in China than in Canada, so China has a comparative advantage in producing T-shirts. The opportunity cost of producing a regional jet is lower in Canada than in China, so Canada has a comparative advantage in producing these airplanes.

You saw in Chapter 2 how Liz and Joe reap gains from trade by specializing in the production of the good at which they have a comparative advantage and then trading with each other. Both are better off.

This same principle applies to trade among

Economics in Action
Canada's Most Traded Items

The figure shows Canada's four largest exports and imports by value. Crude oil is our biggest export, and machinery and equipment as well as consumer goods are our biggest imports. Trade in automobiles—both exports and imports—has slipped from top spot in earlier years.

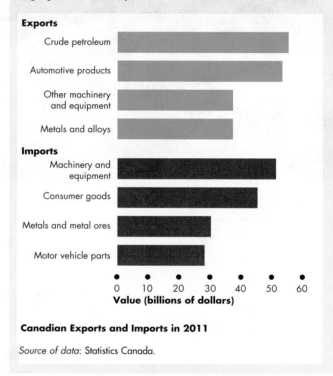

Canadian Exports and Imports in 2011

Source of data: Statistics Canada.

nations. Because China has a comparative advantage at producing T-shirts and Canada has a comparative advantage at producing regional jets, the people of both countries can gain from specialization and trade. China can buy airplanes from Canada at a lower opportunity cost than that at which Chinese firms can produce them. And Canadians can buy T-shirts from China for a lower opportunity cost than that at which Canadian firms can produce them. Also, through international trade, Chinese producers can get higher prices for their T-shirts and Bombardier can sell its regional jets for a higher price. Both countries gain from international trade.

Let's now illustrate the gains from trade that we've just described by studying demand and supply in the global markets for T-shirts and regional jets.

Why Canada Imports T-Shirts

Canada imports T-shirts because the rest of the world has a comparative advantage in producing them. Figure 7.1 illustrates how this comparative advantage generates international trade and how trade affects the price of a T-shirt and the quantities produced and bought.

The demand curve D_{Can} and the supply curve S_{Can} show the demand and supply in the Canadian domestic market only. The demand curve tells us the quantity of T-shirts that Canadians are willing to buy at various prices. The supply curve tells us the quantity of T-shirts that Canadian garment makers are willing to sell at various prices—that is, the quantity supplied at each price when all T-shirts sold in Canada are produced in Canada.

Figure 7.1(a) shows what the Canadian T-shirt market would be like with no international trade.

The price of a shirt would be $8 and 4 million shirts a year would be produced by Canadian garment makers and bought by Canadian consumers.

Figure 7.1(b) shows the market for T-shirts with international trade. Now the price of a T-shirt is determined in the world market, not the Canadian domestic market. The world price of a T-shirt is less than $8, which means that the rest of the world has a comparative advantage in producing T-shirts. The world price line shows the world price at $5 a shirt.

The Canadian demand curve, D_{Can}, tells us that at $5 a shirt, Canadians buy 6 million shirts a year. The Canadian supply curve, S_{Can}, tells us that at $5 a shirt, Canadian garment makers produce 2 million T-shirts a year. To buy 6 million T-shirts when only 2 million are produced in Canada, we must import T-shirts from the rest of the world. The quantity of T-shirts imported is 4 million a year.

FIGURE 7.1   A Market with Imports

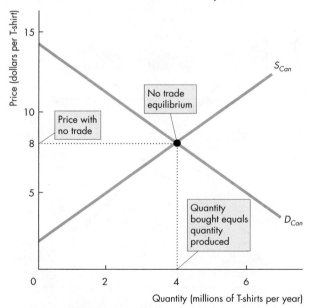

(a) Equilibrium with no international trade

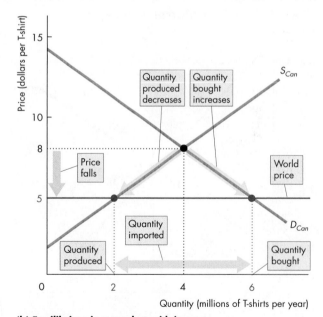

(b) Equilibrium in a market with imports

Part (a) shows the Canadian market for T-shirts with no international trade. The Canadian domestic demand curve D_{Can} and Canadian domestic supply curve S_{Can} determine the price of a T-shirt at $8 and the quantity of T-shirts produced and bought in Canada at 4 million a year.

Part (b) shows the Canadian market for T-shirts with

international trade. World demand and world supply determine the world price of a T-shirt, which is $5. The price in the Canadian market falls to $5 a shirt. Canadian purchases of T-shirts increase to 6 million a year, and Canadian production of T-shirts decreases to 2 million a year. Canada imports 4 million T-shirts a year.

Why Canada Exports Regional Jets

Figure 7.2 illustrates international trade in regional jets. The demand curve D_{Can} and the supply curve S_{Can} show the demand and supply in the Canadian domestic market only. The demand curve tells us the quantity of regional jets that Canadian airlines are willing to buy at various prices. The supply curve tells us the quantity of regional jets that Canadian aircraft makers are willing to sell at various prices.

Figure 7.2(a) shows what the Canadian market for regional jets would be like with no international trade. The price of a regional jet would be $100 million and 40 a year would be produced by Bombardier and bought by Canadian airlines.

Figure 7.2(b) shows the Canadian market for regional jets with international trade. Now the price of a regional jet is determined in the world market and the world price is higher than $100 million, which means that Canada has a comparative advantage in producing regional jets. The world price line shows the world price at $150 million.

The Canadian demand curve, D_{Can}, tells us that at $150 million each, Canadian airlines buy 20 regional jets a year. The Canadian supply curve, S_{Can}, tells us that at $150 million each, Bombardier produces 70 regional jets a year. The quantity produced in Canada (70 a year) minus the quantity purchased by Canadian airlines (20 a year) is the quantity exported, which is 50 regional jets a year.

REVIEW QUIZ

1 Describe the situation in the market for a good or service that Canada imports.
2 Describe the situation in the market for a good or service that Canada exports.

You can work these questions in Study Plan 7.1 and get instant feedback.

———————————————— MyEconLab ◆

FIGURE 7.2   A Market with Exports

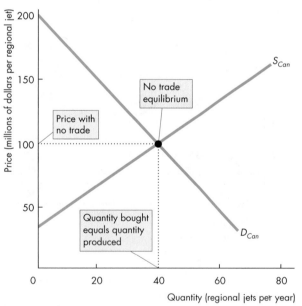

(a) Equilibrium without international trade

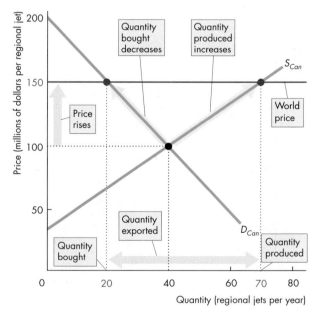

(b) Equilibrium in a market with exports

In part (a), the Canadian market with no international trade, the domestic demand curve D_{Can} and domestic supply curve S_{Can} determine the price of a regional jet at $100 million with 40 regional jets produced and bought each year.

In part (b), with international trade, world demand and world supply determine the world price of a regional jet, which is $150 million. The price in Canada rises to the world price. Canadian production increases to 70 a year, and Canadian purchases decrease to 20 a year. Canada exports 50 regional jets a year.

———————————————— MyEconLab   animation ◆

Winners, Losers, and the Net Gain from Trade

In Chapter 1 (see p. 5), we asked whether globalization is in the social interest—in the self-interest of *both* the low-wage worker in Malaysia who sews your new running shoes and a shoemaker in Toronto. We're now going to answer these questions. You will learn why producers complain about cheap foreign imports, but consumers never complain.

Gains and Losses from Imports

We measure the gains and losses from imports by examining their effect on consumer surplus, producer surplus, and total surplus. In the importing country the winners are those whose surplus increases and the losers are those whose surplus decreases.

Figure 7.3(a) shows what consumer surplus and producer surplus would be with no international trade in T-shirts. Domestic demand, D_{Can}, and domestic supply, S_{Can}, determine the price and quantity. The green area shows consumer surplus and the blue area shows producer surplus. Total surplus is the sum of consumer surplus and producer surplus.

Figure 7.3(b) shows how these surpluses change when the Canadian market opens to imports. The Canadian price falls to the world price. The quantity bought increases to the quantity demanded at the world price and consumer surplus expands from area A to the larger green area $A + B + D$. The quantity produced in Canada decreases to the quantity Canadian producers supply at the world price and producer surplus shrinks to the smaller blue area C.

Part of the gain in consumer surplus, the area B, is a loss of producer surplus—a redistribution of total surplus. But the other part of the increase in consumer surplus, the area D, is a net gain. This increase in total surplus results from the lower price and increased purchases and is the gain from imports.

FIGURE 7.3   Gains and Losses in a Market with Imports

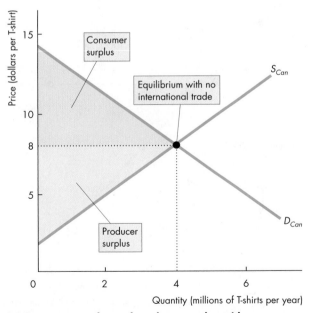

(a) Consumer surplus and producer surplus with no international trade

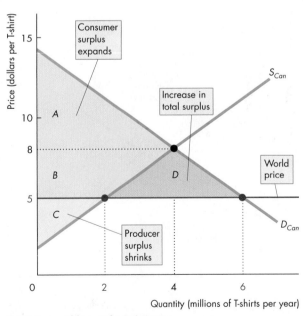

(b) Gains and losses from imports

In part (a), with no international trade, the green area shows the consumer surplus and the blue area shows the producer surplus.

In part (b), with international trade, the price falls to the world price of $5 a shirt. Consumer surplus expands from area A to the area $A + B + D$. Producer surplus shrinks to area C. Area B is a transfer of surplus from producers to consumers. Area D is an increase in total surplus—the gain from imports.

Gains and Losses from Exports

We measure the gains and losses from exports just like we measured those from imports, by their effect on consumer surplus, producer surplus, and total surplus.

Figure 7.4(a) shows the situation with no international trade. Domestic demand, D_{Can}, and domestic supply, S_{Can}, determine the price and quantity, the consumer surplus, and the producer surplus.

Figure 7.4(b) shows how the consumer surplus and producer surplus change when the good is exported. The price rises to the world price. The quantity bought decreases to the quantity demanded at the world price and the consumer surplus shrinks to the green area A. The quantity produced increases to the quantity supplied at the world price and the producer surplus expands to the blue area $B + C + D$.

Part of the gain in producer surplus, the area B, is a loss in consumer surplus—a redistribution of the total surplus. But the other part of the increase in producer surplus, the area D, is a net gain. This increase in total surplus results from the higher price and increased production and is the gain from exports.

Gains for All

You've seen that both imports and exports bring gains. Because one country's exports are other countries' imports, international trade brings gain for all countries. International trade is a win-win game.

REVIEW QUIZ

1 How is the gain from imports distributed between consumers and domestic producers?
2 How is the gain from exports distributed between consumers and domestic producers?
3 Why is the net gain from international trade positive?

You can work these questions in Study Plan 7.2 and get instant feedback.

──────── MyEconLab ◆

FIGURE 7.4 Gains and Losses in a Market with Exports

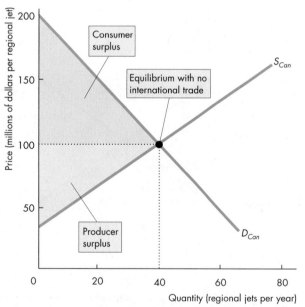

(a) Consumer surplus and producer surplus with no international trade

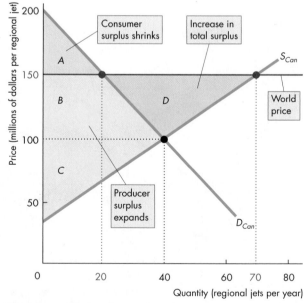

(b) Gains and losses from exports

In part (a), the Canadian market with no international trade, the green area shows the consumer surplus and the blue area shows the producer surplus. In part (b), the Canadian market with international trade, the price rises to the world price. Consumer surplus shrinks to area A. Producer surplus expands from area C to the area $B + C + D$. Area B is a transfer of surplus from consumers to producers. Area D is an increase in total surplus—the gain from exports.

──────── MyEconLab animation ◆

◆ International Trade Restrictions

Governments use four sets of tools to influence international trade and protect domestic industries from foreign competition. They are

- Tariffs
- Import quotas
- Other import barriers
- Export subsidies

Tariffs

A **tariff** is a tax on a good that is imposed by the importing country when an imported good crosses its international boundary. For example, the government of India imposes a 100 percent tariff on wine imported from Ontario. So when an Indian imports a $10 bottle of Ontario wine, he pays the Indian government a $10 import duty.

Tariffs raise revenue for governments and serve the self-interest of people who earn their incomes in import-competing industries. But as you will see, restrictions on free international trade decrease the gains from trade and are not in the social interest.

The Effects of a Tariff To see the effects of a tariff, let's return to the example in which Canada imports T-shirts. With free trade, the T-shirts are imported and sold at the world price. Then, under pressure from Canadian garment makers, the Canadian government imposes a tariff on imported T-shirts. Buyers of T-shirts must now pay the world price plus the tariff. Several consequences follow and Fig. 7.5 illustrates them.

Figure 7.5(a) shows the situation with free international trade. At the world price of $5 a shirt, Canada produces 2 million T-shirts a year and imports 4 million a year. Figure 7.5(b) shows what happens with a tariff set at $2 per T-shirt.

FIGURE 7.5   The Effects of a Tariff

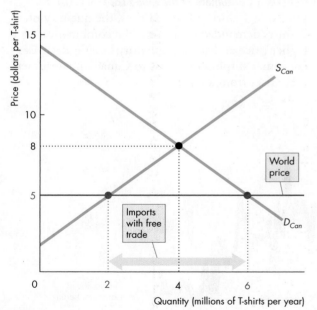

(a) Free trade

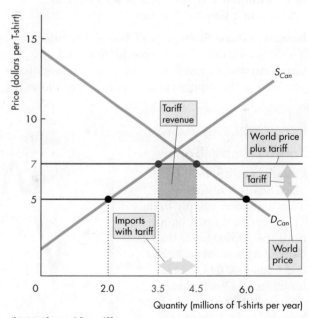

(b) Market with tariff

The world price of a T-shirt is $5. With free trade in part (a), Canadians buy 6 million T-shirts a year. Canadian garment makers produce 2 million T-shirts a year and Canada imports 4 million a year.

With a tariff of $2 per T-shirt in part (b), the price in

the Canadian market rises to $7 a T-shirt. Canadian production increases, Canadian purchases decrease, and the quantity imported decreases. The Canadian government collects a tariff revenue of $2 on each T-shirt imported, which is shown by the purple rectangle.

The following changes occur in the market for T-shirts:

- The price of a T-shirt in Canada rises by $2.
- The quantity of T-shirts bought in Canada decreases.
- The quantity of T-shirts produced in Canada increases.
- The quantity of T-shirts imported into Canada decreases.
- The Canadian government collects a tariff revenue.

Rise in Price of a T-Shirt To buy a T-shirt, Canadians must pay the world price plus the tariff, so the price of a T-shirt rises by the $2 tariff to $7. Figure 7.5(b) shows the new domestic price line, which lies $2 above the world price line. The price rises by the full amount of the tariff. The buyer pays the entire tariff because supply from the rest of the world is perfectly elastic (see Chapter 6, p. 137).

Decrease in Purchases The higher price of a T-shirt brings a decrease in the quantity demanded along the demand curve. Figure 7.5(b) shows the decrease from 6 million T-shirts a year at $5 a shirt to 4.5 million a year at $7 a shirt.

Increase in Domestic Production The higher price of a T-shirt stimulates domestic production, and Canadian garment makers increase the quantity supplied along the supply curve. Figure 7.5(b) shows the increase from 2 million T-shirts at $5 a shirt to 3.5 million a year at $7 a shirt.

Decrease in Imports T-shirt imports decrease by 3 million, from 4 million to 1 million a year. Both the decrease in Canadian purchases and the increase in domestic production contribute to this decrease in Canadian imports.

Tariff Revenue The government's tariff revenue is $2 million—$2 per shirt on 1 million imported shirts—shown by the purple rectangle.

Winners, Losers, and the Social Loss from a Tariff

A tariff on an imported good creates winners and losers and a social loss. When the Canadian government imposes a tariff on an imported good,

- Canadian consumers of the good lose.
- Canadian producers of the good gain.
- Canadian consumers lose more than Canadian producers gain.
- Society loses: A deadweight loss arises.

Canadian Consumers of the Good Lose Because the price of a T-shirt in Canada rises, the quantity of T-shirts demanded decreases. The combination of a higher price and smaller quantity bought decreases consumer surplus—the loss to Canadian consumers that arises from a tariff.

Economics in Action

Tariffs Almost Gone

Canadian tariffs were in place before Confederation. They increased sharply in the 1870s and remained high until the 1930s. Since the **General Agreement on Tariffs and Trade (GATT)** was established in 1947 to reduce international tariffs, tariffs have fallen in a series of negotiating rounds, the most significant of which are identified in the figure. Tariffs have almost gone, but import quotas and other trade barriers persist.

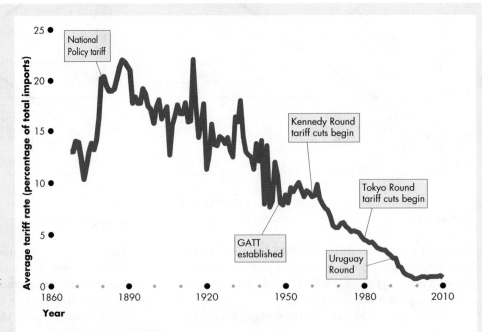

Canadian Tariffs: 1867–2010

Sources of data: Statistics Canada, Historical Statistics of Canada, Catalogue 11-516, July 1999 and CANSIM Tables 380-0002 and 380-0034.

Canadian Producers of the Good Gain Because the price of an imported T-shirt rises by the amount of the tariff, Canadian T-shirt producers are now able to sell their T-shirts for the world price plus the tariff so the quantity of T-shirts supplied by Canadian producers increases. The combination of a higher price and larger quantity produced increases producer surplus—the gain to Canadian producers from the tariff.

Canadian Consumers Lose More Than Canadian Producers Gain Consumer surplus decreases for four reasons: Some becomes producer surplus, some is lost in a higher cost of production (domestic producers have higher costs than foreign producers), some is lost because imports decrease, and some goes to the government as tariff revenue. Figure 7.6 shows these sources of lost consumer surplus.

Figure 7.6(a) shows the consumer surplus and producer surplus with free international trade in T-shirts. Figure 7.6(b) shows the consumer surplus and producer surplus with a $2 tariff on imported T-shirts. By comparing Fig. 7.6(b) with Fig. 7.6(a), you can see how a tariff changes these surpluses.

Consumer surplus—the green area—shrinks for four reasons. First, the higher price transfers surplus from consumers to producers. The blue area *B* represents this loss (and gain of producer surplus). Second, domestic production costs more than imports. The supply curve S_{Can} shows the higher cost of production and the grey area *C* shows this loss of consumer surplus. Third, some of the consumer surplus is transferred to the government. The purple area *D* shows this loss (and gain of government revenue). Fourth, some of the consumer surplus is lost because imports decrease. The grey area *E* shows this loss.

Society Loses: A Deadweight Loss Arises Some of the loss of consumer surplus is transferred to producers and some is transferred to the government and spent on government programs that people value. But the increase in production cost and the loss from decreased imports is transferred to no one: It is a social loss—a deadweight loss. The grey areas labelled *C* and *E* represent this deadweight loss. Total surplus decreases by the area *C* + *E*.

FIGURE 7.6   The Winners and Losers from a Tariff

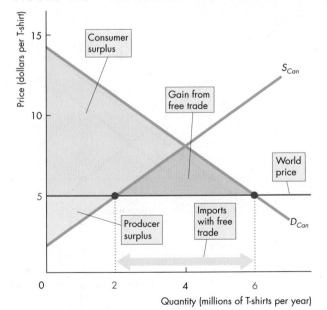

(a) Free trade

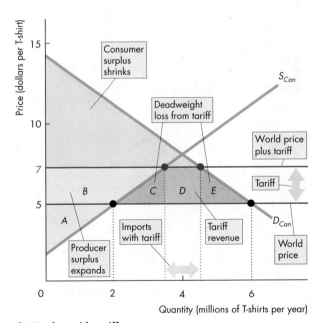

(b) Market with tariff

The world price of a T-shirt is $5. In part (a), with free trade, Canada imports 4 million T-shirts. Consumer surplus, producer surplus, and the gains from free trade are as large as possible.

In part (b), a tariff of $2 per T-shirt raises the

Canadian price of a T-shirt to $7. The quantity imported decreases. Consumer surplus shrinks by the areas *B*, *C*, *D*, and *E*. Producer surplus expands by area *B*. The government's tariff revenue is area *D*, and the tariff creates a deadweight loss equal to the area *C* + *E*.

Import Quotas

We now look at the second tool for restricting trade: import quotas. An **import quota** is a restriction that limits the maximum quantity of a good that may be imported in a given period.

Most countries impose import quotas on a wide range of items. Canada imposes them on food products such as meat, eggs, and dairy and manufactured goods such as textiles and steel.

Import quotas enable the government to satisfy the self-interest of the people who earn their incomes in the import-competing industries. But you will discover that like a tariff, an import quota decreases the gains from trade and is not in the social interest.

The Effects of an Import Quota The effects of an import quota are similar to those of a tariff. The price rises, the quantity bought decreases, and the quantity produced in Canada increases. Figure 7.7 illustrates the effects.

Figure 7.7(a) shows the situation with free international trade. Figure 7.7(b) shows what happens with an import quota of 1 million T-shirts a year. The Canadian supply curve of T-shirts becomes the domestic supply curve, S_{Can}, plus the quantity that the import quota permits. So the Canadian supply curve becomes $S_{Can} + quota$. The price of a T-shirt rises to $7, the quantity of T-shirts bought in Canada decreases to 4.5 million a year, the quantity of T-shirts produced in Canada increases to 3.5 million a year, and the quantity of T-shirts imported into Canada decreases to the quota quantity of 1 million a year. All the effects of this quota are identical to the effects of a tariff of $2 per T-shirt, as you can check in Fig. 7.5(b).

Winners, Losers, and the Social Loss from an Import Quota An import quota creates winners and losers that are similar to those of a tariff but with an interesting difference.

FIGURE 7.7   The Effects of an Import Quota

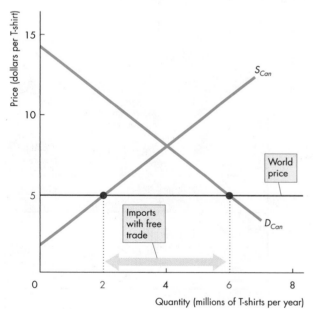

(a) Free trade

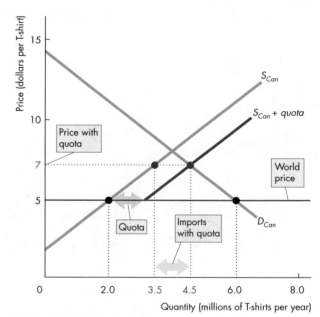

(b) Market with import quota

With free international trade, in part (a), Canadians buy 6 million T-shirts at the world price. Canada produces 2 million T-shirts and imports 4 million a year. With an import quota of 1 million T-shirts a year, in part (b), the

supply of T-shirts in Canada is shown by the curve $S_{Can} + quota$. The price in Canada rises to $7 a T-shirt. Canadian production increases, Canadian purchases decrease, and the quantity of T-shirts imported decreases.

When the government imposes an import quota,

- Canadian consumers of the good lose.
- Canadian producers of the good gain.
- Importers of the good gain.
- Society loses: A deadweight loss arises.

Figure 7.8 shows these gains and losses from an import quota. By comparing Fig. 7.8(b) with a quota and Fig. 7.8(a) with free trade, you can see how an import quota of 1 million T-shirts a year changes the consumer and producer surpluses.

Consumer surplus—the green area—shrinks. This decrease is the loss to consumers from the import quota. The decrease in consumer surplus is made up of four parts. First, some of the consumer surplus is transferred to producers. The blue area *B* represents this loss of consumer surplus (and gain of producer surplus). Second, part of the consumer surplus is lost because the domestic cost of production is higher

than the world price. The grey area *C* represents this loss. Third, part of the consumer surplus is transferred to importers who buy T-shirts for $5 (the world price) and sell them for $7 (the Canadian domestic price). The two blue areas *D* represent this loss of consumer surplus and profit for importers. Fourth, part of the consumer surplus is lost because imports decrease. The grey area *E* represents this loss.

The losses of consumer surplus from the higher cost of production and the decrease in imports is a social loss—a deadweight loss. The grey areas labelled *C* and *E* represent this deadweight loss. Total surplus decreases by the area *C + E*.

You can now see the one difference between an import quota and a tariff. A tariff brings in revenue for the government while a quota brings a profit for the importers. All the other effects are the same, provided the quota is set at the same quantity of imports that results from the tariff.

FIGURE 7.8   The Winners and Losers from an Import Quota

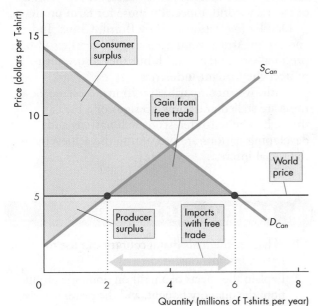

(a) Free trade

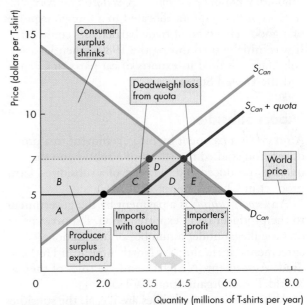

(b) Market with import quota

The world price of a T-shirt is $5. In part (a), with free trade, Canada produces 2 million T-shirts a year and imports 4 million T-shirts. Consumer surplus, producer surplus, and the gain from free international trade (darker green area) are as large as possible. In part (b), the

import quota raises the price of a T-shirt to $7. The quantity imported decreases. Consumer surplus shrinks by the areas B, C, D, and E. Producer surplus expands by area B. Importers' profit is the two areas D, and the quota creates a deadweight loss equal to C + E.

Other Import Barriers

Two sets of policies that influence imports are

- Health, safety, and regulation barriers
- Voluntary export restraints

Health, Safety, and Regulation Barriers Thousands of detailed health, safety, and other regulations restrict international trade. For example, Canadian food imports are examined by the Canadian Food Inspection Agency, which is "mandated to safeguard Canada's food supply and the plants and animals upon which safe and high-quality food depends." The discovery of BSE (mad cow disease) in just one cow in 2003 was enough to close down international trade in Canadian beef. The European Union bans imports of most genetically modified foods, such as Canadian-produced soybeans. Although regulations of the type we've just described are not designed to limit international trade, they have that effect.

Voluntary Export Restraints A *voluntary export restraint* is like a quota allocated to a foreign exporter of a good. This type of trade barrier isn't common. It was initially used during the 1980s when Japan voluntarily limited its exports of car parts to Canada and the United States.

Export Subsidies

A *subsidy* is a payment by the government to a producer. You studied the effects of a subsidy on the quantity produced and the price of a subsidized farm product in Chapter 6, pp. 140–141.

An *export subsidy* is a payment by the government to the producer of an exported good. Export subsidies are illegal under a number of international agreements, including the North American Free Trade Agreement (NAFTA), and the rules of the World Trade Organization (WTO).

Although export subsidies are illegal, the subsidies that the Canadian and European Union governments pay to farmers end up increasing domestic production, some of which gets exported. These exports of subsidized farm products make it harder for producers in other countries, notably in Africa and Central and South America, to compete in global markets. Export subsidies bring gains to domestic producers, but they result in inefficient underproduction in the rest of the world and create a deadweight loss.

Economics in Action
Self-Interest Beats the Social Interest

The **World Trade Organization (WTO)** is an international body established by the world's major trading nations for the purpose of supervising international trade and lowering the barriers to trade.

In 2001, at a meeting of trade ministers from all the WTO member-countries held in Doha, Qatar, an agreement was made to begin negotiations to lower tariff barriers and quotas that restrict international trade in farm products and services. These negotiations are called the **Doha Development Agenda** or the **Doha Round**.

In the period since 2001, thousands of hours of conferences in Cancún in 2003, Geneva in 2004, and Hong Kong in 2005, and ongoing meetings at WTO headquarters in Geneva, costing millions of taxpayers' dollars, have made little progress.

Rich nations, led by the United States, the European Union, and Japan, want greater access to the markets of developing nations in exchange for allowing those nations greater access to the markets of the rich world, especially those for farm products.

Developing nations, led by Brazil, China, India, and South Africa, want access to the markets of farm products of the rich world, but they also want to protect their infant industries.

With two incompatible positions, these negotiations are stalled and show no signs of a breakthrough. The self-interests of rich nations and developing nations are preventing the achievement of the social interest.

REVIEW QUIZ

1 What are the tools that a country can use to restrict international trade?
2 Explain the effects of a tariff on domestic production, the quantity bought, and the price.
3 Explain who gains and who loses from a tariff and why the losses exceed the gains.
4 Explain the effects of an import quota on domestic production, consumption, and price.
5 Explain who gains and who loses from an import quota and why the losses exceed the gains.

You can work these questions in Study Plan 7.3 and get instant feedback.

————————————————— MyEconLab ◆

◆ The Case Against Protection

For as long as nations and international trade have existed, people have debated whether a country is better off with free international trade or with protection from foreign competition. The debate continues, but for most economists, a verdict has been delivered and is the one you have just seen. Free trade promotes prosperity for all countries; protection is inefficient. We've seen the most powerful case for free trade—it brings gains for consumers that exceed any losses incurred by producers, so there is a net gain for society.

But there is a broader range of issues in the free trade versus protection debate. Let's review these issues.

Two classical arguments for restricting international trade are

- The infant-industry argument
- The dumping argument

The Infant-Industry Argument

The **infant-industry argument** for protection is that it is necessary to protect a new industry to enable it to grow into a mature industry that can compete in world markets. The argument is based on the idea that comparative advantage changes or is dynamic and that on-the-job experience—*learning-by-doing*—is an important source of changes in comparative advantage. The fact that learning-by-doing can change comparative advantage doesn't justify protecting an infant industry.

First, the infant-industry argument is not valid if the benefits of learning-by-doing accrue *only* to the firms in the infant industry. The reason is that these firms will anticipate and reap the benefits of learning-by-doing without the additional incentive of protection from foreign competition.

For example, there are huge productivity gains from learning-by-doing in the manufacture of aircraft, but these gains benefit Bombardier and other aircraft producers. Because the people making the decisions are the ones who benefit, they take the future gains into account when they decide on the scale of their activities. No benefits accrue to firms in other industries or other parts of the economy, so there is no need for government assistance to achieve an efficient outcome.

Second, even if the case is made for protecting an infant industry, it is more efficient to do so by giving the firms in the industry a subsidy, which is financed out of taxes. Such a subsidy would encourage the industry to mature and to compete with efficient world producers and keep the price faced by consumers at the world price.

The Dumping Argument

Dumping occurs when a foreign firm sells its exports at a lower price than its cost of production. Dumping might be used by a firm that wants to gain a global monopoly. In this case, the foreign firm sells its output at a price below its cost to drive domestic firms out of business. When the domestic firms have gone, the foreign firm takes advantage of its monopoly position and charges a higher price for its product. Dumping is illegal under the rules of the WTO and is usually regarded as a justification for temporary tariffs, which are called *countervailing duties.*

But there are powerful reasons to resist the dumping argument for protection. First, it is virtually impossible to detect dumping because it is hard to determine a firm's costs. As a result, the test for dumping is whether a firm's export price is below its domestic price. But this test is a weak one because it can be rational for a firm to charge a low price in a market in which the quantity demanded is highly sensitive to price and a higher price in a market in which demand is less price-sensitive.

Second, it is hard to think of a good that is produced by a *global* monopoly. So even if all the domestic firms in some industry were driven out of business, it would always be possible to find alternative foreign sources of supply and to buy the good at a price determined in a competitive market.

Third, if a good or service were a truly global monopoly, the best way of dealing with it would be by regulation—just as in the case of domestic monopolies (see Chapter 13, pp. 313–315). Such regulation would require international cooperation.

The two arguments for protection that we've just examined have an element of credibility. The counterarguments are in general stronger, however, so these arguments do not make the case for protection. But they are not the only arguments that you might encounter. There are many other new arguments against globalization and for protection.

The most common ones are that protection

- Saves jobs
- Allows us to compete with cheap foreign labour
- Penalizes lax environmental standards
- Prevents rich countries from exploiting developing countries

Saves Jobs

First, free trade does cost some jobs, but it also creates other jobs. It brings about a global rationalization of labour and allocates labour resources to their highest-valued activities. International trade in textiles has cost tens of thousands of jobs in Canada as textile mills and other factories closed. But tens of thousands of jobs have been created in other countries as textile mills opened. And many thousands of Canadian workers got better-paying jobs than as textile workers because Canadian export industries expanded and created new jobs. More jobs have been created than destroyed.

Although protection does save particular jobs, it does so at a high cost. For example, until 2005, U.S. textile jobs were protected by an international agreement called the Multifibre Arrangement. The U.S. International Trade Commission (ITC) has estimated that because of import quotas, 72,000 jobs existed in the textile industry that would otherwise have disappeared and that the annual clothing expenditure in the United States was $15.9 billion ($160 per family) higher than it would have been with free trade. Equivalently, the ITC estimated that each textile job saved cost $221,000 a year.

Imports don't only destroy jobs. They create jobs for retailers that sell imported goods and for firms that service those goods. Imports also create jobs by creating income in the rest of the world, some of which is spent on Canadian-made goods and services.

Allows Us to Compete with Cheap Foreign Labour

With the removal of tariffs on trade between Canada, the United States, and Mexico, people said we would hear a "giant sucking sound" as jobs rushed to Mexico. Let's see what's wrong with this view.

The labour cost of a unit of output equals the wage rate divided by labour productivity. For example, if a Canadian autoworker earns $40 an hour and produces 20 units of output an hour, the average labour cost of a unit of output is $2. If a Mexican auto assembly worker earns $4 an hour and produces 1 unit of output an hour, the average labour cost of a unit of output is $4. Other things remaining the same, the higher a worker's productivity, the higher is the worker's wage rate. High-wage workers have high productivity; low-wage workers have low productivity.

Although high-wage Canadian workers are more productive than low-wage Mexican workers, there are differences across industries. Canadian labour is relatively more productive in some activities than in others. For example, the productivity of Canadian workers in producing movies, financial services, and customized computer chips is relatively higher than their productivity in the production of metals and some standardized machine parts. The activities in which Canadian workers are *relatively* more productive than their Mexican counterparts are those in which Canada has a *comparative advantage*. By engaging in free trade, increasing our production and exports of the goods and services in which we have a comparative advantage, and decreasing our production and increasing our imports of the goods and services in which our trading partners have a comparative advantage, we can make ourselves and the citizens of other countries better off.

Penalizes Lax Environmental Standards

Another argument for protection is that many poorer countries, such as China and Mexico, do not have the same environmental policies that we have and, because they are willing to pollute and we are not, we cannot compete with them without tariffs. So if poorer countries want free trade with the richer and "greener" countries, they must raise their environmental standards.

This argument for protection is weak. First, a poor country cannot afford to be as concerned about its environmental standard as a rich country can. Today, some of the worst air and water pollution is found in China, Mexico, and Eastern Europe. But only a few decades ago, London and Los Angeles topped the pollution league chart. The best hope for cleaner air in Beijing and Mexico City is rapid income growth. And free trade contributes to that growth. As incomes in developing countries grow, they will have the *means* to match their desires to improve their environment.

Second, a poor country may have a comparative advantage at doing "dirty" work, which helps it to raise its income and at the same time enables the global economy to achieve higher environmental standards than would otherwise be possible.

Prevents Rich Countries from Exploiting Developing Countries

Another argument for protection is that international trade must be restricted to prevent the people of the rich industrial world from exploiting the poorer people of the developing countries and forcing them to work for slave wages.

Child labour and near-slave labour are serious problems that are rightly condemned. But by trading with poor countries, we increase the demand for the goods that these countries produce and, more significantly, we increase the demand for their labour. When the demand for labour in developing countries increases, the wage rate also increases. So, rather than exploiting people in developing countries, trade can improve their opportunities and increase their wages.

All these arguments for protection leave free-trade unscathed, but a new phenomenon is at work: *offshore outsourcing*. Surely we need protection from this new source of foreign competition. Let's investigate.

Offshore Outsourcing

Roots, Canadian Tire, and BlackBerry: What do these Canadian icons have in common? They all send jobs that could be done in Canada to China, India, Thailand, or even the United States—they are offshoring. What exactly is offshoring?

What Is Offshoring? A firm in Canada can obtain the goods and services that it sells in any of four ways:

1. Hire Canadian labour and produce in Canada.
2. Hire foreign labour and produce in other countries.
3. Buy finished goods, components, or services from other firms in Canada.
4. Buy finished goods, components, or services from other firms in other countries.

Activities 3 and 4 are **outsourcing**, and activities 2 and 4 are **offshoring**. Activity 4 is **offshore outsourcing**. Notice that offshoring includes activities that take place inside Canadian firms. If a Canadian firm opens its own facilities in another country, then it is offshoring.

Offshoring has been going on for hundreds of years, but it expanded rapidly and became a source of concern during the 1990s as many Canadian firms moved information technology services and general office services such as finance, accounting, and human resources management overseas.

Why Did Offshoring of Services Boom During the 1990s? The gains from specialization and trade that you saw in the previous section must be large enough to make it worth incurring the costs of communication and transportation. If the cost of producing a T-shirt in China isn't lower than the cost of producing the T-shirt in Canada by more than the cost of transporting the shirt from China to Canada, then it is more efficient to produce shirts in Canada and avoid the transportation costs.

The same considerations apply to trade in services. If services are to be produced offshore, then the cost of delivering those services must be low enough to leave the buyer with an overall lower price. Before the 1990s, the cost of communicating across large distances was too high to make the offshoring of business services efficient. But during the 1990s, when satellites, fibre-optic cables, and computers cut the price of a phone call between Canada and India to less than a dollar an hour, a huge base of offshore resources became competitive with similar resources in Canada.

What Are the Benefits of Offshoring? Offshoring brings gains from trade identical to those of any other type of trade. We could easily change the names of the items traded from T-shirts and airplanes (the examples in the previous sections of this chapter) to banking services and call centre services (or any other pair of services). A Canadian bank might export banking services to Indian firms, and Indians might provide call centre services to Canadian firms. This type of trade would benefit both Canadians and Indians provided Canada has a comparative advantage in banking services and India has a comparative advantage in call centre services.

Comparative advantages like these emerged during the 1990s. India has the world's largest educated English-speaking population and is located in a time zone half a day ahead of the Canadian east coast and midway between Asia and Europe, which facilitates 24/7 operations. When the cost of communicating with a worker in India was several dollars a minute, as it was before the 1990s, tapping these vast resources was just too expensive. But at today's price of a long-distance telephone call or Internet connection, resources in India can be used to produce services in Canada at a lower cost than those services can be produced by using resources located in Canada. And with the incomes that Indians earn from exporting services, some of the services (and goods) that Indians buy are produced in Canada.

Why Is Offshoring a Concern? Despite the gain from specialization and trade that offshoring brings, many people believe that it also brings costs that eat up the gains. Why?

A major reason is that offshoring is taking jobs in services. The loss of manufacturing jobs to other countries has been going on for decades, but the Canadian service sector has always expanded by enough to create new jobs to replace the lost manufacturing jobs. Now that service jobs are also going overseas, the fear is that there will not be enough jobs for Canadians. This fear is misplaced.

Some service jobs are going overseas, while others are expanding at home. Canada imports call centre services, but it exports education, health care, legal, financial, and a host of other types of services. Jobs in these service sectors are expanding and will continue to do so.

The exact number of jobs that have moved to lower-cost offshore locations is not known, and estimates vary. But even the highest estimate is a tiny number compared to the normal rate of job creation.

Winners and Losers Gains from trade do not bring gains for every single person. Canadians, on average, gain from offshore outsourcing, but some people lose. The losers are those who have invested in the human capital to do a specific job that has now gone offshore.

Unemployment benefits provide short-term temporary relief for these displaced workers. But the long-term solution requires retraining and the acquisition of new skills.

Beyond providing short-term relief through unemployment benefits, there is a large role for government in the provision of education and training to enable the labour force of the twenty-first century to be capable of ongoing learning and rapid retooling to take on new jobs that today we can't foresee.

Schools, colleges, and universities will expand and get better at doing their job of producing a highly educated and flexible labour force.

Avoiding Trade Wars

We have reviewed the arguments commonly heard in favour of protection and the counterarguments against it. There is one counterargument that is general and quite overwhelming: Protection invites retaliation and can trigger a trade war.

The best example of a trade war occurred during the Great Depression of the 1930s when the United States introduced the Smoot-Hawley tariff. Country after country retaliated with its own tariff, and in a short period, world trade had almost disappeared. The costs to all countries were large and led to a renewed international resolve to avoid such self-defeating moves in the future. The costs also led to the creation of GATT and are the impetus behind current attempts to liberalize trade.

Why Is International Trade Restricted?

Why, despite all the arguments against protection, is trade restricted? There are two key reasons:

- Tariff revenue
- Rent seeking

Tariff Revenue Government revenue is costly to collect. In developed countries such as Canada, a well-organized tax collection system is in place that can generate billions of dollars of income tax and sales tax revenues. This tax collection system is made possible by the fact that most economic transactions are done by firms that must keep properly audited financial records. Without such records, revenue collection agencies (such as Canada Revenue Agency) would be severely hampered in their work. Even with audited financial accounts, some potential tax revenue is lost. Nonetheless, for industrialized countries, the income tax and sales taxes are the major sources of revenue and tariffs play a very small role.

But governments in developing countries have a difficult time collecting taxes from their citizens. Much economic activity takes place in an informal economy with few financial records, so only a small amount of revenue is collected from income taxes and sales taxes. The one area in which economic transactions are well recorded and audited is international trade. So this activity is an attractive base for tax collection in these countries and is used much more extensively than it is in developed countries.

Rent Seeking Rent seeking is the major reason why international trade is restricted. **Rent seeking** is lobbying for special treatment by the government to create economic profit or to divert consumer surplus or producer surplus away from others. Free trade increases consumption possibilities *on average*, but not everyone shares in the gain and some people even lose. Free trade brings benefits to some and imposes costs on others, with total benefits exceeding total costs. The uneven distribution of costs and benefits is the principal obstacle to achieving more liberal international trade.

Returning to the example of trade in T-shirts and airplanes, the benefits from free trade accrue to all the producers of airplanes and to those producers of T-shirts that do not bear the costs of adjusting to a smaller garment industry. These costs are transition costs, not permanent costs. The costs of moving to free trade are borne by the garment producers and their employees who must become producers of other goods and services in which Canada has a comparative advantage.

The number of winners from free trade is large, but because the gains are spread thinly over a large number of people, the gain per person is small. The winners could organize and become a political force lobbying for free trade. But political activity is costly. It uses time and other scarce resources and the gains per person are too small to make the cost of political activity worth bearing.

In contrast, the number of losers from free trade is small, but the loss per person is large. Because the loss per person is large, the people who lose *are* willing to incur considerable expense to lobby against free trade.

Both the winners and losers weigh the benefits and costs. Those who gain from free trade weigh the benefits it brings against the cost of achieving it. Those who lose from free trade and gain from protection weigh the benefit of protection against the cost of maintaining it. The protectionists undertake a larger quantity of political lobbying than the free traders.

Compensating Losers

If, in total, the gains from free international trade exceed the losses, why don't those who gain compensate those who lose so that everyone is in favour of free trade?

Some compensation does take place. When Canada entered into the North American Free Trade Agreement

(NAFTA) with the United States and Mexico, the United States created a fund to support and retrain U.S. workers who lost their jobs as a result of the new trade agreement. During NAFTA's first six months, only 5,000 workers applied for benefits under this scheme. The losers from international trade are also compensated indirectly through the normal unemployment compensation arrangements. But only limited attempts are made to compensate those who lose.

The main reason why full compensation is not attempted is that the costs of identifying all the losers and estimating the value of their losses would be enormous. Also, it would never be clear whether a person who has fallen on hard times is suffering because of free trade or for other reasons that might be largely under her or his control. Furthermore, some people who look like losers at one point in time might, in fact, end up gaining. The young autoworker who loses his job in Windsor and gets a job on Alberta's oil patch might resent the loss of work and the need to move. But a year later, looking back on events, he counts himself fortunate. And his kids are delighted to be living in Calgary.

Because we don't in general compensate the losers from free international trade, protectionism is a popular and permanent feature of our national economic and political life and discussion.

REVIEW QUIZ

1 What are the infant-industry and dumping arguments for protection? Are they correct?
2 Can protection save jobs and the environment and prevent workers in developing countries from being exploited?
3 What is offshore outsourcing? Who benefits from it and who loses?
4 What are the main reasons for imposing a tariff?
5 Why don't the winners from free trade win the political argument?

You can work these questions in Study Plan 7.4 and get instant feedback.

―――――――――――――― MyEconLab ◆

◆ We end this chapter on global markets in action in *Reading Between the Lines* on pp. 168–169, where we apply what you've learned by looking at the effects of a Canadian tariff on imports of ski jackets from China.

A Tariff on Ski Jackets

Why This Ski Jacket Still Costs More Here

Toronto Star
January 22, 2011

A Karbon brand ski jacket made in China for a company in Toronto costs more to buy in Canada than in the United States. ...

The gap has closed in the three years since the dollar first hit parity with its U.S. counterpart, but only by about 10 percent, says Hugh Schure, president of Schure Sports, the Toronto-based designer of Karbon brand skiwear. ...

A Karbon ski jacket from its Graphite Alpha Stretch collection that will retail next fall for $550 in Canada will be priced at just $450 in the United States, a $100 difference.

Schure blames Canada's higher tariffs, which can add as much as 16 percent to the cost of importing an outwear item into Canada compared to the United States.

That additional cost gets magnified as the jacket makes its way through the supply chain, as first the wholesaler and then the retailer add their markups, he explained.

"An item with a $50 price difference at wholesale is going to have a $100 difference at retail," he said.

On items with lower tariffs, such as inner layers worn under jackets, cross-border prices are closer to parity, he says.

His manufacturer's suggested retail price on a Karbon brand mid-layer jacket, called the Force, will be $110 in Canada this fall and $100 in the United States, he said. ...

Reprinted with permission—Torstar Syndication Services.

ESSENCE OF THE STORY

- Canada's tariff on outwear is 16 percent higher than the equivalent U.S. tariff.

- The additional cost gets magnified by higher wholesale and retail costs in Canada.

- A Karbon Graphite Alpha Stretch ski jacket made in China for a Toronto company costs $550 in Canada and $450 in the United States.

- A Karbon mid-layer Force ski jacket costs $110 in Canada and $100 in the United States.

ECONOMIC ANALYSIS

- This news article illustrates the effects of a tariff on a Canadian import and also illustrates the distinction between the importer–manufacturer market for a good and the retail market for the good.

- The tariff on imports of ski jackets into Canada is 18 percent of the value imported.

- We don't know the price that Schure Sports pays the Chinese manufacturer, but it is probably about $140, in which case, the import duty is 18 percent of this price—a tariff of approximately $25—and the supply price of a jacket to Canada is $165.

- If you buy the same jacket from a U.S. retailer, you pay $450 to the store and an import duty of 18 percent on this price—a tariff of $81—for a total of $531.

- How does a $140 jacket become a $450 jacket in the United States and a $550 jacket in Canada?

- The answer is that a jacket in a store is a combination of a jacket and the retail (and wholesale and transportation) services that make it available to the final buyer. The retail price includes the costs of these additional services (and the profit on them).

- Figure 1 shows the market for Karbon Graphite Alpha Stretch ski jackets in Canada. Without the tariff, the jacket would be retailed for $525. With the tariff, the price is $550. The deadweight loss from the tariff is small.

- The retail (and wholesale and transportation) markets in the United States are more competitive and efficient than those in Canada, and this fact accounts for most of the lower price in the United States.

- Figure 1 shows the deadweight loss from inefficient Canadian retailing. Notice that this deadweight loss is greater than the deadweight loss arising from the tariff.

- Figure 2 shows the market for Karbon Graphite Alpha Stretch ski jackets if they are bought by Canadians from U.S. stores. The jacket is supplied in retail stores for $450 and at that price, quantity *C* would be bought. But with a tariff of $81 per jacket, the quantity bought is *B* and a large deadweight loss from the tariff arises.

- Would Canadians buy their jackets in Canada or the United States? Most likely the answer is in Canada. The price difference of $19 per jacket is probably not enough to justify the additional time and effort needed to make a purchase in the United States.

- A Canadian importer might decide to smuggle (avoid paying customs duty), but that illegal transaction incurs the cost of breaking the law explained in Chapter 6 (see pp. 142–143.)

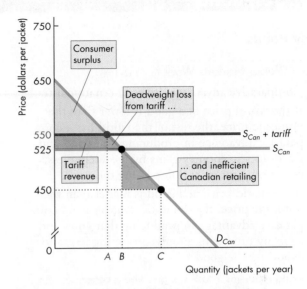

Figure 1 Canadians Buy Ski Jackets in Canada

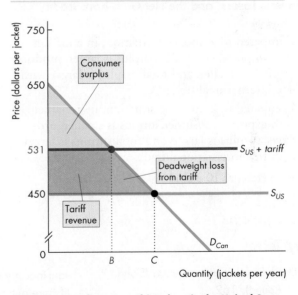

Figure 2 Canadians Buy Ski Jackets in the United States

- Notice that the price to a Canadian buyer is similar regardless of where the jacket is bought. Hugh Schure's suggestion that "additional cost gets magnified as the jacket makes its way through the supply chain, as first the wholesaler and then the retailer add their markups" isn't convincing because it doesn't explain why the costs get magnified. Market forces and the $81 tariff on an imported ski jacket by a Canadian consumer is what drives the Canadian retail price to $550.

169

SUMMARY

Key Points

How Global Markets Work (pp. 152–154)

- Comparative advantage drives international trade.
- If the world price of a good is lower than the domestic price, the rest of the world has a comparative advantage in producing that good and the domestic country gains by producing less, consuming more, and importing the good.
- If the world price of a good is higher than the domestic price, the domestic country has a comparative advantage in producing that good and gains by producing more, consuming less, and exporting the good.

Working Problems 1 to 9 will give you a better understanding of how global markets work.

Winners, Losers, and the Net Gain from Trade (pp. 155–156)

- Compared to a no-trade situation, in a market with imports, consumer surplus is larger, producer surplus is smaller, and total surplus is larger with free international trade.
- Compared to a no-trade situation, in a market with exports, consumer surplus is smaller, producer surplus is larger, and total surplus is larger with free international trade.

Working Problems 10 and 11 will give you a better understanding of winners, losers, and the net gains from trade.

International Trade Restrictions (pp. 157–162)

- Countries restrict international trade by imposing tariffs, import quotas, and other import barriers.
- Trade restrictions raise the domestic price of imported goods, lower the quantity imported, decrease consumer surplus, increase producer surplus, and create a deadweight loss.

Working Problems 12 to 21 will give you a better understanding of international trade restrictions.

The Case Against Protection (pp. 163–167)

- Arguments that protection is necessary for infant industries and to prevent dumping are weak.
- Arguments that protection saves jobs, allows us to compete with cheap foreign labour, is needed to penalize lax environmental standards, and prevents exploitation of developing countries are flawed.
- Offshore outsourcing is just a new way of reaping gains from trade and does not justify protection.
- Trade restrictions are popular because protection brings a small loss per person to a large number of people and a large gain per person to a small number of people. Those who gain have a stronger political voice than those who lose and it is too costly to identify and compensate losers.

Working Problem 22 will give you a better understanding of the case against protection.

Key Terms

Doha Development Agenda (Doha Round), 162
Dumping, 163
Exports, 152
General Agreement on Tariffs and Trade (GATT), 158
Import quota, 160
Imports, 152

Infant-industry argument, 163
Offshore outsourcing, 165
Offshoring, 165
Outsourcing, 165
Rent seeking, 167
Tariff, 157
World Trade Organization (WTO) 162

SCAN THIS

STUDY PLAN PROBLEMS AND APPLICATIONS

MyEconLab ◆ You can work Problems 1 to 22 in Chapter 7 Study Plan and get instant feedback.

How Global Markets Work (Study Plan 7.1)

Use the following information to work Problems 1 to 3.

Canada produces both lumber and wine, it exports lumber, and it imports wine. The rest of the world imports Canadian lumber and exports wine to Canada.

1. a. If Canada did not trade with the rest of the world, compare the equilibrium prices of lumber and wine in Canada with the world prices of lumber and wine.

   b. Does Canada or the rest of the world have a comparative advantage in producing lumber? Does Canada or the rest of the world have a comparative advantage in producing wine?

2. a. Compare the quantities of wine that Canadian wineries produce and that Canadians buy with and without trade with the rest of the world.

   b. Compare the quantities of lumber that the rest of the world produces and that it buys with and without trade with Canada.

3. What are the gains from the trade in lumber and wine between Canada and the rest of the world?

Use the following information to work Problems 4 to 6.

Wholesalers of roses (the firms that supply your local flower shop with roses for Valentine's Day) buy and sell roses in containers that hold 120 stems. The table provides information about the North American wholesale market for roses. The demand schedule is the wholesalers' demand and the supply schedule is the North American rose growers' supply.

Price (dollars per container)	Quantity demanded	Quantity supplied
	(millions of containers per year)	
100	15	0
125	12	2
150	9	4
175	6	6
200	3	8
225	0	10

Wholesalers can buy roses at auction in Aalsmeer, Holland, for $125 per container.

4. a. Without international trade, what would be the price of a container of roses and how many containers of roses a year would be bought and sold in North America?

   b. At the price in your answer to part (a), does North America or the rest of the world have a comparative advantage in producing roses?

5. If North American wholesalers buy roses at the lowest possible price, how many do they buy from local growers and how many do they import?

6. Draw a graph to illustrate the North American wholesale market for roses. Show the market equilibrium with no international trade and the market equilibrium with free trade. Mark the quantity of roses produced by local growers, the quantity imported, and the total quantity bought.

Use the following news clip to work Problems 7 and 8.

Underwater Oil Discovery to Transform Brazil into a Major Exporter

A huge underwater oil field discovered late last year has the potential to transform Brazil into a sizable exporter. Fifty years ago, Petrobras was formed as a trading company to import oil to support Brazil's growing economy. Two years ago, Brazil reached its long-sought goal of energy self-sufficiency.

Source: *International Herald Tribune*, January 11, 2008

7. Describe Brazil's comparative advantage in producing oil and explain why its comparative advantage has changed.

8. a. Draw a graph to illustrate the Brazilian market for oil and explain why Brazil was an importer of oil until a few years ago.

   b. Draw a graph to illustrate the Brazilian market for oil and explain why Brazil may become an exporter of oil in the near future.

9. **Postcard: Bangalore. Hearts Set on Joining the Global Economy, Indian IT Workers Are Brushing Up on Their Interpersonal Skills**

The huge number of Indian workers staffing the world's tech firms and call centres possess cutting-edge technical knowledge, but their interpersonal and communication skills lag far behind. Enter Bangalore's finishing schools.

Source: *Time*, May 5, 2008

a. What comparative advantages does this news clip identify?

b. Using the information in this news clip, what services do you predict Bangalore (India) exports and what services do you predict it imports?

Winners, Losers, and the Net Gain from Trade

(Study Plan 7.2)

10. In the news clip in Problem 9, who will gain and who will lose from the trade in services that the news clip predicts?

11. Use the information on the North American wholesale market for roses in Problem 4 to

a. Explain who gains and who loses from free international trade in roses compared to a situation in which North Americans buy only roses grown locally.

b. Draw a graph to illustrate the gains and losses from free trade.

c. Calculate the gain from international trade.

International Trade Restrictions (Study Plan 7.3)

Use the information on the North American wholesale market for roses in Problem 4 to work Problems 12 to 17.

12. If a tariff of $25 per container is imposed on imports of roses, what happens to the price of roses in North America, the quantity of roses bought, the quantity produced locally, and the quantity imported?

13. Who gains and who loses from this tariff?

14. Draw a graph to illustrate the gains and losses from the tariff and on the graph identify the gains and losses, the tariff revenue, and the deadweight loss.

15. If an import quota of 5 million containers is imposed on roses, what happens to the price of roses in North America, the quantity of roses bought, the quantity produced locally, and the quantity imported?

16. Who gains and who loses from this quota?

17. Draw a graph to illustrate the gains and losses from the import quota and on the graph identify the gains and losses, the importers' profit, and the deadweight loss.

Use the following news clip to work Problems 18 and 19.

Car Sales Go Up as Prices Tumble

Car affordability in Australia is now at its best in 20 years, fuelling a surge in sales as prices tumble. In 2000, Australia cut the tariff to 15 percent and on January 1, 2005, it cut the tariff to 10 percent.

Source: *Courier Mail*, February 26, 2005

18. Explain who gains and who loses from the lower tariff on imported cars.

19. Draw a graph to show how the price of a car, the quantity of cars bought, the quantity of cars produced in Australia, and the quantity of cars imported into Australia changed.

Use the following news clip to work Problems 20 and 21.

Why the World Can't Afford Food

As [food] stocks dwindled, some countries placed export restrictions on food to protect their own supplies. This in turn drove up prices, punishing countries—especially poor ones—that depend on imports for much of their food.

Source: *Time*, May 19, 2008

20. a. What are the benefits to a country from importing food?

b. What costs might arise from relying on imported food?

21. If a country restricts food exports, what effect does this restriction have in that country on the price of food, the quantity of food it produces, the quantity of food it consumes, and the quantity of food it exports?

The Case Against Protection (Study Plan 7.4)

22. **Chinese Tire Maker Rejects U.S. Charge of Defects**

U.S. regulators ordered the recall of more than 450,000 faulty tires. The Chinese tire producer disputed the allegations and hinted that the recall might be an effort by foreign competitors to hamper Chinese exports to the United States. Mounting scrutiny of Chinese-made goods has fuelled worries among U.S. regulators, corporations, and consumers about the risks associated with many products imported from China.

Source: *International Herald Tribune*, June 26, 2007

a. What does the information in the news clip imply about the comparative advantage of producing tires in the United States and China?

b. Could product quality be a valid argument against free trade?

c. How would the product-quality argument against free trade be open to abuse by domestic producers of the imported good?

ADDITIONAL PROBLEMS AND APPLICATIONS

MyEconLab ◆ You can work these problems in MyEconLab if assigned by your instructor.

How Global Markets Work

23. Suppose that the world price of eggs is $1 a dozen, Canada does not trade internationally, and the equilibrium price of eggs in Canada is $3 a dozen. Canada then begins to trade internationally.

    a. How does the price of eggs in Canada change?

    b. Do Canadians buy more or fewer eggs?

    c. Do Canadian egg farmers produce more or fewer eggs?

    d. Does Canada export or import eggs and why?

    e. Would employment in the Canadian egg industry change? If so, how?

24. Suppose that the world price of steel is $100 a tonne, India does not trade internationally, and the equilibrium price of steel in India is $60 a tonne. India then begins to trade internationally.

    a. How does the price of steel in India change?

    b. How does the quantity of steel produced in India change?

    c. How does the quantity of steel bought by India change?

25. A semiconductor is a key component in your laptop, cell phone, and iPod. The table provides information about the market for semiconductors in Canada.

Price (dollars per unit)	Quantity demanded	Quantity supplied
	(billions of units per year)	
10	25	0
12	20	20
14	15	40
16	10	60
18	5	80
20	0	100

    Producers of semiconductors can get $18 a unit on the world market.

    a. With no international trade, what would be the price of a semiconductor and how many semiconductors a year would be bought and sold in Canada?

    b. Does Canada have a comparative advantage in producing semiconductors?

26. **Act Now, Eat Later**

    The hunger crisis in poor countries has its roots in U.S. and European policies of subsidizing the diversion of food crops to produce biofuels such as corn-based ethanol. That is, doling out subsidies to put the world's dinner into the gas tank.

    Source: *Time*, May 5, 2008

    a. What is the effect on the world price of corn of the increased use of corn to produce ethanol in the United States and Europe?

    b. How does the change in the world price of corn affect the quantity of corn produced in a poor developing country with a comparative advantage in producing corn, the quantity it consumes, and the quantity that it either exports or imports?

Winners, Losers, and the Net Gain from Trade

27. Use the news clip in Problem 26. Draw a graph of the market for corn in a poor developing country to show the changes in consumer surplus, producer surplus, and deadweight loss.

Use the following news clip to work Problems 28 and 29.

South Korea Agrees on Terms to Lift Eight-Year Ban on Canada Beef Imports

South Korea agrees to lift the ban on beef imports from Canada, which was imposed after the outbreak of mad-cow disease in 2003. Before the ban, South Korea was the fourth-biggest market for Canadian beef, with exports valued at C$50 million a year.

Source: Bloomberg, June 28, 2011

28. a. Explain how South Korea's import ban on Canadian beef affected beef producers and consumers in South Korea.

    b. Draw a graph of the market for beef in South Korea to illustrate your answer to part (a). Identify the changes in consumer surplus, producer surplus, and deadweight loss.

29. a. Assuming that South Korea is the only importer of Canadian beef, explain how South Korea's import ban affected Canadian beef producers and consumers.

    b. Draw a graph of the Canadian market for beef to illustrate your answer to part (a). Identify the changes in consumer surplus, producer surplus, and deadweight loss.

International Trade Restrictions

Use the following information to work Problems 30 to 32.

Before 1995, trade between Canada and Mexico was subject to tariffs. In 1995, Mexico joined NAFTA and all Canadian and Mexican tariffs have gradually been removed.

30. Explain how the price that Canadians pay for goods from Mexico and the quantity of Canadian imports from Mexico have changed. Who are the winners and who are the losers from this free trade?

31. Explain how the quantity of Canadian exports to Mexico and the Canadian government's tariff revenue from trade with Mexico have changed.

32. Suppose that in 2012, tomato growers in Ontario lobby the Canadian government to impose an import quota on Mexican tomatoes. Explain who in Canada would gain and who would lose from such a quota.

Use the following information to work Problems 33 and 34.

Suppose that in response to huge job losses in the Canadian textile industry, the Government of Canada imposes a 100 percent tariff on imports of textiles from China.

33. Explain how the tariff on textiles will change the price that Canadians pay for textiles, the quantity of textiles imported, and the quantity of textiles produced in Canada.

34. Explain how the Canadian and Chinese gains from trade will change. Who in Canada will lose and who will gain?

Use the following information to work Problems 35 and 36.

With free trade between Australia and Canada, Australia would export beef to Canada, but Canada imposes an import quota on Australian beef.

35. Explain how this quota influences the price that Canadian consumers pay for beef, the quantity of beef produced in Canada, and the Canadian and the Australian gains from trade.

36. Explain who in Canada gains from the quota on beef imports and who loses.

The Case Against Protection

37. **Trading Up**

The cost of protecting jobs in uncompetitive sectors through tariffs is high: Saving a job in the sugar industry costs American consumers

$826,000 in higher prices a year; saving a dairy industry job costs $685,000 per year; and saving a job in the manufacturing of women's handbags costs $263,000.

> Source: *The New York Times*, June 26, 2006

a. What are the arguments for saving the jobs mentioned in this news clip?

b. Explain why these arguments are faulty.

c. Is there any merit to saving these jobs?

Economics in the News

38. After you have studied *Reading Between the Lines* on pp. 168–169, answer the following questions.

a. What is the distinction between a good (such as a ski jacket) and wholesale and retail services?

b. When an imported good has a tariff imposed on it, does the tariff apply to the manufacturer's price, or the wholesale price, or the retail price of the item?

c. Why are Canadian retail services less efficient than U.S. retail services? Can these services be traded internationally?

d. Draw a graph to illustrate the effects of removing the tariff on ski jackets.

e. What is Mr. Schure's explanation for the price gap between Canada and the United States?

f. Draw a graph to illustrate the effects of removing the tariff on ski jackets if Mr. Schure's explanation for the price gap between Canada and the United States is correct.

39. **E.U. Agrees Trade Deal with South Korea**

Italy has dropped its resistance to a E.U. trade agreement with South Korea, which will wipe out $2 billion in annual duties on E.U. exports. Italians argued that the agreement, which eliminates E.U. duties on South Korean cars, would put undue pressure on its own automakers.

> Source: *The Financial Times*, September 16, 2010

a. What is a free-trade agreement? What is its aim?

b. Explain how a tariff on E.U. car imports changes E.U. production of cars, purchases of cars, and imports of cars.

c. Illustrate your answer to part (b) with an appropriate graphical analysis.

d. Show on a graph the changes in consumer surplus and producer surplus that result from free trade in cars.

e. Explain why Italian automakers opposed cuts in car import tariffs.

The Amazing Market

The five chapters that you've just studied explain how markets work. The market is an amazing instrument. It enables people who have never met and who know nothing about each other to interact and do business. It also enables us to allocate our scarce resources to the uses that we value most highly. Markets can be very simple or highly organized. Markets are ancient and they are modern.

A simple and ancient market is one that the American historian Daniel J. Boorstin describes in *The Discoverers* (p. 161). In the late fourteenth century,

> *The Muslim caravans that went southward from Morocco across the Atlas Mountains arrived after twenty days at the shores of the Senegal River. There the Moroccan traders laid out separate piles of salt, of beads from Ceutan coral, and cheap manufactured goods. Then they retreated out of sight. The local tribesmen, who lived in the strip mines where they dug their gold, came to the shore and put a heap of gold beside each pile of Moroccan goods. Then they, in turn, went out of view, leaving the Moroccan traders either to take the gold offered for a particular pile or to reduce the pile of their merchandise to suit the offered price in gold. Once again the Moroccan traders withdrew, and the process went on. By this system of commercial etiquette, the Moroccans collected their gold.*

An organized and modern market is an auction at which the U.S. government sells rights to cell phone companies for the use of the airwaves.

Everything and anything that can be exchanged is traded in markets to the benefit of both buyers and sellers.

Alfred Marshall *(1842–1924) grew up in an England that was being transformed by the railroad and by the expansion of manufacturing. Mary Paley was one of Marshall's students at Cambridge, and when Alfred and Mary married in 1877, celibacy rules barred Alfred from continuing to teach at Cambridge. By 1884, with more liberal rules, the Marshalls returned to Cambridge, where Alfred became Professor of Political Economy.*

Many economists had a hand in refining the demand and supply model, but the first thorough and complete statement of the model as we know it today was set out by Alfred Marshall, with the help of Mary Paley Marshall. Published in 1890, this monumental treatise, The Principles of Economics, *became the textbook on economics on both sides of the Atlantic for almost half a century.*

> The forces to be dealt with are ... so numerous, that it is best to take a few at a time .... Thus we begin by isolating the primary relations of supply, demand, and price.
>
> **ALFRED MARSHALL**
> *The Principles of Economics*

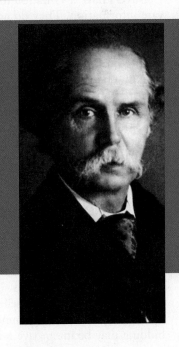

What sparked your interest in economics?

I was studying mathematics and computer science, but I felt that the subjects were not as relevant as I would like.

I discovered economics through a research assistantship with a professor who was working on auctions. I had a summer job working for a firm that sold computers to the government through auctions. Eventually my professor, Bob Marshall, wrote two articles on the topic and testified before Congress to help reform the system for government procurement of computers. That really inspired me and showed me the power of economic ideas to change the world and to make things work more efficiently.

This original inspiration has remained and continues to drive much of your research. Can you explain how economists study auctions?

The study of the design of markets and auction-based marketplaces requires you to use all of the different tools that economics offers.

An auction is a well-defined game. You can write down the rules of the game and a formal theoretical model does a great job capturing the real problem that the players face. And theories do an excellent job predicting behaviour.

Buyers have a valuation for an object that is private information. They do not know the valuations of other bidders, and sometimes they don't even know their own valuation. For example, if they're buying oil rights, there may be uncertainty about how much oil there is in the ground. In that case, information about the amount of oil available is dispersed among the bidders, because each bidder has done their own survey. The bidders face a strategic problem of bidding, and they face an informational problem of trying to draw inferences about how valuable the object will be if they win.

Bidders need to recognize that their bid only matters when they win the auction, and they only win when they bid the most. The knowledge that they were the most optimistic of all the competitors should cause them to revise their beliefs.

From the seller's perspective, there are choices about how an auction is designed—auctions can use sealed bidding, where the seller receives bids and then opens them at a pre-determined time, or alternatively bidding may be interactive, where each bidder has an

opportunity to outbid the previous high bidder. There are also different ways to use bids received by the auctioneer to determine the price. The seller may consider revenue, though governments are often most concerned about efficient allocation.

Both revenue and efficiency are affected by auction design. One key question the seller must con-

> **Both revenue and efficiency are affected by auction design.**

sider is how the design will affect the participation of bidders, as this will determine how competitive bidding will be as well as whether the object gets to the potential bidder who values the item the most.

What must the designer of an auction-based marketplace take into account?

An example of an auction-based marketplace is eBay, where the market designer sets the rules for buyers and sellers to interact.

SUSAN ATHEY is Professor of Economics at Harvard University. Born in 1970 in Boston and growing up in Rockville, Maryland, she completed high school in three years, wrapped up three majors—in economics, mathematics, and computer science—at Duke University at 20, completed her Ph.D. at Stanford University at 24, and was voted tenure at MIT and Stanford at 29. After teaching at MIT for six years and Stanford for five years, she moved to Harvard in 2006. Among her many honours and awards, the most prestigious is the John Bates Clark Medal given to the best economist under 40. She is the first woman to receive this award.

Professor Athey's research is broad both in scope and style. A government that wants to auction natural resources will turn to her fundamental discoveries (and possibly consult with her) before deciding how to organize the auction. An economist who wants to test a theory using a large data set will use her work on statistics and econometrics.

Michael Parkin and Robin Bade talked with Susan Athey about her research, the progress that economists have made in understanding and designing markets, and her advice to students.

When you design an auction-based marketplace, you have a whole new set of concerns. The buyers and sellers themselves are independent agents, each acting in their own interest. The design is a two-step process: You need to design an auction that is going to achieve an efficient allocation; and you need to design both the auction and the overall structure of the marketplace to attract participation.

In the case of eBay, the platform itself chooses the possible auction formats: Auctions take place over time and bidders have the opportunity to outbid the standing high bidder during that time. The platform also allows sellers to use the "buy it now" option. The platform also makes certain tools and services available, such as the ability to search for items in various ways, track auctions, provide feedback, and monitor reputation. The sellers can select the level of the reserve price, whether they want to have a secret reserve price, how long the auction will last, whether to use "buy it now," what time of day the auction closes, how much information to provide, how many pictures they post.

These are all factors that impact participation of bidders and the revenue the seller will receive. The success of the platform hinges on both buyers and sellers choosing to participate.

Does auction theory enable us to predict the differences in the outcomes of an open ascending-bid English auction and a sealed-bid auction?

Sure. In some of my research, I compared open ascending auctions and pay-your-bid, sealed-bid auctions. I showed

> ... sealed-bid auctions can do a better job of deterring collusion ... [and] generate larger revenue.

how the choice of auction format can make a big difference when you have small bidders bidding against larger, stronger bidders who usually (but not always) have higher valuations.

In an open ascending auction, it is hard for a small weaker bidder to ever win, because a stronger bidder can see their bids, respond to them, and outbid them.

But in a pay-your-bid, sealed-bid auction, bidders shade their bids—they bid less than their value, assuring themselves of some profit if they win—and a large bidder doesn't have the opportunity to see and respond to an unusually high bid from a weak bidder. Strong bidders realize that their competition is weak, and they shade their bids a lot—they bid a lot less than their value. That gives a small bidder the opportunity to be aggressive and outbid a larger bidder, even if it has a lower value. So what that does is encourage entry of small bidders. I found empirically that this entry effect was important and it helps sealed-bid auctions generate larger revenue than open ascending-bid auctions.

Does a sealed-bid auction always generate more revenue, other things equal, than an open ascending-bid auction?

Only if you have asymmetric bidders—strong large bidders and weaker small bidders—and even then the effect is ambiguous. It's an empirical question, but it tends to be true. We also showed that sealed-bid auctions can do a better job of deterring collusion. There are theoretical reasons to suggest that sealed bid auctions are more difficult to collude at than open ascending auctions, since at open ascending auctions, bidders can detect an opponent who is bidding higher than an agreement specifies and then respond to that. We found empirically in U.S. Forest Service timber auctions that the gap between sealed-bid auctions and ascending auctions was even greater than what a competitive model would predict, suggesting that some collusion may be at work.

What is the connection between auctions and the supply and demand model?

The basic laws of supply and demand can be seen in evidence in a market like eBay. The more sellers that are selling similar products, the lower the prices they can expect to achieve. Similarly the more buyers there are demanding those objects, the higher the prices the sellers can achieve.

> **The basic laws of supply and demand can be seen in evidence in a market like eBay.**

An important thing for an auction marketplace is to attract a good balance of buyers and sellers so that both the buyers and the sellers find it more profitable to transact in that marketplace rather than using some other mechanism. From a seller's perspective, the more bidders there are on the platform, the greater the demand and the higher the prices. And from the buyer's perspective, the more sellers there are on the platform, the greater the supply and the lower the prices.

Can we think of this thought experiment you just described as discovering demand and supply curves?

Exactly. When you study supply and demand curves, you wave your hands about how the prices actually get set. In different kinds of market settings, the actual mechanisms for setting prices are different. One way of setting prices is through auctions. But we tend to use auctions in settings where there are unique objects, so there isn't just one market price for the thing you are selling. If you were selling something that had lots of market substitutes, you can think of there being a market price in which this object can transact. An auction is a way to find a market price for something where there might not be a fixed market.

Can we think of an auction as a mechanism for finding the equilibrium price and quantity?

Exactly. We can think of the whole collection of auctions on eBay as being a mechanism to discover a market clearing price, and individual items might sell a little higher or a little lower but overall we believe that the prices on eBay auctions will represent market-clearing (equilibrium) prices.

Is economics a good subject in which to major? What subjects work well as complements with economics?

Of course I think economics is a fabulous major and I am passionate about it. I think it's a discipline that trains you to think rigorously. And if you apply yourself you'll finish an economics major with a more disciplined mind than when you started. Whether you go into the business world or academics, you'll be able to confront and think in a logical and structured way about whether a policy makes sense, a business model makes sense, or an industry structure is likely to be sustainable. You should look for that in an undergraduate major. You should not be looking to just absorb facts, but you should be looking to train your mind and to think in a way that you will be able to apply to the rest of your career. I think that economics combines well with statistics and mathematics or with more policy-oriented disciplines.

Do you have anything special to say to women who might be making a career choice? Why is economics a good field for a woman?

On the academic side, economics is a fairly objective field, where the best ideas win, so it's a level playing field. Academics is not very family friendly before you get tenured and extremely family friendly after. Within academics or outside of it, there are a wide range of fairly high-paying jobs that still allow some autonomy over your schedule and that have a deeper and more compelling meaning. For both men and women, if you choose to have a family, you reevaluate your career choices, and the tradeoff between time and money changes. And you're more likely to stick with and excel in a career if you find some meaning in it. So economics combines some of the advantages of having a strong job market and opportunities to have a large enough salary to pay for child care, and makes it economically worthwhile to stay in the workforce, without sacrificing the sense of the greater good.

CHAPTER 8

Utility and Demand

After studying this chapter, you will be able to

◆ Explain the limits to consumption and describe preferences using the concept of utility

◆ Explain the marginal utility theory of consumer choice

◆ Use marginal utility theory to predict the effects of changes in prices and incomes and to explain the paradox of value

◆ Describe some new ways of explaining consumer choices

You want Ke$ha's album *Animal*. Will you buy the CD version from Amazon or will you download it from the iTunes Store? What determines our choices as buyers of recorded music? Also, how much better off are we because we can download an album for less than $10 and some songs for less than $1?

You know that nurses who save people's lives get paid a tiny fraction of what a National Hockey League player earns. Do we really place less value on the people who take care of the injured and the sick than we place on those who provide us with entertaining hockey games?

The theory of consumer choice that you're going to study in this chapter answers questions like the ones we've just posed, and *Reading Between the Lines* at the end of the chapter looks at the nurse and hockey player paradox of value.

◆ Consumption Choices

The choices that you make as a buyer of goods and services—your consumption choices—are influenced by many factors. We can summarize them under two broad headings:

- Consumption possibilities
- Preferences

Consumption Possibilities

Your consumption possibilities are all the things that you can afford to buy. You can afford many different combinations of goods and services, but they are all limited by your income and by the prices that you must pay. For example, you might decide to spend a big part of your income on a gym membership and personal trainer and little on movies and music, or you might spend lots on movies and music and use the free gym at school.

The easiest way to describe consumption possibilities is to consider a model consumer who buys only two items. That's what we'll now do. We'll study the consumption possibilities of Lisa, who buys only movies and pop.

A Consumer's Budget Line Consumption possibilities are limited by income and by the prices of movies and pop. When Lisa spends all her income, she reaches the limits to her consumption possibilities. We describe this limit with a **budget line**, which marks the boundary between those combinations of goods and services that a household can afford to buy and those that it cannot afford.

Figure 8.1 illustrates Lisa's consumption possibilities of movies and pop and her budget line. Lisa has an income of $40 a month, the price of a movie is $8, and the price of pop is $4 a case. Rows *A* through *F* in the table show six possible ways of allocating $40 to these two goods. For example, in row *A* Lisa buys 10 cases of pop and sees no movies; in row *F* she sees 5 movies and buys no pop; and in row *C* she sees 2 movies and buys 6 cases of pop.

Points *A* through *F* in the graph illustrate the possibilities presented in the table, and the line passing through these points is Lisa's budget line.

The budget line constrains choices: It marks the boundary between what is affordable and unafford-able. Lisa can afford all the points on the budget line and inside it. Points outside the line are unaffordable.

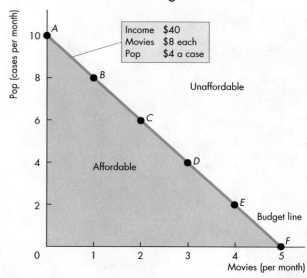

FIGURE 8.1   Lisa's Budget Line

Income $40
Movies $8 each
Pop $4 a case

Possibility	Movies		Pop	
	Quantity	Expenditure (dollars)	Cases	Expenditure (dollars)
A	0	0	10	40
B	1	8	8	32
C	**2**	**16**	**6**	**24**
D	3	24	4	16
E	4	32	2	8
F	5	40	0	0

The graph and the table show six possible ways in which Lisa can allocate $40 to movies and pop. In row *C* and at point *C*, she sees 2 movies and buys 6 cases of pop. The line *AF* is Lisa's budget line and is a boundary between what she can afford and what she cannot afford. Her choices must lie along the line *AF* or inside the orange area.

━━━━━━━ MyEconLab (animation) ◆

Changes in Consumption Possibilities Consumption possibilities change when income or prices change. A rise in income shifts the budget line outward but leaves its slope unchanged. A change in a price changes the slope of the line[1]. Our goal is to predict the effects of such changes on consumption choices. To do so, we must determine the choice a consumer makes. The budget line shows what is possible;

---

[1] Chapter 9 explains an alternative model of consumer choice and pp. 203–204 provide some detail on how changes in income and prices change the budget line.

preferences determine which possibility is chosen. We'll now describe a consumer's preferences.

Preferences

Lisa's income and the prices that she faces limit her consumption choices, but she still has lots of choice. The choice that she makes depends on her preferences—a description of her likes and dislikes.

You saw one way that economists describe **preferences** in Chapter 2 (p. 34), the concept of *marginal benefit* and the *marginal benefit curve*. But you also saw in Chapter 5 (p. 108) that a marginal benefit curve is also a demand curve. The goal of a theory of consumer choice is to derive the demand curve from a deeper account of how consumers make their buying plans. That is, we want to *explain what determines demand and marginal benefit.*

To achieve this goal, we need a deeper way of describing preferences. One approach to this problem uses the idea of utility, and defines **utility** as the benefit or satisfaction that a person gets from the consumption of goods and services. We distinguish two utility concepts:

- Total utility
- Marginal utility

Total Utility The total benefit that a person gets from the consumption of all the different goods and services is called **total utility**. Total utility depends on the level of consumption—more consumption generally gives more total utility.

To illustrate the concept of total utility, think about Lisa's choices. We tell Lisa that we want to measure her utility from movies and pop. We can use any scale that we wish to measure her total utility and we give her two starting points: (1) We will call the total utility from no movies and no pop zero utility; and (2) We will call the total utility she gets from seeing 1 movie a month 50 units.

We then ask Lisa to tell us, using the same scale, how much she would like 2 movies, and more, up to 10 movies a month. We also ask her to tell us, on the same scale, how much she would like 1 case of pop a month, 2 cases, and more, up to 10 cases a month.

In Table 8.1, the columns headed "Total utility" show Lisa's answers. Looking at those numbers, you can say a lot about how much Lisa likes pop and movies. She says that 1 case of pop gives her 75 units of utility—50 percent more than the utility that she gets from seeing 1 movie. You can also see that her total utility from pop climbs more slowly than her

TABLE 8.1 Lisa's Utility from Movies and Pop

Movies			Pop		
Quantity (per month)	Total utility	Marginal utility	Cases (per month)	Total utility	Marginal utility
0	0		0	0	
		 50			 75
1	50		1	75	
		 40			 48
2	90		2	123	
		 32			 36
3	122		3	159	
		 28			 24
4	150		4	183	
		 26			 22
5	176		5	205	
		 24			 20
6	200		6	225	
		 22			 13
7	222		7	238	
		 20			 10
8	242		8	248	
		 17			 7
9	259		9	255	
		 16			 5
10	275		10	260	

total utility from movies. This difference turns on the second utility concept: *marginal utility*.

Marginal Utility We define **marginal utility** as the *change* in total utility that results from a one-unit increase in the quantity of a good consumed.

In Table 8.1, the columns headed "Marginal utility" show Lisa's marginal utility from movies and pop. You can see that if Lisa increases the pop she buys from 1 to 2 cases a month, her total utility from pop increases from 75 units to 123 units. For Lisa, the marginal utility from the second case each month is 48 units (123 – 75).

The marginal utility numbers appear midway between the quantities of pop because it is the *change* in the quantity she buys from 1 to 2 cases that produces the marginal utility of 48 units.

Marginal utility is *positive,* but it *diminishes* as the quantity of a good consumed increases.

Positive Marginal Utility All the things that people enjoy and want more of have a positive marginal utility. Some objects and activities can generate negative marginal utility—and lower total utility. Two examples are hard labour and polluted air. But all the goods and services that people value and that we are thinking about here have positive marginal utility: Total utility increases as the quantity consumed increases.

Diminishing Marginal Utility As Lisa sees more movies, her total utility from movies increases but her

FIGURE 8.2   Total Utility and Marginal Utility

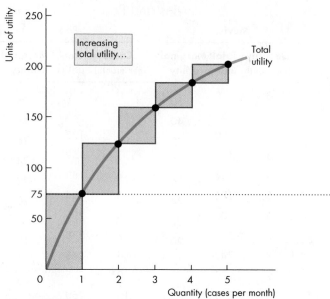

(a) Total utility

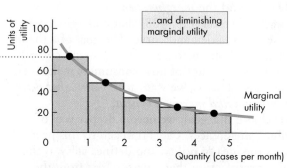

(b) Marginal utility

The figure graphs Lisa's total utility and marginal utility from pop based on the numbers for the first 5 cases of pop a month in Table 8.1. Part (a) shows her total utility—increasing total utility. The bars along the total utility curve show the extra total utility from each additional case of pop—marginal utility. Part (b) shows Lisa's diminishing marginal utility from pop.

MyEconLab   animation

marginal utility from movies decreases. Similarly, as she consumes more pop, her total utility from pop increases but her marginal utility from pop decreases.

The tendency for marginal utility to decrease as the consumption of a good increases is so general and universal that we give it the status of a *principle*—the principle of **diminishing marginal utility**.

You can see Lisa's diminishing marginal utility by calculating a few numbers. Her marginal utility from pop decreases from 75 units from the first case to 48 units from the second case and to 36 units from the third. Her marginal utility from movies decreases from 50 units for the first movie to 40 units for the second and 32 units for the third. Lisa's marginal utility diminishes as she buys more of each good.

Your Diminishing Marginal Utility You've been studying all day and into the evening, and you've been too busy finishing an assignment to shop for pop. A friend drops by with a can of pop. The utility you get from that pop is the marginal utility from your first pop of the day—from *one* can. On another day you've been on a pop binge. You've been working on an assignment, but you've guzzled 10 cans of pop while doing so, and are now totally wired. You are happy enough to have one more can, but the thrill that you get from it is not very large. It is the marginal utility from the *eleventh* can in a day.

Graphing Lisa's Utility Schedules Figure 8.2(a) illustrates Lisa's total utility from pop. The more pop Lisa consumes in a month, the more total utility she gets. Her total utility curve slopes upward.

Figure 8.2(b) illustrates Lisa's marginal utility from pop. It is a graph of the marginal utility numbers in Table 8.1. This graph shows Lisa's diminishing marginal utility from pop. Her marginal utility curve slopes downward as she consumes more pop.

We've described Lisa's consumption possibilities and preferences. Your next task is to see how Lisa chooses what to consume.

◆ REVIEW QUIZ

1   Explain how a consumer's income and the prices of goods limit consumption possibilities.
2   What is utility and how do we use the concept of utility to describe a consumer's preferences?
3   What is the distinction between total utility and marginal utility?
4   What is the key assumption about marginal utility?

You can work these questions in Study Plan 8.1 and get instant feedback.

MyEconLab ◆

Utility-Maximizing Choice

Consumers want to get the most utility possible from their limited resources. They make the choice that maximizes utility. To discover this choice, we combine the constraint imposed by the budget and the consumer's preferences and find the point on the budget line that gives the consumer the maximum attainable utility. Let's find Lisa's utility-maximizing choice.

A Spreadsheet Solution

Lisa's most direct way of finding the quantities of movies and pop that maximize her utility is to make a table in a spreadsheet with the information and calculations shown in Table 8.2. Let's see what that table tells us.

Find the Just-Affordable Combinations Table 8.2 shows the combinations of movies and pop that Lisa can afford and that exhaust her $40 income. For example, in row A, Lisa buys only pop and at $4 a case she can buy 10 cases. In row B, Lisa sees 1 movie and buys 8 cases of pop. She spends $8 on the movie. At $4 a case, she spends $32 on pop and can buy 8 cases. The combination in row B just exhausts her $40. The combinations shown in the table are the same as those plotted on her budget line in Fig. 8.1.

We noted that the budget line shows that Lisa can also afford any combination *inside* the budget line. The quantities in those combinations would be smaller than the ones shown in Table 8.2 and they do not exhaust her $40. But smaller quantities don't maximize her utility. Why? The marginal utilities of movies and pop are positive, so the more of each that Lisa buys, the more total utility she gets.

Find the Total Utility for Each Just-Affordable Combination

Table 8.2 shows the total utility that Lisa gets from the just-affordable quantities of movies and pop. The second and third columns show the numbers for movies and the fourth and fifth columns show those for pop. The centre column adds the total utility from movies to the total utility from pop. This number, the total utility from movies *and* pop, is what Lisa wants to maximize.

In row A of the table, Lisa sees no movies and buys 10 cases of pop. She gets no utility from movies and 260 units of utility from pop. Her total utility from movies and pop (the centre column) is 260 units.

TABLE 8.2   Lisa's Utility-Maximizing Choice

Movies $8		Total utility from movies and pop	Pop $4	
Quantity (per month)	Total utility		Total utility	Cases (per month)
A	0	0	260	260	10
B	1	50	298	248	8
C	2	90	315	225	6
D	3	122	305	183	4
E	4	150	273	123	2
F	5	176	176	0	0

In row C of the table, Lisa sees 2 movies and buys 6 cases of pop. She gets 90 units of utility from movies and 225 units of utility from pop. Her total utility from movies and pop is 315 units. This combination of movies and pop maximizes Lisa's total utility. That is, given the prices of movies and pop, Lisa's best choice when she has $40 to spend is to see 2 movies and buy 6 cases of pop.

If Lisa sees 1 movie, she can buy 8 cases of pop, but she gets only 298 units of total utility—17 units less than the maximum attainable. If she sees 3 movies, she can buy only 4 cases of pop. She gets 305 units of total utility—10 units less than the maximum attainable.

Consumer Equilibrium We've just described Lisa's consumer equilibrium. A **consumer equilibrium** is a situation in which a consumer has allocated all of his or her available income in the way that maximizes his or her total utility, given the prices of goods and services. Lisa's consumer equilibrium is 2 movies and 6 cases of pop.

To find Lisa's consumer equilibrium, we did something that an economist might do but that a consumer is not likely to do: We measured her total utility from all the affordable combinations of movies and pop and then, by inspection of the numbers, selected the combination that gives the highest total utility. There is a more natural way of finding a consumer's equilibrium—a way that uses the idea that choices are made at the margin, as you first met in Chapter 1. Let's look at this approach.

Choosing at the Margin

When you go shopping you don't do utility calculations. But you do decide how to allocate your budget, and you do so in a way that you think is best for you. If you could make yourself better off by spending a few more dollars on an extra unit of one item and the same number of dollars less on something else, you would make that change. So, when you've allocated your budget in the best possible way, you can't make yourself better off by spending more on one item and less on others.

Marginal Utility per Dollar Economists interpret your best possible choice by using the idea of marginal utility per dollar. *Marginal utility* is the increase in total utility that results from consuming *one more unit* of a good. **Marginal utility per dollar** is the *marginal utility* from a good that results from spending *one more dollar* on it.

The distinction between these two marginal concepts is clearest for a good that is infinitely divisible, such as gasoline. You can buy gasoline by the smallest fraction of a gallon and literally choose to spend one more or one less dollar at the pump. The increase in total utility that results from spending one more dollar at the pump is the marginal utility per dollar from gasoline. When you buy a movie ticket or a case of pop, you must spend your dollars in bigger lumps. To buy our marginal movie ticket or case of pop, you must spend the price of one unit and your total utility increases by the marginal utility from that item. So to calculate the marginal utility per dollar for movies (or pop), we must divide marginal utility from the good by its price.

Call the marginal utility from movies MU_M and the price of a movie P_M. Then the *marginal utility per dollar from movies* is

$$MU_M/P_M.$$

Call the marginal utility from pop MU_P and the price of a case of pop P_P. Then the *marginal utility per dollar from pop* is

$$MU_P/P_P.$$

By comparing the marginal utility per dollar from all the goods that a person buys, we can determine whether the budget has been allocated in the way that maximizes total utility.

Let's see how we use the marginal utility per dollar to define a utility-maximizing rule.

Utility-Maximizing Rule A consumer's total utility is maximized by following the rule:

- Spend all the available income.
- Equalize the marginal utility per dollar for all goods.

Spend All the Available Income Because more consumption brings more utility, only those choices that exhaust income can maximize utility. For Lisa, combinations of movies and pop that leave her with money to spend don't give her as much total utility as those that exhaust her $40 per month income.

Equalize the Marginal Utility per Dollar The basic idea behind this rule is to move dollars to good A from good B if doing so increases the utility from good A by more than it decreases the utility from good B. Such a utility-increasing move is possible if the marginal utility per dollar from good A exceeds that from good B.

But buying more of good A decreases its marginal utility. And buying less of good B increases its marginal utility. So by moving dollars from good A to good B, total utility rises, but the gap between the marginal utilities per dollar gets smaller.

As long as the gap exists—as long as the marginal utility per dollar from good A exceeds that from good B—total utility can be increased by spending more on A and less on B. But when enough dollars have been moved from B to A to make the two marginal utilities per dollar equal, total utility cannot be increased further. Total utility is maximized.

Lisa's Marginal Calculation Let's apply the basic idea to Lisa. To calculate Lisa's marginal utility per dollar, we divide her marginal utility numbers for each quantity of each good by the price of the good. The table in Fig. 8.3 shows these calculations for Lisa, and the graph illustrates the situation on Lisa's budget line. The rows of the table are three of her affordable combinations of movies and pop.

Too Much Pop and Too Few Movies In row B, Lisa sees 1 movie a month and consumes 8 cases of pop a month. Her marginal utility from seeing 1 movie a month is 50 units. Because the price of a movie is $8, Lisa's marginal utility per dollar from movies is 50 units divided by $8, or 6.25 units of utility per dollar.

Lisa's marginal utility from pop when she consumes 8 cases of pop a month is 10 units. Because the price of pop is $4 a case, Lisa's marginal utility per dollar from pop is 10 units divided by $4, or 2.50 units of utility per dollar.

When Lisa sees 1 movie and consumes 8 cases of pop a month, her marginal utility per dollar from pop is *less than* her marginal utility per dollar from movies. That is,

$$MU_P/P_P < MU_M/P_M.$$

If Lisa spent an extra dollar on movies and a dollar less on pop, her total utility would increase. She would get 6.25 units from the extra dollar spent on movies and lose 2.50 units from the dollar less spent on pop. Her total utility would increase by 3.75 units (6.25 – 2.50).

Too Little Pop and Too Many Movies In row *D*, Lisa sees 3 movies a month and consumes 4 cases of pop. Her marginal utility from seeing the third movie a month is 32 units. At a price of $8 a movie, Lisa's marginal utility per dollar from movies is 32 units divided by $8, or 4 units of utility per dollar.

Lisa's marginal utility from pop when she buys 4 cases a month is 24 units. At a price of $4 a case, Lisa's marginal utility per dollar from pop is 24 units divided by $4, or 6 units of utility per dollar.

When Lisa sees 3 movies and consumes 4 cases of pop a month, her marginal utility from pop *exceeds* her marginal utility from movies. That is,

$$MU_P/P_P > MU_M/P_M.$$

If Lisa spent an extra dollar on pop and a dollar less on movies, her total utility would increase. She would get 6 units from the extra dollar spent on pop and she would lose 4 units from the dollar less spent on movies. Her total utility would increase by 2 units (6 – 4).

Utility-Maximizing Movies and Pop In Fig. 8.3, if Lisa moves from row *B* to row *C*, she increases the movies she sees from 1 to 2 a month and decreases the pop she consumes from 8 to 6 cases a month. Her marginal utility per dollar from movies falls to 5 and her marginal utility per dollar from pop rises to 5.

Similarly, if Lisa moves from row *D* to row *C*, she decreases the movies she sees from 3 to 2 a month and increases the pop she consumes from 4 to 6 cases a month. Her marginal utility per dollar from movies rises to 5 and her marginal utility per dollar from pop falls to 5.

When Lisa sees 2 movies and consumes 6 cases of pop a month, her marginal utility per dollar from

pop *equals* her marginal utility per dollar from movies. That is,

$$MU_P/P_P = MU_M/P_M.$$

Lisa can't move from this allocation of her budget without making herself worse off.

FIGURE 8.3   Equalizing Marginal Utilities per Dollar

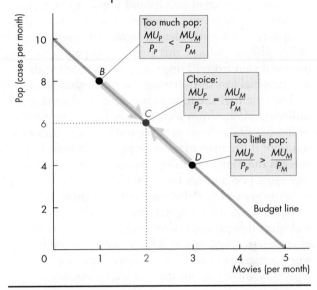

	Movies ($8 each)			Pop ($4 per case)		
	Quantity	Marginal utility	Marginal utility per dollar	Cases	Marginal utility	Marginal utility per dollar
B	1	50	6.25	8	10	2.50
C	2	40	5.00	6	20	5.00
D	3	32	4.00	4	24	6.00

The graph shows Lisa's budget line and identifies three points on it. The rows of the table describe these points.

At point *B* (row *B*), with 1 movie and 8 cases of pop, Lisa's marginal utility per dollar from pop is less than that from movies: Buy less pop and see more movies.

At point *D* (row *D*), with 3 movies and 4 cases of pop, Lisa's marginal utility per dollar from pop is greater than that from movies: Buy more pop and see fewer movies.

At point *C* (row *C*), with 2 movies and 6 cases of pop, Lisa's marginal utility per dollar from pop is equal to that from movies: Lisa's utility is maximized.

MyEconLab   animation

The Power of Marginal Analysis

The method we've just used to find Lisa's utility-maximizing choice of movies and pop is an example of the power of marginal analysis. Lisa doesn't need a computer and a spreadsheet program to maximize utility. She can achieve this goal by comparing the marginal gain from having more of one good with the marginal loss from having less of another good.

The rule that she follows is simple: If the marginal utility per dollar from movies exceeds the marginal utility per dollar from pop, see more movies and buy less pop; if the marginal utility per dollar from pop exceeds the marginal utility per dollar from movies, buy more pop and see fewer movies.

More generally, if the marginal gain from an action exceeds the marginal loss, take the action. You will meet this principle time and again in your study of economics, and you will find yourself using it when you make your own economic choices, especially when you must make big decisions.

Revealing Preferences

When we introduced the idea of utility, we arbitrarily chose 50 units as Lisa's total utility from 1 movie, and we pretended that we asked Lisa to tell us how many units of utility she got from different quantities of pop and movies.

You're now about to discover that we don't need to ask Lisa to tell us her preferences. We can figure them out for ourselves by observing what she buys at various prices.

Also, the units in which we measure Lisa's preferences don't matter. Any arbitrary units will work. In this respect, utility is like temperature. Predictions about the freezing point of water don't depend on the temperature scale; and predictions about a household's consumption choice don't depend on the units of utility.

Lisa's Preferences In maximizing total utility by making the marginal utility per dollar equal for all goods, the units in which utility is measured do not matter.

You've seen that when Lisa maximizes her total utility, her marginal utility per dollar from pop, MU_P/P_P, equals her marginal utility per dollar from movies, MU_M/P_M. That is,

$$MU_P/P_P = MU_M/P_M.$$

Multiply both sides of this equation by the price of pop, P_P, to obtain

$$MU_P = MU_M \times (P_P/P_M).$$

This equation says that the marginal utility from pop, MU_P, is equal to the marginal utility from movies, MU_M, multiplied by the ratio of the price of pop, P_P, to the price of a movie, P_M.

The ratio P_P/P_M is the relative price of pop in terms of movies: It is the number of movies that must be forgone to get 1 case of pop. It is also the opportunity cost of pop. (See Chapter 2, p. 31 and Chapter 3, p. 56.)

For Lisa, when $P_M = \$8$ and $P_P = \$4$ we observe that in a month she goes to the movies twice and buys 6 cases of pop. So we know that her MU_P from 6 cases of pop equals her MU_M from 2 movies multiplied by $\$4/\$8$, or 0.5. That is, for Lisa, the marginal utility from 6 cases of pop equals one-half of the marginal utility from 2 movies.

If we observe the choices that Lisa makes at more prices, we can find more rows in her utility schedule. By her choices, Lisa reveals her preferences.

Units of Utility Don't Matter Lisa's marginal utility from 2 movies is half of her marginal utility from 6 cases of pop. So if the marginal utility from the second movie is 40 units, then the marginal utility from the sixth case of pop is 20 units. But if we call the marginal utility from the second movie 50 units, then the marginal utility from the sixth case of pop is 25 units. The units of utility are arbitrary.

 REVIEW QUIZ

1 Why does a consumer spend the entire budget?
2 What is the marginal utility per dollar and how is it calculated?
3 What two conditions are met when a consumer is maximizing utility?
4 Explain why equalizing the marginal utility per dollar for all goods maximizes utility.

You can work these questions in Study Plan 8.2 and get instant feedback.

——————————————————— MyEconLab ◆

You now understand the marginal utility theory of consumer choices. Your next task is to see what the theory predicts.

Predictions of Marginal Utility Theory

We're now going to use marginal utility theory to make some predictions. You will see that marginal utility theory predicts the law of demand. The theory also predicts that a fall in the price of a substitute of a good decreases the demand for the good and that for a normal good, a rise in income increases demand. All these effects, which in Chapter 3 we simply assumed, are predictions of marginal utility theory.

To derive these predictions, we will study the effects of three events:

- A fall in the price of a movie
- A rise in the price of pop
- A rise in income

A Fall in the Price of a Movie

With the price of a movie at $8 and the price of pop at $4, Lisa is maximizing utility by seeing 2 movies and buying 6 cases of pop each month. Then, with no change in her $40 income and no change in the price of pop, the price of a movie falls from $8 to $4. How does Lisa change her buying plans?

Finding the New Quantities of Movies and Pop You can find the effect of a fall in the price of a movie on the quantities of movies and pop that Lisa buys in a three-step calculation.

1. Determine the just-affordable combinations of movies and pop at the new prices.
2. Calculate the new marginal utilities per dollar from the good whose price has changed.
3. Determine the quantities of movies and pop that make their marginal utilities per dollar equal.

Affordable Combinations The lower price of a movie means that Lisa can afford more movies or more pop. Table 8.3 shows her new affordable combinations. In row *A*, if she continues to see 2 movies a month, she can now afford 8 cases of pop, and in row *B*, if she continues to buy 6 cases of pop, she can now afford 4 movies. Lisa can afford any of the combinations shown in the rows of Table 8.3.

The next step is to find her new marginal utilities per dollar from movies.

New Marginal Utilities per Dollar from Movies A person's preferences don't change just because a price has changed. With no change in her preferences, Lisa's marginal utilities in Table 8.3 are the same as those in Table 8.1. But because the price of a movie has changed, the marginal utility *per dollar* from movies changes. In fact, with a halving of the price of a movie from $8 to $4, the marginal utility per dollar from movies has doubled.

The numbers in Table 8.3 show Lisa's new marginal utility per dollar from movies for each quantity of movies. The table also shows Lisa's marginal utility per dollar from pop for each quantity.

Equalizing the Marginal Utilities per Dollar You can see that if Lisa continues to see 2 movies a month and buy 6 cases of pop, her marginal utility per dollar from movies (row *A*) is 10 units and her marginal utility per dollar from pop (row *B*) is 5 units. Lisa is buying too much pop and too few movies. If she spends a dollar more on movies and a dollar less on pop, her total utility increases by 5 units (10 − 5).

If Lisa continues to buy 6 cases of pop and increases the number of movies to 4 (row *B*), her

---

TABLE 8.3 How a Change in the Price of Movies Affects Lisa's Choices

	Movies ($4 each)			Pop ($4 per case)		
	Quantity	Marginal utility	Marginal utility per dollar	Cases	Marginal utility	Marginal utility per dollar
	0	0		10	5	1.25
	1	50	12.50	9	7	1.75
A	2	40	**10.00**	8	10	2.50
	3	32	8.00	7	13	3.25
B	4	28	7.00	**6**	20	**5.00**
	5	26	6.50	5	22	5.50
C	6	24	**6.00**	4	24	6.00
	7	22	5.50	3	36	9.00
	8	20	5.00	2	48	12.00
	9	17	4.25	1	75	18.75
	10	16	4.00	0	0	

marginal utility per dollar from movies falls to 7 units, but her marginal utility per dollar from pop is 5 units. Lisa is still buying too much pop and seeing too few movies. If she spends a dollar more on movies and a dollar less on pop, her total utility increases by 2 units (7 − 5).

But if Lisa sees 6 movies and buys 4 cases of pop a month (row *C*), her marginal utility per dollar from movies (6 units) equals her marginal utility per dollar from pop and she is maximizing utility. If Lisa moves from this allocation of her budget in either direction, her total utility decreases.

Lisa's increased purchases of movies results from a substitution effect—she substitutes the now lower-priced movies for pop—and an income effect—she can afford more movies.

A Change in the Quantity Demanded Lisa's increase in the quantity of movies that she sees is a change in the quantity demanded. It is the change in the quantity of movies that she plans to see each month when the price of a movie changes and all other influences on buying plans remain the same. We illustrate a change in the quantity demanded by a movement along a demand curve.

Figure 8.4(a) shows Lisa's demand curve for movies. When the price of a movie is $8, Lisa sees 2 movies a month. When the price of a movie falls to $4, she sees 6 movies a month. Lisa moves downward along her demand curve for movies.

The demand curve traces the quantities that maximize utility at each price, with all other influences remaining the same. You can also see that utility-maximizing choices generate a downward-sloping demand curve. Utility maximization with diminishing marginal utility implies the law of demand.

A Change in Demand The decrease in the quantity of pop that Lisa buys is the change in the quantity of pop that she plans to buy at a given price of pop when the price of a movie changes. It is a change in her demand for pop. We illustrate a change in demand by a shift of a demand curve.

Figure 8.4(b) shows Lisa's demand curve for pop. The price of pop is fixed at $4 a case. When the price of a movie is $8, Lisa buys 6 cases of pop on demand curve D_0. When the price of a movie falls to $4, Lisa buys 4 cases of pop on demand curve D_1. The fall in the price of a movie decreases Lisa's demand for pop. Her demand curve for pop shifts leftward. For Lisa, pop and movies are substitutes.

FIGURE 8.4   A Fall in the Price of a Movie

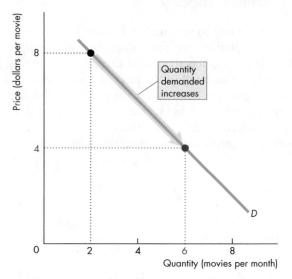

(a) Demand for movies

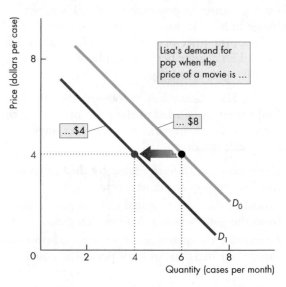

(b) Demand for pop

When the price of a movie falls and the price of pop remains the same, the quantity of movies demanded by Lisa increases, and in part (a), Lisa moves along her demand curve for movies. Also, when the price of a movie falls, Lisa's demand for pop decreases, and in part (b), her demand curve for pop shifts leftward. For Lisa, pop and movies are substitutes.

A Rise in the Price of Pop

Now suppose that with the price of a movie at $4, the price of pop rises from $4 to $8 a case. How does this price change influence Lisa's buying plans? We find the answer by repeating the three-step calculation with the new price of pop.

Table 8.4 shows Lisa's new affordable combinations. In row *A*, if she continues to buy 4 cases of pop a month, she can afford to see only 2 movies; and in row *B*, if she continues to see 6 movies a month, she can afford only 2 cases of pop.

Table 8.4 shows Lisa's marginal utility per dollar from pop for each quantity of pop when the price is $8 a case. The table also shows Lisa's marginal utility per dollar from movies for each quantity.

If Lisa continues to buy 4 cases of pop (row *A*), her marginal utility per dollar from pop is 3. But she must cut the movies she sees to 2, which increases her marginal utility per dollar from movies to 10. Lisa is buying too much pop and too few movies. If she spends a dollar less on pop and a dollar more on movies, her utility increases by 7 units (10 − 3).

But if Lisa sees 6 movies a month and cuts her pop to 2 cases (row *B*), her marginal utility per dollar from movies (6 units) equals her marginal utility per dollar from pop. She is maximizing utility.

Lisa's decreased purchases of pop result from an income effect—she can afford fewer cases and she buys fewer cases. But she continues to buy the same quantity of movies.

Lisa's Demand for Pop   Now that we've calculated the effect of a change in the price of pop on Lisa's buying plans when income and the price of movies remain the same, we have found two points on her demand curve for pop: When the price of pop is $4 a case, Lisa buys 4 cases a month; and when the price of pop is $8 a case, she buys 2 cases a month.

Figure 8.5 shows these points on Lisa's demand curve for pop. It also shows the change in the quantity of pop demanded when the price of pop rises and all other influences on Lisa's buying plans remain the same.

In this example, Lisa continues to buy the same quantity of movies, but this outcome does not always occur. It is a consequence of Lisa's preferences. With different marginal utilities, she might have decreased or increased the quantity of movies that she sees when the price of pop changes.

You've seen that marginal utility theory predicts the law of demand—the way in which the quantity demanded of a good changes when its price changes. Next, we'll see how marginal utility theory predicts the effect of a change in income on demand.

TABLE 8.4   How a Change in the Price of Pop Affects Lisa's Choices

	Movies ($4 each)			Pop ($8 per case)		
	Quantity	Marginal utility	Marginal utility per dollar	Cases	Marginal utility	Marginal utility per dollar
	0	0		5	22	2.75
A	2	40	10.00	**4**	24	**3.00**
	4	28	7.00	3	36	4.50
B	6	24	6.00	**2**	48	**6.00**
	8	20	5.00	1	75	9.38
	10	16	4.00	0	0	

FIGURE 8.5   A Rise in the Price of Pop

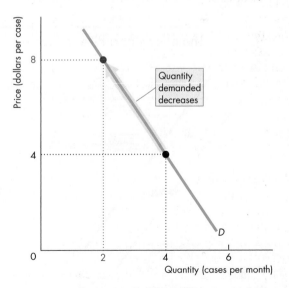

When the price of pop rises and the price of a movie and Lisa's income remain the same, the quantity of pop demanded by Lisa decreases. Lisa moves along her demand curve for pop.

A Rise in Income

Suppose that Lisa's income increases from $40 to $56 a month and that the price of a movie is $4 and the price of pop is $4 a case. With these prices and with an income of $40 a month, Lisa sees 6 movies and buys 4 cases of pop a month (Table 8.3). How does the increase in Lisa's income from $40 to $56 change her buying plans?

Table 8.5 shows the calculations needed to answer this question. If Lisa continues to see 6 movies a month, she can now afford to buy 8 cases of pop (row *A*); if she continues to buy 4 cases of pop, she can now afford to see 10 movies (row *C*).

In row *A*, Lisa's marginal utility per dollar from movies is greater than her marginal utility per dollar from pop. She is buying too much pop and too few movies. In row *C*, Lisa's marginal utility per dollar from movies is less than her marginal utility per dollar from pop. She is buying too little pop and too many movies. But in row *B*, when Lisa sees 8 movies a month and buys 6 cases of pop, her marginal utility per dollar from movies equals that from pop. She is maximizing utility.

Figure 8.6 shows the effects of the rise in Lisa's income on her demand curves for movies and pop. The price of each good is $4. When Lisa's income

TABLE 8.5   Lisa's Choices with an Income of $56 a Month

		Movies ($4 each)			Pop ($4 per case)	
	Quantity	Marginal utility	Marginal utility per dollar	Cases	Marginal utility	Marginal utility per dollar
	4	28	7.00	10	5	1.25
	5	26	6.50	9	7	1.75
A	6	24	**6.00**	8	10	2.50
	7	22	5.50	7	13	3.25
B	8	20	**5.00**	6	20	**5.00**
	9	17	4.25	5	22	5.50
C	10	16	**4.00**	4	24	**6.00**

rises to $56 a month, she sees 2 more movies and buys 2 more cases of pop. Her demand curves for both movies and pop shift rightward—her demand for both movies and pop increases. With a larger income, the consumer always buys more of a *normal* good. For Lisa, movies and pop are normal goods.

FIGURE 8.6   The Effects of a Rise in Income

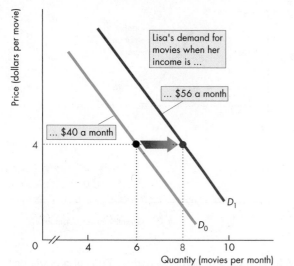

(a) Demand for movies

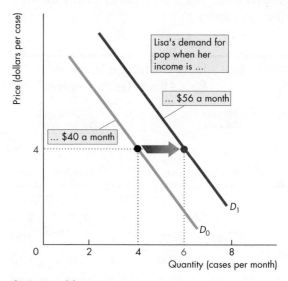

(b) Demand for pop

When Lisa's income increases, her demand for movies and her demand for pop increase. Lisa's demand curves for

movies, in part (a), and for pop, in part (b), shift rightward. For Lisa, movies and pop are normal goods.

The Paradox of Value

The price of water is low and the price of a diamond is high, but water is essential to life while diamonds are used mostly for decoration. How can valuable water be so cheap while a relatively useless diamond is so expensive? This so-called *paradox of value* has puzzled philosophers for centuries. Not until the theory of marginal utility had been developed could anyone give a satisfactory answer.

The Paradox Resolved The paradox is resolved by distinguishing between *total* utility and *marginal* utility. The total utility that we get from water is enormous. But remember, the more we consume of something, the smaller is its marginal utility.

We use so much water that its marginal utility—the benefit we get from one more glass of water or another 30 seconds in the shower—diminishes to a small value.

Diamonds, on the other hand, have a small total utility relative to water, but because we buy few diamonds, they have a high marginal utility.

When a household has maximized its total utility, it has allocated its income in the way that makes the marginal utility per dollar equal for all goods. That is, the marginal utility from a good divided by the price of the good is equal for all goods.

This equality of marginal utilities per dollar holds true for diamonds and water: Diamonds have a high price and a high marginal utility. Water has a low price and a low marginal utility. When the high marginal utility from diamonds is divided by the high price of a diamond, the result is a number that equals the low marginal utility from water divided by the low price of water. The marginal utility per dollar is the same for diamonds and water.

Value and Consumer Surplus Another way to think about the paradox of value and illustrate how it is resolved uses *consumer surplus*. Figure 8.7 explains the paradox of value by using this idea. The supply of water in part (a) is perfectly elastic at price P_W, so the quantity of water consumed is Q_W and the large green area shows the consumer surplus from water. The supply of diamonds in part (b) is perfectly inelastic at the quantity Q_D, so the price of a diamond is P_D and the small green area shows the consumer surplus from diamonds. Water is cheap, but brings a large consumer surplus; diamonds are expensive, but bring a small consumer surplus.

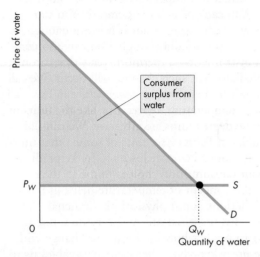

FIGURE 8.7   The Paradox of Value

(a) Water

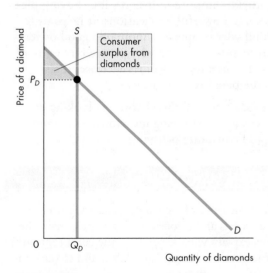

(b) Diamonds

Part (a) shows the demand for and supply of water. Supply is perfectly elastic at the price P_W. At this price, the quantity of water consumed is Q_W and the large green triangle shows consumer surplus. Part (b) shows the demand for and supply of diamonds. Supply is perfectly inelastic at the quantity Q_D. At this quantity, the price of a diamond is P_D and the small green triangle shows consumer surplus. Water is valuable—has a large consumer surplus—but cheap. Diamonds are less valuable than water—have a smaller consumer surplus—but are expensive.

MyEconLab   animation

Temperature: An Analogy

Utility is similar to temperature—both are abstract concepts. You can't *observe* temperature. You can observe water turning to steam if it is hot enough or turning to ice if it is cold enough. You can also construct an instrument—a thermometer—that can help you to predict when such changes will occur. We call the scale on the thermometer *temperature* and we call the units of temperature *degrees*. But like the units of utility, these degree units are arbitrary. We can use Celsius units or Fahrenheit units or some other units.

The concept of utility helps us to make predictions about consumption choices in much the same way that the concept of temperature helps us to make predictions about physical phenomena.

Admittedly, marginal utility theory does not enable us to predict how buying plans change with the same precision that a thermometer enables us to predict when water will turn to ice or steam. But the theory provides important insights into buying plans and has some powerful implications. It helps us to understand why people buy more of a good or service when its price falls and why people buy more of most goods when their incomes increase. It also resolves the paradox of value.

We're going to end this chapter by looking at some new ways of studying individual economic choices and consumer behaviour.

◆ REVIEW QUIZ

1   When the price of a good falls and the prices of other goods and a consumer's income remain the same, explain what happens to the consumption of the good whose price has fallen and to the consumption of other goods.

2   Elaborate on your answer to the previous question by using demand curves. For which good does demand change and for which good does the quantity demanded change?

3   If a consumer's income increases and if all goods are normal goods, explain how the quantity bought of each good changes.

4   What is the paradox of value and how is the paradox resolved?

5   What are the similarities between utility and temperature?

You can work these questions in Study Plan 8.3 and get instant feedback.

———————————————— MyEconLab ◆

Economics in Action

Maximizing Utility from Recorded Music

In 2010, total expenditure on recorded music was $6.9 billion, down from $14 billion in 2000. But the combined quantity of discs and downloads bought increased from 1 billion in 2000 to 1.7 billion in 2010 and the average price of a unit of recorded music fell from $14 to $4.

The average price fell because the mix of formats bought changed dramatically. In 2000, we bought 940 million CDs; in 2010, we bought only 225 million CDs and downloaded 1.3 billion music files.

Figure 1 shows the longer history of the changing formats of recorded music.

The music that we buy isn't just one good—it is several goods. Singles and albums are different goods; downloads and discs are different goods; and downloads to a computer and downloads to a cell phone are different goods. There are three major categories and the table shows the quantities of each that we bought in 2010.

Format	Singles	Albums
	(millions in 2010)	
Disc	1.5	225
Download	1,162	83
Mobile	220	–

Source of data: Recording Industry Association of America.

Most people buy all their music in digital form, but many still buy physical CDs and some people buy both downloads and CDs.

We get utility from the singles and albums that we buy, and the more songs and albums we have, the more utility we get. But our marginal utility from songs and albums decreases as the quantity that we own increases.

We also get utility from convenience. A song that we can buy with a mouse click and play with the spin of a wheel is more convenient both to buy and to use than a song on a CD. The convenience of songs downloaded over the Internet means that, song for song, we get more utility from a song downloaded than we get from a song on a physical CD.

But most albums are still played at home on a CD player. So for most people, a physical CD is a more convenient medium for delivering an album. Album for album, people on average get more utility from a CD than from a download.

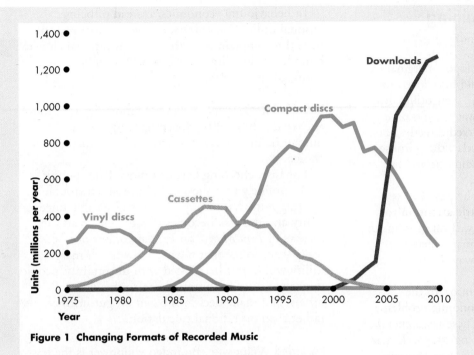

Figure 1 Changing Formats of Recorded Music

In the 1970s, recorded music came on vinyl discs. Cassettes gradually replaced vinyl, then compact discs (CDs) gradually replaced cassettes, and today, digital files downloaded to computers and mobile devices are replacing physical CDs.

When we decide how many singles and albums to download and how many to buy on CD, we compare the marginal utility per dollar from each type of music in each format. We make the marginal utility per dollar from each type of music in each format equal, as the equations below show.

The market for single downloads has created an enormous consumer surplus. The table shows that the quantity of single downloads demanded at 99¢ each was 1,162 million in 2010, and the quantity of singles on a disc demanded at $4.75 a disc was 1.5 million in 2010. If we assume that $4.75 is the most that anyone would pay for a single download (probably an underestimate), the demand curve for single downloads is that shown in Fig. 2.

With the price of a single download at $0.99, consumer surplus (the area of the green triangle in Fig. 2) is $1.5 billion.

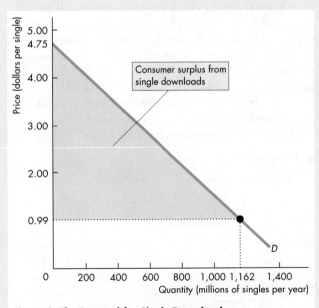

Figure 2 The Demand for Single Downloads

$$\frac{MU_{single\ downloads}}{P_{single\ downloads}} = \frac{MU_{album\ downloads}}{P_{album\ downloads}} = \frac{MU_{physical\ singles}}{P_{physical\ singles}} = \frac{MU_{physical\ albums}}{P_{physical\ albums}} = \frac{MU_{mobile}}{P_{mobile}}$$

$$\frac{MU_{single\ downloads}}{\$0.99} = \frac{MU_{album\ downloads}}{\$10} = \frac{MU_{physical\ singles}}{\$4.75} = \frac{MU_{physical\ albums}}{\$15} = \frac{MU_{mobile}}{\$2.50}$$

◆ New Ways of Explaining Consumer Choices

When William Stanley Jevons developed marginal utility theory in the 1860s, he would have loved to look inside people's brains and "see" their utility. But he believed that the human brain was the ultimate black box that could never be observed directly. For Jevons, and for most economists today, the purpose of marginal utility theory is to explain our *actions*, not what goes on inside our brains.

Economics has developed over the past 150 years with little help from and paying little attention to advances being made in psychology. Both economics and psychology seek to explain human behaviour, but they have developed different ways of attacking the challenge.

A few researchers *have* paid attention to the potential payoff from exploring economic problems by using the tools of psychology. These researchers, some economists and some psychologists, think that marginal utility theory is based on a view of how people make choices that attributes too much to reason and rationality. They propose an alternative approach based on the methods of psychology.

Other researchers, some economists and some neuroscientists, are using new tools to look inside the human brain and open up Jevons' "black box."

This section provides a very brief introduction to these new and exciting areas of economics. We'll explore the two related research agendas:

- Behavioural economics
- Neuroeconomics

Behavioural Economics

Behavioural economics studies the ways in which limits on the human brain's ability to compute and implement rational decisions influence economic behaviour—both the decisions that people make and the consequences of those decisions for the way markets work.

Behavioural economics starts with observed behaviour. It looks for anomalies—choices that do not seem to be rational. It then tries to account for the anomalies by using ideas developed by psychologists that emphasize features of the human brain that limit rational choice.

In behavioural economics, instead of being rational utility maximizers, people are assumed to have three impediments that prevent rational choice: bounded rationality, bounded willpower, and bounded self-interest.

Bounded Rationality Bounded rationality is rationality that is limited by the computing power of the human brain. We can't always work out the rational choice.

For Lisa, choosing between movies and pop, it seems unlikely that she would have much trouble figuring out what to buy. But toss Lisa some uncertainty and the task becomes harder. She's read the reviews of *Iron Man 2* on Fandango, but does she really want to see that movie? How much marginal utility will it give her? Faced with uncertainty, people might use rules of thumb, listen to the views of others, and make decisions based on gut instinct rather than on rational calculation.

Bounded Willpower Bounded willpower is the less-than-perfect willpower that prevents us from making a decision that we know, at the time of implementing the decision, we will later regret.

Lisa might be feeling particularly thirsty when she passes a pop vending machine. Under Lisa's rational utility-maximizing plan, she buys her pop at the discount store, where she gets it for the lowest possible price. Lisa has already bought her pop for this month, but it is at home. Spending $1 on a can now means giving up a movie later this month.

Lisa's rational choice is to ignore the temporary thirst and stick to her plan. But she might not possess the willpower to do so—sometimes she will and sometimes she won't.

Bounded Self-Interest Bounded self-interest is the limited self-interest that results in sometimes suppressing our own interests to help others.

A hurricane hits the Florida coast and Lisa, feeling sorry for the victims, donates $10 to a fund-raiser. She now has only $30 to spend on movies and pop this month. The quantities that she buys are not, according to her utility schedule, the ones that maximize her utility.

The main applications of behavioural economics are in two areas: finance, where uncertainty is a key factor in decision making, and savings, where the future is a key factor. But one behaviour observed by behavioural economists is more general and might affect your choices. It is called the endowment effect.

The Endowment Effect   The endowment effect is the tendency for people to value something more highly simply because they own it. If you have allocated your income to maximize utility, then the price you would be willing to accept to give up something that you own (for example, your coffee mug) should be the same as the price you are willing to pay for an identical one.

In experiments, students seem to display the endowment effect: The price they are willing to pay for a coffee mug that is identical to the one they own is less than the price they would be willing to accept to give up the coffee mug that they own. Behavioural economists say that this behaviour contradicts marginal utility theory.

Neuroeconomics

Neuroeconomics is the study of the activity of the human brain when a person makes an economic decision. The discipline uses the observational tools and ideas of neuroscience to obtain a better understanding of economic decisions.

Neuroeconomics is an experimental discipline. In an experiment, a person makes an economic decision and the electrical or chemical activity of the person's brain is observed and recorded using the same type of equipment that neurosurgeons use to diagnose brain disorders.

The observations provide information about which regions of the brain are active at different points in the process of making an economic decision.

Observations show that some economic decisions generate activity in the area of the brain (called the prefrontal cortex) where we store memories, analyse data, and anticipate the consequences of our actions. If people make rational utility-maximizing decisions, it is in this region of the brain that the decision occurs.

But observations also show that some economic decisions generate activity in the region of the brain (called the hippocampus) where we store memories of anxiety and fear. Decisions that are influenced by activity in this part of the brain might not be rational and might be driven by fear or panic.

Neuroeconomists are also able to observe the amount of a brain hormone (called dopamine), the quantity of which increases in response to pleasurable events and decreases in response to disappointing events. These observations might one day enable neuroeconomists to actually measure utility and shine a bright light inside what was once believed to be the ultimate black box.

Controversy

The new ways of studying consumer choice that we've briefly described here are being used more widely to study business decisions and decisions in financial markets, and this type of research is surely going to become more popular.

But behavioural economics and neuroeconomics generate controversy. Most economists hold the view of Jevons that the goal of economics is to explain the decisions that we observe people making and not to explain what goes on inside people's heads.

Most economists would prefer to probe apparent anomalies more deeply and figure out why they are not anomalies after all.

Economists also point to the power of marginal utility theory and its ability to explain consumer choice and demand as well as resolve the paradox of value.

REVIEW QUIZ

1   Define behavioural economics.
2   What are the three limitations on human rationality that behavioural economics emphasizes?
3   Define neuroeconomics.
4   What do behavioural economics and neuroeconomics seek to achieve?

You can work these questions in Study Plan 8.4 and get instant feedback.
─────────────── MyEconLab ◆

◆   You have now completed your study of marginal utility theory and some new ideas about how people make economic choices. You can see marginal utility theory in action once again in *Reading Between the Lines* on pp. 196–197, where it is used to explain why nurses who save people's lives earn so much less than hockey players who merely provide entertainment.

A Paradox of Value: Nurses and Hockey Players

Nurses Blast McGuinty for Two-Tier Pay Scale

Toronto Star
September 2, 2010

Thousands of Ontario nurses who work at some non-unionized hospitals complain they're getting the cold shoulder from Premier Dalton McGuinty's public sector pay freeze. ...

While 50,000 unionized nurses at dozens of hospitals got 3 per cent raises April 1 as previously negotiated by their Ontario Nurses' Association union, the traditional matching raises never came for several thousand nurses at other hospitals. ...

"We've always been paid the same. This will cost us big money," said Julia Fisher, day surgery nurse at Trillium with 34 years of experience.

At the current rate of $40.65 hourly, a 3 per cent raise would bring an extra $49 for a 40-hour week or $2,537 annually. ...

Reprinted with permission—Torstar Syndication Services.

Kesler Was To Be Restricted Free Agent

sports.espn.go.com
March 19, 2010

Canucks centre Ryan Kesler signed a six-year, $30 million [U.S] contract extension Friday that will keep him in Vancouver through the 2015–16 season.

In his sixth season with the Canucks, the 25-year-old Kesler already has set a new career high with 66 points in 71 games, exceeding the 59 points he recorded last season, when he was a Selke Trophy finalist as the NHL's top defensive forward.

"Ryan Kesler has excelled as a two-way player and in his role as an alternate captain," general manager Mike Gillis said in a statement. "Ryan has showcased his ability to perform under extreme pressure and we are looking forward to continuing to see Ryan develop into one of the League's premier players."

Associated Press, 2010

ESSENCE OF THE STORIES

- In Ontario, nurses earn $40.65 per hour.

- Ryan Kesler has a 5-year contract with the Canucks that will earn him $30 million (U.S.).

- If resources are used efficiently, the marginal utility per dollar from the services of a nurse, MU_N/P_N, equals the marginal utility per dollar from the services of a hockey player, MU_H/P_H. That is,

$$\frac{MU_N}{P_N} = \frac{MU_H}{P_H}.$$

- A nurse in Ontario earns $40.65 an hour, which for a year of 40-hour weeks is $84,552.

- Ryan Kesler earns $30 million over 6 years, or $5 million a year.

- If we put these numbers into the above formula, we get

$$\frac{MU_N}{\$84,552} = \frac{MU_H}{\$5,000,000}.$$

Equivalently,

$$\frac{MU_H}{MU_N} = 59.$$

- Is the marginal utility from Ryan Kesler's services really 59 times that from a nurse's services?

- The answer is no. A nurse might serve about 40 people a day, or perhaps 10,000 in a year; a hockey player like Ryan Kesler serves millions of people a year.

- If a nurse serves 10,000 people a year, then the price of a nurse's service per customer is $84,552/10,000, which equals $8.46.

- If Ryan Kesler serves 2,000,000 people a year, then the price of his service per customer is $5,000,000/2,000,000, which equals $2.50.

- Using these prices of the services per customer, a nurse is worth 3.4 times as much as a hockey player—the marginal utility from the services of a nurse is 3.4 times that from a hockey player.

- Figure 1 shows the market for nurses. The equilibrium quantity is 100,000 workers, and the wage rate is $84,552 a year.

- Figure 2 shows the market for professional hockey players. The equilibrium quantity is 750 players and the average wage rate is $2,000,000 a year. (Ryan Kesler earns more than the average player.)

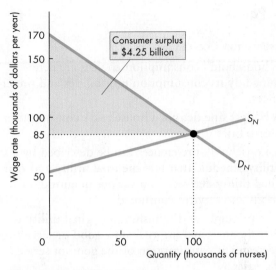

Figure 1 The Value of Nurses

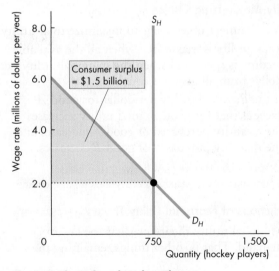

Figure 2 The Value of Hockey Players

- Not only is the marginal utility from a nurse greater than that from a hockey player, but nurses also create a greater consumer surplus.

SUMMARY

Key Points

Consumption Choices (pp. 180–182)

- A household's consumption choices are determined by its consumption possibilities and preferences.
- A budget line defines a household's consumption possibilities.
- A household's preferences can be described by a utility schedule that lists the total utility and marginal utility derived from various quantities of goods and services consumed.
- The principle of diminishing marginal utility is that the marginal utility from a good or service decreases as consumption of the good or service increases.

Working Problems 1 to 7 will give you a better understanding of consumption choices.

Utility-Maximizing Choice (pp. 183–186)

- A consumer's objective is to maximize total utility.
- Total utility is maximized when all the available income is spent and when the marginal utility per dollar from all goods is equal.
- If the marginal utility per dollar for good *A* exceeds that for good *B*, total utility increases if the quantity purchased of good *A* increases and the quantity purchased of good *B* decreases.

Working Problems 8 to 13 will give you a better understanding of a consumer's utility-maximizing choice.

Predictions of Marginal Utility Theory (pp. 187–193)

- Marginal utility theory predicts the law of demand. That is, other things remaining the

same, the higher the price of a good, the smaller is the quantity demanded of that good.
- Marginal utility theory also predicts that, other things remaining the same, an increase in the consumer's income increases the demand for a normal good.
- Marginal utility theory resolves the paradox of value.
- Total value is *total* utility or consumer surplus. But price is related to *marginal* utility.
- Water, which we consume in large amounts, has a high total utility and a large consumer surplus, but the price of water is low and the marginal utility from water is low.
- Diamonds, which we buy in small quantities, have a low total utility and a small consumer surplus, but the price of a diamond is high and the marginal utility from diamonds is high.

Working Problems 14 to 21 will give you a better understanding of the predictions of marginal utility theory.

New Ways of Explaining Consumer Choices (pp. 194–195)

- Behavioural economics studies limits on the ability of the human brain to compute and implement rational decisions.
- Bounded rationality, bounded willpower, and bounded self-interest are believed to explain some choices.
- Neuroeconomics uses the ideas and tools of neuroscience to study the effects of economic events and choices inside the human brain.

Working Problems 22 to 24 will give you a better understanding of the new ways of explaining consumer choices.

Key Terms

Behavioural economics, 194
Budget line, 180
Consumer equilibrium, 183
Diminishing marginal utility, 182
Marginal utility, 181

Marginal utility per dollar, 184
Neuroeconomics, 195
Preferences, 181
Total utility, 181
Utility, 181

SCAN THIS

STUDY PLAN PROBLEMS AND APPLICATIONS

MyEconLab ◆ You can work Problems 1 to 24 in Chapter 8 Study Plan and get instant feedback.

Consumption Choices (Study Plan 8.1)

Use this information to answer Problems 1 and 2.

Jerry has $12 a week to spend on yogurt and magazines. The price of yogurt is $2, and the price of a magazine is $4.

1. List the combinations of yogurt and magazines that Jerry can afford. Draw a graph of Jerry's budget line with the quantity of magazines plotted on the x-axis.

2. Describe how Jerry's consumption possibilities change if, other things remaining the same, (i) the price of a magazine falls and (ii) Jerry's income increases.

Use this information to answer Problems 3 and 4.

Amy has $12 a week to spend on coffee and pop. The price of coffee is $2 a cup, and pop is $1 a can.

3. Draw a graph of Amy's budget line. Can Amy buy 7 cans of pop and 2 cups of coffee a week? Can she buy 7 cups of coffee and 2 cans of pop a week? What is the relative price of a cup of coffee?

4. Suppose that the price of pop remains at $1 a can but the price of coffee rises to $3 a cup. How has the relative price of coffee changed? If she buys 6 cans of pop, what is the maximum number of cups of coffee she can buy in a week? Draw Amy's new budget line.

Use the following data to work Problems 5 to 7.

Max enjoys windsurfing and snorkelling. Max has $35 a day to spend, and he can spend as much time as he likes on his leisure pursuits. The price of renting equipment for windsurfing is $10 an hour and for snorkelling is $5 an hour. The table shows the total utility Max gets from each activity.

Hours per day	Total utility from windsurfing	Total utility from snorkelling
1	120	40
2	220	76
3	300	106
4	360	128
5	396	140
6	412	150
7	422	158

5. Calculate Max's marginal utility from windsurfing at each number of hours per day. Does Max's marginal utility from windsurfing obey the principle of diminishing marginal utility?

6. Calculate Max's marginal utility from snorkelling at each number of hours per day. Does Max's marginal utility from snorkelling obey the principle of diminishing marginal utility?

7. Which does Max enjoy more: his 6th hour of windsurfing or his 6th hour of snorkelling?

Utility-Maximizing Choice (Study Plan 8.2)

Use the data in Problem 5 to work Problems 8 to 11.

8. Make a table that shows the various combinations of hours spent windsurfing and snorkelling that Max can afford.

9. In a table that shows the various combinations of hours spent windsurfing and snorkelling that Max can afford, and add in each row Max's marginal utility per dollar from windsurfing and from snorkelling.

10. a. How many hours does Max windsurf and how many hours does he snorkel to maximize his utility?

b. If Max spent a dollar more on windsurfing and a dollar less on snorkelling than in part (a), by how much would his total utility change?

c. If Max spent a dollar less on windsurfing and a dollar more on snorkelling than in part (a), by how much would his total utility change?

11. Explain why, if Max equalized the marginal utility per hour from windsurfing and from snorkelling, he would *not* maximize his utility.

12. Statistics Canada figures showed on Wednesday, July 7, 2011: The price of fresh milk was 4.3 percent higher, the price of bread was up 10.6 percent, meat prices rose 5.4 percent, and the gasoline price rose 8.3 percent over the year.

a. In terms of fresh milk, what was the change in the relative prices of bread, meat, and gasoline?

b. What do the prices per unit reported by Statistics Canada tell you about the marginal utility from a carton of milk, a loaf of bread, a serving of meat, and a litre of gasoline?

13. **Can Money Buy Happiness?**

Whoever said money can't buy happiness isn't spending it right. There must be some connection, but once your basic human needs are met, does more money buy more happiness? An increase in income from $20,000 a year to $50,000 makes you twice as likely to be happy, but the payoff from more than $90,000 is slight.

Source: CNN, July 18, 2006

a. What does the fundamental assumption of marginal utility theory suggest about the connection between money and happiness?

b. Explain why this news clip is consistent with marginal utility theory.

Predictions of Marginal Utility Theory (Study Plan 8.3)

Use the data in Problem 5 to work Problems 14 to 18.

14. Max is offered a special deal: The price of renting windsurfing equipment is cut to $5 an hour. How many hours does Max spend windsurfing and how many hours does he spend snorkelling?

15. Draw Max's demand curve for rented windsurfing equipment. Over the price range from $5 to $10 an hour, is Max's demand for windsurfing equipment elastic or inelastic?

16. How does Max's demand for snorkelling equipment change when the price of windsurfing equipment falls? What is Max's cross elasticity of demand for snorkelling with respect to the price of windsurfing? Are windsurfing and snorkelling substitutes or complements for Max?

17. If Max's income increases from $35 to $55 a day, how does his demand for rented windsurfing equipment change? Is windsurfing a normal good or an inferior good for Max? Explain.

18. If Max's income increases from $35 to $55 a day, how does his demand for rented snorkelling equipment change? Is snorkelling a normal good or an inferior good for Max? Explain.

Use the following news clip to work Problems 19 to 21.

Exclusive Status: It's in the Bag; $52,500 Purses. 24 Worldwide. 1 in Washington.

Forget your Coach purse. Put away your Kate Spade. Even Hermès's famous Birkin bag seems positively discount. The Louis Vuitton Tribute Patchwork is this summer's ultimate status bag, ringing in at $52,500, and the company is offering only five for sale in North America and 24 worldwide.

Source: *The Washington Post*, August 21, 2007

19. Use marginal utility theory to explain the facts reported in the news clip.

20. If Louis Vuitton offered 500 Tribute Patchwork bags in North America and 2,400 worldwide, what do you predict would happen to the price that buyers would be willing to pay and what would happen to the consumer surplus?

21. If the Tribute Patchwork bag is copied and thousands are sold illegally, what do you predict would happen to the price that buyers would be willing to pay for a genuine bag and what would happen to the consumer surplus?

New Ways of Explaining Consumer Choices
(Study Plan 8.4)

Use the following news clip to work Problems 22 and 23.

Eating Away the Innings in Baseball's Cheap Seats

Baseball and gluttony, two of North America's favourite pastimes, are merging and taking hold at Major League Baseball stadiums: all-you-can-eat seats. Some fans try to "set personal records" during their first game in the section, but by their second or third time in such seats they eat just as they would normally at a game.

Source: *USA Today*, March 6, 2008

22. a. What conflict might exist between utility-maximization and setting "personal records" for eating?

b. What does the fact that fans eat less at subsequent games indicate about the marginal utility from ballpark food as the quantity consumed increases?

23. a. How can setting personal records for eating be reconciled with marginal utility theory?

b. Which ideas of behavioural economics are consistent with the information in the news clip?

24. **Toronto's "Buy Local" Food Policy Under Attack**

The city spends $11 million a year on food for care homes, shelters and daycares. It contracts with food-service distributors who will buy local if it's cheaper. But that might be difficult, noting that last weekend Ontario strawberries were $4 a pint versus $2.50 for California-sourced berries.

Source: *Toronto Star*, June 28, 2011

What conflict might exist between utility-maximization and the decision to allocate the city's budget on the basis of "buy local"?

ADDITIONAL PROBLEMS AND APPLICATIONS

MyEconLab ◆ You can work these problems in MyEconLab if assigned by your instructor.

Consumption Choices

25. Tim buys 2 pizzas and sees 1 movie a week when he has $16 to spend. The price of a movie ticket is $8, and the price of a pizza is $4. Draw Tim's budget line. If the price of a movie ticket falls to $4, describe how Tim's consumption possibilities change.

26. In a week, Erin buys 1 six-pack of pop and sees 2 movies when a movie ticket is $10, pop is $5 a six-pack, and she has $25 to spend. If her budget increases and she has $50 to spend on pop and movies, what is the change in the relative price of a movie ticket? Describe how her consumption possibilities will change.

27. Cindy has $70 a month to spend, and she can spend as much time as she likes playing golf and tennis. The price of an hour of golf is $10, and the price of an hour of tennis is $5. The table shows Cindy's marginal utility from each sport.

Hours per month	Marginal utility from golf	Marginal utility from tennis
1	80	40
2	60	36
3	40	30
4	30	10
5	20	5
6	10	2
7	6	1

Make a table that shows Cindy's consumption possibilities. If Cindy increases her expenditure to $100, describe how her consumption possibilities change.

Utility-Maximizing Choice

Use the data in Problem 27 to work Problems 28 and 29.

28. a. When Cindy has $70 to spend on golf and tennis, how many hours of golf and how many hours of tennis does she play to maximize her utility?

   b. Compared to part (a), if Cindy spent a dollar more on golf and a dollar less on tennis, by how much would her total utility change?

   c. Compared to part (a), if Cindy spent a dollar less on golf and a dollar more on tennis, by how much would her total utility change?

29. Explain why, if Cindy equalized the marginal utility per hour of golf and tennis, she would *not* maximize her utility.

Predictions of Marginal Utility Theory

Use the data in Problem 27 to work Problems 30 to 34.

30. Cindy's tennis club raises its price of an hour of tennis to $10. The price of golf remains at $10 an hour and Cindy continues to spend $70 on tennis and golf.

   a. List the combinations of hours spent playing golf and tennis that Cindy can now afford.

   b. Along with the combinations in part (a), list Cindy's marginal utility per dollar from golf and from tennis.

   c. How many hours does Cindy now spend playing golf and how many hours does she spend playing tennis?

31. Use your answers to Problems 28a and 30 to draw Cindy's demand curve for tennis. Over the price range of $5 to $10 an hour of tennis, is Cindy's demand for tennis elastic or inelastic?

32. Use your answers to Problems 28(a) and 30 to explain how Cindy's demand for golf changed when the price of an hour of tennis increased. What is Cindy's cross elasticity of demand for golf with respect to the price of tennis? Are tennis and golf substitutes or complements for Cindy?

33. Cindy loses her math tutoring job and the amount she has to spend on golf and tennis falls to $35 a month. How does Cindy's demand for golf change? For Cindy, is golf a normal good or an inferior good? Is tennis a normal good or an inferior good?

34. Cindy takes a Club Med vacation, the cost of which includes unlimited sports activities. With no extra charge for golf and tennis, Cindy allocates a total of 4 hours a day to these activities.

   a. How many hours does Cindy play golf and how many hours does she play tennis?

   b. What is Cindy's marginal utility from golf and from tennis?

   c. Why does Cindy equalize the marginal utilities rather than the marginal utility per dollar from golf and from tennis?

35. **Blu-Ray Format Expected to Dominate, but When?**

    Blu-ray stomped HD DVD to become the standard format for high-definition movie discs, but years may pass before it can claim victory over the good old DVD. The people who bought $2,000, 40-inch TVs are the ones that will lead the charge. Everyone else will come along when the price falls. Blu-ray machine prices are now starting to drop and Wal-Mart Stores Inc. began stocking a $298 Magnavox model. That's cheaper than most alternatives, but a hefty price hike from a typical $50 DVD player.

    Source: CNN, June 2, 2008

    a. What does marginal utility theory predict about the marginal utility from a Magnavox Blu-ray machine compared to the marginal utility from a typical DVD player?

    b. What will have to happen to the marginal utility from a Blu-ray machine before it is able to "claim victory over the good old DVD"?

36. Ben spends $50 a year on 2 bunches of flowers and $50 a year on 10,000 litres of tap water. Ben is maximizing utility and his marginal utility from water is 0.5 unit per litre.

    a. Are flowers or water more valuable to Ben?

    b. Explain how Ben's expenditure on flowers and water illustrates the paradox of value.

New Ways of Explaining Consumer Choices

Use the following news clip to work Problems 37 to 39.

Putting a Price on Human Life

Researchers at Stanford and the University of Pennsylvania estimated that a healthy human life is worth about $129,000. Using Medicare records on treatment costs for kidney dialysis as a benchmark, the authors tried to pinpoint the threshold beyond which ensuring another "quality" year of life was no longer financially worthwhile. The study comes amid debate over whether Medicare should start rationing health care on the basis of cost effectiveness.

Source: *Time*, June 9, 2008

37. Why might Medicare ration health care according to treatment that is "financially worthwhile" as opposed to providing as much treatment as is needed by a patient, regardless of cost?

38. What conflict might exist between a person's valuation of his or her own life and the rest of society's valuation of that person's life?

39. How does the potential conflict between self-interest and the social interest complicate setting a financial threshold for Medicare treatments?

Economics in the News

40. After you have studied *Reading Between the Lines* (pp. 196–197), answer the following questions.

    a. If a wave of natural disasters put nurses in the news and a large number of people decide to try to get jobs as nurses, how does

    (i) The marginal utility of the services of a nurse change?

    (ii) Consumer surplus in the market for the services of nurses change?

    b. If television advertising revenues during hockey games double, how does

    (i) The marginal utility of the services of a hockey player change?

    (ii) Consumer surplus in the market for the services of hockey players change?

Use the following news clip to work Problems 41 and 42.

How to Buy Happiness. Cheap

At any day, the rich tend to be a bit happier than the poor, but across-the-board increases in living standards don't seem to make people happier. As living standards increase, most of us respond by raising our own standards: Things that once seemed luxuries now are necessities. As a result, we're working harder than ever to buy stuff that satisfies us less and less.

Source: CNN, October 1, 2004

41. According to the news clip, how do widespread increases in living standards influence total utility?

42. a. What does the news clip imply about how the total utility from consumption changes over time?

    b. What does the news clip imply about how the marginal utility from consumption changes over time?

43. **Five Signs You Have Too Much Money**

    The drink of choice among image-conscious status seekers in Los Angeles is Bling H2O, which costs $38 a bottle. It's not the water that accounts for its cost, but the "limited edition" bottle decked out in Swarovski crystals.

    Source: CNN, January 17, 2006

    a. Assuming that the price of a bottle of Bling H2O is $38 in all the major U.S. cities, what might its popularity in Los Angeles reveal about consumers' incomes or preferences in Los Angeles relative to other U.S. cities?

    b. Why might the marginal utility from a bottle of Bling H2O decrease more rapidly than the marginal utility from ordinary bottled water?

Possibilities, Preferences, and Choices

After studying this chapter, you will be able to

◆ Describe a household's budget line and show how it changes when prices or income change

◆ Use indifference curves to map preferences and explain the principle of diminishing marginal rate of substitution

◆ Predict the effects of changes in prices and income on consumption choices

As the price of a DVD rental has fallen we're renting ever more of them, but we're also going to movie theatres in ever-greater numbers. Why are we going to the movies more when it is so cheap and easy to rent a DVD?

As the prices of music downloads and e-books have fallen, we're downloading ever more songs and books. But e-books have made a smaller inroad into the overall market for books than downloads have in the market for recorded music. Why?

In this chapter, we're going to study a model of choice that answers questions like the ones just posed. We'll use this model to explain the choices we make about movies, and, at the end of the chapter in *Reading Between the Lines*, to explain why e-books are only slowly replacing printed books.

Consumption Possibilities

Consumption choices are limited by income and by prices. A household has a given amount of income to spend and cannot influence the prices of the goods and services it buys. A household's **budget line** describes the limits to its consumption choices.

Let's look at Lisa's budget line.* Lisa has an income of $40 a month to spend. She buys two goods: movies and pop. The price of a movie is $8, and the price of pop is $4 a case.

Figure 9.1 shows alternative combinations of movies and pop that Lisa can afford. In row *A*, she sees no movies and buys 10 cases of pop. In row *F*, she sees 5 movies and buys no pop. Both of these combinations of movies and pop exhaust the $40 available. Check that the combination of movies and pop in each of the other rows also exhausts Lisa's $40 of income. The numbers in the table and the points *A* through *F* in the graph describe Lisa's consumption possibilities.

Divisible and Indivisible Goods Some goods—called divisible goods—can be bought in any quantity desired. Examples are gasoline and electricity. We can best understand household choice if we suppose that all goods and services are divisible. For example, Lisa can see half a movie a month on average by seeing one movie every two months. When we think of goods as being divisible, the consumption possibilities are not only the points *A* through *F* shown in Fig. 9.1, but also all the intermediate points that form the line running from *A* to *F*. This line is Lisa's budget line.

Affordable and Unaffordable Quantities Lisa's budget line is a constraint on her choices. It marks the boundary between what is affordable and what is unaffordable. She can afford any point on the line and inside it. She cannot afford any point outside the line. The constraint on her consumption depends on the prices and her income, and the constraint changes when the price of a good or her income changes. To see how, we use a budget equation.

---

* If you have studied Chapter 8 on marginal utility theory, you have already met Lisa. This tale of her thirst for pop and zeal for movies will sound familiar to you—up to a point. In this chapter, we're going to explore her budget line in more detail and use a different method for representing preferences—one that does not require the idea of utility.

FIGURE 9.1 The Budget Line

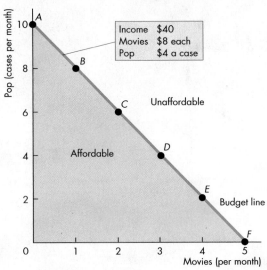

Consumption possibility	Movies (per month)	Pop (cases per month)
A	0	10
B	1	8
C	2	6
D	3	4
E	4	2
F	5	0

Lisa's budget line shows the boundary between what she can and cannot afford. The rows of the table list Lisa's affordable combinations of movies and pop when her income is $40, the price of pop is $4 a case, and the price of a movie is $8. For example, row *A* tells us that Lisa spends all of her $40 income when she buys 10 cases of pop and sees no movies. The figure graphs Lisa's budget line. Points *A* through *F* in the graph represent the rows of the table. For divisible goods, the budget line is the continuous line *AF*. To calculate the equation for Lisa's budget line, start with expenditure equal to income:

$$\$4Q_P + \$8Q_M = \$40.$$

Divide by $4 to obtain

$$Q_P + 2Q_M = 10.$$

Subtract $2Q_M$ from both sides to obtain

$$Q_P = 10 - 2Q_M.$$

MyEconLab   animation

Budget Equation

We can describe the budget line by using a *budget equation*. The budget equation starts with the fact that

$$\text{Expenditure} = \text{Income.}$$

Expenditure is equal to the sum of the price of each good multiplied by the quantity bought. For Lisa,

$$\text{Expenditure} = (\text{Price of pop} \times \text{Quantity of pop})$$
$$+ (\text{Price of movie} \times \text{Quantity of movies}).$$

Call the price of pop P_P, the quantity of pop Q_P, the price of a movie P_M, the quantity of movies Q_M, and income Y. We can now write Lisa's budget equation as

$$P_P Q_P + P_M Q_M = Y.$$

Or, using the prices Lisa faces, $4 a case of pop and $8 a movie, and Lisa's income, $40, we get

$$\$4 Q_P + \$8 Q_M = \$40.$$

Lisa can choose any quantities of pop (Q_P) and movies (Q_M) that satisfy this equation. To find the relationship between these quantities, divide both sides of the equation by the price of pop (P_P) to get

$$Q_P + \frac{P_M}{P_P} \times Q_M = \frac{Y}{P_P}.$$

Now subtract the term $(P_M/P_P) \times Q_M$ from both sides of this equation to get

$$Q_P = \frac{Y}{P_P} - \frac{P_M}{P_P} \times Q_M.$$

For Lisa, income (Y) is $40, the price of a movie (P_M) is $8, and the price of pop (P_P) is $4 a case. So Lisa must choose the quantities of movies and pop to satisfy the equation

$$Q_P = \frac{\$40}{\$4} - \frac{\$8}{\$4} \times Q_M,$$

or

$$Q_P = 10 - 2 Q_M.$$

To interpret the equation, look at the budget line in Fig. 9.1 and check that the equation delivers that budget line. First, set Q_M equal to zero. The budget equation tells us that Q_P, the quantity of pop, is Y/P_P, which is 10 cases. This combination of Q_M and Q_P is the one shown in row *A* of the table in Fig. 9.1. Next set Q_M equal to 5. Q_P now equals zero (row *F* of the table). Check that you can derive the other rows.

The budget equation contains two variables chosen by the household (Q_M and Q_P) and two variables that the household takes as given (Y/P_P and P_M/P_P). Let's look more closely at these variables.

Real Income A household's **real income** is its income expressed as a quantity of goods that the household can afford to buy. Expressed in terms of pop, Lisa's real income is Y/P_P. This quantity is the maximum quantity of pop that she can buy. It is equal to her money income divided by the price of pop. Lisa's money income is $40 and the price of pop is $4 a case, so her real income in terms of pop is 10 cases, which is shown in Fig. 9.1 as the point at which the budget line intersects the y-axis.

Relative Price A **relative price** is the price of one good divided by the price of another good. In Lisa's budget equation, the variable P_M/P_P is the relative price of a movie in terms of pop. For Lisa, P_M is $8 a movie and P_P is $4 a case, so P_M/P_P is equal to 2 cases of pop per movie. That is, to see 1 movie, Lisa must give up 2 cases of pop.

You've just calculated Lisa's opportunity cost of seeing a movie. Recall that the opportunity cost of an action is the best alternative forgone. For Lisa to see 1 more movie a month, she must forgo 2 cases of pop. You've also calculated Lisa's opportunity cost of pop. For Lisa to buy 2 more cases of pop a month, she must forgo seeing 1 movie. So her opportunity cost of 2 cases of pop is 1 movie.

The relative price of a movie in terms of pop is the magnitude of the slope of Lisa's budget line. To calculate the slope of the budget line, recall the formula for slope (see the Chapter 1 Appendix): Slope equals the change in the variable measured on the y-axis divided by the change in the variable measured on the x-axis as we move along the line. In Lisa's case (Fig. 9.1), the variable measured on the y-axis is the quantity of pop and the variable measured on the x-axis is the quantity of movies. Along Lisa's budget line, as pop decreases from 10 to 0 cases, movies increase from 0 to 5. So the magnitude of the slope of the budget line is 10 cases divided by 5 movies, or 2 cases of pop per movie. The magnitude of this slope is exactly the same as the relative price we've just calculated. It is also the opportunity cost of a movie.

A Change in Prices When prices change, so does the budget line. The lower the price of the good measured on the x-axis, other things remaining the same, the flatter is the budget line. For example, if the price of a movie falls from $8 to $4, real income

FIGURE 9.2 Changes in Prices and Income

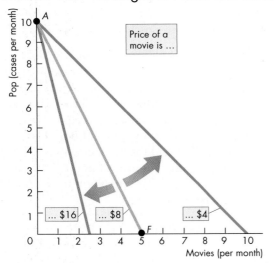

(a) A change in price

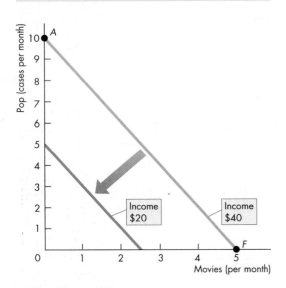

(b) A change in income

In part (a), the price of a movie changes. A fall in the price from $8 to $4 rotates the budget line outward and makes it flatter. A rise in the price from $8 to $16 rotates the budget line inward and makes it steeper.

In part (b), income falls from $40 to $20 while the prices of movies and pop remain the same. The budget line shifts leftward, but its slope does not change.

MyEconLab animation ◆

in terms of pop does not change but the relative price of a movie falls. The budget line rotates outward and becomes flatter, as Fig. 9.2(a) illustrates. The higher the price of the good measured on the *x*-axis, other things remaining the same, the steeper is the budget line. For example, if the price of a movie rises from $8 to $16, the relative price of a movie increases. The budget line rotates inward and becomes steeper, as Fig. 9.2(a) illustrates.

A Change in Income A change in money income changes real income but does not change the relative price. The budget line shifts, but its slope does not change. An increase in money income increases real income and shifts the budget line rightward. A decrease in money income decreases real income and shifts the budget line leftward.

Figure 9.2(b) shows the effect of a change in money income on Lisa's budget line. The initial budget line when Lisa's income is $40 is the same as in Fig. 9.1. The new budget line shows how much Lisa can buy if her income falls to $20 a month. The two budget lines have the same slope because the relative price is the same. The new budget line is closer to the origin because Lisa's real income has decreased.

REVIEW QUIZ

1 What does a household's budget line show?
2 How does the relative price and a household's real income influence its budget line?
3 If a household has an income of $40 and buys only bus rides at $2 each and magazines at $4 each, what is the equation of the household's budget line?
4 If the price of one good changes, what happens to the relative price and the slope of the household's budget line?
5 If a household's money income changes and prices do not change, what happens to the household's real income and budget line?

You can work these questions in Study Plan 9.1 and get instant feedback.

MyEconLab ◆

We've studied the limits to what a household can consume. Let's now learn how we can describe preferences and make a map that contains a lot of information about a household's preferences.

Preferences and Indifference Curves

You are going to discover a very cool idea: that of drawing a map of a person's preferences. A preference map is based on the intuitively appealing idea that people can sort all the possible combinations of goods into three groups: preferred, not preferred, and indifferent. To make this idea more concrete, let's ask Lisa to tell us how she ranks various combinations of movies and pop.

Figure 9.3 shows part of Lisa's answer. She tells us that she currently sees 2 movies and buys 6 cases of pop a month at point *C*. She then lists all the combinations of movies and pop that she says are just as acceptable to her as her current situation. When we plot these combinations of movies and pop, we get the green curve in Fig. 9.3(a). This curve is the key element in a preference map and is called an indifference curve.

An **indifference curve** is a line that shows combinations of goods among which a consumer is *indifferent*. The indifference curve in Fig. 9.3(a) tells us that Lisa is just as happy to see 2 movies and buy 6 cases of pop a month at point *C* as she is to have the combination of movies and pop at point *G* or at any other point along the curve.

Lisa also says that she prefers all the combinations of movies and pop above the indifference curve in Fig. 9.3(a)—the yellow area—to those on the indifference curve. And she prefers any combination on the indifference curve to any combination in the grey area below the indifference curve.

The indifference curve in Fig. 9.3(a) is just one of a whole family of such curves. This indifference curve appears again in Fig. 9.3(b), labelled I_1. The curves labelled I_0 and I_2 are two other indifference curves. Lisa prefers any point on indifference curve I_2 to any point on indifference curve I_1, and she prefers any point on I_1 to any point on I_0. We refer to I_2 as being a higher indifference curve than I_1 and I_1 as being higher than I_0.

A preference map is a series of indifference curves that resemble the contour lines on a map. By looking at the shape of the contour lines on a map, we can draw conclusions about the terrain. Similarly, by looking at the shape of the indifference curves, we can draw conclusions about a person's preferences.

Let's learn how to "read" a preference map.

FIGURE 9.3   A Preference Map

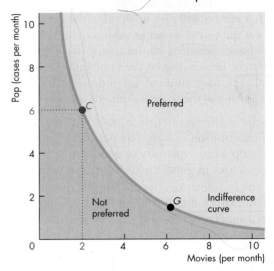

(a) An indifference curve

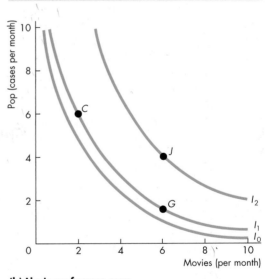

(b) Lisa's preference map

Part (a) shows one of Lisa's indifference curves. She is indifferent between point *C* (with 2 movies and 6 cases of pop) and all other points on the green indifference curve, such as *G*. She prefers points above the indifference curve (in the yellow area) to points on it, and she prefers points on the indifference curve to points below it (in the grey area).

Part (b) shows three of the indifference curves—I_0, I_1, and I_2—in Lisa's preference map. She prefers point *J* to point *C* or *G*, and she prefers all the points on I_2 to those on I_1.

MyEconLab   animation

Marginal Rate of Substitution

The **marginal rate of substitution** (*MRS*) is the rate at which a person will give up good y (the good measured on the y-axis) to get an additional unit of good x (the good measured on the x-axis) while remaining indifferent (remaining on the same indifference curve). The magnitude of the slope of an indifference curve measures the marginal rate of substitution.

■ If the indifference curve is *steep*, the marginal rate of substitution is *high*. The person is willing to give up a large quantity of good y to get an additional unit of good x while remaining indifferent.

■ If the indifference curve is *flat*, the marginal rate of substitution is *low*. The person is willing to give up a small amount of good y to get an additional unit of good x while remaining indifferent.

Figure 9.4 shows you how to calculate the marginal rate of substitution.

At point C on indifference curve I_1, Lisa buys 6 cases of pop and sees 2 movies. Her marginal rate of substitution is the magnitude of the slope of the indifference curve at point C. To measure this magnitude, place a straight line against, or tangent to, the indifference curve at point C. Along that line, as the quantity of pop decreases by 10 cases, the number of movies increases by 5—or 2 cases per movie. At point C, Lisa is willing to give up pop for movies at the rate of 2 cases per movie—a marginal rate of substitution of 2.

At point G on indifference curve I_1, Lisa buys 1.5 cases of pop and sees 6 movies. Her marginal rate of substitution is measured by the slope of the indifference curve at point G. That slope is the same as the slope of the tangent to the indifference curve at point G. Now, as the quantity of pop decreases by 4.5 cases, the number of movies increases by 9—or 1/2 case per movie. At point G, Lisa is willing to give up pop for movies at the rate of 1/2 case per movie—a marginal rate of substitution of 1/2.

As Lisa sees more movies and buys less pop, her marginal rate of substitution diminishes. Diminishing marginal rate of substitution is the key assumption about preferences. A **diminishing marginal rate of substitution** is a general tendency for a person to be willing to give up less of good y to get one more unit of good x, while at the same time remaining indifferent as the quantity of x increases. In Lisa's case, she is less willing to give up pop to see one more movie as the number of movies she sees increases.

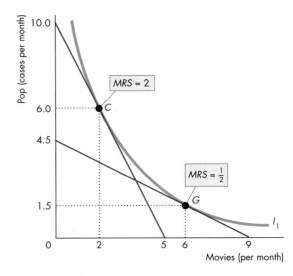

FIGURE 9.4   The Marginal Rate of Substitution

The magnitude of the slope of an indifference curve is called the marginal rate of substitution (*MRS*). The red line at point C tells us that Lisa is willing to give up 10 cases of pop to see 5 movies. Her marginal rate of substitution at point C is 10 divided by 5, which equals 2. The red line at point G tells us that Lisa is willing to give up 4.5 cases of pop to see 9 movies. Her marginal rate of substitution at point G is 4.5 divided by 9, which equals 1/2.

— MyEconLab   animation ◆

Your Diminishing Marginal Rate of Substitution

Think about your own diminishing marginal rate of substitution. Imagine that in a week, you drink 10 cases of pop and see no movies. Most likely, you are willing to give up a lot of pop so that you can see just 1 movie. But now imagine that in a week, you buy 1 case of pop and see 6 movies. Most likely, you will now not be willing to give up much pop to see a 7th movie. As a general rule, the greater the number of movies you see, the smaller is the quantity of pop you are willing to give up to see one additional movie.

The shape of a person's indifference curves incorporates the principle of the diminishing marginal rate of substitution because the curves are bowed towards the origin. The tightness of the bend of an indifference curve tells us how willing a person is to substitute one good for another while remaining indifferent. Let's look at some examples that make this point clear.

Degree of Substitutability

Most of us would not regard movies and pop as being *close* substitutes, but they are substitutes. No matter how much you love pop, some increase in the number of movies you see will compensate you for being deprived of a can of pop. Similarly, no matter how much you love going to the movies, some number of cans of pop will compensate you for being deprived of seeing one movie. A person's indifference curves for movies and pop might look something like those for most ordinary goods and services shown in Fig. 9.5(a).

Close Substitutes Some goods substitute so easily for each other that most of us do not even notice which we are consuming. The different brands of marker pens and pencils are examples. Most people don't care which brand of these items they use or where they buy them. A marker pen from the campus bookstore is just as good as one from the local grocery store. You would be willing to forgo a pen from the campus store if you could get one more pen from the local grocery store. When two goods are perfect substitutes, their indifference curves are straight lines that slope downward, as Fig. 9.5(b) illustrates. The marginal rate of substitution is constant.

Complements Some goods do not substitute for each other at all. Instead, they are complements. The complements in Fig. 9.5(c) are left and right running shoes. Indifference curves of perfect complements are L-shaped. One left running shoe and one right running shoe are as good as one left shoe and two right shoes. Having two of each is preferred to having one of each, but having two of one and one of the other is no better than having one of each.

The extreme cases of perfect substitutes and perfect complements shown here don't often happen in reality, but they do illustrate that the shape of the indifference curve shows the degree of substitutability between two goods. The closer the two goods are to perfect substitutes, the closer the marginal rate of substitution is to being constant (a straight line), rather than diminishing (a curved line). Indifference

---

FIGURE 9.5 The Degree of Substitutability

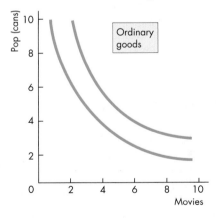

(a) Ordinary goods

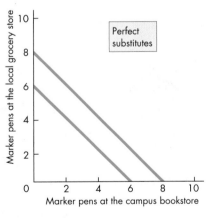

(b) Perfect substitutes

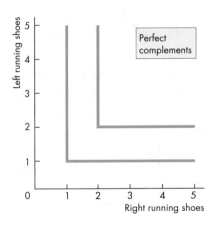

(c) Perfect complements

The shape of the indifference curves reveals the degree of substitutability between two goods. Part (a) shows the indifference curves for two ordinary goods: movies and pop. To drink less pop and remain indifferent, one must see more movies. The number of movies that compensates for a reduction in pop increases as less pop is consumed. Part (b) shows the indifference curves for two perfect substitutes. For the consumer to remain indifferent, one fewer marker pen from the local grocery store must be replaced by one extra marker pen from the campus bookstore. Part (c) shows two perfect complements—goods that cannot be substituted for each other at all. Having two left running shoes with one right running shoe is no better than having one of each. But having two of each is preferred to having one of each.

"With the pork I'd recommend an Alsatian white or a Coke."

© The New Yorker Collection 1988
Robert Weber from cartoonbank.com. All Rights Reserved.

curves for poor substitutes are tightly curved and lie between the shapes of those shown in Figs. 9.5(a) and 9.5(c).

As you can see in the cartoon, according to the waiter's preferences, Coke and Alsatian white wine are perfect substitutes and each is a complement of pork. We hope the customers agree with him.

REVIEW QUIZ

1 What is an indifference curve and how does a preference map show preferences?
2 Why does an indifference curve slope downward and why is it bowed towards the origin?
3 What do we call the magnitude of the slope of an indifference curve?
4 What is the key assumption about a consumer's marginal rate of substitution?

You can work these questions in Study Plan 9.2 and get instant feedback.

━━━━━ MyEconLab ◆

The two components of the model of household choice are now in place: the budget line and the preference map. We will now use these components to work out a household's choice and to predict how choices change when prices and income change.

◆ Predicting Consumer Choices

We are now going to predict the quantities of movies and pop that Lisa chooses to buy. We're also going to see how these quantities change when a price changes or when Lisa's income changes. Finally, we're going to see how the *substitution effect* and the *income effect*, two ideas that you met in Chapter 3 (see p. 57), guarantee that for a normal good, the demand curve slopes downward.

Best Affordable Choice

When Lisa makes her best affordable choice of movies and pop, she spends all her income and is on her highest attainable indifference curve. Figure 9.6 illustrates this choice: The budget line is from Fig. 9.1 and the indifference curves are from Fig. 9.3(b). Lisa's best affordable choice is 2 movies and 6 cases of pop at point *C*—the *best affordable point*.

FIGURE 9.6   The Best Affordable Choice

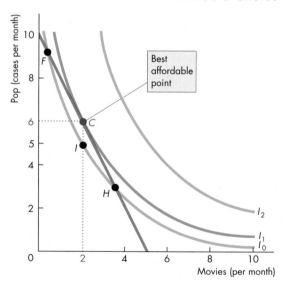

Lisa's best affordable choice is at point *C*, the point on her budget line and on her highest attainable indifference curve. At point *C*, Lisa's marginal rate of substitution between movies and pop (the magnitude of the slope of the indifference curve I_1) equals the relative price of movies and pop (the slope of the budget line).

━━━━━ MyEconLab   animation ◆

On the Budget Line The best affordable point is on the budget line. For every point inside the budget line, such as point *I*, there are points on the budget line that Lisa prefers. For example, she prefers all the points on the budget line between *F* and *H* to point *I*, so she chooses a point on the budget line.

On the Highest Attainable Indifference Curve Every point on the budget line lies on an indifference curve. For example, points *F* and *H* lie on the indifference curve I_0. By moving along her budget line from either *F* or *H* towards *C*, Lisa reaches points on ever-higher indifference curves that she prefers to points *F* or *H*. When Lisa gets to point *C*, she is on the highest attainable indifference curve.

Marginal Rate of Substitution Equals Relative Price At point *C*, Lisa's marginal rate of substitution between movies and pop (the magnitude of the slope of the indifference curve) is equal to the relative price of movies and pop (the magnitude of the slope of the budget line). Lisa's willingness to pay for a movie equals her opportunity cost of a movie.

Let's now see how Lisa's choices change when a price changes.

A Change in Price

The effect of a change in the price of a good on the quantity of the good consumed is called the **price effect**. We will use Fig. 9.7(a) to work out the price effect of a fall in the price of a movie. We start with the price of a movie at $8, the price of pop at $4 a case, and Lisa's income at $40 a month. In this situation, she buys 6 cases of pop and sees 2 movies a month at point *C*.

Now suppose that the price of a movie falls to $4. With a lower price of a movie, the budget line rotates outward and becomes flatter. The new budget line is the darker orange one in Fig. 9.7(a). For a refresher on how a price change affects the budget line, check back to Fig. 9.2(a).

Lisa's best affordable point is now point *J*, where she sees 6 movies and drinks 4 cases of pop. Lisa drinks less pop and watches more movies now that movies are cheaper. She cuts her pop purchases from 6 to 4 cases and increases the number of movies she sees from 2 to 6 a month. When the price of a movie falls and the price of pop and her income remain constant, Lisa substitutes movies for pop.

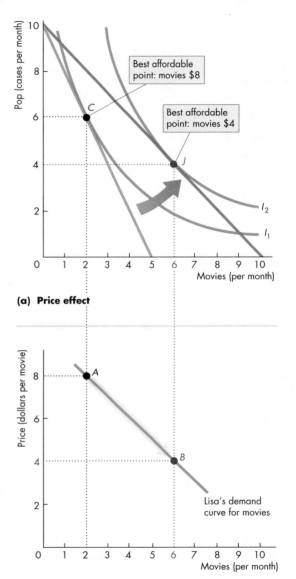

FIGURE 9.7   Price Effect and Demand Curve

(a) Price effect

(b) Demand curve

Initially, Lisa's best affordable point is *C* in part (a). If the price of a movie falls from $8 to $4, Lisa's best affordable point is *J*. The move from *C* to *J* is the price effect.

At a price of $8 a movie, Lisa sees 2 movies a month, at point *A* in part (b). At a price of $4 a movie, she sees 6 movies a month, at point *B*. Lisa's demand curve for movies traces out her best affordable quantity of movies as the price of a movie varies.

MyEconLab   animation

Economics in Action

Best Affordable Choice of Movies and DVDs

Between 2006 and 2011, box-office receipts increased by more than 20 percent. During that same period, the average price of a movie ticket increased by 6 percent. So most of the increase in box-office receipts occurred because people went to the movies more often.

Why is movie-going booming? One answer is that the consumer's experience has improved. Movies in 3-D such as *Avatar* and *Alice in Wonderland* play much better on the big screen than at home. Also, movie theatres are able to charge a higher price for 3-D films, which further boosts receipts. But there is another answer, and at first thought an unlikely one: Events in the market for DVD rentals and downloads have influenced going to the movies. To see why, let's look at the recent history of the DVD rentals market.

Back in 2005, Blockbuster was the main player and the price of a DVD rental was around $4 a night and you needed to make a trip to the store to pick up your disc. Today, you can download a movie from Netflix, the iTunes Store, or Amazon for $1 a night or even less with a monthly subscription.

The easy access to DVDs at $1 a night transformed the markets for movie watching and the figure shows why.

A student has a budget of $40 a month to allocate to movies. To keep the story clear, we'll suppose that the price of a movie ticket was $8 in both 2005 and 2011. The price of a DVD rental in 2005 was $4, so the student's budget line is the one that runs from 5 movies on the *y*-axis to 10 DVD rentals on the

x-axis. The student's best affordable point is 2 movies and 6 rentals a month.

In 2011, the price of a rental falls to $1 a night but the price of a movie ticket remains at $8. So the budget line rotates outward. The student's best affordable point is now at 3 movies and 16 rentals a month. (This student loves movies!)

Many other things changed between 2005 and 2011 that influenced the markets for movies and DVD rentals, but the fall in the price of a DVD rental was the biggest influence.

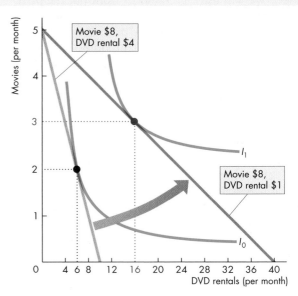

Best Affordable Movies and DVD Rentals

The Demand Curve In Chapter 3, we asserted that the demand curve slopes downward. We can now derive a demand curve from a consumer's budget line and indifference curves. By doing so, we can see that the law of demand and the downward-sloping demand curve are consequences of a consumer's choosing her or his best affordable combination of goods.

To derive Lisa's demand curve for movies, lower the price of a movie and find her best affordable point at different prices. We've just done this for two movie prices in Fig. 9.7(a). Figure 9.7(b) highlights these two prices and two points that lie on Lisa's demand curve for movies. When the price of a movie is $8, Lisa sees 2 movies a month at point *A*. When the price falls to $4, she increases the number of movies she sees to 6 a month at point *B*. The demand curve is made up of these two points plus all the other points that tell us Lisa's best affordable quantity of movies at each movie price, with the price of pop and Lisa's income remaining the same. As you can see, Lisa's demand curve for movies slopes downward—the lower the price of a movie, the more movies she sees. This is the law of demand.

Next, let's see how Lisa changes her purchases of movies and pop when her income changes.

A Change in Income

The effect of a change in income on buying plans is called the **income effect**. Let's work out the income effect by examining how buying plans change when income changes and prices remain constant. Figure 9.8 shows the income effect when Lisa's income falls. With an income of $40, the price of a movie at $4, and the price of pop at $4 a case, Lisa's best afford-able point is *J*—she buys 6 movies and 4 cases of pop. If her income falls to $28, her best affordable point is *K*—she sees 4 movies and buys 3 cases of pop. When Lisa's income falls, she buys less of both goods. Movies and pop are normal goods.

The Demand Curve and the Income Effect A change in income leads to a shift in the demand curve, as shown in Fig. 9.8(b). With an income of $40, Lisa's demand curve for movies is D_0, the same as in Fig. 9.7(b). But when her income falls to $28, she plans to see fewer movies at each price, so her demand curve shifts leftward to D_1.

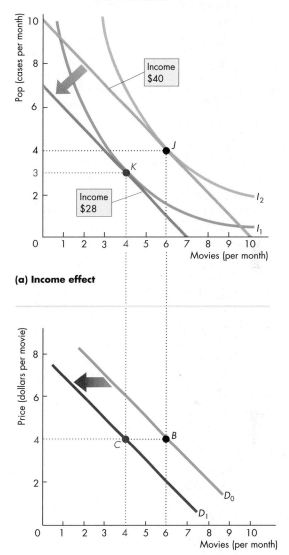

FIGURE 9.8   Income Effect and Change in Demand

(a) Income effect

(b) Demand curve for movies

A change in income shifts the budget line, changes the best affordable point, and changes demand.

In part (a), when Lisa's income decreases from $40 to $28, she sees fewer movies and buys less pop.

In part (b), when Lisa's income is $40, her demand curve for movies is D_0. When Lisa's income falls to $28, her demand curve for movies shifts leftward to D_1. For Lisa, going to the movies is a normal good. Her demand for movies decreases because she now sees fewer movies at each price.

MyEconLab   animation ◆

Substitution Effect and Income Effect

For a normal good, a fall in its price *always* increases the quantity bought. We can prove this assertion by dividing the price effect into two parts:

- Substitution effect
- Income effect

Figure 9.9(a) shows the price effect and Figs. 9.9(b) and 9.9(c) show the two parts into which we separate the price effect.

Substitution Effect   The **substitution effect** is the effect of a change in price on the quantity bought when the consumer (hypothetically) remains indifferent between the original situation and the new one. To work out Lisa's substitution effect when the price of a movie falls, we must lower her income by enough to keep her on the same indifference curve as before.

Figure 9.9(a) shows the price effect of a fall in the price of a movie from $8 to $4. The number of movies increases from 2 to 6 a month. When the price falls, suppose (hypothetically) that we cut Lisa's income to $28. What's special about $28? It is the

income that is just enough, at the new price of a movie, to keep Lisa's best affordable point on the same indifference curve (I_1) as her original point C. Lisa's budget line is now the medium orange line in Fig. 9.9(b). With the lower price of a movie and a smaller income, Lisa's best affordable point is K. The move from C to K along indifference curve I_1 is the substitution effect of the price change. The substitution effect of the fall in the price of a movie is an increase in the quantity of movies from 2 to 4. The direction of the substitution effect never varies: When the relative price of a good falls, the consumer substitutes more of that good for the other good.

Income Effect   To calculate the substitution effect, we gave Lisa a $12 pay cut. To calculate the income effect, we give Lisa back her $12. The $12 increase in income shifts Lisa's budget line outward, as shown in Fig. 9.9(c). The slope of the budget line does not change because both prices remain the same. This change in Lisa's budget line is similar to the one shown in Fig. 9.8. As Lisa's budget line shifts outward, her consumption possibilities expand and her best affordable point becomes J on indifference curve

---

FIGURE 9.9   Substitution Effect and Income Effect

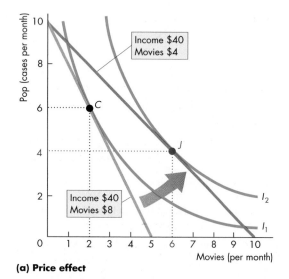

(a) Price effect

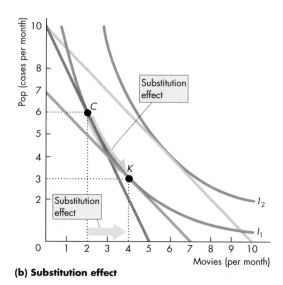

(b) Substitution effect

When the price of a movie falls from $8 to $4, Lisa moves from point C to point J in part (a). The price effect is an increase in the number of movies from 2 to 6 a month. This price effect is separated into a substitution effect in part (b) and an income effect in part (c).

To isolate the substitution effect, we confront Lisa with the new price but keep her on her original indifference curve, I_1. The substitution effect is the move from C to K along indifference curve I_1—an increase from 2 to 4 movies a month.

I_2. The move from K to J is the income effect of the price change.

As Lisa's income increases, she sees more movies. For Lisa, a movie is a normal good. For a normal good, the income effect *reinforces* the substitution effect. Because the two effects work in the same direction, we can be sure that the demand curve slopes downward. But some goods are inferior goods. What can we say about the demand for an inferior good?

Inferior Goods Recall that an *inferior good* is a good for which *demand decreases* when *income increases*. For an inferior good, the income effect is negative, which means that a lower price does not inevitably lead to an increase in the quantity demanded. The substitution effect of a fall in the price increases the quantity demanded, but the negative income effect works in the opposite direction and offsets the substitution effect to some degree. The key question is to what degree.

If the negative income effect *equals* the positive substitution effect, a fall in the price leaves the quantity bought unchanged. When a fall in price leaves the quantity demanded unchanged, the demand curve is vertical and demand is perfectly inelastic.

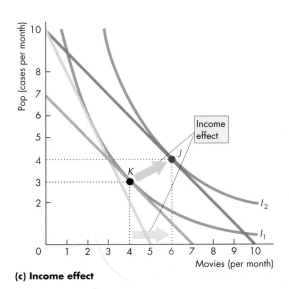

(c) Income effect

To isolate the income effect, we confront Lisa with the new price of movies but increase her income so that she can move from the original indifference curve, I_1, to the new one, I_2. The income effect is the move from K to J—an increase from 4 to 6 movies a month.

MyEconLab   animation ◆

If the negative income effect *is smaller than* the positive substitution effect, a fall in price increases the quantity bought and the demand curve still slopes downward like that for a normal good. But the demand for an inferior good might be less elastic than that for a normal good.

If the negative income effect *exceeds* the positive substitution effect, a fall in the price *decreases* the quantity bought and the demand curve *slopes upward*. This case does not appear to occur in the real world.

You can apply the indifference curve model that you've studied in this chapter to explain the changes in the way we buy recorded music, see movies, and make all our other consumption choices. We allocate our budgets to make our best affordable choices. Changes in prices and incomes change our best affordable choices and change consumption patterns.

REVIEW QUIZ

1 When a consumer chooses the combination of goods and services to buy, what is she or he trying to achieve?

2 Explain the conditions that are met when a consumer has found the best affordable combination of goods to buy. (Use the terms budget line, marginal rate of substitution, and relative price in your explanation.)

3 If the price of a normal good falls, what happens to the quantity demanded of that good?

4 Into what two effects can we divide the effect of a price change?

5 For a normal good, does the income effect reinforce the substitution effect or does it partly offset the substitution effect?

You can work these questions in Study Plan 9.3 and get instant feedback.

━━━━━━━━━━━━━ MyEconLab ◆

◆ *Reading Between the Lines* on pp. 216–217 shows you how the theory of household choice explains why e-books are taking off, and how people choose whether to buy their books in electronic or paper format.

In the chapters that follow, we study the choices that firms make in their pursuit of profit and how those choices determine the supply of goods and services and the demand for productive resources.

Paper Books Versus e-Books

Are e-books at the Tipping Point?

Toronto Star
January 9, 2011

... Sales figures from Amazon ... show e-book sales for the first nine months of 2010 were triple those recorded in the same period last year. Traditional paperbacks led the way, with twice as many e-books bought in this period compared with old-style bound copies. A quick scan of Amazon's top 25, 100, and 1,000 lists further confirms the e-book's new-found dominance: electronic versions now top all three.

While e-book readers have been around for a while—the Kindle was introduced in the U.S. in 2007 and Sony has been selling models since 2006—they are only now becoming a reality for everyday consumers. The Kindle's $399 launch price restricted its initial appeal mainly to well-heeled bookworms who were willing to gamble that Amazon's e-book vision would prevail. ...

The third generation of Amazon's Kindle ... now sells for $139 and is finally available to Canadian consumers. ...

Just before Christmas, Amazon announced it expected to sell 8 million Kindles in 2010, 66 percent more than the 4.8 million initially forecast by analysts. The company also confirmed it had sold more devices in the first 73 days of the holiday quarter than it had sold in all of 2009. American bookseller Barnes & Noble said it sold out its entire inventory of readers during the holidays, and said strong e-reader sales contributed to a 78 percent increase in e-book revenue and a 67 percent rise in overall sales. ...

Carmi Levy is a London, ON-based independent technology analyst and journalist.

ESSENCE OF THE STORY

- Amazon sold three times as many e-books in the first 9 months of 2010 as it sold in the same period of 2009.

- Amazon's e-book reader, Kindle, was introduced in 2007 at $399.

- The third generation of Kindle sells for $139.

- Kindle was launched in the United States and became available to Canadian consumers in 2010.

- Amazon expected to sell 8 million Kindles in 2010, 66 percent more than initially forecast.

ECONOMIC ANALYSIS

- Print books and e-books are substitutes.

- We will assume that print books and e-books are perfect substitutes so that the only feature of them that matters to a buyer is the opportunity cost of books.

- Beth is a lover of books and albums and she spends all her spare budget, which is $500 per year, on these two items.

- When the price of the Kindle reader was $399, Beth didn't buy one and didn't buy e-books. She bought only print books and albums.

- Figure 1 shows why Beth didn't buy a Kindle and ebooks.

- The light orange line is Beth's budget line if she buys a Kindle reader. The price of an album is $10 and the price of an e-book is also $10. So Beth can afford 10 albums if she buys no e-books ($399 + 10 × $10 = $499). Along this budget line, by forgoing 1 album, she can buy 1 e-book.

- The darker orange line is Beth's budget line if she does not buy an e-book reader. She can afford 50 albums (50 × $10 = $500) if she buys no books. If the price of a print book is $50, by forgoing 5 albums, she can buy one print book.

- The red dot shows Beth's best affordable choice. She buys 5 print books and 25 albums: $50 × 5 + $10 × 25 = $500.

- When the price of the Kindle reader falls to $139, Beth buys e-books and albums. Figure 2 shows why.

- The light orange line in Fig. 2 is Beth's budget line if she buys print books. It is the same as the darker orange line in Fig. 1. Nothing has happened (we're assuming) to her budget or the prices of albums and print books, so this budget line is unchanged.

- The darker orange line in Fig. 2 is Beth's budget line if she buys a Kindle and e-books. After paying $139 for a Kindle, she can afford 36 albums (36 × $10 = $360) if she buys no books. Because the price of an album is the same as the price of an e-book, by forgoing 1 album, she can have 1 e-book.

- The red dot in Fig. 2 shows Beth's best affordable choice. She buys 7 e-books and 29 albums ($10 × 7 + $10 × 29 = $360). This expenditure plus $139 for the Kindle reader exhausts her $500 budget.

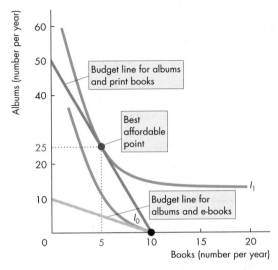

Figure 1 When Kindle Price is $399

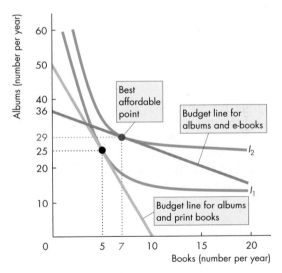

Figure 2 When Kindle Price is $139

SUMMARY

Key Points

Consumption Possibilities (pp. 204–206)

- The budget line is the boundary between what a household can and cannot afford, given its income and the prices of goods.
- The point at which the budget line intersects the *y*-axis is the household's real income in terms of the good measured on that axis.
- The magnitude of the slope of the budget line is the relative price of the good measured on the *x*-axis in terms of the good measured on the *y*-axis.
- A change in the price of one good changes the slope of the budget line. A change in income shifts the budget line but does not change its slope.

Working Problems 1 to 10 will give you a better understanding of consumption possibilities.

Preferences and Indifference Curves (pp. 207–210)

- A consumer's preferences can be represented by indifference curves. The consumer is indifferent among all the combinations of goods that lie on an indifference curve.
- A consumer prefers any point above an indifference curve to any point on it and prefers any point on an indifference curve to any point below it.
- The magnitude of the slope of an indifference curve is called the marginal rate of substitution.

- The marginal rate of substitution diminishes as consumption of the good measured on the *y*-axis decreases and consumption of the good measured on the *x*-axis increases.

Working Problems 11 to 15 will give you a better understanding of preferences and indifference curves.

Predicting Consumer Choices (pp. 210–215)

- A household consumes at its best affordable point. This point is on the budget line and on the highest attainable indifference curve and has a marginal rate of substitution equal to relative price.
- The effect of a price change (the price effect) can be divided into a substitution effect and an income effect.
- The substitution effect is the effect of a change in price on the quantity bought when the consumer (hypothetically) remains indifferent between the original choice and the new choice.
- The substitution effect always results in an increase in consumption of the good whose relative price has fallen.
- The income effect is the effect of a change in income on consumption.
- For a normal good, the income effect reinforces the substitution effect. For an inferior good, the income effect works in the opposite direction to the substitution effect.

Working Problems 16 to 21 will give you a better understanding of predicting consumer choices.

Key Terms

Budget line, 204
Diminishing marginal rate of
   substitution, 208
Income effect, 213
Indifference curve, 207

Marginal rate of substitution, 208
Price effect, 211
Real income, 205
Relative price, 205
Substitution effect, 214

SCAN THIS

STUDY PLAN PROBLEMS AND APPLICATIONS

MyEconLab ◆ You can work Problems 1 to 22 in Chapter 9 Study Plan and get instant feedback.

Consumption Possibilities (Study Plan 9.1)

Use the following information to work Problems 1 to 4.

Sara's income is $12 a week. The price of popcorn is $3 a bag, and the price of a smoothie is $3.

1. Calculate Sara's real income in terms of smoothies. Calculate her real income in terms of popcorn.

2. What is the relative price of smoothies in terms of popcorn? What is the opportunity cost of a smoothie?

3. Calculate the equation for Sara's budget line (with bags of popcorn on the left side).

4. Draw a graph of Sara's budget line with the quantity of smoothies on the x-axis. What is the slope of Sara's budget line? What determines its value?

Use the following information to work Problems 5 to 8.

Sara's income falls from $12 to $9 a week, while the price of popcorn is unchanged at $3 a bag and the price of a smoothie is unchanged at $3.

5. What is the effect of the fall in Sara's income on her real income in terms of smoothies?

6. What is the effect of the fall in Sara's income on her real income in terms of popcorn?

7. What is the effect of the fall in Sara's income on the relative price of a smoothie in terms of popcorn?

8. What is the slope of Sara's new budget line if it is drawn with smoothies on the x-axis?

Use the following information to work Problems 9 and 10.

Sara's income is $12 a week. The price of popcorn rises from $3 to $6 a bag, and the price of a smoothie is unchanged at $3.

9. What is the effect of the rise in the price of popcorn on Sara's real income in terms of smoothies and her real income in terms of popcorn?

10. What is the effect of the rise in the price of popcorn on the relative price of a smoothie in terms of popcorn? What is the slope of Sara's new budget line if it is drawn with smoothies on the x-axis?

Preferences and Indifference Curves (Study Plan 9.2)

11. Draw figures that show your indifference curves for the following pairs of goods:
    - Right gloves and left gloves
    - Coca-Cola and Pepsi
    - Tylenol and acetaminophen (the generic form of Tylenol)
    - Desktop computers and notebook computers
    - Strawberries and ice cream

    For each pair, are the goods perfect substitutes, perfect complements, substitutes, complements, or unrelated?

12. Discuss the shape of the indifference curve for each of the following pairs of goods:
    - Orange juice and smoothies
    - Baseballs and baseball bats
    - Left running shoe and right running shoe
    - Ice cream and fudge sauce
    - Eyeglasses and contact lenses

    Explain the relationship between the shape of the indifference curve and the marginal rate of substitution as the quantities of the two goods change.

Use the following news clip to work Problems 13 and 14.

The Year in Medicine

Sudafed, used by allergy sufferers, contains as the active ingredient pseudoephedrine, which is widely used to make home-made methamphetamine. Allergy sufferers looking to buy Sudafed must now show photo ID, and sign a logbook. The most common alternative, phenylephrine, isn't as effective as pseudoephedrine.

Source: *Time*, December 4, 2006

13. Sketch an indifference curve for Sudafed and phenylephrine that is consistent with this news clip. On your graph, identify combinations that allergy sufferers prefer, do not prefer, and are indifferent among.

14. Explain how the marginal rate of substitution changes as an allergy sufferer increases the consumption of Sudafed.

15. With high gasoline prices, 12 percent of the people surveyed say that they have cancelled their holiday weekend car trip and 11 percent will take shorter outings near home. That may save consumers some money, but it will also likely hurt gas stations, which will sell less gasoline and fewer snacks, and hurt hotels, which will have fewer rooms used and serve fewer casual meals.

Describe the degree of substitutability between holiday weekend car trips and other trip-related goods and services and sketch a consumer's preference map that illustrates your description.

Predicting Consumer Choices (Study Plan 9.3)

16. Use the information in Problem 15.

   a. On a sketch of a consumer's preference map between holiday weekend car trips and other trip-related goods and services, draw a consumer's budget line prior to the rise in the price of gasoline. Mark the consumer's best affordable point.

   b. On your graph, show how the best affordable point changes when the price of gasoline rises.

Use the following information to work Problems 17 and 18.

Pam has chosen her best affordable combination of cookies and granola bars. She spends all of her weekly income on 30 cookies at $1 each and 5 granola bars at $2 each. Next week, people expect the price of a cookie to fall to 50¢ and the price of a granola bar to rise to $5.

17. a. Will Pam be able to buy and want to buy 30 cookies and 5 granola bars next week?

   b. Which situation does Pam prefer: cookies at $1 and granola bars at $2 or cookies at 50¢ and granola bars at $5?

18. a. If Pam changes how she spends her weekly income, will she buy more or fewer cookies and more or fewer granola bars?

   b. When the prices change next week, will there be an income effect, a substitution effect, or both at work?

19. **Canadians' New Focus on Thrift**

   Canadian shoppers' shift to greater thriftiness has been unkind to retailers like Bikini Village and Le Château, which recently posted losses, but it may be a boon for budget stores like

Dollarama Inc., which recently generated double-digit sales.

Source: *The Financial Post*, July 3, 2011

Draw a graph to show the effect of increased thriftiness on sales at (i) Bikini Village and (ii) Dollarama.

Use the following news clip to work Problems 20 and 21.

Boom Time for "Gently Used" Clothes

Most retailers are blaming the economy for their poor sales, but one store chain that sells used name-brand children's clothes, toys, and furniture is boldly declaring that an economic downturn can actually be a boon for its business. Last year, the company took in $20 million in sales, up 5 percent from the previous year. Sales are already up 5 percent this year.

Source: CNN, April 17, 2008

20. a. According to the news clip, is used clothing a normal good or an inferior good?

   b. If the price of used clothing falls and income remains the same, explain how the quantity of used clothing bought changes.

   c. If the price of used clothing falls and income remains the same, describe the substitution effect and the income effect that occur.

21. a. Use a graph to illustrate a family's indifference curves for used clothing and other goods.

   b. In your graph in part (a), draw two budget lines to show the effect of a fall in income on the quantity of used clothing purchased.

Economics in the News (Study Plan 9.EN)

22. **Canada Sees Fewer U.S. Visitors on High Dollar, Gas**

   U.S. tourists making car trips to Canada fell 22 percent from last year. While U.S. visitors traditionally have spent a lot of money here, even more than Canadians do, the manager for the Stratford Shakespeare Festival in Stratford, Ontario, said that its ticket sales have taken a big hit.

Source: Bloomberg News, August 18, 2008

   a. Describe the degree of substitutability between gasoline and Stratford tickets and draw a preference map that illustrates your description.

   b. Draw a budget line for gasoline and Stratford tickets and identify the best affordable point.

   c. Show on your graph how the best affordable point changes when the price of gasoline rises.

ADDITIONAL PROBLEMS AND APPLICATIONS

MyEconLab ◆ You can work these problems in MyEconLab if assigned by your instructor.

Consumption Possibilities

Use the following information to work Problems 23 to 26.

Marc has a budget of $20 a month to spend on root beer and DVDs. The price of root beer is $5 a bottle, and the price of a DVD is $10.

23. What is the relative price of root beer in terms of DVDs and what is the opportunity cost of a bottle of root beer?

24. Calculate Marc's real income in terms of root beer. Calculate his real income in terms of DVDs.

25. Calculate the equation for Marc's budget line (with the quantity of root beer on the left side).

26. Draw a graph of Marc's budget line with the quantity of DVDs on the *x*-axis. What is the slope of Marc's budget line? What determines its value?

Use the following information to work Problems 27 to 30.

Amy has $20 a week to spend on coffee and cake. The price of coffee is $4 a cup, and the price of cake is $2 a slice.

27. Calculate Amy's real income in terms of cake. Calculate the relative price of cake in terms of coffee.

28. Calculate the equation for Amy's budget line (with cups of coffee on the left side).

29. If Amy's income increases to $24 a week and the prices of coffee and cake remain unchanged, describe the change in her budget line.

30. If the price of cake doubles while the price of coffee remains at $4 a cup and Amy's income remains at $20, describe the change in her budget line.

Use the following news clip to work Problems 31 and 32.

Gas Prices Straining Budgets

With gas prices rising, many people say they are staying in and scaling back spending to try to keep within their budget. They are driving as little as possible, cutting back on shopping and eating out, and reducing other discretionary spending.

Source: CNN, February 29, 2008

31. a. Sketch a budget line for a household that spends its income on only two goods: gasoline and restaurant meals. Identify the combinations of gasoline and restaurant meals that are affordable and those that are unaffordable.
   b. Sketch a second budget line to show how a rise in the price of gasoline changes the affordable and unaffordable combinations of gasoline and restaurant meals. Describe how the household's consumption possibilities change.

32. How does a rise in the price of gasoline change the relative price of a restaurant meal? How does a rise in the price of gasoline change real income in terms of restaurant meals?

Preferences and Indifference Curves

Use the following information to work Problems 33 and 34.

Rashid buys only books and CDs and the figure shows his preference map.

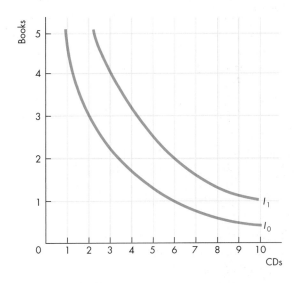

33. a. If Rashid chooses 3 books and 2 CDs, what is his marginal rate of substitution?
   b. If Rashid chooses 2 books and 6 CDs, what is his marginal rate of substitution?

34. Do Rashid's indifference curves display diminishing marginal rate of substitution? Explain why or why not.

35. **You May Be Paid More (or Less) Than You Think**

It's so hard to put a price on happiness, isn't it? But if you've ever had to choose between a job you like and a better-paying one that you like less, you probably wished some economist would tell you how much job satisfaction is worth. Trust in management is by far the biggest component to consider. Say you get a new boss and your trust in management goes up a bit (say, up 1 point on a 10-point scale). That's like getting a 36 percent pay raise. In other words, that increased level of trust will boost your level of overall satisfaction in life by about the same amount as a 36 percent raise would.

Source: CNN, March 29, 2006

a. Measure trust in management on a 10-point scale, measure pay on the same 10-point scale, and think of them as two goods. Sketch an indifference curve (with trust on the x-axis) that is consistent with the news clip.

b. What is the marginal rate of substitution between trust in management and pay according to this news clip?

c. What does the news clip imply about the principle of diminishing marginal rate of substitution? Is that implication likely to be correct?

Predicting Consumer Choices

Use the following information to work Problems 36 and 37.

Jim has made his best affordable choice of muffins and coffee. He spends all of his income on 10 muffins at $1 each and 20 cups of coffee at $2 each. Now the price of a muffin rises to $1.50 and the price of coffee falls to $1.75 a cup.

36. a. Will Jim now be able and want to buy 10 muffins and 20 coffees?

b. Which situation does Jim prefer: muffins at $1 and coffee at $2 a cup or muffins at $1.50 and coffee at $1.75 a cup?

37. a. If Jim changes the quantities that he buys, will he buy more or fewer muffins and more or less coffee?

b. When the prices change, will there be an income effect, a substitution effect, or both at work?

Use the following information to work Problems 38 to 40.

Sara's income is $12 a week. The price of popcorn is $3 a bag, and the price of cola is $1.50 a can. The figure shows Sara's preference map for popcorn and cola.

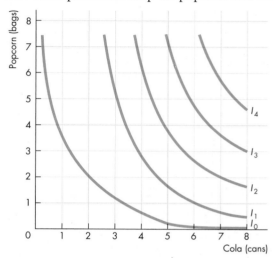

38. What quantities of popcorn and cola does Sara buy? What is Sara's marginal rate of substitution at the point at which she consumes?

39. Suppose that the price of cola rises to $3 a can and the price of popcorn and Sara's income remain the same. What quantities of cola and popcorn does Sara now buy? What are two points on Sara's demand curve for cola? Draw Sara's demand curve.

40. Suppose that the price of cola rises to $3 a can and the price of popcorn and Sara's income remain the same.

a. What is the substitution effect of this price change and what is the income effect of the price change?

b. Is cola a normal good or an inferior good? Explain.

Economics in the News

41. After you have studied *Reading Between the Lines* on pp. 216–217, answer the following questions.

a. How do you buy books?

b. Sketch your budget line for books and other goods.

c. Sketch your indifference curves for books and other goods.

d. Explain why Andy would buy e-books if the price of a reader fell to $100.

Making the Most of Life

UNDERSTANDING HOUSEHOLDS' CHOICES

The powerful forces of demand and supply shape the fortunes of families, businesses, nations, and empires in the same unrelenting way that the tides and winds shape rocks and coastlines. You saw in Chapters 3 through 7 how these forces raise and lower prices, increase and decrease quantities bought and sold, cause revenues to fluctuate, and send resources to their most valuable uses.

These powerful forces begin quietly and privately with the choices that each one of us makes. Chapters 8 and 9 probe these individual choices, offering two alternative approaches to explaining both consumption plans and the allocation of time. These explanations of consumption plans can also explain "noneconomic" choices, such as whether to marry and how many children to have. In a sense, there are no noneconomic choices. If there is scarcity, there must be choice, and economics studies all choices.

The earliest economists (Adam Smith and his contemporaries) did not have a very deep understanding of households' choices. It was not until the nineteenth century that progress was made in this area when Jeremy Bentham (below) introduced the concept of utility and applied it to the study of human choices. Today, Steven Levitt of the University of Chicago, whom you will meet on the following pages, is one of the most influential students of human behaviour.

Jeremy Bentham *(1748–1832), who lived in London, was the son and grandson of lawyers and was himself trained as a barrister. But Bentham rejected the opportunity to maintain the family tradition and, instead, spent his life as a writer, activist, and Member of Parliament in the pursuit of rational laws that would bring the greatest happiness to the greatest number of people.*

Bentham, whose embalmed body is preserved to this day in a glass cabinet in the University of London, was the first person to use the concept of utility to explain human choices. But in Bentham's day, the distinction between explaining and prescribing was not a sharp one, and Bentham was ready to use his ideas to tell people how they ought to behave. He was one of the first to propose pensions for the retired, guaranteed employment, minimum wages, and social benefits such as free education and free medical care.

...It is the greatest happiness of the greatest number that is the measure of right and wrong.

JEREMY BENTHAM
Fragment on Government

Why did you become an economist?

As a freshman in college, I took introductory economics. All the ideas made perfect sense to me—it was the way I naturally thought. My friends were befuddled. I thought, "This is the field for me!"

The idea of rational choice made at the margin lies at the heart of economics. Would you say that your work generally supports that idea or challenges it? Can you provide some examples?

I don't like the word "rational" in this context. I think economists model agents as being rational just for convenience. What really matters is whether people respond to incentives. My work very much supports the idea that humans in all types of circumstances respond strongly to incentives. I've seen it with drug dealers, auto thieves, sumo wrestlers, real estate agents, and elementary school teachers, just to name a few examples.

Can you elaborate? What are the incentives to which drug dealers respond? And does an understanding of these responses tell us anything about how public policy might influence drug use?

The incentives people face differ depending on their particular circumstances. Drug dealers, for instance, want to make money, but they also want to avoid being arrested or even killed. In the data we have on drug sellers, we see that when the drug trade is more lucrative, dealers are willing to take greater risks of arrest to carve out a share of the market. On the other hand, they also do their best to minimize their risks. For example, crack sellers used to carry the crack with them. When laws were passed imposing stiff penalties on anyone caught with anything more than a minimal amount of crack, drug dealers responded by storing the crack somewhere else, and retrieving only the amount being sold to the current client. Sumo wrestlers, on the other hand, care mostly about their official ranking. Sometimes matches occur where one wrestler has more to lose or gain than the other wrestler. We find that sumo wrestlers make corrupt deals to make sure the wrestler who needs the win is the one who actually wins.

Why is an economist interested in crime and cheating?

I think of economics as being primarily about a way of looking at the world and a set of tools for thinking clearly. The topics you apply these tools to are unlimited. That is why I think economics has been so powerful. If you understand economics and use the tools wisely, you will be a better business person, doctor, public servant, parent.

> I think of economics as being primarily about a way of looking at the world and a set of tools for thinking clearly.

STEVEN D. LEVITT is Alvin H. Baum Professor of Economics at the University of Chicago. Born in Minneapolis, he was an undergraduate at Harvard and a graduate student at MIT. Among his many honours, he was recently awarded the John Bates Clark Medal, given to the best economist under 40.

Professor Levitt has studied an astonishingly wide range of human choices and their outcomes. He has examined the effects of policing on crime, shown that real estate agents get a higher price when they sell their own homes than when they sell other people's, devised a test to detect cheating teachers, and studied the choices of drug dealers and gang members. Much of this research has been popularized in *Freakonomics* (Steven D. Levitt and Stephen J. Dubner, HarperCollins, 2005). What unifies this apparently diverse body of research is the use of natural experiments. Professor Levitt has an incredible ability to find just the right set of events and the data the events have generated to enable him to isolate the effect he's looking for.

Michael Parkin and Robin Bade talked with Steven Levitt about his career and the progress that economists have made in understanding how people respond to incentives in all aspects of life.

What is the economic model of crime, and how does it help to design better ways of dealing with criminal activity? Can you illustrate by talking a bit about your work on the behaviour of auto thieves?

The economic model of crime argues that people have a choice of either working for a wage in the legal sector or earning money from illegal activity. The model carefully lays out the set of costs associated with being a criminal (e.g., forgone wages and being punished) and benefits (e.g., the loot) associated with crime and analyses how a maximizing individual will choose whether to commit crimes and how much crime to commit. One reason the model is useful is because it lays out the various ways in which public policy might influence crime rates. For instance, we can increase the probability of a criminal getting caught or make the prison sentence longer for those who are caught. The government might also try to intervene in the labour market to make legal work more attractive—for instance, with a minimum wage.

What is the problem in figuring out whether more police leads to less crime? How did you find the answer?

We think that when you add more police, crime will fall because the cost of being a criminal goes up because of increased detection. From a public policy perspective, understanding how much crime falls in response to police is an important question. In practice, it is hard to answer this question because we don't randomly hire police. Rather, where crime is bad, there is greater demand for police and thus more police. If you just look at different cities, the places with the most police also have the most crime, but it is not because police cause crime, it is because crime causes police to be hired.

> If you just look at different cities, the places with the most police also have the most crime, but it is not because police cause crime, it is because crime causes police to be hired.

To figure out a causal impact of police on crime, you would like to do a randomized experiment where you added a lot of police at random to some cities and took them away in other cities. That is something you cannot really do in real life. So instead, the economist has to look for "natural experiments" to answer the question.

I used the timing of mayoral elections. It turns out that mayors hire a lot of police before elections to "look tough on crime." If elections do not otherwise affect crime, then the election is kind of like a randomizing device that puts more police in some cities every once in a while. Indeed, I found that crime goes down in the year following elections once the police hired are up and running. It is indirect evidence, but it is an example of how economists use their toolbox to handle difficult questions.

Your work shows that legalized abortion leads to less crime. Can you explain how you reach that conclusion? Can you also explain its implications for the pro-life, pro-choice debate?

The theory is simple: Unwanted children have hard lives (including being much more likely to be criminals); after legalized abortion, there are fewer unwanted children. Therefore, there should be less crime (with a 15–20 year lag while the babies grow up and reach high-crime ages).

We looked at what happened to crime 15–20 years after *Roe v. Wade*, in states with high and low abortion rates and in states that legalized abortion a few years earlier than the rest of the country. We could even look at people born immediately before or after abortion became legal.

All the evidence pointed the same way: Crime fell a lot because abortion was legalized.

Our results, however, don't have large implications for the abortion debate. If abortion is murder, as pro-life advocates argue, then the changes in crime we see are trivial in comparison. If a woman simply has the right to control her body, as pro-choice advocates argue, then our estimates about crime are likewise irrelevant.

Our results have more to say about unwantedness: There are big benefits to making sure that children who are brought into the world are wanted and well cared for, through either birth control, adoption, abortion, or parental education.

Terrorism is on everyone's minds these days. And presumably, terrorists respond to incentives. Have you thought about how we might be able to use the insights of economics to better understand and perhaps even combat terrorism?

Terrorism is an unusually difficult question to tackle through incentives. The religious terrorists we are most worried about are willing to give up their lives to carry out terrorist acts. So the only punishment we can really offer is preventing them from committing the act by catching them beforehand or maybe minimizing the damage they can do. Unlike typical criminals, the threat of punishing them after the fact will not help deter the crime. Luckily, even among extremists, there are not many people willing to give their lives for a cause.

Can a student learn how to use natural experiments or do you have a gift that is hard to teach?

I don't think I have such a gift. Most people who are good at something are good because they have worked hard and practiced. That is certainly true with me.

For a while, I just walked around and every time I observed anything in the world I asked myself, "Is that a natural experiment?" Every once in a while I stumbled onto one because I was on the lookout.

> . . . every time I observed anything in the world I asked myself, "Is that a natural experiment?"

What else can a student who wants to become a natural experimenting economist or broader social scientist do to better prepare for that career?

I would say that the best thing students can do is to try to really apply what they are learning to their lives, rather than just memorizing for an exam and quickly forgetting. If you are passionate about economics (or anything else for that matter), you are way ahead of others who are just trying to get by.

CHAPTER
10

Organizing Production

After studying this chapter, you will be able to

◆ Explain what a firm is and describe the economic problem that all firms face

◆ Distinguish between technological efficiency and economic efficiency

◆ Define and explain the principal–agent problem and describe how different types of business organizations cope with this problem

◆ Describe and distinguish between the types of markets in which firms operate

◆ Explain why markets coordinate some economic activities and why firms coordinate others

When Tim Berners-Lee invented the World Wide Web in 1990, he paved the way for the creation of thousands of profitable businesses that include Facebook, Twitter, Apple, Microsoft, Google, and Yahoo!

Some of these successful dot.com firms sell goods and others sell services, but many firms don't *make* the things they sell: They *buy* them from other firms. For example, Apple doesn't make the iPhone!

How do Facebook, Twitter, Apple, Microsoft, Google, Yahoo! and the millions of other firms make their business decisions?

In this chapter, you're going to learn about firms and the choices they make. In *Reading Between the Lines* at the end of the chapter, we'll apply some of what you've learned and look at some of the choices made by Facebook and Yahoo! in the Internet advertising game.

◆ The Firm and Its Economic Problem

The 2 million firms in Canada differ in size and in the scope of what they do, but they all perform the same basic economic functions. Each **firm** is an institution that hires factors of production and organizes those factors to produce and sell goods and services. Our goal is to predict firms' behaviour. To do so, we need to know a firm's goal and the constraints it faces. We start with the goal.

The Firm's Goal

When economists ask entrepreneurs what they are trying to achieve, they get many different answers. Some talk about making a high-quality product, others about business growth, others about market share, others about the job satisfaction of their workforce, and an increasing number today talk about social and environmental responsibility. All of these goals are pursued by firms, but they are not the fundamental goal: They are the means to that goal.

A firm's goal is to maximize profit. A firm that does not seek to maximize profit either fails or is taken over by a firm that does seek that goal.

What is the profit that a firm seeks to maximize? To answer this question, we'll look at Campus Sweaters, Inc., a small producer of knitted sweaters owned and operated by Cindy.

Accounting Profit

In 2011, Campus Sweaters received $400,000 for the sweaters it sold and paid out $80,000 for wool, $20,000 for utilities, $120,000 for wages, $5,000 for the lease of a computer, and $5,000 in interest on a bank loan. These expenses total $230,000, so the firm had a cash surplus of $170,000.

To measure the profit of Campus Sweaters, Cindy's accountant subtracted $20,000 for the depreciation of buildings and knitting machines from the $170,000 cash surplus. *Depreciation* is the fall in the value of a firm's capital. To calculate depreciation, accountants use Revenue Canada rules based on standards established by the accounting profession. Using these rules, Cindy's accountant calculated that Campus Sweaters made a profit of $150,000 in 2011.

Economic Accounting

Accountants measure a firm's profit to ensure that the firm pays the correct amount of income tax and to show its investors how their funds are being used.

Economists measure a firm's profit to enable them to predict the firm's decisions, and the goal of these decisions is to maximize *economic profit*. **Economic profit** is equal to total revenue minus total cost, with total cost measured as the *opportunity cost of production*.

A Firm's Opportunity Cost of Production

The *opportunity cost* of any action is the highest-valued alternative forgone. The *opportunity cost of production* is the value of the best alternative use of the resources that a firm uses in production.

A firm's opportunity cost of production is the value of real alternatives forgone. We express opportunity cost in money units so that we can compare and add up the value of the alternatives forgone.

A firm's opportunity cost of production is the sum of the cost of using resources

- Bought in the market
- Owned by the firm
- Supplied by the firm's owner

Resources Bought in the Market A firm incurs an opportunity cost when it buys resources in the market. The amount spent on these resources is an opportunity cost of production because the firm could have bought different resources to produce some other good or service. For Campus Sweaters, the resources bought in the market are wool, utilities, labour, a leased computer, and a bank loan. The $230,000 spent on these items in 2011 could have been spent on something else, so it is an opportunity cost of producing sweaters.

Resources Owned by the Firm A firm incurs an opportunity cost when it uses its own capital. The cost of using capital owned by the firm is an opportunity cost of production because the firm could sell the capital that it owns and rent capital from another firm. When a firm uses its own capital, it implicitly rents it from itself. In this case, the firm's opportunity cost of using the capital it owns is called the implicit rental rate of capital. The **implicit rental rate** of capital has two components: economic depreciation and forgone interest.

Economic Depreciation Accountants measure *depreciation*, the fall in the value of a firm's capital, using formulas that are unrelated to the change in the market value of capital. **Economic depreciation** is the fall in the *market value* of a firm's capital over the year: the market price of the capital at the start of the year minus the market price of the capital at the end of the year.

Suppose that Campus Sweaters could have sold its buildings and knitting machines on January 1, 2011, for $400,000 and that it can sell the same capital on December 31, 2011, for $375,000. The firm's economic depreciation during 2011 is $25,000 ($400,000 − $375,000). This forgone $25,000 is an opportunity cost of production.

Forgone Interest The funds used to buy capital could have been used for some other purpose, and in their next best use, they would have earned interest. This forgone interest is an opportunity cost of production.

Suppose that Campus Sweaters used $300,000 of its own funds to buy capital. If the firm invested its $300,000 in bonds instead of a knitting factory (and rented the capital it needs to produce sweaters), it would have earned $15,000 a year in interest. This forgone interest is an opportunity cost of production.

Resources Supplied by the Firm's Owner A firm's owner might supply *both* entrepreneurship and labour.

Entrepreneurship The factor of production that organizes a firm and makes its decisions might be supplied by the firm's owner or by a hired entrepreneur. The return to entrepreneurship is profit, and the profit that an entrepreneur earns *on average* is called **normal profit**. Normal profit is the cost of entrepreneurship and is an opportunity cost of production.

If Cindy supplies entrepreneurial services herself, and if the normal profit she can earn on these services is $45,000 a year, this amount is an opportunity cost of production at Campus Sweaters.

Owner's Labour Services *In addition* to supplying entrepreneurship, the owner of a firm might supply labour but not take a wage. The opportunity cost of the owner's labour is the wage income forgone by not taking the best alternative job. For example, if Cindy supplies labour to Campus Sweaters, and if the wage she can earn on this labour at another firm is $55,000 a year, this amount of wages forgone is an opportunity cost of production at Campus Sweaters.

Economic Accounting: A Summary

Table 10.1 summarizes the economic accounting. Campus Sweaters' total revenue is $400,000; its opportunity cost of production is $370,000; and its economic profit is $30,000.

Cindy's personal income is the $30,000 of economic profit plus the $100,000 that she earns by supplying resources to Campus Sweaters.

Decisions

To achieve the objective of maximum economic profit, a firm must make five decisions:

1. What to produce and in what quantities
2. How to produce
3. How to organize and compensate its managers and workers
4. How to market and price its products
5. What to produce itself and buy from others

In all these decisions, a firm's actions are limited by the constraints that it faces. Your next task is to learn about these constraints.

TABLE 10.1   Economic Accounting

Item		Amount
Total Revenue		**$400,000**
Cost of Resources Bought in Market		
Wool	$80,000	
Utilities	20,000	
Wages	120,000	
Computer lease	5,000	
Bank interest	5,000	$230,000
Cost of Resources Owned by Firm		
Economic depreciation	$25,000	
Forgone interest	15,000	$40,000
Cost of Resources Supplied by Owner		
Cindy's normal profit	$45,000	
Cindy's forgone wages	55,000	$100,000
Opportunity Cost of Production		**$370,000**
Economic Profit		**$30,000**

The Firm's Constraints

Three features of a firm's environment limit the maximum economic profit it can make. They are

- Technology constraints
- Information constraints
- Market constraints

Technology Constraints Economists define technology broadly. A **technology** is any method of producing a good or service. Technology includes the detailed designs of machines and the layout of the workplace. It includes the organization of the firm. For example, the shopping mall is one technology for producing retail services. It is a different technology from the catalogue store, which in turn is different from the downtown store.

It might seem surprising that a firm's profit is limited by technology because it seems that technological advances are constantly increasing profit opportunities. Almost every day, we learn about some new technological advance that amazes us. With computers that speak and recognize our own speech and cars that can find the address we need in a city we've never visited, we can accomplish more than ever.

Technology advances over time. But at each point in time, to produce more output and gain more revenue, a firm must hire more resources and incur greater costs. The increase in profit that a firm can achieve is limited by the technology available. For example, by using its current plant and workforce, Ford can produce some maximum number of cars per day. To produce more cars per day, Ford must hire more resources, which increases its costs and limits the increase in profit that it can make by selling the additional cars.

Information Constraints We never possess all the information we would like to have to make decisions. We lack information about both the future and the present. For example, suppose you plan to buy a new computer. When should you buy it? The answer depends on how the price is going to change in the future. Where should you buy it? The answer depends on the prices at hundreds of different computer stores. To get the best deal, you must compare the quality and prices in every store. But the opportunity cost of this comparison exceeds the cost of the computer!

A firm is constrained by limited information about the quality and efforts of its workforce, the current and future buying plans of its customers, and the plans of its competitors. Workers might make too little effort, customers might switch to competing suppliers, and a competitor might enter the market and take some of the firm's business.

To address these problems, firms create incentives to boost workers' efforts even when no one is monitoring them, conduct market research to lower uncertainty about customers' buying plans, and "spy" on each other to anticipate competitive challenges. But these efforts don't eliminate incomplete information and uncertainty, which limit the economic profit that a firm can make.

Market Constraints The quantity each firm can sell and the price it can obtain are constrained by its customers' willingness to pay and by the prices and marketing efforts of other firms. Similarly, the resources that a firm can buy and the prices it must pay for them are limited by the willingness of people to work for and invest in the firm. Firms spend billions of dollars a year marketing and selling their products. Some of the most creative minds strive to find the right message that will produce a knockout television advertisement. Market constraints and the expenditures firms make to overcome them limit the profit a firm can make.

REVIEW QUIZ

1 What is a firm's fundamental goal and what happens if the firm doesn't pursue this goal?
2 Why do accountants and economists calculate a firm's cost and profit in different ways?
3 What are the items that make opportunity cost differ from the accountant's measure of cost?
4 Why is normal profit an opportunity cost?
5 What are the constraints that a firm faces? How does each constraint limit the firm's profit?

You can work these questions in Study Plan 10.1 and get instant feedback.

─────────────────── MyEconLab ◆

In the rest of this chapter and in Chapters 11 through 14, we study the choices that firms make. You're going to learn how we can predict a firm's decisions as those that maximize profit given the constraints the firm faces. We begin by taking a closer look at a firm's technology constraints.

Technological and Economic Efficiency

RIM employs a large workforce, and most RIM workers possess a large amount of human capital. But the firm uses a small amount of physical capital. In contrast, a coal-mining company employs a huge amount of mining equipment (physical capital) and almost no labour. Why? The answer lies in the concept of efficiency. There are two concepts of production efficiency: technological efficiency and economic efficiency. **Technological efficiency** occurs when the firm produces a given output by using the least amount of inputs. **Economic efficiency** occurs when the firm produces a given output at the least cost. Let's explore the two concepts of efficiency by studying an example.

Suppose that there are four alternative techniques for making TVs:

A. *Robot production.* One person monitors the entire computer-driven process.
B. *Production line.* Workers specialize in a small part of the job as the emerging TV passes them on a production line.
C. *Hand-tool production.* A single worker uses a few hand tools to make a TV.
D. *Bench production.* Workers specialize in a small part of the job but walk from bench to bench to perform their tasks.

Table 10.2 sets out the amounts of labour and capital required by each of these four methods to make 10 TVs a day.

Which of these alternative methods are technologically efficient?

Technological Efficiency

Recall that *technological efficiency* occurs when the firm produces a given output by using the least amount of inputs. Look at the numbers in the table and notice that method *A* uses the most capital and the least labour. Method *C* uses the most labour and the least capital. Method *B* and method *D* lie between the two extremes. They use less capital and more labour than method *A* and less labour but more capital than method *C*.

Compare methods *B* and *D*. Method *D* requires 100 workers and 10 units of capital to produce

TABLE 10.2   Four Ways of Making 10 TVs a Day

		Quantities of inputs	
	Method	Labour	Capital
A	Robot production	1	1,000
B	Production line	10	10
C	Hand-tool production	1,000	1
D	Bench production	100	10

10 TVs. Those same 10 TVs can be produced by method *B* with 10 workers and the same 10 units of capital. Because method *D* uses the same amount of capital and more labour than method *B*, method *D* is not technologically efficient.

Are any of the other methods not technologically efficient? The answer is no. Each of the other methods is technologically efficient. Method *A* uses more capital but less labour than method *B*, and method *C* uses more labour but less capital than method *B*.

Which of the methods are economically efficient?

Economic Efficiency

Recall that *economic efficiency* occurs when the firm produces a given output at the least cost.

Method *D*, which is technologically inefficient, is also economically inefficient. It uses the same amount of capital as method *B* but 10 times as much labour, so it costs more. A technologically inefficient method is never economically efficient.

One of the three technologically efficient methods is economically efficient. The other two are economically inefficient. But which method is economically efficient depends on factor prices.

In Table 10.3(a), the wage rate is $75 per day and the rental rate of capital is $250 per day. By studying Table 10.3(a), you can see that method *B* has the lowest cost and is the economically efficient method.

In Table 10.3(b), the wage rate is $150 a day and the rental rate of capital is $1 a day. Looking at Table 10.3(b), you can see that method *A* has the lowest cost and is the economically efficient method. In this case, capital is so cheap relative to labour that the

TABLE 10.3   The Costs of Different Ways of Making 10 TVs a Day

(a) Wage rate $75 per day; Capital rental rate $250 per day

Method	Inputs Labour	Capital	Labour cost ($75 per day)		Capital cost ($250 per day)		Total cost
A	1	1,000	$75	+	$250,000	=	$250,075
B	10	10	750	+	2,500	=	3,250
C	1,000	1	75,000	+	250	=	75,250

(b) Wage rate $150 per day; Capital rental rate $1 per day

Method	Inputs Labour	Capital	Labour cost ($150 per day)		Capital cost ($1 per day)		Total cost
A	1	1,000	$150	+	$1,000	=	$1,150
B	10	10	1,500	+	10	=	1,510
C	1,000	1	150,000	+	1	=	150,001

(c) Wage rate $1 per day; Capital rental rate $1,000 per day

Method	Inputs Labour	Capital	Labour cost ($1 per day)		Capital cost ($1,000 per day)		Total cost
A	1	1,000	$1	+	$1,000,000	=	$1,000,001
B	10	10	10	+	10,000	=	10,010
C	1,000	1	1,000	+	1,000	=	2,000

method that uses the most capital is the economically efficient method.

In Table 10.3(c), the wage rate is $1 a day and the rental rate of capital is $1,000 a day. You can see that method C has the lowest cost and is the economically efficient method. In this case, labour is so cheap relative to capital that the method that uses the most labour is the economically efficient method.

Economic efficiency depends on the relative costs of resources. The economically efficient method is the one that uses a smaller amount of the more expensive resource and a larger amount of the less expensive resource.

A firm that is not economically efficient does not maximize profit. Natural selection favours efficient firms and inefficient firms disappear. Inefficient firms go out of business or are taken over by firms that produce at lower costs.

REVIEW QUIZ

1 Is a firm technologically efficient if it uses the latest technology? Why or why not?

2 Is a firm economically inefficient if it can cut its costs by producing less? Why or why not?

3 Explain the key distinction between technological efficiency and economic efficiency.

4 Why do some firms use a lot of capital and a small amount of labour while others use a small amount of capital and a lot of labour?

You can work these questions in Study Plan 10.2 and get instant feedback.

━━━━━━━━━━━━━━━━━━━━━━ MyEconLab ◆

Next we study the information constraints that firms face and the wide array of organization structures these constraints generate.

◆ Information and Organization

Each firm organizes the production of goods and services by combining and coordinating the productive resources it hires. But there is variety across firms in how they organize production. Firms use a mixture of two systems:

■ Command systems
■ Incentive systems

Command Systems

A **command system** is a method of organizing production that uses a managerial hierarchy. Commands pass downward through the hierarchy, and information passes upward. Managers spend most of their time collecting and processing information about the performance of the people under their control and making decisions about what commands to issue and how best to get those commands implemented.

The military uses the purest form of command system. A commander-in-chief (in Canada, the prime minister) makes the big decisions about strategic goals. Beneath this highest level, generals organize their military resources. Beneath the generals, successively lower ranks organize smaller and smaller units but pay attention to ever-increasing degrees of detail. At the bottom of the managerial hierarchy are the people who operate weapons systems.

Command systems in firms are not as rigid as those in the military, but they share some similar features. A chief executive officer (CEO) sits at the top of a firm's command system. Senior executives who report to and receive commands from the CEO specialize in managing production, marketing, finance, personnel, and perhaps other aspects of the firm's operations. Beneath these senior managers might be several tiers of middle management ranks that stretch downward to the managers who supervise the day-to-day operations of the business. Beneath these managers are the people who operate the firm's machines and who make and sell the firm's goods and services.

Small firms have one or two layers of managers, while large firms have several layers. As production processes have become ever more complex, management ranks have swollen. Today, more people have management jobs than ever before, even though the information revolution slowed the growth of management. In some industries, the information revolution reduced the number of layers of managers and brought a shakeout of middle managers.

Managers make enormous efforts to be well informed. They try hard to make good decisions and issue commands that end up using resources efficiently. But managers always have incomplete information about what is happening in the divisions of the firm for which they are responsible. For this reason, firms use incentive systems as well as command systems to organize production.

Incentive Systems

An **incentive system** is a method of organizing production that uses a market-like mechanism inside the firm. Instead of issuing commands, senior managers create compensation schemes to induce workers to perform in ways that maximize the firm's profit.

Selling organizations use incentive systems most extensively. Sales representatives who spend most of their working time alone and unsupervised are induced to work hard by being paid a small salary and a large performance-related bonus.

But incentive systems operate at all levels in a firm. The compensation plan of a CEO includes a share in the firm's profit, and factory floor workers sometimes receive compensation based on the quantity they produce.

Mixing the Systems

Firms use a mixture of commands and incentives, and they choose the mixture that maximizes profit. Firms use commands when it is easy to monitor performance or when a small deviation from an ideal performance is very costly. They use incentives when it is either not possible to monitor performance or too costly to be worth doing.

For example, Bombardier can easily monitor the performance of workers on a production line. If one person works too slowly, the entire line slows, so a production line is organized with a command system.

In contrast, it is costly to monitor a CEO. For example, what does Larry Page, the CEO of Google Inc., contribute to its success? This question can't be answered with certainty, yet Google's stockholders have to put someone in charge and provide that person with an incentive to maximize stockholders' returns. The performance of Google illustrates a general problem: the principal–agent problem.

The Principal–Agent Problem

The **principal–agent problem** is the problem of devising compensation rules that induce an *agent* to act in the best interest of a *principal.* For example, the stockholders of RIM are *principals,* and the firm's managers are *agents.* The stockholders of RIM (the principals) must induce the managers (agents) to act in the stockholders' best interest. Similarly, Mike Lazaridis (a principal) must induce the designers who are working on the next generation BlackBerry (agents) to work efficiently.

Agents, whether they are managers or workers, pursue their own goals and often impose costs on a principal. For example, the goal of stockholders of CIBC (principals) is to maximize the firm's profit—its true profit, not some fictitious paper profit. But the firm's profit depends on the actions of its managers (agents), and they have their own goals. Perhaps a bank manager takes a customer to a hockey game on the pretense that she is building customer loyalty, when in fact she is simply enjoying on-the-job leisure. This same manager is also a principal, and her tellers are agents. The manager wants the tellers to work hard and attract new customers so that she can meet her operating targets. But the workers enjoy conversations with each other and take on-the-job leisure. Nonetheless, the firm constantly strives to find ways of improving performance and increasing profits.

Coping with the Principal–Agent Problem

Issuing commands does not address the principal–agent problem. In most firms, the shareholders can't monitor the managers and often the managers can't monitor the workers. Each principal must create incentives that induce each agent to work in the interests of the principal. Three ways of attempting to cope with the principal–agent problem are

- Ownership
- Incentive pay
- Long-term contracts

Ownership By assigning ownership (or part-ownership) of a business to managers or workers, it is sometimes possible to induce a job performance that increases a firm's profits. Part-ownership is quite common for senior managers but less common for workers. WestJet offers its employees an Employee Share Purchase Plan, so most of its employees are owners of the company.

Incentive Pay Incentive pay—pay related to performance—is very common. Incentives are based on a variety of performance criteria such as profits, production, or sales targets. Promoting an employee for good performance is another example of the use of incentive pay.

Long-Term Contracts Long-term contracts tie the long-term fortunes of managers and workers (agents) to the success of the principal(s)—the owner(s) of the firm. For example, a multiyear employment contract for a CEO encourages that person to take a long-term view and devise strategies that achieve maximum profit over a sustained period.

These three ways of coping with the principal–agent problem give rise to different types of business organization. Each type of business organization is a different response to the principal–agent problem. Each type uses a different combination of ownership, incentives, and long-term contracts. Let's look at the main types of business organization.

Types of Business Organization

The three main types of business organization are

- Sole proprietorship
- Partnership
- Corporation

Sole Proprietorship A *sole proprietorship* is a firm with a single owner—a proprietor—who has unlimited liability. *Unlimited liability* is the legal responsibility for all the debts of a firm up to an amount equal to the entire wealth of the owner. If a sole proprietorship cannot pay its debts, those to whom the firm owes money can claim the personal property of the owner.

Businesses of some farmers, computer programmers, and artists are examples of sole proprietorships. The proprietor makes management decisions, receives the firm's profits, and is responsible for its losses. Profits from a sole proprietorship are taxed at the same rate as other sources of the proprietor's personal income.

Partnership A *partnership* is a firm with two or more owners who have unlimited liability. Partners must agree on an appropriate management structure and on how to divide the firm's profits among themselves. The profits of a partnership are taxed as the personal income of the owners, but each partner is legally liable for all the debts of the partnership (limited only by the wealth of that individual partner). Liability for the full debts of the partnership is called *joint unlimited liability*. Most law firms are partnerships.

Corporation   A *corporation* is a firm owned by one or more limited liability stockholders. *Limited liability* means that the owners have legal liability only for the value of their initial investment. This limitation of liability means that if the corporation becomes bankrupt, its owners are not required to use their personal wealth to pay the corporation's debts.

Corporations' profits are taxed independently of stockholders' incomes. Stockholders pay tax on dividends and a capital gains tax on the profit they earn when they sell a stock for a higher price than they paid for it. Corporate stocks generate capital gains when a corporation retains some of its profit and reinvests it in profitable activities. So retained earnings are taxed twice because the capital gains they generate are taxed.

Pros and Cons of Different Types of Firms

The different types of business organization arise from firms trying to cope with the principal–agent problem. Each type has advantages in particular situations and because of its special advantages, each type continues to exist. Each type of business organization also has disadvantages.

Table 10.4 summarizes these advantages and disadvantages and other pros and cons of the different types of firms.

TABLE 10.4   The Pros and Cons of Different Types of Firms

Type of Firm	Pros	Cons
Sole Proprietorship	■ Easy to set up ■ Simple decision making ■ Profits taxed only once as owner's income	■ Bad decisions not checked; no need for consensus ■ Owner's entire wealth at risk ■ Firm dies with owner ■ Cost of capital and labour is high relative to that of a corporation
Partnership	■ Easy to set up ■ Diversified decision making ■ Can survive withdrawal of partner ■ Profits taxed only once as owners' incomes	■ Achieving consensus may be slow and expensive ■ Owners' entire wealth at risk ■ Withdrawal of partner may create capital shortage ■ Cost of capital and labour is high relative to that of a corporation
Corporation	■ Owners have limited liability ■ Large-scale, low-cost capital available ■ Professional management not restricted by ability of owners ■ Perpetual life ■ Long-term labour contracts cut labour costs	■ Complex management structure can make decisions slow and expensive ■ Retained profits taxed twice: as company profit and as stockholders' capital gains

Economics in Action
The Size Distribution of Firms in Canada

Industry Canada counts the number of establishments in the Canadian economy and classifies them by size measured by the number of employees. An establishment is not the same as a firm. Some firms operate several, or even many, establishments. For example, Loblaw Companies Limited operates 1,690 grocery stores across Canada. So one large firm operates many small establishments. Keep this fact in mind as you review the data in the figure.

Most establishments in Canada (58 percent of the total) are very small and employ fewer than 5 people. Most of the rest (38 percent of the total) employ between 5 and 99 people. Only 4 percent of establishments employ more than 100 people and only 2,700 establishments (0.3 percent of the total) employ more than 500 people.

The figure shows the distribution of the size of establishments across major industry classes. Most of the largest establishments, shown by the red bars, are found in public administration (government), utilities, and education. Manufacturing, information and culture, and mining, oil, and gas extraction also have some large establishments.

Micro establishments, shown by the blue bars, dominate in agriculture (a group that includes forestry, fishing, and hunting) and professional services, which includes lawyers, accountants, and other types of professional and scientific services.

Most firms in Canada today, regardless of size, are corporations. Many of the very small firms that employ fewer than 5 people find it advantageous to incorporate.

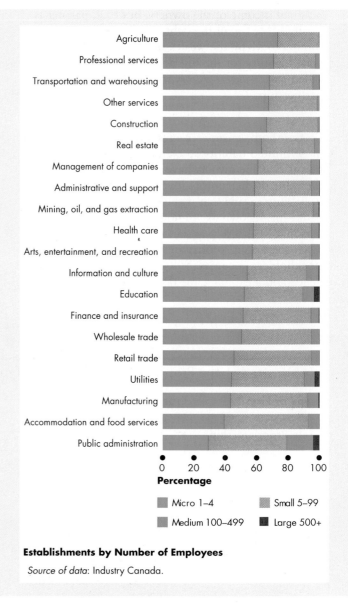

Establishments by Number of Employees

Source of data: Industry Canada.

REVIEW QUIZ

1 Explain the distinction between a command system and an incentive system.
2 What is the principal–agent problem? What are three ways in which firms try to cope with it?
3 What are the three types of firms? Explain the major advantages and disadvantages of each.
4 Why do all three types of firms survive and in which sectors is each type most prominent?

You can work these questions in Study Plan 10.3 and get instant feedback.

MyEconLab ◆

You've now seen how technology constraints and information constraints influence the way firms operate. You've seen why some firms operate with a large amount of labour and human capital and a small amount of physical capital. You've also seen how firms use a mixture of command and incentive systems and employ different types of business organization to cope with the principal–agent problem.

Your next task is to look at the variety of market situations in which firms operate and classify the different market environments in which firms do business.

Markets and the Competitive Environment

The markets in which firms operate vary a great deal. Some are highly competitive, and profits in these markets are hard to come by. Some appear to be almost free from competition, and firms in these markets earn large profits. Some markets are dominated by fierce advertising campaigns in which each firm seeks to persuade buyers that it has the best products. And some markets display the character of a strategic game.

Economists identify four market types:

1. Perfect competition
2. Monopolistic competition
3. Oligopoly
4. Monopoly

Perfect competition arises when there are many firms, each selling an identical product, many buyers, and no restrictions on the entry of new firms into the industry. The many firms and buyers are all well informed about the prices of the products of each firm in the industry. The worldwide markets for corn, rice, and other grain crops are examples of perfect competition.

Monopolistic competition is a market structure in which a large number of firms compete by making similar but slightly different products. Making a product slightly different from the product of a competing firm is called **product differentiation**. Product differentiation gives a firm in monopolistic competition an element of market power. The firm is the sole producer of the particular version of the good in question. For example, in the market for pizzas, hundreds of firms make their own version of the perfect pizza. Each of these firms is the sole producer of a particular brand. Differentiated products are not necessarily different products. What matters is that consumers perceive them to be different. For example, different brands of potato chips and ketchup might be almost identical but perceived by consumers to be different.

Oligopoly is a market structure in which a small number of firms compete. Computer software, airplane manufacture, and international air transportation are examples of oligopolistic industries. Oligopolies might produce almost identical products, such as the colas produced by Coke and Pepsi. Or they might produce differentiated products such as Boeing and Airbus aircraft.

Monopoly is a market structure in which there is only one firm and it produces a good or service that has no close substitutes, and the firm is protected by a barrier preventing the entry of new firms. In some places, the phone, gas, electricity, cable television, and water suppliers are local monopolies—monopolies restricted to a given location. Microsoft Corporation, the software developer that created Windows and Vista, is an example of a global monopoly.

Perfect competition is the most extreme form of competition. Monopoly is the most extreme absence of competition. The other two market types fall between these extremes.

Many factors must be taken into account to determine which market structure describes a particular real-world market. One of these factors is the extent to which a small number of firms dominates the market. To measure this feature of markets, economists use indexes called measures of concentration. Let's look at these measures.

Measures of Concentration

Economists use two measures of concentration:

- The four-firm concentration ratio
- The Herfindahl-Hirschman Index

The Four-Firm Concentration Ratio The **four-firm concentration ratio** is the percentage of the value of sales accounted for by the four largest firms in an industry. The range of the concentration ratio is from almost zero for perfect competition to 100 percent for monopoly. This ratio is the main measure used to assess market structure.

Table 10.5 shows two calculations of the four-firm concentration ratio: one for tire makers and one for printers. In this example, 14 firms produce tires. The largest four have 80 percent of the sales, so the four-firm concentration ratio is 80 percent. In the printing industry, with 1,004 firms, the largest four firms have only 0.5 percent of the sales, so the four-firm concentration ratio is 0.5 percent.

A low concentration ratio indicates a high degree of competition, and a high concentration ratio indicates an absence of competition. A monopoly has a concentration ratio of 100 percent—the largest (and only) firm has 100 percent of the sales. A four-firm concentration ratio that exceeds 60 percent is regarded as an indication of a market that is highly concentrated and dominated by a few firms in an oligopoly. A ratio of less than 60 percent is regarded as an indication of a competitive market.

The Herfindahl-Hirschman Index The **Herfindahl-Hirschman Index**—also called the HHI—is the square of the percentage market share of each firm summed over the largest 50 firms (or summed over all the firms if there are fewer than 50) in a market. For example, if there are four firms in a market and the market shares of the firms are 50 percent, 25 percent, 15 percent, and 10 percent, the Herfindahl-Hirschman Index is

$$\text{HHI} = 50^2 + 25^2 + 15^2 + 10^2 = 3,450.$$

TABLE 10.5   Calculating the Four-Firm Concentration Ratio

Tire makers		Printers	
Firm	**Sales** (millions of dollars)	**Firm**	**Sales** (millions of dollars)
Top, Inc.	200	Fran's	2.5
ABC, Inc.	250	Ned's	2.0
Big, Inc.	150	Tom's	1.8
XYZ, Inc.	100	Jill's	1.7
Largest 4 firms	700	Largest 4 firms	8.0
Other 10 firms	175	Other 1,000 firms	1,592.0
Industry	875	Industry	1,600.0

Four-firm concentration ratios:

Tire makers: $\dfrac{700}{875} \times 100 = 80$ percent

Printers: $\dfrac{8}{1,600} \times 100 = 0.5$ percent

Economics in Action

Concentration in the Canadian Economy

Statistics Canada calculates and publishes data showing the four-firm concentration ratio for each industry in Canada. The bars in the figure show the four-firm concentration ratio.

Sugar production is highly concentrated and almost a monopoly. Other industries that have a high degree of concentration produce tobacco, beer, tires, and soft drinks and ice. These industries are oligopolies.

Industries that produce clothing, bakery items, textiles, fabrics, boats, and printing have low concentration measures and are highly competitive.

Industries that produce women's and girls' shirts, pharmaceutical products, and wooden windows and doors are moderately concentrated. These industries are examples of monopolistic competition.

Concentration measures are useful indicators of the degree of competition in a market, but they must be supplemented by other information to determine the structure of the market.

Newspapers and automobiles are examples of how the concentration measures give a misleading reading of the degree of competition.

Most newspapers are local. They serve a single city or even smaller area. So despite the low concentration measure, newspapers are concentrated in their own local areas.

Automobiles are traded internationally and foreign cars are freely imported into Canada. Despite the high concentration measure, the automobile industry is competitive.

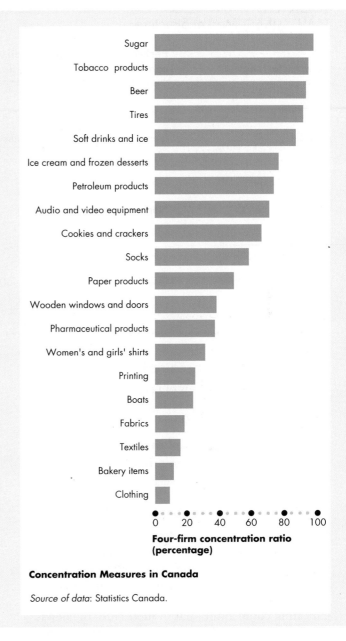

Concentration Measures in Canada

Source of data: Statistics Canada.

In perfect competition, the HHI is small. For example, if each of the largest 50 firms in an industry has a market share of 0.1 percent, then the HHI is $0.1^2 \times 50$, which equals 0.5. At the other extreme in monopoly, the HHI is 10,000. There is only one firm and it has 100 percent of the market, so the HHI is 100^2, which equals 10,000.

The HHI can be used to classify markets across a spectrum of types. A market in which the HHI is less than 1,000 is regarded as being competitive. A market in which the HHI lies between 1,000 and 1,800 is regarded as being moderately competitive— a form of monopolistic competition. A market in which the HHI exceeds 1,800 is regarded as being uncompetitive and a potential matter of concern for regulators.

TABLE 10.6   Market Structure

Characteristics	Perfect competition	Monopolistic competition	Oligopoly	Monopoly
Number of firms in industry	Many	Many	Few	One
Product	Identical	Differentiated	Either identical or differentiated	No close substitutes
Barriers to entry	None	None	Moderate	High
Firm's control over price	None	Some	Considerable	Considerable or regulated
Concentration ratio	0	Low	High	100
HHI (approx. ranges)	Less than 100	101 to 1,800	More than 1,800	10,000
Examples	Wheat, corn	Food, clothing	Computer chips	Local water supply

Limitations of a Concentration Measure

The three main limitations of using only concentration measures as determinants of market structure are their failure to take proper account of

- The geographical scope of the market
- Barriers to entry and firm turnover
- The correspondence between a market and an industry

Geographical Scope of Market   Concentration measures take a national view of the market. Many goods are sold in a *national* market, but some are sold in a *regional* market and some in a *global* one. The concentration measures for newspapers are low, indicating competition, but in most cities the newspaper industry is highly concentrated. The concentration measures for automobiles is high, indicating little competition, but the biggest three North American car makers compete with foreign car makers in a highly competitive global market.

Barriers to Entry and Firm Turnover   Some markets are highly concentrated but entry is easy and the turnover of firms is large. For example, small towns have few restaurants, but no restrictions hinder a new restaurant from opening and many attempt to do so.

Also, a market with only a few firms might be competitive because of *potential entry*. The few firms in a market face competition from the many potential firms that will enter the market if economic profit opportunities arise.

Market and Industry Correspondence   To calculate concentration ratios, Statistics Canada classifies each firm as being in a particular industry. But markets do not always correspond closely to industries for three reasons.

First, markets are often narrower than industries. For example, the pharmaceutical industry, which has a low concentration ratio, operates in many separate markets for individual products—for example, measles vaccine and AIDS-fighting drugs. These drugs do not compete with each other, so this industry, which looks competitive, includes firms that are monopolies (or near monopolies) in markets for individual drugs.

Second, most firms make several products. For example, Westinghouse makes electrical equipment and, among other things, gas-fired incinerators and plywood. So this one firm operates in at least three separate markets, but Statistics Canada classifies Westinghouse as being in the electrical goods and equipment industry. The fact that Westinghouse competes with other producers of plywood does not

Economics in Action

A Competitive Environment

How competitive are markets in North America? Do most firms operate in competitive markets, in monopolistic competition, in oligopoly, or in monopoly markets?

The data needed to answer these questions are hard to get. The last attempt to answer the questions, in a study by William G. Shepherd, an economics professor at the University of Massachusetts at Amherst, covered the years from 1939 to 1980. The figure shows what he discovered.

In 1980, three-quarters of the value of goods and services bought and sold in North America were traded in markets that are essentially competitive—markets that have almost perfect competition or monopolistic competition. Monopoly and the dominance of a single firm accounted for about 5 percent of sales. Oligopoly, which is found mainly in manufacturing, accounted for about 18 percent of sales.

Over the period studied, the economy became increasingly competitive. The percentage of output sold by firms operating in competitive markets (blue bars) expanded most, and the percentage of output sold by firms operating in oligopoly markets (red bars) shrunk most.

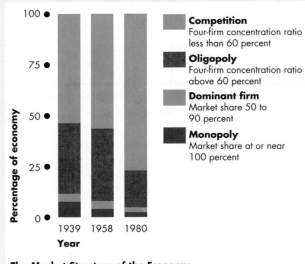

The Market Structure of the Economy

Source of data: William G. Shepherd, "Causes of Increased Competition in the U.S. Economy, 1939–1980," *Review of Economics and Statistics*, 64:4, November 1982, pp. 613–626. © 1982 by the President and Fellows of Harvard College.

During the past decades, the economy has become much more exposed to competition from the rest of the world. The data used by William G. Shepherd don't capture this international competition, so the data probably understate the degree of true competition in the North American economy.

show up in the concentration numbers for the plywood market.

Third, firms switch from one market to another depending on profit opportunities. For example, Canadian Pacific Ltd., which today produces hotel services, forest products, coal and petroleum products, as well as rail services, has diversified from being just a railroad company. Bombardier started producing snowmobiles in 1937. Today, it produces aircraft and rail equipment. Publishers of newspapers, magazines, and textbooks are today rapidly diversifying into Internet and multimedia products. These switches among markets show that there is much scope for entering and exiting a market, and so measures of concentration have limited usefulness.

Despite their limitations, concentration measures do provide a basis for determining the degree of competition in a market when they are combined with information about the geographical scope of the market, barriers to entry, and the extent to which large, multiproduct firms straddle a variety of markets.

REVIEW QUIZ

1 What are the four market types? Explain the distinguishing characteristics of each.

2 What are the two measures of concentration? Explain how each measure is calculated.

3 Under what conditions do the measures of concentration give a good indication of the degree of competition in a market?

4 Is our economy competitive? Is it becoming more competitive or less competitive?

You can work these questions in Study Plan 10.4 and get instant feedback.

—————————— MyEconLab ◆

You now know the variety of market types and how we identify them. Our final question in this chapter is: What determines the things that firms decide to buy from other firms rather than produce for themselves?

◆ Produce or Outsource? Firms and Markets

To produce a good or service, even a simple one such as a shirt, factors of production must be hired and their activities coordinated. To produce a good as complicated as an iPhone, an enormous range of specialist factors of production must be coordinated.

Factors of production can be coordinated either by firms or markets. We'll describe these two ways of organizing production and then see why firms play a crucial role in achieving an efficient use of resources.

Firm Coordination

Firms hire labour, capital, and land, and by using a mixture of command systems and incentive systems (see p. 233) organize and coordinate their activities to produce goods and services.

Firm coordination occurs when you take your car to the garage for an oil change, brake check, and service. The garage owner hires a mechanic and tools and coordinates all the activities that get your car serviced. Firms also coordinate the production of cornflakes, golf clubs, and a host of other items.

Market Coordination

Markets coordinate production by adjusting prices and making the decisions of buyers and sellers of factors of production and components consistent.

Markets can coordinate production.

Market coordination occurs to produce a rock concert. A promoter books a stadium, rents some stage equipment, hires some audio and video recording engineers and technicians, and engages some rock groups, a superstar, a publicity agent, and a ticket agent. The promoter sells tickets to thousands of rock fans, audio rights to a recording company, and video and broadcasting rights to a television network. All these transactions take place in markets that coordinate this huge variety of factors of production.

Outsourcing—buying parts or products from other firms—is another example of market coordination. Dell outsources the production of all the components of its computers. Automakers outsource the production of windshields, windows, transmission systems, engines, tires, and many other auto parts. Apple outsources the entire production of iPods and iPhones.

Why Firms?

What determines whether a firm or a market coordinates a particular set of activities? How does a firm decide whether to buy an item from another firm or manufacture it itself? The answer is cost. Taking account of the opportunity cost of time as well as the costs of the other inputs, a firm uses the method that costs least. In other words, it uses the economically efficient method.

If a task can be performed at a lower cost by markets than by a firm, markets will do the job, and any attempt to set up a firm to replace such market activity will be doomed to failure.

Firms coordinate economic activity when a task can be performed more efficiently by a firm than by markets. In such a situation, it is profitable to set up a firm. Firms are often more efficient than markets as coordinators of economic activity because they can achieve

- Lower transactions costs
- Economies of scale
- Economies of scope
- Economies of team production

Transactions Costs Firms eliminate transactions costs. **Transactions costs** are the costs that arise from finding someone with whom to do business, of reaching an agreement about the price and other aspects of the exchange, and of ensuring that the terms of the agreement are fulfilled. Market transactions require buyers and sellers to get together and to negotiate the terms and conditions of their trading. Sometimes, lawyers have to be hired to draw up contracts. A broken contract leads to still more expense. A firm can lower such transactions costs by reducing the number of individual transactions undertaken.

Imagine getting your car fixed using market coordination. You hire a mechanic to diagnose the problems and make a list of the parts and tools needed to fix them. You buy the parts from several dealers, rent the tools from ABC Rentals, hire an auto mechanic, return the tools, and pay your bills. You can avoid all these transactions and the time they cost you by letting your local garage fix the car.

Economies of Scale When the cost of producing a unit of a good falls as its output rate increases, **economies of scale** exist. An automaker experiences economies of scale because as the scale of production increases, the firm can use cost-saving equipment

Economics in Action

Apple Doesn't Make the iPhone!

Apple designed the iPhone and markets it, but Apple doesn't manufacture it. Why? Apple wants to produce the iPhone at the lowest possible cost. Apple achieves its goal by assigning the production task to more than 30 firms, some of which are listed in the table opposite. These 30 firms produce the components in Asia, Europe, and North America and then the components are assembled in the familiar case by Foxconn and Quanta in Taiwan.

Most electronic products—TVs, DVD players, iPods and iPads, and personal computers—are produced in a similar way to the iPhone with a combination of firm and market coordination. Hundreds of little-known firms compete fiercely to get their components into well-known consumer products.

Altus-Tech	Taiwan
Balda	Germany
Broadcom	United States
Cambridge Silicon Radio	UK
Catcher	Taiwan
Cyntec	Taiwan
Delta Electronics	Taiwan
Epson	Japan
Foxconn	Taiwan
Infineon Technology	Germany
Intel	United States
Largan Precision	Taiwan
Lite On	Taiwan
Marvell	United States
Micron	United States
National Semiconductor	United States
Novatek	Taiwan
Primax	Taiwan
Quanta	Taiwan
Samsung	Korea
Sanyo	Japan
Sharp	Japan
Taiwan Semiconductor	Taiwan
TMD	Japan

and highly specialized labour. An automaker that produces only a few cars a year must use hand-tool methods that are costly. Economies of scale arise from specialization and the division of labour that can be reaped more effectively by firm coordination rather than market coordination.

Economies of Scope A firm experiences *economies of scope* when it uses specialized (and often expensive) resources to produce a *range of goods and services*. For example, Toshiba uses its designers and specialized equipment to make the hard drive for the iPod. But it makes many different types of hard drives and other related products. As a result, Toshiba produces the iPod hard drive at a lower cost than a firm making only the iPod hard drive could achieve.

Economies of Team Production A production process in which the individuals in a group specialize in mutually supportive tasks is *team production*. Sports provide the best examples of team activity. In baseball, some team members specialize in pitching and others in fielding. In basketball, some team members specialize in defense and some in offense. The production of goods and services offers many examples of team activity. For example, production lines in a TV manufacturing plant work most efficiently when individual activity is organized in teams, each worker specializing in a few tasks. You can also think of an entire firm as being a team. The team has buyers of raw materials and other inputs, production workers,

and salespeople. Each individual member of the team specializes, but the value of the output of the team and the profit that it earns depend on the coordinated activities of all the team's members.

Because firms can economize on transactions costs, reap economies of scale and economies of scope, and organize efficient team production, it is firms rather than markets that coordinate most of our economic activity.

REVIEW QUIZ

1 What are the two ways in which economic activity can be coordinated?

2 What determines whether a firm or markets coordinate production?

3 What are the main reasons why firms can often coordinate production at a lower cost than markets can?

You can work these questions in Study Plan 10.5 and get instant feedback.

———————————————— MyEconLab ◆

◆ *Reading Between the Lines* on pp. 244–245 explores the market for Internet advertising. In the next four chapters, we continue to study firms and their decisions. In Chapter 11, we learn about the relationships between cost and output at different output levels. These relationships are common to all types of firms in all types of markets. We then turn to problems that are specific to firms in different types of markets.

Battling for Markets in Internet Advertising

Facebook Makes Gains in Web Ads

http://online.wsj.com
May 12, 2010

Facebook Inc. is catching up to rivals Yahoo Inc. and Microsoft Corp. in selling display ads.

In the first quarter, Facebook pulled ahead of Yahoo for the first time and delivered more banner ads to its U.S. users than any other Web publisher, according to market-research firm comScore Inc. ...

By revenue, Facebook has a long way to go to catch up to its more established rivals. The social-networking site earned more than $500 million in revenue in 2009 and is forecasting revenue of more than $1 billion in 2010, according to people familiar with the matter. Yahoo earned $6.5 billion in revenue in 2009, mostly from advertising. ...

Nielsen Co., another measurement firm, found that Facebook's share of the U.S. display-ad market grew to 20% in April 2010, up from 2% in April 2009. Nielsen still shows Yahoo in the lead, with 34% of all display ads in April 2010, compared with 35% in April 2009. ...

Facebook's rise could help fuel an already rebounding online-advertising market, which shrank during the recession. Display ads have recently shown strong growth as budgets have returned and technology companies have developed new ways to measure the effectiveness of graphical ads. Overall display impressions grew to 1.1 trillion in the first quarter of 2010, up from 944 billion in the first quarter of 2009, according to comScore.

Wall Street Journal, excerpted from "Facebook Makes Gains in Web Ads" by Jessica E. Vascellaro. Copyright 2010 by Dow Jones & Company, Inc. Reproduced with permission of Dow Jones & Company, Inc. via Copyright Clearance Center.

ESSENCE OF THE STORY

- Facebook is catching up to rivals in selling display ads and according to comScore Facebook sold more ads than Yahoo in the first quarter of 2010.

- Facebook's total revenue was more than $500 million in 2009 and is forecast to exceed $1 billion in 2010.

- Yahoo's total revenue, mostly from advertising, was $6.5 billion in 2009.

- Nielsen says that Facebook's share of U.S. display-ads grew from 2 percent to 20 percent in the year to April 2010 while Yahoo's shrank slightly from 35 percent to 34 percent in the same period.

- Display-ads are growing because technology companies have developed new ways to measure the effectiveness of graphical ads.

ECONOMIC ANALYSIS

- Like all firms, Facebook and Yahoo aim to maximize profit.

- Facebook provides social networking services and Yahoo provides an Internet search service.

- Facebook and Yahoo face constraints imposed by the market and technology.

- People who use social networks and search engines demand these services, and Facebook and Yahoo supply them.

- MySpace is Facebook's biggest competitor and Wikipedia lists 189 other social networking sites.

- Google is Yahoo's largest competitor, but another 58 search engines compete for attention.

- The equilibrium price of social networking services and search engine services to their users is zero.

- But social networks and Internet search providers enjoy economies of scope: They produce advertising services as well as their other service.

- To generate revenue and profit, social networks and Internet search providers sell advertising services.

- To attract advertising revenue, a social network or search site must be able to offer the advertiser access to a large potential customer base and target the people most likely to buy the advertised product or service.

- Facebook and Yahoo are attractive to advertisers because they are able to deliver both of these features: hundreds of millions of users, identified by their interests and likely buying patterns.

- To maximize the use of their services, Facebook and Yahoo offer a variety of enticements to users.

- One enticement is the quality of the primary service: social networking or Internet search. Facebook innovates to make its social networking services better than those of MySpace; and Yahoo tries to make its search technology as good as that of Google.

- Another enticement is a variety of related attractions. Yahoo's photo-sharing service is an example.

- Facebook aims to attract even more users and to offer advertisers the most effective return on their marketing dollar.

- Although Facebook has seen explosive growth in users, Fig. 1 shows that it is not generating

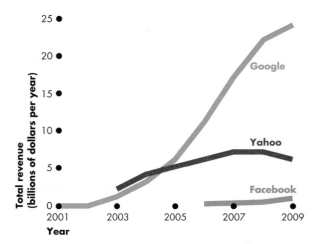

Figure 1 Total Revenue Comparison

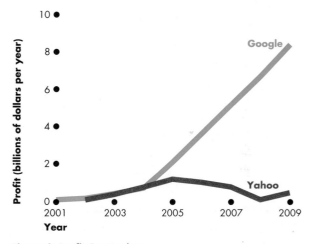

Figure 2 Profit Comparison

revenues on the scale of Google and Yahoo. (No data are available for Facebook profit.)

- Figures 1 and 2 show that Yahoo is not maintaining its position in the market for Internet search.

- The data shown in Figs. 1 and 2 suggest that Internet search is a more effective tool for generating revenue and profit than social networking.

- The data also suggest that Google's expansion is tightening the market constraint that Yahoo faces.

SUMMARY

Key Points

The Firm and Its Economic Problem (pp. 228–230)

- Firms hire and organize factors of production to produce and sell goods and services.
- A firm's goal is to maximize economic profit, which is total revenue minus total cost measured as the opportunity cost of production.
- A firm's opportunity cost of production is the sum of the cost of the resources bought in the market, and the costs of using the firm's own resources and the resources supplied by the firm's owner.
- Normal profit is the opportunity cost of entrepreneurship and is part of the firm's opportunity cost.
- Technology, information, and markets limit the economic profit that a firm can make.

Working Problems 1 and 2 will give you a better understanding of the firm and its economic problem.

Technological and Economic Efficiency (pp. 231–232)

- A method of production is technologically efficient when a firm uses the least amount of inputs to produce a given output.
- A method of production is economically efficient when the cost of producing a given output is as low as possible.

Working Problems 3 and 4 will give you a better understanding of technological and economic efficiency.

Information and Organization (pp. 233–236)

- Firms use a combination of command systems and incentive systems to organize production.
- Faced with incomplete information and uncertainty, firms induce managers and workers to perform in ways consistent with the firms' goals.
- Sole proprietorships, partnerships, and corporations use ownership, incentive pay, and long-term contracts to cope with the principal–agent problem.

Working Problems 5 to 8 will give you a better understanding of information and organization.

Markets and the Competitive Environment (pp. 237–241)

- In perfect competition, many sellers offer an identical product to many buyers and entry is free.
- In monopolistic competition, many sellers offer slightly different products to many buyers and entry is free.
- In oligopoly, a small number of sellers compete and barriers to entry limit the number of firms.
- In monopoly, one firm produces an item that has no close substitutes and the firm is protected by a barrier to entry that prevents the entry of competitors.

Working Problems 9 and 10 will give you a better understanding of markets and the competitive environment.

Produce or Outsource? Firms and Markets (pp. 242–243)

- Firms coordinate economic activities when they can perform a task more efficiently—at lower cost—than markets can.
- Firms economize on transactions costs and achieve the benefits of economies of scale, economies of scope, and economies of team production.

Working Problems 11 and 12 will give you a better understanding of firms and markets.

Key Terms

Command system, 233
Economic depreciation, 229
Economic efficiency, 231
Economic profit, 228
Economies of scale, 242
Firm, 228
Four-firm concentration ratio, 238
Herfindahl-Hirschman Index, 238
Implicit rental rate, 228
Incentive system, 233

Monopolistic competition, 237
Monopoly, 237
Normal profit, 229
Oligopoly, 237
Perfect competition, 237
Principal–agent problem, 234
Product differentiation, 237
Technological efficiency, 231
Technology, 230
Transactions costs, 242

SCAN THIS

STUDY PLAN PROBLEMS AND APPLICATIONS

MyEconLab ◆ You can work Problems 1 to 13 in Chapter 10 Study Plan and get instant feedback.

The Firm and Its Economic Problem (Study Plan 10.1)

1. One year ago, Jack and Jill set up a vinegar-bottling firm (called JJVB). Use the following information to calculate JJVB's opportunity cost of production during its first year of operation:
   - Jack and Jill put $50,000 of their own money into the firm.
   - They bought equipment for $30,000.
   - They hired one employee to help them for an annual wage of $20,000.
   - Jack gave up his previous job, at which he earned $30,000, and spent all his time working for JJVB.
   - Jill kept her old job, which paid $30 an hour, but gave up 10 hours of leisure each week (for 50 weeks) to work for JJVB.
   - JJVB bought $10,000 of goods and services from other firms.
   - The market value of the equipment at the end of the year was $28,000.
   - Jack and Jill have a $100,000 home loan on which they pay interest of 6 percent a year.

2. Joe, who has no skills, no job experience, and no alternative employment, runs a shoeshine stand at the airport. Operators of other shoeshine stands earn $10,000 a year. Joe pays rent to the airport of $2,000 a year, and his total revenue from shining shoes is $15,000 a year. Joe spent $1,000 on a chair, polish, and brushes, using his credit card to buy them. The interest on a credit card balance is 20 percent a year. At the end of the year, Joe was offered $500 for his business and all its equipment. Calculate Joe's opportunity cost of production and his economic profit.

Technological and Economic Efficiency (Study Plan 10.2)

3. Alternative ways of laundering 100 shirts are

Method	Labour (hours)	Capital (machines)
A	1	10
B	5	8
C	20	4
D	50	1

   a. Which methods are technologically efficient?
   b. Which method is economically efficient if the hourly wage rate and the implicit rental rate of

   capital are as follows:
   (i)   Wage rate $1, rental rate $100?
   (ii) Wage rate $5, rental rate $50?
   (iii) Wage rate $50, rental rate $5?

4. **John Deere's Farm Team**

   Deere opened up the Pune [India] centre in 2001. Deere's move was unexpected: Deere is known for its heavy-duty farm equipment and big construction gear whereas many of India's 300 million farmers still use oxen-pulled plows.

   Source: *Fortune*, April 14, 2008

   a. Why do many Indian farmers still use oxen-pulled plows? Are they efficient or inefficient? Explain.
   b. How might making John Deere farm equipment available to Indian farmers change the technology constraint they face?

Information and Organization (Study Plan 10.3)

5. **Here It Is. Now, You Design It!**

   The idea is that the most successful companies no longer invent new products and services on their own. They create them along with their customers, and they do it in a way that produces a unique experience for each customer. The important corollary is that no company owns enough resources—or can possibly own enough—to furnish unique experiences for each customer, so companies must organize a constantly shifting global web of suppliers and partners to do the job.

   Source: *Fortune*, May 26, 2008

   a. Describe this method of organizing and coordinating production: Does it use a command system or incentive system?
   b. How does this method of organizing and coordinating production help firms achieve lower costs?

6. **Rewarding Failure**

   Over the past 25 years CEO pay has risen faster than corporate profits, economic growth, or average wages. A more sensible alternative to the current compensation system would require CEOs to own a lot of company stock. If the stock is given to the boss, his salary and bonus should be docked to reflect its value. As for bonuses, they should be based on improving a company's cash earnings relative to its cost of capital, not to more easily manipulated measures like earnings per share. Bonuses should not be capped, but they should be unavailable to the CEO for some period of years.

Source: *Fortune*, April 28, 2008

a. What is the economic problem that CEO compensation schemes are designed to solve?

b. How do the proposed changes to CEO compensation outlined in the news clip address the problem you described in part (a)?

Use the following news clip to work Problems 7 and 8.

Steps to Creating a Super Startup

Starting a business is a complicated and risky task. Just two-thirds of new small businesses survive at least two years, and only 44 percent survive at least four years. Most entrepreneurs start their businesses by dipping into their savings, borrowing from the family, and using the founder's credit cards. Getting a bank loan is tough unless you have assets—and that often means using your home as collateral.

Source: CNN, October 18, 2007

7. When starting a business, what are the risks and potential rewards identified in the news clip that are associated with a sole proprietorship?

8. How might (i) a partnership and (ii) a corporation help to overcome the risks identified in the news clip?

Markets and the Competitive Environment
(Study Plan 10.4)

9. Sales of the firms in the tattoo industry are

Firm	Sales (dollars per year)
Bright Spots	450
Freckles	325
Love Galore	250
Native Birds	200
Other 15 firms	800

Calculate the four-firm concentration ratio. What is the structure of the tattoo industry?

10. **GameStop Racks Up the Points**

No retailer has more cachet among gamers than GameStop. For now, only Wal-Mart has a larger market share—21.3% last year. GameStop's share was 21.1% last year, and may overtake Wal-Mart this year. But if new women gamers prefer shopping at Target to GameStop, Wal-Mart and Target might erode GameStop's market share.

Source: *Fortune*, June 9, 2008

a. According to the news clip, what is the structure of the U.S. retail video-game market?

b. Estimate a range for the four-firm concentration ratio and the HHI for the game market in the United States based on the information provided in this news clip.

Produce or Outsource? Firms and Markets
(Study Plan 10.5)

11. American automakers buy auto parts from independent suppliers rather than produce the parts themselves. In the 1980s, Chrysler got about 70 percent of its auto parts from independent suppliers, while Ford got about 60 percent and General Motors got 25 percent. A decade earlier, the proportions were 50 percent at Chrysler, 5 percent at Ford, and 20 percent at General Motors.

Source: The Cato Institute Policy Analysis, 1987

a. Why did American automakers decide to outsource most of their parts production?

b. Explain why independent producers of auto parts are more efficient than the automakers.

12. Federal Express enters into contracts with independent truck operators who offer FedEx service and who are rewarded by the volume of packages they carry. Why doesn't FedEx buy more trucks and hire more drivers? What incentive problems might arise from this arrangement?

Economics in the News (Study Plan 10.EN)

13. Lego, the Danish toymaker, incurred economic losses in 2003 and 2004. Lego faced competition from low-cost copiers of its products and a fall in demand. In 2004, to restore profits, Lego fired 3,500 of its 8,000 workers; closed factories in Switzerland and the United States; opened factories in Eastern Europe and Mexico; and introduced performance-based pay for its managers. Lego returned to profit in 2005.

Based on **Picking Up the Pieces**,
The Economist, October 28, 2006

a. Describe the problems that Lego faced in 2003 and 2004, using the concepts of the three types of constraints that all firms face.

b. Which of the actions that Lego took to restore profits addressed an inefficiency? How did Lego seek to achieve economic efficiency?

c. Which of Lego's actions addressed an information and organization problem? How did Lego change the way in which it coped with the principal–agent problem?

d. In what type of market does Lego operate?

ADDITIONAL PROBLEMS AND APPLICATIONS

MyEconLab ◆ You can work these problems in MyEconLab if assigned by your instructor.

The Firm and Its Economic Problem

Use the following information to work Problems 14 and 15.

Lee is a computer programmer who earned $35,000 in 2009. But on January 1, 2010, Lee opened a body board manufacturing business. At the end of the first year of operation, he submitted the following information to his accountant:

- He stopped renting out his cottage for $3,500 a year and used it as his factory. The market value of the cottage increased from $70,000 to $71,000.
- He spent $50,000 on materials, phone, etc.
- He leased machines for $10,000 a year.
- He paid $15,000 in wages.
- He used $10,000 from his savings account, which earns 5 percent a year interest.
- He borrowed $40,000 at 10 percent a year.
- He sold $160,000 worth of body boards.
- Normal profit is $25,000 a year.

14. Calculate Lee's opportunity cost of production and his economic profit.

15. Lee's accountant recorded the depreciation on his cottage during 2010 as $7,000. According to the accountant, what profit did Lee make?

16. In 2009, Toni taught music and earned $20,000. She also earned $4,000 by renting out her basement. On January 1, 2010, she quit teaching, stopped renting out her basement, and began to use it as the office for her new Web site design business. She took $2,000 from her savings account to buy a computer. During 2010, she paid $1,500 for the lease of a Web server and $1,750 for high-speed Internet service. She received a total revenue from Web site designing of $45,000 and earned interest at 5 percent a year on her savings account balance. Normal profit is $55,000 a year. At the end of 2010, Toni could have sold her computer for $500. Calculate Toni's opportunity cost of production and her economic profit in 2010.

17. **The Colvin Interview: Chrysler**

The key driver of profitability will be that the focus of the company isn't on profitability. Our focus is on the customer. If we can find a way to give customers what they want better than anybody else, then what can stop us?

Source: *Fortune*, April 14, 2008

a. In spite of what Chrysler's vice chairman and co-president claims, why is Chrysler's focus actually on profitability?

b. What would happen to Chrysler if it didn't focus on maximizing profit, but instead focused its production and pricing decisions to "give customers what they want"?

18. **Must Watches**

Stocks too volatile? Bonds too boring? Then try an alternative investment—one you can wear on your wrist. The typical return on a watch over five to ten years is roughly 10%. You could do better in an index fund, but what other investment is so wearable?

Source: *Fortune*, April 14, 2008

a. What is the cost of buying a watch?

b. What is the opportunity cost of owning a watch?

c. Does owning a watch create an economic profit opportunity?

Technological and Economic Efficiency

Use the following information to work Problems 19 and 20.

Four methods of completing a tax return and the time taken by each method are: with a PC, 1 hour; with a pocket calculator, 12 hours; with a pocket calculator and paper and pencil, 12 hours; and with a pencil and paper, 16 hours. The PC and its software cost $1,000, the pocket calculator costs $10, and the pencil and paper cost $1.

19. Which, if any, of the methods is technologically efficient?

20. Which method is economically efficient if the wage rate is
(i) $5 an hour?
(ii) $50 an hour?
(iii) $500 an hour?

21. **A Medical Sensation**

Hospitals are buying da Vinci surgical robots. Surgeons, sitting comfortably at a da Vinci console, can use various robotic attachments to perform even the most complex procedures.

Source: *Fortune*, April 28, 2008

a. Assume that performing a surgery with a surgical robot requires fewer surgeons and nurses. Is using the surgical robot technologically efficient?

b. What additional information would you need to be able to say that switching to surgical robots is economically efficient for a hospital?

Information and Organization

22. Loblaws has more than 1,000 stores from coast to coast, more than 140,000 employees, and total revenues of close to $30 billion. Penny and David Chapman run the family-owned Chapman's Ice Cream in Markdale, Ontario, which employs local people and supplies Loblaws with ice cream.

   a. How does Loblaws coordinate its activities? Is it likely to use mainly a command system or also incentive systems? Explain.

   b. How do you think Penny and David Chapman coordinate the activities of Chapman's Ice Cream? Are they likely to use mainly a command system or also incentive systems? Why?

   c. Describe, compare, and contrast the principal–agent problems faced by Loblaws and Chapman's Ice Cream. How might these firms cope with their principal–agent problems?

23. **Where Does Google Go Next?**

   Google gives its engineers one day a week to work on whatever project they want. A couple of colleagues did what many of the young geniuses do at Google: They came up with a cool idea. At Google, you often end up with a laissez-faire mess instead of resource allocation.

   Source: *Fortune*, May 26, 2008

   a. Describe Google's method of organizing production with its software engineers.

   b. What are the potential gains and opportunity costs associated with this method?

Markets and the Competitive Environment

24. The market shares of chocolate makers are

Firm	Market share (percent)
Truffles, Inc.	25
Magic, Inc.	20
All Natural, Inc.	15
Mayfair, Inc.	15
Gold, Inc.	15
Bond, Inc.	10

a. Calculate the Herfindahl-Hirschman Index.

b. What is the structure of the chocolate industry?

Produce or Outsource? Firms and Markets

Use the following information to work Problems 25 to 27.

Two leading design firms, Astro Studios of San Francisco and Hers Experimental Design Laboratory, Inc. of Osaka, Japan, worked with Microsoft to design the Xbox 360 video game console. IBM, ATI, and SiS designed the Xbox 360's hardware. Three firms—Flextronics, Wistron, and Celestica—manufacture the Xbox 360 at their plants in China and Taiwan.

25. Describe the roles of market coordination and coordination by firms in the design, manufacture, and marketing of the Xbox 360.

26. a. Why do you think Microsoft works with a large number of other firms, rather than performing all the required tasks itself?

   b. What are the roles of transactions costs, economies of scale, economies of scope, and economies of team production in the design, manufacture, and marketing of the Xbox?

27. Why do you think the Xbox is designed in the United States and Japan but built in China?

Economics in the News

28. After you have studied *Reading Between the Lines* on pp. 244–245, answer the following questions.

   a. What products do Facebook and Yahoo sell?

   b. In what types of markets do Facebook and Yahoo compete?

   c. How do social networks and Internet search providers generate revenue?

   d. What is special about social networking sites that make them attractive to advertisers?

   e. What is special about Internet search providers that make them attractive to advertisers?

   f. What technological changes might increase the profitability of social networks and Internet search providers?

CHAPTER 11

Output and Costs

After studying this chapter, you will be able to

◆ Distinguish between the short run and the long run

◆ Explain the relationship between a firm's output and labour employed in the short run

◆ Explain the relationship between a firm's output and costs in the short run and derive a firm's short-run cost curves

◆ Explain the relationship between a firm's output and costs in the long run and derive a firm's long-run average cost curve

What do a big electricity supplier in Canada, Hydro One, and Campus Sweaters, a small (fictional) producer of knitwear, have in common? Like every firm, each of these firms must decide how much to produce, how many people to employ, and how much and what type of capital equipment to use. How do firms make these decisions?

Hydro One and the other electric utilities face a demand that fluctuates across the day and from day to day depending on the temperature. How do electric utilities cope with these demand fluctuations?

We are going to answer these questions in this chapter.

To explain the basic ideas, we focus on the economic decisions of Campus Sweaters, Inc. Studying how this firm copes with its economic problems will give us a clear view of the problems faced by all firms. We'll then apply what we learn to the real-world costs of producing cars and electricity. In *Reading Between the Lines*, we'll look at the effects of a new generation of "smart" meters that encourage users to even out electricity consumption across the day.

Decision Time Frames

People who operate firms make many decisions, and all of their decisions are aimed at achieving one over-riding goal: maximum attainable profit. But not all decisions are equally critical. Some decisions are big ones. Once made, they are costly (or impossible) to reverse. If such a decision turns out to be incorrect, it might lead to the failure of the firm. Other decisions are small. They are easily changed. If one of these decisions turns out to be incorrect, the firm can change its actions and survive.

The biggest decision that an entrepreneur makes is in what industry to establish a firm. For most entrepreneurs, their background knowledge and interests drive this decision. But the decision also depends on profit prospects—on the expectation that total revenue will exceed total cost.

Cindy has already decided to set up Campus Sweaters. She has also decided the most effective method of organizing the firm. But she has not decided the quantity to produce, the factors of production to hire, or the price to charge for sweaters.

Decisions about the quantity to produce and the price to charge depend on the type of market in which the firm operates. Perfect competition, monopolistic competition, oligopoly, and monopoly all confront the firm with their own special problems. Decisions about *how* to produce a given output do not depend on the type of market in which the firm operates. *All* types of firms in *all* types of markets make similar decisions about how to produce.

The actions that a firm can take to influence the relationship between output and cost depend on how soon the firm wants to act. A firm that plans to change its output rate tomorrow has fewer options than one that plans to change its output rate six months or six years from now.

To study the relationship between a firm's output decision and its costs, we distinguish between two decision time frames:

- The short run
- The long run

The Short Run

The **short run** is a time frame in which the quantity of at least one factor of production is fixed. For most firms, capital, land, and entrepreneurship are fixed factors of production and labour is the variable factor of production. We call the fixed factors of production the firm's *plant*. In the short run, a firm's plant is fixed.

For Campus Sweaters, the fixed plant is its factory building and its knitting machines. For an electric power utility, the fixed plant is its buildings, generators, computers, and control systems.

To increase output in the short run, a firm must increase the quantity of a variable factor of production, which is usually labour. So to produce more output, Campus Sweaters must hire more labour and operate its knitting machines for more hours a day. Similarly, an electric power utility must hire more labour and operate its generators for more hours a day.

Short-run decisions are easily reversed. The firm can change its output in the short run by changing the quantity of labour it employs.

The Long Run

The **long run** is a time frame in which the quantities of *all* factors of production can be varied. That is, the long run is a period in which the firm can change its *plant*.

To increase output in the long run, a firm can change its plant as well as the quantity of labour it hires. Campus Sweaters can decide whether to install more knitting machines, use a new type of machine, reorganize its management, or hire more labour. Long-run decisions are *not* easily reversed. Once a plant decision is made, the firm usually must live with it for some time. To emphasize this fact, we call the past expenditure on a plant that has no resale value a **sunk cost**. A sunk cost is irrelevant to the firm's current decisions. The only costs that influence its current decisions are the short-run cost of changing its labour inputs and the long-run cost of changing its plant.

REVIEW QUIZ

1 Distinguish between the short run and the long run.
2 Why is a sunk cost irrelevant to a firm's current decisions?

You can work these questions in Study Plan 11.1 and get instant feedback.

 —MyEconLab ◆

We're going to study costs in the short run and the long run. We begin with the short run and describe a firm's technology constraint.

◆ Short-Run Technology Constraint

To increase output in the short run, a firm must increase the quantity of labour employed. We describe the relationship between output and the quantity of labour employed by using three related concepts:

1. Total product
2. Marginal product
3. Average product

These product concepts can be illustrated by either product schedules or product curves. Let's look first at the product schedules.

Product Schedules

Table 11.1 shows some data that describe Campus Sweaters' total product, marginal product, and average product. The numbers tell us how the quantity of sweaters produced increases as Campus Sweaters employs more workers. The numbers also tell us about the productivity of the labour that Campus Sweaters employs.

Focus first on the columns headed "Labour" and "Total product." **Total product** is the maximum output that a given quantity of labour can produce. You can see from the numbers in these columns that as Campus Sweaters employs more labour, total product increases. For example, when 1 worker is employed, total product is 4 sweaters a day, and when 2 workers are employed, total product is 10 sweaters a day. Each increase in employment increases total product.

The **marginal product** of labour is the increase in total product that results from a one-unit increase in the quantity of labour employed, with all other inputs remaining the same. For example, in Table 11.1, when Campus Sweaters increases employment from 2 to 3 workers and does not change its capital, the marginal product of the third worker is 3 sweaters—total product increases from 10 to 13 sweaters.

Average product tells how productive workers are on average. The **average product** of labour is equal to total product divided by the quantity of labour employed. For example, in Table 11.1, the average product of 3 workers is 4.33 sweaters per worker— 13 sweaters a day divided by 3 workers.

If you look closely at the numbers in Table 11.1, you can see some patterns. As Campus Sweaters hires

TABLE 11.1   Total Product, Marginal Product, and Average Product

Labour (workers per day)	Total product (sweaters per day)	Marginal product (sweaters per additional worker)	Average product (sweaters per worker)
A 0	0		
		4	
B 1	4		4.00
		6	
C 2	10		5.00
		3	
D 3	13		**4.33**
		2	
E 4	15		3.75
		1	
F 5	16		3.20

Total product is the total quantity of sweaters produced. Marginal product is the change in total product that results from a one-unit increase in labour. For example, when labour increases from 2 to 3 workers a day (row C to row D), total product increases from 10 to 13 sweaters a day. The marginal product of going from 2 to 3 workers is 3 sweaters. Average product is total product divided by the quantity of labour employed. For example, 3 workers produce 13 sweaters, so the average product of 3 workers is 4.33 sweaters per worker.

more labour, marginal product increases initially, and then begins to decrease. For example, marginal product increases from 4 sweaters a day for the first worker to 6 sweaters a day for the second worker and then decreases to 3 sweaters a day for the third worker. Average product also increases at first and then decreases. You can see the relationships between the quantity of labour hired and the three product concepts more clearly by looking at the product curves.

Product Curves

The product curves are graphs of the relationships between employment and the three product concepts you've just studied. They show how total product, marginal product, and average product change as employment changes. They also show the relationships among the three concepts. Let's look at the product curves.

Total Product Curve

Figure 11.1 shows Campus Sweaters' total product curve, *TP*, which is a graph of the total product schedule. Points *A* through *F* correspond to rows *A* through *F* in Table 11.1. To graph the entire total product curve, we vary labour by hours rather than whole days.

Notice the shape of the total product curve. As employment increases from zero to 1 worker a day, the curve becomes steeper. Then, as employment increases to 3, 4, and 5 workers a day, the curve becomes less steep.

The total product curve is similar to the *production possibilities frontier* (explained in Chapter 2). It separates the attainable output levels from those that are unattainable. All the points that lie above the curve are unattainable. Points that lie below the curve, in the orange area, are attainable, but they are inefficient—they use more labour than is necessary to produce a given output. Only the points *on* the total product curve are technologically efficient.

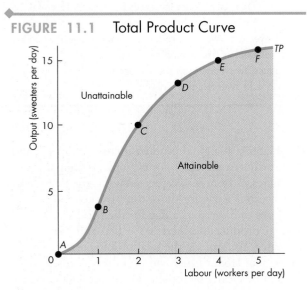

FIGURE 11.1   Total Product Curve

The total product curve, *TP*, is based on the data in Table 11.1. The total product curve shows how the quantity of sweaters produced changes as the quantity of labour employed changes. For example, 2 workers can produce 10 sweaters a day (point *C*). Points *A* through *F* on the curve correspond to the rows of Table 11.1. The total product curve separates attainable outputs from unattainable outputs. Points below the *TP* curve are inefficient.

━━━━━━━━━━━━━━ MyEconLab animation ◆

Marginal Product Curve

Figure 11.2 shows Campus Sweaters' marginal product of labour with 1 knitting machine. Part (a) reproduces the total product curve from Fig. 11.1 and part (b) shows the marginal product curve, *MP*.

In part (a), the orange bars illustrate the marginal product of labour. The height of a bar measures marginal product. Marginal product is also measured by the slope of the total product curve. Recall that the slope of a curve is the change in the value of the variable measured on the *y*-axis—output—divided by the change in the variable measured on the *x*-axis—labour—as we move along the curve. A one-unit increase in labour, from 2 to 3 workers, increases output from 10 to 13 sweaters, so the slope from point *C* to point *D* is 3 sweaters per additional worker, the same as the marginal product we've just calculated.

Again varying the amount of labour in the smallest units possible, we can draw the marginal product curve shown in Fig. 11.2(b). The *height* of this curve measures the *slope* of the total product curve at a point. Part (a) shows that an increase in employment from 2 to 3 workers increases output from 10 to 13 sweaters (an increase of 3). The increase in output of 3 sweaters appears on the *y*-axis of part (b) as the marginal product of going from 2 to 3 workers. We plot that marginal product at the midpoint between 2 and 3 workers. Notice that the marginal product shown in Fig. 11.2(b) reaches a peak at 1.5 workers, and at that point, marginal product is 6 sweaters per additional worker. The peak occurs at 1.5 workers because the total product curve is steepest when employment increases from 1 worker to 2 workers.

The total product and marginal product curves differ across firms and types of goods. Hydro One's product curves are different from those of an automobile producer, whose curves in turn are different from those of Campus Sweaters. But the shapes of the product curves are similar because almost every production process has two features:

- Increasing marginal returns initially
- Diminishing marginal returns eventually

Increasing Marginal Returns   Increasing marginal returns occur when the marginal product of an additional worker exceeds the marginal product of the previous worker. Increasing marginal returns arise from increased specialization and division of labour in the production process.

FIGURE 11.2   Total Product and Marginal Product

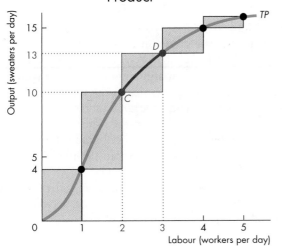

(a) Total product

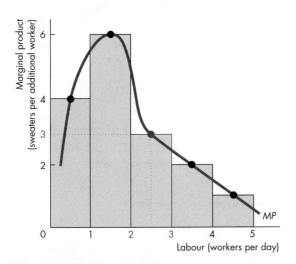

(b) Marginal product

Marginal product is illustrated by the orange bars. For example, when labour increases from 2 to 3 workers a day, marginal product is the orange bar whose height is 3 sweaters. (Marginal product is shown midway between the quantities of labour to emphasize that marginal product results from *changing* the quantity of labour.) The steeper the slope of the total product curve (*TP*) in part (a), the larger is marginal product (*MP*) in part (b). Marginal product increases to a maximum (in this example, when 1.5 workers a day are employed) and then declines—diminishing marginal product.

— MyEconLab   animation   ◆

For example, if Campus Sweaters employs one worker, that person must learn all the aspects of sweater production: running the knitting machines, fixing breakdowns, packaging and mailing sweaters, buying and checking the type and colour of the wool. All these tasks must be performed by that one person.

If Campus Sweaters hires a second person, the two workers can specialize in different parts of the production process and can produce more than twice as much as one worker. The marginal product of the second worker is greater than the marginal product of the first worker. Marginal returns are increasing.

Diminishing Marginal Returns   Most production processes experience increasing marginal returns initially, but all production processes eventually reach a point of *diminishing* marginal returns. **Diminishing marginal returns** occur when the marginal product of an additional worker is less than the marginal product of the previous worker.

Diminishing marginal returns arise from the fact that more and more workers are using the same capital and working in the same space. As more workers are added, there is less and less for the additional workers to do that is productive. For example, if Campus Sweaters hires a third worker, output increases but not by as much as it did when it hired the second worker. In this case, after two workers are hired, all the gains from specialization and the division of labour have been exhausted. By hiring a third worker, the factory produces more sweaters, but the equipment is being operated closer to its limits. There are even times when the third worker has nothing to do because the machines are running without the need for further attention. Hiring more and more workers continues to increase output but by successively smaller amounts. Marginal returns are diminishing. This phenomenon is such a pervasive one that it is called a "law"—the **law of diminishing returns**. The law of diminishing returns states that

> As a firm uses more of a variable factor of production with a given quantity of the fixed factor of production, the marginal product of the variable factor eventually diminishes.

You are going to return to the law of diminishing returns when we study a firm's costs, but before we do that, let's look at the average product of labour and the average product curve.

Average Product Curve

Figure 11.3 illustrates Campus Sweaters' average product of labour and shows the relationship between average product and marginal product. Points *B* through *F* on the average product curve *AP* correspond to those same rows in Table 11.1. Average product increases from 1 to 2 workers (its maximum value at point *C*) but then decreases as yet more workers are employed. Notice also that average product is largest when average product and marginal product are equal. That is, the marginal product curve cuts the average product curve at the point of maximum average product. For the number of workers at which marginal product exceeds average product, average product is *increasing*. For the number of workers at which marginal product is less than average product, average product is *decreasing*.

The relationship between the average product and marginal product is a general feature of the relationship between the average and marginal values of any variable—even your grades.

FIGURE 11.3   Average Product

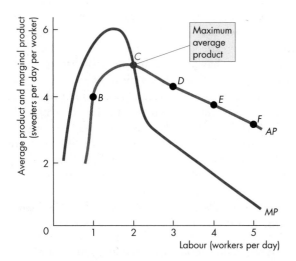

The figure shows the average product of labour and the connection between average product and marginal product. With 1 worker, marginal product exceeds average product, so average product is increasing. With 2 workers, marginal product equals average product, so average product is at its maximum. With more than 2 workers, marginal product is less than average product, so average product is decreasing.

——— MyEconLab   animation   ◆

Economics in Action
How to Pull Up Your Average

Do you want to pull up your average grade? Then make sure that the grade on your next test is better than your current average! Your next test is your marginal test. If your marginal grade exceeds your average grade (like Economics in the figure), your average will rise. If your marginal grade equals your average grade (like English in the figure), your average won't change. If your marginal grade is below your average grade (like History in the figure), your average will fall.

The relationship between your marginal grade and average grade is exactly the same as that between marginal product and average product.

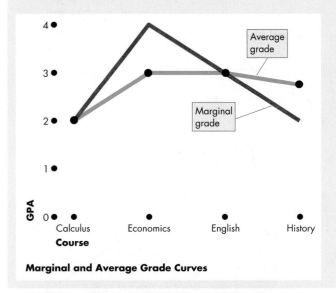

Marginal and Average Grade Curves

◢ REVIEW QUIZ

1. Explain how the marginal product and average product of labour change as the labour employed increases (a) initially and (b) eventually.
2. What is the law of diminishing returns? Why does marginal product eventually diminish?
3. Explain the relationship between marginal product and average product.

You can work these questions in Study Plan 11.2 and get instant feedback.

——————————————— MyEconLab ◆

Campus Sweaters' product curves influence its costs, as you are now going to see.

Short-Run Cost

To produce more output in the short run, a firm must employ more labour, which means that it must increase its costs. We describe the relationship between output and cost by using three cost concepts:

- Total cost
- Marginal cost
- Average cost

Total Cost

A firm's **total cost** (*TC*) is the cost of *all* the factors of production it uses. We separate total cost into total *fixed* cost and total *variable* cost.

Total fixed cost (*TFC*) is the cost of the firm's fixed factors. For Campus Sweaters, total fixed cost includes the cost of renting knitting machines and *normal profit*, which is the opportunity cost of Cindy's entrepreneurship (see Chapter 10, p. 229). The quantities of fixed factors don't change as output changes, so total fixed cost is the same at all outputs.

Total variable cost (*TVC*) is the cost of the firm's variable factors. For Campus Sweaters, labour is the variable factor, so this component of cost is its wage bill. Total variable cost changes as output changes.

Total cost is the sum of total fixed cost and total variable cost. That is,

$$TC = TFC + TVC.$$

The table in Fig. 11.4 shows total costs. Campus Sweaters rents one knitting machine for $25 a day, so its *TFC* is $25. To produce sweaters, the firm hires labour, which costs $25 a day. *TVC* is the number of workers multiplied by $25. For example, to produce 13 sweaters a day, in row *D*, the firm hires 3 workers and *TVC* is $75. *TC* is the sum of *TFC* and *TVC*, so to produce 13 sweaters a day, *TC* is $100. Check the calculations in the other rows of the table.

Figure 11.4 shows Campus Sweaters' total cost curves, which graph total cost against output. The green *TFC* curve is horizontal because total fixed cost ($25 a day) does not change when output changes. The purple *TVC* curve and the blue *TC* curve both slope upward because to increase output, more labour must be employed, which increases total variable cost. Total fixed cost equals the vertical distance between the *TVC* and *TC* curves.

Let's now look at a firm's marginal cost.

FIGURE 11.4   Total Cost Curves

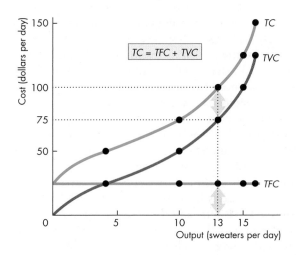

$$TC = TFC + TVC$$

Labour (workers per day)	Output (sweaters per day)	Total fixed cost (*TFC*)	Total variable cost (*TVC*)	Total cost (*TC*)
		(dollars per day)		
A 0	0	25	0	25
B 1	4	25	25	50
C 2	10	25	50	75
D 3	**13**	**25**	**75**	**100**
E 4	15	25	100	125
F 5	16	25	125	150

Campus Sweaters rents a knitting machine for $25 a day, so this cost is the firm's total fixed cost. The firm hires workers at a wage rate of $25 a day, and this cost is its total variable cost. For example, in row *D*, Campus Sweaters employs 3 workers and its total variable cost is 3 × $25, which equals $75. Total cost is the sum of total fixed cost and total variable cost. For example, when Campus Sweaters employs 3 workers, total cost is $100—total fixed cost of $25 plus total variable cost of $75.

The graph shows Campus Sweaters' total cost curves. Total fixed cost is constant—the *TFC* curve is a horizontal line. Total variable cost increases as output increases, so the *TVC* curve and the *TC* curve increase as output increases. The vertical distance between the *TC* curve and the *TVC* curve equals total fixed cost, as illustrated by the two arrows.

MyEconLab   animation

Marginal Cost

Figure 11.4 shows that total variable cost and total cost increase at a decreasing rate at small outputs but eventually, as output increases, total variable cost and total cost increase at an increasing rate. To understand this pattern in the change in total cost as output increases, we need to use the concept of *marginal cost.*

A firm's **marginal cost** is the increase in total cost that results from a one-unit increase in output. We calculate marginal cost as the increase in total cost divided by the increase in output. The table in Fig. 11.5 shows this calculation. When, for example, output increases from 10 sweaters to 13 sweaters, total cost increases from $75 to $100. The change in output is 3 sweaters, and the change in total cost is $25. The marginal cost of one of those 3 sweaters is ($25 ÷ 3), which equals $8.33.

Figure 11.5 graphs the marginal cost data in the table as the red marginal cost curve, *MC.* This curve is U-shaped because when Campus Sweaters hires a second worker, marginal cost decreases, but when it hires a third, a fourth, and a fifth worker, marginal cost successively increases.

At small outputs, marginal cost decreases as output increases because of greater specialization and the division of labour. But as output increases further, marginal cost eventually increases because of the *law of diminishing returns.* The law of diminishing returns means that the output produced by each additional worker is successively smaller. To produce an additional unit of output, ever more workers are required, and the cost of producing the additional unit of output—marginal cost—must eventually increase.

Marginal cost tells us how total cost changes as output increases. The final cost concept tells us what it costs, on average, to produce a unit of output. Let's now look at Campus Sweaters' average costs.

Average Cost

Three average costs of production are

1. Average fixed cost
2. Average variable cost
3. Average total cost

Average fixed cost (*AFC*) is total fixed cost per unit of output. **Average variable cost** (*AVC*) is total variable cost per unit of output. **Average total cost** (*ATC*) is total cost per unit of output. The average cost con-

cepts are calculated from the total cost concepts as follows:

$$TC = TFV + TVC.$$

Divide each total cost term by the quantity produced, *Q,* to get,

$$\frac{TC}{Q} = \frac{TFC}{Q} + \frac{TVC}{Q},$$

or

$$ATC = AFC + AVC.$$

The table in Fig. 11.5 shows the calculation of average total cost. For example, in row *C,* output is 10 sweaters. Average fixed cost is ($25 ÷ 10), which equals $2.50, average variable cost is ($50 ÷ 10), which equals $5.00, and average total cost is ($75 ÷ 10), which equals $7.50. Note that average total cost is equal to average fixed cost ($2.50) plus average variable cost ($5.00).

Figure 11.5 shows the average cost curves. The green average fixed cost curve (*AFC*) slopes downward. As output increases, the same constant total fixed cost is spread over a larger output. The blue average total cost curve (*ATC*) and the purple average variable cost curve (*AVC*) are U-shaped. The vertical distance between the average total cost and average variable cost curves is equal to average fixed cost—as indicated by the two arrows. That distance shrinks as output increases because average fixed cost declines with increasing output.

Marginal Cost and Average Cost

The marginal cost curve (*MC*) intersects the average variable cost curve and the average total cost curve *at their minimum points.* When marginal cost is less than average cost, average cost is decreasing, and when marginal cost exceeds average cost, average cost is increasing. This relationship holds for both the *ATC* curve and the *AVC* curve. It is another example of the relationship you saw in Fig. 11.3 for average product and marginal product and in your average and marginal grades.

Why the Average Total Cost Curve Is U-Shaped

Average total cost is the sum of average fixed cost and average variable cost, so the shape of the *ATC* curve

FIGURE 11.5   Marginal Cost and Average Costs

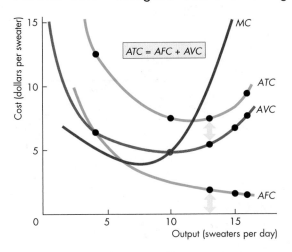

Marginal cost is calculated as the change in total cost divided by the change in output. When output increases from 4 to 10 sweaters, an increase of 6 sweaters, total cost increases by $25. Marginal cost is $25 ÷ 6, which is $4.17.

Each average cost concept is calculated by dividing the related total cost by output. When 10 sweaters are produced, AFC is $2.50 ($25 ÷ 10), AVC is $5 ($50 ÷ 10), and ATC is $7.50 ($75 ÷ 10).

The graph shows that the MC curve is U-shaped and intersects the AVC curve and the ATC curve at their minimum points. The average fixed cost curve (AFC) is downward-sloping. The ATC curve and AVC curve are U-shaped. The vertical distance between the ATC curve and the AVC curve is equal to average fixed cost, as illustrated by the two arrows.

	Labour (workers per day)	Output (sweaters per day)	Total fixed cost (TFC)	Total variable cost (TVC)	Total cost (TC)	Marginal cost (MC) (dollars per additional sweater)	Average fixed cost (AFC)	Average variable cost (AVC)	Average total cost (ATC)
			(dollars per day)				(dollars per sweater)		
A	0	0	25	0	25		—	—	—
						.... 6.25			
B	1	4	25	25	50		6.25	6.25	12.50
						.... 4.17			
C	2	10	25	50	75		2.50	5.00	7.50
						.... 8.33			
D	3	13	25	75	100		1.92	5.77	7.69
						.......12.50			
E	4	15	25	100	125		1.67	6.67	8.33
						.......25.00			
F	5	16	25	125	150		1.56	7.81	9.38

combines the shapes of the *AFC* and *AVC* curves. The U shape of the *ATC* curve arises from the influence of two opposing forces:

1. Spreading total fixed cost over a larger output
2. Eventually diminishing returns

When output increases, the firm spreads its total fixed cost over a larger output and so its average fixed cost decreases—its *AFC* curve slopes downward.

Diminishing returns means that as output increases, ever-larger amounts of labour are needed to produce an additional unit of output. So as output increases, average variable cost decreases initially but eventually increases, and the *AVC* curve slopes upward. The *AVC* curve is U-shaped.

The shape of the *ATC* curve combines these two effects. Initially, as output increases, both average fixed cost and average variable cost decrease, so average total cost decreases. The *ATC* curve slopes downward.

But as output increases further and diminishing returns set in, average variable cost starts to increase. With average fixed cost decreasing more quickly than average variable cost is increasing, the *ATC* curve continues to slope downward. Eventually, average variable cost starts to increase more quickly than average fixed cost decreases, so average total cost starts to increase. The *ATC* curve slopes upward.

Cost Curves and Product Curves

The technology that a firm uses determines its costs. Figure 11.6 shows the links between the firm's product curves and its cost curves. The upper graph shows the average product curve, *AP*, and the marginal product curve, *MP*—like those in Fig. 11.3. The lower graph shows the average variable cost curve, *AVC*, and the marginal cost curve, *MC*—like those in Fig. 11.5.

As labour increases up to 1.5 workers a day (upper graph), output increases to 6.5 sweaters a day (lower graph). Marginal product and average product rise and marginal cost and average variable cost fall. At the point of maximum marginal product, marginal cost is at a minimum.

As labour increases from 1.5 workers to 2 workers a day, (upper graph) output increases from 6.5 sweaters to 10 sweaters a day (lower graph). Marginal product falls and marginal cost rises, but average product continues to rise and average variable cost continues to fall. At the point of maximum average product, average variable cost is at a minimum. As labour increases further, output increases. Average product falls and average variable cost increases.

Shifts in the Cost Curves

The position of a firm's short-run cost curves depends on two factors:

- Technology
- Prices of factors of production

Technology A technological change that increases productivity increases the marginal product and average product of labour. With a better technology, the same factors of production can produce more output, so the technological advance lowers the costs of production and shifts the cost curves downward.

For example, advances in robot production techniques have increased productivity in the automobile industry. As a result, the product curves of Chrysler, Ford, and GM have shifted upward and their cost curves have shifted downward. But the relationships between their product curves and cost curves have not changed. The curves are still linked in the way shown in Fig. 11.6.

Often, as in the case of robots producing cars, a technological advance results in a firm using more capital, a fixed factor, and less labour, a variable factor.

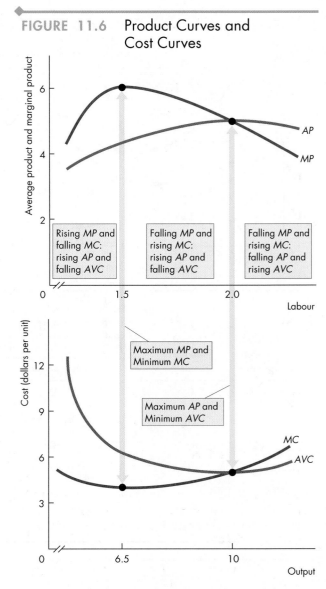

FIGURE 11.6   Product Curves and Cost Curves

A firm's *MP* curve is linked to its *MC* curve. If, as the firm increases its labour from 0 to 1.5 workers a day, the firm's marginal product rises, its marginal cost falls. If marginal product is at a maximum, marginal cost is at a minimum. If, as the firm hires more labour, its marginal product diminishes, its marginal cost rises.

A firm's *AP* curve is linked to its *AVC* curve. If, as the firm increases its labour to 2 workers a day, its average product rises, its average variable cost falls. If average product is at a maximum, average variable cost is at a minimum. If, as the firm hires more labour, its average product diminishes, its average variable cost rises.

MyEconLab   animation ◆

TABLE 11.2   A Compact Glossary of Costs

Term	Symbol	Definition	Equation
Fixed cost		Cost that is independent of the output level; cost of a fixed factor of production	
Variable cost		Cost that varies with the output level; cost of a variable factor of production	
Total fixed cost	TFC	Cost of the fixed factors of production	
Total variable cost	TVC	Cost of the variable factors of production	
Total cost	TC	Cost of all factors of production	$TC = TFC + TVC$
Output (total product)	TP	Total quantity produced (output Q)	
Marginal cost	MC	Change in total cost resulting from a one-unit increase in total product	$MC = \Delta TC \div \Delta Q$
Average fixed cost	AFC	Total fixed cost per unit of output	$AFC = TFC \div Q$
Average variable cost	AVC	Total variable cost per unit of output	$AVC = TVC \div Q$
Average total cost	ATC	Total cost per unit of output	$ATC = AFC + AVC$

Another example is the use of ATMs by banks to dispense cash. ATMs, which are fixed capital, have replaced tellers, which are variable labour. Such a technological change decreases total cost but fixed cost increases and variable cost decreases. This change in the mix of fixed cost and variable cost means that at small outputs, average total cost might increase, while at large outputs, average total cost decreases.

Prices of Factors of Production An increase in the price of a factor of production increases the firm's costs and shifts its cost curves. How the curves shift depends on which factor price changes.

An increase in rent or some other component of *fixed* cost shifts the *TFC* and *AFC* curves upward and shifts the *TC* curve upward but leaves the *AVC* and *TVC* curves and the *MC* curve unchanged. For example, if the interest expense paid by a trucking company increases, the fixed cost of transportation services increases.

An increase in wages, gasoline, or another component of *variable* cost shifts the *TVC* and *AVC* curves upward and shifts the *MC* curve upward but leaves the *AFC* and *TFC* curves unchanged. For example, if

truck drivers' wages or the price of gasoline increases, the variable cost and marginal cost of transportation services increase.

You've now completed your study of short-run costs. All the concepts that you've met are summarized in a compact glossary in Table 11.2.

REVIEW QUIZ

1 What relationships do a firm's short-run cost curves show?

2 How does marginal cost change as output increases (a) initially and (b) eventually?

3 What does the law of diminishing returns imply for the shape of the marginal cost curve?

4 What is the shape of the *AFC* curve and why does it have this shape?

5 What are the shapes of the *AVC* curve and the *ATC* curve and why do they have these shapes?

You can work these questions in Study Plan 11.3 and get instant feedback.

MyEconLab ◆

◆ Long-Run Cost

We are now going to study the firm's long-run costs. In the long run, a firm can vary both the quantity of labour and the quantity of capital, so in the long run, all the firm's costs are variable.

The behaviour of long-run cost depends on the firm's *production function*, which is the relationship between the maximum output attainable and the quantities of both labour and capital.

The Production Function

Table 11.3 shows Campus Sweaters' production function. The table lists total product schedules for four different quantities of capital. The quantity of capital identifies the plant size. The numbers for plant 1 are for a factory with 1 knitting machine—the case we've just studied. The other three plants have 2, 3, and 4 machines. If Campus Sweaters uses plant 2 with 2 knitting machines, the various amounts of labour can produce the outputs shown in the second column of the table. The other two columns show the outputs of yet larger quantities of capital. Each column of the table could be graphed as a total product curve for each plant.

Diminishing Returns   Diminishing returns occur with each of the four plant sizes as the quantity of labour increases. You can check that fact by calculating the marginal product of labour in each of the plants with 2, 3, and 4 machines. With each plant size, as the firm increases the quantity of labour employed, the marginal product of labour (eventually) diminishes.

Diminishing Marginal Product of Capital

Diminishing returns also occur with each quantity of labour as the quantity of capital increases. You can check that fact by calculating the marginal product of capital at a given quantity of labour. The *marginal product of capital* is the change in total product divided by the change in capital when the quantity of labour is constant—equivalently, the change in output resulting from a one-unit increase in the quantity of capital. For example, if Campus Sweaters has 3 workers and increases its capital from 1 machine to 2 machines, output increases from 13 to 18 sweaters a day. The marginal product of the second machine is 5 sweaters a day. If Campus

---

TABLE 11.3   The Production Function

Labour (workers per day)	Output (sweaters per day)			
	Plant 1	Plant 2	Plant 3	Plant 4
1	4	10	13	15
2	10	15	18	20
3	13	18	22	24
4	15	20	24	26
5	16	21	25	27
Knitting machines (number)	1	2	3	4

The table shows the total product data for four quantities of capital (plant sizes). The greater the plant size, the larger is the output produced by any given quantity of labour. For a given plant size, the marginal product of labour diminishes as more labour is employed. For a given quantity of labour, the marginal product of capital diminishes as the quantity of capital used increases.

Sweaters continues to employ 3 workers and increases the number of machines from 2 to 3, output increases from 18 to 22 sweaters a day. The marginal product of the third machine is 4 sweaters a day, down from 5 sweaters a day for the second machine.

Let's now see what the production function implies for long-run costs.

Short-Run Cost and Long-Run Cost

As before, Campus Sweaters can hire workers for $25 a day and rent knitting machines for $25 a day. Using these factor prices and the data in Table 11.3, we can calculate the average total cost and graph the *ATC* curves for factories with 1, 2, 3, and 4 knitting machines. We've already studied the costs of a factory with 1 machine in Figs. 11.4 and 11.5. In Fig. 11.7, the average total cost curve for that case is ATC_1. Figure 11.7 also shows the average total cost curve for a factory with 2 machines, ATC_2, with 3 machines, ATC_3, and with 4 machines, ATC_4.

You can see, in Fig. 11.7, that the plant size has a big effect on the firm's average total cost.

FIGURE 11.7   Short-Run Costs of Four Different Plants

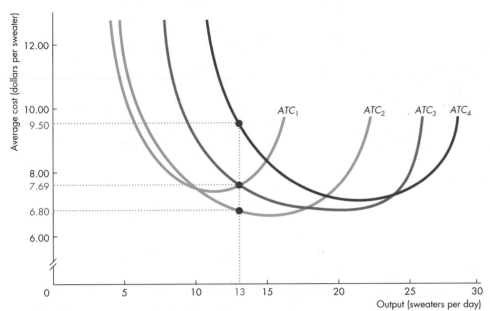

The figure shows short-run average total cost curves for four different quantities of capital at Campus Sweaters. The firm can produce 13 sweaters a day with 1 knitting machine on ATC_1 or with 3 knitting machines on ATC_3 for an average cost of $7.69 a sweater. The firm can produce 13 sweaters a day by using 2 machines on ATC_2 for $6.80 a sweater or by using 4 machines on ATC_4 for $9.50 a sweater.

If the firm produces 13 sweaters a day, the least-cost method of production—*the long-run method*—is with 2 machines on ATC_2.

In Fig. 11.7, two things stand out:

1. Each short-run *ATC* curve is U-shaped.
2. For each short-run *ATC* curve, the larger the plant, the greater is the output at which average total cost is at a minimum.

Each short-run *ATC* curve is U-shaped because, as the quantity of labour increases, its marginal product initially increases and then diminishes. This pattern in the marginal product of labour, which we examined in some detail for the plant with 1 knitting machine on pp. 254–255, occurs at all plant sizes.

The minimum average total cost for a larger plant occurs at a greater output than it does for a smaller plant because the larger plant has a higher total fixed cost and therefore, for any given output, a higher average fixed cost.

Which short-run *ATC* curve a firm operates on depends on the plant it has. In the long run, the firm can choose its plant and the plant it chooses is the one that enables it to produce its planned output at the lowest average total cost.

To see why, suppose that Campus Sweaters plans to produce 13 sweaters a day. In Fig. 11.7, with 1 machine, the average total cost curve is ATC_1 and

the average total cost of 13 sweaters a day is $7.69 a sweater. With 2 machines, on ATC_2, average total cost is $6.80 a sweater. With 3 machines, on ATC_3, average total cost is $7.69 a sweater, the same as with 1 machine. Finally, with 4 machines, on ATC_4, average total cost is $9.50 a sweater.

The economically efficient plant for producing a given output is the one that has the lowest average total cost. For Campus Sweaters, the economically efficient plant to use to produce 13 sweaters a day is the one with 2 machines.

In the long run, a firm chooses the plant that minimizes average total cost. When a firm is producing a given output at the least possible cost, it is operating on its *long-run average cost curve.*

The **long-run average cost curve** is the relationship between the lowest attainable average total cost and output when the firm can change both the plant it uses and the quantity of labour it employs.

The long-run average cost curve is a planning curve. It tells the firm the plant and the quantity of labour to use at each output to minimize average cost. Once the firm chooses a plant, the firm operates on the short-run cost curves that apply to that plant.

The Long-Run Average Cost Curve

Figure 11.8 shows how a long-run average cost curve is derived. The long-run average cost curve, *LRAC*, consists of pieces of the four short-run *ATC* curves. For outputs up to 10 sweaters a day, average total cost is the lowest on *ATC*₁. For outputs between 10 and 18 sweaters a day, average total cost is the lowest on *ATC*₂. For outputs between 18 and 24 sweaters a day, average total cost is the lowest on *ATC*₃. And for outputs in excess of 24 sweaters a day, average total cost is the lowest on *ATC*₄. The piece of each *ATC* curve with the lowest average total cost is highlighted in dark blue in Fig. 11.8. This dark blue scallop-shaped curve made up of the pieces of the four *ATC* curves is the *LRAC* curve.

Economies and Diseconomies of Scale

Economies of scale are features of a firm's technology that make average total cost *fall* as output increases. When economies of scale are present, the *LRAC* curve slopes downward. In Fig. 11.8, Campus Sweaters has economies of scale for outputs up to 15 sweaters a day.

Greater specialization of both labour and capital is the main source of economies of scale. For example, if GM produces 100 cars a week, each worker must perform many different tasks and the capital must be general-purpose machines and tools. But if GM produces 10,000 cars a week, each worker specializes in a small number of tasks, uses task-specific tools, and becomes highly proficient.

Diseconomies of scale are features of a firm's technology that make average total cost *rise* as output increases. When diseconomies of scale are present, the *LRAC* curve slopes upward. In Fig. 11.8, Campus Sweaters experiences diseconomies of scale at outputs greater than 15 sweaters a day.

The challenge of managing a large enterprise is the main source of diseconomies of scale.

Constant returns to scale are features of a firm's technology that keep average total cost constant as output increases. When constant returns to scale are present, the *LRAC* curve is horizontal.

Economies of Scale at Campus Sweaters The economies of scale and diseconomies of scale at Campus Sweaters arise from the firm's production function in Table 11.3. With 1 machine and 1 worker, the firm produces 4 sweaters a day. With 2 machines and 2 workers, total cost doubles but

FIGURE 11.8   Long-Run Average Cost Curve

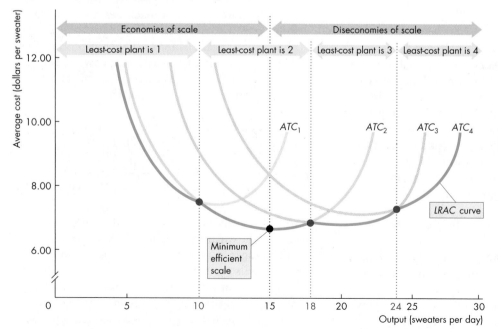

The long-run average cost curve traces the lowest attainable *ATC* when both labour and capital change. The green arrows highlight the output range over which each plant achieves the lowest *ATC*. Within each range, to change the quantity produced, the firm changes the quantity of labour it employs.

Along the *LRAC* curve, economies of scale occur if average cost falls as output increases; diseconomies of scale occur if average cost rises as output increases. Minimum efficient scale is the output at which average cost is lowest—15 sweaters a day.

Economics in Action
Produce More to Cut Cost

Why do GM, Ford, and the other automakers have expensive equipment lying around that isn't fully used? You can answer this question with what you've learned in this chapter.

The basic answer is that auto production enjoys economies of scale. A larger output rate brings a lower long-run average cost—the firm's *LRAC* curve slopes downward.

An auto producer's average total cost curves look like those in the figure. To produce 20 vehicles an hour, the firm installs the plant with the short-run average total cost curve ATC_1. The average cost of producing a vehicle is $20,000.

Producing 20 vehicles an hour doesn't use the plant at its lowest possible average total cost. If the firm could sell enough cars for it to produce 40 vehicles an hour, the firm could use its current plant and produce at an average cost of $15,000 a vehicle.

But if the firm planned to produce 40 vehicles an hour, it would not stick with its current plant. The firm would install a bigger plant with the short-run average total cost curve ATC_2, and produce 40 vehicles an hour for $10,000 a car.

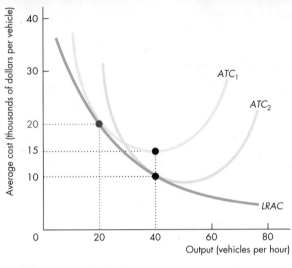

Automobile Plant Average Cost Curves

output more than doubles to 15 sweaters a day, so average cost decreases and Campus Sweaters experiences economies of scale. With 4 machines and 4 workers, total cost doubles again but output less than doubles to 26 sweaters a day, so average cost increases and the firm experiences diseconomies of scale.

Minimum Efficient Scale A firm's **minimum efficient scale** is the *smallest* output at which long-run average cost reaches its lowest level. At Campus Sweaters, the minimum efficient scale is 15 sweaters a day.

The minimum efficient scale plays a role in determining market structure. In a market in which the minimum efficient scale is small relative to market demand, the market has room for many firms, and the market is competitive. In a market in which the minimum efficient scale is large relative to market demand, only a small number of firms, and possibly only one firm, can make a profit and the market is either an oligopoly or a monopoly. We will return to this idea in the next three chapters.

REVIEW QUIZ

1 What does a firm's production function show and how is it related to a total product curve?
2 Does the law of diminishing returns apply to capital as well as to labour? Explain your answer.
3 What does a firm's *LRAC* curve show? How is it related to the firm's short-run *ATC* curves?
4 What are economies of scale and diseconomies of scale? How do they arise? What do they imply for the shape of the *LRAC* curve?
5 What is a firm's minimum efficient scale?

You can work these questions in Study Plan 11.4 and get instant feedback.
———————————————— MyEconLab ◆

◆ *Reading Between the Lines* on pp. 266–267 applies what you've learned about a firm's cost curves. It looks at the cost of producing electricity and explains how the use of smart meters can lower average variable cost.

Cutting the Cost of Producing Electricity

Electricity Prices Set for Small Drop

The Toronto Star
October 19, 2010

Householders who buy their electricity direct from utilities will see their monthly power costs decline by $1 to $3, starting Nov. 1. ...

That's because the times for peak rates of 9.9 cents per kilowatt hour (kwh) shift on Nov. 1 to a winter schedule between 7 and 11 a.m. and again from 5 to 9 p.m. During the summer and early fall, peak period has been 11 a.m. to 5 p.m. ...

The new prices affect those who have already been switched to time-of-use rates, and those who remain on the old system of "tiered pricing."

Households on time-of-use pricing will see the off-peak rate dip 0.2 cents a kwh to 5.1 cents; the mid-peak price drops 0.1 cent to 8.1 cents; and the peak price remains steady at 9.9 cents. ...

Households on tiered pricing will pay 6.4 cents a kwh for the first 1,000 kwh they use each month, and 7.4 cents a kwh for power above that amount. Both prices are down 0.1 cents per kwh from the current level. ...

When prices were last changed six months ago, the energy board had narrowed the gap between peak and off-peak prices, drawing criticism that it was decreasing the incentive for consumers to change their behaviour. ...

Since nearly everyone in the province now has a smart meter that enables time-of-use pricing, the switch-to-time of use pricing is in itself a subtle rate increase, he noted. ...

Time-of-use rates are supposed to encourage consumers to use more power in off-peak periods. But since they were introduced in 2006, off-peak rates have surged 46 percent higher while the peak price has actually dropped 8 percent.

ESSENCE OF THE STORY

- Electricity prices fell slightly in November 2010 with the introduction of a winter schedule for peak rates.

- The new prices affect both the old system of tiered pricing and the new system of time-of-use pricing.

- Nearly everyone in the province has a smart meter that enables time-of-use pricing.

- Tiered pricing rates are 6.4 cents a kWh for the first 1,000 kWh in a month and 7.4 cents a kWh above that amount.

- Time-of-use pricing rates are 5.1 cents a kWh off-peak rate; 8.1 cents mid-peak; and 9.9 cents peak.

- The energy board has narrowed the gap between peak and off-peak prices.

- Time-of-use rates are supposed to encourage more off-peak use, but off-peak rates have increased by 46 percent while the peak price has dropped 8 percent.

ECONOMIC ANALYSIS

- The average variable cost of producing electricity depends on the technology used and on the quantity of electricity produced.

- Figure 1 shows some of the cost differences that arise from using different technologies.

- Electric power utilities use the lowest-cost technologies to meet normal demand and where possible to meet peak demand. At very high peak demand, they also use turbines that burn a high-cost gasoline fuel.

- For a given technology, average variable cost depends on the quantity produced, and Fig. 2 illustrates this relationship.

- In the example in Fig. 2, the plant is designed to produce at minimum *AVC* when it produces 60 percent of its physical maximum output.

- If production could be held steady at 60 percent of the plant's physical maximum output, the cost of producing electricity is minimized.

- But if, to meet peak demand, production increases to the physical limit of the plant, the cost of production increases along the rising *AVC* curve and *MC* curve.

- When electricity is sold for a single price, consumers have no incentive to limit their peak-hour usage.

- By introducing smart meters that enable time-of-day pricing of electricity, consumers can be confronted with the marginal cost of their choices.

A smart meter being installed

- By raising the price during the peak hours and lowering the price during off-peak hours, electricity consumption can be kept more even over the day and closer to the quantity at minimum average variable cost.

- The price differences needed to smooth electricity consumption can be determined by experimenting. Ontario's price differences have narrowed, and it might be necessary to widen them from the current 5.1 cents to 9.9 cents to encourage consumers to even out their electricity usage across the day.

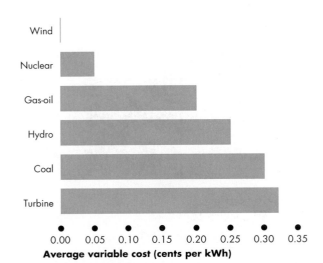

Figure 1 Average Variable Costs of Alternative Technologies

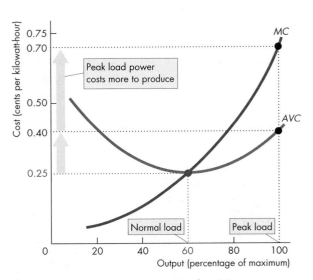

Figure 2 Cost Curves for Generating Electricity

SUMMARY

Key Points

Decision Time Frames (p. 252)

- In the short run, the quantity of at least one factor of production is fixed and the quantities of the other factors of production can be varied.
- In the long run, the quantities of all factors of production can be varied.

Working Problems 1 and 2 will give you a better understanding of a firm's decision time frames.

Short-Run Technology Constraint (pp. 253–256)

- A total product curve shows the quantity a firm can produce with a given quantity of capital and different quantities of labour.
- Initially, the marginal product of labour increases as the quantity of labour increases, because of increased specialization and the division of labour.
- Eventually, marginal product diminishes because an increasing quantity of labour must share a fixed quantity of capital—the law of diminishing returns.
- Initially, average product increases as the quantity of labour increases, but eventually average product diminishes.

Working Problems 3 to 8 will give you a better understanding of a firm's short-run technology constraint.

Short-Run Cost (pp. 257–261)

- As output increases, total fixed cost is constant, and total variable cost and total cost increase.
- As output increases, average fixed cost decreases and average variable cost, average total cost, and marginal cost decrease at low outputs and increase at high outputs. These cost curves are U-shaped.

Working Problems 9 to 14 will give you a better understanding of a firm's short-run cost.

Long-Run Cost (pp. 262–265)

- A firm has a set of short-run cost curves for each different plant. For each output, the firm has one least-cost plant. The larger the output, the larger is the plant that will minimize average total cost.
- The long-run average cost curve traces out the lowest attainable average total cost at each output when both capital and labour inputs can be varied.
- With economies of scale, the long-run average cost curve slopes downward. With diseconomies of scale, the long-run average cost curve slopes upward.

Working Problems 15 to 20 will give you a better understanding of a firm's long-run cost.

Key Terms

Average fixed cost, 258
Average product, 253
Average total cost, 258
Average variable cost, 258
Constant returns to scale, 264
Diminishing marginal returns, 255
Diseconomies of scale, 264
Economies of scale, 264
Law of diminishing returns, 255
Long run, 252

Long-run average cost curve, 263
Marginal cost, 258
Marginal product, 253
Minimum efficient scale, 265
Short run, 252
Sunk cost, 252
Total cost, 257
Total fixed cost, 257
Total product, 253
Total variable cost, 257

SCAN THIS

STUDY PLAN PROBLEMS AND APPLICATIONS

MyEconLab ◆ You can work Problems 1 to 21 in Chapter 11 Study Plan and get instant feedback.

Decision Time Frames (Study Plan 11.1)

1. Which of the following news items involves a short-run decision and which involves a long-run decision? Explain.

   January 31, 2008: Starbucks will open 75 more stores abroad than originally predicted, for a total of 975.

   February 25, 2008: For three hours on Tuesday, Starbucks will shut down every single one of its 7,100 stores so that baristas can receive a refresher course.

   June 2, 2008: Starbucks replaces baristas with vending machines.

   July 18, 2008: Starbucks is closing 616 stores by the end of March.

2. **Final Year for Canada's Tobacco Farmers?**

   Ontario set aside $50 million in a transition fund for tobacco farmers looking to get out of the business and pursue alternative crops such as beans and sweet potatoes. But the farmers say much of the infrastructure designed for tobacco farming can't be used for any other crops.

   Source: CBC News, September 18, 2005

   a. How does offering farmers a payment to exit tobacco growing influence the opportunity cost of growing tobacco?

   b. What is the opportunity cost of using the equipment owned by a tobacco farmer?

Short-Run Technology Constraint (Study Plan 11.2)

Use the following table to work Problems 3 to 7. The table sets out Sue's Surfboards' total product schedule.

Labour (workers per week)	Output (surfboards per week)
1	30
2	70
3	120
4	160
5	190
6	210
7	220

3. Draw the total product curve.

4. Calculate the average product of labour and draw the average product curve.

5. Calculate the marginal product of labour and draw the marginal product curve.

6. a. Over what output range does Sue's Surfboards enjoy the benefits of increased specialization and division of labour?

   b. Over what output range does the firm experience diminishing marginal product of labour?

   c. Over what output range does the firm experience an increasing average product of labour but a diminishing marginal product of labour?

7. Explain how it is possible for a firm to experience simultaneously an increasing *average* product but a diminishing *marginal* product.

8. **Business Boot Camp**

   At a footwear company called Caboots, sales rose from $160,000 in 2000 to $2.3 million in 2006, but in 2007 sales dipped to $1.5 million. Joey and Priscilla Sanchez, who run Caboots, blame the decline partly on a flood that damaged the firm's office and sapped morale.

   Source: CNN, April 23, 2008

   If the Sanchezes are correct in their assumptions and the prices of footwear didn't change

   a. Explain the effect of the flood on the total product curve and marginal product curve at Caboots.

   b. Draw a graph to show the effect of the flood on the total product curve and marginal product curve at Caboots.

Short-Run Cost (Study Plan 11.3)

Use the following data to work Problems 9 to 13. Sue's Surfboards, in Problem 3, hires workers at $500 a week and its total fixed cost is $1,000 a week.

9. Calculate total cost, total variable cost, and total fixed cost of each output in the table. Plot these points and sketch the short-run total cost curves passing through them.

10. Calculate average total cost, average fixed cost, average variable cost, and marginal cost of each output in the table. Plot these points and sketch the short-run average and marginal cost curves passing through them.

11. Illustrate the connection between Sue's *AP*, *MP*, *AVC*, and *MC* curves in graphs like those in Fig. 11.6.

12. Sue's Surfboards rents a factory building. If the rent is increased by $200 a week and other things remain the same, how do Sue's Surfboards' short-run average cost curves and marginal cost curve change?

13. Workers at Sue's Surfboards negotiate a wage increase of $100 a week for each worker. If other things remain the same, explain how Sue's Surfboards' short-run average cost curves and marginal cost curve change.

14. **Grain Prices Go the Way of the Oil Price**

Every morning millions of people confront the latest trend in commodities markets at their kitchen table. Rising prices for crops have begun to drive up the cost of breakfast.

Source: *The Economist*, July 21, 2007

Explain how the rising price of crops affects the average total cost and marginal cost of producing breakfast cereals.

Long-Run Cost (Study Plan 11.4)

Use the table in Problem 3 and the following information to work Problems 15 and 16.

Sue's Surfboards buys a second plant and the output produced by each worker increases by 50 percent. The total fixed cost of operating each plant is $1,000 a week. Each worker is paid $500 a week.

15. Calculate the average total cost of producing 180 and 240 surfboards a week when Sue's Surfboards operates two plants. Graph these points and sketch the *ATC* curve.

16. a. To produce 180 surfboards a week, is it efficient to operate one or two plants?
    b. To produce 160 surfboards a week, is it efficient for Sue's to operate one or two plants?

Use the following table to work Problems 17 to 20. The table shows the production function of Jackie's Canoe Rides.

Labour (workers per day)	Output (rides per day)			
	Plant 1	Plant 2	Plant 3	Plant 4
10	20	40	55	65
20	40	60	75	85
30	65	75	90	100
40	75	85	100	110
Canoes	**10**	**20**	**30**	**40**

Jackie's pays $100 a day for each canoe it rents and $50 a day for each canoe operator it hires.

17. Graph the *ATC* curves for Plant 1 and Plant 2. Explain why these *ATC* curves differ.

18. Graph the *ATC* curves for Plant 3 and Plant 4. Explain why these *ATC* curves differ.

19. a. On Jackie's *LRAC* curve, what is the average cost of producing 40, 75, and 85 rides a week?
    b. What is Jackie's minimum efficient scale?

20. a. Explain how Jackie's uses its *LRAC* curve to decide how many canoes to rent.
    b. Does Jackie's production function feature economies of scale or diseconomies of scale?

Economics in the News (Study Plan 11.EN)

21. **Airlines Seek Out New Ways to Save on Fuel as Costs Soar**

The financial pain of higher fuel prices is particularly acute for airlines because it is their single biggest expense. Airlines pump about 7,000 gallons into a Boeing 737 and about 60,000 gallons into the bigger 747 jet. Each generation of aircraft is more efficient: An Airbus A330 long-range jet uses 38 percent less fuel than the DC-10 it replaced, while the Airbus A319 medium-range jet is 27 percent more efficient than the DC-9 it replaced.

Source: *The New York Times*, June 11, 2008

a. Is the price of fuel a fixed cost or a variable cost for an airline?

b. Explain how an increase in the price of fuel changes an airline's total costs, average costs, and marginal cost.

c. Draw a graph to show the effects of an increase in the price of fuel on an airline's *TFC, TVC, AFC, AVC,* and *MC* curves.

d. Explain how a technological advance that makes an airplane engine more fuel efficient changes an airline's total product, marginal product, and average product.

e. Draw a graph to illustrate the effects of a more fuel-efficient aircraft on an airline's *TP, MP,* and *AP* curves.

f. Explain how a technological advance that makes an airplane engine more fuel efficient changes an airline's average variable cost, marginal cost, and average total cost.

g. Draw a graph to illustrate how a technological advance that makes an airplane engine more fuel efficient changes an airline's *AVC, MC,* and *ATC* curves.

ADDITIONAL PROBLEMS AND APPLICATIONS

MyEconLab ◆ You can work these problems in MyEconLab if assigned by your instructor.

Decision Time Frames

22. A Bakery on the Rise

Some 500 customers a day line up to buy Avalon's breads, scones, muffins, and coffee. Staffing and management are worries. Avalon now employs 35 and plans to hire 15 more. Its payroll will climb by 30 percent to 40 percent. The new CEO has executed an ambitious agenda that includes the move to a larger space, which will increase the rent from $3,500 to $10,000 a month.

Source: CNN, March 24, 2008

a. Which of Avalon's decisions described in the news clip is a short-run decision and which is a long-run decision?

b. Why is Avalon's long-run decision riskier than its short-run decision?

23. The Sunk-Cost Fallacy

You have good tickets to a basketball game an hour's drive away. There's a blizzard raging outside, and the game is being televised. You can sit warm and safe at home and watch it on TV, or you can bundle up, dig out your car, and go to the game. What do you do?

Source: Slate, September 9, 2005

a. What type of cost is your expenditure on tickets?

b. Why is the cost of the ticket irrelevant to your current decision about whether to stay at home or go to the game?

Short-Run Technology Constraint

24. Terri runs a rose farm. One worker produces 1,000 roses a week; hiring a second worker doubles her total product; hiring a third worker doubles her output again; hiring a fourth worker increases her total product but by only 1,000 roses. Construct Terri's marginal product and average product schedules. Over what range of workers do marginal returns increase?

Short-Run Cost

25. Use the events described in the news clip in Problem 22. By how much will Avalon's short-run decision increase its total variable cost? By how much will Avalon's long-run decision increase its monthly total fixed cost? Sketch Avalon's short-run ATC curve before and after the events described in the news clip.

26. Coffee King Starbucks Raises Its Prices

Starbucks is raising its prices because the wholesale price of milk has risen 70 percent and there's a lot of milk in Starbucks lattes.

Source: USA Today, July 24, 2007

Is milk a fixed factor of production or a variable factor of production? Describe how the increase in the price of milk changes Starbucks' short-run cost curves.

27. Bill's Bakery has a fire and Bill loses some of his cost data. The bits of paper that he recovers after the fire provide the information in the following table (all the cost numbers are dollars).

TP	AFC	AVC	ATC	MC
10	120	100	220	
				80
20	*A*	*B*	150	
				90
30	40	90	130	
				130
40	30	*C*	*D*	
				E
50	24	108	132	

Bill asks you to come to his rescue and provide the missing data in the five spaces identified as *A*, *B*, *C*, *D*, and *E*.

Use the following table to work Problems 28 and 29.

ProPainters hires students at $250 a week to paint houses. It leases equipment at $500 a week. The table sets out its total product schedule.

Labour (students)	Output (houses painted per week)
1	2
2	5
3	9
4	12
5	14
6	15

28. If ProPainters paints 12 houses a week, calculate its total cost, average total cost, and marginal cost. At what output is average total cost a minimum?

29. Explain why the gap between ProPainters' total cost and total variable cost is the same no matter how many houses are painted.

Long-Run Cost

Use the table in Problem 28 and the following information to work Problems 30 and 31.

If ProPainters doubles the number of students it hires and doubles the amount of equipment it leases, it experiences diseconomies of scale.

30 Explain how the *ATC* curve with one unit of equipment differs from that when ProPainters uses double the amount of equipment.

31. Explain what might be the source of the diseconomies of scale that ProPainters experiences.

Use the following information to work Problems 32 and 33.

The table shows the production function of Bonnie's Balloon Rides. Bonnie's pays $500 a day to rent a balloon and pays $25 a day for a balloon operator.

Labour (workers per day)	Output (rides per day)			
	Plant 1	Plant 2	Plant 3	Plant 4
10	6	10	13	15
20	10	15	18	20
30	13	18	22	24
40	15	20	24	26
50	16	21	25	27
Balloons (number)	1	2	3	4

32. Graph the *ATC* curves for Plant 1 and Plant 2. Explain why these *ATC* curves differ.

33. Graph the *ATC* curves for Plant 3 and Plant 4. Explain why these *ATC* curves differ.

34. a. On Bonnie's *LRAC* curve, what is the average cost of producing 18 rides and 15 rides a day?
    b. Explain how Bonnie's uses its long-run average cost curve to decide how many balloons to rent.

Use the following news clip to work Problems 35 and 36.

Gap Will Focus on Smaller Scale Stores

Gap has too many stores that are 12,500 square metres. The target store size is 6,000 square metres to 10,000 squaremetres, so Gap plans to combine previously separate concept stores. Some Gap body, adult, maternity, baby and kids stores will be combined in one store.

Source: CNN, June 10, 2008

35. Thinking of a Gap store as a production plant, explain why Gap is making a decision to reduce the size of its stores. Is Gap's decision a long-run decision or a short-run decision?

36. How might combining Gap's concept stores into one store help better take advantage of economies of scale?

Economics in the News

37. After you have studied *Reading Between the Lines* on pp. 266–267, answer the following questions.
    a. Sketch the *AFC*, *AVC*, *ATC*, and *MC* curves for electricity production using the six technologies shown in Fig. 1 on p. 267.
    b. Given the cost differences among the different methods of generating electricity, why do you think we use more than one method? If we could use only one method, which would it be?
    c. Explain how time-of-day pricing that succeeds in smoothing out fluctuations in production across the day lowers the average variable cost and marginal cost of generating electricity.
    d   Draw a graph to illustrate your answer to part (c).

38. **Starbucks Unit Brews Up Self-Serve Espresso Bars**

Automated, self-serve espresso kiosks have appeared in many grocery stores. The machines, which grind their own beans, crank out lattes, and drip coffees take credit and debit cards, and cash. Coinstar buys the kiosks for just under $40,000 per unit, installs them, and provides maintenance. The self-serve kiosks remove the labour costs of having a barista. The kiosks use Starbucks' Seattle's Best Coffee and store personnel handle refills of coffee beans and milk.

Source: MSNBC, June 1, 2008

a. What is Coinstar's total fixed cost of operating one self-serve kiosk?
b. What are Coinstar's variable costs of providing coffee at a self-serve kiosk?
c. Assume that a coffee machine operated by a barista costs less than $40,000. Explain how the fixed costs, variable costs, and total costs of barista-served and self-served coffee differ.
d. Sketch the marginal cost and average cost curves implied by your answer to part (c).

Perfect Competition

After studying this chapter,
you will be able to

◆ Define perfect competition

◆ Explain how a firm makes its output
  decision and why it sometimes shuts
  down temporarily

◆ Explain how price and output are determined in a perfectly competitive market

◆ Explain why firms enter and leave a competitive market and the consequences of
  entry and exit

◆ Predict the effects of a change in demand
  and of a technological advance

◆ Explain why perfect competition is
  efficient

A corn farmer must make many decisions, but figuring out the price to
charge for his corn is not one of them. Corn farmers and the producers of
most crops—among them wheat, soybean, canola—must accept the price
determined by supply and demand.

But the prices that all crop farmers receive fluctuate. What forces in
the world's markets for farm products determine the changes in prices?

We're going to answer this question by studying competitive markets
and building a model of a market in which competition is as fierce and
extreme as possible. We call this situation *perfect* competition.

In *Reading Between the Lines* at the end of the chapter, we'll apply
the model to the global market for corn and see how changes in demand
and fortunate weather bring changes in prices and quantities produced in
this key global agricultural market.

What Is Perfect Competition?

The firms that you study in this chapter face the force of raw competition. We call this extreme form of competition perfect competition. **Perfect competition** is a market in which

- Many firms sell identical products to many buyers.
- There are no restrictions on entry into the market.
- Established firms have no advantage over new ones.
- Sellers and buyers are well informed about prices.

Farming, fishing, wood pulping and paper milling, the manufacture of paper cups and shopping bags, grocery and fresh flower retailing, photo finishing, lawn services, plumbing, painting, dry cleaning, and laundry services are all examples of highly competitive industries.

How Perfect Competition Arises

Perfect competition arises if the minimum efficient scale of a single producer is small relative to the market demand for the good or service. In this situation, there is room in the market for many firms. A firm's *minimum efficient scale* is the smallest output at which long-run average cost reaches its lowest level. (See Chapter 11, p. 265.)

In perfect competition, each firm produces a good that has no unique characteristics, so consumers don't care which firm's good they buy.

Price Takers

Firms in perfect competition are price takers. A **price taker** is a firm that cannot influence the market price because its production is an insignificant part of the total market.

Imagine that you are a wheat farmer in Manitoba. You have 500 hectares planted—which sounds like a lot. But compared to the millions of hectares across the Canadian prairies and the U. S. mid-west as well as the millions more in Argentina, Australia, and Ukraine, your 500 hectares are a drop in the ocean. Nothing makes your wheat any better than any other farmer's, and all the buyers of wheat know the price at which they can do business.

If the market price of wheat is $300 a tonne, then that is the highest price you can get for your wheat. Ask for $310 and no one will buy from you. Offer it for $290 and you'll be sold out in a flash and have given away $10 a tonne. You take the market price.

Economic Profit and Revenue

A firm's goal is to maximize *economic profit*, which is equal to total revenue minus total cost. Total cost is the *opportunity cost* of production, which includes *normal profit*. (See Chapter 10, p. 228.)

A firm's **total revenue** equals the price of its output multiplied by the number of units of output sold (price × quantity). **Marginal revenue** is the change in total revenue that results from a one-unit increase in the quantity sold. Marginal revenue is calculated by dividing the change in total revenue by the change in the quantity sold.

Figure 12.1 illustrates these revenue concepts. In part (a), the market demand curve, *D*, and market supply curve, *S*, determine the market price. The market price is $25 a sweater. Campus Sweaters is just one of many producers of sweaters, so the best it can do is to sell its sweaters for $25 each.

Total Revenue Total revenue is equal to the price multiplied by the quantity sold. In the table in Fig. 12.1, if Campus Sweaters sells 9 sweaters, its total revenue is $225 (9 × $25).

Figure 12.1(b) shows the firm's total revenue curve (*TR*), which graphs the relationship between total revenue and the quantity sold. At point *A* on the *TR* curve, the firm sells 9 sweaters and has a total revenue of $225. Because each additional sweater sold brings in a constant amount—$25—the total revenue curve is an upward-sloping straight line.

Marginal Revenue Marginal revenue is the change in total revenue that results from a one-unit increase in quantity sold. In the table in Fig. 12.1, when the quantity sold increases from 8 to 9 sweaters, total revenue increases from $200 to $225, so marginal revenue is $25 a sweater.

Because the firm in perfect competition is a price taker, the change in total revenue that results from a one-unit increase in the quantity sold equals the market price. *In perfect competition, the firm's marginal revenue equals the market price.* Figure 12.1(c) shows the firm's marginal revenue curve (*MR*) as the horizontal line at the market price.

Demand for the Firm's Product The firm can sell any quantity it chooses at the market price. So the demand curve for the firm's product is a horizontal line at the market price, the same as the firm's marginal revenue curve.

FIGURE 12.1 Demand, Price, and Revenue in Perfect Competition

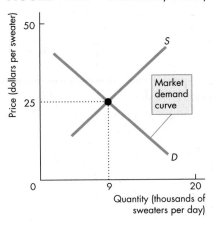

(a) Sweater market

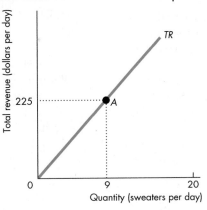

(b) Campus Sweaters' total revenue

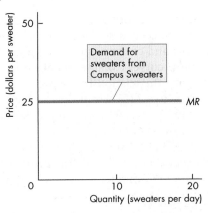

(c) Campus Sweaters' marginal revenue

Quantity sold (Q) (sweaters per day)	Price (P) (dollars per sweater)	Total revenue (TR = P × Q) (dollars)	Marginal revenue (MR = ΔTR/ΔQ) (dollars per additional sweater)
8	25	200	
			 25
9	25	225	
			 25
10	25	250	

In part (a), market demand and market supply determine the market price (and quantity). Part (b) shows the firm's total revenue curve (TR). Point A corresponds to the second row of the table—Campus Sweaters sells 9 sweaters at $25 a sweater, so total revenue is $225. Part (c) shows the firm's marginal revenue curve (MR). This curve is also the demand curve for the firm's sweaters. The demand for sweaters from Campus Sweaters is perfectly elastic at the market price of $25 a sweater.

MyEconLab animation

A horizontal demand curve illustrates a perfectly elastic demand, so the demand for the firm's product is perfectly elastic. A sweater from Campus Sweaters is a *perfect substitute* for a sweater from any other factory. But the *market* demand for sweaters is *not* perfectly elastic: Its elasticity depends on the substitutability of sweaters for other goods and services.

The Firm's Decisions

The goal of the competitive firm is to maximize economic profit, given the constraints it faces. To achieve its goal, a firm must decide

1. How to produce at minimum cost
2. What quantity to produce
3. Whether to enter or exit a market

You've already seen how a firm makes the first decision. It does so by operating with the plant that minimizes long-run average cost—by being on its

long-run average cost curve. We'll now see how the firm makes the other two decisions. We start by looking at the firm's output decision.

REVIEW QUIZ

1 Why is a firm in perfect competition a price taker?
2 In perfect competition, what is the relationship between the demand for the firm's output and the market demand?
3 In perfect competition, why is a firm's marginal revenue curve also the demand curve for the firm's output?
4 What decisions must a firm make to maximize profit?

You can work these questions in Study Plan 12.1 and get instant feedback.

MyEconLab

◆ The Firm's Output Decision

A firm's cost curves (total cost, average cost, and marginal cost) describe the relationship between its output and costs (see pp. 257–261). And a firm's revenue curves (total revenue and marginal revenue) describe the relationship between its output and revenue (p. 275). From the firm's cost curves and revenue curves, we can find the output that maximizes the firm's economic profit.

Figure 12.2 shows how to do this for Campus Sweaters. The table lists the firm's total revenue and total cost at different outputs, and part (a) of the figure shows the firm's total revenue curve, *TR*, and total cost curve, *TC*. These curves are graphs of

numbers in the first three columns of the table.

Economic profit equals total revenue minus total cost. The fourth column of the table in Fig. 12.2 shows the economic profit made by Campus Sweaters, and part (b) of the figure graphs these numbers as its economic profit curve, *EP*.

Campus Sweaters maximizes its economic profit by producing 9 sweaters a day: Total revenue is $225, total cost is $183, and economic profit is $42. No other output rate achieves a larger profit.

At outputs of less than 4 sweaters and more than 12 sweaters a day, the Campus Sweaters would incur an economic loss. At either 4 or 12 sweaters a day, Campus Sweaters would make zero economic profit, called a *break-even point*.

FIGURE 12.2   Total Revenue, Total Cost, and Economic Profit

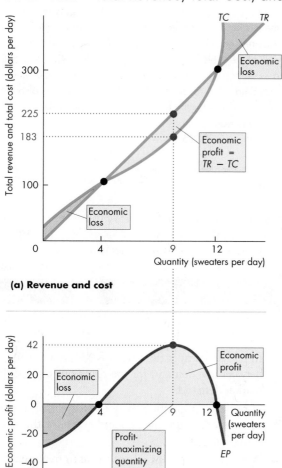

(a) Revenue and cost

(b) Economic profit and loss

Quantity (Q) (sweaters per day)	Total revenue (TR) (dollars)	Total cost (TC) (dollars)	Economic profit (TR − TC) (dollars)
0	0	22	−22
1	25	45	−20
2	50	66	−16
3	75	85	−10
4	100	100	0
5	125	114	11
6	150	126	24
7	175	141	34
8	200	160	40
9	**225**	**183**	**42**
10	250	210	40
11	275	245	30
12	300	300	0
13	325	360	−35

The table lists Campus Sweaters' total revenue, total cost, and economic profit. Part (a) graphs the total revenue and total cost curves and part (b) graphs economic profit.

Campus Sweaters makes maximum economic profit, $42 a day ($225 − $183), when it produces 9 sweaters a day. At outputs of 4 sweaters and 12 sweaters a day, Campus Sweaters makes zero economic profit—these are break-even points. At outputs less than 4 sweaters and greater than 12 sweaters a day, Campus Sweaters incurs an economic loss.

Marginal Analysis and the Supply Decision

Another way to find the profit-maximizing output is to use marginal analysis, which compares marginal revenue, *MR*, with marginal cost, *MC*. As output increases, the firm's marginal revenue is constant but its marginal cost eventually increases.

If marginal revenue exceeds marginal cost (*MR* > *MC*), then the revenue from selling one more unit exceeds the cost of producing it and an increase in output increases economic profit. If marginal revenue is less than marginal cost (*MR* < *MC*), then the revenue from selling one more unit is less than the cost of producing that unit and a *decrease* in output *increases* economic profit. If marginal revenue equals marginal cost (*MR* = *MC*), then the revenue from selling one more unit equals the cost incurred to produce that unit. Economic profit is maximized and either an increase or a decrease in output decreases economic profit.

Figure 12.3 illustrates these propositions. If Campus Sweaters increases its output from 8 sweaters to 9 sweaters a day, marginal revenue ($25) exceeds marginal cost ($23), so by producing the 9th sweater, economic profit increases by $2 from $40 to $42 a day. The blue area in the figure shows the increase in economic profit when the firm increases production from 8 to 9 sweaters per day.

If Campus Sweaters increases its output from 9 sweaters to 10 sweaters a day, marginal revenue ($25) is less than marginal cost ($27), so by producing the 10th sweater, economic profit decreases. The last column of the table shows that economic profit decreases from $42 to $40 a day. The red area in the figure shows the economic loss that arises from increasing production from 9 to 10 sweaters a day.

Campus Sweaters maximizes economic profit by producing 9 sweaters a day, the quantity at which marginal revenue equals marginal cost.

A firm's profit-maximizing output is its quantity supplied at the market price. The quantity supplied at a price of $25 a sweater is 9 sweaters a day. If the price were higher than $25 a sweater, the firm would increase production. If the price were lower than $25 a sweater, the firm would decrease production. These profit-maximizing responses to different market prices are the foundation of the law of supply:

> Other things remaining the same, the higher the market price of a good, the greater is the quantity supplied of that good.

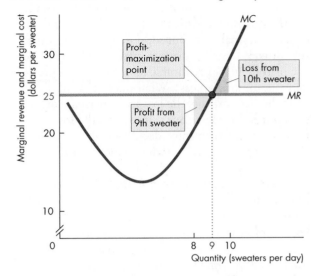

FIGURE 12.3   Profit-Maximizing Output

Quantity (Q) (sweaters per day)	Total revenue (TR) (dollars)	Marginal revenue (MR) (dollars per additional sweater)	Total cost (TC) (dollars)	Marginal cost (MC) (dollars per additional sweater)	Economic profit (TR − TC) (dollars)
7	175		141		34
		25		19	
8	200		160		40
		25		23	
9	225		183		42
		25		27	
10	250		210		40
		25		35	
11	275		245		30

The firm maximizes profit by producing the output at which marginal revenue equals marginal cost and marginal cost is increasing. The table and figure show that marginal cost equals marginal revenue and economic profit is maximized when Campus Sweaters produces 9 sweaters a day.

The table shows that if Campus Sweaters increases output from 8 to 9 sweaters, marginal cost is $23, which is less than the marginal revenue of $25. If output increases from 9 to 10 sweaters, marginal cost is $27 and it exceeds the marginal revenue of $25.

If marginal revenue exceeds marginal cost, an increase in output increases economic profit. If marginal revenue is less than marginal cost, an increase in output decreases economic profit. If marginal revenue equals marginal cost, economic profit is maximized.

MyEconLab   *animation*

Temporary Shutdown Decision

You've seen that a firm maximizes profit by producing the quantity at which marginal revenue (price) equals marginal cost. But suppose that at this quantity, price is less than average total cost. In this case, the firm incurs an economic loss. Maximum profit is a loss (a minimum loss). What does the firm do?

If the firm expects the loss to be permanent, it goes out of business. But if it expects the loss to be temporary, the firm must decide whether to shut down temporarily and produce no output or to keep producing. To make this decision, the firm compares the loss from shutting down with the loss from producing and takes the action that minimizes its loss.

Loss Comparisons A firm's economic loss equals total fixed cost, *TFC*, plus total variable cost minus total revenue. Total variable cost equals average variable cost, *AVC*, multiplied by the quantity produced, *Q*, and total revenue equals price, *P*, multiplied by the quantity *Q*. So

$$\text{Economic loss} = TFC + (AVC - P) \times Q.$$

If the firm shuts down, it produces no output ($Q = 0$). The firm has no variable costs and no revenue but it must pay its fixed costs, so its economic loss equals total fixed cost.

If the firm produces, then in addition to its fixed costs, it incurs variable costs. But it also receives revenue. Its economic loss equals total fixed cost—the loss when shut down—plus total variable cost minus total revenue. If total variable cost exceeds total revenue, this loss exceeds total fixed cost and the firm shuts down. Equivalently, if average variable cost *exceeds* price, this loss exceeds total fixed cost and the firm *shuts down*.

The Shutdown Point A firm's **shutdown point** is the price and quantity at which it is indifferent between producing and shutting down. The shutdown point occurs at the price and the quantity at which average variable cost is a minimum. At the shutdown point, the firm is minimizing its loss and its loss equals total fixed cost. If the price falls below minimum average variable cost, the firm shuts down temporarily and continues to incur a loss equal to total fixed cost. At prices above minimum average variable cost but below average total cost, the firm produces the loss-minimizing output and incurs a loss, but a loss that is less than total fixed cost.

Figure 12.4 illustrates the firm's shutdown decision and the shutdown point that we've just described for Campus Sweaters.

The firm's average variable cost curve is *AVC* and the marginal cost curve is *MC*. Average variable cost has a minimum of $17 a sweater when output is 7 sweaters a day. The *MC* curve intersects the *AVC* curve at its minimum. (We explained this relationship between marginal cost and average cost in Chapter 11; see pp. 258–259.)

The figure shows the marginal revenue curve, *MR*, when the price is $17 a sweater, a price equal to minimum average variable cost.

Marginal revenue equals marginal cost at 7 sweaters a day, so this quantity maximizes economic profit (minimizes economic loss). The *ATC* curve shows that the firm's average total cost of producing 7 sweaters a day is $20.14 a sweater. The firm incurs a loss equal to $3.14 a sweater on 7 sweaters a day, so its loss is $22 a day, which equals total fixed cost.

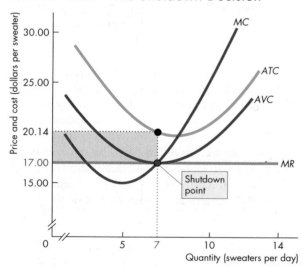

FIGURE 12.4   The Shutdown Decision

The shutdown point is at minimum average variable cost. At a price below minimum average variable cost, the firm shuts down and produces no output. At a price equal to minimum average variable cost, the firm is indifferent between shutting down and producing no output or producing the output at minimum average variable cost. Either way, the firm minimizes its economic loss and incurs a loss equal to total fixed cost.

The Firm's Supply Curve

A perfectly competitive firm's supply curve shows
how the firm's profit-maximizing output varies as the
market price varies, other things remaining the same.
The supply curve is derived from the firm's marginal
cost and average variable cost curves. Figure 12.5
illustrates the derivation of the supply curve.

When the price *exceeds* minimum average variable
cost (more than $17 a sweater), the firm maximizes
profit by producing the output at which marginal
cost equals price. If the price rises, the firm increases
its output—moves up along its marginal cost curve.

When the price is *less than* minimum average variable cost (less than $17 a sweater), the firm maxi-
mizes profit by temporarily shutting down and
producing no output. The firm produces zero output
at all prices below minimum average variable cost.

When the price *equals* minimum average variable
cost, the firm maximizes profit *either* by temporarily
shutting down and producing no output *or* by producing the output at which average variable cost is a
minimum—the shutdown point, *T*. The firm never
produces a quantity between zero and the quantity at
the shutdown point *T* (a quantity greater than zero
and less than 7 sweaters a day).

The firm's supply curve in Fig. 12.5(b) runs along
the *y*-axis from a price of zero to a price equal to
minimum average variable cost, jumps to point *T*,
and then, as the price rises above minimum average
variable cost, follows the marginal cost curve.

REVIEW QUIZ

1 Why does a firm in perfect competition produce
the quantity at which marginal cost equals price?
2 What is the lowest price at which a firm produces
an output? Explain why.
3 What is the relationship between a firm's supply
curve, its marginal cost curve, and its average
variable cost curve?

You can work these questions in Study Plan 12.2
and get instant feedback.

———————————— MyEconLab ◆

So far, we've studied a single firm in isolation.
We've seen that the firm's profit-maximizing decision
depends on the market price, which it takes as given.
How is the market price determined? Let's find out.

FIGURE 12.5   A Firm's Supply Curve

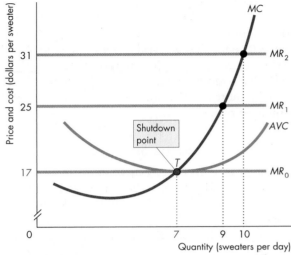

(a) Marginal cost and average variable cost

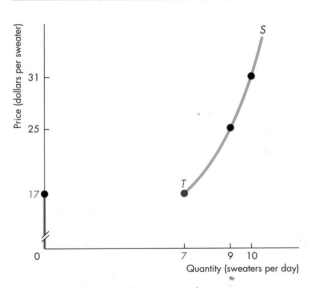

(b) Campus Sweaters' short-run supply curve

Part (a) shows Campus Sweaters' profit-maximizing output
at various market prices. At $25 a sweater, it produces
9 sweaters, and at $17 a sweater, it produces 7 sweaters.
At all prices below $17 a sweater, it produces nothing. Its
shutdown point is *T*. Part (b) shows the firm's supply curve:
the quantity of sweaters it produces at each price. Its supply
curve is made up of the marginal cost curve at all prices
above minimum average variable cost and the vertical axis
at all prices below minimum average variable cost.

———————— MyEconLab animation ◆

Output, Price, and Profit in the Short Run

To determine the price and quantity in a perfectly competitive market, we need to know how market demand and market supply interact. We start by studying a perfectly competitive market in the short run. The short run is a situation in which the number of firms is fixed.

Market Supply in the Short Run

The **short-run market supply curve** shows the quantity supplied by all the firms in the market at each price when each firm's plant and the number of firms remain the same.

You've seen how an individual firm's supply curve is determined. The market supply curve is derived from the individual supply curves. The quantity supplied by the market at a given price is the sum of the quantities supplied by all the firms in the market at that price.

Figure 12.6 shows the supply curve for the competitive sweater market. In this example, the market consists of 1,000 firms exactly like Campus Sweaters. At each price, the quantity supplied by the market is 1,000 times the quantity supplied by a single firm.

The table in Fig. 12.6 shows the firm's and the market's supply schedules and how the market supply curve is constructed. At prices below $17 a sweater, every firm in the market shuts down; the quantity supplied by the market is zero. At $17 a sweater, each firm is indifferent between shutting down and producing nothing or operating and producing 7 sweaters a day. Some firms will shut down, and others will supply 7 sweaters a day. The quantity supplied by each firm is *either* 0 or 7 sweaters, and the quantity supplied by the market is *between* 0 (all firms shut down) and 7,000 (all firms produce 7 sweaters a day each).

The market supply curve is a graph of the market supply schedules and the points on the supply curve *A* through *D* represent the rows of the table.

To construct the market supply curve, we sum the quantities supplied by all the firms at each price. Each of the 1,000 firms in the market has a supply schedule like Campus Sweaters. At prices below $17 a sweater, the market supply curve runs along the *y*-axis. At $17 a sweater, the market supply curve is horizontal—supply is perfectly elastic. As the price

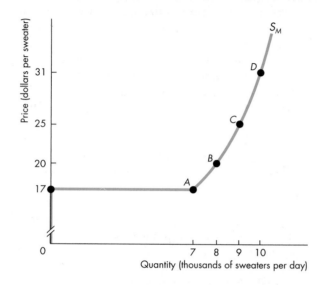

FIGURE 12.6   Short-Run Market Supply Curve

	Price (dollars per sweater)	Quantity supplied by Campus Sweaters (sweaters per day)	Quantity supplied by market (sweaters per day)
A	17	0 or 7	0 to 7,000
B	20	8	8,000
C	25	9	9,000
D	31	10	10,000

The market supply schedule is the sum of the supply schedules of all the individual firms. A market that consists of 1,000 identical firms has a supply schedule similar to that of one firm, but the quantity supplied by the market is 1,000 times as large as that of the one firm (see the table). The market supply curve is S_M. Points A, B, C, and D correspond to the rows of the table. At the shutdown price of $17 a sweater, each firm produces either 0 or 7 sweaters a day and the quantity supplied by the market is between 0 and 7,000 sweaters a day. The market supply is perfectly elastic at the shutdown price.

———————— MyEconLab   animation   ◆

rises above $17 a sweater, each firm increases its quantity supplied and the quantity supplied by the market increases by 1,000 times that of one firm.

Short-Run Equilibrium

Market demand and short-run market supply determine the market price and market output. Figure 12.7(a) shows a short-run equilibrium. The short-run supply curve, S, is the same as S_M in Fig. 12.6. If the market demand curve is D_1, the market price is $20 a sweater. Each firm takes this price as given and produces its profit-maximizing output, which is 8 sweaters a day. Because the market has 1,000 identical firms, the market output is 8,000 sweaters a day.

A Change in Demand

Changes in demand bring changes to short-run market equilibrium. Figure 12.7 shows these changes.

If demand increases and the demand curve shifts rightward to D_2, the market price rises to $25 a sweater. At this price, each firm maximizes profit by increasing its output to 9 sweaters a day. The market output increases to 9,000 sweaters a day.

If demand decreases and the demand curve shifts leftward to D_3, the market price falls to $17. At this price, each firm maximizes profit by decreasing its output. If each firm produces 7 sweaters a day, the market output decreases to 7,000 sweaters a day.

If the demand curve shifts farther leftward than D_3, the market price remains at $17 a sweater because the market supply curve is horizontal at that price. Some firms continue to produce 7 sweaters a day, and others temporarily shut down. Firms are indifferent between these two activities, and whichever they choose, they incur an economic loss equal to total fixed cost. The number of firms continuing to produce is just enough to satisfy the market demand at a price of $17 a sweater.

Profits and Losses in the Short Run

In short-run equilibrium, although the firm produces the profit-maximizing output, it does not necessarily end up making an economic profit. It might do so, but it might alternatively break even or incur an economic loss. Economic profit (or loss) per sweater is price, P, minus average total cost, ATC. So economic profit (or loss) is $(P - ATC) \times Q$. If price equals

---

FIGURE 12.7   Short-Run Equilibrium

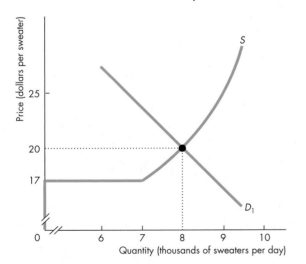

(a) Equilibrium

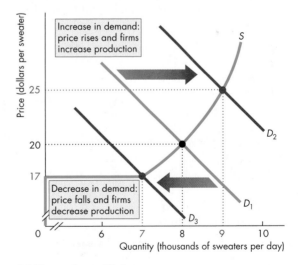

(b) Change in equilibrium

In part (a), the market supply curve is S and the market demand curve is D_1. The market price is $20 a sweater. At this price, each firm produces 8 sweaters a day and the market produces 8,000 sweaters a day.

In part (b), if the market demand increases to D_2, the

price rises to $25 a sweater. Each firm produces 9 sweaters a day and market output is 9,000 sweaters. If market demand decreases to D_3, the price falls to $17 a sweater and each firm decreases its output. If each firm produces 7 sweaters a day, the market output is 7,000 sweaters a day.

average total cost, a firm breaks even—the entrepreneur makes normal profit. If price exceeds average total cost, a firm makes an economic profit. If price is less than average total cost, a firm incurs an economic loss. Figure 12.8 shows these three possible short-run profit outcomes for Campus Sweaters. These outcomes correspond to the three different levels of market demand that we've just examined.

Three Possible Short-Run Outcomes

Figure 12.8(a) corresponds to the situation in Fig. 12.7(a) where the market demand is D_1. The equilibrium price of a sweater is $20 and the firm produces 8 sweaters a day. Average total cost is $20 a sweater. Price equals average total cost (ATC), so the firm breaks even (makes zero economic profit).

Figure 12.8(b) corresponds to the situation in Fig. 12.7(b) where the market demand is D_2. The equilibrium price of a sweater is $25 and the firm produces 9 sweaters a day. Here, price exceeds average total cost, so the firm makes an economic profit. Its economic profit is $42 a day, which equals $4.67 per sweater ($25.00 − $20.33) multiplied by 9, the

profit-maximizing number of sweaters produced. The blue rectangle shows this economic profit. The height of that rectangle is profit per sweater, $4.67, and the length is the quantity of sweaters produced, 9 a day. So the area of the rectangle is economic profit of $42 a day.

Figure 12.8(c) corresponds to the situation in Fig. 12.7(b) where the market demand is D_3. The equilibrium price of a sweater is $17. Here, the price is less than average total cost, so the firm incurs an economic loss. Price and marginal revenue are $17 a sweater, and the profit-maximizing (in this case, loss-minimizing) output is 7 sweaters a day. Total revenue is $119 a day (7 × $17). Average total cost is $20.14 a sweater, so the economic loss is $3.14 per sweater ($20.14 − $17.00). This loss per sweater multiplied by the number of sweaters is $22. The red rectangle shows this economic loss. The height of that rectangle is economic loss per sweater, $3.14, and the length is the quantity of sweaters produced, 7 a day. So the area of the rectangle is the firm's economic loss of $22 a day. If the price dips below $17 a sweater, the firm temporarily shuts down and incurs an economic loss equal to total fixed cost.

FIGURE 12.8   Three Short-Run Outcomes for the Firm

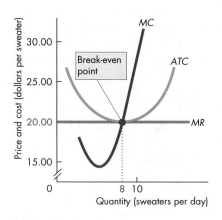

(a) Break even

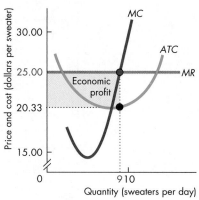

(b) Economic profit

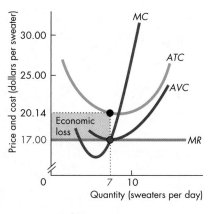

(c) Economic loss

In the short run, the firm might break even (make zero economic profit), make an economic profit, or incur an economic loss. In part (a), the price equals minimum average total cost. At the profit-maximizing output, the firm breaks even and makes zero economic profit. In part (b), the market price is $25 a sweater. At the profit-maximizing output,

the price exceeds average total cost and the firm makes an economic profit equal to the area of the blue rectangle. In part (c), the market price is $17 a sweater. At the profit-maximizing output, the price is below minimum average total cost and the firm incurs an economic loss equal to the area of the red rectangle.

Economics in Action
Production Cutback and Temporary Shutdown

Motor Coach Industries (MCI) employs about 1,000 workers at its Winnipeg plant, where it has been building coaches for more than 70 years. In February 2008, the firm delivered some bad news to labour union head Glen Tomchak: The plant would shut down for a week in April and some workers would be permanently laid off.

MCI officials said that in the current state of the U.S. economy, the demand for coaches was down and prices were depressed.

We can explain this temporary shutdown using the analysis you've learned in this chapter. The shutdown occurred because total revenue was insufficient to cover total *variable* cost.

The firm's permanent cut in its workforce can be explained by the same analysis. The fall in the price of a coach decreased the profit-maximizing quantity of coaches and MCI cut the quantity of labour employed.

◆ REVIEW QUIZ

1 How do we derive the short-run market supply curve in perfect competition?

2 In perfect competition, when market demand increases, explain how the price and each firm's output and profit change in the short run.

3 In perfect competition, when market demand decreases, explain how the price and each firm's output and profit change in the short run.

You can work these questions in Study Plan 12.3 and get instant feedback.

——————————— MyEconLab ◆

◆ Output, Price, and Profit in the Long Run

In short-run equilibrium, a firm might make an economic profit, incur an economic loss, or break even. Although each of these three situations is a short-run equilibrium, only one of them is a long-run equilibrium. The reason is that in the long run, firms can enter or exit the market.

Entry and Exit

Entry occurs in a market when new firms come into the market and the number of firms increases. Exit occurs when existing firms leave a market and the number of firms decreases.

Firms respond to economic profit and economic loss by either entering or exiting a market. New firms enter a market in which existing firms are making an economic profit. Firms exit a market in which they are incurring an economic loss. Temporary economic profit and temporary economic loss don't trigger entry and exit. It's the prospect of persistent economic profit or loss that triggers entry and exit.

Entry and exit change the market supply, which influences the market price, the quantity produced by each firm, and its economic profit (or loss).

If firms enter a market, supply increases and the market supply curve shifts rightward. The increase in supply lowers the market price and eventually eliminates economic profit. When economic profit reaches zero, entry stops.

If firms exit a market, supply decreases and the market supply curve shifts leftward. The market price rises and economic loss decreases. Eventually, economic loss is eliminated and exit stops.

To summarize:

- New firms enter a market in which existing firms are making economic profit.
- As new firms enter a market, the market price falls and the economic profit of each firm decreases.
- Firms exit a market in which they are incurring economic loss.
- As firms leave a market, the market price rises and the economic loss incurred by the remaining firms decreases.
- Entry and exit stop when firms make zero economic profit.

A Closer Look at Entry

The sweater market has 800 firms with cost curves like those in Fig. 12.9(a). The market demand curve is D, the market supply curve is S_1, and the price is $25 a sweater in Fig. 12.9(b). Each firm produces 9 sweaters a day and makes an economic profit.

This economic profit is a signal for new firms to enter the market. As entry takes place, supply increases and the market supply curve shifts rightward towards S^*. As supply increases with no change in demand, the market price gradually falls from $25 to $20 a sweater. At this lower price, each firm makes zero economic profit and entry stops.

Entry results in an increase in market output, but each firm's output *decreases*. Because the price falls, each firm moves down its supply curve and produces less. Because the number of firms increases, the market produces more.

A Closer Look at Exit

The sweater market has 1,200 firms with cost curves like those in Fig. 12.9(a). The market demand curve is D, the market supply curve is S_2, and the price is $17 a sweater in Fig. 12.9(b). Each firm produces 7 sweaters a day and incurs an economic loss.

This economic loss is a signal for firms to exit the market. As exit takes place, supply decreases and the market supply curve shifts leftward towards S^*. As supply decreases with no change in demand, the market price gradually rises from $17 to $20 a sweater. At this higher price, losses are eliminated, each firm makes zero economic profit, and exit stops.

Exit results in a decrease in market output, but each firm's output *increases*. Because the price rises, each firm moves up its supply curve and produces more. Because the number of firms decreases, the market produces less.

FIGURE 12.9   Entry, Exit, and Long-Run Equilibrium

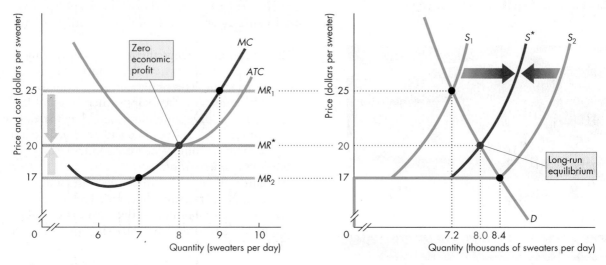

(a) Campus Sweaters

(b) The sweater market

Each firm has cost curves like those of Campus Sweaters in part (a). The market demand curve is D in part (b). When the market supply curve in part (b) is S_1, the market price is $25 a sweater. In part (a), each firm produces 9 sweaters a day and makes an economic profit. Profit triggers the entry of new firms and as new firms enter, the market supply curve shifts rightward, from S_1 towards S^*. The price falls from $25 to $20 a sweater, and the quantity produced increases from 7,200 to 8,000 sweaters. Each firm's output decreases to

8 sweaters a day and economic profit falls to zero.

When the market supply curve is S_2, the price is $17 a sweater. In part (a), each firm produces 7 sweaters a day and incurs an economic loss. Loss triggers exit and as firms exit, the market supply curve shifts leftward, from S_2 towards S^*. The price rises from $17 to $20 a sweater, and the quantity produced decreases from 8,400 to 8,000 sweaters. Each firm's output increases from 7 to 8 sweaters a day and economic profit rises to zero.

Economics in Action
Entry and Exit

An example of entry and falling prices occurred during the 1980s and 1990s in the personal computer market. When IBM introduced its first PC in 1981, IBM had little competition. The price was $7,000 (about $16,850 in today's money) and IBM made a large economic profit selling the new machine.

Observing IBM's huge success, new firms such as Gateway, NEC, Dell, and a host of others entered the market with machines that were technologically identical to IBM's. In fact, they were so similar that they came to be called "clones." The massive wave of entry into the personal computer market increased the market supply and lowered the price. The economic profit for all firms decreased.

Today, a $400 computer is vastly more powerful than its 1981 ancestor that cost 42 times as much.

The same PC market that saw entry during the 1980s and 1990s has seen some exit more recently. In 2001, IBM, the firm that first launched the PC, announced that it was exiting the market. The intense competition from Gateway, NEC, Dell, and others that entered the market following IBM's lead has lowered the price and eliminated the economic profit. So IBM now concentrates on servers and other parts of the computer market.

IBM exited the PC market because it was incurring economic losses. Its exit decreased market supply and made it possible for the remaining firms in the market to make zero economic profit.

International Harvester, a manufacturer of farm equipment, provides another example of exit. For decades, people associated the name "International Harvester" with tractors, combines, and other farm machines. But International Harvester wasn't the only maker of farm equipment. The market became intensely competitive, and the firm began to incur economic losses. Now the firm has a new name, Navistar International, and it doesn't make tractors anymore. After years of economic losses and shrinking revenues, it got out of the farm-machine business in 1985 and started to make trucks.

International Harvester exited because it was incurring an economic loss. Its exit decreased supply and made it possible for the remaining firms in the market to break even.

Long-Run Equilibrium

You've now seen how economic profit induces entry, which in turn eliminates the profit. You've also seen how economic loss induces exit, which in turn eliminates the loss.

When economic profit and economic loss have been eliminated and entry and exit have stopped, a competitive market is in *long-run equilibrium*.

You've seen how a competitive market adjusts towards its long-run equilibrium. But a competitive market is rarely *in* a state of long-run equilibrium. Instead, it is constantly and restlessly evolving towards long-run equilibrium. The reason is that the market is constantly bombarded with events that change the constraints that firms face.

◖ REVIEW QUIZ

1 What triggers entry in a competitive market? Describe the process that ends further entry.
2 What triggers exit in a competitive market? Describe the process that ends further exit.

You can work these questions in Study Plan 12.4 and get instant feedback.

MyEconLab ◆

Markets are constantly adjusting to keep up with changes in tastes, which change demand, and changes in technology, which change costs. In the next sections, we're going to see how a competitive market reacts to changing tastes and technology and how it guides resources to their highest-valued use.

Changing Tastes and Advancing Technology

Increased awareness of the health hazards of smoking has decreased the demand for tobacco products. The development of inexpensive automobile and air transportation during the 1990s decreased the demand for long-distance trains and buses. Solid-state electronics has decreased the demand for TV and radio repair. The development of good-quality inexpensive clothing has decreased the demand for sewing machines. What happens in a competitive market when there is a permanent decrease in the demand for its product?

Microwave food preparation has increased the demand for paper, glass, and plastic cooking utensils and for plastic wrap. The Internet has increased the demand for personal computers and the widespread use of computers has increased the demand for high-speed connections and music downloads. What happens in a competitive market when the demand for its output increases?

Advances in technology are constantly lowering the costs of production. New biotechnologies have dramatically lowered the costs of producing many food and pharmaceutical products. New electronic technologies have lowered the cost of producing just about every good and service. What happens in a competitive market for a good when technological change lowers its production costs?

Let's use the theory of perfect competition to answer these questions.

A Permanent Change in Demand

Figure 12.10(a) shows a competitive market that initially is in long-run equilibrium. The demand curve is D_0, the supply curve is S_0, the market price is P_0, and market output is Q_0. Figure 12.10(b) shows a single firm in this initial long-run equilibrium. The firm produces q_0 and makes zero economic profit.

Now suppose that demand decreases and the demand curve shifts leftward to D_1, as shown in Fig. 12.10(a). The market price falls to P_1, and the quantity supplied by the market decreases from Q_0 to Q_1 as the market moves down along its short-run supply curve S_0. Figure 12.10(b) shows the situation facing a firm. The market price is now below the firm's minimum average total cost, so the firm incurs an economic loss. But to minimize its loss, the firm adjusts its output to keep marginal cost equal to price. At a price of P_1, each firm produces an output of q_1.

The market is now in short-run equilibrium but not long-run equilibrium. It is in short-run equilibrium because each firm is maximizing profit; it is not in long-run equilibrium because each firm is incurring an economic loss—its average total cost exceeds the price.

The economic loss is a signal for some firms to exit the market. As they do so, short-run market supply decreases and the market supply curve gradually shifts leftward. As market supply decreases, the price rises. At each higher price, a firm's profit-maximizing output is greater, so the firms remaining in the market increase their output as the price rises. Each firm moves up along its marginal cost or supply curve in Fig. 12.10(b). That is, as some firms exit the market, market output decreases but the output of the firms that remain in the market increases.

Eventually, enough firms have exited the market for the market supply curve to have shifted to S_1 in Fig. 12.10(a). The market price has returned to its original level, P_0. At this price, the firms remaining in the market produce q_0, the same quantity that they produced before the decrease in demand. Because firms are now making zero economic profit, no firm has an incentive to enter or exit the market. The market supply curve remains at S_1, and market output is Q_2. The market is again in long-run equilibrium.

The difference between the initial long-run equilibrium and the final long-run equilibrium is the number of firms in the market. A permanent decrease in demand has decreased the number of firms. Each firm remaining in the market produces the same output in the new long-run equilibrium as it did initially and makes zero economic profit. In the process of moving from the initial equilibrium to the new one, firms incur economic losses.

We've just worked out how a competitive market responds to a permanent *decrease* in demand. A permanent increase in demand triggers a similar response, except in the opposite direction. The increase in demand brings a higher price, economic profit, and entry. Entry increases market supply and eventually lowers the price to its original level and economic profit to zero.

The demand for Internet service increased permanently during the 1990s and huge profit opportunities arose in this market. The result was a massive

FIGURE 12.10   A Decrease in Demand

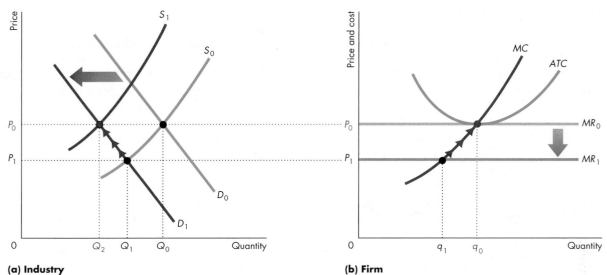

(a) Industry

(b) Firm

A market starts out in long-run competitive equilibrium. Part (a) shows the market demand curve D_0, the market supply curve S_0, the market price P_0, and the equilibrium quantity Q_0. Each firm sells its output at the price P_0, so its marginal revenue curve is MR_0 in part (b). Each firm produces q_0 and makes zero economic profit.

Market demand decreases permanently from D_0 to D_1 in part (a) and the market price falls to P_1. Each firm decreases its output to q_1 in part (b), and the market output

decreases to Q_1 in part (a). Firms now incur economic losses. Some firms exit the market, and as they do so, the market supply curve gradually shifts leftward, from S_0 toward S_1. This shift gradually raises the market price from P_1 back to P_0. While the price is below P_0, firms incur economic losses and some firms exit the market. Once the price has returned to P_0, each firm makes zero economic profit and has no incentive to exit. Each firm produces q_0, and the market output is Q_2.

MyEconLab   animation ◆

rate of entry of Internet service providers. The process of competition and change in the Internet service market is similar to what we have just studied but with an increase in demand rather than a decrease in demand.

We've now studied the effects of a permanent change in demand for a good. In doing so, we began and ended in a long-run equilibrium and examined the process that takes a market from one equilibrium to another. It is this process, not the equilibrium points, that describes the real world.

One feature of the predictions that we have just generated seems odd: In the long run, regardless of whether demand increases or decreases, the market price returns to its original level. Is this outcome inevitable? In fact, it is not. It is possible for the equilibrium market price in the long run to remain the same, rise, or fall.

External Economies and Diseconomies

The change in the long-run equilibrium price depends on external economies and external diseconomies. **External economies** are factors beyond the control of an individual firm that lower the firm's costs as the *market* output increases. **External diseconomies** are factors outside the control of a firm that raise the firm's costs as the *market* output increases. With no external economies or external diseconomies, a firm's costs remain constant as the market output changes.

Figure 12.11 illustrates these three cases and introduces a new supply concept: the long-run market supply curve.

A **long-run market supply curve** shows how the quantity supplied in a market varies as the market price varies after all the possible adjustments have been made, including changes in each firm's plant and the number of firms in the market.

Figure 12.11(a) shows the case we have just studied—no external economies or diseconomies. The long-run market supply curve (LS_A) is perfectly elastic. In this case, a permanent increase in demand from D_0 to D_1 has no effect on the price in the long run. The increase in demand brings a temporary increase in price to P_S and in the short run the quantity increases from Q_0 to Q_S. Entry increases short-run supply from S_0 to S_1, which lowers the price from P_S back to P_0 and increases the quantity to Q_1.

Figure 12.11(b) shows the case of external diseconomies. The long-run market supply curve (LS_B) slopes upward. A permanent increase in demand from D_0 to D_1 increases the price in both the short run and the long run. The increase in demand brings a temporary increase in price to P_S and in the short run the quantity increases from Q_0 to Q_S. Entry increases short-run supply from S_0 to S_2, which lowers the price from P_S to P_2 and increases the quantity to Q_2.

One source of external diseconomies is congestion. The airline market provides a good example. With bigger airline market output, congestion at both airports and in the air increases, resulting in longer delays and extra waiting time for passengers and airplanes. These external diseconomies mean that as the output of air transportation services increases (in the absence of technological advances), average cost increases. As a result, the long-run market supply curve is upward-sloping. A permanent increase in demand brings an increase in quantity and a rise in the price. (Markets with external diseconomies might nonetheless have a falling price because technological advances shift the long-run supply curve downward.)

Figure 12.11(c) shows the case of external economies. The long-run market supply curve (LS_C) slopes downward. A permanent increase in demand from D_0 to D_1 increases the price in the short run and lowers it in the long run. Again, the increase in demand brings a temporary increase in price to P_S and in the short run the quantity increases from Q_0 to Q_S. Entry increases short-run supply from S_0 to S_3, which lowers the price to P_3 and increases the quantity to Q_3.

An example of external economies is the growth of specialist support services for a market as it

FIGURE 12.11   Long-Run Changes in Price and Quantity

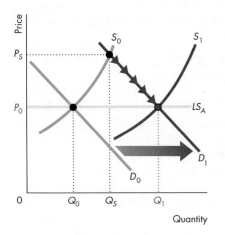

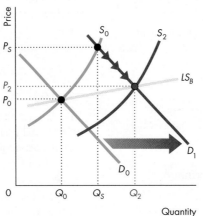

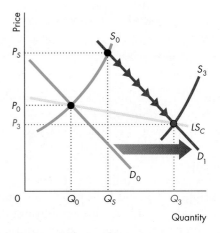

(a) Constant-cost industry

(b) Increasing-cost industry

(c) Decreasing-cost industry

Three possible changes in price and quantity occur in the long run. When demand increases from D_0 to D_1, entry occurs and the market supply curve shifts rightward from S_0 to S_1. In part (a), the long-run market supply curve, LS_A, is horizontal. The quantity increases from Q_0 to Q_1, and the price remains constant at P_0.

In part (b), the long-run market supply curve is LS_B; the price rises to P_2, and the quantity increases to Q_2. This case occurs in industries with external diseconomies. In part (c), the long-run market supply curve is LS_C; the price falls to P_3, and the quantity increases to Q_3. This case occurs in a market with external economies.

MyEconLab   animation ◆

expands. As farm output increased in the nineteenth and early twentieth centuries, the services available to farmers expanded. New firms specialized in the development and marketing of farm machinery and fertilizers. As a result, average farm costs decreased. Farms enjoyed the benefits of external economies. As a consequence, as the demand for farm products increased, the output increased but the price fell.

Over the long term, the prices of many goods and services have fallen, not because of external economies but because of technological change. Let's now study this influence on a competitive market.

Technological Change

Industries are constantly discovering lower-cost techniques of production. Most cost-saving production techniques cannot be implemented, however, without investing in new plant and equipment. As a consequence, it takes time for a technological advance to spread through a market. Some firms whose plants are on the verge of being replaced will be quick to adopt the new technology, while other firms whose plants have recently been replaced will continue to operate with an old technology until they can no longer cover their average variable cost. Once average variable cost cannot be covered, a firm will scrap even a relatively new plant (embodying an old technology) in favour of a plant with a new technology.

New technology allows firms to produce at a lower cost. As a result, as firms adopt a new technology, their cost curves shift downward. With lower costs, firms are willing to supply a given quantity at a lower price or, equivalently, they are willing to supply a larger quantity at a given price. In other words, market supply increases, and the market supply curve shifts rightward. With a given demand, the quantity produced increases and the price falls.

Two forces are at work in a market undergoing technological change. Firms that adopt the new technology make an economic profit, so there is entry by new-technology firms. Firms that stick with the old technology incur economic losses. They either exit the market or switch to the new technology.

As old-technology firms disappear and new-technology firms enter, the price falls and the quantity produced increases. Eventually, the market arrives at a long-run equilibrium in which all the firms use the new technology and make a zero economic profit. Because in the long run competition eliminates economic profit, technological change

brings only temporary gains to producers. But the lower prices and better products that technological advances bring are permanent gains for consumers.

The process that we've just described is one in which some firms experience economic profits and others experience economic losses. It is a period of dynamic change in a market. Some firms do well, and others do badly. Often, the process has a geographical dimension—the expanding new-technology firms bring prosperity to what was once the boondocks, and traditional industrial regions decline. Sometimes, the new-technology firms are in a foreign country, while the old-technology firms are in the domestic economy. The information revolution of the 1990s produced many examples of changes like these. The computer programming industry, traditionally concentrated in the United States, now flourishes in Canada, the United Kingdom, and India. Television shows and movies, traditionally made in Los Angeles and New York, are now made in large numbers in Toronto and Vancouver.

Technological advances are not confined to the information and entertainment industries. Even food production is undergoing a major technological change because of genetic engineering.

REVIEW QUIZ

1   Describe the course of events in a competitive market following a permanent decrease in demand. What happens to output, price, and economic profit in the short run and in the long run?
2   Describe the course of events in a competitive market following a permanent increase in demand. What happens to output, price, and economic profit in the short run and in the long run?
3   Describe the course of events in a competitive market following the adoption of a new technology. What happens to output, price, and economic profit in the short run and in the long run?

You can work these questions in Study Plan 12.5 and get instant feedback.
——————————————— MyEconLab ◆

We've seen how a competitive market operates in the short run and the long run, but is a competitive market efficient?

◆ Competition and Efficiency

A competitive market can achieve an efficient use of resources. You first studied efficiency in Chapter 2. Then in Chapter 5, using only the concepts of demand, supply, consumer surplus, and producer surplus, you saw how a competitive market achieves efficiency. Now that you have learned what lies behind the demand and supply curves of a competitive market, you can gain a deeper understanding of the efficiency of a competitive market.

Efficient Use of Resources

Recall that resource use is efficient when we produce the goods and services that people value most highly (see Chapter 2, pp. 33–35, and Chapter 5, p. 108). If someone can become better off without anyone else becoming worse off, resources are *not* being used efficiently. For example, suppose we produce a computer that no one wants and no one will ever use and, at the same time, some people are clamouring for more video games. If we produce fewer computers and reallocate the unused resources to produce more video games, some people will become better off and no one will be worse off. So the initial resource allocation was inefficient.

In the more technical language that you have learned, resource use is efficient when marginal social benefit equals marginal social cost. In the computer and video games example, the marginal social benefit of a video game exceeds its marginal social cost; the marginal social cost of a computer exceeds its marginal social benefit. So by producing fewer computers and more video games, we move resources towards a higher-valued use.

Choices, Equilibrium, and Efficiency

We can use what you have learned about the decisions made by consumers and competitive firms and market equilibrium to describe an efficient use of resources.

Choices Consumers allocate their budgets to get the most value possible out of them. We derive a consumer's demand curve by finding how the best budget allocation changes as the price of a good changes. So consumers get the most value out of their resources at all points along their demand curves. If the people who consume a good or service are the only ones who benefit from it, then the

market demand curve measures the benefit to the entire society and is the marginal social benefit curve.

Competitive firms produce the quantity that maximizes profit. We derive the firm's supply curve by finding the profit-maximizing quantity at each price. So firms get the most value out of their resources at all points along their supply curves. If the firms that produce a good or service bear all the costs of producing it, then the market supply curve measures the marginal cost to the entire society and the market supply curve is the marginal social cost curve.

Equilibrium and Efficiency Resources are used efficiently when marginal social benefit equals marginal social cost. Competitive equilibrium achieves this efficient outcome because, with no externalities, price equals consumers' marginal social benefit and price equals producers' marginal social cost.

The gains from trade are the sum of consumer surplus and producer surplus. The gains from trade for consumers are measured by *consumer surplus*, which is the area below the demand curve and above the price paid. (See Chapter 5, p. 109.) The gains from trade for producers are measured by *producer surplus*, which is the area above the supply curve and below the price received. (See Chapter 5, p. 111.) The total gains from trade equal total surplus —the sum of consumer surplus and producer surplus. When the market for a good or service is in equilibrium, the gains from trade are maximized.

Illustrating an Efficient Allocation Figure 12.12 illustrates the efficiency of perfect competition in long-run equilibrium. Part (a) shows the individual firm, and part (b) shows the market. The equilibrium market price is P^*. At that price, each firm makes zero economic profit and each firm has the plant that enables it to produce at the lowest possible average total cost. Consumers are as well off as possible because the good cannot be produced at a lower cost and the price equals that least possible cost.

In part (b), consumers get the most out of their resources at all points on the market demand curve, $D = MSB$. Consumer surplus is the green area. Producers get the most out of their resources at all points on the market supply curve, $S = MSC$. Producer surplus is the blue area. Resources are used efficiently at the quantity Q^* and price P^*. At this point, marginal social benefit equals marginal social

FIGURE 12.12   Efficiency of Perfect Competition

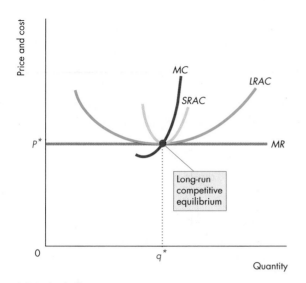

(a) A single firm

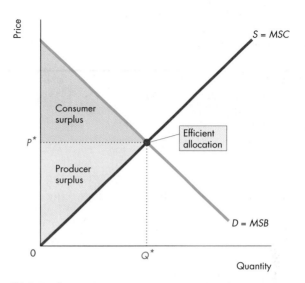

(b) A market

Demand, *D*, and supply, *S*, determine the equilibrium price, *P**. A firm in perfect competition in part (a) produces *q** at the lowest possible long-run average total cost. In part (b), consumers have made the best available choices and are

on the market demand curve, and firms are producing at least cost and are on the market supply curve. With no externalities, marginal social benefit equals marginal social cost, so resources are used efficiently at the quantity *Q**.

MyEconLab   animation ◆

cost, and total surplus (the sum of producer surplus and consumer surplus) is maximized.

When firms in perfect competition are away from long-run equilibrium, either entry or exit is taking place and the market is moving towards the situation depicted in Fig. 12.12. But the market is still efficient. As long as marginal social benefit (on the market demand curve) equals marginal social cost (on the market supply curve), the market is efficient. But it is only in long-run equilibrium that consumers pay the lowest possible price.

◆ You've now completed your study of perfect competition. *Reading Between the Lines* on pp. 292–293 gives you an opportunity to use what you have learned to understand events in the global market for corn during the past few years.

Although many markets approximate the model of perfect competition, many do not. In Chapter 13, we study markets at the opposite extreme of market power: monopoly. Then we'll study markets that lie between perfect competition and monopoly. In

Chapter 14 we study monopolistic competition and in Chapter 15 we study oligopoly. When you have completed this study, you'll have a tool kit that will enable you to understand the variety of real-world markets.

REVIEW QUIZ

1 State the conditions that must be met for resources to be allocated efficiently.
2 Describe the choices that consumers make and explain why consumers are efficient on the market demand curve.
3 Describe the choices that producers make and explain why producers are efficient on the market supply curve.
4 Explain why resources are used efficiently in a competitive market.

You can work these questions in Study Plan 12.6 and get instant feedback.

MyEconLab ◆

Perfect Competition in Corn

Bumper Harvests Bring Stability

www.ft.com
June 1, 2010

There is no better fertilizer than high prices, the old farming adage goes. Trends in agriculture appear to be proving this resoundingly true.

The spike in prices that caused the first global food crisis in 30 years in 2007–08 has led to large increases in production of foods such as corn and wheat. Farmers have responded to higher prices. ...

The U.S. Department of Agriculture said. ... "Higher prices, and thus expanded acreage, in combination with favorable weather, have helped production expand sharply."

Global corn production will hit 835m tonnes in the 2010–11 season, its highest ever level, the USDA forecasts. ... That is likely to lead to a period of relatively stable prices. ...

While prices for the main food and feed grain crops—corn, wheat, and soybeans—are likely to remain steady and low in the next year or so, that does not mean a repeat of the food crisis is impossible. ...

One argument against that view holds that technological gains in response to the crisis have boosted productivity, making farmers more able to deal with increasing consumption.

Some crops, such as corn, saw record yields in the 2009–10 season and the USDA is predicting high yields for next year as well.

But analysts ascribe the gains in productivity more to fortunate weather conditions than a revolution in farming technology. ...

ESSENCE OF THE STORY

- In 2010–11, global corn production will reach its highest ever level at 835 million tonnes.
- High prices in 2007–08 led to large increases in the production of corn and wheat.
- Favourable weather also helped to increase production of these crops.
- Prices for corn, wheat, and soybeans will likely remain low next year, but a future price rise might occur.
- A revolution in farming technology would increase production without raising costs and prices.
- The current gain in productivity is most likely the result of fortunate weather and is likely to be temporary.

- The global market for corn is competitive and the model of perfect competition shows how that market works.

- During 2006 through 2008, increases in demand brought a rising price and an increase in the quantity of corn supplied.

- In 2009 and 2010, good weather conditions brought an increase in the supply of corn and the quantity of corn increased further but its price fell.

- Figure 1 illustrates these events in the market for corn and Fig. 2 their effects on an individual farm.

- From 2006 through 2008, the supply curve of corn was S_0 in Fig. 1. The demand for corn increased and by 2008, the demand curve was D. The price of corn in 2008 was $310 per tonne and 800 million tonnes were produced.

- In 2008, the farm faced a marginal revenue curve MR_0 and had average total cost curve ATC_0 and marginal cost curve MC_0 in Fig. 2.

- The farm maximized profit by producing 8,000 tonnes and (we will assume) made zero economic profit.

- In 2009 and 2010, good weather conditions increased the supply of corn. By 2010–11, the supply curve had shifted rightward to S_1. The price fell to $230 per tonne and production increased to 835 million tonnes.

- Back on the farm in Fig. 2, the lower price decreased marginal revenue and the MR curve shifted downward to MR_1.

- But the fortunate weather increased farm productivity and lowered the cost of producing corn. The average total cost curve shifted downward to ATC_1 and the marginal cost curve shifted downward to MC_1.

- The combination of the lower price and lower costs might leave the farm with an economic profit. In Fig. 2 we're assuming that the farm again made zero economic profit.

- If farms did make a positive (or negative) economic profit, entry (or exit) would eventually return them to a zero economic profit position like that shown in Fig. 2.

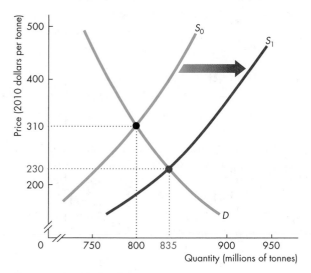

Figure 1 The Market for Corn

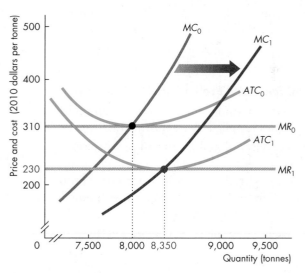

Figure 2 A Corn Farmer

SUMMARY

Key Points

What Is Perfect Competition? (pp. 274–275)

- In perfect competition, many firms sell identical products to many buyers; there are no restrictions on entry; sellers and buyers are well informed about prices.
- A perfectly competitive firm is a price taker.
- A perfectly competitive firm's marginal revenue always equals the market price.

Working Problems 1 to 3 will give you a better understanding of perfect competition.

The Firm's Output Decision (pp. 276–279)

- The firm produces the output at which marginal revenue (price) equals marginal cost.
- In short-run equilibrium, a firm can make an economic profit, incur an economic loss, or break even.
- If price is less than minimum average variable cost, the firm temporarily shuts down.
- At prices below minimum average variable cost, a firm's supply curve runs along the *y*-axis; at prices above minimum average variable cost, a firm's supply curve is its marginal cost curve.

Working Problems 4 to 7 will give you a better understanding of a firm's output decision.

Output, Price, and Profit in the Short Run (pp. 280–283)

- The market supply curve shows the sum of the quantities supplied by each firm at each price.
- Market demand and market supply determine price.
- A firm might make a positive economic profit, zero economic profit, or incur an economic loss.

Working Problems 8 and 9 will give you a better understanding of output, price, and profit in the short run.

Output, Price, and Profit in the Long Run (pp. 283–285)

- Economic profit induces entry and economic loss induces exit.
- Entry increases supply and lowers price and profit. Exit decreases supply and raises price and profit.
- In long-run equilibrium, economic profit is zero. There is no entry or exit.

Working Problems 10 and 11 will give you a better understanding of output, price, and profit in the long run.

Changing Tastes and Advancing Technology (pp. 286–289)

- A permanent decrease in demand leads to a smaller market output and a smaller number of firms. A permanent increase in demand leads to a larger market output and a larger number of firms.
- The long-run effect of a change in demand on price depends on whether there are external economies (the price falls) or external diseconomies (the price rises) or neither (the price remains constant).
- New technologies increase supply and in the long run lower the price and increase the quantity.

Working Problems 12 to 16 will give you a better understanding of changing tastes and advancing technologies.

Competition and Efficiency (pp. 290–291)

- Resources are used efficiently when we produce goods and services in the quantities that people value most highly.
- Perfect competition achieves an efficient allocation. In long-run equilibrium, consumers pay the lowest possible price and marginal social benefit equals marginal social cost.

Working Problems 17 and 18 will give you a better understanding of competition and efficiency.

Key Terms

External diseconomies, 287
External economies, 287
Long-run market supply curve, 287
Marginal revenue, 274
Perfect competition, 274

Price taker, 274
Short-run market supply curve, 280
Shutdown point, 278
Total revenue, 274

SCAN THIS

STUDY PLAN PROBLEMS AND APPLICATIONS

MyEconLab ◆ You can work Problems 1 to 18 in Chapter 12 Study Plan and get instant feedback.

What Is Perfect Competition? (Study Plan 12.1)

Use the following information to work Problems 1 to 3.

Lin's makes fortune cookies that are identical to those made by dozens of other firms, and there is free entry in the fortune cookie market. Buyers and sellers are well informed about prices.

1. In what type of market does Lin's operate? What determines the price of fortune cookies and what determines Lin's marginal revenue from fortune cookies?

2. a. If fortune cookies sell for $10 a box and Lin's offers its cookies for sale at $10.50 a box, how many boxes does it sell?
   b. If fortune cookies sell for $10 a box and Lin's offers its cookies for sale at $9.50 a box, how many boxes does it sell?

3. What is the elasticity of demand for Lin's fortune cookies and how does it differ from the elasticity of the market demand for fortune cookies?

The Firm's Output Decision (Study Plan 12.2)

Use the following table to work Problems 4 to 6. Pat's Pizza Kitchen is a price taker. Its costs are

Output (pizzas per hour)	Total cost (dollars per hour)
0	10
1	21
2	30
3	41
4	54
5	69

4. Calculate Pat's profit-maximizing output and economic profit if the market price is
   (i) $14 a pizza.
   (ii) $12 a pizza.
   (iii) $10 a pizza.

5. What is Pat's shutdown point and what is Pat's economic profit if it shuts down temporarily?

6. Derive Pat's supply curve.

7. The market for paper is perfectly competitive and there are 1,000 firms that produce paper. The table sets out the market demand schedule for paper.

Price (dollars per box)	Quantity demanded (thousands of boxes per week)
3.65	500
5.20	450
6.80	400
8.40	350
10.00	300
11.60	250
13.20	200

Each producer of paper has the following costs when it uses its least-cost plant:

Output (boxes per week)	Marginal cost (dollars per additional box)	Average variable cost	Average total cost
		(dollars per box)	
200	6.40	7.80	12.80
250	7.00	7.00	11.00
300	7.65	7.10	10.43
350	8.40	7.20	10.06
400	10.00	7.50	10.00
450	12.40	8.00	10.22
500	20.70	9.00	11.00

   a. What is the market price of paper?
   b. What is the market's output?
   c. What is the output produced by each firm?
   d. What is the economic profit made or economic loss incurred by each firm?

Output, Price, and Profit in the Short Run

(Study Plan 12.3)

8. In Problem 7, as more and more computer users read documents online rather than print them, the market demand for paper decreases and in the short run the demand schedule becomes

Price (dollars per box)	Quantity demanded (thousands of boxes per week)
2.95	500
4.13	450
5.30	400
6.48	350
7.65	300
8.83	250
10.00	200
11.18	150

If each firm producing paper has the costs set out in Problem 7, what is the market price and the economic profit or loss of each firm in the short run?

9. **Fuel Prices Could Squeeze Cheap Flights**

Airlines are having difficulty keeping prices low, especially as fuel prices keep rising. Airlines have raised fares to make up for the fuel costs. Some airlines have increased the fuel surcharge by $20 a roundtrip.

Source: CNN, June 12, 2008

a. Explain how an increase in fuel prices might cause an airline to change its output (number of flights) in the short run.

b. Draw a graph to show the increase in fuel prices on an airline's output in the short run.

c. Explain why an airline might incur an economic loss in the short run as fuel prices rise.

Output, Price, and Profit in the Long Run

(Study Plan 12.4)

10. The pizza market is perfectly competitive, and all pizza producers have the same costs as Pat's Pizza Kitchen in Problem 4.

a. At what price will some firms exit the pizza market in the long run?

b. At what price will firms enter the pizza market in the long run?

11. In Problem 7, in the long run,

a. Do firms have an incentive to enter or exit the paper market?

b. If firms do enter or exit the market, explain how the economic profit or loss of the remaining paper producers will change.

c. What is the long-run equilibrium market price and the quantity of paper produced? What is the number of firms in the market?

Changing Tastes and Advancing Technology

(Study Plan 12.5)

12. If in the long run, the market demand for paper remains the same as in Problem 8,

a. What is the long-run equilibrium price of paper, the market output, and the economic profit or loss of each firm?

b. Does this market experience external economies, external diseconomies, or constant cost? Illustrate by drawing the long-run supply curve.

Use the following news clip to work Problems 13 and 14.

Coors Brewing Expanding Plant

Coors Brewing Co. of Golden will expand its Virginia packaging plant at a cost of $24 million. The addition will accommodate a new production line, which will bottle beer faster. Coors Brewing employs 470 people at its Virginia plant. The expanded packaging line will add another eight jobs.

Source: *Denver Business Journal*, January 6, 2006

13. a. How will Coors' expansion change its marginal cost curve and short-run supply curve?

b. What does this expansion decision imply about the point on Coors' *LRAC* curve at which the firm was before the expansion?

14. a. If other breweries follow the lead of Coors, what will happen to the market price of beer?

b. How will the adjustment that you have described in part (a) influence the economic profit of Coors and other beer producers?

15. Explain and illustrate graphically how the growing world population is influencing the world market for wheat and a representative individual wheat farmer.

16. Explain and illustrate graphically how the diaper service market has been affected by the decrease in the North American birth rate and the development of disposable diapers.

Competition and Efficiency (Study Plan 12.6)

17. In a perfectly competitive market in long-run equilibrium, can consumer surplus be increased? Can producer surplus be increased? Can a consumer become better off by making a substitution away from this market?

18. **Never Pay Retail Again**

Not only has scouring the Web for the best possible price become standard protocol before buying a big-ticket item, but more consumers are employing creative strategies for scoring hot deals. Comparison shopping, haggling and swapping discount codes are all becoming mainstream marks of savvy shoppers. Online shoppers can check a comparison service like Price Grabber before making a purchase.

Source: CNN, May 30, 2008

a. Explain the effect of the Internet on the degree of competition in the market.

b. Explain how the Internet influences market efficiency.

ADDITIONAL PROBLEMS AND APPLICATIONS

MyEconLab ◆ You can work these problems in MyEconLab if assigned by your instructor.

What Is Perfect Competition?

Use the following news clip to work Problems 19 to 21.

Money in the Tank

Two gas stations stand on opposite sides of the road: Rutter's Farm Store and Sheetz gas station. Rutter's doesn't even have to look across the road to know when Sheetz changes its price of a litre of gas. When Sheetz raises the price, Rutter's pumps are busy. When Sheetz lowers prices, there's not a car in sight. Both gas stations survive but each has no control over the price.

Source: *The Mining Journal*, May 24, 2008

19. In what type of market do these gas stations operate? What determines the price of gasoline and the marginal revenue from gasoline?

20. Describe the elasticity of demand that each of these gas stations faces.

21. Why does each of these gas stations have so little control over the price of the gasoline it sells?

The Firm's Output Decision

22. The figure shows the costs of Quick Copy, one of many copy shops near campus.

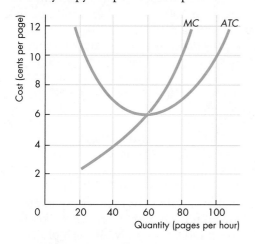

If the market price of copying is 10¢ a page, calculate Quick Copy's

a. Profit-maximizing output.

b. Economic profit.

23. The market for smoothies is perfectly competitive. The following table sets out the market demand schedule.

Price (dollars per smoothie)	Quantity demanded (smoothies per hour)
1.90	1,000
2.00	950
2.20	800
2.91	700
4.25	550
5.25	400
5.50	300

Each of the 100 producers of smoothies has the following costs when it uses its least-cost plant:

Output (smoothies per hour)	Marginal cost (dollars per additional smoothie)	Average variable cost	Average total cost
		(dollars per smoothie)	
3	2.50	4.00	7.33
4	2.20	3.53	6.03
5	1.90	3.24	5.24
6	2.00	3.00	4.67
7	2.91	2.91	4.34
8	4.25	3.00	4.25
9	8.00	3.33	4.44

a. What is the market price of a smoothie?

b. What is the market quantity of smoothies?

c. How many smoothies does each firm sell?

d. What is the economic profit made or economic loss incurred by each firm?

24. **Tembec Takes Axe to Jobs, Costs**

Tembec will permanently close its sawmill in Mattawa, Ontario, which has been idle since July. Earlier, Tembec shut down temporarily facilities in four Canadian provinces in response to depressed market conditions for lumber, pulp, and newsprint. Tembec has also embarked on a cost reduction initiative with suppliers.

Source: *Montreal Gazette*, February 13, 2009

a. Explain how the temporary shutdowns affected Tembec's *TFC*, *TVC*, and *TC*.

b. Under what conditions would the shutdown decision maximize Tembec's economic profit (or minimize its loss)?

c. What will be the effect of the cost reductions on Tembec's economic profit situation?

Output, Price, and Profit in the Short Run

25. **Big Drops in Prices for Crops Make It Tough Down on the Farm**

    Grain prices have fallen roughly 50 percent from earlier this year. With better-than-expected crop yields, world grain production this year will rise 5 percent from 2007 to a record high.

    Source: *USA Today*, October 23, 2008

    Why did grain prices fall in 2008? Draw a graph to show the short-run effect on an individual farmer's economic profit.

Output, Price, and Profit in the Long Run

26. In Problem 23, do firms enter or exit the market in the long run? What is the market price and the equilibrium quantity in the long run?

27. In Problem 24, under what conditions will Tembec exit the sawmilling market?

28. **Exxon Mobil Selling All Its Retail Gas Stations**

    Exxon Mobil is not alone among Big Oil exiting the retail gas business, a market where profits have gotten tougher as crude oil prices have risen. Gas station owners say they're struggling to turn a profit because while wholesale gasoline prices have risen sharply, they've been unable to raise pump prices fast enough to keep pace.

    Source: *Houston Chronicle*, June 12, 2008

    a. Is Exxon Mobil making a shutdown or exit decision in the retail gasoline market?

    b. Under what conditions will this decision maximize Exxon Mobil's economic profit?

    c. How might Exxon Mobil's decision affect the economic profit of other gasoline retailers?

Changing Tastes and Advancing Technology

29. **Another DVD Format, but It's Cheaper**

    New Medium Enterprises claims the quality of its new system, HD VMD, is equal to Blu-ray's but it costs only $199—cheaper than the $300 cost of a Blu-ray player. Chairman of the Blu-ray Disc Association says New Medium will fail because it believes that Blu-ray technology will always be more expensive. But mass production will cut the cost of a Blu-ray player to $90.

    Source: *The New York Times*, March 10, 2008

    a. Explain how technological change in Blu-ray production might support the prediction of lower prices in the long run. Illustrate your explanation with a graph.

    b. Even if Blu-ray prices do drop to $90 in the long run, why might the HD VMD still end up being less expensive at that time?

Competition and Efficiency

30. In a perfectly competitive market, each firm maximizes its profit by choosing only the quantity to produce. Regardless of whether the firm makes an economic profit or incurs an economic loss, the short-run equilibrium is efficient. Is the statement true? Explain why or why not.

Economics in the News

31. After you have studied *Reading Between the Lines* on pp. 292–293, answer the following questions.

    a. What are the features of the global market for corn that make it competitive?

    b. If the increase in production during 2009 and 2010 was due entirely to good weather, what will happen to the price and quantity produced when normal weather returns?

    c. What will happen to an individual farmer's marginal revenue, marginal cost, average total cost, and economic profit if the events in part (b) occur?

    d. If the increase in production during 2009 and 2010 was due mainly to a revolution in farm technology, what will happen to the price and quantity produced when normal weather returns?

32. **Cell phone Sales Hit 1 Billion Mark**

    More than 1.15 billion cell phones were sold worldwide in 2007, a 16 percent increase in a year. Emerging markets, especially China and India, provided much of the growth as many people bought their first phone. Carolina Milanesi, research director for mobile devices at Gartner, reported that in mature markets, such as Japan and Western Europe, consumers' appetite for feature-laden phones was met with new models packed with TV tuners, global positioning satellite functions, touch screens, and cameras.

    Source: *CNET News*, February 27, 2008

    a. Explain the effects of the increase in global demand for cell phones on the market for cell phones and on an individual cell phone producer in the short run.

    b. Draw a graph to illustrate your explanation in part (a).

    c. Explain the long-run effects of the increase in global demand for cell phones on the market for cell phones.

    d. What factors will determine whether the price of a cell phone will rise, fall, or stay the same in the new long-run equilibrium?

Monopoly

**After studying this chapter,
you will be able to**

◆ Explain how monopoly arises and
distinguish between single-price and
price-discriminating monopolies

◆ Explain how a single-price monopoly
determines its output and price

◆ Compare the performance and efficiency
of single-price monopoly and competition

◆ Explain how price discrimination
increases profit

◆ Explain the effects of monopoly
regulation

Google, Microsoft, and eBay are dominant players in the markets they
serve. Because most Web searchers use Google, most advertisers use it
too; because most PCs use Windows, most applications are made for this
operating system; because most online auction buyers use eBay, most
online sellers do too.

These firms are obviously not like firms in perfect competition. How
does their behaviour compare with perfectly competitive firms? Do they
charge prices that are too high and that damage the social interest? What
benefits do they bring?

In this chapter, we study markets in which the firm can influence the
price. We also examine whether monopoly is as efficient as competition.
In *Reading Between the Lines* at the end of the chapter, we'll look at a
claim that Google abuses its market power.

Monopoly and How It Arises

A **monopoly** is a market with a single firm that produces a good or service for which no close substitute exists and that is protected by a barrier that prevents other firms from selling that good or service.

How Monopoly Arises

Monopoly arises for two key reasons:

- No close substitute
- Barrier to entry

No Close Substitute If a good has a close substitute, even though only one firm produces it, that firm effectively faces competition from the producers of the substitute. A monopoly sells a good or service that has no good substitute. Tap water and bottled water are close substitutes for drinking, but tap water has no effective substitute for showering or washing a car and a local public utility that supplies tap water is a monopoly.

Barrier to Entry A constraint that protects a firm from potential competitors is called a **barrier to entry**. The three types of barrier to entry are

- Natural
- Ownership
- Legal

Natural Barrier to Entry A natural barrier to entry creates a **natural monopoly**: a market in which economies of scale enable one firm to supply the entire market at the lowest possible cost. The firms that deliver gas, water, and electricity to our homes are examples of natural monopoly.

In Fig. 13.1 the market demand curve for electric power is *D*, and the long-run average cost curve is *LRAC*. Economies of scale prevail over the entire length of the *LRAC* curve.

One firm can produce 4 million kilowatt-hours at 5¢ a kilowatt-hour. At this price, the quantity demanded is 4 million kilowatt-hours. So if the price was 5¢, one firm could supply the entire market.

If two firms shared the market equally, it would cost each of them 10¢ a kilowatt-hour to produce a total of 4 million kilowatt-hours.

In conditions like those shown in Fig. 13.1, one firm can supply the entire market at a lower cost

FIGURE 13.1   Natural Monopoly

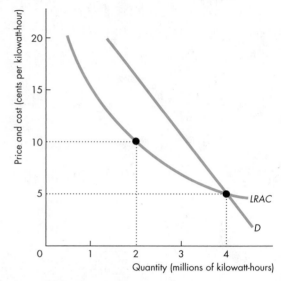

The market demand curve for electric power is *D*, and the long-run average cost curve is *LRAC*. Economies of scale exist over the entire *LRAC* curve. One firm can distribute 4 million kilowatt-hours at a cost of 5¢ a kilowatt-hour. This same total output costs 10¢ a kilowatt-hour with two firms. One firm can meet the market demand at a lower cost than two or more firms can. The market is a natural monopoly.

MyEconLab   animation

than two or more firms can. The market is a natural monopoly.

Ownership Barrier to Entry An ownership barrier to entry occurs if one firm owns a significant portion of a key resource. An example of this type of monopoly occurred during the last century when De Beers controlled up to 90 percent of the world's supply of diamonds. (Today, its share is only 65 percent.)

Legal Barrier to Entry A legal barrier to entry creates a **legal monopoly**: a market in which competition and entry are restricted by the granting of a public franchise, government licence, patent, or copyright.

A *public franchise* is an exclusive right granted to a firm to supply a good or service. An example is Canada Post, which has the exclusive right to deliver residential mail. A *government licence* controls entry into particular occupations, professions, and industries. Examples of this type of barrier to entry occur in medicine, law, dentistry, schoolteaching, architecture, and many other professional services. Licensing does not always create a monopoly, but it does restrict competition.

A *patent* is an exclusive right granted to the inventor of a product or service. A *copyright* is an exclusive right granted to the author or composer of a literary, musical, dramatic, or artistic work. Patents and copyrights are valid for a limited time period that varies from country to country. In Canada, a patent is valid for 20 years. Patents encourage the *invention* of new products and production methods. They also stimulate *innovation*—the use of new inventions—by encouraging inventors to publicize their discoveries and offer them for use under licence. Patents have stimulated innovations in areas as diverse as soybean seeds, pharmaceuticals, memory chips, and video games.

Economics in Action
Information-Age Monopolies

Information-age technologies have created four big natural monopolies. These firms have large plant costs but almost zero marginal cost, so they experience economies of scale.

Microsoft has captured 90 percent of the personal computer operating system market with Windows and 73 percent of the Web browser market with Internet Explorer. eBay has captured 85 percent of the consumer-to-consumer Internet auction market and Google has 78 percent of the search engine market.

New technologies also destroy monopoly. FedEx, Purolator, the fax machine, and e-mail have weakened the monopoly of Canada Post; and the satellite dish has weakened the monopoly of cable television companies.

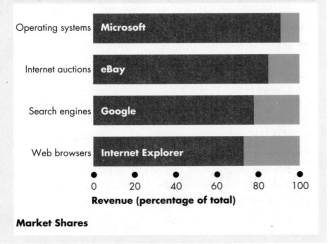

Market Shares

Monopoly Price-Setting Strategies

A major difference between monopoly and competition is that a monopoly sets its own price. In doing so, the monopoly faces a market constraint: To sell a larger quantity, the monopoly must set a lower price. There are two monopoly situations that create two pricing strategies:

- Single price
- Price discrimination

Single Price A **single-price monopoly** is a firm that must sell each unit of its output for the same price to all its customers. De Beers sells diamonds (of a given size and quality) for the same price to all its customers. If it tried to sell at a low price to some customers and at a higher price to others, only the low-price customers would buy from De Beers. Others would buy from De Beers' low-price customers. De Beers is a *single-price* monopoly.

Price Discrimination When a firm practises **price discrimination**, it sells different units of a good or service for different prices. Many firms price discriminate. Microsoft sells its Windows and Office software at different prices to different buyers. Computer manufacturers who install the software on new machines, students and teachers, governments, and businesses all pay different prices. Pizza producers offer a second pizza for a lower price than the first one. These are examples of *price discrimination*.

When a firm price discriminates, it looks as though it is doing its customers a favour. In fact, the firm is charging the highest possible price for each unit sold and making the largest possible profit.

◢ REVIEW QUIZ

1 How does monopoly arise?
2 How does a natural monopoly differ from a legal monopoly?
3 Distinguish between a price-discriminating monopoly and a single-price monopoly.

You can work these questions in Study Plan 13.1 and get instant feedback.

───────────────────────── MyEconLab ◆

We start with a single-price monopoly and see how it makes its decisions about the quantity to produce and the price to charge to maximize its profit.

A Single-Price Monopoly's Output and Price Decision

To understand how a single-price monopoly makes its output and price decision, we must first study the link between price and marginal revenue.

Price and Marginal Revenue

In a monopoly there is only one firm, so the demand curve facing the firm is the market demand curve. Let's look at Bobbie's Barbershop, the sole supplier of haircuts in Trout River, Newfoundland. The table in Fig. 13.2 shows the market demand schedule. At a price of $20, Bobbie sells no haircuts. The lower the price, the more haircuts per hour she can sell. For example, at $12, consumers demand 4 haircuts per hour (row E).

Total revenue (TR) is the price (P) multiplied by the quantity sold (Q). For example, in row D, Bobbie sells 3 haircuts at $14 each, so total revenue is $42. *Marginal revenue* ($MR$) is the change in total revenue (ΔTR) resulting from a one-unit increase in the quantity sold. For example, if the price falls from $16 (row C) to $14 (row D), the quantity sold increases from 2 to 3 haircuts. Total revenue increases from $32 to $42, so the change in total revenue is $10. Because the quantity sold increases by 1 haircut, marginal revenue equals the change in total revenue and is $10. Marginal revenue is placed between the two rows to emphasize that marginal revenue relates to the *change* in the quantity sold.

Figure 13.2 shows the market demand curve and marginal revenue curve (MR) and also illustrates the calculation we've just made. Notice that at each level of output, marginal revenue is less than price—the marginal revenue curve lies below the demand curve. Why is marginal revenue *less* than price? It is because when the price is lowered to sell one more unit, two opposing forces affect total revenue. The lower price results in a revenue loss, and the increased quantity sold results in a revenue gain. For example, at a price of $16, Bobbie sells 2 haircuts (point C). If she lowers the price to $14, she sells 3 haircuts and has a revenue gain of $14 on the third haircut. But she now receives only $14 on the first two haircuts—$2 less than before. As a result, she loses $4 of revenue on the first 2 haircuts. To calculate marginal revenue, she must deduct this amount from the revenue gain of $14. So her marginal revenue is $10, which is less than the price.

FIGURE 13.2   Demand and Marginal Revenue

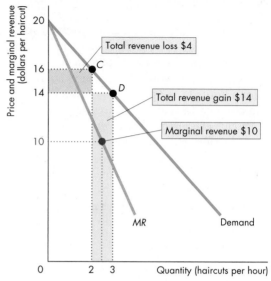

	Price (P) (dollars per haircut)	Quantity demanded (Q) (haircuts per hour)	Total revenue (TR = P × Q) (dollars)	Marginal revenue (MR = ΔTR/ΔQ) (dollars per haircut)
A	20	0	0	
				18
B	18	1	18	
				14
C	**16**	**2**	**32**	
				10
D	**14**	**3**	**42**	
				6
E	12	4	48	
				2
F	10	5	50	

The table shows the demand schedule. Total revenue (TR) is price multiplied by quantity sold. For example, in row C, the price is $16 a haircut, Bobbie sells 2 haircuts, and total revenue is $32. Marginal revenue (MR) is the change in total revenue that results from a one-unit increase in the quantity sold. For example, when the price falls from $16 to $14 a haircut, the quantity sold increases from 2 to 3, an increase of 1 haircut, and total revenue increases by $10. Marginal revenue is $10. The demand curve and the marginal revenue curve, MR, are based on the numbers in the table and illustrate the calculation of marginal revenue when the price falls from $16 to $14 a haircut.

MyEconLab   animation ◆

Marginal Revenue and Elasticity

A single-price monopoly's marginal revenue is related to the *elasticity of demand* for its good. The demand for a good can be *elastic* (the elasticity is greater than 1), *inelastic* (the elasticity is less than 1), or *unit elastic* (the elasticity is equal to 1). Demand is *elastic* if a 1 percent fall in the price brings a greater than 1 percent increase in the quantity demanded. Demand is *inelastic* if a 1 percent fall in the price brings a less than 1 percent increase in the quantity demanded. Demand is *unit elastic* if a 1 percent fall in the price brings a 1 percent increase in the quantity demanded. (See Chapter 4, pp. 84–86.)

If demand is elastic, a fall in the price brings an increase in total revenue—the revenue gain from the increase in quantity sold outweighs the revenue loss from the lower price—and marginal revenue is *positive*. If demand is inelastic, a fall in the price brings a decrease in total revenue—the revenue gain from the increase in quantity sold is outweighed by the revenue loss from the lower price—and marginal revenue is *negative*. If demand is unit elastic, total revenue does not change—the revenue gain from the increase in the quantity sold offsets the revenue loss from the lower price—and marginal revenue is *zero*. (See Chapter 4, p. 88.)

Figure 13.3 illustrates the relationship between marginal revenue, total revenue, and elasticity. As the price gradually falls from $20 to $10 a haircut, the quantity demanded increases from 0 to 5 haircuts an hour. Over this output range, marginal revenue is positive in part (a), total revenue increases in part (b), and the demand for haircuts is elastic. As the price falls from $10 to $0 a haircut, the quantity of haircuts demanded increases from 5 to 10 an hour. Over this output range, marginal revenue is negative in part (a), total revenue decreases in part (b), and the demand for haircuts is inelastic. When the price is $10 a haircut, marginal revenue is zero in part (a), total revenue is at a maximum in part (b), and the demand for haircuts is unit elastic.

In Monopoly, Demand Is Always Elastic The relationship between marginal revenue and elasticity of demand that you've just discovered implies that a profit-maximizing monopoly never produces an output in the inelastic range of the market demand curve. If it did so, it could charge a higher price, produce a smaller quantity, and increase its profit. Let's now look at a monopoly's price and output decision.

FIGURE 13.3   Marginal Revenue and Elasticity

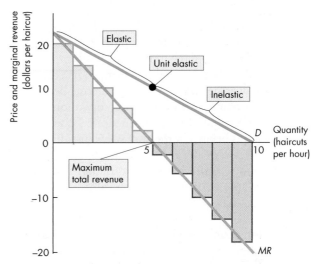

(a) Demand and marginal revenue curves

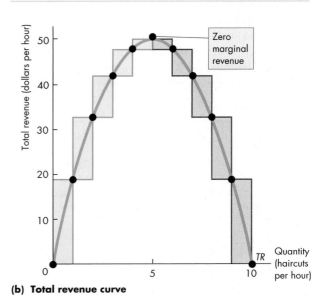

(b) Total revenue curve

In part (a), the demand curve is *D* and the marginal revenue curve is *MR*. In part (b), the total revenue curve is *TR*. Over the range 0 to 5 haircuts an hour, a price cut increases total revenue, so marginal revenue is positive—as shown by the blue bars. Demand is elastic. Over the range 5 to 10 haircuts an hour, a price cut decreases total revenue, so marginal revenue is negative—as shown by the red bars. Demand is inelastic. At 5 haircuts an hour, total revenue is maximized and marginal revenue is zero. Demand is unit elastic.

MyEconLab   animation ◆

Price and Output Decision

A monopoly sets its price and output at the levels that maximize economic profit. To determine this price and output level, we need to study the behaviour of both cost and revenue as output varies. A monopoly faces the same types of technology and cost constraints as a competitive firm, so its costs (total cost, average cost, and marginal cost) behave just like those of a firm in perfect competition. And a monopoly's revenues (total revenue, price, and marginal revenue) behave in the way we've just described.

Table 13.1 provides information about Bobbie's costs, revenues, and economic profit, and Fig. 13.4 shows the same information graphically.

Maximizing Economic Profit   You can see in Table 13.1 and Fig. 13.4(a) that total cost (*TC*) and total revenue (*TR*) both rise as output increases, but *TC* rises at an increasing rate and *TR* rises at a decreasing rate. Economic profit, which equals *TR* minus *TC*, increases at small output levels, reaches a maximum, and then decreases. The maximum profit ($12) occurs when Bobbie sells 3 haircuts for $14 each. If she sells 2 haircuts for $16 each or 4 haircuts for $12 each, her economic profit will be only $8.

Marginal Revenue Equals Marginal Cost   You can see Bobbie's marginal revenue (*MR*) and marginal cost (*MC*) in Table 13.1 and Fig. 13.4(b).

When Bobbie increases output from 2 to 3 haircuts, *MR* is $10 and *MC* is $6. *MR* exceeds *MC* by $4 and Bobbie's profit increases by that amount. If Bobbie increases output yet further, from 3 to 4 haircuts, *MR* is $6 and *MC* is $10. In this case, *MC* exceeds *MR* by $4, so profit decreases by that amount. When *MR* exceeds *MC*, profit increases if output increases. When *MC* exceeds *MR*, profit increases if output *decreases*. When *MC* equals *MR*, profit is maximized.

Figure 13.4(b) shows the maximum profit as price (on the demand curve *D*) minus average total cost (on the *ATC* curve) multiplied by the quantity produced—the blue rectangle.

Maximum Price the Market Will Bear   Unlike a firm in perfect competition, a monopoly influences the price of what it sells. But a monopoly doesn't set the price at the maximum *possible* price. At the maximum possible price, the firm would be able to sell only one unit of output, which in general is less than the profit-maximizing quantity. Rather, a monopoly produces the profit-maximizing quantity and sells that quantity for the highest price it can get.

TABLE 13.1   A Monopoly's Output and Price Decision

Price (P) (dollars per haircut)	Quantity demanded (Q) (haircuts per hour)	Total revenue (TR = P × Q) (dollars)	Marginal revenue (MR = ΔTR/ΔQ) (dollars per haircut)	Total cost (TC) (dollars)	Marginal cost (MC = ΔTC/ΔQ) (dollars per haircut)	Profit (TR − TC) (dollars)
20	0	0		20		−20
			 18		 1	
18	1	18		21		−3
			 14		 3	
16	2	32		24		+8
			 10		 6	
14	3	42		30		+12
			 6		10	
12	4	48		40		+8
			 2		15	
10	5	50		55		−5

This table gives the information needed to find the profit-maximizing output and price. Total revenue (*TR*) equals price multiplied by the quantity sold. Profit equals total revenue minus total cost (*TC*). Profit is maximized when 3 haircuts are sold at a price of $14 each. Total revenue is $42, total cost is $30, and economic profit is $12 ($42 − $30).

FIGURE 13.4   A Monopoly's Output and Price

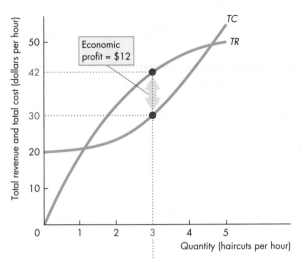

(a) Total revenue and total cost curves

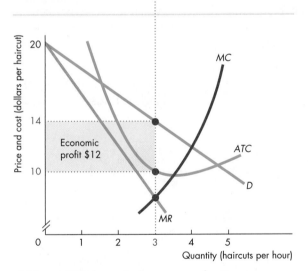

(b) Demand and marginal revenue and cost curves

In part (a), economic profit is the vertical distance equal to total revenue (TR) minus total cost (TC) and it is maximized at 3 haircuts an hour.

In part (b), economic profit is maximized when marginal cost (MC) equals marginal revenue (MR). The profit-maximizing output is 3 haircuts an hour. The price is determined by the demand curve (D) and is $14 a haircut. The average total cost of a haircut is $10, so economic profit, the blue rectangle, is $12—the profit per haircut ($4) multiplied by the quantity (3 haircuts).

MyEconLab animation

All firms maximize profit by producing the output at which marginal revenue equals marginal cost. For a competitive firm, price equals marginal revenue, so price also equals marginal cost. For a monopoly, price exceeds marginal revenue, so price also exceeds marginal cost.

A monopoly charges a price that exceeds marginal cost, but does the monopoly always make an economic profit? In Fig. 13.4(b), Bobbie produces 3 haircuts an hour. Her average total cost is $10 (on the ATC curve) and her price is $14 (on the D curve), so her profit per haircut is $4 ($14 minus $10). Bobbie's economic profit is shown by the area of the blue rectangle, which equals the profit per haircut ($4) multiplied by the number of haircuts (3), for a total of $12.

If firms in a perfectly competitive market make a positive economic profit, new firms enter. That does *not* happen in monopoly. Barriers to entry prevent new firms from entering the market, so a monopoly can make a positive economic profit and might continue to do so indefinitely. Sometimes that economic profit is large, as it is in the international diamond business.

Bobbie makes a positive economic profit. But suppose that Bobbie's landlord increases the rent on her salon. If Bobbie pays an additional $12 an hour for rent, her fixed cost increases by $12 an hour. Her marginal cost and marginal revenue don't change, so her profit-maximizing output remains at 3 haircuts an hour. Her profit decreases by $12 an hour to zero. If Bobbie's salon rent increases by more than $12 an hour, she incurs an economic loss. If this situation were permanent, Bobbie would go out of business.

REVIEW QUIZ

1 What is the relationship between marginal cost and marginal revenue when a single-price monopoly maximizes profit?

2 How does a single-price monopoly determine the price it will charge its customers?

3 What is the relationship between price, marginal revenue, and marginal cost when a single-price monopoly is maximizing profit?

4 Why can a monopoly make a positive economic profit even in the long run?

You can work these questions in Study Plan 13.2 and get instant feedback.

MyEconLab

Single-Price Monopoly and Competition Compared

Imagine a market that is made up of many small firms operating in perfect competition. Then imagine that a single firm buys out all these small firms and creates a monopoly.

What will happen in this market? Will the price rise or fall? Will the quantity produced increase or decrease? Will economic profit increase or decrease? Will either the original competitive situation or the new monopoly situation be efficient?

These are the questions we're now going to answer. First, we look at the effects of monopoly on the price and quantity produced. Then we turn to the questions about efficiency.

Comparing Price and Output

Figure 13.5 shows the market we'll study. The market demand curve is D. The demand curve is the same regardless of how the industry is organized. But the supply side and the equilibrium are different in monopoly and competition. First, let's look at the case of perfect competition.

Perfect Competition   Initially, with many small perfectly competitive firms in the market, the market supply curve is S. This supply curve is obtained by summing the supply curves of all the individual firms in the market.

In perfect competition, equilibrium occurs where the supply curve and the demand curve intersect. The price is P_C, and the quantity produced by the industry is Q_C. Each firm takes the price P_C and maximizes its profit by producing the output at which its own marginal cost equals the price. Because each firm is a small part of the total industry, there is no incentive for any firm to try to manipulate the price by varying its output.

Monopoly   Now suppose that this industry is taken over by a single firm. Consumers do not change, so the market demand curve remains the same as in the case of perfect competition. But now the monopoly recognizes this demand curve as a constraint on the price at which it can sell its output. The monopoly's marginal revenue curve is MR.

The monopoly maximizes profit by producing the quantity at which marginal revenue equals marginal cost. To find the monopoly's marginal cost curve,

first recall that in perfect competition, the market supply curve is the sum of the supply curves of the firms in the industry. Also recall that each firm's supply curve is its marginal cost curve (see Chapter 12, p. 279). So when the market is taken over by a single firm, the competitive market's supply curve becomes the monopoly's marginal cost curve. To remind you of this fact, the supply curve is also labelled MC.

The output at which marginal revenue equals marginal cost is Q_M. This output is smaller than the competitive output Q_C. And the monopoly charges the price P_M, which is higher than P_C. We have established that

> Compared to a perfectly competitive market, a single-price monopoly produces a smaller output and charges a higher price.

We've seen how the output and price of a monopoly compare with those in a competitive market. Let's now compare the efficiency of the two types of market.

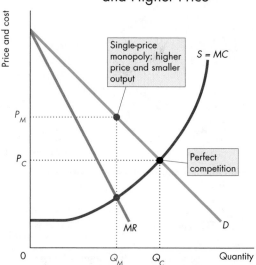

FIGURE   13.5   Monopoly's Smaller Output and Higher Price

A competitive market produces the quantity Q_C at price P_C. A single-price monopoly produces the quantity Q_M at which marginal revenue equals marginal cost and sells that quantity for the price P_M. Compared to perfect competition, a single-price monopoly produces a smaller output and charges a higher price.

MyEconLab   animation   ◆

Efficiency Comparison

Perfect competition (with no externalities) is efficient. Figure 13.6(a) illustrates the efficiency of perfect competition and serves as a benchmark against which to measure the inefficiency of monopoly. Along the demand curve and marginal social benefit curve ($D = MSB$), consumers are efficient. Along the supply curve and marginal social cost curve ($S = MSC$), producers are efficient. In competitive equilibrium, the price is P_C, the quantity is Q_C, and marginal social benefit equals marginal social cost.

Consumer surplus is the area of the green triangle under the demand curve and above the price (see Chapter 5, p. 109). *Producer surplus* is the blue area above the supply curve and below the price (see Chapter 5, p. 111). Total surplus (consumer surplus and producer surplus) is maximized.

Also, in long-run competitive equilibrium, entry and exit ensure that each firm produces its output at the minimum possible long-run average cost.

To summarize: At the competitive equilibrium, marginal social benefit equals marginal social cost; total surplus is maximized; firms produce at the lowest possible long-run average cost; and resource use is efficient.

Figure 13.6(b) illustrates the inefficiency of monopoly and the sources of that inefficiency. A monopoly produces Q_M and sells its output for P_M. The smaller output and higher price drive a wedge between marginal social benefit and marginal social cost and create a *deadweight loss*. The grey triangle shows the deadweight loss and its area is a measure of the inefficiency of monopoly.

Consumer surplus shrinks for two reasons. First, consumers lose by having to pay more for the good. This loss to consumers is a gain for monopoly and increases the producer surplus. Second, consumers lose by getting less of the good, and this loss is part of the deadweight loss.

Although the monopoly gains from a higher price, it loses some producer surplus because it produces a smaller output. That loss is another part of the deadweight loss.

A monopoly produces a smaller output than perfect competition and faces no competition, so it does not produce at the lowest possible long-run average cost. As a result, monopoly damages the social interest in three ways: A monopoly produces less, increases the cost of production, and raises the price by more than the increased cost of production.

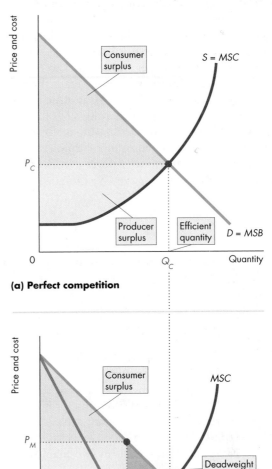

FIGURE 13.6 Inefficiency of Monopoly

(a) Perfect competition

(b) Monopoly

In perfect competition in part (a), output is Q_C and the price is P_C. Marginal social benefit (MSB) equals marginal social cost (MSC); total surplus, the sum of consumer surplus (the green triangle) and producer surplus (the blue area), is maximized; and in the long run, firms produce at the lowest possible average cost. Monopoly in part (b) produces Q_M and raises the price to P_M. Consumer surplus shrinks, the monopoly gains, and a deadweight loss (the grey triangle) arises.

MyEconLab   animation

Redistribution of Surpluses

You've seen that monopoly is inefficient because marginal social benefit exceeds marginal social cost and there is deadweight loss—a social loss. But monopoly also brings a *redistribution* of surpluses.

Some of the lost consumer surplus goes to the monopoly. In Fig. 13.6, the monopoly takes the difference between the higher price, P_M, and the competitive price, P_C, on the quantity sold, Q_M. So the monopoly takes that part of the consumer surplus. This portion of the loss of consumer surplus is not a loss to society. It is redistribution from consumers to the monopoly producer.

Rent Seeking

You've seen that monopoly creates a deadweight loss and is inefficient. But the social cost of monopoly can exceed the deadweight loss because of an activity called rent seeking. Any surplus—consumer surplus, producer surplus, or economic profit—is called **economic rent**. The pursuit of wealth by capturing economic rent is called **rent seeking**.

You've seen that a monopoly makes its economic profit by diverting part of consumer surplus to itself—by converting consumer surplus into economic profit. So the pursuit of economic profit by a monopoly is rent seeking: the attempt to capture consumer surplus.

Rent seekers pursue their goals in two main ways. They might

- Buy a monopoly
- Create a monopoly

Buy a Monopoly To rent seek by buying a monopoly, a person searches for a monopoly that is for sale at a lower price than the monopoly's economic profit. Trading of taxicab licences is an example of this type of rent seeking. In some cities, taxicabs are regulated. The city restricts both the fares and the number of taxis that can operate so that operating a taxi results in economic profit. A person who wants to operate a taxi must buy a licence from someone who already has one. People rationally devote time and effort to seeking out profitable monopoly businesses to buy. In the process, they use up scarce resources that could otherwise have been used to produce goods and services. The value of this lost production is part of the social cost of monopoly.

The amount paid for a monopoly is not a social cost because the payment is just a transfer of an existing producer surplus from the buyer to the seller.

Create a Monopoly Rent seeking by creating a monopoly is mainly a political activity. It takes the form of lobbying and trying to influence the political process. Such influence might be sought by making campaign contributions in exchange for legislative support or by indirectly seeking to influence political outcomes through publicity in the media or more direct contacts with politicians and bureaucrats. An example of a monopoly created in this way is the cable television monopoly created and regulated by the Canadian Radio-Television and Telecommunications Commission (CRTC). Another is a regulation that restricts "split-run" magazines. These regulations restrict output and increase price.

This type of rent seeking is a costly activity that uses up scarce resources. Taken together, firms spend billions of dollars lobbying MPs, MPPs, and bureaucrats in the pursuit of licences and laws that create barriers to entry and establish a monopoly.

Rent-Seeking Equilibrium

Barriers to entry create monopoly. But there is no barrier to entry into rent seeking. Rent seeking is like perfect competition. If an economic profit is available, a new rent seeker will try to get some of it. And competition among rent seekers pushes up the price that must be paid for a monopoly, to the point at which the rent seeker makes zero economic profit by operating the monopoly. For example, competition for the right to operate a taxi leads to a price of $300,000 in Toronto and $200,000 in Montreal for a taxi licence, which is sufficiently high to eliminate the economic profit made by a taxi operator.

Figure 13.7 shows a rent-seeking equilibrium. The cost of rent seeking is a fixed cost that must be added to a monopoly's other costs. Rent seeking and rent-seeking costs increase to the point at which no economic profit is made. The average total cost curve, which includes the fixed cost of rent seeking, shifts upward until it just touches the demand curve. Economic profit is zero. It has been lost in rent seeking.

Consumer surplus is unaffected, but the deadweight loss from monopoly is larger. The deadweight loss now includes the original deadweight loss triangle plus the lost producer surplus, shown by the enlarged grey area in Fig. 13.7.

FIGURE 13.7 Rent-Seeking Equilibrium

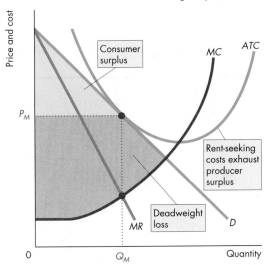

With competitive rent seeking, a monopoly uses all its economic profit to maintain its monopoly. The firm's rent-seeking costs are fixed costs. They add to total fixed cost and to average total cost. The *ATC* curve shifts upward until, at the profit-maximizing price, the firm breaks even.

 MyEconLab   animation ◆

REVIEW QUIZ

1 Why does a single-price monopoly produce a smaller output and charge more than the price that would prevail if the market were perfectly competitive?

2 How does a monopoly transfer consumer surplus to itself?

3 Why is a single-price monopoly inefficient?

4 What is rent seeking and how does it influence the inefficiency of monopoly?

You can work these questions in Study Plan 13.3 and get instant feedback.

━━━━━ MyEconLab ◆

So far, we've considered only a single-price monopoly. But many monopolies do not operate with a single price. Instead, they price discriminate. Let's now see how a price-discriminating monopoly works.

Price Discrimination

You encounter *price discrimination*—selling a good or service at a number of different prices—when you travel, go to the movies, get your hair cut, buy pizza, or visit an art museum or theme park. Many of the firms that price discriminate are not monopolies, but monopolies price discriminate when they can do so.

To be able to price discriminate, a firm must be able to identify and separate different buyer types and sell a product that cannot be resold.

Not all price *differences* are price *discrimination*. Some goods that are similar have different prices because they have different costs of production. For example, the price per 100 grams of cereal is lower if you buy your cereal in a big box than if you buy individual serving size boxes. This price difference reflects a cost difference and is not price discrimination.

At first sight, price discrimination appears to be inconsistent with profit maximization. Why would a movie theatre allow children to see movies at a discount? Why would a hairdresser charge students and senior citizens less? Aren't these firms losing profit by being nice to their customers?

Capturing Consumer Surplus

Price discrimination captures consumer surplus and converts it into economic profit. It does so by getting buyers to pay a price as close as possible to the maximum willingness to pay.

Firms price discriminate in two broad ways. They discriminate

- Among groups of buyers
- Among units of a good

Discriminating Among Groups of Buyers People differ in the value they place on a good—their marginal benefit and willingness to pay. Some of these differences are correlated with features such as age, employment status, and other easily distinguished characteristics. When such a correlation is present, firms can profit by price discriminating among the different groups of buyers.

For example, a face-to-face sales meeting with a customer might bring a large and profitable order. So for salespeople and other business travellers, the marginal benefit from a trip is large and the price that such a traveller is willing to pay for a trip is high. In contrast, for a vacation traveller, any of several different trips and even no vacation trip are options. So for vacation travellers, the marginal benefit of a trip is small and the price that such a traveller is willing to pay for a trip is low. Because business travellers are willing to pay more than vacation travellers are, it is possible for an airline to profit by price discriminating between these two groups.

Discriminating Among Units of a Good   Everyone experiences diminishing marginal benefit and has a downward-sloping demand curve. For this reason, if all the units of the good are sold for a single price, buyers end up with a consumer surplus equal to the value they get from each unit of the good minus the price paid for it.

A firm that price discriminates by charging a buyer one price for a single item and a lower price for a second or third item can capture some of the consumer surplus. Buy one pizza and get a second one free (or for a low price) is an example of this type of price discrimination.

(Note that some discounts for bulk arise from lower costs of production for greater bulk. In these cases, such discounts are not price discrimination.)

Let's see how price discriminating increases economic profit.

Profiting by Price Discriminating

Global Airlines has a monopoly on an exotic route. Figure 13.8 shows the market demand curve (*D*) for travel on this route. It also shows Global Airlines' marginal revenue curve (*MR*), marginal cost curve (*MC*), and average total cost curve (*ATC*).

As a single-price monopoly, Global maximizes profit by producing the quantity at which *MR* equals *MC*, which is 8,000 trips a year, and charging $1,200 per trip. At this quantity, average total cost is $600 per trip, economic profit is $600 a trip, and Global's economic profit is $4.8 million a year, shown by the blue rectangle. Global's customers enjoy a consumer surplus, shown by the green triangle.

Global is struck by the fact that many of its customers are business travellers, and it suspects they are willing to pay more than $1,200 a trip. Global does some market research, which reveals that some business travellers are willing to pay as much as $1,800 a trip. Also, these customers frequently change their travel plans at the last minute. Another group of

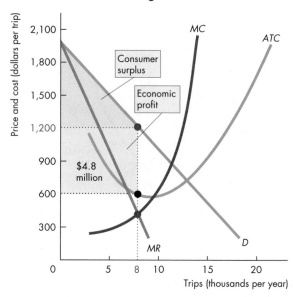

FIGURE 13.8   A Single Price of Air Travel

Global Airlines has a monopoly on an air route. The market demand curve is *D*. Global Airlines' marginal revenue curve is *MR*, its marginal cost curve is *MC*, and its average total cost curve is *ATC*. As a single-price monopoly, Global maximizes profit by selling 8,000 trips a year at $1,200 a trip. Its profit is $4.8 million a year—the blue rectangle. Global's customers enjoy a consumer surplus—the green triangle.

MyEconLab   animation

business travellers is willing to pay $1,600. These customers know a week ahead when they will travel and they never want to stay over a weekend. Yet another group would pay up to $1,400. These travellers know two weeks ahead when they will travel and also don't want to stay away over a weekend.

Global announces a new fare schedule: no restrictions, $1,800; 7-day advance purchase, nonrefundable, $1,600; 14-day advance purchase, nonrefundable, $1,400; 14-day advance purchase, must stay over a weekend, $1,200.

Figure 13.9 shows the outcome with this new fare structure and also shows why Global is pleased with its new fares. It sells 2,000 seats at each of its four prices. Global's economic profit increases by the dark blue steps. Its economic profit is now its original $4.8 million a year plus an additional $2.4 million from its new higher fares. Consumer surplus shrinks to the sum of the smaller green areas.

FIGURE 13.9   Price Discrimination

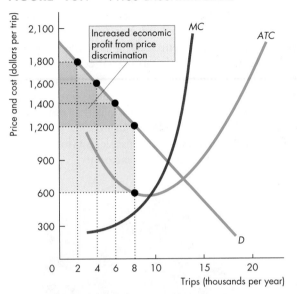

Global revises its fare structure: no restrictions at $1,800, 7-day advance purchase at $1,600, 14-day advance purchase at $1,400, and must stay over a weekend at $1,200. Global sells 2,000 trips at each of its four new fares. Its economic profit increases by $2.4 million a year to $7.2 million a year, which is shown by the original blue rectangle plus the dark blue steps. Global's customers' consumer surplus shrinks.

———————— MyEconLab animation ◆

Perfect Price Discrimination

Perfect price discrimination occurs if a firm is able to sell each unit of output for the highest price anyone is willing to pay for it. In such a case, the entire consumer surplus is eliminated and captured by the producer. To practise perfect price discrimination, a firm must be creative and come up with a host of prices and special conditions, each one of which appeals to a tiny segment of the market.

With perfect price discrimination, something special happens to marginal revenue—the market demand curve becomes the marginal revenue curve. The reason is that when the price is cut to sell a larger quantity, the firm sells only the marginal unit at the lower price. All the other units continue to be sold for the highest price that each buyer is willing to pay. So for the perfect price discriminator, marginal revenue *equals* price and the demand curve becomes the marginal revenue curve.

With marginal revenue equal to price, Global can obtain even greater profit by increasing output up to the point at which price (and marginal revenue) is equal to marginal cost.

So Global seeks new travellers who will not pay as much as $1,200 a trip but who will pay more than marginal cost. Global offers a variety of vacation specials at different low fares that appeal only to new travellers. Existing customers continue to pay the higher fares. With all these fares and specials, Global increases sales, extracts the entire consumer surplus, and maximizes economic profit.

Figure 13.10 shows the outcome with perfect price discrimination. The fares paid by the original travellers extract the entire consumer surplus from this group. The new fares between $900 and $1,200 attract 3,000 additional travellers and also take their entire consumer surplus. Global now makes an economic profit of more than $9 million.

FIGURE 13.10   Perfect Price Discrimination

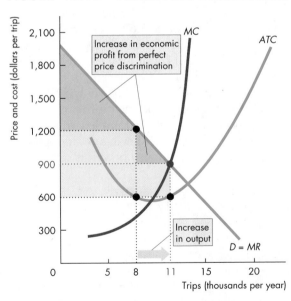

Dozens of fares discriminate among many different types of business traveller, and many new low fares with restrictions appeal to vacation travellers. With perfect price discrimination, the market demand curve becomes Global's marginal revenue curve. Economic profit is maximized when the lowest price equals marginal cost. Global sells 11,000 trips and makes an economic profit of more than $9 million a year.

———————— MyEconLab animation ◆

Efficiency and Rent Seeking with Price Discrimination

With perfect price discrimination, output increases to the point at which price equals marginal cost—where the marginal cost curve intersects the market demand curve (see Fig. 13.10). This output is identical to that of perfect competition. Perfect price discrimination pushes consumer surplus to zero but increases the monopoly's producer surplus to equal the total surplus in perfect competition. With perfect price discrimination, deadweight loss is zero, so perfect price discrimination achieves efficiency.

> The more perfectly the monopoly can price discriminate, the closer its output is to the competitive output and the more efficient is the outcome.

But there are two differences between perfect competition and perfect price discrimination. First,

Economics in Action

Attempting Perfect Price Discrimination

If you want to spend a day at Disney World in Orlando, it will cost you $75.62. You can spend a second (consecutive) day for an extra $72.42. A third day will cost you $68.17. But for a fourth day, you'll pay only $9.59 and for a fifth day, $3.20. For more days all the way up to 10, you'll pay only $2.12 a day.

Disney Corporation hopes that it has read your willingness to pay correctly and not left you with too much consumer surplus. Disney figures though that after three days, your marginal benefit is crashing.

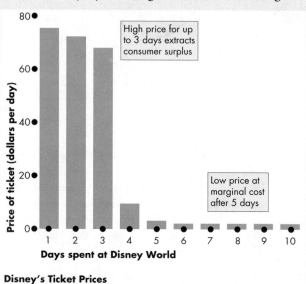

Disney's Ticket Prices

the distribution of the total surplus is different. It is shared by consumers and producers in perfect competition, while the producer gets it all with perfect price discrimination. Second, because the producer grabs all the surplus, rent seeking becomes profitable.

People use resources in pursuit of economic rent, and the bigger the rents, the more resources get used in pursuing them. With free entry into rent seeking, the long-run equilibrium outcome is that rent seekers use up the entire producer surplus.

Real-world airlines are as creative as Global Airlines, as you can see in the cartoon!

Would it bother you to hear how little I paid for this flight?

From William Hamilton, "Voodoo Economics," © 1992 by The Chronicle Publishing Company, p.3. Reprinted with permission of Chronicle Books.

◆ REVIEW QUIZ

1 What is price discrimination and how is it used to increase a monopoly's profit?
2 Explain how consumer surplus changes when a monopoly price discriminates.
3 Explain how consumer surplus, economic profit, and output change when a monopoly perfectly price discriminates.
4 What are some of the ways that real-world airlines price discriminate?

You can work these questions in Study Plan 13.4 and get instant feedback.

———————————————— MyEconLab ◆

You've seen that monopoly is profitable for the monopoly but costly for consumers. It results in inefficiency. Because of these features of monopoly, it is subject to policy debate and regulation. We'll now study the key monopoly policy issues.

◆ Monopoly Regulation

Natural monopoly presents a dilemma. With economies of scale, it produces at the lowest possible cost. But with market power, it has an incentive to raise the price above the competitive price and produce too little—to operate in the self-interest of the monopolist and not in the social interest.

Regulation—rules administered by a government agency to influence prices, quantities, entry, and other aspects of economic activity in a firm or industry—is a possible solution to this dilemma.

To implement regulation, the government establishes agencies to oversee and enforce the rules. For example, the Canadian Transportation Agency regulates transportation under federal jurisdiction, including rail, air, marine transportation and some interprovincial commercial motor transport. The National Energy Board regulates international and interprovincial aspects of the oil, gas, and electric utility industries.

Deregulation is the process of removing regulation of prices, quantities, entry, and other aspects of economic activity in a firm or industry. During the past 30 years, deregulation has occurred in many Canadian markets, including domestic rail and air transportation, telephone service, natural gas, and grain transportation. In 2012, wheat handling and marketing will be deregulated.

Regulation is a possible solution to the dilemma presented by natural monopoly but not a guaranteed solution. There are two theories about how regulation actually works: *the social interest theory* and the *capture theory.*

The **social interest theory** is that the political and regulatory process relentlessly seeks out inefficiency and introduces regulation that eliminates deadweight loss and allocates resources efficiently.

The **capture theory** is that regulation serves the self-interest of the producer, who captures the regulator and maximizes economic profit. Regulation that benefits the producer but creates a deadweight loss gets adopted because the producer's gain is large and visible while each individual consumer's loss is small and invisible. No individual consumer has an incentive to oppose the regulation but the producer has a big incentive to lobby for it.

We're going to examine efficient regulation that serves the social interest and see why it is not a simple matter to design and implement such regulation.

Efficient Regulation of a Natural Monopoly

A cable TV company is a *natural monopoly*—it can supply the entire market at a lower price than two or more competing firms can. Shaw Communications provides cable TV to households in Western Canada. The firm has invested heavily in satellite receiving dishes, cables, and control equipment and so has large fixed costs. These fixed costs are part of the firm's average total cost. Its average total cost decreases as the number of households served increases because the fixed cost is spread over a larger number of households.

Unregulated, Shaw Communications produces the quantity that maximizes profit. Like all single-price monopolies, the profit-maximizing quantity is less than the efficient quantity, and underproduction results in a deadweight loss.

How can Shaw Communications be regulated to produce the efficient quantity of cable TV service? The answer is by being regulated to set its price equal to marginal cost, known as the **marginal cost pricing** rule. The quantity demanded at a price equal to marginal cost is the efficient quantity—the quantity at which marginal benefit equals marginal cost.

Figure 13.11 illustrates the marginal cost pricing rule. The demand curve for cable TV is *D*. Shaw Communications' marginal cost curve is *MC*. That marginal cost curve is (assumed to be) horizontal at $10 per household per month—that is, the cost of providing each additional household with a month of cable programming is $10. The efficient outcome occurs if the price is regulated at $10 per household per month with 10 million households served.

But there is a problem: At the efficient output, average total cost exceeds marginal cost, so a firm that uses marginal cost pricing incurs an economic loss. A cable TV company that is required to use a marginal cost pricing rule will not stay in business for long. How can the firm cover its costs and, at the same time, obey a marginal cost pricing rule?

There are two possible ways of enabling the firm to cover its costs: price discrimination and a two-part price (called a *two-part tariff*).

For example, local telephone companies offer plans at a fixed monthly price that give access to the telephone network and unlimited free calls. The price of a call (zero) equals the marginal cost of a call. Similarly, a cable TV operator can charge a one-time connection fee that covers its fixed cost and then charge a monthly fee equal to marginal cost.

FIGURE 13.11   Regulating a Natural Monopoly

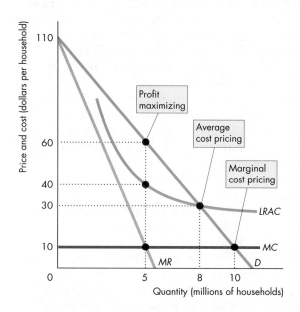

A natural monopoly cable TV supplier faces the demand curve *D*. The firm's marginal cost is constant at $10 per household per month, as shown by the curve labelled *MC*. The long-run average cost curve is *LRAC*.

Unregulated, as a profit-maximizer, the firm serves 5 million households at a price of $60 a month. An efficient marginal cost pricing rule sets the price at $10 a month. The monopoly serves 10 million households and incurs an economic loss. A second-best average cost pricing rule sets the price at $30 a month. The monopoly serves 8 million households and earns zero economic profit.

MyEconLab   animation ◆

Second-Best Regulation of a Natural Monopoly

A natural monopoly cannot always be regulated to achieve an efficient outcome. Two possible ways of enabling a regulated monopoly to avoid an economic loss are

- Average cost pricing
- Government subsidy

Average Cost Pricing   The **average cost pricing rule** sets price equal to average total cost. With this rule the firm produces the quantity at which the average total cost curve cuts the demand curve. This rule

results in the firm making zero economic profit—breaking even. But because for a natural monopoly average total cost exceeds marginal cost, the quantity produced is less than the efficient quantity and a deadweight loss arises.

Figure 13.11 illustrates the average cost pricing rule. The price is $30 a month and the monopoly serves 8 million households.

Government Subsidy   A government subsidy is a direct payment to the firm equal to its economic loss. To pay a subsidy, the government must raise the revenue by taxing some other activity. You saw in Chapter 6 that taxes themselves generate deadweight loss.

And the Second-Best Is ...   Which is the better option, average cost pricing or marginal cost pricing with a government subsidy? The answer depends on the relative magnitudes of the two deadweight losses. Average cost pricing generates a deadweight loss in the market served by the natural monopoly. A subsidy generates deadweight losses in the markets for the items that are taxed to pay for the subsidy. The smaller deadweight loss is the second-best solution to regulating a natural monopoly. Making this calculation in practice is too difficult and average cost pricing is generally preferred to a subsidy.

Implementing average cost pricing presents the regulator with a challenge because it is not possible to be sure what a firm's costs are. So regulators use one of two practical rules:

- Rate of return regulation
- Price cap regulation

Rate of Return Regulation   Under **rate of return regulation**, a firm must justify its price by showing that its return on capital doesn't exceed a specified target rate. This type of regulation can end up serving the self-interest of the firm rather than the social interest. The firm's managers have an incentive to inflate costs by spending on items such as private jets, free hockey tickets (disguised as marketing expenses), and lavish entertainment. Managers also have an incentive to use more capital than the efficient amount. The rate of return on capital is regulated but not the total return on capital, and the greater the amount of capital, the greater is the total return.

Price Cap Regulation   For the reason that we've just examined, rate of return regulation is increasingly being replaced by price cap regulation. A **price cap regulation** is a price ceiling—a rule that specifies the highest price the firm is permitted to set. This type of regulation gives a firm an incentive to operate efficiently and keep costs under control. Price cap regulation has become common for the electricity and telecommunications industries and is replacing rate of return regulation.

To see how a price cap works, let's suppose that the cable TV operator is subject to this type of regulation. Figure 13.12 shows that without regulation, the firm maximizes profit by serving 5 million households and charging a price of $60 a month. If a price cap is set at $30 a month, the firm is permitted to sell

FIGURE 13.12   Price Cap Regulation

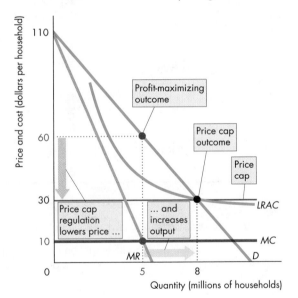

A natural monopoly cable TV supplier faces the demand curve *D*. The firm's marginal cost is constant at $10 per household per month, as shown by the curve labelled *MC*. The long-run average cost curve is *LRAC*.

Unregulated, the firm serves 5 million households at a price of $60 a month. A price cap sets the maximum price at $30 a month. The firm has an incentive to minimize cost and serve the quantity of households that demand service at the price cap. The price cap regulation lowers the price and increases the quantity.

———————————— MyEconLab   animation ◆

any quantity it chooses at that price or at a lower price. At 5 million households, the firm now incurs an economic loss. It can decrease the loss by increasing output to 8 million households. To increase output above 8 million households, the firm would have to lower the price and again it would incur a loss. So the profit-maximizing quantity is 8 million households—the same as with average cost pricing.

Notice that a price cap lowers the price and increases output. This outcome is in sharp contrast to the effect of a price ceiling in a competitive market that you studied in Chapter 6 (pp. 128–130). The reason is that in a monopoly, the unregulated equilibrium output is less than the competitive equilibrium output, and the price cap regulation replicates the conditions of a competitive market.

In Fig. 13.12, the price cap delivers average cost pricing. In practice, the regulator might set the cap too high. For this reason, price cap regulation is often combined with *earnings sharing regulation*—a regulation that requires firms to make refunds to customers when profits rise above a target level.

REVIEW QUIZ

1   What is the pricing rule that achieves an efficient outcome for a regulated monopoly? What is the problem with this rule?
2   What is the average cost pricing rule? Why is it not an efficient way of regulating monopoly?
3   What is a price cap? Why might it be a more effective way of regulating monopoly than rate of return regulation?
4   Compare the consumer surplus, producer surplus, and deadweight loss that arise from average cost pricing with those that arise from profit-maximization pricing and marginal cost pricing.

You can work these questions in Study Plan 13.5 and get instant feedback.
———————————————————— MyEconLab ◆

◆   You've now completed your study of monopoly. *Reading Between the Lines* on pp. 316–317 looks at Google's dominant position in the market for Internet search advertising.

In the next chapter, we study markets that lie between the extremes of perfect competition and monopoly and that blend elements of the two.

Is Google Misusing Monopoly Power?

U.S. to Launch Google Antitrust Probe: Report

Associated Press
June 23, 2011

A published report says U.S. regulators are preparing to issue subpoenas to Google Inc. and other companies as authorities gather information for a broad antitrust probe into the Internet search leader's business practices. ...

The [Federal Trade Commission] FTC is looking into whether Google abuses its dominance of Internet search to extend its influence into other lucrative online markets, such as mapping, comparison shopping and travel. Rivals complain that Google, which handles two out of every three Internet searches in the U.S., manipulates its results to steer users to its own sites and services and bury links to competitors. ...

The European Commission and the Texas attorney general have already opened investigations into whether Google uses its enormous clout as a major gateway to the Internet to stifle competition online. ...

In a statement, FairSearch.org, a coalition of Internet travel companies including Expedia, Hotwire and Kayak, said, "Google's practices are deserving of full-scale investigations by U.S. antitrust authorities."

"Google engages in anti-competitive behaviour across many vertical categories of search that harms consumers by restricting the ability of other companies to compete to put the best products and services in front of Internet users, who should be allowed to pick winners and losers online, not Google," the group said.

...

ESSENCE OF THE STORY

- The FTC will conduct a broad investigation into whether Google has abused its dominance of Internet search.

- Rivals claim that, in two out of every three searches, Google steers users to its own sites and services and buries links to competitors.

- The claim is that Google has grown a large market share in online maps, video, and comparison shopping because its search engine highlights links to these products in search results.

- Google's behaviour harms consumers by restricting the ability of its competitors to put the best products in front of Internet users.

ECONOMIC ANALYSIS

- Google began selling advertisements associated with search keywords in 2000.

- Google sells keywords based on a combination of willingness-to-pay and the number of clicks an advertisement receives, with bids starting at 5¢ per click.

- Google has steadily improved its search engine and refined and simplified its interface with both searchers and advertisers to make searches more powerful and advertising more effective.

- Figure 1 shows Google's extraordinary success in terms of its revenue, cost, and profit.

- Google could have provided a basic search engine with none of the features of today's Google.

- If Google had followed this strategy, people seeking information would have used other search engines and advertisers would have been willing to pay low prices for Google ads.

- Google would have faced the market described in Fig. 2 and earned a small economic profit.

- Instead, Google improved its search and the effectiveness of advertising. The demand for Google ads increased.

- By selling keywords to the highest bidder, Google is able to achieve perfect price discrimination.

- Figure 3 shows the consequences of Google's successful strategy. With perfect price discrimination, Google's producer surplus is maximized. Google produces the efficient quantity of search and advertising by accepting ads as long as price is not less than marginal cost.

- The FTC investigation should find that Google does not appear to be acting against the social interest.

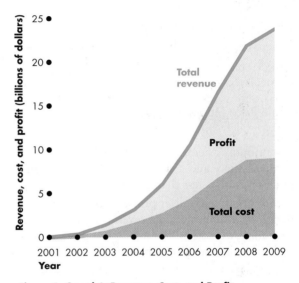

Figure 1 Google's Revenue, Cost, and Profit

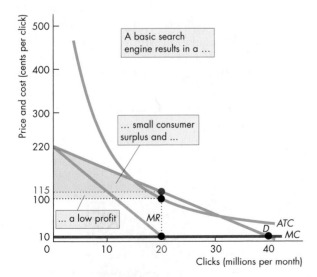

Figure 2 Basic Search Engine

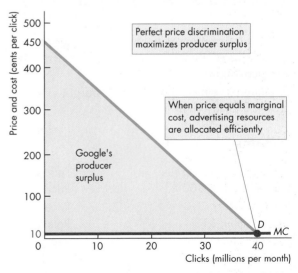

Figure 3 Google with AdWords and Other Features

SUMMARY

Key Points

Monopoly and How It Arises (pp. 300–301)

- A monopoly is a market with a single supplier of a good or service that has no close substitutes and in which barriers to entry prevent competition.
- Barriers to entry may be legal (public franchise, licence, patent, copyright), firm owns control of a resource, or natural (created by economies of scale).
- A monopoly might be able to price discriminate when there is no resale possibility.
- Where resale is possible, a firm charges one price.

Working Problems 1 to 4 will give you a better understanding of monopoly and how it arises.

A Single-Price Monopoly's Output and Price Decision (pp. 302–305)

- A monopoly's demand curve is the market demand curve and a single-price monopoly's marginal revenue is less than price.
- A monopoly maximizes profit by producing the output at which marginal revenue equals marginal cost and by charging the maximum price that consumers are willing to pay for that output.

Working Problems 5 to 9 will give you a better understanding of a single-price monopoly's output and price.

Single-Price Monopoly and Competition Compared (pp. 306–309)

- A single-price monopoly charges a higher price and produces a smaller quantity than a perfectly competitive market.
- A single-price monopoly restricts output and creates a deadweight loss.

- The total loss that arises from monopoly equals the deadweight loss plus the cost of the resources devoted to rent seeking.

Working Problems 10 to 12 will give you a better understanding of the comparison of single-price monopoly and perfect competition.

Price Discrimination (pp. 309–312)

- Price discrimination converts consumer surplus into economic profit.
- Perfect price discrimination extracts the entire consumer surplus; each unit is sold for the maximum price that each consumer is willing to pay; the quantity produced is the efficient quantity.
- Rent seeking with perfect price discrimination might eliminate the entire consumer surplus and producer surplus.

Working Problems 13 to 16 will give you a better understanding of price discrimination.

Monopoly Regulation (pp. 313–315)

- Monopoly regulation might serve the social interest or the interest of the monopoly (the monopoly captures the regulator).
- Price equal to marginal cost achieves efficiency but results in economic loss.
- Price equal to average total cost enables the firm to cover its cost but is inefficient.
- Rate of return regulation creates incentives for inefficient production and inflated cost.
- Price cap regulation with earnings sharing regulation can achieve a more efficient outcome than rate of return regulation.

Working Problems 17 to 19 will give you a better understanding of monopoly regulation.

Key Terms

Average cost pricing rule, 314
Barrier to entry, 300
Capture theory, 313
Deregulation, 313
Economic rent, 308
Legal monopoly, 300
Marginal cost pricing rule, 313
Monopoly, 300
Natural monopoly, 300

Perfect price discrimination, 311
Price cap regulation, 315
Price discrimination, 301
Rate of return regulation, 314
Regulation, 313
Rent seeking, 308
Single-price monopoly, 301
Social interest theory, 313

SCAN THIS

STUDY PLAN PROBLEMS AND APPLICATIONS

MyEconLab ◆ You can work Problems 1 to 19 in Chapter 13 Study Plan and get instant feedback.

Monopoly and How It Arises (Study Plan 13.1)

Use the following information to work Problems 1 to 3.

Canada Post has a monopoly on residential mail delivery. Pfizer Inc. makes LIPITOR, a prescription drug that lowers cholesterol. Rogers Communications is the sole provider of cable television service in some parts of Ontario.

1. a. What are the substitutes, if any, for the goods and services described above?
   b. What are the barriers to entry, if any, that protect these three firms from competition?

2. Which of these three firms, if any, is a natural monopoly? Explain your answer and draw a graph to illustrate it.

3. a. Which of these three firms, if any, is a legal monopoly? Explain your answer.
   b. Which of these three firms are most likely to be able to profit from price discrimination and which are most likely to sell their good or service for a single price?

4. **Air Canada Deal Raises Monopoly Concerns**

   The federal government reacted to a proposed joint venture between Air Canada and United Continental, calling it an "effective merger" on all of their Canadian and U.S. operations. The government said that the venture would create a monopoly on 10 major routes between Canada and the United States and substantially reduce competition on nine others. And consumers will face higher prices and even less choice on key, high demand air routes. The airline said the venture will provide "more convenient service to customers."

   Source: CBC News, June 27, 2011

   a. If this venture gets government approval, what type of monopoly will be created on the 10 major, high demand routes?
   b. With higher prices and restricted choice, what would be the barrier to entry?
   c. How might the venture provide more convenient service?

A Single-Price Monopoly's Output and Price Decision (Study Plan 13.2)

Use the following table to work Problems 5 to 8.

Minnie's Mineral Springs, a single-price monopoly, faces the market demand schedule:

Price (dollars per bottle)	Quantity demanded (bottles per hour)
10	0
8	1
6	2
4	3
2	4
0	5

5. a. Calculate Minnie's total revenue schedule.
   b. Calculate its marginal revenue schedule.

6. a. Draw a graph of the market demand curve and Minnie's marginal revenue curve.
   b. Why is Minnie's marginal revenue less than the price?

7. a. At what price is Minnie's total revenue maximized?
   b. Over what range of prices is the demand for water from Minnie's Mineral Springs elastic?

8. Why will Minnie not produce a quantity at which the market demand for water is inelastic?

9. Minnie's Mineral Springs faces the market demand schedule in Problem 5 and has the following total cost schedule:

Quantity produced (bottles per hour)	Total cost (dollars)
0	1
1	3
2	7
3	13
4	21
5	31

   a. Calculate Minnie's profit-maximizing output and price.
   b. Calculate the economic profit.

Single-Price Monopoly and Competition Compared
(Study Plan 13.3)

Use the following news clip to work Problems 10 to 12.

Zoloft Faces Patent Expiration

Pfizer's antidepressant Zoloft, with $3.3 billion in 2005 sales, loses patent protection on June 30. When a brand name drug loses its patent, both the price of the drug and the dollar value of its sales each tend to drop 80 percent over the next year, as competition opens to a host of generic drugmakers. The real winners are the patients and the insurers, who pay much lower prices. The Food and Drug Administration insists that generics work identically to brand-names.

Source: CNN, June 15, 2006

10. a. Assume that Pfizer has a monopoly in the antidepressant market and that Pfizer cannot price discriminate. Use a graph to illustrate the market price and quantity of Zoloft sold.
    b. On your graph, identify consumer surplus, producer surplus, and deadweight loss.

11. How might you justify protecting Pfizer from competition with a legal barrier to entry?

12. a. Explain how the market for an antidepressant drug changes when a patent expires.
    b. Draw a graph to illustrate how the expiration of the Zoloft patent will change the price and quantity in the market for antidepressants.
    c. Explain how consumer surplus, producer surplus, and deadweight loss change with the expiration of the Zoloft patent.

Price Discrimination (Study Plan 13.4)

Use the following news clip to work Problems 13 and 14.

The Saturday-Night Stay Requirement Is on Its Final Approach

The Saturday-night stay—the requirement that airlines instituted to ensure that business travellers pay an outrageous airfare if he or she wants to go home for the weekend—has gone the way of the dodo bird. Experts agree that low-fare carriers, such as Southwest, are the primary reason major airlines are adopting more consumer-friendly fare structures, which include the elimination of the Saturday-night stay, the introduction of one-way and walk-up fares, and the general restructuring of fares.

Source: Los Angeles Times, August 15, 2004

13. Explain why the opportunity for price discrimination exists for air travel. How does an airline profit from price discrimination?

14. Describe the change in price discrimination in the market for air travel when discount airlines entered the market and explain the effect of discount airlines on the price and the quantity of air travel.

Use the following information to work Problems 15 and 16.

La Bella Pizza can produce a pizza for a marginal cost of $2. Its standard price is $15 a pizza. It offers a second pizza for $5. It also distributes coupons that give a $5 rebate on a standard-priced pizza.

15. How can La Bella Pizza make a larger economic profit with this range of prices than it could if it sold every pizza for $15? Use a graph to illustrate your answer.

16. How might La Bella Pizza make even more economic profit? Would La Bella Pizza then be more efficient than it would be if it charged $15 for each pizza?

Monopoly Regulation (Study Plan 13.5)

Use the following information to work Problems 17 to 19.

The figure shows a situation similar to that of TransCanada, a firm that operates a natural gas distribution system in North America. The firm is a natural monopoly that cannot price discriminate.

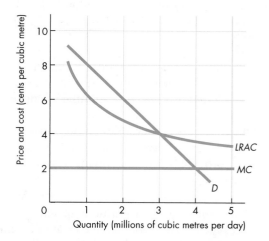

On the graph mark the quantity the firm will produce, the price it will charge, the total surplus, and the deadweight loss if the firm is

17. An unregulated profit-maximizing firm

18. Regulated to make zero economic profit

19. Regulated to be efficient

ADDITIONAL PROBLEMS AND APPLICATIONS

MyEconLab ◆ You can work these problems in MyEconLab if assigned by your instructor.

Monopoly and How It Arises

Use the following list, which gives some information about seven firms, to answer Problems 20 and 21.

- Coca-Cola cuts its price below that of Pepsi-Cola in an attempt to increase its market share.
- A single firm, protected by a barrier to entry, produces a personal service that has no close substitutes.
- A barrier to entry exists, but the good has some close substitutes.
- A firm offers discounts to students and seniors.
- A firm can sell any quantity it chooses at the going price.
- The government issues Nike an exclusive licence to produce golf balls.
- A firm experiences economies of scale even when it produces the quantity that meets the entire market demand.

20. In which of the seven cases might monopoly arise?

21. Which of the seven cases are natural monopolies and which are legal monopolies? Which can price discriminate, which cannot, and why?

A Single-Price Monopoly's Output and Price Decision

Use the following information to work Problems 22 to 26.

Hot Air Balloon Rides is a single-price monopoly. Columns 1 and 2 of the table set out the market demand schedule and columns 2 and 3 set out the total cost schedule:

Price (dollars per ride)	Quantity demanded (rides per month)	Total cost (dollars per month)
220	0	80
200	1	160
180	2	260
160	3	380
140	4	520
120	5	680

22. Construct Hot Air's total revenue and marginal revenue schedules.

23. Draw a graph of the market demand curve and Hot Air's marginal revenue curve.

24. Find Hot Air's profit-maximizing output and price and calculate the firm's economic profit.

25. If the government imposes a tax on Hot Air's profit, how do its output and price change?

26. If instead of taxing Hot Air's profit, the government imposes a sales tax on balloon rides of $30 a ride, what are the new profit-maximizing quantity, price, and economic profit?

27. The figure illustrates the situation facing the publisher of the only newspaper containing local news in an isolated community.

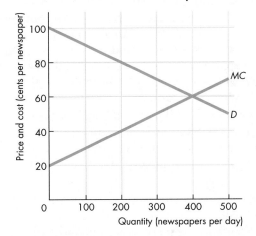

a. On the graph, mark the profit-maximizing quantity and price and the publisher's total revenue per day.

b. At the price charged, is the demand for this newspaper elastic or inelastic? Why?

Single-Price Monopoly and Competition Compared

28. Show on the graph in Problem 27 the consumer surplus from newspapers and the deadweight loss created by the monopoly. Explain why this market might encourage rent seeking.

29. If the newspaper market in Problem 27 were perfectly competitive, what would be the quantity, price, consumer surplus, and producer surplus? Mark each on the graph.

Use the following news clip to work Problems 30 to 32.

Why Your Beer Costs More

Imagine a store where most of the products are kept in the back. You order from the cashier. The products can't be sold below a legislated minimum price. And the overwhelming majority are made by one of three large companies, which also own the store.

In Ontario, that is how $2.5 billion worth of beer is sold each year. The Beer Store in Ontario "is essentially a private monopoly" owned by the province's three largest brewers: Labatt, Molson, and Sleeman.

The brewers, in turn, belong to some of the highest-grossing beer makers in the world—Belgium's Anheuser-Busch InBev, the United States' Molson Coors Brewing Co. and Japan's Sapporo—and they earn about $1 billion a year in profits in Ontario, making the province one of the most lucrative beer markets in the world.

A Beverage Alcohol System Review concluded that Ontario's beer consumers pay higher prices, have less choice, and lack convenience, so it recommended opening beer sales to competition. But government decided against sweeping changes.

A 24-pack of popular brands in Ontario is regularly 25 percent more than in Quebec and New York State, where beer is almost always on sale.

Source: *The Toronto Star*, July 5, 2008

30. Draw a graph to illustrate the market price, quantity of beer sold, and profit that the Beer Store in Ontario makes. On your graph, identify consumer surplus, producer surplus, and deadweight loss.

31. How might the Beer Store's legal monopoly be justified?

32. Explain how the market price, quantity of beer sold, and the Beer Store's profit would change if the Ontario government ended the "essentially a private monopoly." How would consumer surplus, producer surplus, and deadweight loss change?

Price Discrimination

33. **AT&T Moves Away from Unlimited-Data Pricing**

AT&T said it will eliminate its $30 unlimited data plan as the crush of data use from the iPhone has hurt call quality. AT&T is introducing new plans costing $15 a month for 200 megabytes of data traffic or $25 a month for 2 gigabytes. AT&T says those who exceed 2 gigabytes of usage will pay $10 a month for each additional gigabyte. AT&T hopes that these plans will attract more customers.

Source: *The Wall Street Journal*, June 2, 2010

a. Explain why AT&T's new plans might be price discrimination.

b. Draw a graph to illustrate the original plan and the new plans.

Monopoly Regulation

34. **BC Hydro to Cut Proposed Rate Increase Following Government Review**

BC Hydro was asking its regulator, the BC Utilities Commission, to approve rate increases of 9.73-percent per year over three years, or a cumulative 32 percent, and hinted that it would need future increases that would add up to 50 percent over five years.

Premier Christy Clark asked for a review because of concerns about how the rate increase would affect families. The review panel recommended that BC Hydro cut its increases to 8 percent in its first year and 3.9 percent in each of the next two years, which totals almost 17 percent.

Source: *The Vancouver Sun*, August 11, 2011

a. What is the objective of BC Hydro in seeking the price increases reported in the news clip?

b. What is the objective of Premier Clark in asking for a review and expressing concern about the price hike?

c. Draw a graph of the market for hydro in British Columbia to illustrate your answers to the questions in parts (a) and (b).

Economics in the News

35. After you have studied *Reading Between the Lines* on pp. 316–317, answer the following questions.

a. Why do Google's competitors say that Google needs to be investigated? Do you agree? Explain why or why not.

b. Explain why it would be inefficient to regulate Google to make it charge the same price per keyword click to all advertisers.

c. Explain why selling keywords to the highest bidder can lead to an efficient allocation of advertising resources.

36. **Antitrust Inquiry Launched into Intel**

Intel, the world's largest chipmaker, holds 80 percent of the microprocessor market. Advanced Micro Devices complains that Intel stifles competition, but Intel says that the 42.4 percent fall in prices between 2000 and 2007 shows that this industry is fiercely competitive.

Source: *The Washington Post*, June 7, 2008

a. Is Intel a monopoly in the chip market?

b. Evaluate the argument made by Intel that the fall in prices "shows that this industry is fiercely competitive."

Monopolistic Competition

After studying this chapter, you will be able to

◆ Define and identify monopolistic competition

◆ Explain how a firm in monopolistic competition determines its price and output in the short run and the long run

◆ Explain why advertising costs are high and why firms use brand names in monopolistic competition

The online shoe store shoebuy.com lists athletic shoes made by 56 different producers. The store offers 1,401 different types of shoes for women and 1,757 different types for men. The market for athletic shoes is competitive, but it isn't perfectly competitive. Each firm has a monopoly on its own shoe.

Most of the things that you buy are like athletic shoes—they come in many different types. Pizza and cell phones are two more striking examples.

The model of monopolistic competition that is explained in this chapter helps us to understand the competition that we see every day in the markets for athletic shoes, pizza, cell phones, and many other goods and services.

Reading Between the Lines, at the end of this chapter, applies the model to the market for smartphones in which Apple and many others compete.

◆ What Is Monopolistic Competition?

You have studied perfect competition, in which a large number of firms produce at the lowest possible cost, make zero economic profit, and are efficient. You've also studied monopoly, in which a single firm restricts output, produces at a higher cost and price than in perfect competition, and is inefficient.

Most real-world markets are competitive but not perfectly competitive, because firms in these markets have some power to set their prices, as monopolies do. We call this type of market *monopolistic competition*.

Monopolistic competition is a market structure in which

- A large number of firms compete.
- Each firm produces a differentiated product.
- Firms compete on product quality, price, and marketing.
- Firms are free to enter and exit the industry.

Large Number of Firms

In monopolistic competition, as in perfect competition, the industry consists of a large number of firms. The presence of a large number of firms has three implications for the firms in the industry.

Small Market Share   In monopolistic competition, each firm supplies a small part of the total industry output. Consequently, each firm has only limited power to influence the price of its product. Each firm's price can deviate from the average price of other firms by only a relatively small amount.

Ignore Other Firms   A firm in monopolistic competition must be sensitive to the average market price of the product, but the firm does not pay attention to any one individual competitor. Because all the firms are relatively small, no one firm can dictate market conditions, and so no one firm's actions directly affect the actions of the other firms.

Collusion Impossible   Firms in monopolistic competition would like to be able to conspire to fix a higher price—called *collusion*. But because the number of firms in monopolistic competition is large, coordination is difficult and collusion is not possible.

Product Differentiation

A firm practices **product differentiation** if it makes a product that is slightly different from the products of competing firms. A differentiated product is one that is a close substitute but not a perfect substitute for the products of the other firms. Some people are willing to pay more for one variety of the product, so when its price rises, the quantity demanded of that variety decreases, but it does not (necessarily) decrease to zero. For example, Adidas, Asics, Diadora, Etonic, Fila, New Balance, Nike, Puma, and Reebok all make differentiated running shoes. If the price of Adidas running shoes rises and the prices of the other shoes remain constant, Adidas sells fewer shoes and the other producers sell more. But Adidas shoes don't disappear unless the price rises by a large enough amount.

Competing on Quality, Price, and Marketing

Product differentiation enables a firm to compete with other firms in three areas: product quality, price, and marketing.

Quality   The quality of a product is the physical attributes that make it different from the products of other firms. Quality includes design, reliability, the service provided to the buyer, and the buyer's ease of access to the product. Quality lies on a spectrum that runs from high to low. Some firms—such as Dell Computer Corp.—offer high-quality products. They are well designed and reliable, and the customer receives quick and efficient service. Other firms offer a lower-quality product that is poorly designed, that might not work perfectly, and that is not supported by effective customer service.

Price   Because of product differentiation, a firm in monopolistic competition faces a downward-sloping demand curve. So, like a monopoly, the firm can set both its price and its output. But there is a tradeoff between the product's quality and price. A firm that makes a high-quality product can charge a higher price than a firm that makes a low-quality product.

Marketing   Because of product differentiation, a firm in monopolistic competition must market its product. Marketing takes two main forms: advertising and packaging. A firm that produces a high-quality product wants to sell it for a suitably high price. To be able to do so, it must advertise and package its product in a way that convinces buyers that they are getting the higher quality for which they are paying a higher price. For example, pharmaceutical companies advertise and package their brand-name drugs to persuade buyers that these items are superior to the lower-priced generic alternatives. Similarly, a low-quality producer uses advertising and packaging to persuade buyers that although the quality is low, the low price more than compensates for this fact.

Entry and Exit

Monopolistic competition has no barriers to prevent new firms from entering the industry in the long run. Consequently, a firm in monopolistic competition cannot make an economic profit in the long run. When existing firms make an economic profit, new firms enter the industry. This entry lowers prices and eventually eliminates economic profit. When firms incur economic losses, some firms leave the industry in the long run. This exit increases prices and eventually eliminates the economic loss.

In long-run equilibrium, firms neither enter nor leave the industry and the firms in the industry make zero economic profit.

Examples of Monopolistic Competition

Economics in Action below shows 10 industries that are good examples of monopolistic competition. These industries have many firms and the number in each industry is shown in parentheses after industry's name. In the market for upholstered household furniture, the largest 4 firms produce only 30 percent of the industry's total sales and the largest 20 firms produce 69 percent of total sales. The number on the right is the Herfindahl-Hirschman Index. A value below 1,800 is considered to be monopolistic competition.

REVIEW QUIZ

1 What are the distinguishing characteristics of monopolistic competition?
2 How do firms in monopolistic competition compete?
3 Provide some examples of industries near your school that operate in monopolistic competition (excluding those in the figure below).

You can work these questions in Study Plan 14.1 and get instant feedback.

——————— MyEconLab ◆

Economics in Action
Monopolistic Competition Today

These 10 industries operate in monopolistic competition. The number of firms in the industry is shown in parentheses after the name of the industry. The red bars show the percentage of industry sales by the largest 4 firms. The blue bars show the percentage of industry sales by the next 4 largest firms, and the orange bars show the percentage of industry sales by the next 12 largest firms. So the entire length of the combined red, blue, and orange bars shows the percentage of industry sales by the largest 20 firms. The Herfindahl-Hirschman Index is shown on the right.

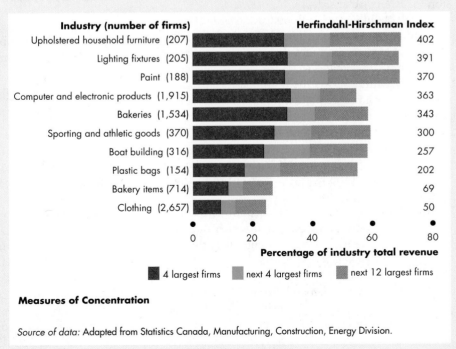

Industry (number of firms)	Herfindahl-Hirschman Index
Upholstered household furniture (207)	402
Lighting fixtures (205)	391
Paint (188)	370
Computer and electronic products (1,915)	363
Bakeries (1,534)	343
Sporting and athletic goods (370)	300
Boat building (316)	257
Plastic bags (154)	202
Bakery items (714)	69
Clothing (2,657)	50

Percentage of industry total revenue

■ 4 largest firms   ■ next 4 largest firms   ■ next 12 largest firms

Measures of Concentration

Source of data: Adapted from Statistics Canada, Manufacturing, Construction, Energy Division.

Price and Output in Monopolistic Competition

Suppose you've been hired by Michael Budman and Don Green, the co-founders of Roots Canada Ltd., to manage the production and marketing of Roots jackets. Think about the decisions that you must make at Roots. First, you must decide on the design and quality of jackets and on your marketing program. Second, you must decide on the quantity of jackets to produce and the price at which to sell them.

We'll suppose that Roots has already made its decisions about design, quality, and marketing and now we'll concentrate on the output and pricing decision. We'll study quality and marketing decisions in the next section.

For a given quality of jackets and marketing activity, Roots faces given costs and market conditions. Given its costs and the demand for its jackets, how does Roots decide the quantity of jackets to produce and the price at which to sell them?

The Firm's Short-Run Output and Price Decision

In the short run, a firm in monopolistic competition makes its output and price decision just like a monopoly firm does. Figure 14.1 illustrates this decision for Roots jackets.

The demand curve for Roots jackets is *D*. This demand curve tells us the quantity of Roots jackets demanded at each price, given the prices of other jackets. It is not the demand curve for jackets in general.

The *MR* curve shows the marginal revenue curve associated with the demand curve for Roots jackets. It is derived just like the marginal revenue curve of a single-price monopoly that you studied in Chapter 13.

The *ATC* curve and the *MC* curve show the average total cost and the marginal cost of producing Roots jackets.

Roots' goal is to maximize its economic profit. To do so, it produces the output at which marginal revenue equals marginal cost. In Fig. 14.1, this output is 125 jackets a day. Roots charges the price that buyers are willing to pay for this quantity, which is determined by the demand curve. This price is $75 per jacket. When Roots produces 125 jackets a day, its average total cost is $25 per jacket and it makes an economic profit of $6,250 a day ($50 per

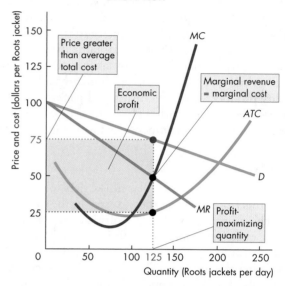

FIGURE 14.1   Economic Profit in the Short Run

Roots maximizes profit by producing the quantity at which marginal revenue equals marginal cost, 125 jackets a day, and charging the price of $75 a jacket. This price exceeds the average total cost of $25 a jacket, so the firm makes an economic profit of $50 a jacket. The blue rectangle illustrates economic profit, which equals $6,250 a day ($50 a jacket multiplied by 125 jackets a day).

——————————— MyEconLab   animation ◆

jacket multiplied by 125 jackets a day). The blue rectangle shows Roots' economic profit.

Profit Maximizing Might Be Loss Minimizing

Figure 14.1 shows that Roots is making a large economic profit. But such an outcome is not inevitable. A firm might face a level of demand for its product that is too low for it to make an economic profit.

Excite@Home was such a firm. Offering high-speed Internet service over the same cable that provides television, Excite@Home hoped to capture a large share of the Internet portal market in competition with AOL, MSN, and a host of other providers.

Figure 14.2 illustrates the situation facing Excite@Home in 2001. The demand curve for its portal service is *D*, the marginal revenue curve is *MR*, the average total cost curve is *ATC*, and the marginal cost curve is *MC*. Excite@Home maximized profit—

FIGURE 14.2 Economic Loss in the Short Run

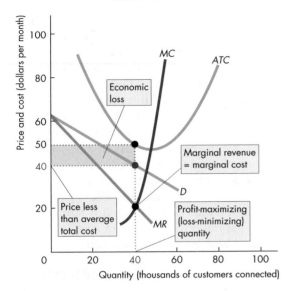

Profit is maximized where marginal revenue equals marginal cost. The loss-minimizing quantity is 40,000 customers. The price of $40 a month is less than the average total cost of $50 a month, so the firm incurs an economic loss of $10 a customer. The red rectangle illustrates economic loss, which equals $400,000 a month ($10 a customer multiplied by 40,000 customers).

—————————————— MyEconLab animation ◆

equivalently, it minimized its loss—by producing the output at which marginal revenue equals marginal cost. In Fig. 14.2, this output is 40,000 customers. Excite@Home charged the price that buyers were willing to pay for this quantity, which was determined by the demand curve and which was $40 a month. With 40,000 customers, Excite@Home's average total cost was $50 per customer, so it incurred an economic loss of $400,000 a month ($10 a customer multiplied by 40,000 customers). The red rectangle shows Excite@Home's economic loss.

So far, the firm in monopolistic competition looks like a single-price monopoly. It produces the quantity at which marginal revenue equals marginal cost and then charges the price that buyers are willing to pay for that quantity, as determined by the demand curve. The key difference between monopoly and monopolistic competition lies in what happens next when firms either make an economic profit or incur an economic loss.

Long Run: Zero Economic Profit

A firm like Excite@Home is not going to incur an economic loss for long. Eventually, it goes out of business. Also, there is no restriction on entry into monopolistic competition, so if firms in an industry are making economic profit, other firms have an incentive to enter that industry.

As Gap and other firms start to make jackets similar to those made by Roots, the demand for Roots jackets decreases. The demand curve for Roots jackets and the marginal revenue curve shift leftward. As these curves shift leftward, the profit-maximizing quantity and price fall.

Figure 14.3 shows the long-run equilibrium. The demand curve for Roots jackets and the marginal revenue curve have shifted leftward. The firm produces 75 jackets a day and sells them for $25 each. At this output level, average total cost is also $25 per jacket.

FIGURE 14.3 Output and Price in the Long Run

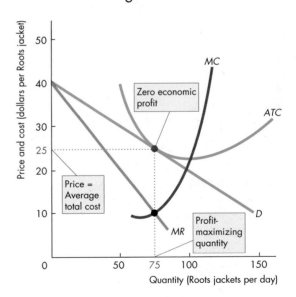

Economic profit encourages entry, which decreases the demand for each firm's product. When the demand curve touches the ATC curve at the quantity at which MR equals MC, the market is in long-run equilibrium. The output that maximizes profit is 75 jackets a day, and the price is $25 per jacket. Average total cost is also $25 per jacket, so economic profit is zero.

—————————————— MyEconLab animation ◆

So Roots is making zero economic profit on its jackets. When all the firms in the industry are making zero economic profit, there is no incentive for new firms to enter.

If demand is so low relative to costs that firms incur economic losses, exit will occur. As firms leave an industry, the demand for the products of the remaining firms increases and their demand curves shift rightward. The exit process ends when all the firms in the industry are making zero economic profit.

Monopolistic Competition and Perfect Competition

Figure 14.4 compares monopolistic competition and perfect competition and highlights two key differences between them:

- Excess capacity
- Markup

Excess Capacity A firm has **excess capacity** if it produces below its **efficient scale**, which is the quantity at which average total cost is a minimum—the quantity at the bottom of the U-shaped *ATC* curve. In Fig. 14.4, the efficient scale is 100 jackets a day. Roots in part (a) produces 75 Roots jackets a day and has *excess capacity* of 25 jackets a day. But if all jackets are alike and are produced by firms in perfect competition, each firm in part (b) produces 100 jackets a day, which is the efficient scale. Average total cost is the lowest possible only in *perfect* competition.

You can see the excess capacity in monopolistic competition all around you. Family restaurants (except for the truly outstanding ones) almost always have some empty tables. You can always get a pizza delivered in less than 30 minutes. It is rare that every pump at a gas station is in use with customers waiting in line. There are always many real estate agents ready to help find or sell a home. These industries are examples of monopolistic competition. The firms

---

FIGURE 14.4   Excess Capacity and Markup

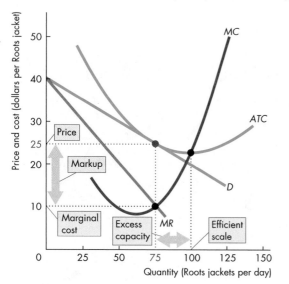

(a) Monopolistic competition

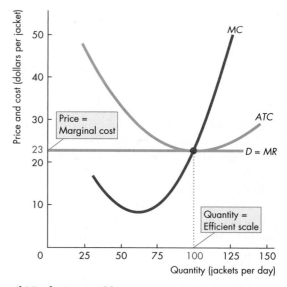

(b) Perfect competition

The efficient scale is 100 jackets a day. In monopolistic competition in the long run, because the firm faces a downward-sloping demand curve for its product, the quantity produced is less than the efficient scale and the firm has excess capacity. Price exceeds marginal cost by the amount of the markup.

In contrast, because in perfect competition the demand for each firm's product is perfectly elastic, the quantity produced in the long run equals the efficient scale and price equals marginal cost. The firm produces at the least possible cost and there is no markup.

MyEconLab   animation   ◆

have excess capacity. They could sell more by cutting their prices, but they would then incur losses.

Markup A firm's **markup** is the amount by which price exceeds marginal cost. Figure 14.4(a) shows Roots' markup. In perfect competition, price always equals marginal cost and there is no markup. Figure 14.4(b) shows this case. In monopolistic competition, buyers pay a higher price than in perfect competition and also pay more than marginal cost.

Is Monopolistic Competition Efficient?

Resources are used efficiently when marginal social benefit equals marginal social cost. Price equals marginal social benefit and the firm's marginal cost equals marginal social cost (assuming there are no external benefits or costs). So if the price of a Roots jacket exceeds the marginal cost of producing it, the quantity of Roots jackets produced is less than the efficient quantity. And you've just seen that in long-run equilibrium in monopolistic competition, price *does* exceed marginal cost. So is the quantity produced in monopolistic competition less than the efficient quantity?

Making the Relevant Comparison Two economists meet in the street, and one asks the other, "How is your husband?" The quick reply is "Compared to what?" This bit of economic wit illustrates a key point: Before we can conclude that something needs fixing, we must check out the available alternatives.

The markup that drives a gap between price and marginal cost in monopolistic competition arises from product differentiation. It is because Roots jackets are not quite the same as jackets from Banana Republic, CK, Diesel, DKNY, Earl Jackets, Gap, Levi's, Ralph Lauren, or any of the other dozens of producers of jackets that the demand for Roots jackets is not perfectly elastic. The only way in which the demand for jackets from Roots might be perfectly elastic is if there is only one kind of jacket and all firms make it. In this situation, Roots jackets are indistinguishable from all other jackets. They don't even have identifying labels.

If there was only one kind of jacket, the total benefit of jackets would almost certainly be less than it is with variety. People value variety—not only because it enables each person to select what he or she likes best but also because it provides an external benefit.

Most of us enjoy seeing variety in the choices of others. Contrast a scene from the China of the 1960s, when everyone wore a Mao tunic, with the China of today, where everyone wears the clothes of their own choosing. Or contrast a scene from the Germany of the 1930s, when almost everyone who could afford a car owned a first-generation Volkswagen Beetle, with the world of today with its enormous variety of styles and types of automobiles.

If people value variety, why don't we see infinite variety? The answer is that variety is costly. Each different variety of any product must be designed, and then customers must be informed about it. These initial costs of design and marketing—called setup costs—mean that some varieties that are too close to others already available are just not worth creating.

The Bottom Line Product variety is both valued and costly. The efficient degree of product variety is the one for which the marginal social benefit of product variety equals its marginal social cost. The loss that arises because the quantity produced is less than the efficient quantity is offset by the gain that arises from having a greater degree of product variety. So compared to the alternative—product uniformity—monopolistic competition might be efficient.

REVIEW QUIZ

1 How does a firm in monopolistic competition decide how much to produce and at what price to offer its product for sale?

2 Why can a firm in monopolistic competition make an economic profit only in the short run?

3 Why do firms in monopolistic competition operate with excess capacity?

4 Why is there a price markup over marginal cost in monopolistic competition?

5 Is monopolistic competition efficient?

You can work these questions in Study Plan 14.2 and get instant feedback.

————————————————— MyEconLab ◆

You've seen how the firm in monopolistic competition determines its output and price in both the short run and the long run when it produces a given product and undertakes a *given* marketing effort. But how does the firm choose its product quality and marketing effort? We'll now study these decisions.

◆ Product Development and Marketing

When Roots made its price and output decision that we've just studied, it had already made its product quality and marketing decisions. We're now going to look at these decisions and see how they influence the firm's output, price, and economic profit.

Innovation and Product Development

The prospect of new firms entering the industry keeps firms in monopolistic competition on their toes! To enjoy economic profits, they must continually seek ways of keeping one step ahead of imitators—other firms that imitate the success of profitable firms.

One major way of trying to maintain economic profit is for a firm to seek out new products that will provide it with a competitive edge, even if only temporarily. A firm that introduces a new and differentiated product faces a demand that is less elastic and is able to increase its price and make an economic profit. Eventually, imitators will make close substitutes for the innovative product and compete away the economic profit arising from an initial advantage. So to restore economic profit, the firm must again innovate.

Profit-Maximizing Product Innovation The decision to innovate and develop a new or improved product is based on the same type of profit-maximizing calculation that you've already studied.

Innovation and product development are costly activities, but they also bring in additional revenues. The firm must balance the cost and revenue at the margin.

The marginal dollar spent on developing a new or improved product is the marginal cost of product development. The marginal dollar that the new or improved product earns for the firm is the marginal revenue of product development. At a low level of product development, the marginal revenue from a better product exceeds the marginal cost. At a high level of product development, the marginal cost of a better product exceeds the marginal revenue.

When the marginal cost and marginal revenue of product development are equal, the firm is undertaking the profit-maximizing amount of product development.

Efficiency and Product Innovation Is the profit-maximizing amount of product innovation also the efficient amount? Efficiency is achieved if the marginal social benefit of a new and improved product equals its marginal social cost.

The marginal social benefit of an innovation is the increase in price that consumers are willing to pay for it. The marginal social cost is the amount that the firm must pay to make the innovation. Profit is maximized when marginal *revenue* equals marginal cost. But in monopolistic competition, marginal revenue is less than price, so product innovation is probably not pushed to its efficient level.

Monopolistic competition brings many product innovations that cost little to implement and are purely cosmetic, such as new and improved packaging or a new scent in laundry powder. And even when there is a genuine improved product, it is never as good as what the consumer is willing to pay for. For example, "The Legend of Zelda: Twilight Princess" is regarded as an almost perfect and very cool game, but users complain that it isn't quite perfect. It is a game whose features generate a marginal revenue equal to the marginal cost of creating them.

Advertising

A firm with a differentiated product needs to ensure that its customers know how its product is different from the competition. A firm also might attempt to create a consumer perception that its product is different from its competitors, even when that difference is small. Firms use advertising and packaging to achieve this goal.

Advertising Expenditures Firms in monopolistic competition incur huge costs to ensure that buyers appreciate and value the differences between their own products and those of their competitors. So a large proportion of the price that we pay for a good covers the cost of selling it, and this proportion is increasing. Advertising in newspapers and magazines and on radio, television, and the Internet is the main selling cost. But it is not the only one. Selling costs include the cost of shopping malls that look like movie sets, glossy catalogues and brochures, and the salaries, airfares, and hotel bills of salespeople.

Advertising expenditures affect the profits of firms in two ways: They increase costs and they change demand. Let's look at these effects.

Economics in Action
The Cost of Selling a Pair of Shoes

When you buy a pair of running shoes that cost you $110, you're paying $14.25 for the materials from which the shoes are made, $4.25 for the services of the Malaysian worker who made the shoes, and $8.25 for the production and transportation services of a manufacturing firm in Asia and a shipping company. These numbers total $26.75. You pay the Canadian government $5.25 in import duty. So we've now accounted for a total of $32. Where did the other $78 go? It is the cost of advertising, retailing, and other sales and distribution services.

The selling costs associated with running shoes are not unusual. Almost everything that you buy includes a selling cost component that exceeds one half of the total cost. Your clothing, food, electronic items, DVDs, magazines, and even your textbooks cost more to sell than they cost to manufacture.

Advertising costs are only a part, and often a small part, of total selling costs. For example, Nike spends about $6.25 on advertising per pair of shoes sold.

For the North American economy as a whole, there are some 20,000 advertising agencies, which employ more than 200,000 people and have sales of $45 billion. These numbers are only part of the total cost of advertising because firms have their own internal advertising departments, the costs of which we can only guess.

But the biggest part of selling costs is not the cost of advertising. It is the cost of retailing services. The retailer's selling costs (and economic profit) are often as much as 50 percent of the price you pay.

| Raw materials $14.25 | Production costs $11.75 | Import duty $5.25 | Selling costs $78 |

Selling Costs and Total Cost Selling costs are fixed costs and they increase the firm's total cost. So like the fixed cost of producing a good, advertising costs per unit decrease as the quantity produced increases.

Figure 14.5 shows how selling costs change a firm's average total cost. The blue curve shows the average total cost of production. The red curve shows the firm's average total cost of production plus advertising. The height of the red area between the two curves shows the average fixed cost of advertising. The *total* cost of advertising is fixed. But the *average* cost of advertising decreases as output increases.

Figure 14.5 shows that if advertising increases the quantity sold by a large enough amount, it can lower average total cost. For example, if the quantity sold increases from 25 jackets a day with no advertising to 100 jackets a day with advertising, average total cost falls from $60 to $40 a jacket. The reason is that although the *total* fixed cost has increased, the greater fixed cost is spread over a greater output, so average total cost decreases.

FIGURE 14.5   Selling Costs and Total Cost

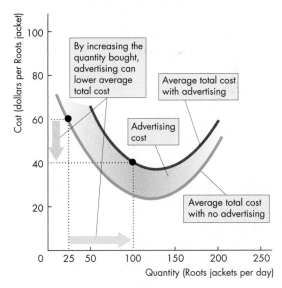

Selling costs such as the cost of advertising are fixed costs. When added to the average total cost of production, selling costs increase average total cost by a greater amount at small outputs than at large outputs. If advertising enables sales to increase from 25 jackets a day to 100 jackets a day, average total cost *falls* from $60 to $40 a jacket.

MyEconLab   animation

Selling Costs and Demand Advertising and other selling efforts change the demand for a firm's product. But how? Does demand increase or does it decrease? The most natural answer is that advertising increases demand. By informing people about the quality of its products or by persuading people to switch from the products of other firms, a firm might expect to increase the demand for its own products.

But all firms in monopolistic competition advertise, and all seek to persuade customers that they have the best deal. If advertising enables a firm to survive, the number of firms in the market might increase. And to the extent that the number of firms does increase, advertising *decreases* the demand faced by any one firm. It also makes the demand for any one firm's product more elastic. So advertising can end up not only lowering average total cost but also lowering the markup and the price.

Figure 14.6 illustrates this possible effect of advertising. In part (a), with no advertising, the demand for Roots jackets is not very elastic. Profit is maxi-

mized at 75 jackets per day, and the markup is large. In part (b), advertising, which is a fixed cost, increases average total cost from ATC_0 to ATC_1 but leaves marginal cost unchanged at MC. Demand becomes much more elastic, the profit-maximizing quantity increases, and the markup shrinks.

Using Advertising to Signal Quality

Some advertising, like the Roger Federer Swiss bank UBS ad in glossy magazines or the huge number of dollars that Coke and Pepsi spend, seems hard to understand. There doesn't seem to be any concrete information about the bank in the smile of a tennis player. And surely, everyone knows about Coke and Pepsi. What is the gain from pouring millions of dollars into advertising these well-known colas?

One answer is that advertising is a signal to the consumer that the product is a high-quality product. A **signal** is an action taken by an informed person (or firm) to send a message to uninformed people. Think about two colas: Coke and Oke. Oke knows

---

FIGURE 14.6   Advertising and the Markup

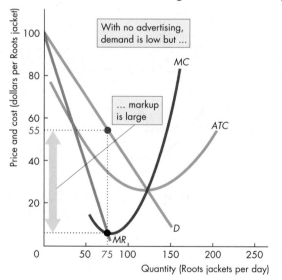

(a) No firms advertise

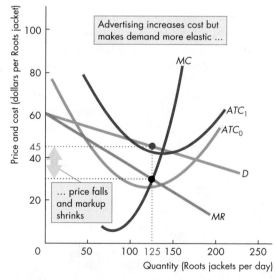

(b) All firms advertise

If no firms advertise, demand for each firm's product is low and not very elastic. The profit-maximizing output is small, the markup is large, and the price is high.

Advertising increases average total cost and shifts the ATC curve upward from ATC_0 to ATC_1. If all firms advertise, the demand for each firm's product becomes more elastic. Output increases, the price falls, and the markup shrinks.

that its cola is not very good and that its taste varies depending on which cheap batch of unsold cola it happens to buy each week. So Oke knows that while it could get a lot of people to try Oke by advertising, they would all quickly discover its poor quality and switch back to the cola they bought before. Coke, in contrast, knows that its product has a high-quality consistent taste and that once consumers have tried it, there is a good chance they'll never drink anything else. On the basis of this reasoning, Oke doesn't advertise but Coke does and it spends a lot of money to make a big splash.

Cola drinkers who see Coke's splashy ads know that the firm would not spend so much money advertising if its product were not truly good. So consumers reason that Coke is indeed a really good product. The flashy expensive ad signals that Coke is really good without saying anything about Coke.

Notice that if advertising is a signal, it doesn't need any specific product information. It just needs to be expensive and hard to miss. That's what a lot of advertising looks like. So the signalling theory of advertising predicts much of the advertising that we see.

Brand Names

Many firms create and spend a lot of money promoting a brand name. Why? What benefit does a brand name bring to justify the sometimes high cost of establishing it?

The basic answer is that a brand name provides information to consumers about the quality of a product, and is an incentive to the producer to achieve a high and consistent quality standard.

To see how a brand name helps the consumer, think about how you use brand names to get information about quality. You're on a road trip, and it is time to find a place to spend the night. You see roadside advertisements for Holiday Inn, Joe's Motel, and Annie's Driver's Stop. You know about Holiday Inn because you've stayed in it before. You've also seen its advertisements and know what to expect. You have no information at all about Joe's and Annie's. They might be better than the lodgings you do know about, but without that knowledge, you're not going to try them. You use the brand name as information and stay at Holiday Inn.

This same story explains why a brand name provides an incentive to achieve high and consistent quality. Because no one would know whether Joe's and Annie's were offering a high standard of service, they

have no incentive to do so. But equally, because everyone expects a given standard of service from Holiday Inn, a failure to meet a customer's expectation would almost surely lose that customer to a competitor. So Holiday Inn has a strong incentive to deliver what it promises in the advertising that creates its brand name.

Efficiency of Advertising and Brand Names

To the extent that advertising and brand names provide consumers with information about the precise nature of product differences and about product quality, they benefit the consumer and enable a better product choice to be made. But the opportunity cost of the additional information must be weighed against the gain to the consumer.

The final verdict on the efficiency of monopolistic competition is ambiguous. In some cases, the gains from extra product variety unquestionably offset the selling costs and the extra cost arising from excess capacity. The tremendous varieties of books and magazines, clothing, food, and drinks are examples of such gains. It is less easy to see the gains from being able to buy a brand-name drug that has a chemical composition identical to that of a generic alternative, but many people do willingly pay more for the brand-name alternative.

 REVIEW QUIZ

1 How, other than by adjusting price, do firms in monopolistic competition compete?
2 Why might product innovation and development be efficient and why might it be inefficient?
3 How do selling costs influence a firm's cost curves and its average total cost?
4 How does advertising influence demand?
5 Are advertising and brand names efficient?

You can work these questions in Study Plan 14.3 and get instant feedback.

——————————————— MyEconLab ◆

◆ Monopolistic competition is one of the most common market structures that you encounter in your daily life. *Reading Between the Lines* on pp. 334–335 applies the model of monopolistic competition to the market for smartphones and shows why you can expect continual innovation and the introduction of new phones from Apple and other producers of smartphones.

Product Differentiation in the Market for Smartphones

Top 10 Apple iPhone 5 Contenders

International Business Times

July 31, 2011

Apple Inc.'s next generation iPhone, dubbed iPhone 5, is facing too much of a competition from Android. It is being speculated that iPhone 5 is scheduled to launch in early September.

The latest rumour comes from the *China Times*, which says that Apple plans to produce 4 million units of the device following a production run of 400,000 test units. That's all to ready the device for a release in the second week of September.

Apple's iPhone 5 is also expected to boast of significant hardware and software upgrades. Upcoming iPhone 5 slated for release in September is expected to have an 8-megapixel camera and the A5 dual-core processor found in the iPad 2 to give stiff competition for other dual-core smartphones found in the market today. And a few analysts predict that the other features of iPhone 5 will most probably remain the same with minor tweaks, ...

[Some of the] ... expected iPhone 5 features are:

—An improved antenna

—Better camera ...

—4G connectivity ...

—Improved speech recognition features

—Wireless charging capability

—Better talk-time and standby time. ...

But does the iPhone 5 have enough firepower to challenge the top 10 new 'super' smartphones that run on Google Inc.'s Android?

The top iPhone 5 contenders are: Samsung Galaxy S2, Google Nexus 4G, Motorola Droid 3, Motorola Photon 4G, Motorola Droid Bionic, HTC myTouch 4G Slide, HTC Blast, HTC Sensation 4G, HTC Evo 3D, and HTC Thunderbolt.

ESSENCE OF THE STORY

- Apple's next generation iPhone, the iPhone 5, is expected in September 2011.

- It is rumoured that Apple will produce 4 million iPhone 5s for the launch.

- The iPhone 5 is expected to have big hardware and software upgrades.

- Among the expected upgrades are an improved camera, a faster processor, wireless charging, and better talk-time and standby time.

- Apple faces competition from smartphones that use Google's Android operating system.

- This competition is coming from Google, HTC, Motorola, Samsung, and others.

- Apple sold its first iPhone in 2007 and has brought successive versions to market, the latest of which was the iPhone 5 in 2011.

- By creating a substantially differentiated product, Apple was able to generate a great deal of interest in smartphones throughout the world.

- As Apple planned the launch of iPhone 4S (called iPhone 5 in the news article), many competing, but differentiated, devices were on the market.

- The monopolistic competition model explains what is happening in the smartphone market.

- Figure 1 shows the market for Apple's iPhone 4S in its first month. (The numbers are assumed.)

- Because Apple's iPhone differs from its competitors and has features that users value, the demand curve, *D*, and marginal revenue curve, *MR*, provide a large short-run profit opportunity.

- The marginal cost curve is *MC* and the average total cost curve is *ATC*. Apple maximizes its economic profit by producing the quantity at which marginal revenue equals marginal cost, which, in this example, is 4 million iPhones a month.

- This quantity of iPhones can be sold for $200 each.

- The blue rectangle shows Apple's economic profit.

- Because this market is profitable, entry takes place. The news article tells us that Google, HTC, Motorola, and Samsung and others have entered the smartphone market.

- Figure 2 shows the the consequences of entry.

- The demand for the iPhone 4S decreases as the market is shared with other smartphones.

- Apple's profit-maximizing price of the iPhone falls, and in the long run, economic profit is eliminated.

- With zero economic profit, Apple has an incentive to develop an even better differentiated phone and start the cycle described here again, making an economic profit with a new phone in the short run.

- You can be sure that the iPhone 4S, isn't Apple's final version and that in 2013 its new differentiated successor will be launched.

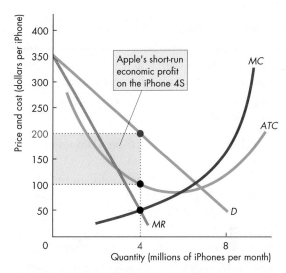

Figure 1 Economic Profit in the Short Run

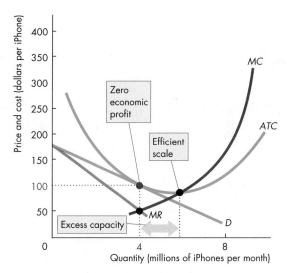

Figure 2 Zero Economic Profit in the Long Run

SUMMARY

Key Points

What Is Monopolistic Competition? (pp. 324–325)

- Monopolistic competition occurs when a large number of firms compete with each other on product quality, price, and marketing.

Working Problems 1 and 2 will give you a better understanding of what monopolistic competition is.

Price and Output in Monopolistic Competition (pp. 326–329)

- Each firm in monopolistic competition faces a downward-sloping demand curve and produces the profit-maximizing quantity.
- Entry and exit result in zero economic profit and excess capacity in long-run equilibrium.

Working Problems 3 to 12 will give you a better understanding of price and output in monopolistic competition.

Product Development and Marketing (pp. 330–333)

- Firms in monopolistic competition innovate and develop new products.
- Advertising expenditures increase total cost, but average total cost might fall if the quantity sold increases by enough.
- Advertising expenditures might increase demand, but demand might decrease if competition increases.
- Whether monopolistic competition is inefficient depends on the value we place on product variety.

Working Problems 13 to 18 will give you a better understanding of product development and marketing.

Key Terms

Efficient scale, 328
Excess capacity, 328
Markup, 329

Monopolistic competition, 324
Product differentiation, 324
Signal, 332

SCAN THIS

MyEconLab ◆ You can work Problems 1 to 19 in Chapter 14 Study Plan and get instant feedback.

STUDY PLAN PROBLEMS AND APPLICATIONS

What Is Monopolistic Competition? (Study Plan 14.1)

1. Which of the following items are sold by firms in monopolistic competition? Explain your selections.
   - Cable television service
   - Wheat
   - Athletic shoes
   - Soft drinks
   - Toothbrushes
   - Ready-mix concrete

2. The four-firm concentration ratio for audio equipment makers is 30 and for electric lamp makers it is 89. The HHI for audio equipment makers it is 415 and for electric lamp makers it is 2,850. Which of these markets is an example of monopolistic competition?

Price and Output in Monopolistic Competition
(Study Plan 14.2)

Use the following information to work Problems 3 and 4.

Sara is a dot.com entrepreneur who has established a Web site at which people can design and buy sweatshirts. Sara pays $1,000 a week for her Web server and Internet connection. The sweatshirts that her customers design are made to order by another firm, and Sara pays this firm $20 a sweatshirt. Sara has no other costs. The table sets out the demand schedule for Sara's sweatshirts.

Price (dollars per sweatshirt)	Quantity demanded (sweatshirts per week)
0	100
20	80
40	60
60	40
80	20
100	0

3. Calculate Sara's profit-maximizing output, price, and economic profit.

4. a. Do you expect other firms to enter the Web sweatshirt business and compete with Sara?
   b. What happens to the demand for Sara's sweatshirts in the long run? What happens to Sara's economic profit in the long run?

Use the following figure, which shows the situation facing a producer of running shoes, to work Problems 5 to 10.

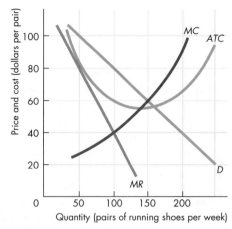

5. What quantity does the firm produce, what price does it charge, and what is its economic profit or economic loss?

6. In the long run, how does the number of firms producing running shoes change?

7. In the long run, how does the price of running shoes and the quantity the firm produces change? What happens to the market output?

8. Does the firm have excess capacity in the long run? If the firm has excess capacity in the long run, why doesn't it decrease its capacity?

9. In the long run, compare the price of a pair of running shoes and the marginal cost of producing the pair.

10. Is the market for running shoes efficient or inefficient in the long run? Explain your answer.

11. **Wake Up and Smell the Coffee**

    Every change that Starbucks made over the past few years—automated espresso machines, preground coffee, drive-throughs, fewer soft chairs and less carpeting—was made for a reason: to smooth operations or boost sales. Those may have been the right choices at the time, but together they ultimately diluted the coffee-centric experience. By 2008, Starbucks experienced a drop in traffic as customers complained that in pursuing rapid growth, the company has strayed too far from its roots. Starbucks will once again grind beans in its stores for drip coffee, give free drip refills, and provide two hours of wi-fi. The company will roll out its new sleek, low-rise espresso machine that makes baristas more visible.

Source: *Time*, April 7, 2008

a. Explain how Starbucks' past attempts to maximize profits ended up eroding product differentiation.

b. Explain how Starbucks' new plan intends to increase economic profit.

12. **The Shoe That Won't Quit**

I finally decided to take the plunge and buy a pair of Uggs, but when I got around to shopping for my Uggs, the style that I wanted was sold out. The scarcity factor was not a glitch in the supply chain, but rather a carefully calibrated strategy by Uggs' parent Deckers Outdoor that is one of the big reasons behind the brand's success. Deckers tightly controls distribution to ensure that supply does not outstrip demand. If Deckers ever opened up the supply of Uggs to meet demand, sales would shoot up like a rocket, but they'd come back down just as fast.

Source: *Fortune*, June 5, 2008

a. Explain why Deckers intentionally restricts the quantity of Uggs that the firm sells.

b. Draw a graph to illustrate how Deckers maximizes the economic profit from Uggs.

Product Development and Marketing (Study Plan 14.3)

Use the following information to work Problems 13 to 16.

Suppose that Tommy Hilfiger's marginal cost of a jacket is a constant $100 and the total fixed cost at one of its stores is $2,000 a day. This store sells 20 jackets a day, which is its profit-maximizing number of jackets. Then the stores nearby start to advertise their jackets. The Tommy Hilfiger store now spends $2,000 a day advertising its jackets, and its profit-maximizing number of jackets sold jumps to 50 a day.

13. a. What is this store's average total cost of a jacket sold before the advertising begins?

b. What is this store's average total cost of a jacket sold after the advertising begins?

14. a. Can you say what happens to the price of a Tommy Hilfiger jacket? Why or why not?

b. Can you say what happens to Tommy's markup? Why or why not?

c. Can you say what happens to Tommy's economic profit? Why or why not?

15. How might Tommy Hilfiger use advertising as a signal? How is a signal sent and how does it work?

16. How does having a brand name help Tommy Hilfiger to increase its economic profit?

Use the following news clip to work Problems 17 and 18.

Food's Next Billion-Dollar Brand?

While it's not the biggest brand in margarine, Smart Balance has an edge on its rivals in that it's made with a patented blend of vegetable and fruit oils that has been shown to help improve consumers' cholesterol levels. Smart Balance sales have skyrocketed while overall sales for margarine have stagnated. It remains to be seen if Smart Balance's healthy message and high price will resound with consumers.

Source: *Fortune*, June 4, 2008

17. How do you expect advertising and the Smart Balance brand name will affect Smart Balance's ability to make a positive economic profit?

18. Are long-run economic profits a possibility for Smart Balance? In long-run equilibrium, will Smart Balance have excess capacity or a markup?

Economics in the News (Study Plan 14.EN)

19. **Computer Makers Prepare to Stake Bigger Claim in Phones**

Emboldened by Apple's success with its iPhone, many PC makers and chip companies are charging into the cellphone business, promising new devices that can pack the horsepower of standard computers into palm-size packages—devices that handle the full glory of the Internet, power two-way video conferences, and stream high-definition movies to your TV. It is a development that spells serious competition for established cellphone makers and phone companies.

Source: *The New York Times*, March 15, 2009

a. Draw a graph of the cost curves and revenue curves of a cell phone company that makes a positive economic profit in the short run.

b. If cell phone companies start to include the popular features introduced by PC makers, explain how this decision will affect their profit in the short run.

c. What do you expect to happen to the cell phone company's economic profit in the long run, given the information in the news clip?

d. Draw a graph to illustrate your answer to part (c).

ADDITIONAL PROBLEMS AND APPLICATIONS

MyEconLab ◆ You can work these problems in MyEconLab if assigned by your instructor.

What Is Monopolistic Competition?

20. Which of the following items are sold by firms in monopolistic competition? Explain your selections.
    - Orange juice
    - Canned soup
    - PCs
    - Chewing gum
    - Breakfast cereals
    - Corn

21. The HHI for automobiles is 2,350, for sporting goods it is 161, for batteries it is 2,883, and for jewelry it is 81. Which of these markets is an example of monopolistic competition?

Price and Output in Monopolistic Competition

Use the following information to work Problems 22 and 23.

Lorie teaches singing. Her fixed costs are $1,000 a month, and it costs her $50 of labour to give one class. The table shows the demand schedule for Lorie's singing lessons.

Price (dollars per lesson)	Quantity demanded (lessons per month)
0	250
50	200
100	150
150	100
200	50
250	0

22. Calculate Lorie's profit-maximizing output, price, and economic profit.

23. a. Do you expect other firms to enter the singing lesson business and compete with Lorie?
    b. What happens to the demand for Lorie's lessons in the long run? What happens to Lorie's economic profit in the long run?

Use the figure in the next column, which shows the situation facing Mike's Bikes, a producer of mountain bikes, to work Problems 24 to 28. The demand and costs of other mountain bike producers are similar to those of Mike's Bikes.

24. What quantity does the firm produce and what is its price? Calculate the firm's economic profit or economic loss.

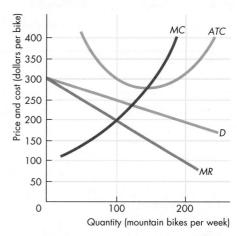

25. What will happen to the number of firms producing mountain bikes in the long run?

26. a. How will the price of a mountain bike and the number of bikes produced by Mike's Bikes change in the long run?
    b. How will the quantity of mountain bikes produced by all firms change in the long run?

27. Is there any way for Mike's Bikes to avoid having excess capacity in the long run?

28. Is the market for mountain bikes efficient or inefficient in the long run? Explain your answer.

Use the following news clip to work Problems 29 and 30.

Groceries for the Gourmet Palate

No food, it seems, is safe from being repackaged to look like an upscale product. Samuel Adams' $120 Utopias, in a ridiculous copper-covered 24-oz. bottle meant to resemble an old-fashioned brew kettle, is barely beer. It's not carbonated like a Bud, but aged in oak barrels like scotch. It has a vintage year, like a Bordeaux, is light, complex, and free of any alcohol sting, despite having six times as much alcohol content as a regular can of brew.

Source: *Time*, April 14, 2008

29. a. Explain how Samuel Adams has differentiated its Utopias to compete with other beer brands in terms of quality, price, and marketing.
    b. Predict whether Samuel Adams produces at, above, or below the efficient scale in the short run.

30. a. Predict whether the $120 price tag on the Utopias is at, above, or below marginal cost:

     (i) In the short run.
     (ii) In the long run.
  b. Do you think that Samuel Adams' Utopias makes the market for beer inefficient?

Use the following news clip to work Problems 31 and 32.

Swinging for Female Golfers

One of the hottest areas of innovation is in clubs for women, who now make up nearly a quarter of the 24 million golfers in the United States. Callaway and Nike, two of the leading golf-equipment manufacturers, recently released new clubs designed specifically for women.

Source: *Time*, April 21, 2008

31. a. How are Callaway and Nike attempting to maintain economic profit?
  b. Draw a graph to illustrate the cost curves and revenue curves of Callaway or Nike in the market for golf clubs for women.
  c. Show on your graph in part (b) the short-run economic profit.

32. a. Explain why the economic profit that Callaway and Nike make on golf clubs for women is likely to be temporary.
  b. Draw a graph to illustrate the cost curves and revenue curves of Callaway or Nike in the market for golf clubs for women in the long run. Mark the firm's excess capacity.

Product Development and Marketing

Use the following information to work Problems 33 to 35.

Bianca bakes delicious cookies. Her total fixed cost is $40 a day, and her average variable cost is $1 a bag. Few people know about Bianca's Cookies, and she is maximizing her profit by selling 10 bags a day for $5 a bag. Bianca thinks that if she spends $50 a day on advertising, she can increase her market share and sell 25 bags a day for $5 a bag.

33. If Bianca's advertising works as she expects, can she increase her economic profit by advertising?

34. If Bianca advertises, will her average total cost increase or decrease at the quantity produced?

35. If Bianca advertises, will she continue to sell her cookies for $5 a bag or will she change her price?

Use the following news clip to work Problems 36 and 37.

Chocolate Market Goes Hi-End

"The demand for premium chocolate continues to grow," said Joan Steuer, founder of Chocolate Marketing. There are two sides to this growth: There's the chocolate confections themselves—fancy artisan chocolates, such as those produced by Gatineau chocolatier Gaetan Tessier; and there's the packaging. Steur says that chocolate confections are being sold in "exquisite" packages that "push the envelope on pricing."

Source: *Vancouver Sun*, March 22, 2008

36. a. Explain how strong demand for premium chocolate without exquisite packaging will affect Tessier's company's economic profit.
  b. Explain how the "exquisite" packages that "push the envelope on pricing" will affect the economic profit made in part (a).

37. Can Tessier's company make a positive economic profit in the long run? Will it have either excess capacity or a markup in the long run?

38. **Under Armour's Big Step Up**

Under Armour, the red-hot athletic-apparel brand, has joined Nike, Adidas, and New Balance as a major player in the market for athletic footwear. Under Armour plans to revive the long-dead cross-training category. But will young athletes really spend $100 for a cross training shoe to lift weights in?

Source: *Time*, May 26, 2008

What factors influence Under Armour's ability to make an economic profit in the cross-training shoe market?

Economics in the News

39. After you have studied *Reading Between the Lines* on pp. 334–335, answer the following questions.
  a. Describe the cost curves (*MC* and *ATC*) and the marginal revenue and demand curves for the iPhone when Apple first introduced it.
  b. How do you think the creation of the iPhone influenced the demand for older-generation cell phones?
  c. Explain the effects of the introduction of the iPhone 5 on HTC and other firms in the market for smartphones. Draw a graph to illustrate your answer.
  d. Explain the effect on Apple of the decisions by Google, HTC, Motorola, and Samsung to bring their own smartphones to market.
  e. Draw a graph to illustrate your answer to part (e).
  f. Do you think the smartphone market is efficient? Explain your answer.
  g. Do you predict that producers of smartphones have excess capacity? Explain your answer.

CHAPTER
15

Oligopoly

After studying this chapter, you will be able to

◆ Define and identify oligopoly

◆ Use game theory to explain how price and output are determined in oligopoly

◆ Use game theory to explain other strategic decisions

◆ Describe the anti-combine law that regulates oligopoly

The chip in your laptop was made by either Intel or Advanced Micro Devices (AMD); the battery in your TV remote is most likely a Duracell or an Energizer. In the markets for computer chips and batteries, as well as in those for high-tech razors and big airplanes, two producers compete for market share in the pursuit of maximum profit. Many other markets have only a few firms.

How does a market work when only a handful of firms compete? To answer this question, we need the models of oligopoly based on game theory, which this chapter explains.

At the end of the chapter, in *Reading Between the Lines*, we'll look at the market for high-tech razors and see the game that Gillette and Schick are playing in their battle for market share and maximum profit.

341

What Is Oligopoly?

Oligopoly, like monopolistic competition, lies between perfect competition and monopoly. The firms in oligopoly might produce an identical product and compete only on price, or they might produce a differentiated product and compete on price, product quality, and marketing. **Oligopoly** is a market structure in which

- Natural or legal barriers prevent the entry of new firms.
- A small number of firms compete.

Barriers to Entry

Natural or legal barriers to entry can create oligopoly. You saw in Chapter 13 how economies of scale and demand form a natural barrier to entry that can create a *natural monopoly*. These same factors can create a *natural oligopoly*.

Figure 15.1 illustrates two natural oligopolies. The demand curve, *D* (in both parts of the figure), shows the demand for taxi rides in a town. If the average

total cost curve of a taxi company is ATC_1 in part (a), the market is a natural **duopoly**—an oligopoly market with two firms. You can probably see some examples of duopoly where you live. Some cities have only two taxi companies, two car rental firms, two copy centres, or two college bookstores.

The lowest price at which the firm would remain in business is $10 a ride. At that price, the quantity of rides demanded is 60 a day, the quantity that can be provided by just two firms. There is no room in this market for three firms. But if there were only one firm, it would make an economic profit and a second firm would enter to take some of the business and economic profit.

If the average total cost curve of a taxi company is ATC_2 in part (b), the efficient scale of one firm is 20 rides a day. This market is large enough for three firms.

A legal oligopoly arises when a legal barrier to entry protects the small number of firms in a market. A city might license two taxi firms or two bus companies, for example, even though the combination of demand and economies of scale leaves room for more than two firms.

FIGURE 15.1   Natural Oligopoly

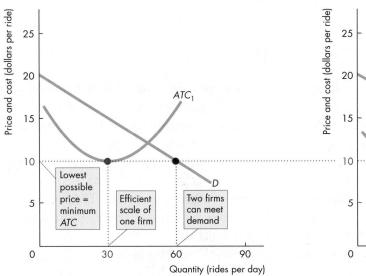

(a) Natural duopoly

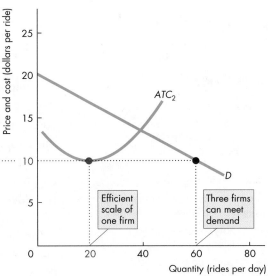

(b) Natural oligopoly with three firms

The lowest possible price is $10 a ride, which is the minimum average total cost. When a firm produces 30 rides a day, the efficient scale, two firms can satisfy the market demand. This natural oligopoly has two firms—a natural duopoly.

When the efficient scale of one firm is 20 rides per day, three firms can satisfy the market demand at the lowest possible price. This natural oligopoly has three firms.

Small Number of Firms

Because barriers to entry exist, oligopoly consists of a small number of firms, each of which has a large share of the market. Such firms are interdependent, and they face a temptation to cooperate to increase their joint economic profit.

Interdependence With a small number of firms in a market, each firm's actions influence the profits of all the other firms. Zola Doré opened her coffee shop in downtown Whitehorse in 2005. In April 2008, Starbucks opened. The number of coffee shops increased to three. There was too much competition for coffee drinkers' dollars in the city of 20,500. Starbucks survived, but Zola went out of business in June 2008. Zola and Starbucks were interdependent.

Temptation to Cooperate When a small number of firms share a market, they can increase their profits by forming a cartel and acting like a monopoly. A **cartel** is a group of firms acting together—colluding—to limit output, raise price, and increase economic profit. Cartels are illegal, but they do operate in some markets. But for reasons that you'll discover in this chapter, cartels tend to break down.

Examples of Oligopoly

Economics in Action below shows some examples of oligopoly. The dividing line between oligopoly and monopolistic competition is hard to pin down. As a practical matter, we identify oligopoly by looking at concentration ratios, the Herfindahl-Hirschman Index, and information about the geographical scope of the market and barriers to entry. The HHI that divides oligopoly from monopolistic competition is generally taken to be 1,800—below 1,800 is usually an example of monopolistic competition and above 1,800 is usually an example of oligopoly.

REVIEW QUIZ

1 What are the two distinguishing characteristics of oligopoly?
2 Why are firms in oligopoly interdependent?
3 Why do firms in oligopoly face a temptation to collude?
4 Can you think of some examples of oligopolies that you buy from?

You can work these questions in Study Plan 15.1 and get instant feedback.

━━━━━━━━━━━━━━━━━━━━━━━ MyEconLab ◆

Economics in Action
Oligopoly Today

These markets are oligopolies. Although in some of them, the number of firms (in parentheses) is large, the share of the market held by the 4 largest firms (the red bars) is close to 100 percent.

The most concentrated markets—cigarettes, motor vehicles, breakfast cereals, chocolates, pet food, and batteries—are dominated by just one or two firms.

If you want to buy an AAA battery for your TV remote or toothbrush, you'll find it hard to avoid buying a Duracell or an Energizer.

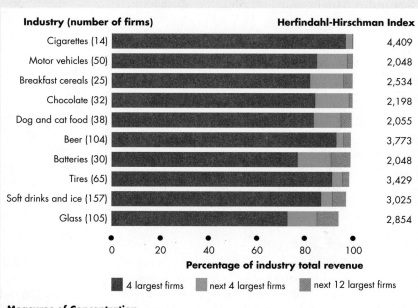

Industry (number of firms)	Herfindahl-Hirschman Index
Cigarettes (14)	4,409
Motor vehicles (50)	2,048
Breakfast cereals (25)	2,534
Chocolate (32)	2,198
Dog and cat food (38)	2,055
Beer (104)	3,773
Batteries (30)	2,048
Tires (65)	3,429
Soft drinks and ice (157)	3,025
Glass (105)	2,854

Percentage of industry total revenue

■ 4 largest firms   ■ next 4 largest firms   ■ next 12 largest firms

Measures of Concentration

Source of data: Adapted from Statistics Canada, Manufacturing, Construction, and Energy Division.

◆ Oligopoly Games

Economists think about oligopoly as a game between two or a few players, and to study oligopoly markets they use game theory. **Game theory** is a set of tools for studying *strategic behaviour*—behaviour that takes into account the expected behaviour of others and the recognition of mutual interdependence. Game theory was invented by John von Neumann in 1937 and extended by von Neumann and Oskar Morgenstern in 1944 (p. 367). Today, it is one of the major research fields in economics.

Game theory seeks to understand oligopoly as well as other forms of economic, political, social, and even biological rivalries by using a method of analysis specifically designed to understand games of all types, including the familiar games of everyday life (see Talking with Thomas Hubbard on pp. 368–370). To lay the foundation for studying oligopoly games, we first think about the features that all games share.

What Is a Game?

What is a game? At first thought, the question seems silly. After all, there are many different games. There are ball games and parlour games, games of chance and games of skill. But what is it about all these different activities that makes them games? What do all these games have in common? All games share four common features:

- Rules
- Strategies
- Payoffs
- Outcome

We're going to look at these features of games by playing at a game called "the prisoners' dilemma." The prisoners' dilemma game displays the essential features of many games, including oligopoly games, and it gives a good illustration of how game theory works and generates predictions.

The Prisoners' Dilemma

Art and Bob have been caught red-handed stealing a car. Facing airtight cases, they will receive a sentence of two years each for their crime. During his interviews with the two prisoners, the Crown attorney begins to suspect that he has stumbled on the two people who were responsible for a multimillion-dollar bank robbery some months earlier. But this is just a suspicion. He has no evidence on which he can convict them of the greater crime unless he can get them to confess. But how can he extract a confession? The answer is by making the prisoners play a game. Let's look at the game they play.

Rules   Each prisoner (player) is placed in a separate room and cannot communicate with the other prisoner. Each is told that he is suspected of having carried out the bank robbery and that

> If both of them confess to the larger crime, each will receive a sentence of 3 years for both crimes.

> If he alone confesses and his accomplice does not, he will receive only a 1-year sentence while his accomplice will receive a 10-year sentence.

Strategies   In game theory, **strategies** are all the possible actions of each player. Art and Bob each have two possible actions:

1. Confess to the bank robbery.
2. Deny having committed the bank robbery.

Because there are two players, each with two strategies, there are four possible outcomes:

1. Both confess.
2. Both deny.
3. Art confesses and Bob denies.
4. Bob confesses and Art denies.

Payoffs   Each prisoner can work out his *payoff* in each of these situations, and we can tabulate the four possible payoffs for each of the prisoners in what is called a payoff matrix for the game. A **payoff matrix** is a table that shows the payoffs for every possible action by each player for every possible action by each other player.

Table 15.1 shows a payoff matrix for Art and Bob. The squares show the payoffs for each prisoner—the red triangle in each square shows Art's and the blue triangle shows Bob's. If both prisoners confess (top left), each gets a prison term of 3 years. If Bob confesses but Art denies (top right), Art gets a 10-year sentence and Bob gets a 1-year sentence. If Art confesses and Bob denies (bottom left), Art gets a 1-year sentence and Bob gets a 10-year sentence. Finally, if both of them deny (bottom right), neither can be convicted of the bank robbery charge but both are sentenced for the car theft—a 2-year sentence.

Outcome The choices of both players determine the outcome of the game. To predict that outcome, we use an equilibrium idea proposed by John Nash of Princeton University (who received the Nobel Prize for Economic Science in 1994 and was the subject of the 2001 movie *A Beautiful Mind*). In **Nash equilibrium**, player *A* takes the best possible action given the action of player *B* and player *B* takes the best possible action given the action of player *A*.

In the case of the prisoners' dilemma, the Nash equilibrium occurs when Art makes his best choice given Bob's choice and when Bob makes his best choice given Art's choice.

To find the Nash equilibrium, we compare all the possible outcomes associated with each choice and eliminate those that are dominated—that are not as good as some other choice. Let's find the Nash equilibrium for the prisoners' dilemma game.

Finding the Nash Equilibrium Look at the situation from Art's point of view. If Bob confesses (top row), Art's best action is to confess because in that case, he is sentenced to 3 years rather than 10 years. If Bob denies (bottom row), Art's best action is still to confess because in that case he receives 1 year rather than 2 years. So Art's best action is to confess.

Now look at the situation from Bob's point of view. If Art confesses (left column), Bob's best action is to confess because in that case, he is sentenced to 3 years rather than 10 years. If Art denies (right column), Bob's best action is still to confess because in that case, he receives 1 year rather than 2 years. So Bob's best action is to confess.

Because each player's best action is to confess, each does confess, each goes to jail for 3 years, and the Crown attorney has solved the bank robbery. This is the Nash equilibrium of the game.

The Nash equilibrium for the prisoners' dilemma is called a **dominant-strategy equilibrium**, which is an equilibrium in which the best strategy of each player is to cheat (confess) *regardless of the strategy of the other player.*

The Dilemma The dilemma arises as each prisoner contemplates the consequences of his decision and puts himself in the place of his accomplice. Each knows that it would be best if both denied. But each also knows that if he denies it is in the best interest of the other to confess. So each considers whether to deny and rely on his accomplice to deny or to

TABLE 15.1   Prisoners' Dilemma Payoff Matrix

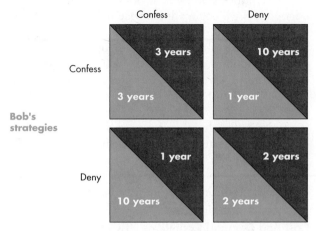

Each square shows the payoffs for the two players, Art and Bob, for each possible pair of actions. In each square, the red triangle shows Art's payoff and the blue triangle shows Bob's. For example, if both confess, the payoffs are in the top left square. The equilibrium of the game is for both players to confess and each gets a 3-year sentence.

confess hoping that his accomplice denies but expecting him to confess. The dilemma leads to the equilibrium of the game.

A Bad Outcome For the prisoners, the equilibrium of the game, with each confessing, is not the best outcome. If neither of them confesses, each gets only 2 years for the lesser crime. Isn't there some way in which this better outcome can be achieved? It seems that there is not, because the players cannot communicate with each other. Each player can put himself in the other player's place, and so each player can figure out that there is a best strategy for each of them. The prisoners are indeed in a dilemma. Each knows that he can serve 2 years *only* if he can trust the other to deny. But each prisoner also knows that it is *not* in the best interest of the other to deny. So each prisoner knows that he must confess, thereby delivering a bad outcome for both.

The firms in an oligopoly are in a similar situation to Art and Bob in the prisoners' dilemma game. Let's see how we can use this game to understand oligopoly.

An Oligopoly Price-Fixing Game

We can use game theory and a game like the prisoners' dilemma to understand price fixing, price wars, and other aspects of the behaviour of firms in oligopoly. We'll begin with a price-fixing game.

To understand price fixing, we're going to study the special case of duopoly—an oligopoly with two firms. Duopoly is easier to study than oligopoly with three or more firms, and it captures the essence of all oligopoly situations. Somehow, the two firms must share the market. And how they share it depends on the actions of each. We're going to describe the costs of the two firms and the market demand for the item they produce. We're then going to see how game theory helps us to predict the prices charged and the quantities produced by the two firms in a duopoly.

Cost and Demand Conditions   Two firms, Trick and Gear, produce switchgears. They have identical costs. Figure 15.2(a) shows their average total cost curve (*ATC*) and marginal cost curve (*MC*). Figure 15.2(b) shows the market demand curve for switchgears (*D*). The two firms produce identical switchgears, so one firm's switchgear is a perfect substitute for the other's, and the market price of each firm's product is identical. The quantity demanded depends on that price—the higher the price, the smaller is the quantity demanded.

This industry is a natural duopoly. Two firms can produce this good at a lower cost than either one firm or three firms can. For each firm, average total cost is at its minimum when production is 3,000 units a week. When price equals minimum average total cost, the total quantity demanded is 6,000 units a week, and two firms can just produce that quantity.

Collusion   We'll suppose that Trick and Gear enter into a collusive agreement. A **collusive agreement** is an agreement between two (or more) producers to form a cartel to restrict output, raise the price, and increase profits. Such an agreement is illegal in Canada and is undertaken in secret. The strategies that firms in a cartel can pursue are to

- Comply
- Cheat

A firm that complies carries out the agreement. A firm that cheats breaks the agreement to its own benefit and to the cost of the other firm.

Because each firm has two strategies, there are four possible combinations of actions for the firms:

1. Both firms comply.
2. Both firms cheat.
3. Trick complies and Gear cheats.
4. Gear complies and Trick cheats.

FIGURE 15.2   Costs and Demand

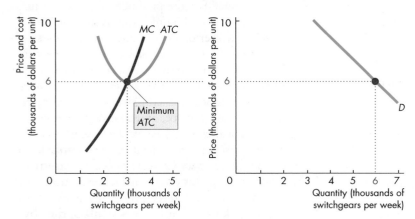

(a) Individual firm

(b) Industry

The average total cost curve for each firm is *ATC*, and the marginal cost curve is *MC* in part (a). Minimum average total cost is $6,000 a unit, and it occurs at a production of 3,000 units a week.

Part (b) shows the market demand curve. At a price of $6,000, the quantity demanded is 6,000 units per week. The two firms can produce this output at the lowest possible average cost. If the market had one firm, it would be profitable for another to enter. If the market had three firms, one would exit. There is room for only two firms in this industry. It is a natural duopoly.

Colluding to Maximize Profits Let's work out the payoffs to the two firms if they collude to make the maximum profit for the cartel by acting like a monopoly. The calculations that the two firms perform are the same calculations that a monopoly performs. (You can refresh your memory of these calculations by looking at Chapter 13, pp. 304–305.) The only thing that the firms in duopoly must do beyond what a monopoly does is to agree on how much of the total output each of them will produce.

Figure 15.3 shows the price and quantity that maximize industry profit for the duopoly. Part (a) shows the situation for each firm, and part (b) shows the situation for the industry as a whole. The curve labelled *MR* is the industry marginal revenue curve. This marginal revenue curve is like that of a single-price monopoly (Chapter 13, p. 302).The curve labelled MC_I is the industry marginal cost curve if each firm produces the same quantity of output. This curve is constructed by adding together the outputs of the two firms at each level of marginal cost. Because the two firms are the same size, at each level of marginal cost, the industry output is twice the output of one firm. The curve MC_I in part (b) is twice as far to the right as the curve *MC* in part (a).

To maximize industry profit, the firms in the duopoly agree to restrict output to the rate that makes the industry marginal cost and marginal revenue equal. That output rate, as shown in part (b), is 4,000 units a week. The demand curve shows that the highest price for which the 4,000 switchgears can be sold is $9,000 each. Trick and Gear agree to charge this price.

To hold the price at $9,000 a unit, production must be 4,000 units a week. So Trick and Gear must agree on output rates for each of them that total 4,000 units a week. Let's suppose that they agree to split the market equally so that each firm produces 2,000 switchgears a week. Because the firms are identical, this division is the most likely.

The average total cost (*ATC*) of producing 2,000 switchgears a week is $8,000, so the profit per unit is $1,000 and economic profit is $2 million (2,000 units × $1,000 per unit). The economic profit of each firm is represented by the blue rectangle in Fig. 15.3(a).

We have just described one possible outcome for a duopoly game: The two firms collude to produce the monopoly profit-maximizing output and divide that output equally between themselves. From the industry point of view, this solution is identical to a monopoly. A duopoly that operates in this way is indistinguishable from a monopoly. The economic profit that is made by a monopoly is the maximum total profit that can be made by the duopoly when the firms collude.

But with price greater than marginal cost, either firm might think of trying to increase profit by cheating on the agreement and producing more than the agreed amount. Let's see what happens if one of the firms does cheat in this way.

FIGURE 15.3   Colluding to Make Monopoly Profits

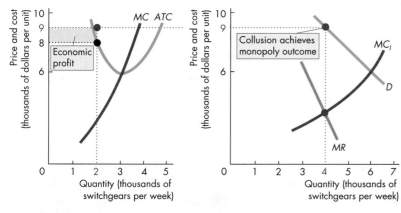

(a) Individual firm   **(b) Industry**

The industry marginal cost curve, MC_I in part (b), is the horizontal sum of the two firms' marginal cost curves, *MC* in part (a). The industry marginal revenue curve is *MR*. To maximize profit, the firms produce 4,000 units a week (the quantity at which marginal revenue equals marginal cost). They sell that output for $9,000 a unit. Each firm produces 2,000 units a week. Average total cost is $8,000 a unit, so each firm makes an economic profit of $2 million (blue rectangle)—2,000 units multiplied by $1,000 profit a unit.

One Firm Cheats on a Collusive Agreement To set the stage for cheating on their agreement, Trick convinces Gear that demand has decreased and that it cannot sell 2,000 units a week. Trick tells Gear that it plans to cut its price so that it can sell the agreed 2,000 units each week. Because the two firms produce an identical product, Gear matches Trick's price cut but still produces only 2,000 units a week.

In fact, there has been no decrease in demand. Trick plans to increase output, which it knows will lower the price, and Trick wants to ensure that Gear's output remains at the agreed level.

Figure 15.4 illustrates the consequences of Trick's cheating. Part (a) shows Gear (the complier); part (b) shows Trick (the cheat); and part (c) shows the industry as a whole. Suppose that Trick increases output to 3,000 units a week. If Gear sticks to the agreement to produce only 2,000 units a week, total output is now 5,000 a week, and, given demand in part (c), the price falls to $7,500 a unit.

Gear continues to produce 2,000 units a week at a cost of $8,000 a unit and incurs a loss of $500 a unit, or $1 million a week. This economic loss is shown by the red rectangle in part (a). Trick produces 3,000 units a week at a cost of $6,000 a unit. With a price

of $7,500, Trick makes a profit of $1,500 a unit and therefore an economic profit of $4.5 million. This economic profit is the blue rectangle in part (b).

We've now described a second possible outcome for the duopoly game: One of the firms cheats on the collusive agreement. In this case, the industry output is larger than the monopoly output and the industry price is lower than the monopoly price. The total economic profit made by the industry is also smaller than the monopoly's economic profit. Trick (the cheat) makes an economic profit of $4.5 million, and Gear (the complier) incurs an economic loss of $1 million. The industry makes an economic profit of $3.5 million. This industry profit is $0.5 million less than the economic profit that a monopoly would make, but it is distributed unevenly. Trick makes a bigger economic profit than it would under the collusive agreement, while Gear incurs an economic loss.

A similar outcome would arise if Gear cheated and Trick complied with the agreement. The industry profit and price would be the same, but in this case, Gear (the cheat) would make an economic profit of $4.5 million and Trick (the complier) would incur an economic loss of $1 million.

Let's next see what happens if both firms cheat.

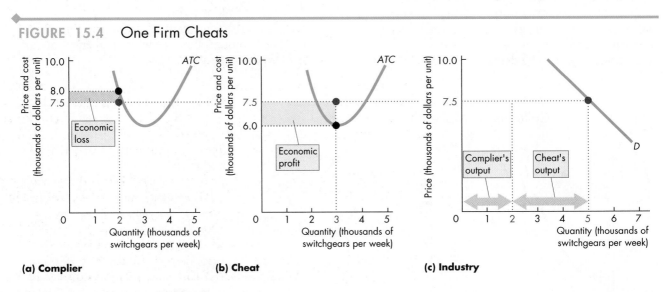

FIGURE 15.4   One Firm Cheats

(a) Complier   **(b) Cheat**   **(c) Industry**

One firm, shown in part (a), complies with the agreement and produces 2,000 units. The other firm, shown in part (b), cheats on the agreement and increases its output to 3,000 units a week. Given the market demand curve, shown in part (c), and with a total production of 5,000 units a week,

the price falls to $7,500 a unit. At this price, the complier in part (a) incurs an economic loss of $1 million ($500 per unit × 2,000 units), shown by the red rectangle. In part (b), the cheat makes an economic profit of $4.5 million ($1,500 per unit × 3,000 units), shown by the blue rectangle.

MyEconLab animation

Both Firms Cheat Suppose that both firms cheat and that each firm behaves like the cheating firm that we have just analysed. Each tells the other that it is unable to sell its output at the going price and that it plans to cut its price. But because both firms cheat, each will propose a successively lower price. As long as price exceeds marginal cost, each firm has an incentive to increase its production—to cheat. Only when price equals marginal cost is there no further incentive to cheat. This situation arises when the price has reached $6,000. At this price, marginal cost equals price. Also, price equals minimum average total cost. At a price less than $6,000, each firm incurs an economic loss. At a price of $6,000, each firm covers all its costs and makes zero economic profit. Also, at a price of $6,000, each firm wants to produce 3,000 units a week, so the industry output is 6,000 units a week. Given the demand conditions, 6,000 units can be sold at a price of $6,000 each.

Figure 15.5 illustrates the situation just described. Each firm, in part (a), produces 3,000 units a week, and its average total cost is a minimum ($6,000 per unit). The market as a whole, in part (b), operates at the point at which the market demand curve (*D*) intersects the industry marginal cost curve (*MC_I*). Each firm has lowered its price and increased its output to try to gain an advantage over the other firm. Each has pushed this process as far as it can without incurring an economic loss.

We have now described a third possible outcome of this duopoly game: Both firms cheat. If both firms cheat on the collusive agreement, the output of each firm is 3,000 units a week and the price is $6,000 a unit. Each firm makes zero economic profit.

The Payoff Matrix Now that we have described the strategies and payoffs in the duopoly game, we can summarize the strategies and the payoffs in the form of the game's payoff matrix. Then we can find the Nash equilibrium.

Table 15.2 sets out the payoff matrix for this game. It is constructed in the same way as the payoff matrix for the prisoners' dilemma in Table 15.1. The squares show the payoffs for the two firms—Gear and Trick. In this case, the payoffs are profits. (For the prisoners' dilemma, the payoffs were losses.)

The table shows that if both firms cheat (top left), they achieve the perfectly competitive outcome—each firm makes zero economic profit. If both firms comply (bottom right), the industry makes the monopoly profit and each firm makes an economic profit of $2 million. The top right and bottom left squares show the payoff if one firm cheats while the other complies. The firm that cheats makes an economic profit of $4.5 million, and the one that complies incurs a loss of $1 million.

Nash Equilibrium in the Duopolists' Dilemma The duopolists have a dilemma like the prisoners' dilemma. Do they comply or cheat? To answer this question, we must find the Nash equilibrium.

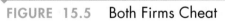

FIGURE 15.5   Both Firms Cheat

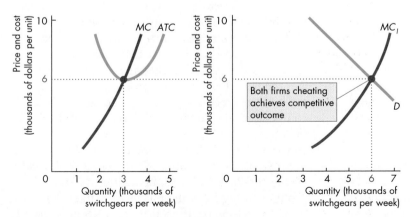

(a) Individual firm   **(b) Industry**

If both firms cheat by increasing production, the collusive agreement collapses. The limit to the collapse is the competitive equilibrium. Neither firm will cut its price below $6,000 (minimum average total cost) because to do so will result in losses.

In part (a), each firm produces 3,000 units a week at an average total cost of $6,000. In part (b), with a total production of 6,000 units, the price falls to $6,000. Each firm now makes zero economic profit. This output and price are the ones that would prevail in a competitive industry.

TABLE 15.2   Duopoly Payoff Matrix

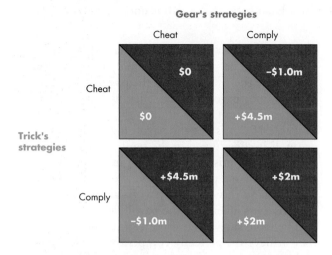

Each square shows the payoffs from a pair of actions. For example, if both firms comply with the collusive agreement, the payoffs are recorded in the bottom right square. The red triangle shows Gear's payoff, and the blue triangle shows Trick's. In Nash equilibrium, both firms cheat.

Look at things from Gear's point of view. Gear reasons as follows: Suppose that Trick cheats. If I comply, I will incur an economic loss of $1 million. If I also cheat, I will make zero economic profit. Zero is better than *minus* $1 million, so I'm better off if I cheat. Now suppose Trick complies. If I cheat, I will make an economic profit of $4.5 million, and if I comply, I will make an economic profit of $2 million. A $4.5 million profit is better than a $2 million profit, so I'm better off if I cheat. So regardless of whether Trick cheats or complies, it pays Gear to cheat. Cheating is Gear's best strategy.

Trick comes to the same conclusion as Gear because the two firms face an identical situation. So both firms cheat. The Nash equilibrium of the duopoly game is that both firms cheat. And although the industry has only two firms, they charge the same price and produce the same quantity as those in a competitive industry. Also, as in perfect competition, each firm makes zero economic profit.

This conclusion is not general and will not always arise. We'll see why not by looking first at some other games that are like the prisoners' dilemma. Then we'll broaden the types of games we consider.

Other Oligopoly Games

Firms in oligopoly must decide whether to mount expensive advertising campaigns; whether to modify their product; whether to make their product more reliable and more durable; whether to price discriminate and, if so, among which groups of customers and to what degree; whether to undertake a large research and development (R&D) effort aimed at lowering production costs; and whether to enter or leave an industry.

All of these choices can be analysed as games that are similar to the one that we've just studied. Let's look at one example: an R&D game.

Economics in Action
An R&D Game in the Market for Diapers

Disposable diapers have been around for a bit more than 40 years. Procter & Gamble (which has a 40 percent market share with Pampers) and Kimberly-Clark (which has a 33 percent market share with Huggies) have always been the market leaders.

When the disposable diaper was first introduced, it had to be cost-effective in competition with reusable, laundered diapers. A costly research and development effort resulted in the development of machines that could make disposable diapers at a low enough cost to achieve that initial competitive edge. But new firms tried to get into the business and take market share away from the two industry leaders, and the industry leaders themselves battled each other to maintain or increase their own market shares.

During the early 1990s, Kimberly-Clark was the first to introduce Velcro closures. And in 1996, Procter & Gamble was the first to introduce "breathable" diapers.

The key to success in this industry (as in any other) is to design a product that people value highly relative to the cost of producing it. The firm that creates the most highly valued product and also develops the least-cost technology for producing it gains a competitive edge, undercutting the rest of the market, increasing its market share, and increasing its profit.

But the R&D that must be undertaken to improve product quality and cut cost is itself costly. So the cost of R&D must be deducted from the profit resulting from the increased market share that lower costs achieve. If no firm does R&D, every firm can be better off, but if one firm initiates the R&D activity, all must follow.

Table 15.3 illustrates the dilemma (with hypothetical numbers) for the R&D game that Kimberly-Clark and Procter & Gamble play. Each firm has two strategies: Spend $25 million a year on R&D or spend nothing on R&D. If neither firm spends on R&D, they make a joint profit of $100 million: $30 million for Kimberly-Clark and $70 million for Procter & Gamble (bottom right of the payoff matrix). If each firm conducts R&D, market shares are maintained but each firm's profit is lower by the amount spent on R&D (top left square of the payoff matrix). If Kimberly-Clark pays for R&D but Procter & Gamble does not, Kimberly-Clark gains a large part of Procter & Gamble's market. Kimberly-Clark profits, and Procter & Gamble loses (top right square of the payoff matrix). Finally, if Procter & Gamble conducts R&D and Kimberly-Clark does not, Procter & Gamble gains market share from Kimberly-Clark, increasing its profit, while Kimberly-Clark incurs a loss (bottom left square).

TABLE 15.3 Pampers Versus Huggies: An R&D Game

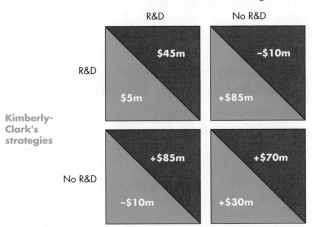

If both firms undertake R&D, their payoffs are those shown in the top left square. If neither firm undertakes R&D, their payoffs are in the bottom right square. When one firm undertakes R&D and the other one does not, their payoffs are in the top right and bottom left squares. The red triangle shows Procter & Gamble's payoff, and the blue triangle shows Kimberly-Clark's. The Nash equilibrium for this game is for both firms to undertake R&D. The structure of this game is the same as that of the prisoners' dilemma.

Confronted with the payoff matrix in Table 15.3, the two firms calculate their best strategies. Kimberly-Clark reasons as follows: If Procter & Gamble does not undertake R&D, we will make $85 million if we do and $30 million if we do not; so it pays us to conduct R&D. If Procter & Gamble conducts R&D, we will lose $10 million if we don't and make $5 million if we do. Again, R&D pays off. So conducting R&D is the best strategy for Kimberly-Clark. It pays, regardless of Procter & Gamble's decision.

Procter & Gamble reasons similarly: If Kimberly-Clark does not undertake R&D, we will make $70 million if we follow suit and $85 million if we conduct R&D. It therefore pays to conduct R&D. If Kimberly-Clark does undertake R&D, we will make $45 million by doing the same and lose $10 million by not doing R&D. Again, it pays us to conduct R&D. So for Procter & Gamble, R&D is also the best strategy.

Because R&D is the best strategy for both players, it is the Nash equilibrium. The outcome of this game is that both firms conduct R&D. They make less profit than they would if they could collude to achieve the cooperative outcome of no R&D.

The real-world situation has more players than Kimberly-Clark and Procter & Gamble. A large number of other firms share a small portion of the market, all of them ready to eat into the market share of Procter & Gamble and Kimberly-Clark. So the R&D efforts by these two firms not only serve the purpose of maintaining shares in their own battle but also help to keep barriers to entry high enough to preserve their joint market share.

The Disappearing Invisible Hand

All the games that we've studied are versions of the prisoners' dilemma. The essence of that game lies in the structure of its payoffs. The worst possible outcome for each player arises from cooperating when the other player cheats. The best possible outcome, for each player to cooperate, is not a Nash equilibrium because it is in neither player's *self-interest* to cooperate if the other one cooperates. It is this failure to achieve the best outcome for both players—the best social outcome if the two players are the entire economy—that led John Nash to claim (as he was portrayed as doing in the movie *A Beautiful Mind*) that he had challenged Adam Smith's idea that we are always guided, as if by an invisible hand, to promote the social interest when we are pursuing our self-interest.

A Game of Chicken

The Nash equilibrium for the prisoners' dilemma is unique: Both players cheat (confess). Not all games have a unique equilibrium, and one that doesn't is a game called "chicken."

An Example of the Game of Chicken A graphic, if disturbing, version of "chicken" has two cars racing towards each other. The first driver to swerve and avoid a crash is the "chicken." The payoffs are a big loss for both if no one "chickens out;" zero for both if both "chicken out;" and zero for the chicken and a gain for the one who stays the course. If player 1 swerves, player 2's best strategy is to stay the course; and if player 1 stays the course, player 2's best strategy is to swerve.

An Economic Example of Chicken An economic game of chicken can arise when R&D creates a new technology that cannot be kept secret or patented, so both firms benefit from the R&D of either firm. The chicken in this case is the firm that does the R&D.

Suppose, for example, that either Apple or Nokia spends $9 million developing a new touch-screen technology that both would end up being able to use regardless of which of them developed it.

Table 15.4 illustrates a payoff matrix for the game that Apple and Nokia play. Each firm has two strategies: Do the R&D ("chicken out") or do not do the R&D. Each entry shows the additional profit (the profit from the new technology minus the cost of the research), given the strategies adopted.

If neither firm does the R&D, each makes zero additional profit. If both firms conduct the R&D, each firm makes an additional $5 million. If one of the firms does the R&D ("chickens out"), the chicken makes $1 million and the other firm makes $10 million. Confronted with these payoffs, the two firms calculate their best strategies. Nokia is better off doing R&D if Apple does no R&D. Apple is better off doing R&D if Nokia does no R&D. There are two Nash equilibrium outcomes: Only one of them does the R&D, but we can't predict which one.

You can see that an outcome with no firm doing R&D isn't a Nash equilibrium because one firm would be better off doing it. Also both firms doing R&D isn't a Nash equilibrium because one firm would be better off *not* doing it. To decide *which* firm does the R&D, the firms might toss a coin, called a mixed strategy.

TABLE 15.4   An R&D Game of Chicken

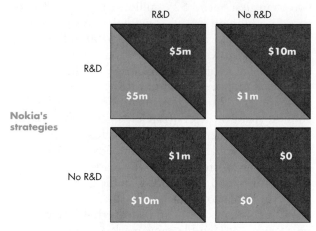

If neither firm does the R&D, their payoffs are in the bottom right square. When one firm "chickens out" and does the R&D while the other does no R&D, their payoffs are in the top right and bottom left squares. When both "chicken out" and do the R&D, the payoffs are in the top left square. The red triangle shows Apple's payoff, and the blue triangle shows Nokia's. The equilibrium for this R&D game of chicken is for only one firm to undertake the R&D. We cannot tell which firm will do the R&D and which will not.

◼ REVIEW QUIZ

1 What are the common features of all games?
2 Describe the prisoners' dilemma game and explain why the Nash equilibrium delivers a bad outcome for both players.
3 Why does a collusive agreement to restrict output and raise price create a game like the prisoners' dilemma?
4 What creates an incentive for firms in a collusive agreement to cheat and increase production?
5 What is the equilibrium strategy for each firm in a duopolists' dilemma and why do the firms not succeed in colluding to raise the price and profits?
6 Describe two structures of payoffs for an R&D game and contrast the prisoners' dilemma and the chicken game.

You can work these questions in Study Plan 15.2 and get instant feedback.

Repeated Games and Sequential Games

The games that we've studied are played just once. In contrast, many real-world games are played repeatedly. This feature of games turns out to enable real-world duopolists to cooperate, collude, and make a monopoly profit.

Another feature of the games that we've studied is that the players move simultaneously. But in many real-world situations, one player moves first and then the other moves—the play is sequential rather than simultaneous. This feature of real-world games creates a large number of possible outcomes.

We're now going to examine these two aspects of strategic decision-making.

A Repeated Duopoly Game

If two firms play a game repeatedly, one firm has the opportunity to penalize the other for previous "bad" behaviour. If Gear cheats this week, perhaps Trick will cheat next week. Before Gear cheats this week, won't it consider the possibility that Trick will cheat next week? What is the equilibrium of this game?

Actually, there is more than one possibility. One is the Nash equilibrium that we have just analysed. Both players cheat, and each makes zero economic profit forever. In such a situation, it will never pay one of the players to start complying unilaterally because to do so would result in a loss for that player and a profit for the other. But a **cooperative equilibrium** in which the players make and share the monopoly profit is possible.

A cooperative equilibrium might occur if cheating is punished. There are two extremes of punishment. The smallest penalty is called "tit for tat." A *tit-for-tat strategy* is one in which a player cooperates in the current period if the other player cooperated in the previous period, but cheats in the current period if the other player cheated in the previous period. The most severe form of punishment is called a trigger strategy. A *trigger strategy* is one in which a player cooperates if the other player cooperates but plays the Nash equilibrium strategy forever thereafter if the other player cheats.

In the duopoly game between Gear and Trick, a tit-for-tat strategy keeps both players cooperating and making monopoly profits. Let's see why with an example.

Table 15.5 shows the economic profit that Trick and Gear will make over a number of periods under two alternative sequences of events: colluding and cheating with a tit-for-tat response by the other firm.

If both firms stick to the collusive agreement in period 1, each makes an economic profit of $2 million. Suppose that Trick contemplates cheating in period 1. The cheating produces a quick $4.5 million economic profit and inflicts a $1 million economic loss on Gear. But a cheat in period 1 produces a response from Gear in period 2. If Trick wants to get back into a profit-making situation, it must return to the agreement in period 2 even though it knows that Gear will punish it for cheating in period 1. So in period 2, Gear punishes Trick and Trick cooperates. Gear now makes an economic profit of $4.5 million, and Trick incurs an economic loss of $1 million. Adding up the profits over two periods of play, Trick would have made more profit by cooperating—$4 million compared with $3.5 million.

What is true for Trick is also true for Gear. Because each firm makes a larger profit by sticking with the collusive agreement, both firms do so and the monopoly price, quantity, and profit prevail.

In reality, whether a cartel works like a one-play game or a repeated game depends primarily on the

TABLE 15.5 Cheating with Punishment

Period of play	Collude		Cheat with tit-for-tat	
	Trick's profit	Gear's profit	Trick's profit	Gear's profit
	(millions of dollars)		(millions of dollars)	
1	2	2	4.5	–1.0
2	2	2	–1.0	4.5
3	2	2	2.0	2.0
4	.	.	.	.

If duopolists repeatedly collude, each makes a profit of $2 million per period of play. If one player cheats in period 1, the other player plays a tit-for-tat strategy and cheats in period 2. The profit from cheating can be made for only one period and must be paid for in the next period by incurring a loss. Over two periods of play, the best that a duopolist can achieve by cheating is a profit of $3.5 million, compared to an economic profit of $4 million by colluding.

number of players and the ease of detecting and punishing cheating. The larger the number of players, the harder it is to maintain a cartel.

Games and Price Wars A repeated duopoly game can help us understand real-world behaviour and, in particular, price wars. Some price wars can be interpreted as the implementation of a tit-for-tat strategy. But the game is a bit more complicated than the one we've looked at because the players are uncertain about the demand for the product.

Playing a tit-for-tat strategy, firms have an incentive to stick to the monopoly price. But fluctuations in demand lead to fluctuations in the monopoly price, and sometimes, when the price changes, it might seem to one of the firms that the price has fallen because the other has cheated. In this case, a price war will break out. The price war will end only when each firm is satisfied that the other is ready to cooperate again. There will be cycles of price wars and the restoration of collusive agreements. Fluctuations in the world price of oil might be interpreted in this way.

Some price wars arise from the entry of a small number of firms into an industry that had previously been a monopoly. Although the industry has a small number of firms, the firms are in a prisoners' dilemma and they cannot impose effective penalties for price cutting. The behaviour of prices and outputs in the computer chip industry during 1995 and 1996 can be explained in this way. Until 1995, the market for Pentium chips for IBM-compatible computers was dominated by one firm, Intel Corporation, which was able to make maximum economic profit by producing the quantity of chips at which marginal cost equalled marginal revenue. The price of Intel's chips was set to ensure that the quantity demanded equalled the quantity produced. Then in 1995 and 1996, with the entry of a small number of new firms, the industry became an oligopoly. If the firms had maintained Intel's price and shared the market, together they could have made economic profits equal to Intel's profit. But the firms were in a prisoners' dilemma, so prices fell towards the competitive level.

Let's now study a sequential game. There are many such games, and the one we'll examine is among the simplest. It has an interesting implication and it will give you the flavour of this type of game. The sequential game that we'll study is an entry game in a contestable market.

A Sequential Entry Game in a Contestable Market

If two firms play a sequential game, one firm makes a decision at the first stage of the game and the other makes a decision at the second stage.

We're going to study a sequential game in a **contestable market**—a market in which firms can enter and leave so easily that firms in the market face competition from *potential* entrants. Examples of contestable markets are routes served by airlines and by barge companies that operate on the major waterways. These markets are contestable because firms could enter if an opportunity for economic profit arose and could exit with no penalty if the opportunity for economic profit disappeared.

If the Herfindahl-Hirschman Index (Chapter 10, p. 238) is used to determine the degree of competition, a contestable market appears to be uncompetitive. But a contestable market can behave as if it were perfectly competitive. To see why, let's look at an entry game for a contestable air route.

A Contestable Air Route Agile Air is the only firm operating on a particular route. Demand and cost conditions are such that there is room for only one airline to operate. Wanabe Inc. is another airline that could offer services on the route.

We describe the structure of a sequential game by using a *game tree* like that in Fig. 15.6. At the first stage, Agile Air must set a price. Once the price is set and advertised, Agile can't change it. That is, once set, Agile's price is fixed and Agile can't react to Wanabe's entry decision. Agile can set its price at either the monopoly level or the competitive level.

At the second stage, Wanabe must decide whether to enter or to stay out. Customers have no loyalty (there are no frequent-flyer programs) and they buy from the lowest-price firm. So if Wanabe enters, it sets a price just below Agile's and takes all the business.

Figure 15.6 shows the payoffs from the various decisions (Agile's in the red triangles and Wanabe's in the blue triangles).

To decide on its price, Agile's CEO reasons as follows: Suppose that Agile sets the monopoly price. If Wanabe enters, it earns 90 (think of all payoff numbers as thousands of dollars). If Wanabe stays out, it earns nothing. So Wanabe will enter. In this case Agile will lose 50.

Now suppose that Agile sets the competitive price. If Wanabe stays out, it earns nothing, and if it

FIGURE 15.6   Agile Versus Wanabe: A Sequential Entry Game in a Contestable Market

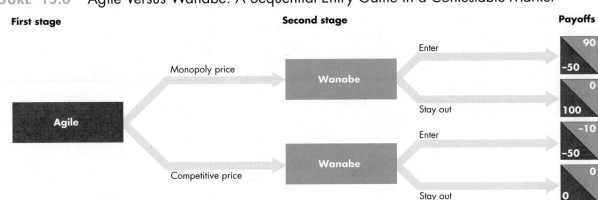

First stage

Second stage

Payoffs

Agile

Monopoly price

Wanabe

Enter — 90 / −50

Stay out — 0 / 100

Competitive price

Wanabe

Enter — −10 / −50

Stay out — 0 / 0

If Agile sets the monopoly price, Wanabe makes 90 (thousand dollars) by entering and earns nothing by staying out. So if Agile sets the monopoly price, Wanabe enters.

If Agile sets the competitive price, Wanabe earns nothing if it stays out and incurs a loss if it enters. So if Agile sets the competitive price, Wanabe stays out.

MyEconLab   animation ◆

enters, it loses 10, so Wanabe will stay out. In this case, Agile will make zero economic profit.

Agile's best strategy is to set its price at the competitive level and make zero economic profit. The option of earning 100 by setting the monopoly price with Wanabe staying out is not available to Agile. If Agile sets the monopoly price, Wanabe enters, undercuts Agile, and takes all the business.

In this example, Agile sets its price at the competitive level and makes zero economic profit. A less costly strategy, called **limit pricing**, sets the price at the highest level that inflicts a loss on an entrant. Any loss is big enough to deter entry, so it is not always necessary to set the price as low as the competitive price. In the example of Agile and Wanabe, at the competitive price, Wanabe incurs a loss of 10 if it enters. A smaller loss would still keep Wanabe out.

This game is interesting because it points to the possibility of a monopoly behaving like a competitive industry and serving the social interest without regulation. But the result is not general and depends on one crucial feature of the setup of the game: At the second stage, Agile is locked in to the price set at the first stage.

If Agile could change its price in the second stage, it would want to set the monopoly price if Wanabe stayed out—100 with the monopoly price beats zero with the competitive price. But Wanabe can figure out what Agile would do, so the price set at the first

stage has no effect on Wanabe. Agile sets the monopoly price and Wanabe might either stay out or enter.

We've looked at two of the many possible repeated and sequential games, and you've seen how these types of games can provide insights into the complex forces that determine prices and profits.

◢ REVIEW QUIZ

1   If a prisoners' dilemma game is played repeatedly, what punishment strategies might the players employ and how does playing the game repeatedly change the equilibrium?

2   If a market is contestable, how does the equilibrium differ from that of a monopoly?

You can work these questions in Study Plan 15.3 and get instant feedback.

MyEconLab ◆

So far, we've studied oligopoly with unregulated market power. Firms like Trick and Gear are free to collude to maximize their profit with no concern for the consumer or the law.

But when firms collude to achieve the monopoly outcome, they also have the same effects on efficiency and the social interest as monopoly. Profit is made at the expense of consumer surplus and a deadweight loss arises. Your next task is to see how Canadian anti-combine law limits market power.

◆ Anti-Combine Law

Anti-combine law is the law that regulates oligopolies and prevents them from becoming monopolies or behaving like monopolies. Anti-combine law can work in the public interest to maximize total surplus or in the self-interest of producers to maximize producer surpluses. We'll describe Canada's anti-combine law and examine some recent cases.

Canada's Anti-Combine Law

Canada's anti-combine law dates from 1889. At that time, monopoly was a major political issue and people were concerned about the absence of competition in industries as diverse as sugar and groceries, biscuits and confectionery, coal, binder twine, agricultural implements, stoves, coffins, eggs, and fire insurance. Canada's anti-combine law today is defined in the Competition Act of 1986, which is described in Table 15.6 on p. 358. The Act established a Competition Bureau and a Competition Tribunal. The Competition Act distinguishes between criminal and noncriminal practices.

Criminal offences include conspiring to fix prices, bid-rigging, and false advertising. It is also a criminal offence for a manufacturer to set the price at which a retailer must sell its products—called *resale price maintenance*. The courts handle alleged criminal offences, and the standard level of proof beyond a reasonable doubt must be established.

Noncriminal offences are mergers, abuse of a dominant market position, refusal to deal, and other actions designed to limit competition such as exclusive dealing. The Director of the Competition Bureau sends alleged violations of a noncriminal nature to the Competition Tribunal for examination.

Some Major Anti-Combine Cases

To see how the Competition Act has been working, we'll look at a few cases. The first case we'll examine is important because it confirms the Competition Tribunal's power to enforce its orders.

Chrysler   In 1986, Chrysler stopped supplying auto parts to Richard Brunet, a Montreal auto dealer. Chrysler also discouraged other dealers from supplying Brunet. The Competition Tribunal claimed that Chrysler wanted Brunet's business for itself and

ordered Chrysler to resume doing business with Brunet. Chrysler did not resume sending supplies and the Tribunal cited Chrysler for contempt. Appeals against this ruling eventually reached the Supreme Court of Canada, which confirmed the Tribunal's power over contempt for its ruling. The Tribunal subsequently dropped its contempt charge.

The second case we'll look at concerns aspartame, the sweetener in many soft drinks.

NutraSweet   NutraSweet, the maker of aspartame, tried to gain a monopoly in aspartame. It did so by licensing the use of its "swirl" only on products for which it had an exclusive deal. On October 4, 1990, the Competition Tribunal ruled that this action was an abuse of dominant position and unduly limited competition. The Competition Tribunal told NutraSweet that it may not enforce existing contracts, enter into new contracts in which it is the exclusive supplier, or give inducements to encourage the display of its "swirl." As a result of this case, competition increased and the price of aspartame fell in Canada.

The third case we'll examine concerns a publication that is now struggling to stay alive: the Yellow Pages.

Bell Canada Enterprises   Two subsidiaries of Bell Canada Enterprises have a 90 percent share of the market for the publication of telephone directories in their territories. These companies tie the sale of advertising services to the sale of advertising space in the Yellow Pages. If you want to advertise in the Yellow Pages, you must buy the advertising services of one of these two companies. As a result, other advertising agencies cannot effectively compete for business in Yellow Pages advertising.

The Director of the Competition Bureau applied for an order prohibiting the tied-sale practice of these two companies.

Other Recent Cases   The Competition Bureau has investigated several high-profile cases in the past few years. These include a movie theatre merger when Cineplex Galaxy acquired Famous Players, a retail gasoline price-fixing cartel in Quebec, two proposed mergers between big Canadian banks, and the ownership transfer and relocation policies of the NHL when Jim Balsillie tried to buy the Nashville Predators.

Economics in Action
Cineplex Galaxy Acquires Famous Players

In 2004, Cineplex Galaxy bought Famous Players. But before the deal could be confirmed, the Competition Bureau needed to vet and approve it.

The Firms The firms in the deal were

1. **Cineplex Galaxy** operated 86 theatres with 775 screens under the Cineplex Odeon and Galaxy brands in British Columbia, Alberta, Saskatchewan, Manitoba, Ontario, and Quebec.
2. **Famous Players** operated 77 theatres and 768 screens in the same six provinces as Cineplex Galaxy. The firm operated a number of brands other than its own name including Coliseum, Colossus, Paramount, and SilverCity.

By number of theatres and screens, Cineplex Galaxy was larger but Famous Players had larger box-office receipts.

The Markets There isn't just one Canadian market for movie theatres. Each urban area is a separate market.

Barriers to Entry The Competition Bureau identified three barriers to entry into the movie-theatre industry:

1. Access to high box-office movies
2. Access to suitable locations
3. Sunk costs and risks

Access to Movies The distribution policies of the major movie studios and distributors make entry risky. A new entrant cannot be sure before entering that the studios and distributors will provide it with movies capable of generating box-office revenue. So entry is highly risky.

Access to Locations During the late 1990s, a major building program created a large number of new stadium theatres, all of which occupied the best sites. As a consequence, it is difficult today to acquire a suitable site or location for a new movie theatre in many urban markets.

Sunk Costs and Risks Most new movie theatres are stadium-seating complexes that are single-purpose buildings. They are costly to build but have no resale

value so the cost of building them is a sunk cost, which makes entry very risky.

Concentration and Competition after the Merger
With Cineplex Galaxy and Famous Players operating as a single firm, many urban markets would become highly concentrated.

The Competition Bureau identified 17 local markets. In seven of them, the new merged firm would have had 100 percent market share and in five others, they would be near monopolies.

A few areas would have competition: in Montreal from Cinémas Guzzo; and in Montreal, Ottawa, and Toronto from AMC, a large U.S. operator. Outside of these major cities, the merged firm would have faced either no competition or very limited competition from small local firms.

The Competition Bureau's Decision The Competition Bureau examined the competitive impact of the merger in each of the cities where Famous Players and Cineplex Galaxy competed and determined that the merger would likely reduce competition substantially in 17 of these areas. The Bureau was concerned about both price and non-price competition on such factors as theatre quality and film choice.

To resolve these concerns, in 17 cities the Bureau required the new firm to sell 35 of its theatres.

The general rule the Bureau employed was to reduce the new firm's market share in each city to a level similar to the pre-merger market share of the larger of Cineplex or Famous Players.

Source: The Competition Bureau, *Acquisition of Famous Players by Cineplex Galaxy.*

◆

TABLE 15.6   Canada's Anti-Combine Law: The Competition Act, 1986

Abuse of Dominant Position

79 (1) Where on application by the Director, the Tribunal finds that:

(a) one or more persons substantially or completely control, throughout Canada or any area thereof, a class or species of business,

(b) that person or those persons have engaged in or are engaging in a practice of anticompetitive acts, and

(c) the practice has had, is having or is likely to have the effect of preventing or lessening competition substantially in a market,

the Tribunal may make an order prohibiting all or any of those persons from engaging in that practice.

Mergers

92 (1) Where on application by the Director, the Tribunal finds that a merger or proposed merger prevents or lessens, or is likely to prevent or lessen, competition substantially ... the Tribunal may... [,]

in the case of a completed merger, order any party to the merger or any other person

(i) to dissolve the merger ...

(ii) to dispose of assets and shares ...

[or]

in the case of a proposed merger, make an order directed against any party to the proposed merger or any other person

(i) ordering the person ... not to proceed with the merger

(ii) ordering the person not to proceed with part of the merger

◆

Economics in Action
Mergers Blocked

In January 1998, the Royal Bank of Canada and the Bank of Montreal announced that they wanted to merge and create a new bank. Soon after, in April 1998, CIBC and TD Bank announced their desire to combine.

After some months of deliberation, in December 1998, the Finance Minister, Paul Martin, told the banks that they could not proceed with their proposed mergers.

Why the Merger Was Blocked The Finance Minister said that the bank mergers were not in the public interest because they would result in

- Too much concentration of economic power in the hands of too few financial institutions

- Reduced competition in the financial services markets
- Reduced Government of Canada flexibility to address future concerns

A Competition Bureau report agreed.

Competition Bureau's View
The Competition Bureau investigated the impact of the proposed bank mergers on competition in the banking industry. The Bureau concluded that the mergers would substantially lessen competition and would result in bank branches being closed. Canadians would end up paying higher prices for reduced banking services.

Bank mergers in Canada are now so politically sensitive that any future attempts to merge will require the sanction of the federal government.

Economics in Action
Price Fixing

In June 2008, during a period of rapidly rising oil and gasoline prices, the Competition Bureau laid criminal charges against a number of individuals and companies in Victoriaville, Thetford Mines, Magog, and Sherbrooke (all in Quebec) for fixing the price of gasoline at the pump.

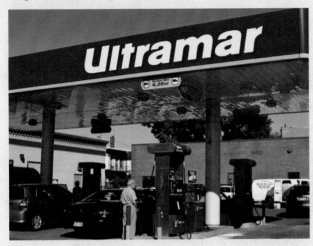

Price-fixing cartels are hard to detect. Evidence of identical prices does *not* prove the operation of a price-fixing agreement. Firms in perfect competition charge identical prices. Canadian law requires the Competition Bureau to provide evidence that proves, beyond a reasonable doubt, that the competitors *have an agreement to fix prices.*

In the Quebec gas prices case, the Competition Bureau used wiretaps and searches and took advantage of an immunity program that encourages people who are themselves breaking the law to provide evidence to investigators.

After extensive investigations, evidence emerged that gas retailers had made agreements by telephone on the prices they would charge. The evidence suggested that the overwhelming majority of gasoline retailers in these markets participated in the cartel.

The Court imposed fines totalling more than $2 million against the companies that pleaded guilty.

The Competition Bureau's investigation into potential price-fixing in the retail gasoline market continues in other markets in Canada.

Source: Adapted from the Competition Bureau, *Competition Bureau Uncovers Gasoline Cartel in Quebec.*

Economics in Action
Abuse of Dominant Position

In May 2007, Jim Balsillie did a tentative deal to buy the NHL team called Nashville Predators with the intention, it was believed, of relocating the team to Hamilton, Ontario.

Locating the Predators in Hamilton would take some of the market from the Toronto Maple Leafs, who would demand compensation. The Buffalo Sabres might also be damaged and demand compensation, although NHL rules do permit relocation outside a radius of 80 kilometres of an existing team.

NHL policy requires that before a relocation can be accepted, a new owner must make a good faith effort to keep the team in its city. Balsillie, it was claimed, had made no such attempt, and the NHL prevented him from completing the deal.

Following intense discussion in the media, the Competition Bureau investigated whether the NHL's transfer of ownership and relocation policies were anticompetitive or merely designed to protect the interests of the league.

After a major and highly detailed investigation, the Competition Bureau concluded that the NHL's policies were not anticompetitive and did not constitute an abuse of a dominant position. Rather, their aim was to maintain healthy rivalries among teams, to attract the largest possible audiences, and to encourage the investment in sports facilities by local governments.

Source: The Competition Bureau, *NHL Ownership Transfer and Relocation Policies.*

REVIEW QUIZ

1 What is the act of Parliament that provides our anti-combine law?
2 What actions violate the anti-combine law?
3 Under what circumstances is a merger unlikely to be approved?

You can work these questions in Study Plan 15.4 and get instant feedback.

━━━━━━━━━━━━━━ MyEconLab ◆

◆ Oligopoly is a market structure that you often encounter in your daily life. *Reading Between the Lines* on pp. 360–361 looks at a game played in the market for high-tech razors.

Gillette and Schick in a Duopoly Game

The Straight Razor Has Been Outdone

Toronto Star

May 15, 2010

The straight razor, that timeless icon of quality men's grooming, is officially a relic.

The latest generations of drugstore razors, born from millions of dollars in research and development, put grandpa's old single blade to ignominious shame.

"I can't compete with this," says straight razor guru Rick Ricci as he holds up the new Schick Hydro, a scruff chopper developed over a seven-year period by engineers in Germany and the United States.

Ricci owns Toronto's Truefitt and Hill, a lavish men's barbershop in Scotia Plaza, where Bay Streeters recline in old school barber chairs for the retro charm of an old school shave.

"We're world-renowned barbers and, I'm telling you, the single blade can't do as well as this."

Ah, these are heady days for shaving technology.

Simultaneous with the Schick launch, Gillette unveiled its latest high-priced offering—the ProGlide.

Billed as a "dramatically better" version of the popular Fusion razor (which is advertised on television about every 15 seconds), the ProGlide is the product of 30,000 customer trials involving "precise measurement instrumentation used in the aerospace, semiconductor, and medical imaging categories," says a release.

The thrust: Thinner, finer blades reduce tug-and-pull and unlock the secret to irritation-free closeness. ...

The modern man is motivated unlike ever before in modern history to step up his grooming game. ...

Reprinted with permission—Torstar Syndication Services.

ESSENCE OF THE STORY

- Schick developed a new razor called the Hydro.
- Schick spent seven years working with engineers in Germany and the United States on its new razor.
- Gillette also developed a new razor, the Fusion ProGlide.
- The ProGlide was developed with advanced technology and 30,000 user trials.
- The ProGlide has thinner blades than its predecessor.
- Gillette advertises heavily on television.

ECONOMIC ANALYSIS

- The global market in high-tech razors (razors with multiple blades, a battery, and other aids to comfort) is dominated by two brands: Gillette, made by Procter & Gamble (P&G), and Schick, made by Energizer.

- Figure 1 shows the shares in this market. You can see that Gillette has 70 percent of the market, Schick 20 percent, and others only 10 percent.

- In 2010, P&G and Energizer increased the intensity of their competition by spending hundreds of millions of dollars developing and marketing more advanced razors: the Gillette ProGlide and the Schick Hydro.

- We can interpret this competition as a prisoners' dilemma game.

- Table 1 shows the payoff matrix (millions of dollars of profit) for the game played by P&G and Energizer. (The numbers are hypothetical.)

- This game is a prisoners' dilemma like that on p. 345 and has a dominant-strategy Nash equilibrium.

- If P&G develops and markets a new razor, Energizer makes a larger profit by also developing and marketing a new razor (+$30 million versus –$60 million); and if P&G *doesn't* develop and market a new razor, Energizer again makes a larger profit by developing and marketing a new razor (+$90 million versus +$50 million).

- So Energizer's best strategy is to develop and market a new razor.

- If Energizer develops and markets a new razor, P&G makes a larger profit by also developing and marketing a new razor (+$75 million versus –$40 million); and if Energizer *doesn't* develop and market a new razor, P&G again makes a larger profit by developing and marketing a new razor (+$275 million versus +$175 million).

- So P&G's best strategy is to develop and market a new razor.

- Because both firms' best strategy is to develop and market a new razor, that is the equilibrium of the game.

- The firms are in a prisoners' dilemma because each would be better off avoiding the costly development and marketing costs and continuing to sell large quantities of their older style razor.

- With neither firm bringing the new razor to market, P&G would gain $100 million ($175 million versus $75 million) and Energizer would gain $20 million ($50 million versus $30 million).

- But each firm can see that if it doesn't bring a new razor to market, the other firm will and the consequence for the one that doesn't have a new razor will be a large loss.

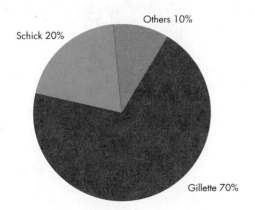

Figure 1 Market Shares in the High-Tech Razor Market

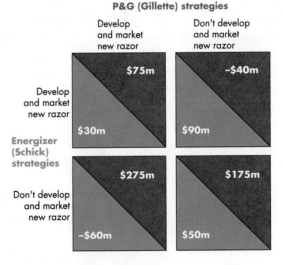

Table 1 P&G and Energizer in a Prisoners' Dilemma

SUMMARY

Key Points

What Is Oligopoly? (pp. 342–343)

- Oligopoly is a market in which a small number of firms compete.

Working Problems 1 to 3 will give you a better understanding of what oligopoly is.

Oligopoly Games (pp. 344–352)

- Oligopoly is studied by using game theory, which is a method of analysing strategic behaviour.
- In a prisoners' dilemma game, two prisoners acting in their own self-interest harm their joint interest.
- An oligopoly (duopoly) price-fixing game is a prisoners' dilemma in which the firms might collude or cheat.
- In Nash equilibrium, both firms cheat and output and price are the same as in perfect competition.
- Firms' decisions about advertising and R&D can be studied by using game theory.

Working Problems 4 to 7 will give you a better understanding of oligopoly games.

Repeated Games and Sequential Games (pp. 353–355)

- In a repeated game, a punishment strategy can produce a cooperative equilibrium in which price and output are the same as in a monopoly.
- In a sequential contestable market game, a small number of firms can behave like firms in perfect competition.

Working Problem 8 will give you a better understanding of repeated and sequential games.

Anti-Combine Law (pp. 356–359)

- Anti-combine law provides an alternative way for government to control monopoly and monopolistic practices.
- The Competition Act of 1986 sets out Canada's anti-combine law and established a Competition Bureau and a Competition Tribunal.
- Criminal activity is handled by the courts; violations of a noncriminal nature are examined by the Competition Tribunal.

Working Problems 9 to 11 will give you a better understanding of anti-combine law.

Key Terms

Anti-combine law, 356
Cartel, 343
Collusive agreement, 346
Contestable market, 354
Cooperative equilibrium, 353
Dominant-strategy equilibrium, 345
Duopoly, 342

Game theory, 344
Limit pricing, 355
Nash equilibrium, 345
Oligopoly,   342
Payoff matrix,   344
Strategies,   344

SCAN THIS

STUDY PLAN PROBLEMS AND APPLICATIONS

MyEconLab ◆ You can work Problems 1 to 12 in Chapter 15 Study Plan and get instant feedback.

What Is Oligopoly? (Study Plan 15.1)

1. Two firms make most of the chips that power a PC: Intel and Advanced Micro Devices. What makes the market for PC chips a duopoly? Sketch the market demand curve and cost curves that describe the situation in this market and that prevent other firms from entering.

2. **Sparks Fly for Energizer**

   Energizer is gaining market share against competitor Duracell and its profit is rising despite the sharp rise in the price of zinc, a key battery ingredient.

   Source: businessweek.com, August 2007

   In what type of market are batteries sold? Explain your answer.

3. **Oil City**

   In the late 1990s, Reliance spent $6 billion to build a world-class oil refinery at Jamnagar, India. Now Reliance is more than doubling the size of the facility, which will make it the world's biggest producer of gasoline —1.2 million gallons of gasoline per day, or about 5% of global capacity. Reliance plans to sell the gasoline in the United States and Europe where it's too expensive and politically difficult to build new refineries. The bulked-up Jamnagar will be able to move the market and Singapore traders expect a drop in fuel prices as soon as it's going at full steam.

   Source: *Fortune*, April 28, 2008

   a. Explain why the news clip claims that the global market for gasoline is not perfectly competitive.

   b. What barriers to entry might limit competition in this market and give a firm such as Reliance power to influence the market price?

Oligopoly Games (Study Plan 15.2)

4. Consider a game with two players who cannot communicate, and in which each player is asked a question. The players can answer the question honestly or lie. If both answer honestly, each receives $100. If one player answers honestly and the other lies, the liar receives $500 and the honest player gets nothing. If both lie, then each receives $50.

   a. Describe the strategies and payoffs of this game.

   b. Construct the payoff matrix.

   c. What is the equilibrium of this game?

   d. Compare this game to the prisoners' dilemma. Are the two games similar or different? Explain.

Use the following information to work Problems 5 and 6.

Soapy Inc. and Suddies Inc. are the only producers of soap powder. They collude and agree to share the market equally. If neither firm cheats on the agreement, each makes $1 million profit. If either firm cheats, the cheat makes a profit of $1.5 million, while the complier incurs a loss of $0.5 million. If both cheat, they break even. Neither firm can monitor the other's actions.

5. a. What are the strategies in this game?

   b. Construct the payoff matrix for this game.

6. a. What is the equilibrium of this game if it is played only once?

   b. Is the equilibrium a dominant-strategy equilibrium? Explain.

7. **The World's Largest Airline**

   On May 3, 2010, United Airlines and Continental Airlines announced a $3 billion merger that would create the world's biggest airline. The deal was completed in a remarkably short three weeks, and would give the airlines the muscle to fend off low-cost rivals at home and to take on foreign carriers abroad. For consumers, the merger could eventually result in higher prices although the new company does not intend to raise fares. One of the rationales for airline mergers is to cut capacity.

   Source: *The New York Times*, June 7, 2010

   a. Explain how this airline merger might increase air travel prices.

   b. Explain how this airline merger might lower air travel production costs.

   c. Explain how cost savings arising from a cut in capacity might get passed on to travellers and might boost producers' profits. Which do you predict will happen from this airline merger and why?

Repeated Games and Sequential Games
(Study Plan 15.3)

8. If Soapy Inc. and Suddies Inc. repeatedly play the duopoly game that has the payoffs described in Problem 5, on each round of play:
   a. What are the strategies that each firm might adopt?
   b. Can the firms adopt a strategy that gives the game a cooperative equilibrium?
   c. Would one firm still be tempted to cheat in a cooperative equilibrium? Explain your answer.

Anti-Combine Law (Study Plan 15.4)

9. **Rogers Woos iPhone Users with Discount Package; $30 a Month**

   Rogers Wireless Inc. caved to consumer pressure, temporarily slashing data fees on its smartphone plans just ahead of the carrier's launch of the iPhone 3G. Customers who sign up for the new iPhone between July 11, when it goes on sale, and the end of August will pay just $30 a month for access to six gigabytes of data usage. The 6-GB plan would enable a customer to send and receive more than 157,000 e-mails a month, or visit more than 35,000 Web pages. Users can now use the iPhone the way it was intended, but buyers will still have to sign a three-year contract with Rogers, and the new offer would be in addition to any voice plan a wireless customer subscribes to.

   Source: *The National Post*, July 10, 2008

   a. How does this arrangement between Rogers and Apple regarding the iPhone affect competition in the market for cell phone service?
   b. Does the iPhone arrangement between Rogers and Apple violate Canada's anti-combine law? Explain.

10. **Watchdog Impedes Airline Venture**

    The Competition Bureau has called a proposed joint venture between Air Canada and United Continental "effectively a merger" because it would create a monopoly on 10 major transborder routes and substantially reduce competition on nine others. A sufficient barrier to entry on 10 routes includes a lack of availability of landing slots, that would prevent new competitors from entering the market. The airlines argue that consumers would benefit from lower fares, improved schedules and more choice.

    Source: *The Financial Post*, June 28, 2011

    a. Think about the market for air travel on the 10 routes between Canada and the United States mentioned in the news clip and describe the game played by Air Canada and United Continental on these routes.
    b. With no merger between the two airlines, what would you expect the equilibrium price and output to be in this market?
    c. With a merger, how would you expect the equilibrium price and output to change?
    d. Would you expect a merger of the two airlines to be in the social interest? Explain.

11. **Competition Bureau Takes on Visa, MasterCard**

    Canada's largest credit card companies are facing a challenge from the Competition Bureau over fees they charge to merchants. Every time a transaction is processed, the credit card companies collect between 1.5 and 3 percent of the total amount of the transaction. The rules have eliminated competition between the rivals and driven up the cost to merchants, which ultimately affects the prices consumers pay.

    a. Think about the market for credit card payment services and describe the game played by Visa and MasterCard in this market.
    b. Explain why Visa and MasterCard might be able to operate in violation of the anti-combine law in this market.

Economics in the News (Study Plan 15.EN)

12. **Wireless Old Guard Faces New Rivals**

    Rogers, Bell, and Telus with 93 percent of the now $18-billion mobile industry are facing unexpectedly high pressure to slash fees on voice plans, in some cases offering customers unlimited calling time. Wind Mobile and Vidéotron have undercut them. Consumers are the beneficiaries, as they were intended to be when federal officials set course five years ago to jolt what many believed to be a static, overpriced sector into renewed competition by allowing a slew of new players to buy licences to operate.

    Source: *The Financial Post*, August 11, 2011

    a. What strategy is the owners of the new licences using to gain market share? What strategies are Rogers, Bell, and Telus using to counter the new competition?
    b. Explain the likely outcome of this increased competition in the long run on the price, quantity, and efficiency.

ADDITIONAL PROBLEMS AND APPLICATIONS

MyEconLab ◆ You can work these problems in MyEconLab if assigned by your instructor.

What Is Oligopoly?

13. **An Energy Drink with a Monster of a Stock**

    The $5.7 billion energy-drink category, in which Monster holds the No. 2 position behind industry leader Red Bull, has slowed down as copycat brands jostle for shelf space. Over the past five years Red Bull's market share in dollar terms has gone from 91 percent to well under 50 percent and much of that loss has been Monster's gain.

    Source: *Fortune*, December 25, 2006

    a. Describe the structure of the energy-drink market. How has that structure changed over the past few years?

    b. If Monster and Red Bull formed a cartel, how would the price charged for energy drinks and the profits made change?

Oligopoly Games

Use the following information to work Problems 14 and 15.

Bud and Wise are the only two producers of aniseed beer, a New Age product designed to displace root beer. Bud and Wise are trying to figure out how much of this new beer to produce. They know:

(i) If they both limit production to 10,000 litres a day, they will make the maximum attainable joint profit of $200,000 a day—$100,000 a day each.

(ii) If either firm produces 20,000 litres a day while the other produces 10,000 a day, the one that produces 20,000 litres will make an economic profit of $150,000 and the other one will incur an economic loss of $50,000.

(iii) If both increase production to 20,000 litres a day, each firm will make zero economic profit.

14. Construct a payoff matrix for the game that Bud and Wise must play.

15. Find the Nash equilibrium of the game that Bud and Wise play.

16. **Asian Rice Exporters to Discuss Cartel**

    The rice-exporting nations Thailand, Cambodia, Laos, and Myanmar planned to discuss a proposal by Thailand, the world's largest rice exporter, that they form a cartel. Ahead of the meeting, the countries said that the purpose of the rice cartel would be to contribute to ensuring food stability, not just in an individual country but also to address food shortages in the

region and the world. The cartel will not hoard rice and raise prices when there are shortages.

The Philippines says that it is a bad idea. It will create an oligopoly, and the cartel could price the grain out of reach for millions of people.

Source: CNN, May 6, 2008

a. Assuming the rice-exporting nations become a profit-maximizing colluding oligopoly, explain how they would influence the global market for rice and the world price of rice.

b. Assuming the rice-exporting nations become a profit-maximizing colluding oligopoly, draw a graph to illustrate their influence on the global market for rice.

c. Even in the absence of international anti-combine law, why might it be difficult for this cartel to successfully collude? Use the ideas of game theory to explain.

17. Suppose that Mozilla and Microsoft each develop their own versions of an amazing new Web browser that allows advertisers to target consumers with great precision. Also, the new browser is easier and more fun to use than existing browsers. Each firm is trying to decide whether to sell the browser or to give it away. What are the likely benefits from each action? Which action is likely to occur?

18. Why do Coca-Cola and PepsiCo spend huge amounts on advertising? Do they benefit? Does the consumer benefit? Explain your answer by constructing a game to illustrate the choices Coca-Cola and PepsiCo make.

Use the following information to work Problems 19 and 20.

Microsoft with Xbox 360, Nintendo with Wii, and Sony with PlayStation 3 are slugging it out in the market for the latest generation of video game consoles. Xbox 360 was the first to market; Wii has the lowest price; PS3 uses the most advanced technology and has the highest price.

19. a. Thinking of the competition among these firms in the market for consoles as a game, describe the firms' strategies concerning design, marketing, and price.

    b. What, based on the information provided, turned out to be the equilibrium of the game?

20. Can you think of reasons why the three consoles are so different?

Repeated Games and Sequential Games

21. If Bud and Wise in Problem 15 play the game repeatedly, what is the equilibrium of the game?

22. Agile Airlines' profit on a route on which it has a monopoly is $10 million a year. Wanabe Airlines is considering entering the market and operating on this route. Agile warns Wanabe to stay out and threatens to cut the price so that if Wanabe enters it will make no profit. Wanabe determines that the payoff matrix for the game in which it is engaged with Agile is shown in the table.

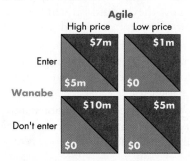

Does Wanabe believe Agile's assertion? Does Wanabe enter or not? Explain.

23. **Oil Trading Probe May Uncover Manipulation**

Amid soaring oil prices the Commodity Futures Trade Commission (CFTC) is looking into manipulation of the oil market—withholding oil in an attempt to drive prices higher. The CFTC has found such evidence in the past and it's likely it will find evidence again. But it is unlikely that a single player acting alone would be able to run the price up from $90 to $135.

Source: CNN, May 30, 2008

What type of market does the news clip imply best describes the U.S. oil market?

Anti-Combine Law

Use the following news clip to work Problems 24 and 25.

Gadgets for Sale … or Not

How come the prices of some gadgets, like the iPod, are the same no matter where you shop? No, the answer isn't that Apple illegally manages prices. In reality, Apple uses an accepted retail strategy called minimum advertised price to discourage resellers from discounting. The minimum advertised price (MAP) is the absolute lowest price of a product that resellers can advertise. MAP is usually enforced through marketing subsidies offered by a manufacturer to its resellers that keep the price at or above the MAP. Stable prices are important to the company that is both a manufacturer and a retailer. If Apple resellers advertised the iPod below cost, they could squeeze the Apple Stores out of their own markets. The downside to the price stability is that by limiting how low sellers can go, MAP keeps prices artificially high (or at least higher than they might otherwise be with unfettered price competition).

Source: *Slate*, December 22, 2006

24. a. Describe the practice of resale price maintenance that violates the anti-combine law.

    b. Describe the MAP strategy used by iPod and explain how it differs from a resale price maintenance agreement that would violate the anti-combine law.

25. Why might the MAP strategy be against the social interest and benefit only the producer?

Economics in the News

26. After you have studied *Reading Between the Lines* on pp. 360–361, answer the following questions.

    a. What are the strategies of P&G and Energizer in the market for high-tech razors?

    b. Why, according to the news article, would Energizer have a hard time competing with P&G?

    c. Why wouldn't Energizer stick with its old razor and leave P&G to incur the cost of developing and marketing a new one on its own?

    d. Could Energizer do something that would make the Schick Hydro the market leader? Would that action maximize Energizer's profit?

27. **Boeing and Airbus Predict Asian Sales Surge**

Airlines in the Asia-Pacific region are emerging as the biggest customers for aircraft makers Boeing and Airbus. The two firms predict that over the next 20 years, more than 8,000 planes worth up to $1.2 trillion will be sold there.

Source: BBC News, February 3, 2010

    a. In what type of market are big airplanes sold?

    b. Thinking of competition between Boeing and Airbus as a game, what are the strategies and the payoffs?

    c. Set out a hypothetical payoff matrix for the game you've described in part (b). What is the equilibrium of the game?

    d. Do you think the market for big airplanes is efficient? Explain and illustrate your answer.

Managing Change and Limiting Market Power

Our economy is constantly changing. Every year, new goods appear and old ones disappear. New firms are born and old ones die. This process of change is initiated and managed by firms operating in markets.

When a new product appears, just one or two firms sell it: Apple and IBM were the only producers of personal computers; Microsoft was (and almost still is) the only producer of the PC operating system; Intel was the only producer of the PC chip. These firms had enormous power to determine the quantity to produce and the price of their products.

In many markets, entry eventually brings competition. Even with just two rivals, the industry changes its face in a dramatic way. *Strategic interdependence* is capable of leading to an outcome like perfect competition.

With the continued arrival of new firms in an industry, the market becomes competitive. But in most markets, the competition isn't perfect: it becomes *monopolistic competition* with each firm selling its own differentiated product.

Often, an industry that is competitive becomes less so as the bigger and more successful firms in the industry begin to swallow up the smaller firms, either by driving them out of business or by acquiring their assets. Through this process, an industry might return to oligopoly or even monopoly. You can see such a movement in the auto and banking industries today.

By studying firms and markets, we gain a deeper understanding of the forces that allocate resources and begin to see the invisible hand at work.

John von Neumann *was one of the great minds of the twentieth century. Born in Budapest, Hungary, in 1903, Johnny, as he was known, showed early mathematical brilliance. He was 25 when he published the article that changed the social sciences and began a flood of research on* **game theory**—*a flood that has not subsided. In that article, von Neumann proved that in a zero-sum game (such as sharing a pie), there exists a best strategy for each player.*

Von Neumann did more than invent game theory: He also invented and built the first practical computer, and he worked on the Manhattan Project, which developed the atomic bomb during World War II.

Von Neumann believed that the social sciences would progress only if they used their own mathematical tools, not those of the physical sciences.

Real life consists of bluffing, of little tactics of deception, of asking yourself what is the other man going to think I mean to do.

JOHN VON NEUMANN, told to Jacob Bronowski (in a London taxi) and reported in *The Ascent of Man*

Professor Hubbard, why did you decide to become an economist and what attracted you to the empirical study of firms and markets? And why your special interest in the role of information?

I became an economist a little bit by accident. My first job coming out of undergrad was in an economic consulting firm. I'd never considered doing a PhD in economics before then. I didn't know any PhDs growing up. I don't come from an academic background. But working with PhD economists, I noticed that they were doing some pretty interesting things. They were looking at anti-competitive practices and regulatory stuff associated with the television and casino industries. What I saw when doing this work made me think that an academic job would be even better. I figured I'd go to graduate school to think about all of these interesting things.

When I went to graduate school I got interested in industrial organization. Now I did take a side trip. After doing my first year of graduate school, I took a year off. I spent it on the President's Council of Economic Advisers. That was loads of fun because it reminded me about what I like most about economics—applying it to understanding real-world problems. A typical first-year PhD program doesn't give you that sense. You are learning a lot of method and technique. But being thrust into a world where you have to skilfully use econ concepts has you very quickly using them and applying them to real-world policy discussions. I worked on the policy discussion surrounding environmental issues and that led to my dissertation.

Some economists who specialize in the study of firms and markets focus on theory and in particular game theory. Others, like you, have an empirical, data-driven approach. How do you see these two ways of studying, and seeking to understand, how firms and markets work?

I don't think my approach is all that data driven. It's problem driven. I think the core of economics is theory, not data. I think what I try to do is to be a strong consumer of theory, at least the theory that is relevant to the problems that I'm interested in. What I try to do with respect to my research is to find a circumstance where the theory is a good fit for the data and the data are a good fit for the theory. Both are good fits for the general question at hand.

My dissertation was about the expert services market. Famous examples of these are doctors and lawyers, but I looked at auto repair guys. In these markets, doctors know more than their patients about the patient's condition; lawyers know more than their clients about the client's condition. A lot of people have tried to study these markets in these contexts—especially the medical context. Well, coming out of my experience at the Council of Economic Advisers, I was exposed to a lower-brow expert service market—the market for auto emissions inspection.

> The core of economics is theory, not data. ... I try to be a ... consumer of ... the theory that is relevant to the problems that I'm interested in.

The basic economic issues for auto repair are pretty similar to the set of issues that doctors face. But data on auto repairers are far superior to data on physicians' services. When you investigate a specific expert services question with lots of good data you can discover how the organizational structure of firms and

THOMAS HUBBARD is the John L. and Helen Kellogg Distinguished Professor of Management and Strategy at the Kellogg School of Management, Northwestern University, and a research fellow at the National Bureau of Economic Research.

Professor Hubbard is an empirical economist. His work is driven by data. The central problems that unify much of his work are the limits to information and the fact that information is costly to obtain. Professor Hubbard studies the ways in which information problems influence the organization of firms; the extent to which firms make or buy what they sell; and the structure and performance of markets.

His work appears in the leading journals such as the *American Economic Review*, the *Quarterly Journal of Economics*, and the *Rand Journal of Economics*. He is a co-editor of the *Journal of Industrial Economics*.

Michael Parkin talked with Thomas Hubbard about his research and what we learn from it about the choices that firms make and their implications for market structure and performance.

the information environment affect the economic outcome. Doing things like that appeals to me.

Same way with trucking: I wrote a whole mass of papers about trucking. I was interested in the organization of firms and the organizational tradeoffs in the context of trucking happen to be manifested in very easy-to-understand and obvious ways. And you could get extremely good data, essentially close to the level of individual transactions.

Some people are good at creating theory and we need that work. But as I see it, good problem-driven economics needs three things: understanding the theory, understanding the institutional structure and evidence at hand, and integrating theory with institutional structure and data. It's fascinating when you can triangulate.

You have made important contributions to our understanding of the factors that determine whether a firm will make or buy. Can you summarize what we know about this question?

If there is one thing that Coase (Ronald Coase, see p. 411) taught us about the boundaries of the firm, it is that thinking about whether to do something internally or to outsource it is a very useful starting point is to make the decision on a transaction-by-transaction basis.

Most firms probably don't think at that level of detail. But still it's the right starting point because it gets you to think about the useful fact that activities have to be performed and they have to be performed either internally or externally. The way I like to think about it is to boil it down to the theory of markets and incentives.

Markets provide strong incentives but not necessarily good incentives. So when you outsource something, you rely on a market mechanism rather than on something within a firm that is less than a market mechanism. By outsourcing, you expose people to a strong market incentive. Now that can be good, and it is good most of the time. Strong market incentives get people to do things that the market rewards. Market rewards are generally quite valuable, but in some circumstances what the market rewards isn't what the buyer would want to reward. So there's a tradeoff. Strong incentives are sometimes good and sometimes bad. Therefore, keeping things inside the firm provides a weaker incentive. Sometimes that is good.

> Markets provide strong incentives but not necessarily good incentives.

Can you provide an example?

Think about McDonald's. McDonald's is not one firm. It is many firms because a lot of the outlets are owned and managed by franchisees and some are owned and managed internally by McDonald's.

McDonald's thinks about whether to run one of its restaurants itself or franchise it out. One thing that it has in mind is if it franchises it out, then the franchisor is going to be exposed to very strong market incentives. Now under some circumstances this is great. The franchisee treats the business as if he owns it. So the good part about it is the franchisee works hard to try to develop his business.

But there is a flip side to the franchisee treating the business as his own that can be harmful for the chain. For example, a franchisee might want to install a menu item that is locally popular but not globally accepted. Or putting this item on the menu might cause logistical problems elsewhere. There could be externalities, in other words. So a restaurant owned by a franchisee might not be the best option even though it provides good incentives in one dimension. Therefore, you might bring it inside and own the place yourself.

You've used the construction of the interstate highway system as a natural experiment through which to study the structure of the market for gasoline. Can you describe the question you posed and what you discovered?

The question is really pretty simple: How does an industry respond to an anticipated increase in demand? And how does this response differ depending on whether demand is in the same place—new demanders have the same preferences as older demanders did—or is in a different place—new demanders have different preferences than what the existing demanders have?

So I got thinking about this question and realized that the construction of the interstate highways provided a way of addressing it. The U.S. interstate highway system, an enormous public works project, was built slowly and steadily over the course of 20 years. Sometimes a new interstate highway would be close and parallel to an existing road and sometimes it would be several miles away from the road it replaced. So when a new highway was opened, it did either one or two things: When it was close by, it increased demand; when it was far away, it both increased demand and shifted demand spatially.

If the new highway was parallel to an existing road, it increased the volume of traffic along the route and increased the demand for gasoline in the corridor in which the highway was built. But when a new highway was some miles distant from the route it replaced, it shifted demand as well as increasing demand.

The unique thing about this research is we know exactly when a new highway opened, so we know the exact day that demand changed. We also know how many gas stations there were in that area and the time and the distribution of those gas stations. We can watch this over time. We can do this not just for one town. We can do this for hundreds of places as the highways developed over time.

So what we found is that the timing and the margin of the adjustment differed depending on whether the new highway was close to or far away from the old highway. When the highway was close, all the adjustment in demand was in larger firms, larger service stations. You didn't see any new service stations. You just saw bigger service stations. And

when the new highway was far away, you saw the adjustment to be in more service stations. So if you are a businessperson you're thinking about changes in demand and if entry opportunities occur when new demand comes, will they tend to occur when the new demanders have different demands than the existing ones?

As far as timing goes we saw something a little surprising. When the highway was opened near the existing route, you see that the adjustment takes place before the highway even opened. When I said that you saw larger gas stations once the highway is opened close to the old route, you saw this starting to happen two to three years before the highway actually opened. By the time the highway opened, most of the adjustments had already taken place.

But when the highway was opened far from the existing road, the opposite was true—all the action happened after the highway opened.

You've given us a wonderful glimpse into the fascinating research of a problem-driven economist who creatively finds rich data. Let's end with your advice to a student who is just starting to study economics. What makes it a good subject in which to major?

Watch what I do, not what I say! When I took my first economics course in my freshman year my reaction to it was "Wow, this explains everything." I took an undergraduate micro course. Just seeing supply curves and demand curves was wonderful. I thought economics explained things in ways that other disciplines didn't do. And the truth is although I'm a specialist in industrial organization and we've been talking about game theory and so on and so forth, the power of introductory micro is astounding. In most of the economic questions that I encounter outside of my role as a researcher, essentially I'm deploying undergraduate introductory microeconomics but at a really high level. So understanding microeconomics extremely deeply is going to be useful to anybody that works for a living. You always have to deal with your demanders. You always have to deal with prices and competition. You'll take your first course and you'll have some ability to use these tools. But understanding at some extraordinary deep level takes a career to do really well, but the returns are always positive.

> ... understanding microeconomics is useful to anybody that works for a living.

PART FIVE Market Failure and Government

CHAPTER
16

Externalities

After studying this chapter, you will be able to

◆ Explain how externalities arise

◆ Explain why negative externalities lead to inefficient overproduction and the actions that might achieve an efficient outcome

◆ Explain why positive externalities lead to inefficient underproduction and the actions that might achieve an efficient outcome

We burn huge quantities of fossil fuels—coal, natural gas, and oil—that increase the amount of carbon dioxide in our atmosphere. How can we take account of our carbon footprint when we turn on our heating or air-conditioning or take a trip by car, bus, or airplane?

Everyone benefits from the discoveries of smart scientists and engineers, and from living with other well-educated people. Do we spend enough on education and research to enjoy enough of these benefits?

In this chapter, we study the problems that arise because many of our actions impose costs on or bring benefits to other people in ways that we don't take into account when we make our own choices. In *Reading Between the Lines* at the end of the chapter, we look at the effects of a carbon tax designed to lower carbon emissions and address climate change.

Externalities in Our Lives

An **externality** is a *cost or a benefit* that arises from *production* and falls on someone other than the producer, or a *cost or benefit* that arises from *consumption* and falls on someone other than the consumer. We call an externality that imposes a cost a **negative externality**; and we call an externality that provides a benefit a **positive externality**.

We identify externalities as four types:

- Negative production externalities
- Negative consumption externalities
- Positive production externalities
- Positive consumption externalities

Negative Production Externalities

Congestion, pollution, and carbon emission are the sources of the most costly and widespread negative production externalities.

Congestion Every weekday morning and afternoon, Highway 401, which runs across the north of Toronto, slows to a crawl as trucks and commuters compete for position on what looks like an extensive parking lot.

The costs of congestion are time costs and fuel costs. Drivers and their passengers spend extra hours sitting in stalled traffic, burning additional fuel. Each rush-hour user of Highway 401 imposes a cost on the other users. This cost is a negative production externality.

The economic analysis of externalities looks at alternative ways of dealing with problems such as the cost of congestion on Highway 401.

Pollution and Carbon Emission When you run your air-conditioning, use hot water, drive a car, take a trip by airplane, or even ride a bus or train, your action contributes to pollution and increases your carbon footprint.

Economic activity pollutes air, water, and land, and these individual areas of pollution interact through the *ecosystem*.

Air Pollution Sixty percent of our air pollution comes from road transportation and industrial processes. Only 20 percent arises from electric power generation. See the trends in U.S. air pollution since 1980 in *Economics in Action* below.

A common belief is that air pollution is getting worse. In many developing countries, air pollution is getting worse. The rapid economic development of

Economics in Action
Air Pollution Trends: Cleaner and Safer

The figure shows the percentage changes in the concentrations of six air pollutants between 1990 and 2008 and their economic sources. All of these pollutants decreased.

These reductions in air pollution are more impressive when they are seen against the trends in economic activity. Between 1990 and 2008, total production in the United States increased by 66 percent, vehicle miles travelled increased by 40 percent, and the population increased by 20 percent.

The U.S. Clean Air Act has brought regulations that cut emissions of carbon monoxide, volatile organic compounds, oxides of nitrogen, sulphur dioxide, and particulate matter to around a half of their 1990 levels. And economic actions that you will learn about in this chapter almost eliminated lead from highways and industrial processes.

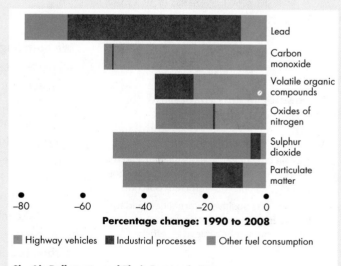

Six Air Pollutants and Their Economic Sources

Source of data: Latest Findings on National Air Quality: Status and Trends through 2008, United States Environmental Protection Agency, www.epa.gov/air/airtrends/2010/report/airpollution.pdf.

China has created a serious air quality problem for Beijing. During the 2008 Olympics, construction activity was halted and factories closed in an attempt to provide temporary relief from air that would endanger the health of athletes.

But air pollution in the world's richest countries is getting less severe for most substances. Air pollution has been on a downward trend for more than 30 years.

In contrast to the trends in air pollution, carbon emissions and emissions of other global warming gases such as methane are on the increase, and consequently the carbon dioxide concentration in the Earth's atmosphere is increasing at an unprecedented pace.

The costs of air pollution and carbon emission are high and widespread. Sulphur dioxide and nitrogen oxide emissions from coal-fired and oil-fired generators of electric utilities cause acid rain, which damages trees and crops. Airborne substances such as lead from leaded gasoline are believed to cause cancer and other life-threatening conditions. Depletion of the ozone layer exposes us to higher doses of cancer-causing ultraviolet rays from the sun. And most costly of all, the increased carbon concentration is bringing global warming and potentially extremely costly climate change.

Some technological changes to cut costs, lessen air pollution, and slow the carbon build up are possible either now or with further research and development.

Road vehicles can be made "greener" with new fuels including ethanol, alcohol, natural gas, propane and butane, and hydrogen. Vehicles can also be powered by electricity or batteries. But whether this change lessens air pollution and carbon emissions depends on how electricity is produced.

Economics in Action
The Greatest Market Failure?

British economist Nicholas Stern reviewed the science and economics of global warming and climate change for the United Kingdom government and his report, the *Stern Review on the Economics of Climate Change,* attracted much attention. Stern calls climate change "the greatest market failure the world has ever seen."

As the figure shows, global temperature and carbon dioxide (CO_2) trends are starkly upward. Stern says that to avoid the risk of catastrophic climate change, this upward trend must be stopped.

Scientists debate the contribution of human economic activity to these trends, but most say it is the major source. Although ice-core estimates show long swings in CO_2 concentration, the recent increase is the most rapid recorded.

The cost of achieving Stern's target is high, estimated at 1 percent of the value of global production. If this cost is to be met by the people who live in the rich countries, and realistically they are the only ones who can afford to pay, it will cost about $750 per person every year.

Some economists question Stern's assumptions and conclusions and argue that the cost of reducing emissions will be much lower if we go a bit more slowly and take advantage of future technological

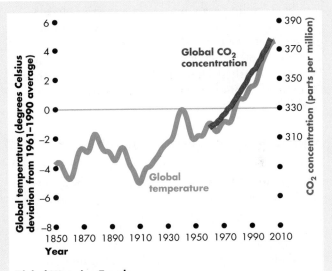

Global Warming Trends

Sources of data: Met Office Hadley Centre and Scripps Institution of Oceanography.

advances that will lower the cost of renewable energy sources—the sun, tide, and wind.

All economists agree that solving the global warming problem will require changes in the incentives that people face. The cost of carbon-emitting activities must rise and the cost of the search for new energy technologies must fall. A carbon tax or tradeable carbon permits are two possible ways of addressing this problem.

Pollution-free electricity can be generated by harnessing wind power, solar power, tidal power, or geothermal power. Another alternative is nuclear power. This method is good for air pollution but creates a potential long-term problem for land and water pollution because there is no known entirely safe method of disposing of spent nuclear fuel.

Water Pollution The dumping of industrial waste and untreated sewage and the runoff from fertilizers pollute oceans, lakes, and rivers. There are two main alternatives to polluting the waterways and oceans. One is the chemical processing of waste to render it inert or biodegradable. The other, in wide use for nuclear waste, is to use land sites for storage in secure containers.

Land Pollution Land pollution arises from dumping toxic waste products. Ordinary household garbage does not pose a pollution problem unless contaminants from dumped garbage seep into the water supply. Recycling is an apparently attractive alternative, but it requires an investment in new technologies to be effective. Incineration is a high-cost alternative to landfill, and it produces air pollution. Furthermore, these alternatives are not free, and they become efficient only when the cost of using landfill is high.

Negative Consumption Externalities

Negative consumption externalities are a source of irritation for most of us. Smoking tobacco in a confined space creates fumes that many people find unpleasant and that pose a health risk. Smoking creates a negative consumption externality. To deal with this externality, in many places and in almost all public places, smoking is banned. But banning smoking imposes a negative consumption externality on smokers! The majority imposes a cost on the minority—the smokers who would prefer to consume tobacco while dining or taking a plane trip.

Noisy parties and outdoor rock concerts are other examples of negative consumption externalities. They are also examples of the fact that a simple ban on an activity is not a solution. Banning noisy parties avoids the external cost on sleep-seeking neighbours, but it results in the sleepers imposing an external cost on the fun-seeking partygoers.

Permitting dandelions to grow in lawns, not picking up leaves in the fall, and allowing a dog to bark loudly or to foul a neighbour's lawn are other sources of negative consumption externalities.

Positive Production Externalities

If a honey farmer places beehives beside an orange grower's orchard, two positive production externalities arise. The honey farmer gets a positive production externality from the orange grower because the bees collect pollen and nectar from orange blossoms. And the orange grower gets a positive production externality because the bees pollinate the blossoms.

Positive Consumption Externalities

When you get a flu vaccination, you lower your risk of getting infected this winter. But if you avoid the flu, your neighbour who didn't get vaccinated has a better chance of avoiding it too. Flu vaccination generates positive consumption externalities.

When the owner of a historic building restores it, everyone who sees the building gets pleasure from it. Similarly, when someone erects a spectacular house—such as those built in Montreal's "Golden Square Mile" in the 1800s—or another exciting building—such as the CN Tower in Toronto—an external consumption benefit flows to everyone who has an opportunity to view it. Education, which we examine in this chapter, is another example of this type of externality.

◣ REVIEW QUIZ

1 What are the four types of externality?
2 Provide an example of each type of externality that is different from the ones described above.
3 How are the externalities you've identified addressed, either by the market or by public policy?

You can work these questions in Study Plan 16.1 and get instant feedback.

───────────────────── MyEconLab ◆

We've described the four types of externalities and provided some examples of each. Pollution is the most important of the negative externalities and it is this example that we use to study the economics of external costs.

Negative Externality: Pollution

To study the economics of negative externalities that arise from pollution, we distinguish between the private cost and the social cost of production.

Private Cost and Social Cost

A *private cost* of production is a cost that is borne by the producer of a good or service. *Marginal cost* is the cost of producing an *additional unit* of a good or service. So **marginal private cost** (*MC*) is the cost of producing an additional unit of a good or service that is borne by its producer.

An *external cost* is a cost of producing a good or service that is *not* borne by the producer but borne by other people. A **marginal external cost** is the cost of producing an additional unit of a good or service that falls on people other than the producer.

Marginal social cost (*MSC*) is the marginal cost incurred by the producer and by everyone else on whom the cost falls—by society. It is the sum of marginal private cost and marginal external cost. That is,

$$MSC = MC + \text{Marginal external cost.}$$

We express costs in dollars, but we must always remember that a cost is an opportunity cost—something real, such as clean air or a clean river, is given up to get something.

Valuing an External Cost Economists use market prices to put a dollar value on the cost of pollution. For example, suppose that there are two similar rivers, one polluted and the other clean. Five hundred identical homes are built along the side of each river. The homes on the clean river rent for $2,500 a month, and those on the polluted river rent for $1,500 a month. If the pollution is the only detectable difference between the two rivers and the two locations, the rent decrease of $1,000 per month is the cost of the pollution. With 500 homes on the polluted river, the external cost of pollution is $500,000 a month.

External Cost and Output Figure 16.1 shows an example of the relationship between output and cost in a chemical industry that pollutes. The marginal cost curve, *MC*, describes the marginal private cost borne by the firms that produce the chemical. Marginal cost increases as the quantity of chemical

produced increases. If the firms dump waste into a river, they impose an external cost that increases with the amount of the chemical produced. The marginal social cost curve, *MSC*, is found by adding the marginal external cost to the marginal private cost. So a point on the *MSC* curve shows the sum of the marginal private cost of producing a given output and marginal external cost created. For example, when the chemical industry produces 4,000 tonnes of chemical a month, its marginal private cost is $100 a tonne and the marginal external cost is $125 a tonne, so the marginal social cost is $225 a tonne.

In Fig. 16.1, when the quantity of chemical produced increases, the amount of pollution increases and the external cost of pollution increases.

Figure 16.1 shows the relationship between the quantity of chemical produced and the cost of the pollution it creates, but it doesn't tell us how much pollution the chemical industry creates. That quantity depends on the quantity of the chemical produced, which depends on supply and demand in the market for the chemical. We now look at that market.

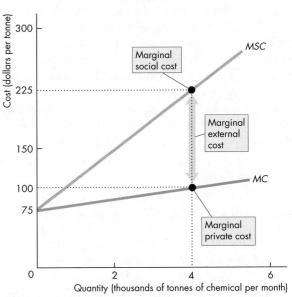

FIGURE 16.1   An External Cost

The *MC* curve shows the marginal private cost borne by the factories that produce a chemical. The *MSC* curve shows the sum of marginal private cost and marginal external cost. When output is 4,000 tonnes of chemical a month, marginal private cost is $100 a tonne, marginal external cost is $125 a tonne, and marginal social cost is $225 a tonne.

MyEconLab animation

Production and Pollution: How Much?

When an industry is unregulated and free to pollute, the amount of pollution it creates depends on the market equilibrium price and quantity of the good produced. In Fig. 16.2, the demand curve for a pollution-creating chemical is *D*. This curve also measures the marginal social benefit, *MSB*, from the chemical. The supply curve of the chemical is *S*. This curve also measures the producers' marginal private cost, *MC*. The supply curve is the marginal private cost curve because when firms make their production and supply decisions, they consider only the costs that they will bear. Market equilibrium occurs at a price of $100 a tonne and 4,000 tonnes of chemical a month.

This equilibrium is inefficient. You learned in Chapter 5 that the allocation of resources is efficient when marginal social benefit equals marginal social cost. But we must count *all* the costs—private and external—when we compare marginal social benefit and marginal social cost. So with an external cost, the allocation is efficient when marginal social benefit equals marginal *social* cost. This outcome occurs when the quantity of chemical produced is 2,000 tonnes a month. The unregulated market overproduces by 2,000 tonnes of chemical a month and creates a deadweight loss shown by the grey triangle.

How can the people who live by the polluted river get the chemical factories to decrease their output of chemical and create less pollution? If some method can be found to achieve this outcome, everyone—the owners of the chemical factories and the residents of the riverside homes—can gain. Let's explore some solutions.

Property Rights

Sometimes it is possible to reduce the inefficiency arising from an external cost by establishing a property right where one does not currently exist. **Property rights** are legally established titles to the ownership, use, and disposal of factors of production and goods and services that are enforceable in the courts.

Suppose that the chemical factories own the river and the 500 homes alongside it. The rent that people are willing to pay depends on the amount of pollution. Using the earlier example, people are willing to pay $2,500 a month to live alongside a pollution-free river but only $1,500 a month to live with the pollution created by 4,000 tonnes of chemical a month. If the factories produce this quantity, they

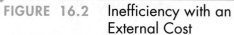

FIGURE 16.2   Inefficiency with an External Cost

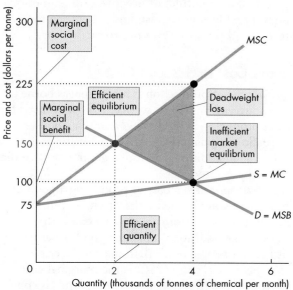

The market supply curve is the factories' marginal private cost curve, *S = MC*. The market demand curve is the marginal social benefit curve, *D = MSB*. The market equilibrium occurs at a price of $100 a tonne and 4,000 tonnes of chemical a month This market outcome is inefficient because marginal social cost exceeds marginal social benefit. The efficient quantity of chemical is 2,000 tonnes a month. The grey triangle shows the deadweight loss created by the pollution.

MyEconLab   animation

lose $1,000 a month for each home for a total of $500,000 a month. The chemical factories are now confronted with the cost of their pollution—forgone rent from the people who live by the river.

Figure 16.3 illustrates the outcome by using the same example as in Fig. 16.2. With property rights in place, the *MC* curve no longer measures all the costs that the factories face in producing the chemical. It excludes the pollution costs that they must now bear. The *MSC* curve now becomes the factories' marginal private cost curve *MC*. The factories bear all the costs, so the market supply curve based on all the costs is the curve labelled *S = MC = MSC*.

Market equilibrium now occurs at a price of $150 a tonne and 2,000 tonnes of chemical a month. This outcome is efficient. The factories still produce some pollution, but it is the efficient quantity.

FIGURE 16.3   Property Rights Achieve an Efficient Outcome

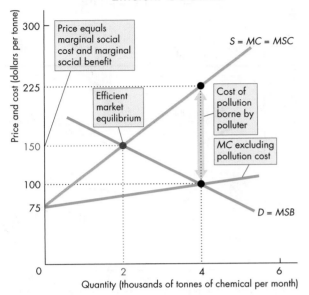

With property rights, the marginal cost curve that excludes pollution costs shows only part of the producers' marginal cost. The marginal cost of producing the chemical now includes the cost of pollution—the external cost. So the producers' supply curve is $S = MC = MSC$. The market equilibrium now occurs at a price of $150 a tonne and 2,000 tonnes of chemical a month. This outcome is efficient because marginal social cost equals marginal social benefit. The pollution created is not zero, but it is the efficient quantity.

————— MyEconLab   animation ◆

The Coase Theorem

Does it matter how property rights are assigned? Does it matter whether the polluter or the victim of the pollution owns the resource that might be polluted? Until 1960, everyone thought that it did matter. But in 1960, Ronald Coase (see p. 413) had a remarkable insight, now called the Coase theorem.

The **Coase theorem** is the proposition that if property rights exist, if only a small number of parties are involved, and if transactions costs are low, then private transactions are efficient. There are no externalities because the transacting parties take all the costs and benefits into account. Furthermore, it doesn't matter who has the property rights.

Application of the Coase Theorem In the example that we've just studied, the factories own the river and the homes. Suppose that instead, the residents own their homes and the river. Now the factories must pay a fee to the homeowners for the right to dump their waste. The greater the quantity of waste dumped into the river, the more the factories must pay. So again, the factories face the opportunity cost of the pollution they create. The quantity of chemical produced and the amount of waste dumped are the same whoever owns the homes and the river. If the factories own them, they bear the cost of pollution because they receive a lower income from home rents. If the residents own the homes and the river, the factories bear the cost of pollution because they must pay a fee to the homeowners. In both cases, the factories bear the cost of their pollution and dump the efficient amount of waste into the river.

The Coase solution works only when transactions costs are low. **Transactions costs** are the opportunity costs of conducting a transaction. For example, when you buy a house, you incur a series of transactions costs. You might pay a realtor to help you find the best place and a lawyer to run checks that assure you that the seller owns the property and that after you've paid for it, the ownership has been properly transferred to you.

In the example of the homes alongside a river, the transactions costs that are incurred by a small number of chemical factories and a few homeowners might be low enough to enable them to negotiate the deals that produce an efficient outcome. But in many situations, transactions costs are so high that it would be inefficient to incur them. In these situations, the Coase solution is not available.

Suppose, for example, that everyone owns the airspace above their homes up to, say, 10 kilometres. If someone pollutes your airspace, you can charge a fee. But to collect the fee, you must identify who is polluting your airspace and persuade them to pay you. Imagine the costs of negotiating and enforcing agreements with the 300 million people who live in Canada and the United States and the several thousand factories that emit sulphur dioxide and create acid rain that falls on your property! In this situation, we use public choices to cope with external costs. But the transactions costs that block a market solution are real costs, so attempts by the government to deal with external costs offer no easy solution. Let's look at some of these attempts.

Government Actions in a Market with External Costs

The three main methods that governments use to cope with external costs are

- Taxes
- Emission charges
- Cap-and-trade

Taxes   The government can use taxes as an incentive for producers to cut back the pollution they create. Taxes used in this way are called **Pigovian taxes**, in honour of Arthur Cecil Pigou, the British economist who first worked out this method of dealing with external costs during the 1920s.

By setting the tax equal to the marginal external cost, firms can be made to behave in the same way as they would if they bore the cost of the externality directly. To see how government actions can change the outcome in a market with external costs, let's return to the example of the chemical factories and the river.

Assume that the government has assessed the marginal external cost accurately and imposes a tax on the factories that exactly equals this cost. Figure 16.4 illustrates the effects of this tax.

The demand curve and marginal social benefit curve, $D = MSB$, and the firms' marginal cost curve, MC, are the same as in Fig. 16.2. The pollution tax equals the marginal external cost of the pollution. We add this tax to the marginal private cost to find the market supply curve. This curve is the one labelled $S = MC + tax = MSC$. This curve is the market supply curve because it tells us the quantity supplied at each price given the firms' marginal cost and the tax they must pay. This curve is also the marginal social cost curve because the pollution tax has been set equal to the marginal external cost.

Demand and supply now determine the market equilibrium price at $150 a tonne and a quantity of 2,000 tonnes of chemical a month. At this quantity of chemical production, the marginal social cost is $150 and the marginal social benefit is $150, so the outcome is efficient. The firms incur a marginal private cost of $88 a tonne and pay a tax of $62 a tonne. The government collects tax revenue of $124,000 a month.

Emission Charges   Emission charges are an alternative to a tax for confronting a polluter with the external cost of pollution. The government sets a

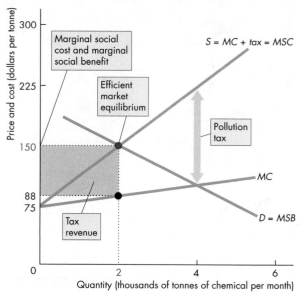

FIGURE 16.4   A Pollution Tax to Achieve an Efficient Outcome

When the government imposes a pollution tax equal to the marginal external cost of pollution, the supply curve becomes the marginal private cost curve, MC, plus the tax—the curve $S = MC + tax$. Market equilibrium occurs at a price of $150 a tonne and a quantity of 2,000 tonnes of chemical a month. This equilibrium is efficient because marginal social cost equals marginal social benefit. The purple rectangle shows the government's tax revenue.

──────── MyEconLab   ⬤animation ◆

price per unit of pollution. The more pollution a firm creates, the more it pays in emission charges. This method of dealing with pollution externalities has been used only modestly in North America but is common in Europe where, for example, France, Germany, and the Netherlands make water polluters pay a waste disposal charge.

To work out the emission charge that achieves efficiency, the government needs information about the polluting industry that, in practice, is rarely available.

Cap-and-Trade   Instead of taxing or imposing emission charges on polluters, each potential polluter might be assigned a permitted pollution limit. Each firm knows its own costs and its benefits from pollution, and making pollution limits marketable is a clever way of using this private information that is unknown to the government. The government issues each firm a permit to emit a certain amount of pollution, and firms can trade these permits. Firms that have a low marginal cost of reducing pollution sell their permits, and firms that have a high marginal cost of reducing pollution buy permits. The market in permits determines the price at which firms trade permits. Each firm buys or sells permits until its marginal cost of pollution equals the market price of a permit.

This method of dealing with pollution provides an even stronger incentive than emission charges to find lower-polluting technologies because the price of a pollution permit rises as the demand for permits increases.

A Real-World Market for Emission Permits

Environment Canada has not used marketable permits, but the Environmental Protection Agency (EPA) in the United States has. The EPA first implemented air quality programs following the passage of the Clean Air Act in 1970.

Trading in lead pollution permits became common during the 1980s, and this marketable permit program has been rated a success. It enabled lead to be virtually eliminated from the atmosphere. But this success might not easily translate to other situations because lead pollution has some special features. First, most lead pollution came from a single source: leaded gasoline. Second, lead in gasoline is easily monitored. Third, the objective was clear: to eliminate lead in gasoline. The EPA is now considering using marketable permits to promote efficiency in the control of chlorofluorocarbons—the gases that are believed to damage the ozone layer.

REVIEW QUIZ

1 What is the distinction between private cost and social cost?
2 How do external costs prevent a competitive market from allocating resources efficiently?
3 How can external costs be eliminated by assigning property rights?
4 How do taxes help us to cope with external costs? At what level must a pollution tax be set to be efficient?
5 How do emission charges and marketable pollution permits work?

You can work these questions in Study Plan 16.2 and get instant feedback.

━━━━━━━━━━ MyEconLab ◆

◆ Positive Externality: Knowledge

Knowledge comes from education and research. To study the economics of knowledge, we distinguish between private benefits and social benefits.

Private Benefits and Social Benefits

A *private benefit* is a benefit that the consumer of a good or service receives. *Marginal benefit* is the benefit from an *additional unit* of a good or service. So **marginal private benefit** (*MB*) is the benefit that the consumer of a good or service receives from an additional unit of it.

The *external benefit* from a good or service is the benefit that someone other than the consumer of the good or service receives. University graduates generate many external benefits. On average, they are better citizens, have lower crime rates, and are more tolerant of the views of others. They enable the success of high quality newspapers and television channels, music, theatre, and other organized social activities that bring benefits to many other people.

A **marginal external benefit** is the benefit from an additional unit of a good or service that people *other than its consumer* enjoy. The benefit that your friends and neighbours get from your university education is its marginal external benefit.

Marginal social benefit (*MSB*) is the marginal benefit enjoyed by society—by the consumer of a good or service (marginal private benefit) and by others (the marginal external benefit). That is,

$$MSB = MB + \text{Marginal external benefit}.$$

Figure 16.5 shows an example of the relationship between marginal private benefit, marginal external benefit, and marginal social benefit. The marginal benefit curve, *MB*, describes the marginal private benefit enjoyed by the people who receive a university education. Marginal private benefit decreases as the number of students enrolled increases.

In the example in Fig. 16.5, when 15 million students enroll in university, the marginal external benefit is $15,000 per student per year. The marginal social benefit curve, *MSB*, is the sum of marginal private benefit and marginal external benefit at each number of students. For example, when 15 million students a year enroll, the marginal private benefit is $10,000 per student and the marginal external benefit is $15,000 per student, so the marginal social benefit is $25,000 per student.

FIGURE 16.5 An External Benefit

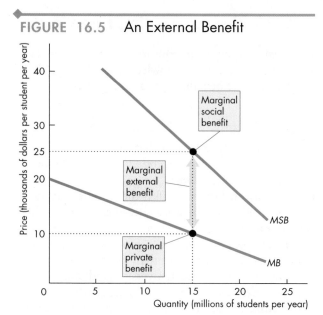

The *MB* curve shows the marginal private benefit enjoyed by the people who receive a college education. The *MSB* curve shows the sum of marginal private benefit and marginal external benefit. When 15 million students attend university, the marginal private benefit is $10,000 per student, the marginal external benefit is $15,000 per student, and the marginal social benefit is $25,000 per student.

——————MyEconLab animation ◆

FIGURE 16.6 Inefficiency with an External Benefit

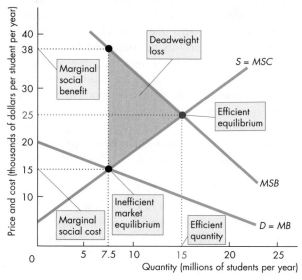

The market demand curve is the marginal private benefit curve, *D = MB*. The supply curve is the marginal social cost curve, *S = MSC*. Market equilibrium at a tuition of $15,000 a year and 7.5 million students is inefficient because marginal social benefit exceeds marginal social cost. The efficient quantity is 15 million students. A deadweight loss arises (grey triangle) because too few students enroll in college.

——————MyEconLab animation ◆

When people make schooling decisions, they ignore its external benefits and consider only their private benefits. So if education were provided by private schools that charged full-cost tuition, the market would produce too few graduates.

Figure 16.6 illustrates this private underprovision. The supply curve is the marginal social cost curve, *S = MSC*. The demand curve is the marginal *private* benefit curve, *D = MB*. Market equilibrium occurs at a tuition of $15,000 per student per year with 7.5 million students per year. At this equilibrium, the marginal social benefit of $38,000 per student exceeds the marginal social cost by $23,000 per student. Too few students enroll in university. The efficient number is 15 million per year, where marginal social benefit equals marginal social cost. The grey triangle shows the deadweight loss created.

Underproduction similar to that in Fig. 16.6 would occur in elementary school and high school if public education was left to an unregulated market. When children learn basic reading, writing, and number skills, they receive the private benefit of increased earning power. But even these basic skills bring the external benefit of developing better citizens.

External benefits also arise from the discovery of new knowledge. When Isaac Newton worked out the formulas for calculating the rate of response of one variable to another—calculus—everyone was free to use his method. When a spreadsheet program called VisiCalc was invented, Lotus Corporation and Microsoft were free to copy the basic idea and create 1-2-3 and Excel. When the first shopping mall was built and found to be a successful way of arranging retailing, everyone was free to copy the idea, and malls sprouted like mushrooms.

Once someone has discovered a basic idea, others can copy it. Because they do have to work to copy an idea, they face an opportunity cost, but they do not usually have to pay a fee for the idea. When people make decisions, they ignore the external benefits and consider only the private benefits.

When people make decisions about the amount of education or research to undertake, they balance the marginal private cost against the marginal private benefit. They ignore the external benefit. As a result, if we left education and research to unregulated market forces, we would get too little of these activities.

To get closer to producing the efficient quantity of a good with an external benefit, we make public choices, through governments, to modify the market outcome.

Government Actions in the Face of External Benefits

Four devices that governments can use to achieve a more efficient allocation of resources in the presence of external benefits are

- Public production
- Private subsidies
- Vouchers
- Patents and copyrights

Public Production   With **public production**, a good or service is produced by a public authority that receives its revenue from the government. The education services produced by public universities and colleges and public schools are examples of public production.

Figure 16.7(a) shows how public production might overcome the underprovision that arises in

---

FIGURE 16.7   Public Production or Private Subsidy to Achieve an Efficient Outcome

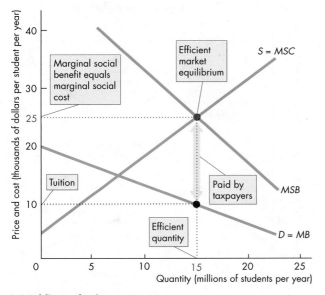

(a) Public production

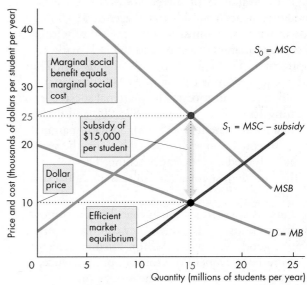

(b) Private subsidy

In part (a), marginal social benefit equals marginal social cost with 15 million students enrolled per year, the efficient quantity. Tuition is set at $10,000 per student per year equal to marginal private benefit. Taxpayers cover the other $15,000 of cost per student per year.

In part (b), with a subsidy of $15,000 per student, the supply curve is $S_1 = MSC -$ subsidy. The equilibrium price is $10,000 per year, and the market equilibrium is efficient with 15 million students enrolled per year. Marginal social benefit equals marginal social cost.

Fig. 16.6. Public provision cannot lower the cost of production, so marginal social cost is the same as before. Marginal private benefit and marginal external benefit are also the same as before.

The efficient quantity occurs where marginal social benefit equals marginal social cost. In Fig. 16.7(a), this quantity is 15 million students. Tuition is set to ensure that the efficient number of students enrolls. That is, tuition is set equal to the marginal private benefit at the efficient quantity. In Fig. 16.7(a), tuition is $10,000 a year. The rest of the cost of the public university is borne by the taxpayers and, in this example, is $15,000 per student per year.

Private Subsidies A **subsidy** is a payment that the government makes to private producers. By making the subsidy depend on the level of output, the government can induce private decision makers to consider external benefits when they make their choices.

Figure 16.7(b) shows how a subsidy to private colleges works. In the absence of a subsidy, the market supply curve is $S_0 = MSC$. The demand curve is the marginal private benefit curve, $D = MB$. If the government provides a subsidy to colleges of $15,000 per student per year, we must subtract the subsidy from the colleges' marginal cost to find the new market supply curve. That curve is $S_1 = MSC - subsidy$. The market equilibrium is tuition of $10,000 a year and 15 million students a year. The marginal social cost of educating 15 million students is $25,000 and the marginal social benefit is $25,000. So with marginal social cost equal to marginal social benefit, the subsidy has achieved an efficient outcome. The tuition and the subsidy just cover the colleges' marginal cost.

Vouchers A **voucher** is a token that the government provides to households, which they can use to buy specified goods or services. Milton Friedman, recipient of the 1976 Nobel Prize for economic science, long advocated vouchers as a means of providing parents with greater choice and control over the education of their children. Some people advocate them for college and university so that students can both receive financial help and exercise choice.

A school voucher allows parents to choose the school their children will attend and to use the voucher to pay part of the cost. The school cashes the vouchers to pay its bills. A voucher provided to a university student would work in a similar way. Because vouchers can be spent only on a specified

item, they increase the willingness to pay for that item and so increase the demand for it.

Figure 16.8 shows how a voucher system works. The government provides a voucher per student equal to the marginal external benefit. Parents (or students) use these vouchers to supplement the dollars they pay for education. The marginal social benefit curve becomes the demand for college education, $D = MSB$. The market equilibrium occurs at a price of $25,000 per student per year, and 15 million students attend college. Each student pays $10,000 tuition, and schools collect an additional $15,000 per student from the voucher.

If the government estimates the value of the external benefit correctly and makes the value of the voucher equal the marginal external benefit, the outcome from the voucher scheme is efficient. Marginal social cost equals marginal social benefit, and the deadweight loss is eliminated.

FIGURE 16.8   An Efficient Outcome with an External Benefit

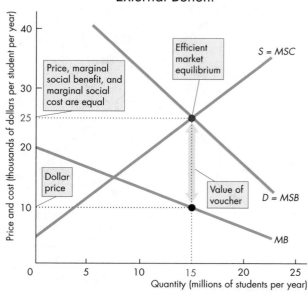

The efficient number of students is 15 million, where marginal social benefit equals marginal social cost. With the demand and marginal private benefit curve, $D = MB$, the price at which the efficient number will enroll is $10,000 per year. If students pay this price, the taxpayer must somehow pay the rest, which equals the marginal external cost at the efficient quantity—$15,000 per student per year.

MyEconLab   animation   ◆

Vouchers are similar to subsidies, but their advocates say that they are more efficient than subsidies because the consumer can monitor school performance more effectively than the government can.

Patents and Copyrights Knowledge might be an exception to the principle of diminishing marginal benefit. Additional knowledge (about the right things) makes people more productive. And there seems to be no tendency for the additional productivity from additional knowledge to diminish.

For example, in just 15 years, advances in knowledge about microprocessors have given us a sequence of processor chips that has made our personal computers increasingly powerful. Each advance in knowledge about how to design and manufacture a processor chip has brought ever larger increments in performance and productivity. Similarly, each advance in knowledge about how to design and build an airplane has brought apparently ever larger increments in performance: Orville and Wilbur Wright's 1903 Flyer was a one-seat plane that could hop a farmer's field. The Lockheed Constellation, designed in 1949, was an airplane that could fly 120 passengers from New York to London, but with two refuelling stops in Newfoundland and Ireland. Today, a Boeing 747 can carry 400 people nonstop from Singapore to New York (flights of 15,325 kilometres that take 20 hours). Similar examples can be found in agriculture, biogenetics, communications, engineering, entertainment, and medicine.

One reason why the stock of knowledge increases without diminishing returns is the sheer number of different techniques that can in principle be tried. Paul Romer, an economist at Stanford University, explains this fact. "Suppose that to make a finished good, 20 different parts have to be attached to a frame, one at a time. A worker could proceed in numerical order, attaching part one first, then part two. ... Or the worker could proceed in some other order, starting with part 10, then adding part seven ... With 20 parts, ... there are [more] different sequences ... than the total number of seconds that have elapsed since the big bang created the universe, so we can be confident that in all activities, only a very small fraction of the possible sequences have ever been tried."[1]

---

[1] Paul Romer, "Ideas and Things," in *The Future Surveyed*, supplement to *The Economist*, September 11, 1993, pp. 71–72.

Think about all the processes, all the products, and all the different bits and pieces that go into each, and you can see that we have only begun to scratch the surface of what is possible.

Because knowledge is productive and generates external benefits, it is necessary to use public policies to ensure that those who develop new ideas have incentives to encourage an efficient level of effort. The main way of providing the right incentives uses the central idea of the Coase theorem and assigns property rights—called **intellectual property rights**—to creators. The legal device for establishing intellectual property rights is the patent or copyright. A **patent** or **copyright** is a government-sanctioned exclusive right granted to the inventor of a good, service, or productive process to produce, use, and sell the invention for a given number of years. A patent enables the developer of a new idea to prevent others from benefiting freely from an invention for a limited number of years.

Although patents encourage invention and innovation, they do so at an economic cost. While a patent is in place, its holder has a monopoly. And monopoly is another source of inefficiency (which is explained in Chapter 13). But without a patent, the effort to develop new goods, services, or processes is diminished and the flow of new inventions is slowed. So the efficient outcome is a compromise that balances the benefits of more inventions against the cost of temporary monopoly in new inventions.

REVIEW QUIZ

1 What is special about knowledge that creates external benefits?

2 How might governments use public provision, private subsidies, and vouchers to achieve an efficient amount of education?

3 How might governments use public provision, private subsidies, vouchers, and patents and copyrights to achieve an efficient amount of research and development?

You can work these questions in Study Plan 16.3 and get instant feedback.

─── MyEconLab ◆

Reading Between the Lines on pp. 384–385 looks at the effects of a carbon tax in British Columbia on the efficient production of plywood.

A Carbon Tax

The Carbon Tax Is Working Nicely

Sydney Morning Herald

July 25, 2011

... Heard the one about the carbon tax working perfectly nicely, enjoying popular approval, reducing emissions, not killing capitalism? No, it's not a joke, or a fantasy—it's British Columbia. ...

This week's *Economist* magazine notes that, since introducing the tax in 2008, the B.C. economy has done well, outperforming the rest of Canada with slightly higher growth, slightly lower unemployment, and lower income taxes. And the carbon tax has the support of the majority of the citizenry.

This is a tax that was introduced at $C10 a tonne, rising by $C5 a year to be $C30 next year. ...

And the B.C. government didn't wimp out on applying the tax to fuel either—the *Economist* reports that the tax adds 5 cents a litre to the price of petrol. Fuel consumption per head in "British Columbia has shown the rest of Canada, a country with high carbon emissions per head, that a carbon tax can achieve multiple benefits at minimal cost," opines the *Economist*. ...

Only environmentalists were enthusiastic. Businesses feared it would add to costs and slow the economy. The leftish New Democratic Party (NDP) worried it would hurt the poor. But these fears have proved groundless.

"The carbon tax has been good for the environment, good for taxpayers, and it hasn't hurt the economy," says Stewart Elgie, a professor of law and economics at the University of Ottawa.

"It helped that the law introducing the levy required its proceeds to be recycled back to individuals and companies as cuts in income taxes." ...

ESSENCE OF THE STORY

- British Columbia introduced a carbon tax in 2008.

- Since 2008, the BC economy has had faster growth and lower unemployment than the rest of Canada.

- This is a tax that was introduced at $10 a tonne and will be $30 a tonne next year.

- The tax applies to gasoline and has added 5¢ a litre to its price.

- Economist Stewart Elgie says the carbon tax is good for the environment and for taxpayers and it hasn't hurt the economy.

- British Columbia's tax on carbon is a Pigovian tax designed to confront fuel users with the marginal social cost of their carbon emissions and to change behaviour.

- The tax will be $30 per tonne of carbon-dioxide equivalent emissions in 2012.

- Some fuel users will cut back their consumption and production. Others will switch to cleaner fuels.

- One firm that has chosen to switch to a cleaner fuel is the Richmond Plywood Corporation.

- Richmond Plywood's fuel cost depends on the quantity produced—it is a marginal cost—so a carbon tax increases a firm's marginal cost of production (MC), which decreases its supply.

- A decrease in supply raises the price and decreases the quantity produced.

- Figure 1 shows the effects of the B.C. carbon tax on the market for plywood. Without the tax, marginal cost, MC, determines the supply curve S_0. The equilibrium price is $25 per square metre and 20 million square metres of plywood per month are produced.

- The carbon tax decreases the supply of plywood and shifts the supply curve to S_1. The price rises to $25.50 per square metre and the quantity produced decreases to 19 million square metres of plywood per month.

- Figure 2 shows what is happening at Richmond Plywood. (All values are assumed and don't represent this firm's actual situation.)

- The firm is a price taker and it maximizes profit by producing the quantity at which MC equals marginal revenue and price, MR. With no carbon tax, the firm produces 20,000 square metres per month at the intersection of MR_0 and MC_{gas}.

- When the carbon tax is introduced, the price rises and marginal revenue rises to MR_1. Firms must chose between two alternatives: (1) Pay the tax or (2) Switch from using gas to burning its own wood waste and avoid the tax.

- In the example in Fig. 2, if the firm keeps using gas, it faces a marginal cost of $MC_{gas} + tax$ and cuts production to 19,000 square metres of plywood per month.

- If the firm switches to wood, its marginal cost becomes MC_{wood} and the firm maximizes profit by producing 20,000 square metres of plywood per month.

- If Richmond Plywood is the only firm that switches to wood, that is the end of the story. If all firms switch to wood, the price of plywood falls below $25.50 per square metre and Richmond produces between 19,000 and 20,000 square metres per month.

- The tax decreases B.C. carbon emissions by decreasing the quantity produced of some goods and by changing the fuels used to produce some goods.

- As the news article reports and as the example of Richmond Plywood shows, Pigovian taxes work.

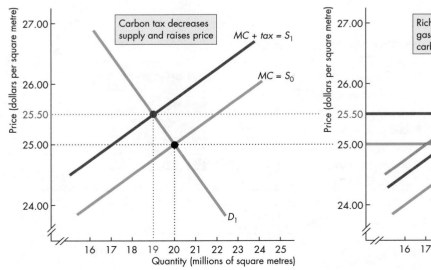

Figure 1 The Market for Plywood

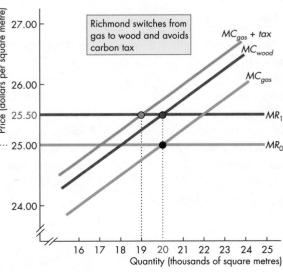

Figure 2 Richmond Plywood Corporation

SUMMARY

Key Points

Externalities in Our Lives (pp. 372–374)

- An externality can arise from either a production activity or a consumption activity.
- A negative externality imposes an external cost.
- A positive externality provides an external benefit.

Working Problem 1 will give you a better understanding of externalities in our lives.

Negative Externality: Pollution (pp. 375–379)

- A competitive market would produce too much of a good that has external production costs.
- External costs are costs of production that fall on people other than the producer of a good or service. Marginal social cost equals marginal private cost plus marginal external cost.
- Producers take account only of marginal private cost and produce more than the efficient quantity when there is a marginal external cost.
- Sometimes it is possible to overcome a negative externality by assigning a property right.
- When property rights cannot be assigned, governments might overcome externalities by using taxes, emission charges, or marketable permits.

Working Problems 2 to 12 will give you a better understanding of the external costs of pollution.

Positive Externality: Knowledge (pp. 379–383)

- External benefits are benefits that are received by people other than the consumer of a good or service. Marginal social benefit equals marginal private benefit plus marginal external benefit.
- External benefits from education arise because better-educated people tend to be better citizens, commit fewer crimes, and support social activities.
- External benefits from research arise because once someone has worked out a basic idea, others can copy it.
- Vouchers or subsidies to schools or the provision of public education below cost can achieve a more efficient provision of education.
- Patents and copyrights create intellectual property rights and an incentive to innovate. But they do so by creating a temporary monopoly, the cost of which must be balanced against the benefit of more inventive activity.

Working Problems 13 to 17 will give you a better understanding of the external benefits of knowledge.

Key Terms

Coase theorem, 377
Copyright, 383
Externality, 372
Intellectual property rights, 383
Marginal external benefit, 379
Marginal external cost, 375
Marginal private benefit, 379
Marginal private cost, 375
Marginal social benefit, 379
Marginal social cost, 375

Negative externality, 372
Patent, 383
Pigovian taxes, 378
Positive externality, 372
Property rights, 376
Public production, 381
Subsidy, 382
Transactions costs, 377
Voucher, 382

SCAN THIS

STUDY PLAN PROBLEMS AND APPLICATIONS

MyEconLab ◆ You can work Problems 1 to 18 in Chapter 16 Study Plan and get instant feedback.

Externalities in Our Lives (Study Plan 16.1)

1. Consider each of the following activities or events and say for each one whether it is an externality. If so, say whether it is a positive or negative production or consumption externality.
   - Airplanes take off from Pearson International Airport during the Canadian Open tennis tournament, which is taking place nearby
   - A sunset over the Pacific Ocean
   - An increase in the number of people who are studying for graduate degrees
   - A person wears strong perfume while attending an orchestra concert
   - A homeowner plants an attractive garden in front of his house
   - A person talks on a cell phone while driving
   - A bakery bakes bread

Negative Externality: Pollution (Study Plan 16.2)

Use the following figure to work Problems 2 to 6. The figure illustrates the market for tomatoes.

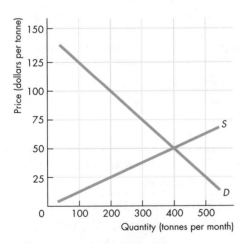

A small town is surrounded by a large tomato farm. The tomato grower sprays the plants with chemicals to control disease and the chemical waste flows into the river passing through the town. The marginal external cost of the chemical waste is equal to the marginal private cost of producing tomatoes.

2. If no one owns the river and the town takes no action to control the waste, what is the quantity of tomatoes and the deadweight loss created?

3. a. If the town owns the river and makes the tomato grower pay the cost of pollution, how many tomatoes are produced? What does the grower pay the town per tonne of tomatoes produced?
   b. If the tomato grower owns the river and rents it to the town, how many tomatoes are produced? How is the rent paid by the town to the grower (per tonne of tomatoes produced) influenced by tomato growing?
   c. Compare the quantities of tomatoes produced in parts (a) and (b) and explain the relationship between these quantities.

4. If no one owns the river and the city introduces a pollution tax, what is the tax per tonne of tomatoes produced that achieves an efficient outcome?

5. Compare the outcomes when property rights exist and when the pollution tax achieves the efficient amount of waste.

6. Suppose that no one owns the river and the government issues two marketable pollution permits: one to the tomato grower and one to the city. Each permit allows the same amount of pollution of the river, and the total pollution created is the efficient amount. What is the quantity of tomatoes produced and what is the market price of a pollution permit? Who buys and who sells a permit?

Use the following new clip to work Problems 7 and 8.

Waste Plan Pits City Against Industry

A battle is brewing between the city of Toronto and the city's coffee shops. Not to mention the interest groups behind plastic water bottles, taxpayer rights, and restaurants. Toronto is targeting in-store packaging—disposable coffee cups, takeout food containers, water bottles and plastic bags. Businesses don't want to change. The city will ban non-recyclable coffee cups and bags and give customers who use their own coffee cups a 20-cent discount. Sales of bottled water at Toronto City Hall are also banned.

Source: TheStar.com, November 6, 2008

7. a. Describe the externality that arises from plastic containers and bags.

b. Draw a graph to illustrate how plastic containers and bags create deadweight loss.

8. a. Explain why a complete ban on plastic containers and bags might be inefficient.

   b. Explain the effects on the use of plastic containers of Toronto's suggested policy of making manufacturers pay for recycling.

Use the following news clip to work Problems 9 to 11.

The Year in Medicine: Cell phones

Talking on a hands-free cell phone while driving might seem safe, but think again. People who used hands-free cell phones in simulation trials exhibited slower reaction times and took longer to hit the brakes than drivers who weren't otherwise distracted. Data from real-life driving tests show that cell phone use rivals drowsy driving as a major cause of accidents.

Source: *Time*, December 4, 2006

9. a. Explain the external costs that arise from using a cell phone while driving.

   b. Explain why the market for cell phone service creates a deadweight loss.

10. Draw a graph to illustrate how a deadweight loss arises from the use of cell phones.

11. Explain how government intervention might improve the efficiency of cell phone use.

12. **Pollution Rules Squeeze Strawberry Crop**

Last year, Ventura County farmers harvested nearly 12,000 acres of strawberries valued at more than $323 million. To comply with the federal Clean Air Act, growers must use 50 percent less pesticide. It is estimated that strawberry output will fall by 60 percent.

Source: *USA Today*, February 29, 2008

Explain how a limit on pesticide will change the efficiency of the strawberry industry. Would a cap-and-trade scheme be more efficient?

Positive Externality: Knowledge (Study Plan 16.3)

13. **Tuition Hikes, Not Loan Access, Should Frighten Students**

The real danger during a recession is a hike in tuition, not a cut in student loans. In past recessions, states have cut funding for colleges and increased tuition. The Cato Institute says a better policy would be for states to maintain the subsidies to colleges and increase their deficits.

Source: *USA Today*, October 22, 2008

If government cuts the subsidy to colleges, why will tuition rise and the number of students

enrolled decrease? Why is it a better policy for government to maintain the subsidy to colleges?

Use the figure, which shows the marginal private benefit from college education, to work Problems 14 to 17.

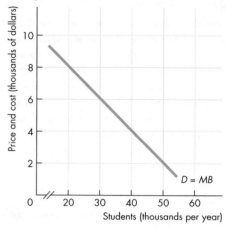

The marginal cost of a college education is a constant $6,000 per student per year. The marginal external benefit from a college education is a constant $4,000 per student per year.

14. What is the efficient number of students? If all colleges are private, how many people enroll in college and what is the tuition?

15. If the government decides to provide public colleges, what tuition will these colleges charge to achieve the efficient number of students? How much will taxpayers have to pay?

16. If the government decides to subsidize private colleges, what subsidy will achieve the efficient number of college students?

17. If the government offers vouchers to those who enroll at a college and no subsidy, what is the value of the voucher that will achieve the efficient number of students?

Economics in the News (Study Plan 16.EN)

18. **Global Solutions for Local Gridlock**

Gridlock costs Toronto $6 billion a year, with average commutes of 80 minutes. By 2031, an additional 27 minutes will be added to the daily grind. Civic leaders are looking at road tolls, a regional gas tax, and parking levies.

Source: *The Toronto Star*, June 24, 2011

Will road tolls, a regional gas tax, and parking levies make Toronto streets less congested? If the new charges cut commute times, will the Toronto road system be more efficient? Explain.

ADDITIONAL PROBLEMS AND APPLICATIONS

MyEconLab ◆ You can work these problems in MyEconLab if assigned by your instructor.

Externalities in Our Lives

19. What externalities arise from smoking tobacco products and how do we deal with them?

20. What externalities arise from beautiful and ugly buildings and how do we deal with them?

Negative Externality: Pollution

21. Betty and Anna work at the same office in Calgary. They both must attend a meeting in Edmonton, so they decide to drive to the meeting together. Betty is a cigarette smoker and her marginal benefit from smoking a package of cigarettes a day is $40. Cigarettes are $6 a pack. Anna dislikes cigarette smoke, and her marginal benefit from a smoke-free environment is $50 a day. What is the outcome if
    a. Betty drives her car with Anna as a passenger?
    b. Anna drives her car with Betty as a passenger?

Use the following information and the figure, which illustrates the market for a pesticide with no government intervention, to work Problems 21 to 24.

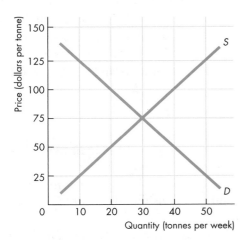

When factories produce pesticide, they also create waste, which they dump into a lake on the outskirts of the town. The marginal external cost of the waste is equal to the marginal private cost of producing the pesticide (that is, the marginal social cost of producing the pesticide is double the marginal private cost).

22. What is the quantity of pesticide produced if no one owns the lake and what is the efficient quantity of pesticide?

23. If the residents of the town own the lake, what is the quantity of pesticide produced and how much do residents of the town charge the factories to dump waste?

24. If the pesticide factories own the lake, how much pesticide is produced?

25. If no one owns the lake and the government levies a pollution tax, what is the tax that achieves the efficient outcome?

Use the following table to work Problems 26 to 28.

The first two columns of the table show the demand schedule for electricity from a coal burning utility; the second and third columns show the utility's cost of producing electricity. The marginal external cost of the pollution created is equal to the marginal cost.

Price (cents per kilowatt)	Quantity (kilowatts per day)	Marginal cost (cents per kilowatt)
4	500	10
8	400	8
12	300	6
16	200	4
20	100	2

26. With no government action to control pollution, what is the quantity of electricity produced, the price of electricity, and the marginal external cost of the pollution generated?

27. With no government action to control pollution, what is the marginal social cost of the electricity generated and the deadweight loss created?

28. Suppose that the government levies a pollution tax, such that the utility produces the efficient quantity. What is the price of electricity? What is the tax levied, and the government's tax revenue per day?

Positive Externality: Knowldege

Use the following news clip to work Problems 29 and 30.

Light Bulbs: Shining a Light on Bulb Recycling

We've received several questions about recycling light bulbs, ranging from regular incandescents to compact fluorescents (CFLs). First off, recycling incandescent bulbs is not on the priority list, because they don't contain toxic materials and don't offer much in the way of recoverable resources. It is important to recycle the far more energy-efficient CFLs.

Home Depot Canada is aiming to recycle 1.5 million bulbs by 2011 and says all components from the bulbs will be reused in creating a host of new products, including glass bottles and jars, baseball bats and products for the lighting industry. Lasting six to 10 times longer than the average incandescent bulb and using up to 75 percent less electricity, CFLs save on power consumption and cut your electricity bill. When properly recycled, CFLs are definitely your best bet for the environment—and your pocketbook.

Source: *Calgary Herald*, March 27, 2008

29. a. Relative to incandescents, what is the external benefit associated with CFLs?

   b. Draw a graph to illustrate and explain why the market for CFLs is inefficient.

30. Draw a graph to illustrate and explain how government actions might achieve an efficient outcome in the market for bulbs.

Use the following figure and information to work Problems 31 to 34.

The marginal cost of educating a student is a constant $4,000 a year and the figure shows the students' marginal benefit curve. Suppose that college education creates an external benefit of a constant $2,000 per student per year.

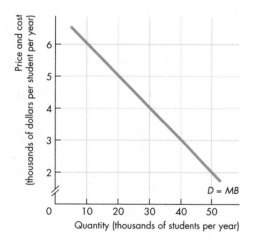

31. If all colleges are private and the market for education is competitive, how many students enroll, what is the tuition, and what is the deadweight loss created?

32. If the government decides to provide public colleges, what tuition will these colleges charge to achieve the efficient number of students? How much will taxpayers have to pay?

33. If the government decides to subsidize private colleges, what subsidy will achieve the efficient number of college students?

34. If the government offers vouchers to those who enroll at a college and no subsidy, what is the value of the voucher that will achieve the efficient number of students?

Use the following news clip to work Problems 35 to 37.

How Arts Funding Is Done Elsewhere

When Rick van der Ploege became Holland's secretary of culture in 1998, he launched an arts-funding revolution that alarmed his quiet, multicultural country—but also became a potential model for smaller-population countries such as Canada. Bursaries for about $100,000 a year were offered to foreign graduate students. Foreign filmmakers could also receive funding—as long as it met Dutch content requirement. More contentiously, artists would have to prove that there was a market for their creations if they wanted a subsidy. "My argument has always been to get the best people in the world. ... Whether they be Canadian, Japanese, and maybe the Dutch, bring them together, and the locals would then have to compete on a global scale."

Source: *National Post*, September 26, 2008

35. What external benefits are associated with the arts?

36. Draw a graph to illustrate and explain why the market for arts creates a deadweight loss.

37. Draw a graph to illustrate and explain how bursaries for foreign graduate students might improve efficiency.

Economics in the News

38. After you have studied *Reading Between the Lines* on pp. 384–385, answer the following questions:

   a. What is British Columbia doing to cut carbon emissions that the rest of Canada is not doing?

   b. Explain and illustrate with appropriate graphs the effects of the B.C. carbon tax on production and carbon emissions.

   c. Which holds the greater promise as a method of lowering carbon emissions: actions that decrease the demand for carbon emitting fuels or actions that decrease the supply of these fuels? Explain.

   d. Why might a carbon cap-and-trade program be preferred to a carbon tax?

Public Goods and Common Resources

After studying this chapter, you will be able to

- Distinguish among private goods, public goods, and common resources
- Explain how the free-rider problem arises and how the quantity of public goods is determined
- Explain the tragedy of the commons and its possible solutions

Why don't we let private firms produce weather forecasting, national defence, or police services and sell their products in the market? What can be done to prevent the extinction of fish species in the Atlantic Ocean resulting from overfishing? These are the two big questions of this chapter.

In *Reading Between the Lines* at the end of the chapter, we look at a pressing tragedy of the commons in the world today: the overuse of the tropical rain forests.

Classifying Goods and Resources

Good, services, and resources differ in the extent to which people can be *excluded* from consuming them and the extent to which one person's consumption *rivals* the consumption of others.

Excludable

A good is **excludable** if it is possible to prevent someone from enjoying its benefits. Brink's security services, Cooke Aquaculture's fish, and a U2 concert are examples. People must pay to consume them.

A good is **nonexcludable** if it is impossible (or extremely costly) to prevent anyone from benefiting from it. The services of the Calgary police, fish in the Atlantic Ocean, and a concert on network television are examples. When a police cruiser enforces the speed limit, everyone on the highway benefits; anyone with a boat can fish in the ocean; and anyone with a TV can watch a network broadcast.

Rival

A good is **rival** if one person's use of it decreases the quantity available for someone else. A Brink's truck can't deliver cash to two banks at the same time. A fish can be consumed only once.

A good is **nonrival** if one person's use of it does not decrease the quantity available for someone else. The services of the police and a concert on network television are nonrival. One person's benefit doesn't lower the benefit of others.

A Fourfold Classification

Figure 17.1 classifies goods, services, and resources into four types.

Private Goods A **private good** is both rival and excludable. A can of Coke and a fish on Cooke Aquaculture's farm are examples of private goods.

Public Goods A **public good** is both nonrival and nonexcludable. A public good can be consumed simultaneously by everyone, and no one can be excluded from enjoying its benefits. National defence is the best example of a public good. Another is weather forecasting.

Common Resources A **common resource** is rival and nonexcludable. A unit of a common resource can be

FIGURE 17.1   Fourfold Classification of Goods

	Excludable	Nonexcludable
Rival	**Private goods** Food and drink Car House	**Common resources** Fish in ocean Atmosphere City parks
Nonrival	**Natural monopoly goods** iTunes song Cable television Bridge or tunnel	**Public goods** National defence The law Weather forecasting

A private good is one for which consumption is rival and from which consumers can be excluded. A public good is one for which consumption is nonrival and from which it is impossible to exclude a consumer. A common resource is one that is rival but nonexcludable. A good that is nonrival but excludable is a good produced by a natural monopoly.

———————————— MyEconLab animation ◆

used only once, but no one can be prevented from using what is available. Ocean fish are a common resource. They are rival because a fish taken by one person isn't available for anyone else, and they are nonexcludable because it is difficult to prevent people from catching them.

Natural Monopoly Good A **natural monopoly good** is nonrival and excludable. When buyers can be excluded if they don't pay but the good is nonrival, marginal cost is zero. The fixed cost of producing such a good is usually high, so economies of scale exist over the entire range of output for which there is a demand (see p. 300). An iTunes song and cable television are examples of natural monopoly goods.

 REVIEW QUIZ

1 Distinguish among public goods, private goods, common resources, and natural monopolies.
2 Provide examples of goods (or services or resources) in each of the four categories that differ from the examples in this section.

You can work these questions in Study Plan 17.1 and get instant feedback.

———————————— MyEconLab ◆

◆ Public Goods

Why does the government provide our weather forecasting? Why don't we buy our weather forecasts from North Pole Weather, Inc., a private firm that competes for our dollars in the marketplace in the same way that McDonald's does? The answer is that weather forecasting is a public good—nonexcludable and nonrival—and it has a free-rider problem.

The Free-Rider Problem

A *free rider* enjoys the benefits of a good or service without paying for it. Because a public good is provided for everyone to use and no one can be excluded from its benefits, no one has an incentive to pay his or her share of the cost. Everyone has an incentive to free ride. The **free-rider problem** is that the market would provide an inefficiently small quantity of a public good. Marginal social benefit from the public good would exceed its marginal social cost and a deadweight loss would arise.

Let's look at the marginal social benefit and marginal social cost of a public good.

Marginal Social Benefit from a Public Good

Lisa and Max (the only people in an imagined society) value weather forecasts. Figures 17.2(a) and 17.2(b) graph their marginal benefits from a weather satellite system as MB_L for Lisa and MB_M for Max. A person's marginal benefit from a public good, like that from a private good, diminishes as the quantity of the good increases—the marginal benefit curves slope downward.

Figure 17.2(c) shows the marginal *social* benefit curve, *MSB*. Because everyone gets the same quantity of a public good, its marginal social benefit curve is the sum the marginal benefits of all individuals at each *quantity*—it is the *vertical* sum of the individual *MB* curves. So the *MSB* curve in part (c) is the marginal social benefit curve for the economy made up of Lisa and Max. For each satellite, Lisa's marginal benefit is added to Max's marginal benefit to calculate the marginal social benefit from that satellite.

Contrast the *MSB* curve for a public good with that of a private good. To obtain the economy's *MSB* curve for a private good, we *sum the quantities demanded* by all individuals at each price—we sum the individual marginal benefit curves *horizontally* (see Chapter 5, p. 108).

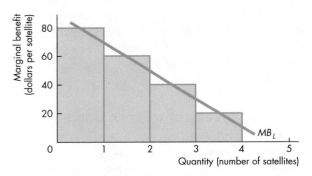

(a) Lisa's marginal benefit

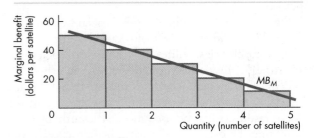

(b) Max's marginal benefit

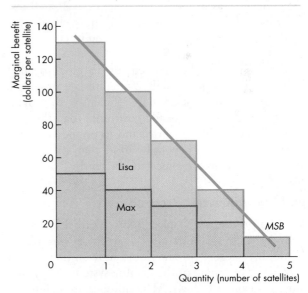

(c) Economy's marginal social benefit

The marginal social benefit at each quantity of the public good is the sum of the marginal benefits of all individuals. The marginal benefit curves are MB_L for Lisa and MB_M for Max. The economy's marginal social benefit curve is *MSB*.

──────── MyEconLab animation ◆

Marginal Social Cost of a Public Good

The marginal social cost of a public good is determined in exactly the same way as that of a private good—see p. 110. The principle of increasing marginal cost applies to the marginal cost of a public good and the marginal social cost curve of a public good slopes upward.

Efficient Quantity of a Public Good

To determine the efficient quantity of a public good, we use the same principles that you learned in Chapter 5 and have used repeatedly: Find the quantity at which marginal social benefit equals marginal social cost.

Figure 17.3 shows the marginal social benefit curve, *MSB*, and the marginal social cost curve, *MSC*, for defence satellites. (Now think of society as consisting of Lisa and Max and 30 million others.)

If marginal social benefit exceeds marginal social cost, as it does when fewer than 2 satellites are provided, resources can be used more efficiently by increasing the quantity. The extra benefit exceeds the extra cost. If marginal social cost exceeds marginal social benefit, as it does when more than 2 satellites are provided, resources can be used more efficiently by decreasing the quantity. The saving in cost exceeds the loss of benefit.

If marginal social benefit equals marginal social cost, as it does when exactly 2 satellites are provided, resources cannot be used more efficiently. To provide more than 2 satellites would cost more than the additional coverage is worth, and to provide fewer satellites lowers the benefit by more than its cost saving. Resources are allocated efficiently.

Inefficient Private Provision

Could a private firm—North Pole Weather, Inc.—deliver the efficient quantity of satellites? Most likely it couldn't because no one would have an incentive to buy his or her share of the satellite system. Everyone would reason as follows: "The number of satellites provided by North Pole Weather, Inc., is not affected by my decision to pay my share or not. But my own private consumption will be greater if I free ride and do not pay my share of the cost of the satellite system. If I don't pay, I enjoy the same level of security and I can buy more private goods. I will spend my money on private goods and free ride on the

FIGURE 17.3 The Efficient Quantity of a Public Good

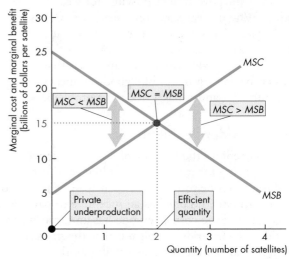

With fewer than 2 satellites, marginal social benefit, *MSB*, exceeds marginal social cost, *MSC*. With more than 2 satellites, *MSC* exceeds *MSB*. Only with 2 satellites is *MSC* equal to *MSB* and the number of satellites efficient.

————————— MyEconLab animation ◆

public good." Such reasoning is the free-rider problem. If everyone reasons the same way, North Pole Weather, Inc., has no revenue and so provides no satellites. Because the efficient level is 2 satellites, private provision is inefficient.

Efficient Public Provision

The political process might be efficient or inefficient. We look first at an efficient outcome. There are two political parties: Greens and Blues. They agree on all issues except for the number of satellites. The Greens want 3 satellites, and the Blues want 1 satellite. But both parties want to get elected, so they run a voter survey and discover the marginal social benefit curve of Fig. 17.4. They also consult with satellite producers to establish the marginal cost schedule. The parties then do a "what-if" analysis. If the Greens propose 3 satellites and the Blues propose 1 satellite, the voters will be equally unhappy with both parties. Compared to the efficient quantity, the Blues want an underprovision of 1 satellite and the Greens want an overprovision of 1 satellite. The deadweight losses are equal. So the election would be too close to call.

FIGURE 17.4   An Efficient Political Outcome

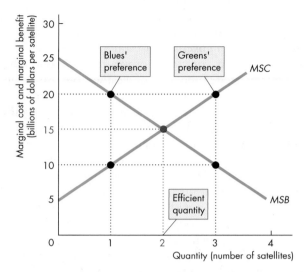

The Blues would like to provide 1 satellite and the Greens would like to provide 3 satellites. The political outcome is 2 satellites because unless each party proposes 2 satellites, the other party will beat it in an election.

———— MyEconLab animation ◆

Contemplating this outcome, the Greens realize that they are too hawkish to get elected. They figure that if they scale back to 2 satellites, they will win the election if the Blues propose 1 satellite. The Blues reason in a similar way and figure that if they increase the number of satellites to 2, they can win the election if the Greens propose 3 satellites.

So they both propose 2 satellites. The voters are indifferent between the parties, and each party receives 50 percent of the vote.

Regardless of which party wins the election, 2 satellites are provided and this quantity is efficient. Competition in the political marketplace results in the efficient provision of a public good.

The Principle of Minimum Differentiation The tendency for competitors to make themselves similar to appeal to the maximum number of clients or voters is called the **principle of minimum differentiation**. This principle describes the behaviour of political parties. It also explains why fast-food restaurants cluster in the same block and even why new auto models have similar features. If McDonald's opens a new restaurant, it is likely that Wendy's will open near to McDonald's rather than a kilometre down the road. If Chrysler designs a new van with a sliding door on the driver's side, most likely Ford will too.

For the political process to deliver the efficient outcome that you've just seen, voters must be well informed, evaluate the alternatives, and vote in the election. Political parties must be well informed about voter preferences. As the next section shows, we can't expect to achieve this outcome.

Inefficient Public Overprovision

If competition between two political parties is to deliver the efficient quantity of a public good, bureaucrats must cooperate and help to achieve this outcome. In the case of satellites, bureaucrats in the Department of Weather Forecasting (DWF) must cooperate and accept this outcome.

Objective of Bureaucrats Bureaucrats want to maximize their department's budget because a bigger budget brings greater status and more power. So the DWF's objective is to maximize the defence budget.

Figure 17.5 shows the outcome if the DWF is successful in the pursuit of its goal. The DWF might

FIGURE 17.5   Bureaucratic Overprovision

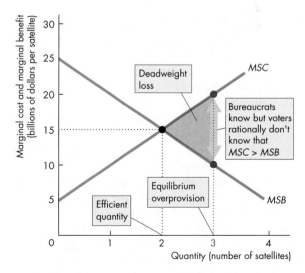

Well-informed bureaucrats want to maximize their budget and rationally ignorant voters enable the bureaucrats to go some way towards achieving their goal. A public good might be inefficiently overprovided with a deadweight loss.

———— MyEconLab animation ◆

try to persuade the politicians that 2 satellites cost more than the originally budgeted amount; or the DWF might press its position more strongly and argue for more than 2 satellites. In Fig. 17.5, the DWF persuades the politicians to go for 3 satellites.

Why don't the politicians block the DWF? Won't overproducing satellites cost future votes? It will if voters are well informed and know what is best for them. But voters might not be well informed, and well-informed interest groups might enable the DWF to achieve its objective and overcome the objections of the politicians.

Rational Ignorance   A principle of the economic analysis of public choices is that it is rational for a voter to be ignorant about an issue unless that issue has a perceptible effect on the voter's economic welfare. **Rational ignorance** is the decision not to acquire information because the cost of doing so exceeds the expected benefit.

For example, each voter knows that he or she can make virtually no difference to the Government of Canada's weather forecasting. Each voter also knows that it would take an enormous amount of time and effort to become even moderately well informed about alternative weather technologies. So voters remain relatively uninformed about the technicalities of weather issues. Although we are using weather forecasting as an example, the same reasoning applies to all aspects of government economic activity.

All voters are consumers of weather forecasts. But not all voters are producers of weather forecasts. Only a small number of voters are in this latter category. Voters who own or work for firms that produce components of satellites have a direct personal interest in defence because it affects their incomes and careers. These voters have an incentive to become well informed about defence issues and to operate a political lobby aimed at furthering their own self-interests.

In collaboration with the bureaucrats who are responsible for the provision of a public good, informed voters who produce that public good exert a larger influence than do the relatively uninformed voters who only use the public good.

When the rationality of the uninformed voter and special interest groups are taken into account, the political equilibrium provides public goods in excess of the efficient quantity. So in the satellite example, 3 or more satellites might be installed rather than the efficient quantity of 2 satellites.

Economics in Action

Is a Lighthouse a Public Good?

Canada's first lighthouse was built at Louisbourg, Nova Scotia, in 1730.

For two centuries, economists used the lighthouse as an example of a public good. No one can be prevented from seeing its warning light—*nonexcludable*—and one person seeing its light doesn't prevent someone else from doing so too—*nonrival.*

Ronald Coase, who won the 1991 Nobel Prize for ideas he first developed when he was an undergraduate at the London School of Economics, discovered that before the nineteenth century, lighthouses in England were built and operated by private corporations that earned profits by charging tolls on ships docking at nearby ports. A ship that refused to pay the lighthouse toll was *excluded* from the port.

So the benefit arising from the services of a lighthouse is *excludable*. Because the services provided by a lighthouse are nonrival but excludable, a lighthouse is an example of a natural monopoly good and not a public good.

Two Types of Political Equilibrium

We've seen that two types of political equilibrium are possible: efficient and inefficient. These two types of political equilibrium correspond to two theories of government:

- Social interest theory
- Public choice theory

Social Interest Theory Social interest theory predicts that governments make choices that achieve an efficient provision of public goods. This outcome occurs in a perfect political system in which voters are fully informed about the effects of policies and refuse to vote for outcomes that can be improved upon.

Public Choice Theory Public choice theory predicts that governments make choices that result in inefficient overprovision of public goods. This outcome occurs in political markets in which voters are rationally ignorant and base their votes only on issues that they know affect their own net benefit. Voters pay more attention to their self-interests as producers than their self-interests as consumers, and public officials also act in their own self-interest. The result is government failure that parallels market failure.

Why Government Is Large and Growing

Now that we know how the quantity of public goods is determined, we can explain part of the reason for the growth of government. Government grows in part because the demand for some public goods increases at a faster rate than the demand for private goods. There are two possible reasons for this growth:

- Voter preferences
- Inefficient overprovision

Voter Preferences The growth of government can be explained by voter preferences in the following way. As voters' incomes increase (as they do in most years), the demand for many public goods increases more quickly than income. (Technically, the income elasticity of demand for many public goods is greater than one—see Chapter 4, pp. 92–93.) These goods include public health, education, weather forecasting, highways, airports, and air-traffic control systems. If politicians did not support increases in expenditures on these items, they would not get elected.

Inefficient Overprovision Inefficient overprovision might explain the size of government but not its growth rate. It (possibly) explains why government is larger than its efficient scale, but it does not explain why governments use an increasing proportion of total resources.

Voters Strike Back

If government grows too large relative to the value that voters place on public goods, there might be a voter backlash against government programs and a large bureaucracy. Electoral success during the 1990s at the provincial and federal levels required politicians of all parties to embrace smaller, leaner, and more efficient government. The September 11 attacks have led to a greater willingness to pay for security but have probably not lessened the desire for lean government.

Another way in which voters—and politicians—can try to counter the tendency of bureaucrats to expand their budgets is to privatize the production of public goods. Government provision of a public good does not automatically imply that a government-operated bureau must produce the good. Garbage collection (a public good) is often done by a private firm, and experiments are being conducted with even private prisons.

 REVIEW QUIZ

1 What is the free-rider problem and why does it make the private provision of a public good inefficient?

2 Under what conditions will competition among politicians for votes result in an efficient provision of a public good?

3 How do rationally ignorant voters and budget-maximizing bureaucrats prevent the political marketplace from delivering the efficient quantity of a public good?

You can work these questions in Study Plan 17.2 and get instant feedback.

————————————————— MyEconLab ◆

You've seen how public goods create a free-rider problem that would result in the underprovision of such goods. We're now going to learn about common resources and see why they result in the opposite problem—the overuse of such resources.

Common Resources

Overgrazing the pastures around a village in Middle Ages England and overfishing the cod stocks of the North Atlantic Ocean during the recent past are tragedies of the commons. The **tragedy of the commons** is the overuse of a common resource that arises when its users have no incentive to conserve it and use it sustainably.

To study the tragedy of the commons and its possible remedies, we'll focus on the recent and current tragedy—overfishing and depleting the stock of Atlantic cod. We begin by thinking about the sustainable use of a renewable resource.

Sustainable Use of a Renewable Resource

A *renewable natural resource* is one that replenishes itself by the birth and growth of new members of the population. Fish, trees, and the fertile soil are all examples of this type of resource.

Focusing on fish, the sustainable catch is the quantity that can be caught year after year without depleting the stock. This quantity depends on the stock and in the interesting way illustrated in Fig. 17.6.

If the stock of fish is small, the quantity of new fish born is also small, so the sustainable catch is small.

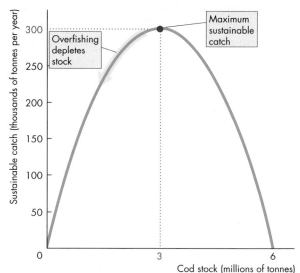

FIGURE 17.6   Sustainable Catch

As the stock of fish increases (on the *x*-axis), the sustainable catch (on the *y*-axis) increases to a maximum. Beyond that number, more fish must compete for food and the sustainable catch falls.

If the catch exceeds the sustainable catch, the fish stock diminishes.

— MyEconLab   animation ◆

Economics in Action
The Original Tragedy of the Commons

The term "tragedy of the commons" comes from fourteenth-century England, where areas of rough grassland surrounded villages. The commons were open to all and used for grazing cows and sheep owned by the villagers.

Because the commons were open to all, no one had an incentive to ensure that the land was not overgrazed. The result was a severe overgrazing situation. Because the commons were overgrazed, the quantity of cows and sheep that they could feed kept falling, the longer the overgrazing continued.

During the sixteenth century, the price of wool increased and England became a wool exporter to the world. Sheep farming became profitable, and sheep owners wanted to gain more effective control of the land they used. So the commons were gradually privatized and enclosed. Overgrazing ended, and land use became more efficient.

Economics in Action

One of Today's Tragedies of the Commons

Before 1970, Atlantic cod was abundant. It was fished for many centuries and was a major food source for the first European settlers in North America. During the sixteenth century, hundreds of European ships caught large quantities of cod in the northwest Atlantic off the coast of what is now New England and Newfoundland. By 1620, there were more than 1,000 fishing boats in the waters off Newfoundland, and in 1812 about 1,600 boats. During these years, cod were huge fish, typically weighing in at more than 110 kilograms and measuring 1-2 metres in length.

Most of the fishing during these years was done using lines and productivity was low. But low productivity limited the catch and enabled cod to be caught sustainably over hundreds of years.

The situation changed dramatically during the 1960s with the introduction of high-efficiency nets (called trawls, seines, and gill nets), sonar technology to find fish concentrations, and large ships with efficient processing and storage facilities. These technological advances brought soaring cod harvests. In less than a decade, cod landings increased from less than 300,000 tonnes a year to 800,000 tonnes.

This volume of cod could not be taken without a serious collapse in the remaining stock and by the 1980s it became vital to regulate cod fishing. But regulation was of limited success and stocks continued to fall.

In 1992, a total ban on cod fishing in the North Atlantic stabilized the population but at a very low level. Two decades of ban have enabled the species to repopulate, and it is now hoped that one day cod fishing will return but at a low and sustainable rate.

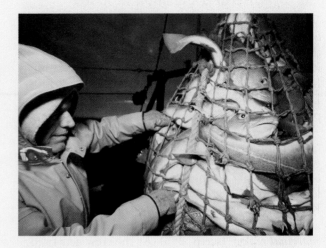

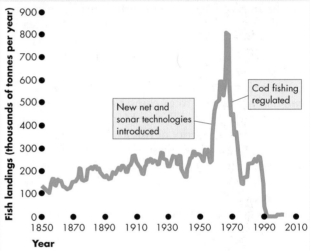

The Atlantic Cod Catch: 1850–2005

Source of data for graph: Millenium Ecosystem Assessment.
Source of information: Codfishes—Atlantic cod and its fishery, science.jrank.org.

If the fish stock is large, many fish are born, but they must compete with each other for food so only a small number survive to reproduce and to grow large enough to catch.

Between a small and a large stock is a quantity of fish stock that maximizes the sustainable catch. In Fig. 17.6, this fish stock is 3 million tonnes and the sustainable catch is 300,000 tonnes a year. The maximum sustainable catch arises from a balancing of the birth of new fish from the stock and the availability of food to sustain the fish popuation.

If the quantity of fish caught is less than the sustainable catch, the fish stock grows; if the quantity caught exceeds the sustainable catch, the fish stock shrinks; and if the quantity caught equals the sustainable catch, the fish stock remains constant and is available for future generations of fishers in the same quantity that is available today.

If the fish stock exceeds the level that maximizes the sustainable catch, overfishing isn't a problem. But if the fish stock is less than the level that maximizes the sustainable catch, overfishing depletes the stock.

The Overuse of a Common Resource

Why might a fish stock be overused? Why might overfishing occur? The answer is that fishers face only their own private cost and don't face the cost they impose on others—external cost. The *social* cost of fishing combines the *private* cost and *external* cost. Let's examine the costs of catching fish to see how the presence of external cost brings overfishing.

Marginal Private Cost You can think of the *marginal private cost* of catching fish as the additional cost incurred by keeping a boat and crew at sea for long enough to increase the catch by one tonne. Keeping a fishing boat at sea for an additional amount of time eventually runs into *diminishing marginal returns* (see p. 253). As the crew gets tired and the storage facilities get overfull, the catch per hour decreases. The cost of keeping the boat at sea for an additional hour is constant so the marginal cost of catching fish increases as the quantity caught increases.

You've just seen that the *principle of increasing marginal cost* applies to catching fish just as it applies to other production activities: Marginal private cost increases as the quantity of fish caught increases.

The marginal private cost of catching fish determines an individual fisher's supply of fish. A profit-maximizing fisher is willing to supply the quantity at which the market price of fish covers the marginal private cost. And the market supply is the sum of the quantities supplied by each individual fisher.

Marginal External Cost The marginal external cost of catching fish is the cost per additional tonne that one fisher's production imposes on all other fishers. This additional cost arises because one fisher's catch decreases the remaining stock, which in turn decreases the renewal rate of the stock and makes it harder for others to find and catch fish.

Marginal external cost also increases as the quantity of fish caught increases. If the quantity of fish caught is so large that it drives the species to near extinction, the marginal external cost becomes infinitely large.

Marginal Social Cost The *marginal social cost* of catching fish is the marginal private cost plus the marginal external cost. Because both of its components increase as the quantity caught increases, marginal social cost also increases with the quantity of fish caught.

Marginal Social Benefit and Demand The marginal social benefit from fish is the price that consumers are willing to pay for an additional kilogram of fish. Marginal social benefit decreases as the quantity of fish consumed increases, so the demand curve, which is also the marginal social benefit curve, slopes downward.

Overfishing Equilibrium Figure 17.7 illustrates overfishing and how it arises. The market demand curve for fish is the marginal social benefit curve, *MSB*. The market supply curve is the marginal *private* cost curve, *MC*. Market equilibrium occurs at the intersection point of these two curves. The equilibrium quantity is 800,000 tonnes per year and the equilibrium price is $10 per kilogram.

At this market equilibrium, overfishing is running down the fish stock. Figure. 17.7 illustrates why

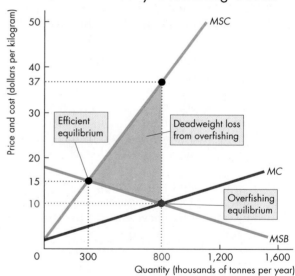

FIGURE 17.7   Why Overfishing Occurs

The supply curve is the marginal private cost curve, *MC*. The demand curve is the marginal social benefit curve, *MSB*. Market equilibrium occurs at a quantity of 800,000 tonnes and a price of $10 per kilogram.

The marginal social cost curve is *MSC* and at the market equilibrium there is overfishing—marginal social cost exceeds marginal social benefit.

The quantity at which *MSC* equals *MSB* is the efficient quantity, 300,000 tonnes per year. The grey triangle shows the deadweight loss from overfishing.

MyEconLab   animation   ◆

overfishing occurs. At the market equilibrium quantity, marginal social benefit (and willingness to pay) is $10 per kilogram, but the marginal social cost exceeds this amount. The marginal external cost is the cost of running down the fish stock.

Efficient Equilibrium   What is the efficient use of a common resource? It is the use of the resource that makes the marginal social benefit from the resource equal to the marginal social cost of using it.

In Fig. 17.7, the efficient quantity of fish is 300,000 tonnes per year—the quantity that makes marginal social cost (on the *MSC* curve) equal to marginal social benefit (on the *MSB* curve). At this quantity, the marginal catch of each individual fisher costs society what people are willing to pay for it.

Deadweight Loss from Overfishing   Deadweight loss measures the cost of overfishing. The grey triangle in Fig. 17.7 illustrates this loss. It is the marginal social cost minus the marginal social benefit from all the fish caught in excess of the efficient quantity.

Achieving an Efficient Outcome

Defining the conditions under which a common resource is used efficiently is easier than delivering those conditions. To use a common resource efficiently, it is necessary to design an incentive mechanism that confronts the users of the resource with the marginal *social* consequences of their actions. The same principles apply to common resources as those that you met earlier in Chapter 10 when you studied the external cost of pollution.

The three main methods that might be used to achieve the efficient use of a common resource are

- Property rights
- Production quotas
- Individual transferable quotas (ITQs)

Property Rights   A common resource that no one owns and that anyone is free to use contrasts with *private property*, which is a resource that *someone* owns and has an incentive to use in the way that maximizes its value. One way of overcoming the tragedy of the commons is to convert a common resource to private property. By assigning private property rights to what was previously a common resource, its owner faces the same conditions as

society faces. It doesn't matter who owns the resource.

The users of the resource will be confronted with the full cost of using it because they either own it or pay a fee to the owner for permission to use it.

When private property rights over a resource are established and enforced, the *MSC* curve becomes the marginal *private* cost curve, and the use of the resource is efficient.

Figure 17.8 illustrate an efficient outcome with property rights. The supply curve $S = MC = MSC$ and the demand curve $D = MSB$ determine the equilibrium price and quantity. The price equals both marginal social benefit and marginal social cost and the quantity is efficient.

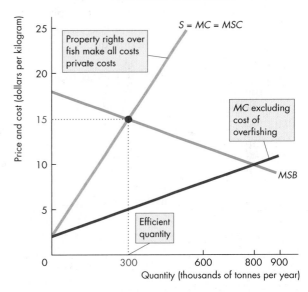

FIGURE 17.8   Property Rights Achieve an Efficient Outcome

With private property rights, fishers pay the owner of the fish stock for permission to fish and face the full social cost of their actions. The marginal cost curve includes the external cost, so the supply curve is the marginal private cost curve and the marginal social cost curve, $S = MC = MSC$.

Market equilibrium occurs at $15 per kilogram and at that price, the quantity is 300,000 tonnes per year. At this quantity, marginal social cost equals marginal social benefit, and the quantity of fish caught is efficient.

The property rights convert the fish stock from a common resource to a private resource and it is used efficiently.

MyEconLab   animation

The private property solution to the tragedy of the commons *is* available in some cases. It was the solution to the original tragedy of the commons in England's Middle Ages. It is also a solution that has been used to prevent overuse of the airwaves that carry cell phone services. The right to use this space (called the frequency spectrum) has been auctioned by governments to the highest bidders. The owner of each part of the spectrum is the only one permitted to use it (or to license someone else to use it).

But assigning private property rights is not always feasible. It would be difficult, for example, to assign private property rights to the oceans. It would not be impossible, but the cost of enforcing private property rights over thousands of hectares of ocean would be high. It would be even more difficult to assign and protect private property rights to the atmosphere.

In some cases, there is an emotional objection to assigning private property rights. Critics of it have a moral objection to someone owning a resource that they regard as public. In the absence of property rights, some form of government intervention is used, one of which is a production quota.

Production Quota A *production quota* is an upper limit to the quantity of a good that may be produced in a specified period. The quota is allocated to individual producers, so each producer has its own quota.

You studied the effects of a production quota in Chapter 6 (pp. 139–140) and learned that a quota can drive a wedge between marginal social benefit and marginal social cost and create deadweight loss. In that earlier example, the market was efficient without a quota. But in the case of common resources, the market overuses the resource and produces an inefficient quantity. A production quota in this market brings a move towards a more efficient outcome.

Figure 17.9 shows a quota that achieves an efficient outcome. The quota limits the catch (production) to 300,000 tonnes, the efficient quantity at which marginal social benefit, *MSB*, equals marginal social cost, *MSC*. If everyone sticks to their own quota, the outcome is efficient. But implementing a production quota has two problems.

First, it is in every fisher's self-interest to catch more fish than the quantity permitted under the quota. The reason is that price exceeds marginal private cost, so by catching more fish, a fisher gets a higher income. If enough fishers break the quota, overfishing and the tragedy of the commons remain.

Second, marginal cost is not, in general, the same for all producers—as we're assuming here. Efficiency

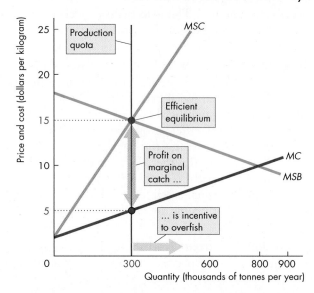

FIGURE 17.9   A Production Quota to Use a Common Resource Efficiently

A quota of 300,000 tonnes that limits production to this quantity raises the price to $15 per kilogram, and lowers marginal cost to $5 per kilogram. A fisher who cheats and produces more that the alloted quota increases his profit by $10 per kilogram. If all (or most) fishers cheat, production exceeds the quota and there is a return to overfishing.

━━━ MyEconLab (animation) ◆

requires that the quota be allocated to the producers with the lowest marginal cost. But bureaucrats who allocate quotas do not have information about the marginal cost of individual producers. Even if they tried to get this information, producers would have an incentive to lie about their costs so as to get a bigger quota.

So where producers are difficult, or very costly, to monitor or where marginal cost varies across producers, a production quota cannot achieve an efficient outcome.

Individual Transferable Quotas Where producers are difficult to monitor or where marginal cost varies across producers, a more sophisticated quota system can be effective. It is an **individual transferable quota (ITQ)**, which is a production limit that is assigned to an individual who is then free to transfer (sell) the quota to someone else. A market in ITQs emerges and ITQs are traded at their market price.

The market price of an ITQ is the highest price that someone is willing to pay for one. That price is marginal social benefit minus marginal cost. The price of an ITQ will rise to this level because fishers who don't have a quota would be willing to pay this amount to get one.

A fisher with an ITQ could sell it for the market price, so by not selling the ITQ the fisher incurs an opportunity cost. The marginal cost of fishing, which now includes the opportunity cost of the ITQ, equals the marginal social benefit from the efficient quantity.

Figure 17.10 illustrates how ITQs work. Each fisher receives an allocation of ITQs and the total catch permitted by the ITQs is 300,000 tonnes per year. Fishers trade ITQs: Those with low marginal cost buy ITQs from those with high marginal cost and the market price of an ITQ settles at $10 per kilogram of fish. The marginal private cost of fishing now becomes the original marginal private cost, *MC*, plus the price of the ITQ. The marginal private cost curve shifts upward from *MC* to *MC* + *price of ITQ* and each fisher is confronted with the marginal *social* cost of fishing. No one has an incentive to exceed the quota because to do so would send marginal cost above price and result in a loss on the marginal catch. The outcome is efficient.

FIGURE 17.10 ITQs to Use a Common Resource Efficiently

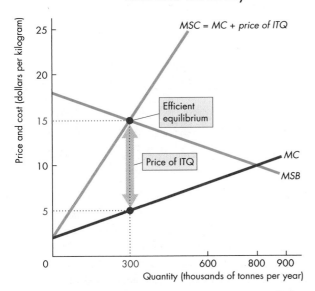

ITQs are issued on a scale that keeps output at the efficient level. The market price of an ITQ equals the marginal social benefit minus marginal cost. Because each user of the common resource faces the opportunity cost of using the resource, self-interest achieves the social interest.

———— MyEconLab animation ◆

Economics in Action

ITQs Work

Iceland introduced the first ITQs in 1984 to conserve its stocks of lobster. In 1986, New Zealand and a bit later Australia introduced ITQs to conserve fish stocks in the South Pacific and Southern Oceans. The evidence from these countries suggests that ITQs work well.

ITQs help maintain fish stocks, but they also reduce the size of the fishing industry. This consequence of ITQs puts them against the self-interest of fishers. In all countries, the fishing industry opposes restrictions on its activities, but in Australia and New Zealand, the opposition is not strong enough to block ITQs.

In the United States the opposition has been harder to overcome and in 1996, Congress passed the Sustainable Fishing Act that put a moratorium on ITQs. This moratorium was lifted in 2004 and since then, ITQs have been applied to 28 fisheries from the Gulf of Alaska to the Gulf of Mexico. Economists have studied the effects of ITQs extensively and agree that they work. ITQs offer an effective tool for achieving an efficient use of the stock of ocean fish.

Opposition to ITQs has prevented them from being adopted in Canada. One Parliamentary committee in Ottawa even went so far as to argue that evidence from Australia and New Zealand should not be used to justify ITQs in Canada.

REVIEW QUIZ

1 What is the tragedy of the commons? Give two examples, including one from your province.
2 Describe the conditions under which a common resource is used efficiently.
3 Review three methods that might achieve the efficient use of a common resource and explain the obstacles to efficiency.

You can work these questions in Study Plan 17.3 and get instant feedback.
———————————————— MyEconLab ◆

◆ *Reading Between the Lines* on pp. 404–405 looks at one of today's tragedies of the commons: the overuse of tropical rainforests.

A Tragedy of the Commons

Premier Clark: Protect the Great Bear Rainforest, …

savethegreatbear.org
April 1, 2011

Environmental organizations working to protect tropical rainforests around the equator have asked the British Columbia government to take the necessary steps to protect the Great Bear Rainforest in British Columbia, as announced on March 31, 2009. …

"The Great Bear Rainforest is Canada's Amazon and one the best carbon vaults of the planet. People around the world care about the fate of the rare white spirit bear as much as they care about Orangutans and panthers" said Cesar Moran-Cahusac from the Amazon Conservation Association.

"The world is looking for solutions of the kind that are being developed in the Great Bear Rainforest—addressing conservation, Aboriginal land rights and economic activities that respect the limits of nature," said Henry Cirhuza, Congolese Programme Manager for The Gorilla Organization, DRC. …

The letter comes on the second anniversary of the signing of the landmark Great Bear Rainforest Agreements, and serves as a reminder to the new premier that there is still much work left to be done. …

The Great Bear Rainforest is the largest remaining intact coastal temperate rainforest in the world and home to the rare white Spirit Bear, Grizzly Bears and rich runs of salmon. The agreements, announced March 31 2009 by the B.C. government, First Nations, environmental groups and logging companies, included a five-year plan to ensure ecological integrity by implementing further conservation steps and improving human well-being in coastal communities. …

ESSENCE OF THE STORY

- The Great Bear Rainforest is the world's largest remaining intact temperate rainforest.

- It is home to the white Spirit Bear.

- The B.C. government, First Nations, environmental groups, and logging companies have agreed on a five-year plan to protect the Great Bear Rainforest.

- Environmental organizations around the world have asked the B.C. government to ensure the agreement works.

ECONOMIC ANALYSIS

- The Great Bear Rainforest of British Columbia and Alaska is a source of timber and is also a natural resource enjoyed by thousands of people who appreciate its natural beauty and the wide range of trees, animals, and birds that it supports.

- The forest is home to rare and ancient species of trees and is a carbon-dioxide sink that helps to maintain the Earth's atmosphere.

- The forest is common property but subject to laws and regulations made by the province of British Columbia and the state of Alaska.

- The private incentive to exploit the timber resources of this forest is strong.

- Because no logging company owns the forests, there is no incentive to conserve the resources and use them on a sustainable basis.

- The result is a danger of overuse, just like the overuse of the commons of England in the Middle Ages.

- The figures illustrate the tragedy of the commons in the Great Bear Rainforest.

- Figure 1 shows the relationship between its sustainable production of timber and the density of the forest. With no regulation, loggers would deplete the forest; the efficient use of the forest does *not* maximize sustainable timber production.

- Figure 2 explains why the efficient use doesn't maximize sustainable production.

- It shows the marginal private cost of a logging company. It also shows the marginal social (and private) benefit from timber and the marginal social cost of timber.

- The producers' marginal cost of harvesting timber is assumed to be $40 per tonne on the MC curve.

- The MSB curve shows the marginal social benefit of timber.

- If the logging companies and the government make a deal that ignores the value of the rainforest to those who enjoy visiting it, production is 16 tonnes per year (an assumed number), which is the maximum sustainable output of the rainforest.

- Adding the cost of destruction of the rainforest to the marginal cost gives the marginal social cost of timber, which is assumed to be $60 per tonne.

- If environmental groups and the government make a deal that correctly values the rainforest as a natural resource to be enjoyed, production is 8 tonnes per year.

- Producing the maximum sustainable quantity is overproduction and creates the deadweight loss shown in Fig. 2.

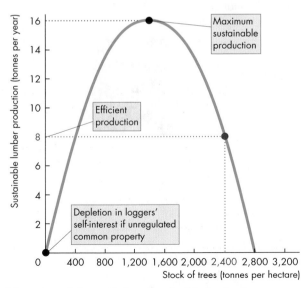

Figure 1 Rainforest Timber Sustainable Production

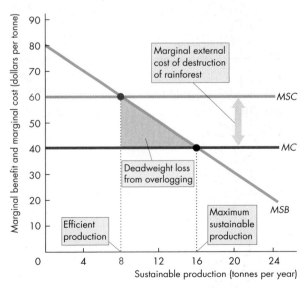

Figure 2 Marginal Benefit and Marginal Cost

SUMMARY

Key Points

Classifying Goods and Resources (pp. 392)

- A private good is a good or service that is rival and excludable.
- A public good is a good or service that is nonrival and nonexcludable.
- A common resource is a resource that is rival but nonexcludable.

Working Problems 1 and 2 will give you a better understanding of classifying goods and resources.

Public Goods (pp. 393–397)

- Because a public good is a good or service that is *nonrival* and *nonexcludable*, it creates a *free-rider* problem: No one has an incentive to pay their share of the cost of providing a public good.
- The efficient level of provision of a public good is that at which marginal social benefit equals marginal social cost.
- Competition between political parties can lead to the efficient scale of provision of a public good.

- Bureaucrats who maximize their budgets and voters who are rationally ignorant can lead to the inefficient overprovision of a public good—government failure.

Working Problems 3 to 11 will give you a better understanding of providing public goods.

Common Resources (pp. 398–403)

- Common resources create a problem that is called the tragedy of the commons—no one has a private incentive to conserve the resources and use them at an efficient rate.
- A common resource is used to the point at which the marginal social (private) benefit equals the marginal private cost.
- A common resource might be used efficiently by creating a private property right, setting a quota, or issuing individual transferable quotas.

Working Problems 12 to 18 will give you a better understanding of common resources.

Key Terms

Common resource, 392
Excludable, 392
Free-rider problem, 393
Individual transferable quota (ITQ), 402
Natural monopoly good, 392
Nonexcludable, 392
Nonrival, 392

Principle of minimum differentiation, 395
Private good, 392
Public good, 392
Rational ignorance, 396
Rival, 392
Tragedy of the commons, 398

SCAN THIS

STUDY PLAN PROBLEMS AND APPLICATIONS

MyEconLab ◆ You can work Problems 1 to 18 in Chapter 17 Study Plan and get instant feedback.

Classifying Goods and Resources (Study Plan 17.1)

1. Classify each of the following items as excludable, nonexcludable, rival, or nonrival.
   - eBay
   - A mouse
   - A Twitter page
   - MyEconLab Web site

2. Classify each of the following items as a public good, a private good, a natural monopoly good, or a common resource.
   - Highway control services
   - City sidewalks
   - Canada Post
   - Purolator courier service

Public Goods (Study Plan 17.2)

3. For each of the following goods, explain whether there is a free-rider problem. If there is no such problem, how is it avoided?
   - July 1st fireworks display
   - TransCanada Highway in rural Manitoba
   - Wireless Internet access in hotels
   - The public library in your city

4. The table sets out the marginal benefits that Terri and Sue receive from police officers on duty on the university campus:

Police officers on duty (number per night)	Marginal benefit	
	Terri	Sue
	(dollars per police officer)	
1	18	22
2	14	18
3	10	14
4	6	10
5	2	6

   a. If the police officers are provided by the city government, is the presence of the police on campus a private good or a public good?
   b. Suppose that Terri and Sue are the only students on the campus at night. Draw a graph to show the marginal social benefit from on-campus police officers on duty at night.

5. For each of the following goods and services, explain whether there is a free-rider problem. If there is no such problem, how is it avoided?
   - Canadian Hurricane Centre
   - Ambulance service
   - Road safety signs
   - The Canadian Coast Guard

6. **Vaccination Dodgers**

   Doctors struggle to eradicate polio worldwide, but one of the biggest problems is persuading parents to vaccinate their children. Since the discovery of the vaccine, polio has been eliminated from Europe and the law requires everyone to be vaccinated. People who refuse to be vaccinated are "free riders."

   Source: *USA Today*, March 12, 2008

   Explain why someone who has not opted out on medical or religious grounds and refuses to be vaccinated is a "free rider."

Use the following figure to work Problems 7 to 9.

The figure provides information about a waste disposal system that a city of 1 million people is considering installing.

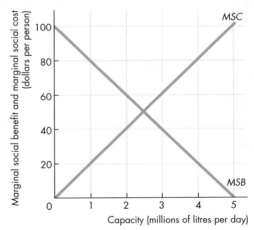

7. What is the efficient capacity of the disposal system? How much will each person have to pay in taxes for the city to install the efficient capacity?

8. What is the political equilibrium if voters are well informed?

9. What is the political equilibrium if voters are rationally ignorant and bureaucrats achieve the highest attainable budget?

Use the data on a mosquito control program in the following table to work Problems 10 and 11.

Quantity (hectares sprayed per day)	Marginal social cost	Marginal social benefit
	(thousands of dollars per day)	
1	2	10
2	4	8
3	6	6
4	8	4
5	10	2

10. What quantity of spraying would a private mosquito control program provide? What is the efficient quantity of spraying? In a single-issue election on the quantity of spraying, what quantity would the winner of the election provide?

11. If the government sets up a Department of Mosquito Control and appoints a bureaucrat to run it, would mosquito spraying most likely be underprovided, overprovided, or provided at the efficient quantity?

Common Resources (Study Plan 17.3)

Use the following figure to work Problems 12 to 14. The figure shows the market for North Atlantic tuna.

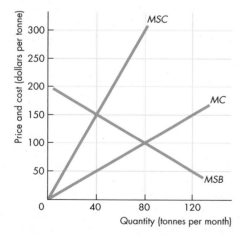

12. a. What is the quantity of tuna that fishers catch and the price of tuna? Is the tuna stock being used efficiently? Explain why or why not.
    b. What would be the price of tuna, if the stock of tuna is used efficiently?

13. a. With a quota of 40 tonnes a month for the tuna fishing industry, what is the equilibrium price of tuna and the quantity of tuna that fishers catch?
    b. Is the equilibrium an overfishing equilibrium?

14. If the government issues ITQs to individual fishers that limit the total catch to the efficient quantity, what is the market price of an ITQ?

15. **Whaling "Hurts Tourist Industry"**

    Leah Garces, the director of programs at the World Society for the Protection of Animals, reported that whale watching is more economically significant and sustainable to people and communities than whaling. The global whale-watching industry is estimated to be a $1.25 billion business enjoyed by over 10 million people in more than 90 countries each year.

    Source: BBC, June 2, 2009

    Describe the tradeoff facing communities that live near whaling areas. How might a thriving whale-watching industry avoid the tragedy of the commons?

Use the following information to work Problems 16 to 18.

A natural spring runs under land owned by 10 people. Each person has the right to sink a well and can take water from the spring at a constant marginal cost of $5 a litre. The table sets out the external cost and the social benefit of water.

Quantity of water (litres per day)	Marginal external cost (dollars per litre)	Marginal social benefits (dollars per litre)
10	1	10
20	2	9
30	3	8
40	4	7
50	5	6
60	6	5
70	7	4

16. Draw a graph to illustrate the market equilibrium. On your graph, show the efficient quantity of water taken.

17. If the government sets a quota on the total amount of water such that the spring is used efficiently, what would that quota be?

18. If the government issues ITQs to landowners that limit the total amount of water taken to the efficient quantity, what is the market price of an ITQ?

ADDITIONAL PROBLEMS AND APPLICATIONS

MyEconLab ◆ You can work these problems in MyEconLab if assigned by your instructor.

Classifying Goods and Resources

19. Classify each of the following items as excludable, nonexcludable, rival, or nonrival.
    - Firefighting service
    - A Starbucks coffee
    - A view of Niagara Falls
    - Jasper National Park
    - A Google search

20. Classify each of the following items as a public good, a private good, a natural monopoly good, or a common resource.
    - Car licences
    - Tuna in the Pacific Ocean
    - Air service within Canada
    - Local storm-water system

Public Goods

Use the following news clip to work Problems 21 and 22.

"Free Riders" Must be Part of Health Debate

President Obama insists that "the reason people don't have health insurance isn't because they don't want it, it's because they can't afford it." There are 47 million uninsured Americans and of these, 16 percent earn more than $75,000 a year and 15 percent earn between $50,000 and $75,000 a year. About 16 percent of those who received "free" medical care in 2004 had incomes at least four times the federal poverty level.

Source: *Los Angeles Times*, March 4, 2008

21. Explain why government-subsidized health-care services can create a free-rider problem.

22. Explain the evidence the news clip presents to contradict the argument that "the reason people don't have health insurance isn't because they don't want it, it's because they can't afford it."

23. The table sets out the marginal benefits that Sam and Nick receive from the town's street lighting:

| Number of street lights | Marginal benefit | |
| | Sam | Nick |
	(dollars per street light)	
1	10	12
2	8	9
3	6	6
4	4	3
5	2	0

a. Is the town's street lighting a private good or a public good?

b. Suppose that Sam and Nick are the only residents of the town. Draw a graph to show the marginal social benefit from the town's street lighting.

24. What is the principle of diminishing marginal benefit? Does Sam's, Nick's, or the society's marginal benefit diminish faster?

Use the following news clip to work Problems 25 and 26.

A Bridge Too Far Gone

Gas taxes have paid most of America's freeway system. Now motorists pay about one-third as much in the gas taxes to drive a mile as they did in the 1960s. Raising gas taxes is politically tricky, but it wouldn't matter if private cash was flooding into infrastructure, or if new ways were being found to control demand. Neither is happening, and private companies building toll roads brings howls of outrage.

Source: *The Economist*, August 9, 2007

25. Why is it "politically tricky" to raise gas taxes to finance infrastructure?

26. What in this news clip points to a distinction between public *production* of a public good and public *provision*? Give examples of three public goods that are *produced* by private firms but *provided* by government and paid for with taxes.

Common Resources

27. **In Quebec, an Economic Plan**

    As the polar ice caps recede, Canada plans Asian shipping routes and sustainable developments for its northern lands. "We're building a parallel canal to the Panama Canal for Chinese and Indian ships, so they can accelerate the transport of goods," says Jean Charest, the Premier of Québec. Charest announced Québec's Plan Nord: a plan to develop the north by opening mines, building infrastructure to mines, boosting tourism, and establishing sustainable logging.

    Source: *Fortune*, June 3, 2011

    Which items in the news clip are common resources? Which items are public goods? Which activities are likely to increase climate change? Explain your answer.

28. If hikers were required to pay a fee to use the Overlander Trail in Jasper National Park,
    a. Would the use of this common resource be more efficient?
    b. Would it be even more efficient if the most popular spots along the trail had the highest prices?
    c. Why do you think we don't see more market solutions to the tragedy of the commons?

Use the following information to work Problems 29 to 31.

A spring runs under a village. Everyone can sink a well on her or his land and take water from the spring. The following figure shows the marginal social benefit from water and the marginal cost of taking it.

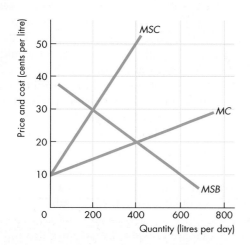

29. What is the quantity of water taken and what is the private cost of the water taken?

30. What is the efficient quantity of water taken and the marginal social cost at the efficient quantity?

31. If the village council sets a quota on the total amount of water such that the spring is used efficiently, what would be the quota and the market value of the water taken per day?

32. **Polar Ice Cap Shrinks Further and Thins**

    With the warming of the planet, the polar ice cap is shrinking and the Arctic Sea is expanding. As the ice cap shrinks further, more and more underwater mineral resources will become accessible. Many countries are staking out territorial claims to parts of the polar region.

    Source: *The Wall Street Journal*, April 7, 2009

Explain how ownership of these mineral resources will influence the amount of damage done to the Arctic Sea and its wildlife.

Economics in the News

33. After you have studied *Reading Between the Lines* on pp. 404–405, answer the following questions:
    a. What are the competing uses of the Great Bear Rainforest?
    b. If the Great Bear Rainforest was owned by logging companies, and assuming the number in the graphs on p. 405, how much logging would be done, what would be the price of timber, and what would be the deadweight loss from logging?
    c. If the Great Bear Rainforest was owned by eco-vacation companies, and assuming the number in the graphs on p. 405, how much logging would be done, what would be the price of timber, and what would be the dead-weight loss from logging?
    d. How might the use of ITQs in logging be used to achieve an efficient use of the Great Bear Rainforest? Why might that be a better solution than the regulations described in the news article?

34. **Who's Hiding under the U.S. Umbrella?**

    Students of the Cold War learn that, to deter possible Soviet aggression, the United States placed a "strategic umbrella" over NATO Europe and Japan, with the United States providing most of their national security. Under President Ronald Reagan, the United States spent 6 percent of GDP on defence, whereas the Europeans spent only 2 to 3 percent and the Japanese spent only 1 percent, although all faced a common enemy. Thus the U.S. taxpayer paid a disproportionate share of the overall defence spending, whereas NATO Europe and Japan spent more on consumer goods or saved.

    Source: *International Herald Tribune*, January 30, 2008

    a. Explain the free-rider problem described in this news clip.
    b. Does the free-rider problem in international defence mean that the world has too little defence against aggression?
    c. How do nations try to overcome the free-rider problem among nations?

Making the Rules

Creating a system of responsible democratic government is a huge enterprise and one that could easily go wrong. Creating a constitution that made despotic and tyrannical rule impossible was relatively easy. And we achieved such a constitution for Canada by using some sound economic ideas. We've designed a sophisticated system of incentives—of carrots and sticks—to make the government responsive to public opinion and to limit the ability of individual self-interests to gain at the expense of the majority. But we were not able to create a constitution that effectively blocks the ability of special interest groups to capture the consumer and producer surpluses that result from specialization and exchange.

We have created a system of government to deal with four market failures: (1) monopoly; (2) externalities; (3) public goods; and (4) common resources.

Government might help cope with these market failures, but as the founding fathers knew well, government does not eliminate the pursuit of self-interest. Voters, politicians, and bureaucrats pursue their self-interest, sometimes at the expense of the social interest, and instead of market failure, we get government failure.

Many economists have thought long and hard about the problems discussed in this part. But none has had as profound an effect on our ideas in this area as Ronald Coase.

Ronald Coase *(1910–), was born in England and educated at the London School of Economics, where he was deeply influenced by his teacher, Arnold Plant, and by the issues of his youth: communist central planning versus free markets.*

Professor Coase has lived in the United States since 1951. He first visited America as a 20-year-old on a travelling scholarship during the depths of the Great Depression. It was on this visit, and before he had completed his bachelor's degree, that he conceived the ideas that 60 years later were to earn him the 1991 Nobel Prize for Economic Science.

Ronald Coase discovered and clarified the significance of transactions costs and property rights for the functioning of the economy. He has revolutionized the way we think about property rights and externalities and has opened up the growing field of law and economics.

The question to be decided is: Is the value of fish lost greater or less than the value of the product which contamination of the stream makes possible?

RONALD H. COASE
The Problem of Social Cost

Why did you decide to become an economist?

I've wanted to be an economist from about the age of 13. That was when I took my first class in economics (an interesting story in itself) and discovered that all of the thoughts swimming around in my head belonged to a "science" and there was an entire body of people who understood this science—a lot better than I did, anyway. I can still recall reading *The Wealth of Nations* for the first time; it was a revelation.

What drew you to study the economics of education?

We all care about education, perhaps because it is the key means by which opportunity is (or should be) extended to all. Also, nearly everyone now acknowledges that highly developed countries like the United States and Canada rely increasingly on education as the engine of economic growth. Thus, one reason I was drawn to education is its importance. However, what primarily drew me was that education issues were so clearly begging for economic analysis and that there was so little of it. I try hard to understand educational institutions and problems, but I insist on bringing economic logic to bear on educational issues.

Why is education different from fast food? Why don't we just let people buy it from private firms that are regulated to maintain quality standards analogous to the safety standards that the FDA imposes on fast-food producers?

The thing that makes education different from fast food is not that we cannot buy it from private institutions that are regulated to maintain quality standards. We do this all the time—think of private schools and colleges. What makes education different is that it is (a) an investment, not consumption, and (b) the capital markets for financing the investments work poorly when left on their own. Essentially, our country has an interest in every person investing optimally in his or her education. To make investments, however, people need funds that allow them to attend good schools and take time away from work. Children don't have these funds and cannot arrange for loans that they may or may not pay off decades later. Therefore, children depend on their families for funds, and families do not necessarily have the funds to invest optimally or the right incentives to do so.

Society has a role in filling the gaps in the capital market; it fills this role by public funding of elementary and secondary education, government guaranteed loans, college savings programs, and so on. There is no particular reason, however, why government needs to actually run schools; it can provide the funding without actually providing schooling.

In one of your papers, you posed the question: Does competition among public schools benefit students or taxpayers? What are the issues, what was your answer, and how did you arrive at it?

We are all familiar with the fact that families choose public schools when they choose where to live. This traditional form is by far the most pervasive form of school choice in the United States, and few parents who exercise it would be willing to give it up. Yet, until quite recently, we did not know whether having such traditional school choice was good for students (high achievement) or taxpayers (more efficient schools). It is important to know because some people in the United States, especially poor people who live in central cities, are unable to exercise this form of school choice. Economists hypothesized that this lack of choice might be a reason why many children from poor, central city families receive such a deficient education, especially considering the dollars spent in their schools (which spend significantly more than the median school).

To investigate this hypothesis, I examined all of the metropolitan areas in the United States. They vary a great deal in the degree of traditional choice available to parents. On one extreme, there is a group of metropolitan areas with hundreds of school districts. On the other extreme, there is a group of metropolitan areas with only one school district. Most are somewhere in between. A family in a metropolitan area with one district may have no easy way of "escaping" a badly run district administration. A family in a metropolitan area with hundreds of districts can choose among several districts that match well with its job location, housing preferences, and so on.

Looking across metropolitan areas with many districts (lots of potential competition from traditional school choice) and few districts (little potential competition), I found that areas with greater competition had substantially higher student achievement for any given level of school spending. This suggests that schools are more efficient producers of achievement when they face competition.

What do we know about the relative productivity of public and private schools?

It is somewhat difficult to say whether achievement is higher at public or private schools in the United States. The best studies use randomly assigned private school scholarships, follow the same children over time, or use "natural experiments" in which some areas accidentally end up with more private schools than others. These studies tend to find that, for the same student, private schools produce achievement that is up to 10 percent higher. However, for understanding which type of school is more productive, we actually do not need private schools to have higher achievement. For the sake of argument, let's "call it a draw" on the achievement question.

In recent studies comparing achievement in public and private schools, the public schools spent an average of $9,662 per student and the private schools spent an average of $2,427 per student. These spending numbers, combined with achievement that we will call equal, suggest that the private schools were 298 percent more productive. I would not claim that this number is precisely correct; we could think of some minor adjustments. But it is difficult not to conclude that the private schools are significantly more productive. They produce equal achievement for a fraction of the cost.

> Economists should say to policy makers: "Tell me your goals; I'll design you a voucher."

What can economists say about the alternative methods of financing education? Is there a voucher solution that could work?

There is definitely a voucher solution that could work because vouchers are inherently an extremely flexible policy. People often see the word "voucher" and think of, say, a $2000 voucher being given to a small share of children. But this need not be so. Anything that we can do with public school financing we can do better with a voucher because vouchers can be specific to a student, whereas the government can never ensure that funds get to an individual student by giving those funds to his or her district.

Any well-designed voucher system will give schools an incentive to compete. However, when designing vouchers, we can also build in remedies for a variety of educational problems. Vouchers can be used to ensure that disabled children get the funding they need and the program choices they need. Compared to current school finance programs, vouchers can do a better job of ensuring that low-income families have sufficient funds to invest in the child's education. Well-designed vouchers can encourage schools to make their student bodies socio-economically diverse. Economists should say to policy makers: "Tell me your goals; I'll design you a voucher."

Is there a conflict between efficiency and equity in the provision of quality education?

To raise the public funds that allow all families to invest optimally in their children's education, we have to have taxes. Taxes always create some deadweight loss, so we always create some inefficiency when we raise the funds we need to provide equitable educational opportunities. However, if the funds are used successfully and actually induce people to make optimal investments in their education, we have eliminated much more inefficiency than the taxes created. Thus, in an ideal world, there need not be a conflict between efficiency and equity.

In the real world, public funds are often raised with taxes (creating deadweight loss) and then are not successfully used. If we spend twice as much on public schools and do not have higher achievement to show for it, then there are no efficiency gains to overwhelm the efficiency losses from taxation. In other words, to avoid a conflict between equity and efficiency, we must learn how to use public funds productively in education. This is what the economics of education is all about.

What advice do you have for a student who is just starting to study economics? Is economics a good subject in which to major? What other subjects go well alongside it? And do you have anything special to say to women who are making a career choice? What must we do to get more women involved in our subject?

Students who are just starting to study economics should do two things. First, learn the tools even if they seem abstruse. Once you have mastered the tools, you will be able to "see the forest for the trees." As long as you don't master the tools, you will be in the trees and will find it hard to think about economic problems. Second, think about economic problems! The real world is a great moving textbook of economics, once you have the tools to analyse it.

Economics is a great subject in which to major because it trains you for life, for many careers, and for the thinking that you would need in a leadership position. I think that it is the best training for a future career in business, the law, or policy making. Don't forget nonprofits: Every year, nonprofit organizations try to hire people with economics skills who are also interested in charitable schemes.

Math and statistics courses are complementary to economics because they make it easier for a student to master the tools quickly. Economics goes well with many studies in the arts and sciences, too. It all depends on what you want to use economics for. If you want to do health policy making, take economics along with premedical courses. If you want to be a policy maker in the performing arts, take economics along with music.

I wish that there were more women in economics. Our field loses far too many talented minds. Also, women who need to understand economics for their careers are sometimes without it. To aspiring women economists, I can only say to hang in there. Mastering economics is empowering. You will never have to worry about your opinion not being taken seriously if you are a good economist.

CHAPTER

18

Markets for Factors of Production

After studying this chapter, you will be able to

◆ Describe the anatomy of factor markets

◆ Explain how the value of marginal product determines the demand for a factor of production

◆ Explain how wage rates and employment are determined and how labour unions influence labour markets

◆ Explain how capital and land rental rates and natural resource prices are determined

You know that wage rates vary a lot. A server at McDonald's earns $10 an hour while Jose Bautista, who plays for the Blue Jays, collects a cool $8 million a year. What determines the wages that people earn?

In this chapter, we study labour markets as well as markets for capital and natural resources. You will learn how the prices and quantities of factors of production are determined. In *Reading Between the Lines* at the end of the chapter, we look at the factor markets of Alberta and see how they constantly reallocate resources.

◆ The Anatomy of Factor Markets

The four factors of production are

- Labour
- Capital
- Land (natural resources)
- Entrepreneurship

Let's take a brief look at the anatomy of the markets in which these factors of production are traded.

Markets for Labour Services

Labour services are the physical and mental work effort that people supply to produce goods and services. A labour market is a collection of people and firms who trade labour services. The price of labour services is the wage rate.

Some labour services are traded day by day. These services are called *casual labour.* People who pick fruit and vegetables often just show up at a farm and take whatever work is available that day. But most labour services are traded on a contract, called a **job**.

Most labour markets have many buyers and many sellers and are competitive. In these labour markets, the wage rate is determined by supply and demand, just like the price is determined in any other competitive market.

In some labour markets, a labour union organizes labour, which introduces an element of monopoly on the supply-side of the labour market. In this type of labour market, a bargaining process between the union and the employer determines the wage rate.

We'll study both competitive labour markets and labour unions in this chapter.

Markets for Capital Services

Capital consists of the tools, instruments, machines, buildings, and other constructions that have been produced in the past and that businesses now use to produce goods and services. These physical objects are themselves goods—capital goods. Capital goods are traded in goods markets, just as bottled water and toothpaste are. The price of a dump truck, a capital good, is determined by supply and demand in the market for dump trucks. This market is not a market for capital services.

A market for *capital services* is a *rental market*—a market in which the services of capital are hired.

An example of a market for capital services is the vehicle rental market in which Avis, Budget, Hertz, U-Haul, and many other firms offer automobiles and trucks for hire. The price in a capital services market is a *rental rate.*

Most capital services are not traded in a market. Instead, a firm buys capital and uses it itself. The services of the capital that a firm owns and operates have an implicit price that arises from depreciation and interest costs (see Chapter 10, pp. 228–229). You can think of this price as the implicit rental rate of capital. Firms that buy capital and use it themselves are *implicitly* renting the capital to themselves.

Markets for Land Services and Natural Resources

Land consists of all the gifts of nature—natural resources. The market for land as a factor of production is the market for the *services of land*—the use of land. The price of the services of land is a rental rate.

Most natural resources, such as farm land, can be used repeatedly. But a few natural resources are non-renewable. **Nonrenewable natural resources** are resources that can be used only once. Examples are oil, natural gas, and coal. The prices of nonrenewable natural resources are determined in global *commodity markets* and are called *commodity prices.*

Entrepreneurship

Entrepreneurial services are not traded in markets. Entrepreneurs receive the profit or bear the loss that results from their business decisions.

 REVIEW QUIZ

1 What are the factors of production and their prices?
2 What is the distinction between capital and the services of capital?
3 What is the distinction between the price of capital equipment and the rental rate of capital?

You can work these questions in Study Plan 18.1 and get instant feedback.

———————————————— MyEconLab ◆

The rest of this chapter explores the influences on the demand and supply of factors of production. We begin by studying the demand for a factor of production.

The Demand for a Factor of Production

The demand for a factor of production is a **derived demand**—it is derived from the demand for the goods and services that the labour produces. You've seen, in Chapters 10 through 15, how a firm determines its profit-maximizing output. The quantities of factors of production demanded are a consequence of the firm's output decision. A firm hires the quantities of factors of production that produce the firm's profit-maximizing output.

To decide the quantity of a factor of production to hire, a firm compares the cost of hiring an additional unit of the factor with its value to the firm. The cost of hiring an additional unit of a factor of production is the factor price. The value to the firm of hiring one more unit of a factor of production is called the factor's value of marginal product. We calculate the **value of marginal product** as the price of a unit of output multiplied by the marginal product of the factor of production.

To study the demand for a factor of production, we'll use labour as the example. But what you learn here about the demand for labour applies to the demand for all factors of production.

Value of Marginal Product

Table 18.1 shows you how to calculate the value of marginal product of labour at Angelo's Bakery. The first two columns show Angelo's total product schedule—the number of loaves per hour that each quantity of labour can produce. The third column shows the marginal product of labour—the change in total product that results from a one-unit increase in the quantity of labour employed. (See Chapter 11, pp. 253–256 for a refresher on product schedules.)

Angelo can sell bread at the going market price of $2 a loaf. Given this information, we can calculate the value of marginal product (fourth column). It equals price multiplied by marginal product. For example, the marginal product of hiring the second worker is 6 loaves. Each loaf sold brings in $2, so the value of marginal product of the second worker is $12 (6 loaves at $2 each).

A Firm's Demand for Labour

The value of marginal product of labour tells us what an additional worker is worth to a firm. It tells us the revenue that the firm earns by hiring one more worker. The wage rate tells us what an additional worker costs a firm.

The value of marginal product of labour and the wage rate together determine the quantity of labour demanded by a firm. Because the value of marginal product decreases as the quantity of labour employed increases, there is a simple rule for maximizing profit: Hire the quantity of labour at which the value of marginal product equals the wage rate.

If the value of marginal product of labour exceeds the wage rate, a firm can increase its profit by hiring

---

TABLE 18.1 Value of Marginal Product at Angelo's Bakery

	Quantity of labour (L) (workers)	Total product (TP) (loaves per hour)	Marginal product ($MP = \Delta TP/\Delta L$) (loaves per worker)	Value of marginal product ($VMP = MP \times P$) (dollars per worker)
A	0	0		
			7	14
B	1	7		
			6	**12**
C	**2**	13		
			5	10
D	3	18		
			4	8
E	4	22		
			3	6
F	5	25		

The value of marginal product of labour equals the price of the product multiplied by marginal product of labour. If Angelo's hires 2 workers, the marginal product of the second worker is 6 loaves (in the third column). The price of a loaf is $2, so the value of marginal product of the second worker is $2 a loaf multiplied by 6 loaves, which is $12 (in fourth column).

one more worker. If the wage rate exceeds the value of marginal product of labour, a firm can increase its profit by laying off one worker. But if the wage rate equals the value of marginal product of labour, the firm cannot increase its profit by changing the number of workers it employs. The firm is making the maximum possible profit. So

The quantity of labour demanded by a firm is the quantity at which the value of marginal product of labour equals the wage rate.

A Firm's Demand for Labour Curve

A firm's demand for labour curve is derived from its value of marginal product curve. Figure 18.1 shows these two curves. Figure 18.1(a) shows the value of marginal product curve at Angelo's Bakery. The blue bars graph the numbers in Table 18.1. The curve labelled *VMP* is Angelo's value of marginal product curve.

If the wage rate falls and other things remain the same, a firm hires more workers. Figure 18.1(b) shows Angelo's demand for labour curve.

Suppose the wage rate is $10 an hour. You can see in Fig.18.1(a) that if Angelo hires 2 workers, the value of marginal product of labour is $12 an hour. At a wage rate of $10 an hour, Angelo makes a profit of $2 an hour on the second worker. If Angelo hires a third worker, the value of marginal product of that worker is $10 an hour. So on this third worker, Angelo breaks even.

If Angelo hired 4 workers, his profit would fall. The fourth worker generates a value of marginal product of only $8 an hour but costs $10 an hour, so Angelo does not hire the fourth worker. When the wage rate is $10 an hour, the quantity of labour demanded by Angelo is 3 workers.

Figure 18.1(b) shows Angelo's demand for labour curve, *D*. At $10 an hour, the quantity of labour demanded by Angelo is 3 workers. If the wage rate increased to $12 an hour, Angelo would decrease the quantity of labour demanded to 2 workers. If the wage rate decreased to $8 an hour, Angelo would increase the quantity of labour demanded to 4 workers.

A change in the wage rate brings a change in the quantity of labour demanded and a movement along the demand for labour curve.

A change in any other influence on a firm's labour-hiring plans changes the demand for labour and shifts the demand for labour curve.

FIGURE 18.1   The Demand for Labour at Angelo's Bakery

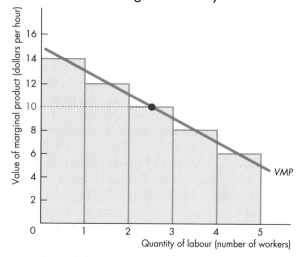

(a) Value of marginal product

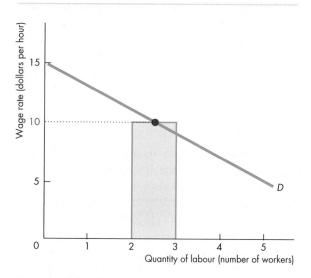

(b) Demand for labour

Angelo's Bakery can sell any quantity of bread at $2 a loaf. The blue bars in part (a) represent the firm's value of marginal product of labour (based on Table 18.1). The line labelled *VMP* is the firm's value of marginal product curve. Part (b) shows Angelo's demand for labour curve. Angelo hires the quantity of labour that makes the value of marginal product equal to the wage rate. The demand for labour curve slopes downward because the value of marginal product diminishes as the quantity of labour employed increases.

MyEconLab   animation

Changes in a Firm's Demand for Labour

A firm's demand for labour depends on

- The price of the firm's output
- The prices of other factors of production
- Technology

The Price of the Firm's Output The higher the price of a firm's output, the greater is the firm's demand for labour. The price of output affects the demand for labour through its influence on the value of marginal product of labour. A higher price for the firm's output increases the value of marginal product of labour. A change in the price of a firm's output leads to a shift in the firm's demand for labour curve. If the price of the firm's output increases, the demand for labour increases and the demand for labour curve shifts rightward.

For example, if the price of bread increased to $3 a loaf, the value of marginal product of Angelo's fourth worker would increase from $8 an hour to $12 an hour. At a wage rate of $10 an hour, Angelo would now hire 4 workers instead of 3.

The Prices of Other Factors of Production If the price of using capital decreases relative to the wage rate, a firm substitutes capital for labour and increases the quantity of capital it uses. Usually, the demand for labour will decrease when the price of using capital falls. For example, if the price of a bread-making machine falls, Angelo might decide to install one machine and lay off a worker. But the demand for labour could increase if the lower price of capital led to a sufficiently large increase in the scale of production. For example, with cheaper machines available, Angelo might install a machine and hire more labour to operate it. This type of factor substitution occurs in the long run when the firm can change the size of its plant.

Technology New technologies decrease the demand for some types of labour and increase the demand for other types. For example, if a new automated bread-making machine becomes available, Angelo might install one of these machines and lay off most of his workforce—a decrease in the demand for bakery workers. But the firms that manufacture and service automated bread-making machines hire more labour, so there is an increase in the demand for this type of labour. An event similar to this one occurred during the 1990s when the introduction of electronic telephone exchanges decreased the demand for telephone operators and increased the demand for computer programmers and electronics engineers.

Table 18.2 summarizes the influences on a firm's demand for labour.

TABLE 18.2   A Firm's Demand for Labour

The Law of Demand

(Movements along the demand curve for labour)

The quantity of labour demanded by a firm

Decreases if:	Increases if:
■ The wage rate increases	■ The wage rate decreases

Changes in Demand

(Shifts in the demand curve for labour)

A firm's demand for labour

Decreases if:	Increases if:
■ The price of the firm's output decreases	■ The price of the firm's output increases
■ The price of a substitute for labour falls	■ The price of a substitute for labour rises
■ The price of a complement of labour rises	■ The price of a complement of labour falls
■ A new technology or new capital decreases the marginal product of labour	■ A new technology or new capital increases the marginal product of labour

REVIEW QUIZ

1 What is the value of marginal product of labour?
2 What is the relationship between the value of marginal product of labour and the marginal product of labour?
3 How is the demand for labour derived from the value of marginal product of labour?
4 What are the influences on the demand for labour?

You can work these questions in Study Plan 18.2 and get instant feedback.

Labour Markets

Labour services are traded in many different labour markets. Examples are markets for bakery workers, van drivers, crane operators, computer support specialists, air traffic controllers, surgeons, and economists. Some of these markets, such as the market for bakery workers, are local. They operate in a given urban area. Some labour markets, such as the market for air traffic controllers, are national. Firms and workers search across the nation for the right match of worker and job. And some labour markets are global, such as the market for superstar hockey, basketball, and soccer players.

We'll look at a local market for bakery workers as an example. First, we'll look at a *competitive* labour market. Then, we'll see how monopoly elements can influence a labour market.

A Competitive Labour Market

A competitive labour market is one in which many firms demand labour and many households supply labour.

Market Demand for Labour Earlier in the chapter, you saw how an individual firm decides how much labour to hire. The market demand for labour is derived from the demand for labour by individual firms. We determine the market demand for labour by adding together the quantities of labour demanded by all the firms in the market at each wage rate. (The market demand for a good or service is derived in a similar way—see Chapter 5, p. 107.)

Because each firm's demand for labour curve slopes downward, the market demand for labour curve also slopes downward.

The Market Supply of Labour The market supply of labour is derived from the supply of labour decisions made by individual households.

Individual's Labour Supply Decision People can allocate their time to two broad activities: labour supply and leisure. (Leisure is a catch-all term. It includes all activities other than supplying labour.) For most people, leisure is more fun than work so to induce them to work they must be offered a wage.

Think about the labour supply decision of Jill, one of the workers at Angelo's Bakery. Let's see how the wage rate influences the quantity of labour she is willing to supply.

Reservation Wage Rate Jill enjoys her leisure time, and she would be pleased if she didn't have to spend her time working at Angelo's Bakery. But Jill wants to earn an income, and as long as she can earn a wage rate of at least $5 an hour, she's willing to work. This wage is called her *reservation wage*. At any wage rate above her reservation wage, Jill supplies some labour.

The wage rate at Angelo's is $10 an hour, and at that wage rate, Jill chooses to work 30 hours a week. At a wage rate of $10 an hour, Jill regards this use of her time as the best available. Figure 18.2 illustrates.

Backward-Bending Labour Supply Curve If Jill were offered a wage rate between $5 and $10 an hour, she would want to work fewer hours. If she were offered a wage rate above $10 an hour, she would want to work more hours, but only up to a point. If Jill could earn $25 an hour, she would be willing to

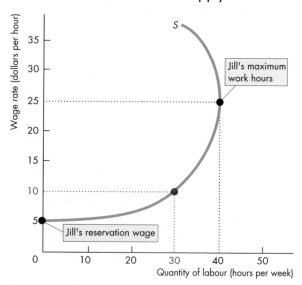

FIGURE 18.2   Jill's Labour Supply Curve

Jill's labour supply curve is *S*. Jill supplies no labour at wage rates below her reservation wage of $5 an hour. As the wage rate rises above $5 an hour, the quantity of labour that Jill supplies increases to a maximum of 40 hours a week at a wage rate of $25 an hour. As the wage rate rises above $25 an hour, Jill supplies a decreasing quantity of labour: her labour supply curve bends backward. The income effect on the demand for leisure dominates the substitution effect.

—————————————— MyEconLab animation ◆

work 40 hours a week (and earn $1,000 a week). But at a wage rate above $25 an hour, with the goods and services that Jill can buy for $1,000, her priority would be a bit more leisure time. So if the wage rate increased above $25 an hour, Jill would cut back on her work hours and take more leisure. Jill's labour supply curve eventually bends backward.

Jill's labour supply decisions are influenced by a substitution effect and an income effect.

Substitution Effect At wage rates below $25 an hour, the higher the wage rate Jill is offered, the greater is the quantity of labour that she supplies. Jill's wage rate is her *opportunity cost of leisure*. If she quits work an hour early to catch a movie, the cost of that extra hour of leisure is the wage rate that Jill forgoes. The higher the wage rate, the less willing Jill is to forgo the income and take the extra leisure time. This tendency for a higher wage rate to induce Jill to work longer hours is a *substitution effect*.

Income Effect The higher Jill's wage rate, the higher is her income. A higher income, other things remaining the same, induces Jill to increase her demand for most goods and services. Leisure is one of those goods. Because an increase in income creates an increase in the demand for leisure, it also creates a decrease in the quantity of labour supplied.

Market Supply Curve Jill's supply curve shows the quantity of labour supplied by Jill as her wage rate changes. Most people behave like Jill and have a backward-bending labour supply curve, but they have different reservation wage rates and wage rates at which their labour supply curves bend backward.

A market supply curve shows the quantity of labour supplied by all households in a particular job market. It is found by adding together the quantities of labour supplied by all households to a given job market at each wage rate.

Also, along a supply curve in a particular job market, the wage rates available in other job markets remain the same. For example, along the supply curve of car-wash workers, the wage rates of car salespeople, mechanics, and all other labour are constant.

Despite the fact that an individual's labour supply curve eventually bends backward, the market supply curve of labour slopes upward. The higher the wage rate for car-wash workers, the greater is the quantity of labour supplied in that labour market.

Let's now look at labour market equilibrium.

Competitive Labour Market Equilibrium Labour market equilibrium determines the wage rate and employment. In Fig. 18.3, the market demand curve for bakery workers is D and the market supply curve of bakery workers is S. The equilibrium wage rate is $10 an hour, and the equilibrium quantity is 300 bakery workers. If the wage rate exceeded $10 an hour, there would be a surplus of bakery workers. More people would be looking for jobs in bakeries than firms were willing to hire. In such a situation, the wage rate would fall as firms found it easy to hire people at a lower wage rate. If the wage rate were less than $10 an hour, there would be a shortage of bakery workers. Firms would not be able to fill all the positions they had available. In this situation, the wage rate would rise as firms found it necessary to offer higher wages to attract labour. Only at a wage rate of $10 an hour are there no forces operating to change the wage rate.

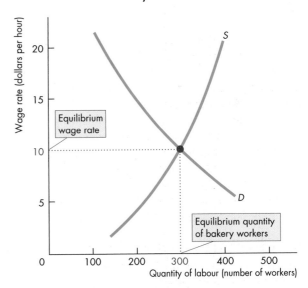

FIGURE 18.3   The Market for Bakery Workers

A competitive labour market coordinates firms' and households' plans. The market is in equilibrium—the quantity of labour demanded equals the quantity supplied at a wage rate of $10 an hour when 300 workers are employed. If the wage rate exceeds $10 an hour, the quantity supplied exceeds the quantity demanded and the wage rate will fall. If the wage rate is below $10 an hour, the quantity demanded exceeds the quantity supplied and the wage rate will rise.

MyEconLab   animation

A Labour Market with a Union

A **labour union** is an organized group of workers that aims to increase the wage rate and influence other job conditions. Let's see what happens when a union enters a competitive labour market.

Influences on Labour Supply   One way of raising the wage rate is to decrease the supply of labour. In some labour markets, a union can restrict supply by controlling entry into apprenticeship programs or by influencing job qualification standards. Markets for skilled workers, doctors, dentists, and lawyers are the easiest ones to control in this way.

If there is an abundant supply of nonunion labour, a union can't decrease supply. For example, in the market for farm labour in southern Ontario, the flow of nonunion labour from Jamaica makes it difficult for a union to control the supply.

On the demand side of the labour market, the union faces a tradeoff: The demand for labour curve slopes downward, so restricting supply to raise the wage rate costs jobs. For this reason, unions also try to influence the demand for union labour.

Influences on Labour Demand   A union tries to increase the demand for the labour of its members in four main ways:

1. Increasing the value of marginal product of its members by organizing and sponsoring training schemes and apprenticeship programs, and by professional certification.
2. Lobbying for import restrictions and encouraging people to buy goods made by unionized workers.
3. Supporting minimum wage laws, which increase the cost of employing low-skilled labour and lead firms to substitute high-skilled union labour for low-skilled nonunion labour.
4. Lobbying for restrictive immigration laws to decrease the supply of foreign workers.

Labour Market Equilibrium with a Union   Figure 18.4 illustrates what happens to the wage rate and employment when a union successfully enters a competitive labour market. With no union, the demand curve is D_C, the supply curve is S_C, the wage rate is $10 an hour, and 300 workers have jobs.

Now a union enters this labour market. First, look at what happens if the union has sufficient control

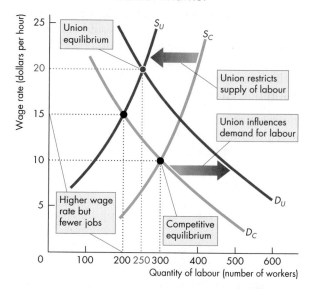

FIGURE 18.4   A Union Enters a Competitive Labour Market

In a competitive labour market, the demand curve is D_C and the supply curve is S_C. The wage rate is $10 an hour and 300 workers are employed. If a union decreases the supply of labour and the supply of labour curve shifts to S_U, the wage rate rises to $15 an hour and employment decreases to 200 workers. If the union can also increase the demand for labour and shift the demand for labour curve to D_U, the wage rate rises to $20 an hour and 250 workers are employed.

MyEconLab   animation

over the supply of labour to be able to restrict supply below its competitive level—to S_U. If that is all the union is able to do, employment falls to 200 workers and the wage rate rises to $15 an hour.

Suppose now that the union is also able to increase the demand for labour to D_U. The union can get an even bigger increase in the wage rate and with a smaller fall in employment. By maintaining the restricted labour supply at S_U, the union increases the wage rate to $20 an hour and achieves an employment level of 250 workers.

Because a union restricts the supply of labour in the market in which it operates, the union's actions spill over into nonunion markets. Workers who can't get union jobs must look elsewhere for work. This action increases the supply of labour in nonunion markets and lowers the wage rate in those markets. This spillover effect further widens the gap between union and nonunion wages.

Monopsony in the Labour Market Not all labour markets in which unions operate are competitive. Rather, some are labour markets in which the employer possesses market power and the union enters to try to counteract that power.

A market in which there is a single buyer is called a **monopsony**. A monopsony labour market has one employer. In some parts of the country, managed health-care organizations are the major employer of health-care professionals. In some communities, Wal-Mart is the main employer of sales clerks. These firms have monopsony power.

A monopsony acts on the buying side of a market in a similar way to a monopoly on the selling side. The firm maximizes profit by hiring the quantity of labour that makes the marginal cost of labour equal to the value of marginal product of labour and by paying the lowest wage rate at which it can attract this quantity of labour.

Figure 18.5 illustrates a monopsony labour market. Like all firms, a monopsony faces a downward-sloping value of marginal product curve, VMP, which is its demand for labour curve, D—the curve labelled $VMP = D$ in the figure.

What is special about monopsony is the marginal cost of labour. For a firm in a competitive labour market, the marginal cost of labour is the wage rate. For a monopsony, the marginal cost of labour exceeds the wage rate. The reason is that being the only buyer in the market, the firm faces an upward-sloping supply of labour curve—the curve S in the figure.

To attract one more worker, the monopsony must offer a higher wage rate. But it must pay this higher wage rate to all its workers, so the marginal cost of a worker is the wage rate plus the increased wage bill that arises from paying all the workers the higher wage rate.

The supply curve is now the average cost of labour curve and the relationship between the supply curve and the marginal cost of labour curve, MCL, is similar to that between a monopoly's demand curve and marginal revenue curve (see p. 302). The relationship between the supply curve and the MCL curve is also similar to that between a firm's average cost curve and marginal cost curve (see pp. 258–259).

To find the profit-maximizing quantity of labour to hire, the monopsony sets the marginal cost of labour equal to the value of marginal product of labour. In Fig. 18.5, this outcome occurs when the firm employs 100 workers.

To hire 100 workers, the firm must pay $10 an hour (on the supply of labour curve). Each worker is paid $10 an hour, but the value of marginal product of labour is $20 an hour, so the firm makes an economic profit of $10 an hour on the marginal worker.

If the labour market in Fig. 18.5 were competitive, the equilibrium wage rate and employment would be determined by the demand and supply curves. The wage rate would be $15 an hour, and 150 workers would be employed. So compared with a competitive labour market, a monopsony pays a lower wage rate and employs fewer workers.

A Union and a Monopsony A union is like a monopoly. If the union (monopoly seller) faces a monopsony buyer, the situation is called **bilateral monopoly**. The National Hockey League (the owners) and the National Hockey League Players Association (the union of players) is an example of bilateral

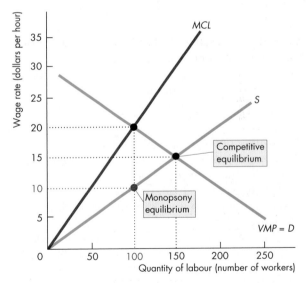

FIGURE 18.5 A Monopsony Labour Market

A monopsony is a market structure in which there is a single buyer. A monopsony in the labour market has a value of marginal product curve VMP and faces a labour supply curve S. The marginal cost of labour curve is MCL. Making the marginal cost of labour equal to the value of marginal product maximizes profit. The monopsony hires 100 hours of labour and pays the lowest wage rate for which that quantity of labour will work, which is $10 an hour.

MyEconLab   animation

monopoly. The NHL and the NHLPA negotiate a multi-year salary deal.

The outcome of bargaining depends on the costs that each party can inflict on the other. The firm can shut down the plant and lock out its workers, and the workers can shut down the plant by striking. Each party estimates the other's strength and what it will lose if it does not agree to the other's demands.

Usually, an agreement is reached without a strike or a lockout. The threat is usually enough to bring the bargaining parties to an agreement. When a strike or lockout does occur, it is because one party has misjudged the costs each party can inflict on the other. Such an event occurred on September 15, 2004, when negotiations failed and the owners locked out the players. The 88th NHL season was cancelled. Teams lost an estimated $2 billion in revenue from tickets, media, sponsorships, and concessions, while players gave up about $1 billion in lost salaries.

In the example in Fig. 18.5, if the union and employer are equally strong, and each party knows the strength of the other, they will agree to split the gap between $10 (the wage rate on the supply curve) and $20 (the wage rate on the demand curve) and agree to a wage rate of $15 an hour.

You've now seen that in a monopsony, a union can bargain for a higher wage rate without sacrificing jobs. A similar outcome can arise in a monopsony labour market when a minimum wage law is enforced. Let's look at the effect of a minimum wage.

Monopsony and the Minimum Wage In a competitive labour market, a minimum wage that exceeds the equilibrium wage decreases employment (see Chapter 6, pp. 131–132). In a monopsony labour market, a minimum wage can increase both the wage rate and employment. Let's see how.

Figure 18.6 shows a monopsony labour market without a union. The wage rate is $10 an hour and 100 workers are employed.

A minimum wage law is passed that requires employers to pay at least $15 an hour. The monopsony now faces a perfectly elastic supply of labour at $15 an hour up to 150 workers (along the minimum wage line). To hire more than 150 workers, a wage rate above $15 an hour must be paid (along the supply curve). Because the wage rate is $15 an hour up to 150 workers, so is the marginal cost of labour $15 an hour up to 150 workers. To maximize profit, the monopsony sets the marginal cost of labour

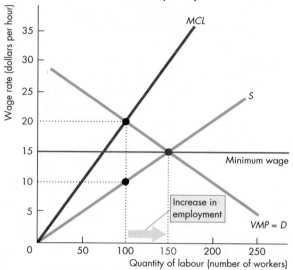

FIGURE 18.6 Minimum Wage Law in Monopsony

In a monopsony labour market, the wage rate is $10 an hour and 100 workers are hired. If a minimum wage law increases the wage rate to $15 an hour, the wage rate rises to this level and employment increases to 150 workers.

———————————— MyEconLab animation ◆

equal to the value of marginal product of labour (on the demand curve). That is, the monopsony hires 150 workers and pays $15 an hour. The minimum wage law has succeeded in raising the wage rate and increasing the number of workers employed.

Scale of the Union–Nonunion Wage Gap

You've seen how a union can influence the wage rate, but how much of a difference to wage rates do unions actually make? This question is difficult to answer. To measure the difference in wages attributable to unions, economists have looked at the wages of unionized and nonunionized workers who do similar work and have similar skills.

The evidence based on these comparisons is that the union–nonunion wage gap lies between 10 and 25 percent of the wage. For example, unionized airline pilots earn about 25 percent more than nonunion pilots with the same level of skill. In markets that have only a union wage rate, we might presume that the wage rate is 10 to 25 percent higher than it would be in the absence of a union.

Economics in Action
Wage Rates in Canada

In 2010, the average wage rate in Canada was $960 a week. The figure shows the *average weekly wage rates* for 25- to 54-year-olds in 15 jobs.

You can see that a senior manager, on average, earns more than three times as much per week as a chef or cook and more than twice as much as machine operators. Remember that these numbers are averages. Individual managers earn much more or much less than the average manager.

Many more occupations earn a wage rate below the national average than above it. And most of the occupations that earn more than the national average require a university degree and postgraduate training.

Earning differences are explained by differences in the value of marginal product of the skills in the various occupations and in market power.

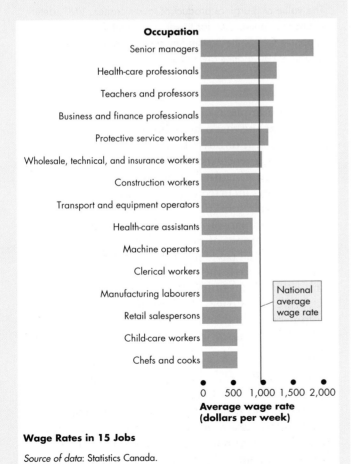

Wage Rates in 15 Jobs

Source of data: Statistics Canada.

Trends and Differences in Wage Rates

You can use what you've learned about labour markets to explain the trend in wage rates and differences between wage rates.

Wage rates increase over time—trend upward. The reason is that the value of marginal product of labour trends upward. Technological change and the new types of capital that it brings make workers more productive. With greater labour productivity, the demand for labour increases and so does the average wage rate. Even jobs in which productivity doesn't increase experience an increase in the *value* of marginal product. Child care is an example. A child-care worker can't care for an increasing number of children, but an increasing number of parents who earn high wages are willing to hire child-care workers. The *value* of marginal product of these workers increases.

Wage rates are unequal, and in recent years they have become increasingly unequal. High wage rates have increased rapidly while low wage rates have stagnated or even fallen. The reasons are complex and not fully understood.

One reason is that the new technologies of the 1990s and 2000s made skilled workers more productive and destroyed some low-skilled jobs. An example is the ATM, which took the jobs and lowered the wage rate of bank tellers and created the jobs and increased the wage rates of computer programmers and electronic engineers. Another reason is that globalization has brought increased competition for low-skilled workers and opened global markets for high-skilled workers.

◆ REVIEW QUIZ

1 What determines the amount of labour that households plan to supply?
2 How is the wage rate and employment determined in a competitive labour market?
3 How do labour unions influence wage rates?
4 What is a monopsony and why is a monopsony able to pay a lower wage rate than a firm in a competitive labour market?
5 How is the wage rate determined when a union faces a monopsony?
6 What is the effect of a minimum wage law in a monopsony labour market?

You can work these questions in Study Plan 18.3 and get instant feedback.

Capital and Natural Resource Markets

The markets for capital and land can be understood by using the same basic ideas that you've seen when studying a competitive labour market. But markets for nonrenewable natural resources are different. We'll now examine three groups of factor markets:

- Capital rental markets
- Land rental markets
- Nonrenewable natural resource markets

Capital Rental Markets

The demand for capital is derived from the *value of marginal product of capital*. Profit-maximizing firms hire the quantity of capital services that makes the value of marginal product of capital equal to the *rental rate of capital*. The *lower* the rental rate of capital, other things remaining the same, the *greater* is the quantity of capital demanded. The supply of capital responds in the opposite way to the rental rate. The *higher* the rental rate, other things remaining the same, the *greater* is the quantity of capital supplied. The equilibrium rental rate makes the quantity of capital demanded equal to the quantity supplied.

Figure 18.7 illustrates the rental market for tower cranes—capital used to construct high-rise buildings. The value of marginal product and the demand curve is *VMP = D*. The supply curve is *S*. The equilibrium rental rate is $1,000 per day and 100 tower cranes are rented.

Rent-Versus-Buy Decision Some capital services are obtained in a rental market like the market for tower cranes. Just as construction companies rent tower cranes, many of the world's largest airlines rent their airplanes. But not all capital services are obtained in a rental market. Instead, firms buy the capital equipment that they use. You saw in Chapter 10 (pp. 226–227) that the cost of the services of the capital that a firm owns and operates itself is an implicit rental rate that arises from depreciation and interest costs. Firms that buy capital *implicitly* rent the capital to themselves.

The decision to obtain capital services in a rental market rather than buy capital and rent it implicitly is made to minimize cost. The firm compares the cost of explicitly renting the capital and the cost of

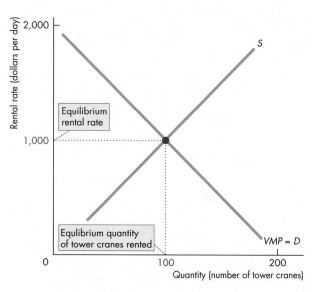

FIGURE 18.7 A Rental Market for Capital

The value of marginal product of tower cranes, *VMP*, determines the demand, *D*, for tower crane rentals. With the supply curve, *S*, the equilibrium rental rate is $1,000 a day and 100 cranes are rented.

MyEconLab animation

buying and implicitly renting it. This decision is the same as the one that a household makes in deciding whether to rent or buy a home.

To make a rent-versus-buy decision, a firm must compare a cost incurred in the *present* with a stream of rental costs incurred over some *future* period. The Mathematical Note (pp. 432–433) explains how to make this comparison by calculating the *present value* of a future amount of money. If the *present value* of the future rental payments of an item of capital equipment exceeds the cost of buying the capital, the firm will buy the equipment. If the *present value* of the future rental payments of an item of capital equipment is less than the cost of buying the capital, the firm will rent (or lease) the equipment.

Land Rental Markets

The demand for land, like the demand for labour and the demand for capital, is a derived demand and is based on the *value of marginal product of land*. Profit-maximizing firms rent the quantity of land at which the value of marginal product of land is equal to the *rental rate of land*. The *lower* the rental rate, other things remaining the same, the *greater* is the quantity of land demanded.

But the supply of land is special: Its quantity is fixed, so the quantity supplied cannot be changed by people's decisions. The supply of each particular block of land is perfectly inelastic.

The equilibrium rental rate makes the quantity of land demanded equal to the quantity available. Figure 18.8 illustrates the market for a 1-hectare block of land in Toronto. The quantity supplied is fixed and the supply curve is *S*. The value of marginal product and the demand curve is *VMP = D*. The equilibrium rental rate is $1,000 a hectare per day.

The rental rate of land is high on Bloor Street, Toronto, because the willingness to pay for the services produced by that land is high, which in turn makes the *VMP* of land high. A Big Mac costs more at McDonald's on Bloor Street than at McDonald's on Mountain Road, Moncton, but not because the rental rate of land is higher in Toronto. The rental rate of land is higher in Toronto because of the greater willingness to pay for a Big Mac (and other goods and services) in Toronto.

FIGURE 18.8   A Rental Market for Land

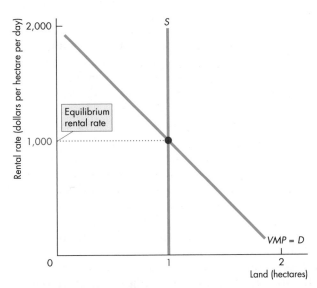

The value of marginal product of a 1-hectare block, *VMP*, determines the rental demand, *D*, for this land. With the supply curve, *S*, the block rents for $1,000 a day.

───────── MyEconLab animation ◆

Nonrenewable Natural Resource Markets

The nonrenewable natural resources are oil, gas, and coal. Burning one of these fuels converts it to energy and other by-products, and the used resource cannot be re-used. The natural resources that we use to make metals are also nonrenewable, but they can be used again, at some cost, by recycling them.

Oil, gas, and coal are traded in global commodity markets. The price of a given grade of crude oil is the same in Calgary, London, and Singapore. Traders, linked by telephone and the Internet, operate these markets around the clock every day of the year.

Demand and supply determine the prices and the quantities traded in these commodity markets. We'll look at the influences on demand and supply by considering the global market for crude oil.

The Demand for Oil   The two key influences on the demand for oil are

1. The *value of marginal product* of oil
2. The expected future price of oil

The value of marginal product of oil is the *fundamental* influence on demand. It works in exactly the same way for a nonrenewable resource as it does for any other factor of production. The greater the quantity of oil used, the smaller is the value of marginal product of oil. Diminishing value of marginal product makes the demand curve slope downward. The lower the price, the greater is the quantity demanded.

The higher the expected future price of oil, the greater is the present demand for oil. The expected future price is a *speculative* influence on demand. Oil in the ground and oil in storage tanks are inventories that can be held or sold. A trader might plan to buy oil to hold now and to sell it later for a profit. Instead of buying oil to hold and sell later, the trader could buy a bond and earn interest. The interest forgone is the opportunity cost of holding the oil. If the price of oil is expected to rise by a bigger percentage than the interest rate, a trader will hold oil and incur the opportunity cost. In this case, the return from holding oil exceeds the return from holding bonds.

The Supply of Oil   The three key influences on the supply of oil are

1. The known oil reserves
2. The scale of current oil production facilities
3. The expected future price of oil

Known oil reserves are the oil that has been discovered and can be extracted with today's technology. This quantity increases over time because advances in technology enable ever-less accessible sources to be discovered. The greater the size of known reserves, the greater is the supply of oil. But this influence on supply is small and indirect. It operates by changing the expected distant future price of oil. Even a major new discovery of oil would have a negligible effect on the current supply of oil.

The scale of current oil production facilities is the *fundamental* influence on the supply of oil. Producing oil is like any production activity: It is subject to increasing marginal cost. The increasing marginal cost of extracting oil means that the supply curve of oil slopes upward. The higher the price of oil, the greater is the quantity supplied. When new oil wells are sunk or when new faster pumps are installed, the supply of oil increases. When existing wells run dry, the supply of oil decreases. Over time, the factors that increase supply are more powerful than those that decrease supply, so changes in the fundamental influence increase the supply of oil.

Speculative forces based on expectations about the future price also influence the supply of oil. The *higher* the expected future price of oil, the *smaller* is the present supply of oil. A trader with an oil inventory might plan to sell now or to hold and sell later. You've seen that interest forgone is the opportunity cost of holding the oil. If the price of oil is expected to rise by a bigger percentage than the interest rate, it is profitable to incur the opportunity cost of holding oil rather than selling it immediately.

The Equilibrium Price of Oil

The demand for oil and the supply of oil determine the equilibrium price and quantity traded. Figure 18.9 illustrates the market equilibrium.

The value of marginal product of oil, *VMP*, is the *fundamental determinant of demand*, and the marginal cost of extraction, *MC*, is the *fundamental determinant of supply*. Together, they determine the *market fundamentals price*.

If expectations about the future price are also based on fundamentals, the equilibrium price is the market fundamentals price. But if expectations about the future price of oil depart from what the market fundamentals imply, *speculation* can drive a wedge between the equilibrium price and the market fundamentals price.

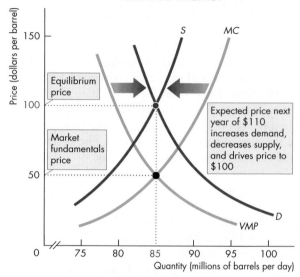

FIGURE 18.9   A Nonrenewable Natural Resource Market

The value of marginal product of a natural resource, *VMP*, and the marginal cost of extraction, *MC*, determine the *market fundamentals price*. Demand, *D*, and supply, *S*, which determine the equilibrium price, are influenced by the expected future price. Speculation can bring a gap between the market fundamentals price and the equilibrium price.

─────── MyEconLab   animation   ◆

The Hotelling Principle

Harold Hotelling, an economist at Columbia University, had an incredible idea: Traders expect the price of a nonrenewable natural resource to rise at a rate equal to the interest rate. We call this idea the **Hotelling Principle**. Let's see why it is correct.

You've seen that the interest rate is the opportunity cost of holding an oil inventory. If the price of oil is expected to rise at a rate that exceeds the interest rate, it is profitable to hold a bigger inventory. Demand increases, supply decreases, and the price rises. If the interest rate exceeds the rate at which the price of oil is expected to rise, it is not profitable to hold an oil inventory. Demand decreases, supply increases, and the price falls. But if the price of oil is expected to rise at a rate equal to the interest rate, holding an inventory of oil is just as good as holding bonds. Demand and supply don't change and the price does not change. Only when the price of oil is expected to rise at a rate equal to the interest rate is the price at its equilibrium.

Economics in Action
The World and Canadian Markets for Oil

The world produced 30 billion barrels of oil in 2011 and the price per barrel increased from $80 in 2010 to $100 in mid-2011. Canada produced 1.1 billion barrels in 2011, which is close to 4 percent of global production. This quantity is more than enough for Canada's use of crude oil. But we sell more than two-thirds our production to the United States and we buy almost one half of the oil that we use from Africa, Europe, the Middle East, Mexico, and Venezuela (see Fig. 1).

Transportation costs explain these movements of oil. It is easy and cheap to pipe oil from Alberta into the United States and Western Canada; and to transport oil in tankers from the rest of the world to Eastern Canada.

As a net exporter, Canada benefits from a high oil price and the Hotelling Principle tells us that we can expect that price to rise at a rate equal to the interest rate. That doesn't mean that the price *will* rise at this rate. As you can see in Fig. 2, the price of oil over the past 60 years has fluctuated a lot.

At some times, such as the 1970s and 2000s, the price of oil has soared. At other times, such as the 1980s and the recent years of global financial crisis, the price has plunged.

Changes in expectations about the future change demand and supply in the present and bring swings

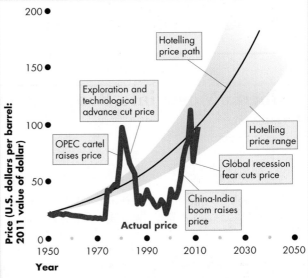

Figure 2 The Price of Oil and Its Hotelling Path

Source of data: U.S. Energy Information Administration.

in the price. But despite its wild fluctuations, the price of oil keeps returning to the Hotelling path and in 2011, the real price of oil was almost exactly on the path predicted by the Hotelling Principle.

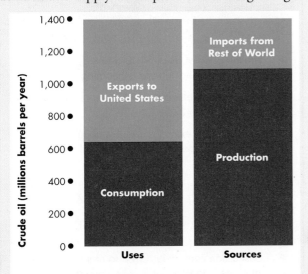

Figure 1 Canada's Uses and Sources of Oil

Sources of data: Statistics Canada and National Energy Board.

REVIEW QUIZ

1 What determines demand and supply in rental markets for capital and land?
2 What determines the demand for a nonrenewable natural resource?
3 What determines the supply of a nonrenewable natural resource?
4 What is the market fundamentals price and how might it differ from the equilibrium price?
5 Explain the Hotelling Principle.

You can work these questions in Study Plan 18.4 and get instant feedback.
———————————————— MyEconLab ◆

◆ *Reading Between the Lines* on pp. 430–431 focuses on the factor markets of Alberta and the way in which they allocate resources and labour.

The next chapter looks at how the market economy distributes income and explains the trends in the distribution of income. The chapter also looks at the efforts by governments to redistribute income and modify the market outcome.

Resources and Labour Interact

Alberta Moves into Boom Territory

Toronto Star

June 7, 2011

We're hearing the "B" word in Alberta again: some are calling it a bubble, others a boom.

But there's no question that the rising price of oil is fuelling optimism about the province's economic prospects even though the rest of the world is still in the doldrums.

Oilsands developments, both current and projected, are the main source of optimism. A recent report by the Calgary-based Canadian Energy Research Institute estimates that oilsands related jobs in Canada will jump from the current 75,000 to 905,000 over the next 25 years. And for every two jobs created in Canada, one will be created in the United States.

Even the ever-shrinking pool of conventional light crude oil is attracting investors who want to get it out of the ground and to market as soon as possible. In a new drilling forecast, the Canadian Association of Oilwell Drilling Contractors said it now expects drilling activity in Western Canada during the last three quarters of 2011 to be 24 percent higher than anticipated last fall.

Economic forecasts haven't been all that reliable in the past few years. And all the current forecasts for Alberta depend on oil prices remaining in the $100-a-barrel zone, or higher. But even if they dip, current bitumen producers can be profitable with the oil price in the $40 to $75 range.

Some in the resource industries are even predicting a labour shortage by next year. They will be looking for skilled workers and those with the latest technological training since getting oil out of the ground is more complicated than ever. But construction companies are also hiring: Ledcor, one of the industry giants, recently launched its first full-scale hiring campaign in an effort to find 9,000 workers for projects across Western Canada. ...

ESSENCE OF THE STORY

- With the price of oil at $100 a barrel, oilsands are profitable and Alberta is booming.

- Production is profitable with a price of oil in the range of $40 to $75.

- New drilling to extract conventional light crude oil is set to be 24 percent higher than anticipated last fall.

- Jobs in the oil industry are expected to grow from 75,000 in 2011 to 905,000 by 2036.

- Oil producers will be hiring increasingly skilled workers.

- Construction companies are also hiring and one firm alone is looking for 9,000 workers.

ECONOMIC ANALYSIS

- The market for oil is a global market, and demand and supply in the global oil market determine the price.

- Both demand and supply depend on expectations of the future price of oil, which results in a highly volatile price.

- But in the long run and on the average, the price of oil is determined by fundamentals: the value of marginal product (VMP) of oil and the marginal cost (MC) of extracting it.

- The market fundamentals price rises at a rate equal to the interest rate—the Hotelling Principle.

- The sources of oil used change in the long run as the price changes. Conventional crude oil reserves are used at a low price and oilsands are used when the price rises to or exceeds the marginal cost of extracting oil from them.

- Figure 1 shows how an increase in the VMP and demand for oil bring a higher price and an increase in Alberta's production.

- With VMP and demand at $VMP_0 = D_0$, the price of oil is $80 a barrel and conventional reserves of crude oil are used.

- With demand at $VMP_1 = D_1$, the price of oil rises to $100 a barrel and the higher marginal cost oilsands are now used.

- As the price of oil keeps rising above $100 a barrel, Alberta's oilsands projects expand and the quantity of oil produced steadily increases.

- The market for oil and the Alberta labour market interact.

- With an expansion of the oilsands development, the demand for labour in Alberta increases. At first, to meet this increase in demand, the wage rate rises and the quantity of labour supplied increases.

- The higher wages and better jobs available in Alberta induce a migration from Eastern Canada westward. This migration brings an increase in the supply of labour in Alberta, which lowers the wage rate but continues to increase the quantity of labour employed.

- Figure 2 illustrates these labour market developments. Initially the demand for labour is LD_0 and the supply of labour is LS_0.

- The higher price of oil increases the value of marginal product of oil workers and the demand for labour increases. The demand curve shifts rightward to LD_1.

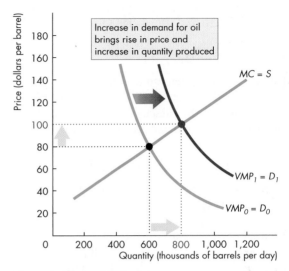

Figure 1 Alberta Oil Market

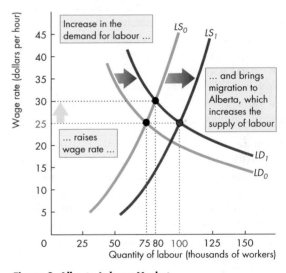

Figure 2 Alberta Labour Market

- The wage rate rises and the higher wage rate increases the quantity of labour supplied.

- The higher wage rate and better employment prospects in Alberta induce people to leave Eastern Canada and move west to Alberta.

- As people move, the supply of labour increases and the supply curve shifts rightward from LS_0 to LS_1.

- The increase in supply increases employment further but lowers the wage rate. In this example, the wage rate returns to its original level.

MATHEMATICAL NOTE

Present Value and Discounting

Rent-Versus-Buy Decision

To decide whether to rent an item of capital equipment or to buy the capital and implicitly rent it, a firm must compare the present expenditure on the capital with the future rental cost of the capital.

Comparing Current and Future Dollars

To compare a present expenditure with a future expenditure, we convert the future expenditure to its "present value."

The **present value** of a future amount of money is the amount that, if invested today, will grow to be as large as that future amount when the interest that it will earn is taken into account.

So the present value of a future amount of money is smaller than the future amount. The calculation that we use to convert a future amount of money to its present value is called **discounting**.

The easiest way to understand discounting and present value is to first consider its opposite: How a present value grows to a future amount of money because of *compound interest.*

Compound Interest

Compound interest is the interest on an initial investment plus the interest on the interest that the investment has previously earned. Because of compound interest, a present amount of money (a present value) grows into a larger future amount. The future amount is equal to the present amount (present value) plus the interest it will earn in the future. That is,

Future amount = Present value + Interest income.

The interest in the first year is equal to the present value multiplied by the interest rate, r, so

Amount after 1 year = Present value +
$\qquad$ ($r \times$ Present value).

or

Amount after 1 year = Present value $\times$ (1 + r).

If you invest $100 today and the interest rate is 10 percent a year ($r = 0.1$), 1 year from today you will have $110—the original $100 plus $10 interest.

Check that the above formula delivers that answer:

$$\$100 \times 1.1 = \$110.$$

If you leave this $110 invested to earn 10 percent during a second year, at the end of that year you will have

Amount after 2 years = Present value $\times$ (1 + r)^2.

With the numbers of the previous example, you invest $100 today at an interest rate of 10 percent a year ($r = 0.1$). After 1 year you will have $110—the original $100 plus $10 interest. And after the second year, you will have $121. In the second year, you earned $10 on your initial $100 plus $1 on the $10 interest that you earned in the first year.

Check that the above formula delivers that answer:

$$\$100 \times (1.1)^2 = \$100 \times 1.21 = \$121.$$

If you leave your $100 invested for n years, it will grow to

Amount after n years = Present value $\times$ (1 + r)^n.

With an interest rate of 10 percent a year, your $100 will grow to $195 after 7 years ($n = 7$)—almost double the present value of $100.

Discounting a Future Amount

We have just calculated future amounts 1 year, 2 years, and n years in the future, knowing the present value and the interest rate. To calculate the present value of these future amounts, we just work backward.

To find the present value of an amount 1 year in the future, we divide the future amount by (1 + r).

That is,

$$\text{Present value} = \frac{\substack{\text{Amount of money} \\ \text{1 year in future}}}{(1 + r)}.$$

Let's check that we can use the present value formula by calculating the present value of $110 1 year from now when the interest rate is 10 percent a year.

You'll be able to guess that the answer is $100 because we just calculated that $100 invested today at 10 percent a year becomes $110 in 1 year. So the present value of $110 1 year from today is $100. But let's use the formula. Putting the numbers into the above formula, we have

$$\text{Present value} = \frac{\$110}{(1 + 0.1)}$$

$$= \frac{\$110}{1.1} = \$100.$$

To calculate the present value of an amount of money 2 years in the future, we use the formula:

$$\text{Present value} = \frac{\text{Amount of money}}{(1 + r)^2}.$$

Use this formula to calculate the present value of $121 2 years from now at an interest rate of 10 percent a year. With these numbers, the formula gives

$$\text{Present value} = \frac{\$121}{(1 + 0.1)^2}$$

$$= \frac{\$121}{(1.1)^2}$$

$$= \frac{\$121}{1.21}$$

$$= \$100.$$

We can calculate the present value of an amount of money n years in the future by using the general formula

$$\text{Present value} = \frac{\text{Amount of money}}{(1 + r)^n}.$$

For example, if the interest rate is 10 percent a year, $100 to be received 10 years from now has a present value of $38.55. That is, if $38.55 is invested today at 10 percent a year it will accumulate to $100 in 10 years.

Present Value of a Sequence of Future Amounts

You've seen how to calculate the present value of an amount of money 1 year, 2 years, and n years in the future. Most practical applications of present value calculate the present value of a sequence of future amounts of money that are spread over several years. An airline's payment of rent for the lease of airplanes is an example.

To calculate the present value of a sequence of amounts over several years, we use the formula you have learned and apply it to each year. We then sum the present values for all the years to find the present value of the sequence of amounts.

For example, suppose that a firm expects to pay $100 a year for each of the next 5 years and the interest rate is 10 percent a year ($r = 0.1$). The present value (PV) of these 5 payments of $100 each is calculated by using the following formula:

$$PV = \frac{\$100}{1.1} + \frac{\$100}{1.1^2} + \frac{\$100}{1.1^3} + \frac{\$100}{1.1^4} + \frac{\$100}{1.1^5},$$

$$PV = \$90.91 + \$82.64 + \$75.13 + \$68.30 + \$62.09$$

$$= \$379.07.$$

You can see that the firm pays $500 over 5 years. But because the money is paid in the future, it is not worth $500 today. Its present value is only $379.07. And the further in the future the money is paid, the smaller is its present value. The $100 paid 1 year in the future is worth $90.91 today, but the $100 paid 5 years in the future is worth only $62.09 today.

The Decision to Lease or Buy

Suppose that a firm is deciding whether to lease or buy a machine. It can lease for 5 years at $100 a year, or it can buy for $500. The machine will be worthless after 5 years. The firm would jump at leasing. Only if the firm could buy the machine for less than $379.07 would it want to buy.

Many personal and business decisions turn on calculations like the one you've just made. A decision to buy or rent an apartment, to lease or rent a car, to pay off a student loan or let the loan run another year can all be made using the above calculation.

SUMMARY

Key Points

The Anatomy of Factor Markets (pp. 416)

- The factor markets are: job markets for labour; rental markets (often implicit rental markets) for capital and land; and global commodity markets for nonrenewable natural resources.
- The services of entrepreneurs are not traded on a factor market.

Working Problem 1 will give you a better understanding of the anatomy of factor markets.

The Demand for a Factor of Production (pp. 417–419)

- The value of marginal product determines the demand for a factor of production.
- The value of marginal product decreases as the quantity of the factor employed increases.
- The firm employs the quantity of each factor of production that makes the value of marginal product equal to the factor price.

Working Problems 2 to 8 will give you a better understanding of the demand for a factor of production.

Labour Markets (pp. 420–425)

- The value of marginal product of labour determines the demand for labour. A rise in the wage rate brings a decrease in the quantity demanded.
- The quantity of labour supplied depends on the wage rate. At low wage rates, a rise in the wage rate increases the quantity supplied. Beyond a high enough wage rate, a rise in the wage rate decreases the quantity supplied—the supply curve eventually bends backward.

- Demand and supply determine the wage rate in a competitive labour market.
- A labour union can raise the wage rate by restricting the supply or increasing the demand for labour.
- A monopsony can lower the wage rate below the competitive level.
- A union or a minimum wage in a monopsony labour market can raise the wage rate without a fall in employment.

Working Problems 9 to 11 will give you a better understanding of labour markets.

Capital and Natural Resource Markets (pp. 426–429)

- The value of marginal product of capital (and land) determines the demand for capital (and land).
- Firms make a rent-versus-buy decision by choosing the option that minimizes cost.
- The supply of land is inelastic and the demand for land determines the rental rate.
- The demand for a nonrenewable natural resource depends on the value of marginal product and on the expected future price.
- The supply of a nonrenewable natural resource depends on the known reserves, the cost of extraction, and the expected future price.
- The price of nonrenewable natural resources can differ from the market fundamentals price because of speculation based on expectations about the future price.
- The price of a nonrenewable natural resource is expected to rise at a rate equal to the interest rate.

Working Problems 12 to 17 will give you a better understanding of capital and natural resource markets.

Key Terms

Bilateral monopoly, 423
Compound interest, 432
Derived demand, 417
Discounting, 432
Hotelling Principle, 428
Job, 416

Labour union, 422
Monopsony, 423
Nonrenewable natural resources, 416
Present value, 432
Value of marginal product, 417

SCAN THIS

STUDY PLAN PROBLEMS AND APPLICATIONS

MyEconLab ◆ You can work Problems 1 to 18 in Chapter 18 Study Plan and get instant feedback.

The Anatomy of Factor Markets (Study Plan18.1)

1. Tim is opening a new online store. He plans to hire people to key in the data at $10 an hour. Tim is also considering buying or leasing some new computers. The purchase price of a computer is $900 and after three years it is worthless. The annual cost of leasing a computer is $450.
   a. In which factor markets does Tim operate?
   b. What is the price of the capital equipment and the rental rate of capital?

The Demand for a Factor of Production (Study Plan18.2)

Use the following data to work Problems 2 to 7. Wanda owns a fish store. She employs students to sort and pack the fish. Students can pack the following amounts of fish:

Number of students	Quantity of fish (kilograms)
1	20
2	50
3	90
4	120
5	145
6	165
7	180
8	190

The fish market is competitive and the price of fish is 50¢ a kilogram. The market for packers is competitive and their market wage rate is $7.50 an hour.

2. Calculate the marginal product of the students and draw the marginal product curve.
3. Calculate the value of marginal product of labour and draw the value of marginal product curve.
4. a. Find Wanda's demand for labour curve.
   b. How many students does Wanda employ?

Use the following additional information to work Problems 5 and 6.
The market price of fish falls to 33.33¢ a kilogram, but the packers' wage rate remains at $7.50 an hour.

5. a. How does the students' marginal product change?
   b. How does the value of marginal product of labour change?

6. a. How does Wanda's demand for labour change?
   b. What happens to the number of students that Wanda employs?

7. At Wanda's fish store packers' wages increase to $10 an hour, but the price of fish remains at 50¢ a kilogram.
   a. What happens to the value of marginal product of labour?
   b. What happens to Wanda's demand for labour curve?
   c. How many students does Wanda employ?

8. **Canadian Housing Starts Rise in July**
   Housing starts rose in July due to an increase in multiple starts in all regions except Quebec. Quebec was also the only region to have July starts fall behind the 12-month average. The largest gains have been in Ontario and British Columbia, with starts up 42 percent and 34 percent year-over-year respectively.
   Source: *Canadian Real Estate Magazine*, August 10, 2011
   a. Explain how an increase in housing starts (building new homes) influences the market for construction labour.
   b. Draw a graph to illustrate the effect of a rise in housing starts in the market for construction labour.

Labour Markets (Study Plan18.3)

Use the following news clip to work Problems 9 to 11.
Rose City Ford Worker Strike
A picket in front of the Rose City Ford dealership (in Windsor, Ontario) blocked traffic as employees walked off the job. The workers, members of the Canadian Auto Workers (CAW) union, have been without a contract since July 2010. Negotiations to agree to a new contract broke off in July 2011. In a recent vote, 74 percent of the workers backed the union against an attempt to decertify it.
   Source: CBC News, August 17, 2011

9. Why would these workers back the CAW?
10. Why might Rose City Ford oppose the CAW?
11. How can the CAW try to raise the wage rate of the Rose City Ford workers?

Capital and Natural Resource Markets (Study Plan 18.4)

12. Classify the following items as a nonrenewable natural resource, a renewable natural resource, or not a natural resource. Explain your answers.
    a. The CN Tower
    b. Lake Huron
    c. Coal in an Alberta mine
    d. The Internet
    e. Algonquin Park
    f. Power generated by wind turbines

13. **Ford Wants to Speed Up Land Sales to Ease Debt**

    Build Toronto, launched in 2009, controls 40 city properties that are worth more than $200 million, and their value keeps rising. Mayor Rob Ford wants Build Toronto to accelerate sales of these properties and make the land available for development and ease the city's debt.

    Source: *The Toronto Star*, August 3, 2011
    a. Why does the price of land in Toronto keep rising? In your answer include a discussion of the demand for and supply of land.
    b. Use a graph to show why the price of land in Toronto has increased over the past decade.
    c. Is the supply of land in Toronto perfectly inelastic?

14. In the news clip in Problem 8,
    a. Explain how a rise in housing starts influences the market for construction equipment leases.
    b. Draw a graph to illustrate the effect of a rise in housing starts in the market for construction equipment leases.

Use the following news clip to work Problems 15 and 16.

Intensive Farming: Ecologically Sustainable?

According to the European Commission, global agricultural production needs to be doubled by 2050 to feed the world. But at the same time, it says this will have to be done with less water and fewer pesticides and greenhouse gas emissions, amid growing competition for land.

Source: euractiv.com, August 16, 2011

15. a. Is farmland a renewable or nonrenewable resource?
    b. Explain how the growing demand for farm products will affect the market for land and draw a graph to illustrate your answer.

16. How might farmers meet the growing demand for farm products without having to use a greater quantity of farmland?

17. **Wind Giants Rising off British Shores**

    Each blade of a wind turbine is longer than the wingspan of a jumbo jet and the blades are set on towers taller than Big Ben! Thirty turbines built by a Swedish power company are being installed in the Irish Sea at a cost of £500 billion—a cost vastly greater than that of conventional coal fired power stations that would generate the same amount of power. As part of its green energy effort to meet targets for cutting carbon emissions, the UK government plans to generate a quarter of the country's electricity using offshore wind by 2020.

    Source: BBC News, August 15, 2011
    a. Explain how meeting carbon emission targets is influencing the market for wind turbines.
    b. What happens to the value of marginal product of a wind turbine as a power company installs additional turbines?

Mathematical Note (Study Plan 18.MN)

18. Keshia is opening a new bookkeeping service. She is considering buying or leasing some new laptop computers. The purchase price of a laptop is $1,500 and after three years it is worthless. The annual lease rate is $550 per laptop. The value of marginal product of one laptop is $700 a year. The value of marginal product of a second laptop is $625 a year. The value of marginal product of a third laptop is $575 a year. And the value of marginal product of a fourth laptop is $500 a year.
    a. How many laptops will Keshia lease or buy?
    b. If the interest rate is 4 percent a year, will Keshia lease or buy her laptops?
    c. If the interest rate is 6 percent a year, will Keshia lease or buy her laptops?

ADDITIONAL PROBLEMS AND APPLICATIONS

MyEconLab ◆ You can work these problems in MyEconLab if assigned by your instructor.

The Anatomy of Factor Markets

19. Venus is opening a tennis school. She plans to hire a marketing graduate to promote the school and an administrator at $20 an hour. Venus is also considering buying or leasing a new tennis ball machine. The purchase price of the machine is $1,000 and after three years it is worthless. The annual cost of leasing the machine is $500.
    a. In which factor markets does Venus operate?
    b. What is the price of the capital equipment and the rental rate of capital?

The Demand for a Factor of Production

Use the following data to work Problems 20 to 23.
Kaiser's Ice Cream Parlour hires workers to produce smoothies. The market for smoothies is perfectly competitive, and the price of a smoothie is $4. The labour market is competitive, and the wage rate is $40 a day. The table shows the workers' total product schedule.

Number of workers	Quantity produced (smoothies per day)
1	7
2	21
3	33
4	43
5	51
6	55

20. Calculate the marginal product of hiring the fourth worker and the fourth worker's value of marginal product.

21. How many workers will Kaiser's hire to maximize its profit and how many smoothies a day will Kaiser's produce?

22. If the price rises to $5 a smoothie, how many workers will Kaiser's hire?

23. Kaiser's installs a new soda fountain that increases the productivity of workers by 50 percent. If the price of a smoothie remains at $4 and the wage rises to $48 a day, how many workers does Kaiser's hire?

Use the following news clip to work Problems 24 and 25.

New Refinery's Oil Terminal Cleared

Newfoundland and Labrador Refining Corp., in the race to build North America's first new refinery in a generation, has received federal environmental approvals for its marine terminal. The facility proposed will cost $4.6 billion and will process 300,000 barrels of oil per day. A second facility with the same capacity is planned for Saint John, New Brunswick.

Source: *Reuters*, April 30, 2008

24. Explain how a high price of gasoline influences the markets for oil refineries and draw a graph to illustrate the effect.

25. Explain how a high price of gasoline influences the markets for oil refinery labour and draw a graph to illustrate the effect.

Labour Markets

26. **You May Be Paid More (or Less) than You Think**

    It's hard to put a price on happiness, but if you've ever had to choose between a job you like and a better-paying one that you like less, you'd like to know what job satisfaction is worth.

    John Helliwell and Haifang Huang (economists at the University of British Columbia) have estimated four key factors influencing job satisfaction: Trust in management is like a 36 percent pay raise; a job with lots of variety is like a 21 percent pay raise; a job that requires a high level of skill is like a 19 percent pay raise; and a job with enough time to finish your work is like an 11 percent pay raise.

    Source: CNN, March 29, 2006

    a. How might the job characteristics described here affect the supply of labour for different types of jobs?
    b. How might this influence on supply result in different wage rates that reflect the attractiveness of a job's characteristics?

Use the following news clip to work Problems 27 to 30.

The New War over Wal-Mart

Today, Wal-Mart employs more people—1.7 million—than any other private employer in the world. With size comes power: Wal-Mart's prices are lower and workers argue that its wages are also lower than its competitors. Last year, the workers at a Canadian outlet joined the union and Wal-Mart immediately closed the outlet. But does Wal-Mart behave any worse than its competitors? When it comes to payroll, Wal-Mart's median hourly wage tracks the national median wage for general merchandise retail jobs.

Source: *The Atlantic*, June 2006

27. a. Assuming that Wal-Mart has market power in a labour market, explain how the firm could use that market power in setting wages.
    b. Draw a graph to illustrate how Wal-Mart might use labour market power to set wages.

28. a. Explain how a union of Wal-Mart's employees would attempt to counteract Wal-Mart's wage offers (a bilateral monopoly).
    b. Explain the response by the Canadian Wal-Mart to the unionization of employees.

29. Based upon evidence presented in this article, does Wal-Mart function as a monopsony in labour markets, or is the market for retail labour more competitive? Explain.

30. If the market for retail labour is competitive, explain the potential effect of a union on the wage rate. Draw a graph to illustrate your answer.

Capital and Natural Resource Markets

Use the following news clip to work Problems 31 and 32.

Sun About to Shine on Natural Gas

In August 2011, the price of natural gas was roughly 70 percent below its 2008 high, but with the growth of shale gas supplies expected to slow as fracking—using high-pressure water and chemicals to extract natural gas from shale—came under tighter regulation, the price is expected to rise. Conventional natural gas output was falling, U.S. natural gas inventories are low, and the demand for natural gas continues to rise, as the cleaner-burning fuel displaces coal to generate electric power.

Source: *Edmonton Journal*, August 18, 2011

31. a. Is natural gas a renewable or nonrenewable resource? Explain.
    b. Explain the reasons to think the price of natural gas would rise.

32. a. If fracking was completely banned, how would you expect the price of natural gas to respond?
    b. What could cause the price of natural gas to fall in the future?

33. New technology has allowed oil to be pumped from much deeper offshore oil fields than before. For example, 28 deep ocean rigs operate in the deep waters of the Gulf of Mexico.
    a. What effect do you think deep ocean sources have had on the world oil price?
    b. Who will benefit from drilling for oil in the Gulf of Mexico? Explain your answer.

34. Water is a natural resource that is plentiful in Canada but not plentiful in Arizona and southern California.
    a. If Canadians start to export bulk water to Arizona and southern California, what do you predict will be the effect on the price of bulk water?
    b. Will Canada eventually run out of water?
    c. Do you think the Hotelling Principle applies to Canada's water? Explain why or why not.

Economics in the News

35. After you have studied *Reading Between the Lines* on pp. 430–431, answer the following questions.
    a. Why are Alberta's oilsands an attractive target for development when the price of oil exceeds $100 a barrel?
    b. How did the *VMP* of oilsands change during 2010 and 2011? Explain and illustrate your answer with an appropriate graphical analysis.
    c. How does the Hotelling Principle tell us that the Alberta oilsands might eventually be used?
    d. How does the development of oilsands influence the Alberta labour market? Explain and illustrate your answer with an appropriate graphical analysis.
    e. Could the labour market become so tight that it prevents the profitable development of the oilsands?
    f. Could migration into Alberta make the wage rate fall?
    g. How might the development of efficient green energy sources to deal with climate change affect the world price of oil and the development of Alberta's oilsands?
    h. If efficient green energy sources are developed, what will happen to the *VMP* of Alberta's oilsands? Explain and illustrate your answer with an appropriate graphical analysis.

Economic Inequality

Every night, around 2,500 people sleep outside without shelter in
Vancouver, a city with mansions that are home to some of the wealthiest
Canadians. In Toronto, where Isadore Sharp is building a luxury apartment
tower with a penthouse priced at $30 million, more than 5,000 people
seek a bed every night in a shelter for the homeless. Extreme poverty and
extreme wealth exist side by side in every major Canadian city and in most
parts of the world.

In this chapter, we study economic inequality—its extent, its sources,
and the things governments do to make it less extreme. At the end of the
chapter, in *Reading Between the Lines*, we take a close look at poverty
rates across Canada.

Measuring Economic Inequality

Statistics Canada provides measures of economic inequality based on three definitions of income: market income, total income, and after-tax income. **Market income** equals the wages, interest, rent, and profit earned in factor markets before paying income taxes. **Total income** equals market income plus cash payments to households by governments. **After-tax income** equals total income minus tax payments by households to governments.

The Distribution of Income

Figure 19.1 shows the distribution of annual after-tax income across the 14.3 million households in Canada in 2009. Note that the *x*-axis measures household after-tax income and the *y*-axis is percentage of households.

The most common household income, called the *mode* income, was received by the 7 percent of the households whose incomes fell between $30,000 and $34,999.

The middle level of household income in 2009, called the *median* income, was $48,300. Fifty percent of households have an income that exceeds the median and fifty percent have an income below the median.

The *average* household money income in 2009, also called the *mean* income, was $59,700. This number equals total household after-tax income divided by the 14.3 million households.

You can see in Fig. 19.1 that the mode income is less than the median income and that the median income is less than the mean income. This feature of the distribution of income tells us that there are more households with low incomes than with high incomes. It also tells us that some of the high incomes are very high.

The income distribution in Fig. 19.1 is called a *positively skewed* distribution, which means that it has a long tail of high values. This distribution shape contrasts with the bell distribution of people's heights. In a bell-shaped distribution, the mean, median, and mode are all equal.

Another way of looking at the distribution of income is to measure the percentage of total income received by each given percentage of households. Data are reported for five groups—called *quintiles* or fifth shares—each consisting of 20 percent of households.

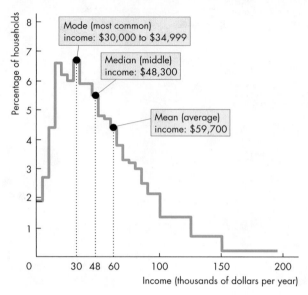

FIGURE 19.1 The Distribution of After-Tax Income in Canada in 2009

Mode (most common) income: $30,000 to $34,999

Median (middle) income: $48,300

Mean (average) income: $59,700

The distribution of after-tax income is positively skewed. The mode (most common) income is less than the median (middle) income, which in turn is less than the mean (average) income. The distribution shown here ends at $200,000 because data above that level are not available, but the distribution goes up to several million dollars a year.

Source of data: Statistics Canada, CANSIM Table 202–0601.

————————————— MyEconLab animation ◆

Figure 19.2 shows the distribution based on these shares in 2009. The poorest 20 percent of households received 4.9 percent of total after-tax income; the second poorest 20 percent received 10.6 percent; the third 20 percent received 16.3 percent; the fourth 20 percent received 24.0 percent; and the highest 20 percent received 44.2 percent of total after-tax income.

The distribution of income in Fig. 19.1 and the quintile shares in Fig. 19.2 tell us that income is distributed unequally. But we need a way of comparing the distribution of income in different periods and using different measures. A clever graphical tool called the *Lorenz curve* enables us to make such comparisons.

FIGURE 19.2   Quintile Shares in Canada in 2009

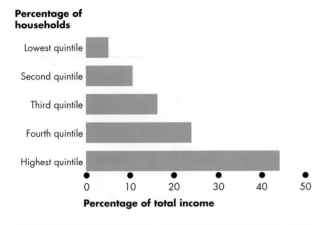

Percentage of households

- Lowest quintile
- Second quintile
- Third quintile
- Fourth quintile
- Highest quintile

Percentage of total income (0 10 20 30 40 50)

Households (percentage)	Income (percentage of total income)
Lowest 20	4.9
Second 20	10.6
Third 20	16.3
Fourth 20	24.0
Highest 20	44.2

In 2009, the poorest 20 percent of households received 4.9 percent of total income; the second poorest 20 percent received 10.6 percent; the third 20 percent received 16.3 percent; the fourth 20 percent received 24.0 percent; and the highest 20 percent received 44.2 percent.

Source of data: Statistics Canada, CANSIM Table 202–0604.

MyEconLab animation

The Income Lorenz Curve

The income **Lorenz curve** graphs the cumulative percentage of income against the cumulative percentage of households. Figure 19.3 shows the income Lorenz curve using the quintile shares from Fig. 19.2. The table shows the percentage of income of each quintile group. For example, row *A* tells us that the lowest quintile of households receives 4.9 percent of total income. The table also shows the *cumulative* percentages of households and income. For example, row *B* tells us that the lowest two quintiles (lowest 40 percent) of households receive 15.5 percent of total income (4.9 percent for the lowest quintile plus 10.6 percent for the next lowest).

FIGURE 19.3   The Income Lorenz Curve in 2009

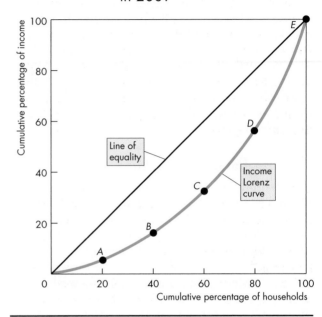

	Households		Income	
	Percentage	Cumulative percentage	Percentage	Cumulative percentage
A	Lowest 20	20	4.9	4.9
B	Second 20	40	10.6	15.5
C	Third 20	60	16.3	31.8
D	Fourth 20	80	24.0	55.8
E	Highest 20	100	44.2	100.0

The cumulative percentage of income is graphed against the cumulative percentage of households. Points *A* through *E* on the Lorenz curve correspond to the rows of the table. If incomes were distributed equally, each 20 percent of households would receive 20 percent of total income and the Lorenz curve would fall along the line of equality. The Lorenz curve shows that income is unequally distributed.

Source of data: Statistics Canada, CANSIM Table 202–0604.

MyEconLab animation

The Lorenz curve provides a direct visual clue about the degree of income inequality by comparing it with the line of equality. This line, identified in Fig. 19.3, shows what the Lorenz curve would be if everyone had the same level of income.

If income were distributed equally across all the households, each quintile would receive 20 percent of total income and the cumulative percentages of income received would equal the cumulative percentages of households, so the Lorenz curve would be the straight line labelled "Line of equality."

The actual distribution of income shown by the curve labelled "Income Lorenz curve" can be compared with the line of equality. The closer the Lorenz curve is to the line of equality, the more equal is the distribution of income.

The Distribution of Wealth

The distribution of wealth provides another way of measuring economic inequality. A household's **wealth** is the value of the things that it owns at a *point in time*. In contrast, income is the amount that the household receives over a given *period of time*.

Figure 19.4 shows the Lorenz curve for wealth in Canada in 1999. The median household wealth in 1999 was $64,000. Wealth is extremely unequally distributed, and for this reason, the data are grouped by seven unequal groups of households. The poorest 40 percent of households owns only 1.1 of total wealth (row A' in the table). The next poorest 10 percent owns only 2.8 percent of total wealth (row B') and the next poorest 10 percent owns only 4.7 percent of total wealth (row C'). So the poorest 60 percent of households owns only 8.6 percent of total wealth. At the other end of the wealth distribution, the wealthiest 10 percent of households owns 55.6 percent of total wealth (row G').

Figure 19.4 shows the income Lorenz curve (from Fig. 19.3) alongside the wealth Lorenz curve. You can see that the Lorenz curve for wealth is much farther away from the line of equality than is the Lorenz curve for income, which means that the distribution of wealth is much more unequal than the distribution of income.

Wealth or Income?

We've seen that wealth is much more unequally distributed than is income. Which distribution provides the better description of the degree of inequality? To answer this question, we need to think about the connection between wealth and income.

Wealth is a stock of assets, and income is the flow of earnings that results from the stock of wealth. Suppose that a person owns assets worth

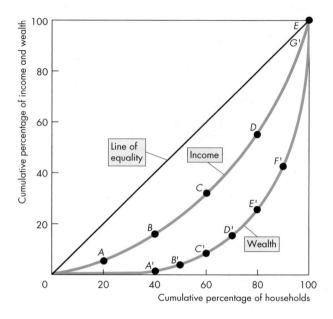

FIGURE 19.4   Lorenz Curves for Income and Wealth in Canada

	Households		Wealth	
	Percentage	Cumulative percentage	Percentage	Cumulative percentage
A' Lowest 40	40	1.1	1.1
B' Next 10	50	2.8	3.9
C' Next 10	60	4.7	8.6
D' Next 10	70	7.4	16.0
E' Next 10	80	11.0	27.0
F' Next 10	90	17.4	44.4
G' Highest 10	100	55.6	100.0

The cumulative percentage of wealth is graphed against the cumulative percentage of households. Points A' through G' on the Lorenz curve for wealth correspond to the rows of the table. By comparing the Lorenz curves for income and wealth, we can see that wealth is distributed much more unequally than is income.

Sources of data: Statistics Canada CANSIM Table 202–0604 and Catalogue 75-202-XIE.

MyEconLab   animation

$1 million—has a wealth of $1 million. If the rate of return on assets is 5 percent a year, then this person receives an income of $50,000 a year from those assets. We can describe this person's economic condition by using either the wealth of $1 million or the income of $50,000. When the rate of return is 5 percent a year, $1 million of wealth equals $50,000 of income in perpetuity. Wealth and income are just different ways of looking at the same thing.

But in Fig. 19.4, the distribution of wealth is more unequal than the distribution of income. Why? It is because the wealth data do not include the value of human capital, while the income data measure income from all wealth, including human capital.

Think about Lee and Peter, two people with equal income and equal wealth. Lee's wealth is human capital and his entire income is from employment. Peter's wealth is investments in stocks and bonds and his entire income is from these investments.

When a Census Bureau agent interviews Lee and Peter in a national income and wealth survey, their incomes are recorded as being equal, but Lee's wealth is recorded as zero, while Peter's wealth is recorded as the value of his investments. Peter looks vastly more wealthy than Lee in the survey data.

Because the national survey of wealth excludes human capital, the income distribution is a more accurate measure of economic inequality than the wealth distribution.

Annual or Lifetime Income and Wealth?

A typical household's income changes over its life cycle. Income starts out low, grows to a peak when the household's workers reach retirement age, and then falls after retirement. Also, a typical household's wealth changes over time. Like income, it starts out low, grows to a peak at the point of retirement, and falls after retirement.

Think about three households with identical lifetime incomes: one young, one middle-aged, and one retired. The middle-aged household has the highest income and wealth, the retired household has the lowest, and the young household falls in the middle. The distributions of annual income and wealth in a given year are unequal, but the distributions of lifetime income and wealth are equal.

The data on inequality share the bias that you've just seen. Inequality in annual income and wealth data overstates lifetime inequality because households are at different stages in their life cycles.

Trends in Inequality

To see trends in the income distribution, we need a measure that enables us to rank distributions on the scale of more equal and less equal. No perfect scale exists, but one that is much used is called the Gini ratio. The **Gini ratio** equals the ratio of the area between the line of equality and the Lorenz curve to the entire area beneath the line of equality. The larger the Gini ratio, the greater is the degree of income inequality. If income is equally distributed, the Lorenz curve is the same as the line of equality, so the Gini ratio is zero. If one person has all the income and everyone else has none, the Gini ratio is 1.

Economics in Action
The Rich Get Richer

The figure shows how the distribution of after-tax income changed between 1976 and 2009. The share of total income received by the richest 20 percent of households increased from 40 percent to 44 percent. The share received by the poorest 20 percent of households remained constant at 5 percent. The shares received by the other three groups decreased, and the share of the third (the middle) 20 percent of households decreased most from 17.9 percent to 16.4 percent. A large amount of research has been done to try to explain these trends.

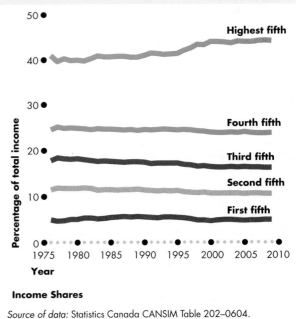

Income Shares

Source of data: Statistics Canada CANSIM Table 202–0604.

Figure 19.5 shows the Canadian Gini ratio from 1976 to 2009. The first thing that stands out in this graph is the rising trend. The Gini ratio increased from about 0.37 to 0.45, a rise of 20 percent, which means that on this measure, incomes became much more unequal.

Looking in more detail at the timing of the rise in the Gini ratio, you can see two bursts. From 1977 to 1989, the ratio increased from 0.37 to 0.39—a modest increase. From 1990 to 1998, it increased from 0.39 to 0.45—a sharp increase. After 2000, the Gini ratio stopped rising, which means that most of the increased inequality occurred during the 1980s and 1990s.

You can see in *Economics in Action* on the previous page some of the details of the increased inequality. The income share of the highest quintile increased while those of the middle quintiles decreased.

No one knows for sure *why* the trend to greater inequality occurred, but we'll explore the most likely explanation later in this chapter (on p. 448).

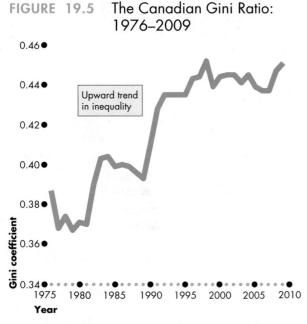

FIGURE 19.5   **The Canadian Gini Ratio: 1976–2009**

Measured by the Gini ratio, the distribution of income in Canada became more unequal from 1976 to 2009. The percentage of income earned by the richest households increased through these years. Some increase in inequality occurred during the 1980s, but most of the increase occurred during the 1990s. Since 2000, the Gini ratio has fluctuated but has not continued an upward trend

Source of data: Statistics Canada, CANSIM Table 202-0705.

MyEconLab   animation ◆

Economics in Action
School Pays

The lowest incomes are earned by people who scratch out a living doing seasonal work on farms. But the poorest Canadians are people who earn nothing and rely on handouts to survive. The incidence of poverty varies systematically depending on household characteristics, and six characteristics stand out:

- Education
- Labour force status
- Source of income
- Household type
- Age of householder
- Number of children

Education   Education makes a huge difference to a household's income and to the risk of being poor. A person who has not completed high school has the highest risk of being poor. University graduates and those with a post-graduate or professional degree have the lowest risk of being poor.

Labour Force Status   Households that are in the labour force, even if unemployed, tend to have higher incomes than those not in the labour force — either they've retired or they have become discouraged by a persistent failure to find a suitable job.

Source of Income   A household that earns its income either by working or from its wealth is unlikely to be poor and a household that receives its income in the form of a transfer payment from the government is more likely to be poor.

Household Type   Households with two parents present are unlikely to be poor. The poorest household is most likely to be one with a single female parent—almost 50 percent of whom are poor.

Age of Householder   The youngest and the oldest households have lower incomes and a greater incidence of poverty than middle-aged households.

Number of Children   On average, the more children in a household, the smaller is the income per person and the more likely the household is to be poor.

Poverty

Poverty is a state in which a family's income is too low to be able to buy the quantities of food, shelter, and clothing that are deemed necessary.

Poverty is both an absolute and a relative concept. Millions of people in Africa and Asia live, barely, in absolute poverty with incomes of less than $400 a year.

In Canada, poverty is identified in relative terms using the concept of the **low-income cut-off**, defined as the income level below which a family normally spends 63.6 percent or more of its income on food, shelter, and clothing. (The low-income cut-off is determined separately for each family type.)

How much poverty (defined as the percentage of families with incomes below the low-income cut-off) is there in Canada, and is the problem getting worse or better? Figure 19.6 answers this question.

The incidence of poverty has fluctuated between a low of 14 percent in 1989 and a high of 20 percent in 1996 and 1997. But there has been no trend in poverty and on the average, 17 percent of Canadian families have incomes below the low-income cut-off.

FIGURE 19.6   The Incidence of Low Income

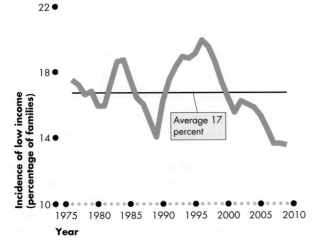

The incidence of low income in Canada has fluctuated between 14 percent and 20 percent of families. On average, 17 percent of families have incomes below the low-income cut-off.

Source of data: Statistics Canada, CANSIM Table 202–0804.

────── MyEconLab   animation   ◆

Economics in Action

How Long Does a Spell of Poverty Last?

Most poverty is temporary and short-lived. The figure shows the numbers: 75 percent of those in poverty remain in that state for less than 1 year and another 8 percent of those in poverty remain so for 1 year. Poverty rates for people who are in that state for 2 years or more are very low.

Given that the average poverty rate is 17 percent of families, around 2 percent of families experience poverty that persists for more than 2 years.

The duration of poverty, like its level, depends on household characteristics, and education is the key. The least well educated tend to be those who experience the most persistent poverty.

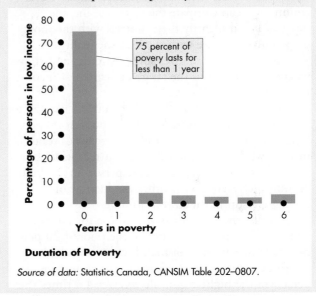

Duration of Poverty

Source of data: Statistics Canada, CANSIM Table 202–0807.

◆ **REVIEW QUIZ**

1 Which is distributed more unequally, income or wealth? Why? Which is the better measure?
2 Has the distribution of income become more equal or more unequal?
3 What are the main characteristics of people who earn large incomes and who earn small incomes?
4 What is poverty and how does its incidence vary across households?

You can work these questions in Study Plan 19.1 and get instant feedback.

────── MyEconLab ◆

Inequality in the World Economy

Which countries have the greatest economic inequality and which have the least and the greatest equality? Where does Canada rank? Is it one of the most equal or most unequal or somewhere in the middle? And how much inequality is there in the world as a whole when we consider the entire world as a single global economy?

We'll answer these questions by first looking at the income distribution in a selection of countries and then by examining features of the global distribution of income.

Income Distributions in Selected Countries

By inspecting the income distribution data for every country, we can compare the degree of income inequality and identify the countries with the most inequality and those with the least inequality.

Figure 19.7 summarizes some extremes and shows where Canada lies in the range of degrees of income inequality.

Look first at the numbers in the table. They tell us that in Brazil and South Africa, the poorest 20 percent of households receive only 2 percent of total income while the highest 20 percent receive 65 percent of total income. An average person in the highest quintile receives 32.5 times the income of an average person in the lowest quintile.

Contrast these numbers with those for Finland and Sweden. In these countries, the poorest 20 percent receive 8 percent of total income and the highest 20 percent receive 35 percent. So an average person in the highest quintile receives 4.4 times the income of an average person in the lowest quintile.

The numbers for Canada lie between these extremes with an average person in the highest quintile receiving just under nine times the income received by an average person in the lowest quintile.

Brazil and South Africa are extremes not matched in any other major country or region. Inequality is large in these countries because they have a relatively small but rich European population and a large and relatively poor indigenous population.

Finland and Sweden are extremes, but they are not unusual. Income distributions similar to these are found in many European countries in which governments pursue aggressive income redistribution policies.

We look next at the global income distribution.

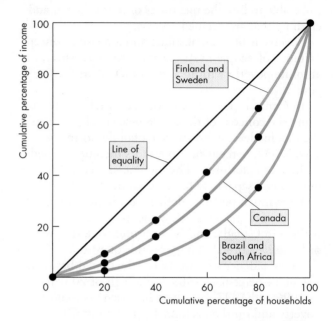

FIGURE 19.7 Lorenz Curves Compared

| Households | Percentage of total income[1] | | |
	Brazil and South Africa	Canada	Finland and Sweden
Lowest 20 percent	2	5	8
Second 20 percent	5	11	14
Third 20 percent	10	16	20
Fourth 20 percent	18	24	23
Highest 20 percent	65	44	35

The table shows the percentages of total income received by each quintile. The figure shows the cumulative percentage of income graphed against the cumulative percentage of households. The data and the Lorenz curves show that income is distributed most unequally in Brazil and South Africa and least unequally in Finland and Sweden. The degree of income inequality in Canada lies between these extremes.

Sources of data: Brazil, South Africa, Finland, and Sweden, Klaus W. Deininger and Lyn Squire, Measuring Income Inequality Database, World Bank, http://go.worldbank.org/. Canada, See Fig. 19.2.

[1]The data are based on income after redistribution. See pp. 453–454 for an account of income redistribution in Canada.

MyEconLab animation ◆

Global Inequality and Its Trends

The global distribution of income is much more unequal than the distribution within any one country. The reason is that many countries, especially in Africa and Asia, are in a pre-industrial stage of economic development and are poor, while industrial countries such as Canada, the United States, and those in Western Europe are rich. When we look at the distribution of income across the entire world population that goes from the low income of the poorest African to the high income of the richest American, we observe a very large degree of inequality.

To put some raw numbers on this inequality, start with the poorest. Measured in the value of the Canadian dollar in 2005, a total of 3 billion people or 50 percent of the world population live on $2.50 a day or less. Another 2 billion people or 30 percent of the world population live on more than $2.50 but less than $10 a day. So 5 billion people or 80 percent of the world population live on $10 a day or less.

In contrast, in rich Canada, the average person has an income of $164 per day and lowest income in the highest income quintile is $240 a day.

So the average Canadian earns 66 times the income of one of the world's 3 billion poorest people and more than 16.4 times the income of 80 percent of the people who live in developing economies. A Canadian with the lowest income in the highest income quintile earns 96 times that of the world's poorest people but only 9 times that of an average Canadian in the lowest quintile.

World Gini Ratio We can compare world inequality with Canadian inequality by comparing Gini ratios. You saw that the Canadian Gini ratio in 2009 was about 0.45. The world Gini ratio is about 0.64. Interpreting the Gini ratio in terms of the Lorenz curve, the world Lorenz curve lies much farther from the line of equality than the Canadian Lorenz curve.

World Trend You saw (in Fig. 19.5 on p. 444) that incomes have become more unequal in Canada—the Gini ratio has increased. The same trends are found in most economies. Increased income inequality is a big issue in two of the world's largest and poorer nations, China and India. In these two economies, urban middle classes are getting richer at a faster pace than the rural farmers.

Despite greater inequality within countries, the world is becoming *less* unequal. Figure 19.8 shows

FIGURE 19.8 The World Gini Ratio: 1970–2000

Measured by the Gini ratio, the distribution of income in the entire world became more equal between 1970 and 2000.

Source of data: Xavier Sala-i-Martin, "The World Distribution of Income: Falling Poverty and . . . Convergence, Period," *Quarterly Journal of Economics*, Vol. 121, No. 2, pp. 351–397, May 2006. Reprinted by permission of MIT Press Journals.

———————— MyEconLab animation ◆

this trend towards less inequality as measured by the world Gini ratio. How can the world income distribution become less unequal while individual countries become more unequal? The answer is that average incomes in poorer countries are rising much faster than average incomes in rich countries. While the gap between rich and poor is widening *within* countries, it is narrowing *across* countries.

◢ REVIEW QUIZ

1 In which countries are incomes distributed most unequally and least unequally?
2 Which income distribution is more unequal and why: the income distribution in Canada or in the entire world?
3 How can incomes become *more* unequally distributed within countries and *less* unequally distributed across countries?

You can work these questions in Study Plan 19.2 and get instant feedback.

———————— MyEconLab ◆

◆ The Sources of Economic Inequality

We've described some key facts about economic inequality and its trends and our task now is to explain those facts. We began this task in Chapter 18 by learning about the forces that influence demand and supply in the markets for labour, capital, and land. We're now going to deepen our understanding of these forces.

Inequality arises from unequal labour market outcomes and from unequal ownership of capital. We'll begin by looking at labour markets and three features of them that contribute to differences in income:

- Human capital
- Discrimination
- Contests among superstars

Human Capital

A clerk in a law firm earns less than one-tenth of the amount earned by the lawyer he assists. An operating room assistant earns less than one-tenth of the amount earned by the surgeon with whom she works. A bank teller earns less than one-tenth of the amount earned by the bank's CEO. Some of the differences in these earnings arise from differences in human capital.

To see the influence of human capital on labour incomes, consider the example of a law clerk and the lawyer he assists. (The same reasoning can be applied to an operating room assistant and surgeon, or a bank teller and bank CEO.)

Demand, Supply, and Wage Rates A lawyer performs many tasks that a law clerk cannot perform. Imagine an untrained law clerk cross-examining a witness in a complicated trial. The tasks that the lawyer performs are valued highly by her clients who willingly pay for her services. Using a term that you learned in Chapter 18, a lawyer has a *high value of marginal product*, and a higher value of marginal product than her law clerk. But you also learned in Chapter 18 that the value of marginal product of labour determines the demand for labour. So, because a lawyer has a high value of marginal product, there is also a high demand for her services.

To become a lawyer, a person must acquire human capital. But human capital is costly to acquire. This cost—an opportunity cost—includes expenditures on tuition and textbooks. It also includes forgone earnings during the years spent in university and law school. It might also include low earnings doing on-the-job training in a law office during the summer.

Because the human capital needed to supply lawyer services is costly to acquire, a person's willingness to supply these services reflects this cost. The supply of lawyer services is smaller than the supply of law-clerk services.

The demand for and supply of each type of labour determine the wage rates that each type earns. Lawyers earn a higher wage rate than law clerks because the demand for lawyers is greater and the supply of lawyers is smaller. The gap between the wage rates reflects the higher value of marginal product of a lawyer (demand) and the cost of acquiring human capital (supply).

Do Education and Training Pay? You know that a lawyer earns much more than a law clerk, but does human capital add more to earning power generally and on average? The answer is that it does. Rates of return on high school and post-secondary education have been estimated to be in the range of 5 percent to 10 percent a year after allowing for inflation, which suggests that a university degree is a better investment than almost any other that a person can undertake.

Human capital differences help to explain much of the inequality that we observe. High-income households tend to be better educated, middle-aged, married couples. Human capital differences are correlated with these household characteristics. Education contributes directly to human capital. Age contributes indirectly to human capital because older workers have more experience than younger workers. Human capital differences can also explain a small part of the inequality associated with sex. A larger proportion of men than women have completed four years of university.

These differences in education levels between the sexes are becoming smaller and today, more women than men are enrolled in university, so this source of differences in average earnings is gradually being eliminated. But it remains a source of the difference in the average earnings of men and women.

Career interruptions can decrease human capital. A person (most often a woman) who interrupts a career to raise young children usually returns to the labour force with a lower earning capacity than a similar person who has kept working. Likewise, a person who has suffered a spell of unemployment often finds a new job at a lower wage rate than that of a similar person who has not been unemployed.

Trends in Inequality Explained by a Race Between Technology and Education You've seen that high-income households have earned an increasing share of total income while lower-income households have earned a decreasing share: Why?

Harvard University economists Claudia Goldin and Lawrence Katz have amassed a heap of data that point towards an answer. They say there is a race between technological change and the education needed to work with the new technologies, and for now, technology is winning.

A related idea is that information technologies such as computers and laser scanners are *substitutes* for low-skilled labour: They perform tasks that previously low-skilled labour did. The introduction of these technologies has lowered the value of marginal product and the demand for low-skilled labour.

These same technologies require high-skilled labour to design, program, and run them. High-skilled labour and the information technologies are *complements*. So the introduction of these technologies has increased the value of marginal product and the demand for high-skilled labour.

As changes in information technology have increased the growth rate of the demand for high-skilled labour, trends in schooling have lowered the growth rate of the supply of high-skilled labour. Since 1995, the trend growth rate of human capital through education has slowed. Before 1995, the percentage of the labour force with a university degree was growing at a rate of 4 percent a year. After 1995, that growth rate slowed to about 2 percent a year.

The combination of the two forces we've just described has lowered the earnings of low-skilled labour and increased the earnings of high-skilled labour.

Figure 19.9 illustrates this outcome. In Fig. 19.9(a), the demand for low-skilled labour decreases from D_0 to D_1 and the supply of low-skilled labour increases from S_0 to S_1. The wage rate falls from $10 per hour to $8 per hour. In Fig. 19.9(b), the demand for high-skilled labour increases from D_0 to D_1 and the supply of high-skilled labour decreases from S_0 to S_1. The wage rate rises from $20 per hour to $25 per hour.

The wider wage gap increases the income share of the highest quintile and lowers the shares of the lower quintiles.

FIGURE 19.9   Explaining the Trend in Income Distribution

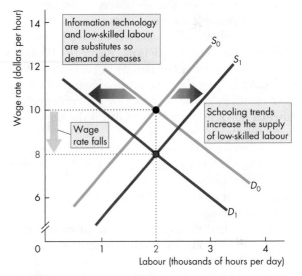

(a) The market for low-skilled labour

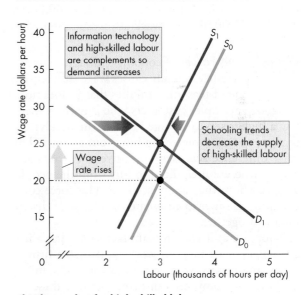

(b) The market for high-skilled labour

In part (a), the demand for low-skilled labour decreases, the supply of low-skilled labour increases, and the wage rate of low-skilled labour falls.

In part (b), the demand for high-skilled labour increases, the supply of high-skilled labour decreases, and the wage rate of high-skilled labour rises. Inequality increases.

MyEconLab   animation

Discrimination

Human capital differences can explain some of the economic inequality that we observe. Discrimination is another possible source of inequality.

Suppose that females and males have identical abilities as investment advisors. Figure 19.10 shows the supply curves of females, S_F in part (a), and of males, S_M in part (b). The value of marginal product of investment advisors, shown by the two curves labelled VMP in parts (a) and (b), is the same for both groups.

If everyone is free of sex-based prejudice, the market determines a wage rate of $40,000 a year for investment advisors. But if the customers are prejudiced against women, this prejudice is reflected in the wage rate and employment.

Suppose that the perceived value of marginal product of the females, when discriminated against, is VMP_{DA}. Suppose that the perceived value of marginal product for males, the group discriminated in favour of, is VMP_{DF}. With these VMP curves, females earn $20,000 a year and only 1,000 females work as investment advisors; males earn $60,000 a year and 3,000 of them work as investment advisors.

Counteracting Forces Economists disagree about whether prejudice actually causes wage differentials, and one line of reasoning implies that it does not. In the above example, customers who buy from men pay a higher service charge for investment advice than do the customers who buy from women. This price difference acts as an incentive to encourage people who are prejudiced to buy from the people against whom they are prejudiced. This force could be strong enough to eliminate the effects of discrimination altogether.

Suppose, as is true in manufacturing, that a firm's customers never meet its workers. If such a firm discriminates against women (or against visible minorities), it can't compete with firms that hire these groups because the firm that discriminates has higher costs than those of the nonprejudiced firms. Only firms that do not discriminate survive in a competitive industry.

Whether because of discrimination or from some other source, women on average do earn lower incomes than men. Another possible source of lower wage rates of women arises from differences in the relative degree of specialization of women and men.

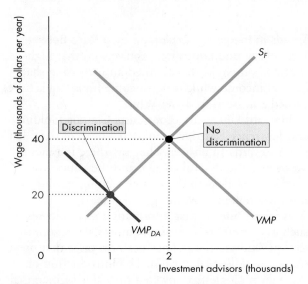

FIGURE 19.10   Discrimination

(a) Females

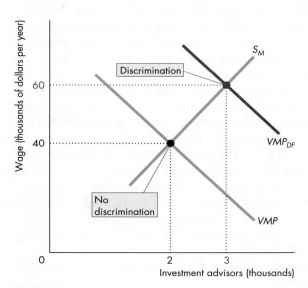

(b) Males

With no discrimination, the wage rate is $40,000 a year and 2,000 of each group are hired. With discrimination against women, the value of marginal product curve in part (a) is VMP_{DA} and that in part (b) is VMP_{DF}. The wage rate for women falls to $20,000 a year, and only 1,000 are employed. The wage rate for men rises to $60,000 a year, and 3,000 are employed.

MyEconLab   animation ◆

Differences in the Degree of Specialization Couples must choose how to allocate their time between working for a wage and doing jobs in the home, such as cooking, cleaning, shopping, organizing vacations, and, most important, bearing and raising children. Let's look at the choices of Bob and Sue.

Bob might specialize in earning an income and Sue in taking care of the home. Or Sue might specialize in earning an income and Bob in taking care of the home. Or both of them might earn an income and share home production jobs.

The allocation they choose depends on their preferences and on their earning potential. The choice of an increasing number of households is for each person to diversify between earning an income and doing some household chores. But in most households, Bob will specialize in earning an income and Sue will both earn an income and bear a larger share of the task of running the home. With this allocation, Bob will probably earn more than Sue. If Sue devotes time and effort to ensuring Bob's mental and physical well-being, the quality of Bob's market labour will be higher than it would be if he were diversified. If the roles were reversed, Sue would be able to supply market labour that earns more than Bob's.

To test whether the degree of specialization accounts for earnings differences between the sexes, economists have compared the incomes of never-married men and women. They have found that, on the average, with equal amounts of human capital, the wages of these two groups are the same.

Contests Among Superstars

The differences in income that arise from differences in human capital are important and affect a large proportion of the population. But human capital differences can't account for some of the really large income differences.

The super rich—those in the top 1 percent of the income distribution—earn vastly more than can be explained by human capital differences. What makes a person super rich?

A clue to the answer is provided by thinking about the super rich in tennis and golf. What makes tennis players and golfers special is that their earnings depend on where they finish in a tournament. When Petra Kvitová won the Wimbledon Championship in 2011, she received £1,100,000 or $1,770,000. The runner-up in this event, Maria Sharapova, received £650,000. So Petra earned 70 percent more than the amount earned by Maria. And she earned 96 times the amount received by the players who lost in the first round of the tournament.

It is true that Petra Kvitová has a lot of human capital. She practices hard and long and is a remarkable athlete. But anyone who is good enough to get into a tennis Grand Slam tournament is similarly well equipped with human capital and has spent a similar number of long hours in training and practice. It isn't human capital that explains the differences in earnings. It is the tournament and the prize differences that accounts for the large differences in earnings.

Three questions jump out: First, why do we reward superstar tennis players (and golfers) with prizes for winning a contest? Second, why are the prizes so different? And third, do the principles that apply on the tennis court (and golf course) apply more generally?

Why Prizes for a Contest? The answer to this question (which was noted in Chapter 5, see p. 104) is that contests with prizes do a good job of allocating scarce resources efficiently when the efforts of the participants are hard to monitor and reward directly. There is only one winner, but many people work hard in an attempt to be that person. So a lot of diligent effort is induced by a contest.

Why Are Prizes So Different? The prizes need to be hugely different to induce enough effort. If the winner received 10 percent more than the runner-up, the gain from being the winner would be insufficient to encourage anyone to work hard enough. Someone would win but no one would put in much effort. Tennis matches would be boring, golf scores would be high, and no one would be willing to pay to see these sports. Big differences are necessary to induce a big enough effort to generate the quality of performance that people are willing to pay to see.

Does the Principle Apply More Generally? Winner-takes-all isn't confined to tennis and golf. Movie stars; superstars in baseball, basketball, football, and ice hockey; and top corporate executives can all be viewed as participants in contests that decide the winners. The prize for the winner is an income around double that of the runner-up and many multiples of the incomes of those who drop out earlier in the tournament.

Do Contests Among Superstars Explain the Trend?

Contests among superstars can explain large differences in incomes. But can contests explain the trend towards greater inequality with an increasing share of total income going to the super rich thereby boosting the income share of the highest quintile?

An idea first suggested by University of Chicago economist Sherwin Rosen suggests that a winner-takes-all contest can explain the trend. The key is that globalization has increased the market reach of the winner and increased the spread between the winner and the runners-up.

Global television audiences now watch all the world's major sporting events and the total revenue generated by advertising spots during these events has increased. Competition among networks and cable and satellite television distributors has increased the fees that event organizers receive. And to attract the top star performers, prize money has increased and the winner gets the biggest share of the prize pot.

So the prizes in sports have become bigger and the share of income going to the "winner" has increased.

A similar story can be told about superstars and the super rich in business. As the cost of doing business on a global scale has fallen, more and more businesses have become global in their reach. Not only are large multinational corporations sourcing their inputs from far afield and selling in every country, they are also recruiting their top executives from a global talent pool. With a larger source of talent, and a larger total revenue, firms must make the "prize"—the reward for the top job—more attractive to compete for the best managers.

We've examined some sources of inequality in the labour market. Let's now look at the way inequality arises from unequal ownership of capital.

Unequal Wealth

You've seen that wealth inequality—excluding human capital—is much greater than income inequality. This greater wealth inequality arises from two sources: life-cycle saving patterns and transfers of wealth from one generation to the next.

Life-Cycle Saving Patterns Over a family's life cycle, wealth starts out at zero or perhaps less than zero. A student who has financed education all the way through graduate school might have lots of human capital and an outstanding student loan of $60,000. This person has negative wealth. Gradually loans get

paid off and a retirement fund is accumulated. At the point of retiring from full-time work, the family has maximum wealth. Then, during its retirement years, the family spends its wealth. This life-cycle pattern means that much of the wealth is owned by people in their sixties.

Intergenerational Transfers Some households inherit wealth from the previous generation. Some save more than enough on which to live during retirement and transfer wealth to the next generation. But these intergenerational transfers of wealth do not always increase wealth inequality. If a generation that has a high income saves a large part of that income and leaves wealth to a succeeding generation that has a lower income, this transfer decreases the degree of inequality. But one feature of intergenerational transfers of wealth leads to increased inequality: wealth concentration through marriage.

Marriage and Wealth Concentration People tend to marry within their own socioeconomic class—a phenomenon called *assortative mating*. In everyday language, "like attracts like." Although there is a good deal of folklore that "opposites attract," perhaps such Cinderella tales appeal to us because they are so rare in reality. Wealthy people seek wealthy partners.

Because of assortative mating, wealth becomes more concentrated in a small number of families and the distribution of wealth becomes more unequal.

REVIEW QUIZ

1 What role does human capital play in accounting for income inequality?

2 What role might discrimination play in accounting for income inequality?

3 What role might contests among superstars play in accounting for income inequality?

4 How might technological change and globalization explain trends in the distribution of income?

5 Does inherited wealth make the distribution of income less equal or more equal?

You can work these questions in Study Plan 19.3 and get instant feedback.

—————————————— MyEconLab ◆

Next, we're going to see how taxes and government programs redistribute income and decrease the degree of economic inequality.

Income Redistribution

The three main ways in which governments in Canada redistribute income are

- Income taxes
- Income maintenance programs
- Subsidized services

Income Taxes

Income taxes may be progressive, regressive, or proportional. A **progressive income tax** is one that taxes income at an average rate that increases as income increases. A **regressive income tax** is one that taxes income at an average rate that decreases as income increases. A **proportional income tax** (also called a *flat-rate income tax*) is one that taxes income at a constant average rate, regardless of the level of income.

The income tax rates that apply in Canada are composed of two parts: federal and provincial taxes. The highest income tax rates are in Quebec and the lowest are in Alberta. There is variety in the detailed tax arrangements in the individual provinces but the tax system, at both the federal and provincial levels, is progressive.

The poorest Canadians pay no income tax. Even those who earn $30,000 a year pay a very low rate of income tax. Those whose incomes are $50,000 a year pay about 21 percent of their income in income taxes; those whose incomes are $100,000 a year pay about 28 percent in income tax; and as incomes increase, the average tax rate increases to 45 percent or higher.

Income Maintenance Programs

Three main types of programs redistribute income by making direct payments (in cash, services, or vouchers) to people in the lower part of the income distribution. They are

- Social security
- Employment insurance
- Welfare

Social Security Four government programs—Old Age Security (OAS), Guaranteed Income Supplement (GIS), the Allowance, and the Allowance for the Survivor (AS)—ensure a minimum level of income for senior citizens. Cash payments to retired or disabled workers or their surviving spouses are paid for by compulsory payroll taxes on both employers and employees. In 2011, the maximum OAS was $533.70 a month, the maximum GIS for a single person was $458.58, the maximum Allowance was $1,013.54, and the maximum AS was $1,134.70.

Employment Insurance To provide an income to unemployed workers, the federal government has established an unemployment compensation program. The Employment Insurance program is funded by employee and employer contributions, and after a qualifying period the worker is entitled to receive a benefit if he or she becomes unemployed. In 2011, the maximum unemployment benefit was 55 percent of gross weekly earnings over the previous 26 weeks, adjusted for the unemployment rate in his or her region of Canada to a maximum of $458 per week.

Welfare Other welfare programs provide income maintenance for families and persons. They are

1. Canada Social Transfer (CST), in support of post-secondary education, social assistance, and social services, including early childhood development, is administered by the provinces and provides basic assistance to cover the cost of food, clothing, personal and household items, and, in some provinces and territories, regularly recurring special needs.
2. Canada/Quebec Pension Plans, funded equally by employee and employer contributions, provide retirement benefits, survivor benefits, disability benefits, and death benefits.
3. Workers' Compensation, a provincial program funded by employers, is designed to provide financial assistance to, as well as medical care and rehabilitation of, workers injured at work.

Subsidized Services

A great deal of redistribution takes place through the provision of subsidized services—services provided by the government at prices below the cost of production. The taxpayers who consume these goods and services receive a transfer in kind from the taxpayers who do not consume them. The two most important areas in which this form of redistribution takes place are education—both kindergarten through grade 12 and college and university—and health care.

Economics in Action

Income Redistribution: Only the Richest Pay

To determine the scale of income redistribution, we need to compare the distribution of *market income* with the distribution of *after-tax income*. The data available on benefits exclude the value of subsidized services (such as the value of university education and health care services), so the resulting distribution might understate the total amount of redistribution from the rich to the poor.

The figures show the scale of redistribution based on the calculations just described. In Fig. 1, the blue Lorenz curve describes the market distribution of income and the green Lorenz curve shows the distribution of income after all taxes and benefits. (The Lorenz curve based on total income—market income plus transfer payments from governments—lies between these two curves.)

The distribution after taxes and benefits is much less unequal than the market distribution. In 2009, the lowest 20 percent of households received only 1.1 percent of market income but 4.9 percent of after-tax income. The second lowest 20 percent of households received 7.2 percent of market income but 10.6 percent of after-tax income. The highest 20 percent of households received 52.4 percent of market income but only 44.2 percent of after-tax income.

Figure 2 highlights the percentage of total income redistributed among the five groups. The share of total income received by the lowest three quintiles (60 percent) of households increased. The share received by the lowest quintile increased by 3.8 percent and the share received by the second lowest quintile increased by 3.4 percent. The share of total income received by the fourth quintile fell slightly. And the share of total income received by the highest quintile fell by 8.2 percent of total income.

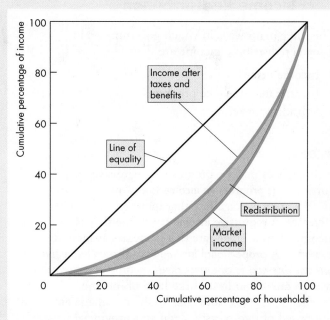

Figure 1   Income Distribution Before and After Redistribution

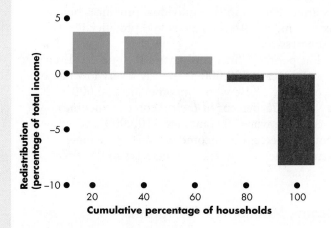

Figure 2   The Scale of Redistribution

Source of data: Statistics Canada CANSIM Table 202–0701.

Canadian students enrolled in the universities in Ontario pay annual tuition fees of around $5,000. This tuition fee is much less than the cost of a year's education. The cost of a year of university education is about $20,000. Thus families with members enrolled in these institutions receive a benefit from the government of about $15,000 per student per year. Those with several college or university students receive proportionately higher benefits.

Government provision of health care to all residents has brought high-quality and high-cost health care to millions of people who earn too little to buy such services themselves. As a result, this program has contributed to reducing inequality.

The Big Tradeoff

The redistribution of income creates what has been called the **big tradeoff**, a tradeoff between equity and efficiency.

You learned in Chapter 5 that there are two views about equity (or fairness): the *fair rules* view and the *fair outcome* view. The fair rules view doesn't present a tradeoff between equity and efficiency because voluntary transactions are efficient and even if they result in inequality, they are considered fair.

The big tradeoff arises from the fair results view of equity. On this view, more equal is fairer: less equal is less fair. But there is a tradeoff—a big tradeoff— because redistributing income and wealth to achieve greater equality ends up creating inefficiencies.

There are two sources of inefficiency from redistributing income and wealth:

- Administrative cost
- Deadweight loss

Administrative Cost   A dollar collected from a rich person does not translate into a dollar received by a poor person. Some of the dollar collected gets used up in the process of redistribution. Tax-collecting agencies such as the Canada Revenue Agency and welfare-administering agencies (as well as tax accountants and lawyers) use skilled labour, computers, and other scarce resources to do their work. The bigger the scale of redistribution, the greater is the opportunity cost of administering it.

But the cost of collecting taxes and making welfare payments is a small part of the total cost of redistribution.

Deadweight Loss   The bigger cost of redistributing income and wealth arises from allocative inefficiency—from deadweight loss—of taxes and benefits.

Greater equality can be achieved only by taxing productive activities—from taxing work and saving. Taxing people's income from their work and saving lowers the after-tax income they receive. This lower after-tax income makes them work and save less, which in turn results in smaller output and less consumption not only for the rich who pay the taxes but also for the poor who receive the benefits.

It is not only taxpayers who face weaker incentives to work. Benefit recipients also face weaker incentives. In fact, under the welfare arrangements that prevail in Canada today, the weakest incentives to work are those faced by households that benefit most from welfare. When a welfare recipient gets a job, benefits are withdrawn and eligibility for support is withdrawn. In effect, these households face a marginal tax rate of more than 100 percent on their earnings. This arrangement locks poor households in a welfare trap.

So the scale and methods of income redistribution must pay close attention to the incentive effects of taxes and benefits.

A Major Welfare Challenge

The poorest people in Canada are women who have not completed high school, have a child (or children), and live without a partner. Single mothers present a major welfare challenge. Their numbers are large— approximately 1 million—and their economic plight and the economic prospects for their children are serious.

For physically fit single mothers, the long-term solution to their problem is education and on-the-job training—acquiring human capital. The short-term solution is welfare. But welfare must be designed to minimize the disincentive to pursue the long-term goal. This is the central challenge in designing an effective welfare program.

◆ REVIEW QUIZ

1 How do governments in Canada redistribute income?
2 Describe the scale of redistribution in Canada.
3 What is one of the major welfare challenges today and how is it being tackled in Canada?

You can work these questions in Study Plan 19.4 and get instant feedback.

———————————————————— MyEconLab ◆

◆ We've examined economic inequality in Canada. We've seen how inequality arises and that inequality has been increasing. *Reading Between the Lines* on pp. 456–457 looks at the increasing incidence of low incomes across Canada and its distribution across the provinces and regions.

Changes in the Poverty Rate

Ontario Poverty Rate Up Since Last Election

Toronto Star
June 18, 2011

Almost 300,000 more Ontarians have sunk into poverty since the McGuinty government was re-elected in 2007 on a pledge to fight the problem, according to the latest Statistics Canada income data from 2009 released this week.

Despite the 2008 recession, which battered Ontario industries, the province's 13.1 percent poverty rate was still slightly below the national average of 13.3 percent, says Ontario's Social Planning Network.

The network of social planning councils crunched the numbers using the after-tax Low Income Measure, the province's new method of measuring poverty.

But Ontario's 17 percent growth in poverty since 2007 was the highest in the country, the group says.

Almost 1.7 million Ontarians are living in poverty, including almost 400,000 children, according to the StatsCan data.

Using the Low Income Measure, an Ontario family of four living on $37,164 or less was considered poor in 2008.

The McGuinty Liberals introduced a Poverty Reduction Act in 2009 aimed at cutting child poverty by 25 percent by 2014. ...

[Social Planning Network] chair Janet Gasparini ... [said] ... "A comprehensive strategy to end poverty among all parts of the population is sorely needed to stem and reverse this direction."

Reprinted with permission—Torstar Syndication Services.

ESSENCE OF THE STORY

- Almost 1.7 million Ontarians, including almost 400,000 children, were living on an income below the Low Income Measure of poverty in 2009.

- The McGuinty Liberal government, re-elected in 2007, pledged to fight poverty and in 2009 introduced a Poverty Reduction Act aimed at cutting child poverty by 25 percent by 2014.

- From 2007 to 2009, the Ontario poverty rate increased and by more than that in any other province.

- Despite the 2008 recession and the large increase, Ontario's poverty rate was below the national average in 2009.

- A comprehensive [government] strategy is needed to reduce poverty in Ontario.

ECONOMIC ANALYSIS

- The news article implies that the poverty rate in Ontario is too high, has risen too much, and is a problem that needs action by the Ontario government.

- The three figures provide some facts about low incomes in Ontario and the other provinces.

- Figure 1 shows three features on the incomes of families in the lowest quintile: redistribution by government, inequality, and after-tax income levels.

- Government redistribution is greatest in the Atlantic provinces and Quebec and least in Alberta. Ontario is in the middle of the pack.

- Inequality, measured by the ratio of average incomes in the highest and lowest quintiles, is greatest in British Columbia and least in Manitoba. Ontario ranks second highest.

- After-tax income of the lowest quintile is greatest in Alberta and least in British Columbia. Again, Ontario is in the middle.

- The data shown in Fig. 1 make it clear that the province with highest income for the poor has the least government redistribution.

- Figure 2 reinforces this conclusion. It shows the poverty rates in 2009. Again, Alberta, the least aggressive in redistributing income, has the lowest poverty rate. Ontario has the third lowest.

- Figure 3 looks at the change in the poverty rates from 2007 to 2009. It is here that Ontario looks worse than the other provinces with a much larger increase in poverty than any other province.

- Alberta, British Columbia, and Manitoba also experienced an increase in their poverty rates.

- The source of these increases in poverty rates is almost certainly a fall in incomes, production, and employment throughout the global economy in 2008.

- Canada shared in this economic contraction and the economically most successful provinces were the hardest hit.

- It is a recovery of the Canadian economy and the global economy that has the best chance to "stem and reverse" Ontario's poverty trend, not more redistribution of income by the government of Ontario.

Three indicators (see legend)

- ■ Redistribution (multiples of market income from government)
- ■ Inequality (ratio of average highest to lowest quintile)
- ■ After-tax income (relative to Canada average × 10)

Figure 1 Three Indicators of Low Income and Inequality

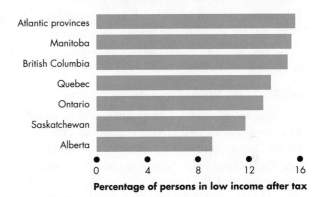

Percentage of persons in low income after tax

Figure 2 Low Income Across the Provinces

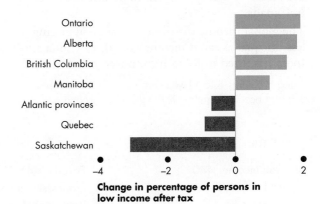

Change in percentage of persons in low income after tax

Figure 3 Changes in Low Income Across the Provinces

Source of data: Statistics Canada CANSIM Table 202–0804.

SUMMARY

Key Points

Measuring Economic Inequality (pp. 440–445)

- In 2009, the mode after-tax household income was between $30,000 and $34,999 a year, the median after-tax income was $48,300, and the mean after-tax income was $59,700.
- The income distribution is positively skewed.
- In 2009, the poorest 20 percent of households received 4.9 percent of total after-tax income and the wealthiest 20 percent received 44.2 percent of total after-tax income.
- Wealth is distributed more unequally than income because the wealth data exclude the value of human capital.
- Between 1976 and 2009, the distribution of income has become more unequal.
- Education, type of household, and age and sex of householder all influence household income.

Working Problems 1 to 7 will give you a better understanding of economic inequality in Canada.

Inequality in the World Economy (pp. 446–447)

- Incomes are distributed most unequally in Brazil and South Africa and least unequally in Finland, Sweden, and some other European economies.
- The Canadian income distribution lies between the extremes.
- The distribution of income across individuals in the global economy is much more unequal than in Canada.
- The global income distribution has been getting less unequal as rapid income growth in China and India has lifted millions from poverty.

Working Problems 8 to 11 will give you a better understanding of economic inequality in the world economy.

The Sources of Economic Inequality (pp. 448–452)

- Inequality arises from differences in human capital and from contests among superstars.
- Trends in the distribution of human capital and in the rewards to superstars that arise from technological change and globalization can explain some of the trend in increased inequality.
- Inequality might arise from discrimination.
- Inequality between men and women might arise from differences in the degree of specialization.
- Intergenerational transfers of wealth lead to increased inequality and assortative mating tends to concentrate wealth.

Working Problems 12 to 15 will give you a better understanding of the sources of economic inequality.

Income Redistribution (pp. 453–455)

- Governments redistribute income through progressive income taxes, income maintenance programs, and subsidized services.
- Redistribution increases the share of total income received by the lowest 60 percent of households and decreases the share of total income received by the two highest quintiles.
- Because the redistribution of income weakens incentives, it creates a tradeoff between equity and efficiency.
- Effective redistribution seeks to support the long-term solution to low income, which is education and job training—acquiring human capital.

Working Problems 16 to 17 will give you a better understanding of income redistribution.

Key Terms

After-tax income, 440	Poverty, 445
Big tradeoff, 455	Progressive income tax, 453
Gini ratio, 443	Proportional income tax, 453
Lorenz curve, 441	Regressive income tax, 453
Low-income cut-off, 445	Total income, 440
Market income, 440	Wealth, 442

SCAN THIS

STUDY PLAN PROBLEMS AND APPLICATIONS

MyEconLab ◆ You can work Problems 1 to 17 in Chapter 19 Study Plan and get instant feedback.

Measuring Economic Inequality (Study Plan 19.1)

1. What is after-tax income? Describe the distribution of after-tax income in Canada in 2009.

2. The table shows after-tax income shares in Canada in 1986.

Households	After-tax income (percent of total)
Lowest 20 percent	5.5
Second 20 percent	11.4
Third 20 percent	17.6
Fourth 20 percent	24.7
Highest 20 percent	40.8

   a. Draw a Lorenz curve for Canada in 1986 and compare it with the Lorenz curve in 2009 shown in Fig. 19.3 on p. 441.

   b. Was Canadian after-tax income distributed more equally or less equally in 2009 than it was in 1986?

Use the following news clip to work Problems 3 to 6.

Canada's Income Gap Widens, Report Says

The income gap between rich and poor in Canada widened in the period from 1993 to 2009, the Conference Board of Canada reported Wednesday.

   Incomes of the poor increased marginally in the period, it said, but the gap between rich and poor widened.

   The average income of the poorest Canadians rose from $12,400 in 1976 to $14,500 in 2009.

   However, the gap between the real average income of the richest 20 per cent of Canadians and the poorest 20 per cent widened from $92,300 in 1976 to $117,500 in 2009.

Source: CBC News, July 13, 2011

3. What are the implications of the information provided in the news clip for the quintile shares of the highest and lowest quintiles?

4. What are the implications of the information provided in the news article for the change in poverty rates between 1976 and 2009?

5. What is excluded from income measures that can lead to a misleading measurement of the degree of economic inequality?

6. Why has the gap between high-income and low-income households grown in recent decades?

7. **Income of Canadians**

   Median after-tax income for Canadian families of two or more people amounted to $63,800 in 2009, virtually unchanged from 2008. This was the second consecutive year without significant change in after-tax income following four years of growth.

   Source: *The Daily*, Statistics Canada, June 15, 2011

   a. What does the information in this news report tell you about the distribution of income in 2008 and 2009?

   b. What additional information would you need to know how the changes described changed the Canadian Lorenz curve?

Inequality in the World Economy (Study Plan 19.2)

8. Incomes in China and India are a small fraction of incomes in the United States. But incomes in China and India are growing at more than twice the rate of those in the United States.

   a. Explain how economic inequality in China and India is changing relative to that in the United States.

   b. How is the world Lorenz curve and world Gini ratio changing?

Use the following table to work Problems 9 to 11. The table shows the income shares in the United States and the United Kingdom.

Households	U.S. income	U.K. income
	(percentage of total)	
Lowest 20 percent	3	3
Second 20 percent	9	5
Third 20 percent	15	14
Fourth 20 percent	23	25
Highest 20 percent	50	53

9. Create a table that shows the cumulative distribution of U.S. and U.K. incomes. Is the distribution of income more unequal in the United States or in the United Kingdom?

10. Draw the U.K. Lorenz curve and compare it with the Lorenz curve in Fig. 19.3 on p. 441. In which country is income less equally distributed?

11. Draw the U.S. Lorenz curve and compare it with the Lorenz curve in Fig. 19.3 on p. 441. In which country is income less equally distributed?

The Sources of Economic Inequality (Study Plan 19.3)

12. The following figure shows the market for low-skilled labour.

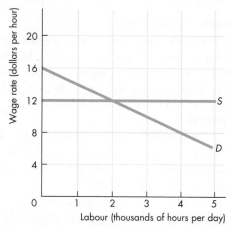

Labour (thousands of hours per day)

The value of marginal product of high-skilled workers is $16 an hour greater than that of low-skilled workers at each quantity of labour. The cost of acquiring human capital adds $12 an hour to the wage that must be offered to attract high-skilled labour.

Compare the equilibrium wage rates of low-skilled labour and high-skilled labour. Explain why the difference between these wage rates equals the cost of acquiring human capital.

Use the following information to work Problems 13 and 14.

In 2011, 3 million Canadians had full-time professional jobs that paid about $800 a week while 1 million Canadians had full-time sales jobs that paid about $530 a week.

13. Explain why professionals are paid more than salespeople and why, despite the higher weekly wage, more people are employed as professionals than as salespeople.

14. If the online shopping trend continues, how do you think the market for salespeople will change in coming years?

15. The figure shows the market for a group of workers who are discriminated against. Suppose that others workers in the same industry are not discriminated against and their value of marginal product is perceived to be twice that of the workers who are discriminated against. Suppose

also that the supply of these other workers is 2,000 hours per day less at each wage rate.

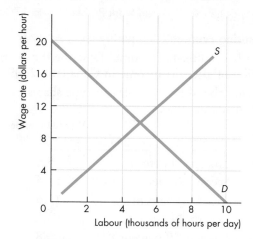

Labour (thousands of hours per day)

a. What is the wage rate of the workers who are discriminated against?
b. What is the quantity of workers employed who are discriminated against?
c. What is the wage rate of the workers who do not face discrimination?
d. What is the quantity of workers employed who do not face discrimination?

Income Redistribution (Study Plan 19.4)

Use the following table to work Problems 16 and 17. The table shows three redistribution schemes.

Before-tax income (dollars)	Plan A tax (dollars)	Plan B tax (dollars)	Plan C tax (dollars)
10,000	1,000	1,000	2,000
20,000	2,000	4,000	2,000
30,000	3,000	9,000	2,000

16. Which scheme has a proportional tax? Which scheme has a regressive tax? Which scheme has a progressive tax?

17. a. Which scheme will increase economic inequality? Explain why.
    b. Which scheme will reduce economic inequality? Explain why.
    c. Which scheme will have no effect on economic inequality? Explain why.

ADDITIONAL PROBLEMS AND APPLICATIONS

MyEconLab ◆ You can work these problems in MyEconLab if assigned by your instructor.

Measuring Economic Inequality

Use the following table to work Problems 18 and 19. The table shows the distribution of market income in Canada in 2009.

Households	Market income (percentage of total)
Lowest 20 percent	1.1
Second 20 percent	7.2
Third 20 percent	14.7
Fourth 20 percent	24.7
Highest 20 percent	52.3

18. a. What is the definition of market income?
    b. Draw the Lorenz curve for the distribution of market income.

19. Compare the distribution of market income with the distribution of after-tax income shown in Fig. 19.3 on p. 441. Which distribution is more unequal and why?

Inequality in the World Economy

Use the following table to work Problems 20 to 22. The table shows shares of income in Australia.

Households	Income share (percentage of total)
Lowest 20 percent	7
Second 20 percent	13
Third 20 percent	18
Fourth 20 percent	24
Highest 20 percent	38

20. Draw the Lorenz curve for the income distribution in Australia and in Brazil and South Africa (use the data in Fig. 19.6 on p. 446). Is income distributed more equally or less equally in Brazil and South Africa than in Australia?

21. Is the Gini ratio for Australia larger or smaller than that for Brazil and South Africa? Explain your answer.

22. What are some reasons for the differences in the distribution of income in Australia and in Brazil and South Africa?

The Sources of Economic Inequality

Use the following news clip to work Problems 23 to 26.

Increased Inequality a Global Phenomenon

The Organization for Economic Cooperation and Development (OECD) held a conference in the summer of 2011 on economic inequality. In a back-grounder to the conference, it published data on changes in the distribution of income over the previous 25 years. Some highlights are:

1. Inequality increased in almost all countries.
2. The increase in inequality in Canada was not exceptionally large or small—it was average.
3. Inequality increased least in Japan and most in Australia.
4. In Japan, the incomes of the lowest group fell but in other countries, they increased.

Source: OECD

23. Explain the main causes of increased income inequality in Canada and other nations.

24. Draw a graph to illustrate how the main causes of increased income inequality generate this outcome.

25. What do the four facts suggest about the causes of the increased inequality?

26. How can income inequality increase if all incomes rise? Why isn't Japan, where the incomes of the lowest group decreased, the only country in which inequality increased?

27. **Where Women's Pay Trumps Men's**
    Men work more than women on the job, at least in terms of overall hours. That's just one reason why in most fields, men's earnings exceed women's earnings. But Warren Farrell found 39 occupations in which women's median earnings exceeded men's earnings by at least 5 percent and in some cases by as much as 43 percent. In fields like engineering, a company may get one woman and seven men applying for a job. If the company wants to hire the woman, it might have to pay a premium to get her. Also, where women can combine technical expertise with people

skills—such as those required in sales and where customers prefer dealing with a woman—that's likely to contribute to a premium in pay.

Source: CNN, March 2, 2006

a. Draw a graph to illustrate why discrimination could result in female workers getting paid more than male workers for some jobs.

b. Explain how market competition could potentially eliminate this wage differential.

c. If customers "prefer dealing with a woman" in some markets, how might that lead to a persistent wage differential between men and women?

Income Redistribution

28. Use the information provided in Problem 18 and in Fig. 19.3 on p. 441.

a. What is the percentage of total income that is redistributed from the highest income group?

b. What percentages of total income are redistributed to the lower income groups?

29. Describe the effects of increasing the amount of income redistribution in Canada to the point at which the lowest income group receives 15 percent of total income and the highest income group receives 30 percent of total income.

Use the following news clip to work Problems 30 and 31.

Income Gap Growing

In 2009, people in the highest quintile had 24.6 times as much market income as those in the lowest quintile, but after taxes and transfers the people in the highest quintile had 9.1 times as much income as those in the lowest quintile.

In 1989, the people in the highest quintile had 7.2 times more income after taxes and transfers than those in the lowest quintile.

In 1990, 82.9 percent of the unemployed received unemployment benefits. In 2009, 47.8 percent of the unemployed received unemployment benefits.

Source: Conference Board of Canada, July 13, 2011

30. Explain what the information provided in the news clip implies about the effects of income redistribution policies on the income gap between the richest and poorest Canadians.

31. How have changes in employment insurance changed the income gap between the richest and the poorest Canadians?

Economics in the News

32. After you have studied *Reading Between the Lines* on pp. 456–457, answer the following questions.

a. What are the broad facts reported in the news article about the changes in the poverty rate in Ontario and what does Social Planning Network chair Janet Gasparini say is the problem and solution?

b. How does the level of the Ontario poverty rate compare with that of the other provinces?

c. How does the *change* in the Ontario poverty rate compare with that of the other provinces?

d. Which provinces redistribute incomes the most and which the least?

e. What are the implications of the cross-province data on poverty and redistribution for the big tradeoff?

33. **The Best and Worst College Degrees by Salary**

Business administration is always a strong contender for honors as the most popular university major. This is no surprise since students think business is the way to make big bucks. But is business administration really as lucrative as students and their parents believe? Nope.

In a new survey by PayScale, Inc. of salaries by college degree, business administration didn't even break into the list of the top 10 or 20 most lucrative college degrees. A variety of engineering majors claim eight of the top 10 salary spots with chemical engineering ($65,700) winning best for starting salaries. Out of 75 undergrad college majors, business administration ($42,900) came in 35th, behind such degrees as occupational therapy ($61,300), information technology ($49,400), and economics ($48,800).

Source: moneywatch.com, July 21, 2009

a. Why do college graduates with different majors have drastically different starting salaries?

b. Draw a graph of the labour markets for economics majors and business administration majors to illustrate your explanation of the differences in the starting salaries of these two groups.

For Whom?

During the past 35 years, the gap between the richest and the poorest in Canada has widened. But millions in Asia have been lifted from poverty and are now enjoying a high and rapidly rising standard of living. What are the forces that generate these trends? The answer to this question is the forces of demand and supply in factor markets. These forces determine wages, interest rates, rents, and the prices of natural resources. These forces also determine people's incomes.

In Canada, human capital and entrepreneurship are the most prized resources, and their incomes have grown most rapidly. In Asia, labour has seen its wage rates transformed. And in all regions rich in oil, incomes have risen on the back of high and fast-rising energy prices.

Many outstanding economists have advanced our understanding of factor markets and the role they play in helping to resolve the conflict between the demands of humans and the resources available. One of them is Thomas Robert Malthus.

Another is Harold Hotelling, whose prediction of an ever-rising price of nonrenewable natural resources implies an ever-falling rate of their use and an intensifying search for substitutes.

Yet another is Julian Simon, who challenged both the Malthusian gloom and the Hotelling Principle. He believed that people are the "ultimate resource" and predicted that a rising population lessens the pressure on natural resources. A bigger population provides a larger number of resourceful people who can discover more efficient ways of using scarce resources.

Thomas Robert Malthus *(1766–1834), an English clergyman and economist, was an extremely influential social scientist. In his best-selling* Essay on the Principle of Population, *published in 1798, he predicted that population growth would outstrip food production and said that wars, famine, and disease were inevitable unless population growth was held in check by marrying at a late age and living a celibate life. (He married at 38 a wife of 27—marriage ages that he recommended for others.)*

Malthus had a profound influence on Charles Darwin, who got the key idea that led him to the theory of natural selection from the Essay on the Principle of Population. *But it was also Malthus' gloomy predictions that made economics the "dismal science."*

The passion between the sexes has appeared in every age to be so nearly the same, that it may always be considered, in algebraic language, as a given quantity.

THOMAS ROBERT MALTHUS
An Essay on the Principle of Population

TALKING WITH David Card

Professor Card, what attracted you to economics?

When I went to university I had no intention of studying economics: I was planning to be a physics major. I was helping a friend with her problem set and started reading the supply and demand section of the textbook. I was impressed with how well the model seemed to describe the paradox that a bumper crop can be bad for farmers. I read most of the book over the next few days. The next year, I signed up as an economics major.

Almost all your work is grounded in data. You are an empirical economist. How do you go about your work, where do your data come from, and how do you use data?

The data I use come from many different sources. I have collected my own data from surveys; transcribed data from historical sources and government publications; and used computerized data files based on records from censuses and surveys in the United States, Canada, Britain, and other countries.

An economist can do three things with data. The first is to develop simple statistics on basic questions such as "What fraction of families live in poverty?" For this, one needs to understand how the data were collected and processed and how the questions were asked. For example, the poverty rate depends on how you define a "family." If a single mother and her child live with the mother's parents, the income of the mother and the grandparents is counted as "family income."

The second thing economists do with data is develop descriptive comparisons. For example, I have compared the wage differences between male and female workers. Again, the details are important. For example, the male-female wage differential is much bigger if you look at annual earnings than at earnings per hour, because women work fewer hours per year.

Once you've established some simple facts, you start to get ideas for possible explanations. You can also rule out a lot of other ideas.

The third and most difficult thing that empirical economists try to do is infer a causal relationship. In rare instances, we have a true experiment in which a random subgroup of volunteers is enrolled in a "treatment group" and the remainder become the

"control group." The Self Sufficiency Program (SSP)— an experimental welfare reform demonstration in Canada—was conducted this way. Because of random assignment, we know that the treatment and control groups would have looked very similar in the absence of the treatment. Thus when we see a difference in behaviour, such as the higher level of work activity by single parents in the treatment group of SSP, we can infer that the financial incentives of SSP caused people to work more.

> The ... most difficult thing that empirical economists try to do is infer a causal relationship.

Most often, we don't have an experiment. We see a group of people who are subject to some "treatment" (such as a higher minimum wage) and we try

David Card is Class of 1950 Professor of Economics at the University of California, Berkeley, and Director of the Labor Studies Program at the U.S. National Bureau of Economic Research.

Born in Canada, Professor Card obtained his B.A. at Queen's University, Kingston, Ontario, in 1977 and his Ph.D. at Princeton University in 1983. He has received many honours, the most notable of which is the American Economic Association's John Bates Clark Prize, awarded to the best economist under 40.

Professor Card's research on labour markets and the effects of public policies on earnings, jobs, and the distribution of income has produced around 150 articles and several books. His most recent book (co-edited with Alan Auerbach and John Quigley) is *Poverty, the Distribution of Income, and Public Policy* (New York: Russell Sage Foundation, 2006). An earlier book (co-authored with Alan B. Krueger), *Myth and Measurement: The New Economics of the Minimum Wage* (Princeton, NJ: Princeton University Press, 1995), made a big splash and upset one of the most fundamental beliefs about the effects of minimum wages.

Michael Parkin and Robin Bade talked with David Card about his work and the progress that economists have made in understanding how public policies can influence the distribution of income and economic well-being.

to construct a comparison group by finding some other group similar to the treatment group who tell us what the treatment group would have looked like in the absence of treatment. If we can't find a compelling comparison group, we have to be cautious.

In your book on the minimum wage with Alan Krueger, you reported that an increase in the minimum wage increased employment—the opposite of the conventional wisdom. How did you reach that conclusion?

We studied several instances where minimum wages were raised in one place but not in another. For example, when we found out that the New Jersey legislature had recently voted to raise the minimum wage, we set up a survey of fast-food restaurants in New Jersey and in nearby parts of Pennsylvania. We surveyed the stores a few months before the New Jersey minimum went up and then again one year later, after the minimum had been raised. The first-round survey found that conditions were very similar in the two states. In the second round, we found that although wages were now higher in New Jersey, employment was also slightly higher. It was very important to have the first-round survey to benchmark any differences that existed prior to the rise in the minimum. Thus, we argued that any differential changes in New Jersey relative to Pennsylvania from the first round to the second round were most plausibly due to the minimum wage.

How did you explain what you found?

We argued that many employers in New Jersey before the rise in the minimum were operating with vacancies and would have liked to hire more workers but could not do so without raising their wages. In this situation, an increase in the minimum wage can cause some employers to hire more and others to hire less. On average, the net effect on employment can be small. What we saw was a rise in wages and a reduction in vacancies in New Jersey, coupled with a small gain in employment.

You've examined just about every labour market policy. Let's talk about welfare payments to single mothers: How do they influence labour market decisions?

The Self Sufficiency Program welfare demonstration in Canada tested an earnings subsidy as an alternative to conventional welfare payments. The problem with conventional welfare is that recipients have no incentive to work: If they earn $1, their payments are reduced by $1. That led Milton Friedman in the early 1950s to advocate an alternative "negative income tax" program, such as SSP, in which recipients who earn more only lose a fraction of their benefits (in the case of SSP, 50 cents per dollar earned). The results showed that this alternative system encourages single parents to work more.

Immigration has been big news in recent years. Can you describe your work on this issue and your findings?

My research has tried to understand whether the arrival of low-skilled immigrants hurts the labour

465

market opportunities for less-skilled natives. One of my papers studies the effect of the Mariel Boatlift, which occurred in 1980 following a political uprising that led Fidel Castro to declare that people who wanted to leave Cuba were free to exit from the port of Mariel. Within days, a flotilla of small boats from the United States began transporting people to Miami, and 150,000 people eventually left. Over one half stayed in Miami, creating a huge "shock" to the supply of low-skilled labour. I studied the effect by looking at wages and unemployment rates for various groups in Miami and in a set of comparison cities that had very similar wage and employment trends in the previous decade. I found that the influx of the boatlift had no discernible effect on wages or unemployment of other workers in Miami. My later work has confirmed that the Miami story seems to hold in most other cities. Cities can absorb big inflows of low-skilled immigrants with remarkably little negative impact on natives.

The distribution of income has become increasingly unequal. Do we know why?

There are many sources. Family incomes have become more unequal in part because of a rise in families with two very high-wage earners. These families have pulled away from the rest, creating a widening distribution. The very richest families, whose incomes are above the 95th or 99th percentile of the income distribution, earn an increasingly large share of national income. The trends in income for this group account for most of the rise in inequality we have seen in the past 10 years.

Unfortunately, it is very hard to study this group because they represent such a small fraction of families, and they are often under-reported on surveys. The best available data, from tax returns, don't tell us much about the sources of this group's success, though it seems to be due to labour market earnings rather than to previous investments or family wealth.

There is a large literature on wage inequality among the larger "middle" of the population: people who earn up to $150,000 per year, for example. Wage inequality for men in this group rose very sharply in the early 1980s in the United States, rose a little more between 1985 and 1990, and was fairly stable (or even decreasing) in the 1990s. Some of the rise in the 1980s was due to decreases in unionization, and some was due to the changing effects of the minimum wage, which fell in real terms in the early 1980s, and then gained in the early to mid-1990s.

Some researchers ascribe the rest of the trend in wage inequality to the spread of computers and increasing demands for highly skilled workers. Others blame international trade and, most recently, immigration. Those explanations are hard to evaluate because we don't really see the forces of new technology or trade that affect any particular worker. One thing we do know is that wage inequality trends were quite different in many other countries. Canada, for instance, had relatively modest rises in inequality in the 1980s.

What advice do you have for someone who is just beginning to study economics? What other subjects do you think work well alongside economics? Do you have some reading suggestions?

The part of economics that most interests me is the behaviour of people in their everyday life. People constantly have to answer questions such as: Should I get more education? How much should I save? Should I send my children to the local public school? It's extremely important to see how these questions are answered by different people: people from poorer families or other countries or who had to make very different choices. Take any opportunity to find out what life is like for other people. You can learn a lot from reading novels, spending a year abroad, or taking classes in sociology or history. The best economists are observant and thoughtful social scientists. My other piece of advice is study mathematics. The more mathematics training you have, the more easily you can understand what economists are doing. Newton invented calculus to study the motion of planets, but economics benefits from the same tools.

> ... find out what life is like for other people. ... The best economists are observant and thoughtful social scientists.

Absolute advantage A person has an absolute advantage if that person is more productive than another person. (p. 38)

After-tax income Total income minus tax payments by households to governments. (p. 440)

Allocative efficiency A situation in which goods and services are produced at the lowest possible cost and in the quantities that provide the greatest possible benefit. We cannot produce more of any good without giving up some of another good that we *value more highly.* (p. 33)

Anti-combine law A law that regulates oligopolies and prevents them from becoming monopolies or behaving like monopolies. (p. 356)

Average cost pricing rule A rule that sets price to cover cost including normal profit, which means setting the price equal to average total cost. (p. 314)

Average fixed cost Total fixed cost per unit of output. (p. 258)

Average product The average product of a factor of production. It equals total product divided by the quantity of the factor employed. (p. 253)

Average total cost Total cost per unit of output. (p. 258)

Average variable cost Total variable cost per unit of output. (p. 258)

Barrier to entry A natural or legal constraint that protects a firm from potential competitors. (p. 300)

Behavioural economics A study of the ways in which limits on the human brain's ability to compute and implement rational decisions influence economic behaviour—both the decisions that people make and the consequences of those decisions for the way markets work. (p. 194)

Benefit The benefit of something is the gain or pleasure that it brings and is determined by preferences. (p. 8)

Big tradeoff The tradeoff between equality and efficiency. (pp. 117, 455)

Bilateral monopoly A situation in which a monopoly seller faces a monopsony buyer. (p. 423)

Black market An illegal market in which the price exceeds the legally imposed price ceiling. (p. 128)

Budget line The limit to a household's consumption choices. It marks the boundary between those combinations of goods and services that a household can afford to buy and those that it cannot afford. (pp. 180, 204)

Capital The tools, equipment, buildings, and other constructions that businesses use to produce goods and services. (p. 4)

Capital accumulation The growth of capital resources, including *human capital.* (p. 36)

Capture theory A theory that regulation serves the self-interest of the producer, who captures the regulator and maximizes economic profit. (p. 313)

Cartel A group of firms acting together—colluding—to limit output, raise the price, and increase economic profit. (p. 343)

Ceteris paribus Other things being equal—all other relevant things remaining the same. (p. 22)

Change in demand A change in buyers' plans that occurs when some influence on those plans other than the price of the good changes. It is illustrated by a shift of the demand curve. (p. 58)

Change in supply A change in sellers' plans that occurs when some influence on those plans other than the price of the good changes. It is illustrated by a shift of the supply curve. (p. 63)

Change in the quantity demanded A change in buyers' plans that occurs when the price of a good changes but all other influences on buyers' plans remain unchanged. It is illustrated by a movement along the demand curve. (p. 61)

Change in the quantity supplied A change in sellers' plans that occurs when the price of a good changes but all other influences on sellers' plans remain unchanged. It is illustrated by a movement along the supply curve. (p. 64)

Coase theorem The proposition that if property rights exist, only a small number of parties are involved, and transactions costs are low, then private transactions are efficient. (p. 377)

Collusive agreement An agreement between two (or more) producers to form a cartel to restrict output, raise the price, and increase profits. (p. 346)

Command system A method of allocating resources by the order (command) of someone in authority. In a firm a managerial hierarchy organizes production. (pp. 106, 233)

Common resource A resource that is rival and nonexcludable. (p. 392)

Comparative advantage A person or country has a comparative advantage in an activity if that person or country can perform the activity at a lower opportunity cost than anyone else or any other country. (p. 38)

Competitive market A market that has many buyers and many sellers, so no single buyer or seller can influence the price. (p. 56)

Complement A good that is used in conjunction with another good. (p. 59)

Compound interest The interest on an initial investment plus the interest on the interest that the investment has previously earned. (p. 432)

Constant returns to scale Features of a firm's technology that lead to constant long-run average cost as output increases. When constant returns to scale are present, the *LRAC* curve is horizontal. (p. 264)

Consumer equilibrium A situation in which a consumer has allocated all his or her available income in the way that, given the prices of goods and services, maximizes his or her total utility. (p. 183)

Consumer surplus The excess of the benefit received from a good over the amount paid for it. It is calculated as the marginal benefit (or value) of a good minus its price, summed over the quantity bought. (p. 109)

Contestable market A market in which firms can enter and leave so easily that firms in the market face competition from *potential* entrants. (p. 354)

Cooperative equilibrium The outcome of a game in which the players make and share the monopoly profit. (p. 353)

Copyright A government-sanctioned exclusive right granted to the inventor of a good, service, or productive process to produce, use, and sell the invention for a given number of years. (p. 383)

Cross elasticity of demand The responsiveness of the demand for a good to a change in the price of a substitute or complement, other things remaining the same. It is calculated as the percentage change in the quantity demanded of the good divided by the percentage change in the price of the substitute or complement. (p. 91)

Deadweight loss A measure of inefficiency. It is equal to the decrease in total surplus that results from an inefficient level of production. (p. 113)

Demand The entire relationship between the price of the good and the quantity demanded of it when all other influences on buyers' plans remain the same. It is illustrated by a demand curve and described by a demand schedule. (p. 57)

Demand curve A curve that shows the relationship between the quantity demanded of a good and its price when all other influences on consumers' planned purchases remain the same. (p. 58)

Deregulation The process of removing regulation of prices, quantities, entry, and other aspects of economic activity in a firm or industry. (p. 313)

Derived demand Demand for a factor of production—it is derived from the demand for the goods and services produced by that factor. (p. 417)

Diminishing marginal rate of substitution The general tendency for a person to be willing to give up less of good y to get one more unit of good x,

while at the same time remaining indifferent as the quantity of good x increases. (p. 208)

Diminishing marginal returns The tendency for the marginal product of an additional unit of a factor of production to be less than the marginal product of the previous unit of the factor. (p. 255)

Diminishing marginal utility The tendency for marginal utility to decrease as the quantity consumed of a good increases. (p. 182)

Direct relationship A relationship between two variables that move in the same direction. (p. 16)

Discounting The calculation we use to convert a future amount of money to its present value. (p. 432)

Diseconomies of scale Features of a firm's technology that make average total cost rise as output increases—the *LRAC* curve slopes upward. (p. 264)

Doha Development Agenda (Doha Round) Negotiations held in Doha, Qatar, to lower tariff barriers and quotas that restrict international trade in farm products and services. (p. 162)

Dominant-strategy equilibrium An equilibrium in which the best strategy for each player is to cheat *regardless of the strategy of the other player.* (p. 345)

Dumping The sale by a foreign firm of exports at a lower price than the cost of production. (p. 163)

Duopoly A market structure in which two producers of a good or service compete. (p. 342)

Economic depreciation The *fall* in the market value of a firm's capital over a given period. (p. 229)

Economic efficiency A situation that occurs when the firm produces a given output at the least cost. (p. 231)

Economic growth The expansion of production possibilities. (p. 36)

Economic model A description of some aspect of the economic world that includes only those features of the world that are needed for the purpose at hand. (p. 10)

Economic profit A firm's total revenue minus its total cost, with total cost measured as the opportunity cost of production. (p. 228)

Economic rent Any surplus—consumer surplus, producer surplus, or economic profit. (p. 308)

Economics The social science that studies the *choices* that individuals, businesses, governments, and entire societies make as they cope with *scarcity* and the *incentives* that influence and reconcile those choices. (p. 2)

Economies of scale Features of a firm's technology that make average total cost fall as output increases—the *LRAC* curve slopes downward. (pp. 242, 264)

Economies of scope Decreases in average total cost that occur when a firm uses specialized resources to produce a range of goods and services. (p. 243)

Efficiency A situation in which the available resources are used to produce goods and services at the lowest possible cost and in quantities that give the greatest value or benefit. (p. 5)

Efficient scale The quantity at which average total cost is a minimum—the quantity at the bottom of the U-shaped *ATC* curve. (p. 328)

Elastic demand Demand with a price elasticity greater than 1; other things remaining the same, the percentage change in the quantity demanded exceeds the percentage change in price. (p. 87)

Elasticity of supply The responsiveness of the quantity supplied of a good to a change in its price, other things remaining the same. (p. 94)

Entrepreneurship The human resource that organizes the other three factors of production: labour, land, and capital. (p. 4)

Equilibrium price The price at which the quantity demanded equals the quantity supplied. (p. 66)

Equilibrium quantity The quantity bought and sold at the equilibrium price. (p. 66)

Excess capacity A firm has excess capacity if it produces below its efficient scale. (p. 328)

Excludable A good or service or a resource is excludable if it is possible to prevent someone from enjoying the benefit of it. (p. 392)

Exports The goods and services that we sell to people in other countries. (p. 152)

External diseconomies Factors outside the control of a firm that raise the firm's costs as the market output increases. (p. 287)

External economies Factors beyond the control of a firm that lower the firm's costs as the market output increases. (p. 287)

Externality A cost (external cost) or a benefit (external benefit) that arises from production or consumption of a private good and that falls on someone other than its producer or consumer. (p. 372)

Factors of production The productive resources used to produce goods and services. (p. 3)

Firm An economic unit that hires factors of production and organizes those factors to produce and sell goods and services. (pp. 41, 228)

Four-firm concentration ratio A measure of market power that is calculated as the percentage of the value of sales accounted for by the four largest firms in an industry. (p. 238)

Free-rider problem The problem that the market would provide an inefficiently small quantity of a public good. (p. 393)

Game theory A set of tools for studying strategic behaviour—behaviour that takes into account the expected behaviour of others and the recognition of mutual interdependence. (p. 344)

General Agreement on Tariffs and Trade (GATT) An international agreement signed in 1947 to reduce tariffs on international trade. (p. 159)

Gini ratio The ratio of the area between the line of equality and the Lorenz curve to the entire area beneath the line of equality. (p. 443)

Goods and services The objects that people value and produce to satisfy human wants. (p. 3)

Herfindahl-Hirschman Index A measure of market power that is calculated as the square of the market share of each firm (as a percentage) summed over the largest 50 firms (or over all firms if there are fewer than 50) in a market. (p. 238)

Hotelling Principle The idea that traders expect the price of a nonrenewable natural resource to rise at a rate equal to the interest rate. (p. 428)

Human capital The knowledge and skill that people obtain from education, on-the-job training, and work experience. (p. 3)

Implicit rental rate The firm's opportunity cost of using its own capital. (p. 228)

Import quota A restriction that limits the maximum quantity of a good that may be imported in a given period. (p. 160)

Imports The goods and services that we buy from people in other countries. (p. 152)

Incentive A reward that encourages an action or a penalty that discourages one. (p. 2)

Incentive system A method of organizing production that uses a market-like mechanism inside the firm. (p. 233)

Income effect The effect of a change in income on buying plans, other things remaining the same. (p. 213)

Income elasticity of demand The responsiveness of demand to a change in income, other things remaining the same. It is calculated as the percentage change in the quantity demanded divided by the percentage change in income. (p. 92)

Indifference curve A line that shows combinations of goods among which a consumer is *indifferent*. (p. 207)

Individual transferable quota (ITQ) A production limit that is assigned to an individual who is free to transfer (sell) the quota to someone else. (p. 402)

Inelastic demand A demand with a price elasticity between 0 and 1; the percentage change in the quantity demanded is less than the percentage change in price. (p. 86)

Infant-industry argument The argument that it is necessary to protect a new industry to enable it to grow into a mature industry that can compete in world markets. (p. 163)

Inferior good A good for which demand decreases as income increases. (p. 60)

Intellectual property rights Property right for discoveries owned by creators of knowledge. (p. 383)

Interest The income that capital earns. (p. 4)

Inverse relationship A relationship between variables that move in opposite directions. (p. 17)

Job A contract for the trade of labour services. (p. 416)

Labour The work time and work effort that people devote to producing goods and services. (p. 3)

Labour union An organized group of workers that aims to increase the wage rate and influence other job conditions. (p. 422)

Land The "gifts of nature" that we use to produce goods and services. (p. 3)

Law of demand Other things remaining the same, the higher the price of a good, the smaller is the quantity demanded of it; the lower the price of a good, the larger is the quantity demanded of it. (p. 57)

Law of diminishing returns As a firm uses more of a variable factor of production with a given quantity of the fixed factor of production, the marginal product of the variable factor of production eventually diminishes. (p. 255)

Law of supply Other things remaining the same, the higher the price of a good, the greater is the quantity supplied of it. (p. 62)

Legal monopoly A market in which competition and entry are restricted by the granting of a public franchise, government license, patent, or copyright. (p. 300)

Limit pricing The practice of setting the price at the highest level that inflicts a loss on an entrant. (p. 355)

Linear relationship A relationship between two variables that is illustrated by a straight line. (p. 16)

Long run The time frame in which the quantities of *all* factors of production can be varied. (p. 252)

Long-run average cost curve The relationship between the lowest attainable average total cost and output when the firm can change both the plant it uses and the quantity of labour it employs. (p. 263)

Long-run market supply curve A curve that shows how the quantity supplied in a market varies as the market price varies after all the possible adjustments have been made, including changes in each firm's plant and the number of firms in the market. (p. 287)

Lorenz curve A curve that graphs the cumulative percentage of income or wealth against the cumulative percentage of households. (p. 441)

Low-income cut-off The income level below which a family normally spends 63.6 percent or more of its income on food, shelter, and clothing. (p. 445)

Macroeconomics The study of the performance of the national economy and the global economy. (p. 2)

Margin When a choice is made by comparing a little more of something with its cost, the choice is made at the margin. (p. 9)

Marginal benefit The benefit that a person receives from consuming one more unit of a good or service. It is measured as the maximum amount that a person is willing to pay for one more unit of the good or service. (pp. 9, 34)

Marginal benefit curve A curve that shows the relationship between the marginal benefit of a good and the quantity of that good consumed. (p. 34)

Marginal cost The *opportunity cost* of producing *one* more unit of a good or service. It is the best alternative forgone. It is calculated as the increase in total cost divided by the increase in output. (pp. 9, 33, 258)

Marginal cost pricing rule A rule that sets the price of a good or service equal to the marginal cost of producing it. (p. 313)

Marginal external benefit The benefit from an additional unit of a good or service that people other than the consumer enjoy. (p. 379)

Marginal external cost The cost of producing an additional unit of a good or service that falls on people other than the producer. (p. 375)

Marginal private benefit The benefit from an additional unit of a good or service that the consumer of that good or service receives. (p. 379)

Marginal private cost The cost of producing an additional unit of a good or service that is borne by the producer of that good or service. (p. 375)

Marginal product The increase in total product that results from a one-unit increase in the variable input, with all other inputs remaining the same. It is calculated as the increase in total product divided by the increase in the variable input employed, when the quantities of all other inputs remain the same. (p. 253)

Marginal rate of substitution The rate at which a person will give up good *y* (the good measured on the *y*-axis) to get an additional unit of good *x* (the good measured on the *x*-axis) while at the same time remaining indifferent (remaining on the same indifference curve) as the quantity of *x* increases. (p. 208)

Marginal revenue The change in total revenue that results from a one-unit increase in the quantity sold. It is calculated as the change in total revenue divided by the change in quantity sold. (p. 274)

Marginal social benefit The marginal benefit enjoyed by society—by the consumer of a good or service (marginal private benefit) plus the marginal benefit enjoyed by others (marginal external benefit). (p. 379)

Marginal social cost The marginal cost incurred by the producer and by everyone else on whom the cost falls—by society. It is the sum of marginal private cost and marginal external cost. (p. 375)

Marginal utility The *change* in total utility resulting from a one-unit increase in the quantity of a good consumed. (p. 181)

Marginal utility per dollar The marginal utility from a good that results from spending one more dollar on it. It is calculated as the marginal utility from the good divided by its price. (p. 184)

Market Any arrangement that enables buyers and sellers to get information and to do business with each other. (p. 42)

Market failure A situation in which a market delivers an inefficient outcome. (p. 113)

Market income The wages, interest, rent, and profit earned in factor markets and before paying income taxes. (p. 440)

Markup The amount by which the firm's price exceeds its marginal cost. (p. 329)

Microeconomics The study of the choices that individuals and businesses make, the way these choices interact in markets, and the influence of governments. (p. 2)

Minimum efficient scale The *smallest* quantity of output at which the long-run average cost reaches its lowest level. (p. 265)

Minimum wage A regulation that makes the hiring of labour below a specified wage rate illegal. The lowest wage at which a firm may legally hire labour. (p. 131)

Money Any commodity or token that is generally acceptable as a means of payment. (pp. 42, 590)

Money price The number of dollars that must be given up in exchange for a good or service. (p. 56)

Monopolistic competition A market structure in which a large number of firms make similar but slightly different products and compete on product quality, price, and marketing, and firms are free to enter or exit the market. (pp. 237, 324)

Monopoly A market structure in which there is only one firm and it produces a good or service that has no close substitutes, and the firm is protected by a barrier preventing the entry of new firms. (pp. 237, 300)

Monopsony A market in which there is a single buyer. (p. 423)

Nash equilibrium The outcome of a game that occurs when player A takes the best possible action given the action of player B and player B takes the best possible action given the action of player A. (p. 345)

Natural monopoly A market in which economies of scale enable one firm to supply the entire market at the lowest possible cost. (p. 300)

Natural monopoly good A good that is nonrival and excludable. When buyers can be excluded if they don't pay but the good is nonrival, marginal cost is zero. (p. 392)

Negative externality An externality that arises from either production or consumption and that imposes an external cost. (p. 372)

Negative relationship A relationship between variables that move in opposite directions. (p. 17)

Neuroeconomics The study of the activity of the human brain when a person makes an economic decision. (p. 195)

Nonexcludable A good or service or a resource is nonexcludable if it is impossible (or extremely costly) to prevent someone from enjoying its benefits. (p. 392)

Nonrenewable natural resources Natural resources that can be used only once. (p. 416)

Nonrival A good or service or a resource is nonrival if its use by one person does not decrease the quantity available for someone else. (p. 392)

Normal good A good for which demand increases as income increases. (p. 60)

Normal profit The return to entrepreneurship is normal profit and it is the profit that an entrepreneur earns *on average*. (p. 229)

Offshore outsourcing A Canadian firm buys finished goods, components, or services from other firms in other countries. (p. 165)

Offshoring A Canadian firm hires foreign labour and produces in a foreign country or a Canadian firm buys finished goods, components, or services from firms in other countries. (p. 165)

Oligopoly A market structure in which a small number of firms compete. (pp. 237, 342)

Opportunity cost The highest-valued alternative that we must give up to get something. (pp. 8, 31)

Outsourcing A Canadian firm buys finished goods, components, or services from other firms in Canada or from firms in other countries. (p. 165)

Patent A government-sanctioned exclusive right granted to the inventor of a good, service, or productive process to produce, use, and sell the invention for a given number of years. (p. 383)

Payoff matrix A table that shows the payoffs for every possible action by each player for every possible action by each other player. (p. 344)

Perfect competition A market in which there are many firms each selling an identical product; there are many buyers; there are no restrictions on entry into the industry; firms in the industry have no advantage over potential new entrants; and firms and buyers are well informed about the price of each firm's product. (pp. 237, 274)

Perfectly elastic demand Demand with an infinite price elasticity; the quantity demanded changes by an infinitely large percentage in response to a tiny price change. (p. 87)

Perfectly inelastic demand Demand with a price elasticity of zero; the quantity demanded remains constant when the price changes. (p. 86)

Perfect price discrimination Price discrimination that occurs when a firm sells each unit of output for the highest price that anyone is willing to pay for it. The firm extracts the entire consumer surplus. (p. 311)

Pigovian taxes Taxes that are used as an incentive for producers to cut back on an activity that creates an external cost. (p. 378)

Positive externality An externality that arises from either production or consumption and that creates an external benefit. (p. 372)

Positive relationship A relationship between two variables that move in the same direction. (p. 16)

Poverty A state in which a household's income is too low to be able to buy the quantities of food, shelter, and clothing that are deemed necessary. (p. 444)

Preferences A description of a person's likes and dislikes and the intensity of those feelings. (pp. 8, 34, 181)

Present value The amount of money that, if invested today, will grow to be as large as a given future amount when the interest that it will earn is taken into account. (p. 432)

Price cap A regulation that makes it illegal to charge a price higher than a specified level. (p. 128)

Price cap regulation A rule that specifies the highest price that the firm is permitted to set—a price ceiling. (p. 315)

Price ceiling A regulation that makes it illegal to charge a price higher than a specified level. (p. 128)

Price discrimination The practice of selling different units of a good or service for different prices. (p. 301)

Price effect The effect of a change in the price of a good on the quantity of the good consumed, other things remaining the same. (p. 211)

Price elasticity of demand A units-free measure of the responsiveness of the quantity demanded of a good to a change in its price, when all other influences on buyers' plans remain the same. (p. 84)

Price floor A regulation that makes it illegal to trade at a price lower than a specified level. (p. 131)

Price taker A firm that cannot influence the price of the good or service it produces. (p. 274)

Principal-agent problem The problem of devising compensation rules that induce an *agent* to act in the best interest of a *principal*. (p. 234)

Principle of minimum differentiation The tendency for competitors to make themselves similar to appeal to the maximum number of clients or voters. (p. 395)

Private good A good or service that is both rival and excludable. (p. 392)

Producer surplus The excess of the amount received from the sale of a good or service over the cost of producing it. It is calculated as the price of a good minus the marginal cost (or minimum supply-price), summed over the quantity sold. (p. 111)

Product differentiation Making a product slightly different from the product of a competing firm. (pp. 237, 324)

Production efficiency A situation in which goods and services are produced at the lowest possible cost. (p. 31)

Production possibilities frontier The boundary between the combinations of goods and services that can be produced and the combinations that cannot. (p. 30)

Production quota An upper limit to the quantity of a good that may be produced in a specified period. (p. 139)

Profit The income earned by entrepreneurship. (p. 4)

Progressive income tax A tax on income at an average rate that increases as income increases. (p. 453)

Property rights The social arrangements that govern the ownership, use, and disposal of anything that people value. Property rights are enforceable in the courts. (pp. 42, 376)

Proportional income tax A tax on income at a constant average rate, regardless of the level of income. (p. 453)

Public good A good or service that is both nonrival and nonexcludable. It can be consumed simultaneously by everyone and no one can be excluded from enjoying its benefits. (p. 392)

Public production The production of a good or service by a public authority that receives its revenue from the government. (p. 381)

Quantity demanded The amount of a good or service that consumers plan to buy during a given time period at a particular price. (p. 57)

Quantity supplied The amount of a good or service that producers plan to sell during a given time period at a particular price. (p. 62)

Rate of return regulation A regulation that requires the firm to justify its price by showing that its return on capital doesn't exceed a specified target rate. (p. 314)

Rational choice A choice that compares costs and benefits and achieves the greatest benefit over cost for the person making the choice. (p. 8)

Rational ignorance The decision not to acquire information because the cost of doing so exceeds the expected benefit. (p. 396)

Real income A household's income expressed as a quantity of goods that the household can afford to buy. (p. 205)

Regressive income tax A tax on income at an average rate that decreases as income increases. (p. 453)

Regulation Rules administered by a government agency to influence prices, quantities, entry, and other aspects of economic activity in a firm or industry. (p. 313)

Relative price The ratio of the price of one good or service to the price of another good or service. A relative price is an opportunity cost. (pp. 56, 205)

Rent The income that land earns. (p. 4)

Rent ceiling A regulation that makes it illegal to charge a rent higher than a specified level. (p. 128)

Rent seeking The lobbying for special treatment by the government to create economic profit or to divert consumer surplus or producer surplus away from others. The pursuit of wealth by capturing economic rent. (pp. 167, 308)

Rival A good, service, or resource is rival if its use by one person decreases the quantity available for someone else. (p. 392)

Scarcity Our inability to satisfy all our wants. (p. 2)

Scatter diagram A graph that plots the value of one variable against the value of another variable for a number of different values of each variable. (p. 14)

Search activity The time spent looking for someone with whom to do business. (p. 128)

Self-interest The choices that you think are the best ones available for you are choices made in your self-interest. (p. 5)

Short run The time frame in which the quantity of at least one factor of production is fixed and the quantities of the other factors can be varied. The fixed factor is usually capital—that is, the firm uses a given plant. (p. 252)

Short-run market supply curve A curve that shows the quantity supplied in a market at each price when each firm's plant and the number of firms remain the same. (p. 280)

Shutdown point The price and quantity at which the firm is indifferent between producing the profit-maximizing output and shutting down temporarily. The shutdown point occurs at the price and the quantity at which average variable cost is a minimum. (p. 278)

Signal An action taken by an informed person (or firm) to send a message to uninformed people. (p. 332)

Single-price monopoly A monopoly that must sell each unit of its output for the same price to all its customers. (p. 301)

Slope The change in the value of the variable measured on the y-axis divided by the change in the value of the variable measured on the x-axis. (p. 20)

Social interest Choices that are the best ones for society as a whole. (p. 5)

Social interest theory A theory that the political and regulatory process relentlessly seeks out inefficiency and introduces regulation that eliminates deadweight loss and allocates resources efficiently. (p. 313)

Strategies All the possible actions of each player in a game. (p. 344)

Subsidy A payment made by the government to a producer. (pp. 140, 382)

Substitute A good that can be used in place of another good. (p. 59)

Substitution effect The effect of a change in price of a good or service on the quantity bought when the consumer (hypothetically) remains indifferent between the original and the new consumption situations—that is, the consumer remains on the same indifference curve. (p. 214)

Sunk cost The past expenditure on a plant that has no resale value. (p. 252)

Supply The entire relationship between the price of a good and the quantity supplied of it when all other influences on producers' planned sales remain the same. It is described by a supply schedule and illustrated by a supply curve. (p. 62)

Supply curve A curve that shows the relationship between the quantity supplied of a good and its price when all other influences on producers' planned sales remain the same. (p. 62)

Symmetry principle A requirement that people in similar situations be treated similarly. (p. 118)

Tariff A tax that is imposed by the importing country when an imported good crosses its international boundary. (p. 157)

Tax incidence The division of the burden of the tax between the buyer and the seller. (p. 133)

Technological change The development of new goods and of better ways of producing goods and services. (p. 36)

Technological efficiency A situation that occurs when the firm produces a given output by using the least amount of inputs. (p. 231)

Technology Any method of producing a good or service. (p. 230)

Total cost The cost of all the productive resources that a firm uses. (p. 257)

Total fixed cost The cost of the firm's fixed inputs. (p. 257)

Total income Market income plus cash payments to households by governments. (p. 440)

Total product The maximum output that a given quantity of labour can produce. (p. 253)

Total revenue The value of a firm's sales. It is calculated as the price of the good multiplied by the quantity sold. (pp. 88, 274)

Total revenue test A method of estimating the price elasticity of demand by observing the change in total revenue that results from a change in the price, when all other influences on the quantity sold remain the same. (p. 88)

Total surplus The sum of consumer surplus and producer surplus. (p. 112)

Total utility The total benefit that a person gets from the consumption of all the different goods and services. (p. 181)

Total variable cost The cost of all the firm's variable inputs. (p. 257)

Tradeoff A constraint that involves giving up one thing to get something else. (p. 8)

Tragedy of the commons The absence of incentives to prevent the overuse and depletion of a commonly owned resource. (p. 398)

Transactions costs The opportunity costs of making trades in a market. The costs that arise from finding someone with whom to do business, of reaching an agreement about the price and other aspects of the exchange, and of ensuring that the terms of the agreement are fulfilled. (pp. 115, 242, 377)

Unit elastic demand Demand with a price elasticity of 1; the percentage change in the quantity demanded equals the percentage change in price. (p. 86)

Utilitarianism A principle that states that we should strive to achieve "the greatest happiness for the greatest number of people." (p. 116)

Utility The benefit or satisfaction that a person gets from the consumption of goods and services. (p. 181)

Value of marginal product The value to the firm of hiring one more unit of a factor of production. It is calculated as the price of a unit of output multiplied by the marginal product of the factor of production. (p. 417)

Voucher A token that the government provides to households, which they can use to buy specified goods and services. (p. 382)

Wages The income that labour earns. (p. 4)

Wealth The value of all the things that people own at a point in time. (p. 442)

World Trade Organization (WTO) An international organization that places obligations on its member countries to observe the GATT rules. (p. 162)

real income, 205
real property, 42
recorded music, 192–193
redistribution of income. *See* income redistribution
redistribution of surpluses, 308
Reebok, 324
refusal to deal, 356
regional market, 240
regressive income tax, 453
regulation, 313
regulatory barriers, 162
related goods, 59, 63
relationship
    direct relationship, 16, 17*f*
    inverse relationship, 17–18, 18*f*
    negative relationship, 17–18, 18*f*, 25, 25*f*
    positive relationship, 16, 17*f*, 25
    slope of a relationship, 20–22
relative price, 56, 57, 205, 211
renewable natural resource, 398–399
rent, 4
rent ceilings, 128–130, 129*f*
rent seeking, 167, 308, 312
rent-seeking equilibrium, 308, 309*f*
rent *vs.* buy decision, 426, 432–433
rental market, 416, 426–427
rental rate, 416, 426–427
repeated game, 353–354
resale price maintenance, 356
reservation wage, 420
resource allocation
    benefit, 108–111
    cost, 108–111
    efficient allocation, 290–291
    fairness and efficiency, 118
    methods, 106–107
    and social interest, 108
    surplus, 108–111
resource allocation methods
    command system, 106
    contest, 106
    first-come, first served method, 106–107
    force, 107
    lottery, 107
    majority rule, 106
    market price, 106
    personal characteristics, 107
resource substitution possibilities, 95–96
resources
    allocation of. *See* resource allocation
    bought in the market, 228
    classification of, 392, 392*f*

common resource, 115, 392, 398–403
    efficient use of, 290
    misallocated resources, 31
    natural resources. *See* natural resources
    owned by the firm, 228
    supplied by firm's owner, 229
    unused resources, 31
revenue
    marginal revenue, 274, 302–303
    perfect competition, 275*f*
    total revenue, 274, 276*f*, 302
rich-poor gap, 463
Richmond Plywood Corporation, 385
RIM, 4, 234
rival, 392
Romer, Paul, 383*n*
Roots, 326, 327–328, 329
Rosen, Sherwin, 452
roses, 120–121
Royal Bank of Canada, 358
Russia, 6, 41, 44

S

safety regulations, 162
Samsung, 334
Samuelson, Paul, 53
scarcity, 2, 30–31
scatter diagram, 14–16, 15*f*
Schick, 360–361
school choice, 412–413
sealed-bid auction, 177–178
search activity, 128
self-interest, 5
    bounded self-interest, 194–195
    discrimination, 130
    vs. selfish actions, 9
    and social interest, 5–7, 9
    vs. social interest, 162
Self Sufficiency Program (SSP), 464, 465
selfish actions, 9
sellers
    illegal goods, 142, 143
    market, 56
    taxes, 133–135, 134*f*
selling costs, 331–332, 331*f*
sequential game, 354–355
services. *See* goods and services
Sharapova, Maria, 451
Shaw Communications, 313
Shepherd, William G., 241
shoebuy.com, 323
Shonkwiler, J. Scott, 99
short run, 252
    losses, 281–282
    output, 280–283
    price, 280–283
    profit, 280–283
short-run cost, 257–261, 263*f*
    average total cost, 263
    and long-run cost, 262–263
short-run equilibrium, 281, 281*f*
short-run market supply curve, 280, 280*f*
short-run supply, 96
short-run technology constraint, 253–256

shortage
    housing shortage, 128, 130
    and prices, 67
shutdown decision, 278, 278*f*, 283
shutdown point, 278
signal, 332–333
Simon, Julian, 463
single-price monopoly, 301
    output and price decision, 302–305, 305*f*
    vs. perfect competition, 306–309
slope, 20
    across an arc, 21–22, 22*f*
    of curved line, 21–22
    negative slope, 20*f*
    at a point (in curved line), 21, 21*f*
    positive slope, 20*f*
    of a relationship, 20–22
    of straight line, 20–21, 20*f*, 24–25
Smith, Adam, 51, 53, 113, 223, 351
Smoot-Hawley tariff, 166
social benefits, 379–381, 400
social cost
    marginal social cost. *See* marginal social cost
    pollution, 375
social interest, 5, 9
    resource allocation, 108
    vs. self-interest, 162
social interest theory, 313, 397
social loss
    see also deadweight loss
    import quota, 160–161
    tariff, 159
social networking sites, 244–245
Social Planning Network, 456
social science, 10
social security, 453
sole proprietorship, 234, 235*t*
South Africa, 141, 162
South America, 141, 162
"spaghetti bowl" problem, 54
specialization, 38
speculation, 427, 428
standard of living, and economic growth, 36
state of nature, 64
Statistics Canada, 239, 240
Stern, Nicholas, 373
straight line
    equations of straight lines, 24–25
    negative relationship, 25, 25*f*
    position of, 25
    positive relationships, 25
    slope of, 20–21, 20*f*, 24–25
straight line, 360
straight razor, 360
strategies, 344
strawberries, 71
subsidized services, 453–454
subsidy, 140–141, **382**
    effects of, 140, 141*f*
    export subsidies, 162
    farm subsidies, 140–141
    increase in supply, 140
    inefficiency, 141

College students (p. 1) Adresr/
Shutterstock
Nike factory (p. 5) Adek Berry/AFP/
Getty Images
Intel chip (p. 6) Christian Prand/
Imagebroker/Alamy
Smokestacks (p. 6) Don B. Stevenson/
Alamy
House for sale sign (p. 7) Toronto Star/
GetStock

Grown for biofuel sign (p. 29) Dave
Reede/All Canada Photos
Jet factory (p. 41) Bloomberg/
Getty Images
Garment worker (p. 41) David R.
Frazier Photolibrary Inc./Alamy
Adam Smith (p. 51) John Kay/
Bettmann/Corbis
Jagdish Bhagwati (p. 52) Courtesy of
Michael Parkin

Coffee shop (p. 55) Image Source/
Getty Images
Ocean oil platform (p. 69) Alberto
Incrocci/Riser/Getty Images
Strawberry picker (p. 71) Chris
O'Meara/AP Images

Frozen tomato plant (p. 83) Chris
O'Meara/AP Images

Woman smelling rose (p. 105) Robert
Lehmann/Alamy
Flower auction (p. 121) Tom Koene/
Picture Contact BV/Alamy

Minimum wage protestors (p. 127)
Charla Jones/Toronto Star/GetStock

FedEx plane (p. 151) Oliver Berg/dpa/
Corbis
Alfred Marshall (p. 175) Public
Domain/Wikipedia

Susan Athey (p. 176) Courtesy of Susan
Athey

Music CD (p. 179) Courtesy of Deepa
Chungi

Reading on the beach (p. 203) Chris
Hackett/Getty Images
Movie box office (p. 212) Corbis
Family watching movie at home
(p. 212) Sean Locke/iStockphoto
Kindle (p. 216) Joshua Kristal/Alamy
Jeremy Bentham (p. 223) Bettmann/
Corbis
Steven D. Levitt (p. 224) Courtesy of
Steven D. Levitt

Computer server room (p. 227) Dana
Neely/Jetta Productions/Blend
Images/Corbis
Wheat field (p. 237) Photodisc/
Getty Images
Pizza dough (p. 237) Michael Newman/
Photo Edit
Boeing and Airbus (p. 237) Bloomberg/
Getty Images
Rogers' satellites (p. 237) Steve White/
CP Images
iPhone (p. 243) Oliver Leedham/Alamy

Hydro dam (p. 251) Bert Hoferichter/
Alamy
Car assembly line (p. 265)
Glowimages/Getty Images
Smart meter (p. 267) Pat Sullivan/
CenterPoint/AP Images

Harvesting wheat (p. 273) Vstock/Tetra
Images/Alamy
Bus (p. 283) Robert Pernell/
Shutterstock
Computer shopping (p. 285) Digital
Vision/Getty Images
Tractor (p. 285) Elena Elisseeva/
Shutterstock

Google headquarters (p. 299) Paul
Sakuma/AP Images

Shoe shopping (p. 323) Jeff Greenberg/
Alamy

AMD and Intel computers (p. 341)
Paul Sakuma/AP Images
Famous Players (p. 357) Steve White/
CP Images
Ultramar gas station (p. 359) Paul
Chiasson/CP Images
John von Neumann (p. 367) Topham/
Image Works
Thomas Hubbard (p. 368) Evanston
Photographic Studios

Smokestacks (p. 371) Gino's Premium
Images/Alamy

Satellite (p. 391) Utah
Images/NASA/Alamy
Fish (p. 391) Gary Stokes/Alamy
Lighthouse (p. 396) Crystal Harris/
Scotiapuzzles.com
Landscape painting (p. 398) Marten
Ryckaert/Christie's Images/
Bridgeman
Fishermen (p. 399) Photonica/
Getty Images
Ronald Coase (p. 411) David Joel
Photography
Caroline M. Hoxby (p. 412) Courtesy
of Caroline M. Hoxby/E.S. Lee

Construction tower (p. 415) Karen
Bleirer/AFP/Getty Images

City streets (p. 439) Bill Brooks/Alamy
Thomas Robert Malthus (p. 463) John
Linnell/Bettmann/Corbis
David Card (p. 464) Stuart Schwartz
Photography Inc.

NOTES

NOTES

READING BETWEEN THE LINES